Engineering the Dutch Empire

Whether the photographs used in this document that are derived from other sources are subject to copyright has been checked, but as far as is known that is not the case. Possible rights holders may contact the author.

ISBN 978-94-6301-166-2

Eburon Academic Publishers, Delft, www.eburon.nl

Cover design: Textcetera, The Hague

Engineering the Dutch Empire

Irrigation, the Colonial State and Ideology in Java 1832-1942

Wim Ravesteijn

Eburon

Delft 2018

To

Maria Adrienne Jacqueline

Contents

Figures

Prologue

Chapters 1-11

Epilogue

Preface

> You, the king, are like a great mountain and your subjects are the trees upon it. It is the balance of harmony between the highest and the lowest that maintains prosperity and happiness (from an old Javan epic, cited by Van Setten van der Meer 1979: 98).

I

This book has a long history. My interest in irrigation drifted in the universe of grand theories on the rise of civilization in river valleys until I came into contact with Harry Lintsen who, in 1989, was made Professor of the History of Technology at Delft University of Technology. It was in consultation with him that I embarked on dissertation research into the development of colonial technology, later specializing in colonial irrigation engineering. It all started with a "case study" but later, because of the sheer volume of the material, it was to become the only sample of colonial technological development in my research (I then went on to focus on a number of cases).

The background to all of this was a project involving research into the history of technological development in the Netherlands. It was Harry Lintsen who headed this project. He was later succeeded by Johan Schot (Lintsen 1992-1995; then Schot 1998-2003). It was thought that a colonial dimension should be added to this research. Gradually my research lost the character of being an historic study pur sang as it started to become more and more of a quest for background information on present-day problems in the field of irrigation in Indonesia. Thanks to my academic supervisor, Frans Hüsken, who unfortunately died far too young, in 2010, much attention was given to the context of irrigation development (especially the state formation aspect) but technology continued to occupy an important place in the study as a whole.

My historical and fieldwork research resulted, in 1997, in a dissertation, entitled *De zegenrijke heeren der wateren. Irrigatie en staat op Java, 1832-1942* ("The Auspicious Lords of the Waters. Irrigation and the Colonial State in Java, 1832-1942"). Since Dutch is not a widely used language it seemed fairly obvious that my thesis should be translated into English and so that soon happened. That process also gave me the opportunity to rectify certain imperfections (including those discovered by a number of reviewers), to delete repetition and to reduce the length of certain passages on theoretical and general backgrounds. What I had been unable to do in 1997 but had been able to do then is this: I have managed to improve upon the text after first having distanced myself from it for a while. However, the manuscript was shelved, waiting for a time when I could make the final touches. There were other challenges too, both substantive and organizational, including a series of follow-up research and book projects initiated by Jan Kop on irrigation and public works in Indonesia.

Ultimately, however, I found the time, the patience and the inspiration to finish this book by editing and revising the text that was already there. Where possible and where necessary, I have used the above-mentioned and other follow-up work to give updates, empirically and theoretically, sometimes replacing parts of the text with references. Since 1997 the scientific community in the domain of irrigation and technology in Indonesia has not been idle either. It has included Maurits Ertsen's dissertation (2005), written as a follow-up to my thesis and under my co-supervision. All the newly published research also enabled me to update the text, include new references and delete some of the more outdated ones.

Last but not least, I took the opportunity to organize my data and arguments in a slightly different way taking a new structuring perspective. The book still describes and analyses the ups and downs of irrigation engineers in the Dutch East Indies from a colonial state formation viewpoint, as did my dissertation. In addition, however, there is a new message: it shows and argues, to a greater extent than did my thesis, the engineering character of the whole Dutch colonial project in the Indonesian archipelago, not only technologically but also ideologically though always from the irrigation angle.

The added value of this study remains its empirical character. Despite all the scientific progress, colonial irrigation in Indonesia is still an underexposed topic in the international scientific literature and by presenting, discussing and analysing a treasure trove of Dutch data this publication aims to rectify matters. Hopefully, it will also stimulate the discussion on technology and colonialism, a subject of research and interpretation infused with sensitivity and swayed by issues of the day.

One of the inspirational sources for the title of my dissertation, which requires a punctuation mark which we do not have to denote irony, was the novel *Heren van de thee* "Lords of the Tea") by Hella Haasse. But there was another source, tapped by my research: the sometimes overconfident but always impressive actions of the colonial engineers.

The Caesarean motto *veni, vidi, vici* would seem to aptly describe the attitude that the Dutch had to Indies irrigation. When the Dutch arrived on the scene, Javanese irrigation technology had a centuries-old history which meant that the techniques employed had become very refined. As inhabitants of a country partly below sea-level and with the Meuse and Rhine deltas the Dutch did, of course, have a long history of experience with water resources development and management but they were unfamiliar with irrigation. In their own country the preoccupation had always been predominantly with flooding, with the battle against water. In the Indies it was more of a battle to obtain water. The climatological circumstances (hot and, during the west monsoon season, much wetter than in the Netherlands), the geographical aspect (large plains similar to the Dutch deltas but also with jungle areas and volcanic hills) and the ecological conditions (rice cultivation) on the other side of the world were quite different from in the Netherlands. Nonetheless, on becoming acquainted with Javanese irrigation methods, the Dutch soon felt inspired to come up with improvements.

For the Javanese people there was something divine about running water and so such water was attributed to the gods. For them the Solo, the biggest river of Java, was the *Bengawan*: the auspicious Lord of the Waters (Van Naerssen 1938: A. 65, cf. Van Setten van der Meer 1979). Dutch irrigation engineers arrived from over the seas to subject these water gods to their regimes. In terms of their own religious beliefs, they went about completing creation in the Indies. In so doing, the engineers were following in the footsteps of the sovereigns of the old Indo-Javanese domains and their ambitious projects. Ironically, as we shall see, it was precisely the Solo that was going to prove too powerful for the engineers!

Though long dubbed "The Auspicious Lords of the Waters", this study now requires a new title that does justice to its unique character. The shift in perspective from engineers simply constructing works to ideology-based engineering in a broader sense, also establishes a better connection with the later Republic of Indonesia, which not only inherited Dutch engineering works, but also the spirit in which they were built.

II

The present monograph concludes a series of volumes on irrigation and public works in Indonesia between 1800 and 2015. It started with my above-mentioned dissertation *De zegenrijke heeren der wateren. Irrigatie en staat op Java, 1832-1942* (Delft 1997) and was followed by a series of follow-up publications, sometimes written together with others. In several scientific papers I have summarized and specified my findings (e.g. Ravesteijn 2002a, 2006 and 2007a) and presented additional data (e.g. Ravesteijn 2000, 2002a and 2002c, Ertsen and Ravesteijn 2008). I also extended some of the theoretical arguments (e.g. Ravesteijn 2002b, 2007b and 2010, Ravesteijn, Hermans and Van der Vleuten 2002).

In addition, and in close cooperation with Jan Kop, I wrote and edited four follow-up books, extending the scope to public works: *Bouwen in de archipel. Burgerlijke Openbare Werken in Nederlands-Indië en Indonesië 1800-2000* ("Building in the Archipelago. Civil Public Works in the Dutch East Indies and Indonesia 1800-2000", Zutphen 2004), *For Profit and Prosperity: The Contribution made by Dutch Engineers to Public Works in Indonesia 1800-2000* (Zaltbommel/Leiden 2008, translation of *Bouwen in de archipel*), *Irrigation Revisited: An Anthology of Indonesian-Dutch Cooperation 1965-2014* (co-edited by Kasper Kop, Delft/Jakarta 2015) and *Tapak Tilas Irigasi: Bunga Rampai Kerja Sama Indonesia-Belanda 1965-2014* (Jakarta 2017, translation of *Irrigation Revisited*). With this study I have come full circle, a virtuous circle of knowledge and insight, driven by 25 years of research into the ups and downs of civil engineers in the Dutch East Indies. It was the English translation of my dissertation that formed the basis for the present publication, but the manuscript has been revised and updated in the light of follow-up research and new insights as well as information obtained from newly published studies.

The historical research as well as the writing of my dissertation has been made possible and has been sustained by the stimulating help and encouragement of many individuals in the Netherlands and in Indonesia. I would like to thank my thesis supervisors, especially Frans Hüsken (1945-2010), who in the many relaxed discussions that we had was perpetually able to refuel my interest and provide me with valuable knowledge. I am equally thankful to Arnold Walravens, Henk Voets and Erik Andriessen for their supervision. Much thanks goes to those who have supplied commentary on parts of the manuscript or on previous chapters or parts: Paul Ankum, Rob Brouwer, Marilyn van Dalen, Jan van den Ende, Maurits Ertsen, Marie-Louise ten Horn-van Nispen, Lucas Horst, Bert de Jager, Frida de Jong and Ton Robben. Once again I would like to thank Lucas Horst for making available to me his Van Blommestein file, which I also used for certain follow-up publications. Finally I would like to thank all of those who made time for informative discussions with me. In the Netherlands some of these people were, alongside some of those already mentioned, H.J. Schoemaker, Nico Schulte Nordholt and Jan Wuisman.

In Indonesia, where I conducted both archival research and fieldwork in the 1990s, I would like to thank the staff of the *DHV* engineering bureau (now part of Royal HaskoningDHV) who were informative or of help in other ways. In that connection I think especially of the engineers Jan Sonneveld and Budi Subroto. My thanks goes also to Jaap Erkelens of the *KITLV* (the Royal Netherlands Institute of Southeast Asian and Caribbean Studies) in Jakarta who helped me greatly by putting me in contact with employees at the Department of Public Works. I am grateful also to the academics at the universities I visited who supplied me with much information, notably Richard Hutapea of the Satya Wacana University in Salatiga and Loekman Soetrisno of the Gadjah Mada University in Yogyakarta. I am furthermore most grateful to the many people – in particular the experts from the Department of Public Works (in Jakarta and elsewhere) and from the Provincial Public Works Departments – who took care of me during my travels, showed me around, informed me and were of help in other ways. It would be impossible to name them all. However, there are several people who should be singled out. I am especially thankful to the engineer Soenarno and the engineer Roedjito who had the authority and readiness to support me, to Tjandra Mualim who proved to be a great travel organizer, to the engineer R. Didiek who reorganised his work for a few days to fit in with my travel scheme, to Djauhari Sumintardja who put me in contact with Soenarno and to the engineers Karwito and Mudjuanto who accompanied me on the road for a full week.

Furthermore, I am indebted to Harry Lintsen, who enabled me to do my dissertation work, though we disagreed on the approach, and to Peter Idenburg who as dean of the Faculty of Technology, Policy and Management made the translation financially possible. Diane Butterman-Dorey took responsibility for the translation work. I look back with satisfaction on our period of co-operation and I am grateful to her for all her efforts. She bears no responsibility for a great deal of the later rewriting of the text, including the new notes and sections, which might explain the Dinglish here and there. I thank her, however, for checking the Prologue and the other short texts at the beginning of this book.

In finishing this book I am thankful to Jeroen van den Hoven, Ibo van de Poel and Sabine Roeser for their supportive attitude. Jan Kop has been an inspirational research and writing partner for many years. Though now an Emeritus Professor, he has put a lot of energy into our research collaboration. With his input and perspective Jan has taught me much not only about civil engineering in the Dutch East Indies, but also about the ins and outs of life in colonial society, or rather, in what was then a significant part of the Netherlands. He was the great stimulator in the last stages of the making of this book who did not stop encouraging me to complete "our trilogy" on civil engineering in the Dutch East Indies for an international public. Jan also critically checked the updated Epilogue, which resulted in many improvements, though I was not able to meet all his expectations. My genuine and sincere thanks go to him!

I thank KITLV/Royal Netherlands Institute of Southeast Asian and Caribbean Studies in Leiden, the Netherlands, for kindly giving me permission to use a number of photos from their collection (which now falls under the Leiden University Libraries). These photos were earlier made available to me for a lecture at the instigation of *KITLV* (in particular Gerrit Knaap) in conjunction with the so-called *Wetenweek* ("Learning week") on October 21, 2005.

Marja Offers was there from the very beginning of this long-lasting research and writing project. Her support goes far beyond encouraging me. She is my partner for better or for worse and I seize this opportunity to express my thanks to her for that.

Wim Ravesteijn
Delft, autumn 2017

Note to the reader

The Indonesian archipelago (comprising some 13,000 islands) constituted the key part of the Dutch colonial empire. It was and still is referred to as the (Dutch or Netherlands) Indies or East Indies, not to be confused with the Dutch West Indies on the other side of the globe. In this book, I prefer to speak of "the Dutch East Indies", shortened to "the Indies". Java is the main island and the region on which I shall focus. The Outlying Regions or Outer Islands, including Sumatra and Celebes (now Sulawesi), constituted the other parts of the "Emerald Belt", the name that the Dutch proudly gave to their colonial possessions in the East. I adhere to the country name "Indonesia" for the independent republic.

Instead of "East Indian" or "Indian", I also use "Indies" as an adjective (without an apostrophe), when referring for instance to the (Dutch) Indies Department of Civil Public Works, "The Indies Guide" (*De Indische Gids*, a Dutch colonial bulletin) and (Dutch) Indies engineers.

The Dutch language is avoided as much as possible in the running text. All Dutch quotations have been translated. Readers interested in the Dutch versions are hereby referred to my earlier-published dissertation. Dutch titles of important Dutch writings have been maintained and are followed by the English translation given (only the first time) in quotation marks and in brackets. Thereafter the English translations are used. The same applies to Dutch journals and similar such sources: the running text contains the original titles together with their English translations; from then on just the translations are used. However, the Dutch titles are retained in the references (with a translation, if used for the first time). See the **Sources** for a list of journals and their translations (and for the abbreviations used in the literature list) and see the Introductory note for similar Dutch sources (as well as all the abbreviations). The yearly report of the Indies Department of Civil Public Works, for example, appears in the text as the "Civil Public Works Report", but in the source references I use *Verslag BOW* (*BOW* is the abbreviation for *het Departement van Burgerlijke Openbare Werken*, or the Department of Civil Public Works). In references to other Dutch sources, the original text has also been honoured with a one-off translation. All of this is repeated in each chapter. Finally, the original Dutch wording is occasionally given in brackets. Note: references to archival sources are only given in English.

Supporting maps and other figures from Dutch sources have been provided with translations of key terms only when deemed strictly necessary.

Confusion might arise in relation to the multitude and diversity of government bodies in the Dutch Indies; the many "departments". Just to clarify matters: there is an administrational line and a technical line. The terms generally used in this book are given in bold print. **The colonial government** (*het gouvernement*), based in Batavia (now Jakarta), constituted the top of the administrational pyramid in the Indies, with the **Dutch government** and the Dutch **Minister of the Colonies** bearing ultimate responsibility. In the course of time, the power balance shifted between the two, but, of course, the motherland remained the most powerful. The colonial government is also referred to as the **Indies government** (especially in the late colonial period, when the term "colony" has been deleted from all official jargon) or the **colonial** or **Indies administration**, the latter involving the whole administrative apparatus. The head of the colonial government was the **Governor-General**, which further consisted of the **Directors** heading the **Directorates** and later various central **Departments**. Examples: the Department of Civil Public Works, the Department of Civil Service and the Department of Agriculture. Shortened forms are used for these departments, e.g. **Civil Public Works**, though not for the Civil Service Department, to avoid confusion with the inland administration.

The Civil Service (*het Binnenlands Bestuur*) or the inland administration, consisted of regional departments, called **Residencies**, which were made up of local departments or **Regencies**, divided into **Districts** (and **Sub-Districts**). The **regional heads of administration** were termed the **Residents**; **Assistant-Residents** were known as the heads of the Regencies, together with the indigenous **Regents** (the latter being termed the "younger brothers" of the Residents). Districts had their indigenous **Chiefs** (***Wedonos***), Sub-Districts their **Assistant-*Wedonos***. Decentralization and emancipation in the late colonial period brought a new generation of government bodies, including the **People's Council** (*Volksraad*) in Batavia and the **Provinces** (headed by **Governors**). Java had three such Provinces consisting of various Residencies. The term "region" is used in a general sense.

The technical line relates to irrigation and public works and the relevant organisations. On the whole this had to do with the Indies **Public Works Organisation** (in Dutch: *de Indische Waterstaat*; comparable to the Dutch State Public Works Organisation: *Rijkswaterstaat*), shortened to **Public Works** (see below). Most importantly: the **Department of Civil Public Works** in Batavia, consisting of various **Divisions** (with their **Heads**), included, for example, the **Technical Division**. This evolved from the **Bureau of Public Works**, and its predecessors into the **Department of Transport and Public Works**. Later, the Provinces got their own **Provincial Public Works Department** (with a **Head**). Regional **Public Works Divisions** (*Waterstaatsafdelingen*) and **Irrigation Divisions** (*Irrigatieafdelingen*) were also established (both with their respective **Heads**) and were divided into **Sections** (not to be confused with the "sections" [with rice fields] of an irrigation area). Earlier Public Works Divisions were also denoted as **Inspectorates** (headed by an **Inspector**). For management purposes, local **Irrigation Commissions** were set up. Finally, there were projects, consisting of irrigation works (e.g. the Pemali Works) and the relevant **(Irrigation) Services**, headed by an engineer (the **Director** of the Service concerned or the **Head of the [Irrigation] Works**) and falling under the Civil Public Works Department or, later, the relevant Provincial Public Works Department. "Irrigation service" or "public works service" are used as general terms, the latter also to denote Public Works (see below).

Civil Service employees are referred to as **administrators** (more in the case of the higher ranks) or (in general) **civil servants**. Employees of other administrative bodies are referred to as **officials**. **Public Works engineers** who were employed by the Civil Public Works Department (or Public Works in general), were officials as well. However, they are referred to in their technical capacity, as engineers ("public works engineers" [*waterstaatsingenieurs*] exist as well, but they are generally referred to as **civil engineers**).

For reasons of clarity and consistency, I have been generous with capital letters for state institutions and official positions. Though this might sometimes be contrary to contemporary language conventions or rules, it does correspond with what I encountered in many Dutch colonial sources. Capital letters are used for the names of government bodies (e.g. Department of Civil Public Works and Provinces) and – if possible – their shortened forms (e.g. Agriculture). "Public Works" is used in a general sense, like "Public Works Organisation" (see above). While comprising, in later times, the Provincial Public Works Departments as well as the central Public Works Department, it previously consisted of the Bureau of Public Works and its predecessors. Capitals are also used for government positions (e.g. Inspector, Director, Clerk and *Mandur*). I have written "works" with a capital in the case of specific irrigation works (e.g. the Pemali Works), though I have not extended this to apply each time various works (without a name) are mentioned.

In colonial bureaucracy, "engineer" was used to denote a technical function. There were Trainee Engineers, First, Second and Third Class Engineers or Chief Engineers. However, the term also came to be used as a title (abbreviated in Dutch to "ir") for technical professionals with higher or academic technical schooling (notably in relation to the engineering training facilities in Delft and later also in Wageningen: agricultural engineers, and Bandung). In this study the term "engineer" is applied in both senses of the word. Generally, "engineer" is written with a small letter, except if used to indicate a specific position.

Dutch, Indonesian and other non-English words are given in italics. For Indies and Indonesian words and geographical names, I have used the current Indonesian spelling, even in colonial quotes.

Dutch or Dutch colonial weights and measures have been used. The Dutch guilder (*f*) was replaced by the euro (€) in 2002 at an exchange rate of 1 euro equalling 2.20 guilders or, conversely, *f* 1.00 equalling € 0.45. In colonial times *bouws* and *pikols* were used, equalling 0.7 hectare and 61.76 kilo respectively.

Prologue: the lens matters!

> You the king are like a great mountain and your subjects are the trees upon it. It is the balance of harmony between the highest and the lowest that maintains prosperity and happiness (from an old Javan epic, cited by Van Setten van der Meer 1979: 98).

> Much of what happens in the Indies is not all that easy to understand (former Minister of the Colonies, Sprenger van Eyk, cited by Van Bosse 1901: 361).

The famous Dutch novelist Hella Haasse (1918-2011) is said to have characterized Dutch colonial interference as being akin to "scratching on a rock". She spoke from experience because she was born in Jakarta, the capital of the Dutch East Indies (then Batavia) and died in Amsterdam, the capital of the Netherlands. Her claim might have applied to the Outer Islands of Indonesia but not to Java, the main island of the Indonesian archipelago. This book shows that Dutch irrigation interference in Java went much further than simply scratching the surface; it was closer to rock-carving and systematically redrawing the map!

Haasse's qualification is repeated in Mrázek's *Engineers of Happy Land*, where he speaks of "flies upon the milk", quoting the Dutch journalist Willem Walraven who made that claim in the 1930's when the numbers of Dutch people in the colony (Mrázek 2002: 9) were limited. Elsewhere Mrázek (p. 35) quotes – apparently with consent – the nationalist Sjafroedddin Prawiranegara who asserted something similar when he predicted that Indonesian blood "will flow, and … creep, like the roots of alang-alang, the coarse tall grass". I much appreciate Haasse's work on the Indies, especially *De heren van de thee* ("The Lords of the Tea"). I have more difficulty with Mrázek's implicit and suggestive history writing (compare Dixon 2003), but I cannot deny that he provides interesting and informative narratives on the basis of great knowledge and insight, especially with regard to the engineering of technological constructions and networks including roads, electricity provision, telephone and architectural structures.

Indeed, if one visits and travels through Indonesia one is impressed by its post-colonial achievements, for instance in the field of architecture in Jakarta. One may think especially of the landmark buildings along the well-known Jalan M.H. Thamrin-Sudirman and in other big cities where modern architecture eclipses most monumental buildings of colonial times. With regard to water control, Indonesia has been a pioneer in rubber dam building, one such dam being in Surabaya. The country definitely has a modern and dynamic appeal. Visitors are overwhelmed by the lively trade and industry and by its people who ambitiously move forward while forging ahead on the ladder of development and progress. In addition to all the modern works, big plans are perpetually being made and executed in the interests of the nation's further advancement. The partly implemented Palapa Ring project will greatly improve connectivity throughout the country. With the Great Garuda Plan where the idea is to close off the Bay of Jakarta and establish a new iconic business centre, Jakarta looks ahead to a bright future.[1] Still, I find it hard to follow the viewpoints of the above-mentioned writers when it comes to the significance of the networks of roads and other public works constructed in colonial times which actually and factually formed the basis of the Indonesian state. If, after having read this book, the reader still thinks that in the field of irrigation, especially in Java, the Dutch contribution was of minor significance that would amaze me. It would furthermore indicate that this study has failed to serve its purpose and fulfil its ambition! How can such big differences in opinions arise?

Since the time of the agricultural revolution in the Middle East and the world population's embarkation on the path known as civilisation, irrigation has been a well-known and important phenomenon. Round 1900 irrigation had become such a topic of fascination that the canals on Mars which had just been discovered were even associated with higher levels of civilisation; indeed with a civilisation which, according to Percival Lowell, was even perceived as being superior to that of societies here on earth (Wanders 1971: 145). The discovery of canals on Mars turned out to be an optical illusion, neither visible through stronger or weaker telescope lenses, but maybe there was more to it. The awareness of a strong link between irrigation and civilisation might have inspired the work of engineers like William Willcocks, who built the Aswan dam (1899-1902), the very first big dam in the world (Courtland Penfield 1899). This connection was later elaborated in, for instance, the work of Gordon Childe (1951 and 1963), and gave rise to the Hydraulic Hypothesis of Karl Wittfogel (1957), who saw in large-scale irrigation the basis for the "total power" of eastern despots. This view could well have acted as an additional trigger for the notion that there were canals on Mars. Could we interpret the downplay of Dutch colonial irrigation interference in the same way? Is it an illusion, optical or otherwise?

If one zooms in on irrigation works, the Dutch effort cannot be ignored or trivialized at all. Dutch Indies irrigation works can be found everywhere in Java, especially in the coastal plains. Whatever town or village one visits on this main island of the Indonesian archipelago, especially in the coastal plains area, the results of Dutch compulsive activity in the field of irrigation are never far away. For instance, one need only think of the weir in the Pemali river (see **Figures 1 and 2**).

This showcase of colonial irrigation engineering is situated in the hinterland of Tegal (see **Figure 3**), its long horizontal lines forming an unnatural but powerful presence in an undulating landscape set against a backdrop of mountains, sharply defined on a hot day in the east monsoon season. In the course of an average day during the west monsoon season, however, dark clouds gather above the mountains in readiness for the next downfall. During the east monsoon period the water level is low in the river with trickles of clear (because free of silt) water pouring down over the several meters high dam. In the rainy season, however, the river swells dangerously and brown-coloured water plummets down over the full width of the river like a wall of water. A man bathing in the water, people washing clothes, a buffalo in the nearby field of stubble, children passing by, a proa packed full with passengers negotiating the waterfall: the scene at the foot of the weir has probably not changed for a hundred and twenty five years. Together with numerous other structural works and a very branched network of canals, the Pemali dam is responsible for ensuring that the *sawas* (wet rice fields) with a collective surface area of thousands of hectares are provided with "life-giving" water, thus contributing significantly to good and certain rice harvests.

---

[1] Both projects have been topics of master thesis research work – the latter also PhD research – conducted by Indonesian students at Delft University of Technology in which I was also involved as a supervisor. Other relevant master's theses and projects I was engaged in include the development of geothermal energy in Indonesia, the extraction of biogas from waste in Java and the modelling of water resources management in the Surabaya river basin.

Figure 1: The weir in the Pemali river in the west monsoon period (photo WR)

Figure 2: The weir in the Pemali river in the east monsoon period (photo WR)

The Pemali weir was completed in 1897; the entire irrigation network in 1903. The engineer A.G. Lamminga (see **Figure 4.2**) is closely linked to these and other works in the region. Born in Friesland in 1855, in the north of the Netherlands, trained at the Polytechnic School in Delft (now Delft University of Technology), he made his name through his engineering activities in the coastal plains of North Java. Through his Pemali-Comal Works, Lamminga was responsible for providing a long stretch of land on the northern coast of Central Java with modern irrigation facilities, including water management regulation. He succeeded where others had failed. In the process, Lamminga gained for himself the status of founder of modern irrigation technology in the Indies. In 1930 a monument was unveiled to this "creative genius" in Tegal, the central town in the area. The whole idea of erecting a commemorative memorial came from the engineers who "had started their Indies career under or who had been educated at the school" of that same creative genius (Lamminga monument 1930: 121). Lamminga was the great example for all the engineers who came after him; he was one of their heroes. His works remain, though his statue has gone. In the place where it once stood another monument can be found that was erected in 1969 in honour of one of the heroes of the republic, Jos. Soedarso, a naval officer.

Figure 3: Map of Java and Madura (cf. **Appendix A**)

Lamminga left more than mere traces. After his return from the Dutch East Indies he was appointed Professor at the Technical College in Delft, which supplanted the school. There he became involved in establishing the Hydraulic Laboratory (now Deltares). Present-day civil engineering students in Delft and other scholars engaged in irrigation or water issues in Indonesia or in other developing countries can now apply for travel and other grants from the Lamminga Foundation that was set up after his death in 1920.

Zooming out on irrigation works always leads to the same result. When one flies over Java the patchwork of rice-fields or *sawas* separated and supported by an intricate web of irrigation canals and works is clearly visible, especially the big weirs controlling the rivers. One may think, for instance, of the movable dam situated in the Cisadane river, created by the Dutch in the 1930s. This remarkable structure is not far from Jakarta, the capital of Indonesia, so that travellers who arrive or leave by plane can, if they are lucky, view it from the air in all its glory (see **Figure 4**). Situated as it is between houses and *sawas* I found this structure to be more impressive from the air than from the ground. In that way I was clearly able to see how this gigantic specimen of engineering, with its ten broad sluices, dominated the river. The river had been reduced to a small stream with water flowing to the *sawas* via two inlet sluices situated on either side of the structure.

However, not everything that the Dutch undertook overseas worked out. For instance, the Solo Valley Works project, started at the end of the nineteenth century, was halted but, had it succeeded, it would undoubtedly have brought forth the most impressive monuments of colonial irrigation prowess (see **Figure 5**). The Solo river, which is known by the Javanese as the *Bengawan* or the "auspicious Lord of the Waters", was too powerful for the colonial irrigation engineers who, in their constructing of massive structural works, could perhaps be likened to the Indo-Javanese monarchs of the past as they walked in the footsteps of the river gods.

Today the river still dominates the area and, despite its beautiful name, poverty is rife there. That particularly applies to the Bengawan Jero, a low-lying area in the Solo Valley (in the Surabaya hinterland). The situation has, however, slightly improved over the course of time. In colonial times some people there lived on their rafts in the rainy season that was dominated by the west monsoon. The raft dwellers are gone now, though the rain still fills the basin that forms the area to the brim, resulting in an extensive flowing plain of water. On their thresholds people remain dry (see **Figure 6**). During the dry east monsoon season the area's dryness is conspicuous, yellow-brown *sawas* prevail. From time to time groups of people can be spotted there, men and women hidden under straw hats busy bringing in the harvest and threshing and winnowing the rice. Their industriousness contrasts sharply with the scorching heat. During the west monsoon season the situation changes dramatically: no labourers are to be seen in dry fields but rather people paddling about in hollowed-out tree trunks.

Elsewhere monumental works have indeed been produced but with poor results. A good example of this is the Sampean area around Situbondo in East Java. In Situbondo there is a small plaque in one of the quayside walls of the local weir that serves to remind one of the very first modern dam in the area that was built in 1832. Various dam constructions were to follow but each time they were seriously damaged by the great force of the river. It was only after much perseverance that the Sampean area was finally equipped with modern irrigation. In the process, the river was diverted and a new weir was constructed at a different point. As a result, the area has become an open air museum – or graveyard – for colonial irrigation technology (see **Figure 7**). In Situbondo, there are even the ruins of inlet sluices to be found between the town's buildings, a dam that has been downgraded to a distribution construction (see **Figure 3.1**) and a riverbed that disintegrated due to colonial intervention.

The dams, canals, sluices, aqueducts, reservoirs and other structural irrigation works, created by Dutch East Indies engineers, comprise an inevitable component of the extensive and refined network of canals in today's Java. This irrigation network is of vital importance. While Indonesia as a whole has some 255 million inhabitants, Java is at present populated by some 148 million people living in close proximity to each other (Demographics of Indonesia, 2016). Rice is the staple diet and roughly half of the island's population is employed in agriculture, especially irrigated rice-cultivation. Irrigation, the artificial watering of agricultural crops is, like rice cultivation itself, something that has a long history going back at least 2000 years in Java. Despite all the things that have in the past gone wrong, the basis for the present system on the main island of the Dutch East Indies or in the Indonesian archipelago was laid in the colonial era, by civil engineers. Around 1940 1.3 of the 3.3 million hectares of agricultural land in Java (i.e. 40%) was in use for irrigated rice cultivation controlled by "technological irrigation".

Figure 4: The weir in the Cisadane river (photo WR)

Figure 5: The site of the planned weir in the Solo river (photo WR)

Figure 6: Flooding in the Solo Valley (photo WR)

Figure 7: Ruins of irrigation work in the Sampean delta (photo WR)

What is the Indonesian perspective? It seems that the people themselves have less difficulty recognizing the full impact of the Dutch efforts, though – or maybe because of that – their turbulent post-colonial history has pushed the Dutch period with all its colonial misery into the background, perhaps even more so than in the Netherlands. People know where their food comes from. Rice is the staple diet and present-day irrigated rice production, enabled by Dutch engineering works and agricultural policies, feeds a significant part of the Indonesian population. The Indonesian engineers who accompanied me during my visits were well aware of this, sometimes they were as impressed by colonial works as I was: "We cannot make works as solid anymore", one engineer said. Non-technical Indonesians are knowledgeable as well, at least in the countryside. I was told, for instance, that local people in the Solo Valley in East Java, had implored the Indonesian government to resume the failed Dutch Solo Works!

Another telling sign was the fact that after independence Dutch plans initially continued to dominate irrigation activities, expanding and rehabilitating colonial works though, at times, the Dutch themselves played a minor role. Sukarno embraced W.J. van Blommestein's East Java welfare plans and ordered the construction of the Jatiluhur reservoir, though it was French engineers who undertook the job.

Like the canals supposedly seen on Mars, another matter may be significant as well, in this case pertaining to the lens of "political correctness". It is no longer acceptable to write about the great achievements of the Dutch in their overseas territories as was customary in the past (Van Helsdingen and Hoogerberk 1941). Colonialism is simply no longer "decent" and emphasizing constructive contributions is labelled as justification and legitimization aimed at covering up evil aspects (Goss 2009). Much of this is understandable and often even, to a certain extent, true but if one goes too far one misses the point, as this study will illustrate in relation to irrigation. (For similar arguments on public works in general, see Ravesteijn and Kop 2004, 2008).

This monograph will investigate the nature and implications of Dutch irrigation intervention in Java while also particularly demonstrating why the Dutch undertook such a tour de force and how they set about the task. The works of the Pemali, Cisadane, Solo Valley and Sampean areas will be extensively examined and other works will be discussed too, but in rather less detail. The development of technological or modern irrigation (i.e. that realised by civil engineers) in colonial Java will not only be described but also analysed and plenty of attention will be devoted to the relationship all of this had to the process of colonial state formation in the Indies at a time when the engineering profession and, to a lesser degree, Indies Hydraulic Engineering was developing. Ideological aspects will be given ample attention. This book shows how the Dutch empire was engineered in the spirit of technological optimism and a solid faith in progress, in which engineers were a main actor, but worked alongside others. Lastly, postcolonial developments in and around the domain of irrigation will also be discussed.

This is a study that falls into the History of Technology field. My theoretical lens derives from the multi-disciplinary field of Science, Technology and Society (STS), in the framework of which the History of Technology as an academic discipline has taken shape and received content. STS is a field that not only brings together technology researchers with various backgrounds but also their views of technological development. All in all, that leads to insight into the differences and similarities between these factions and their outlooks as well as to cross-pollination. It also leads to the development of new "inter-disciplinary" approaches, which reflect ideas that are alive in the STS field of study as a whole. While traditional views on technology development assume and emphasize its autonomous character and its significance for social progress, STS shows the embeddedness of technology in society as well as the interrelationship between technological innovation and social processes of change and transformation, while simultaneously nuancing technology's progressive impact.

This book aims to increase our understanding and knowledge of colonial irrigation from a broad and critical STS-perspective while remaining focussed on irrigation engineering in relation to political conditions and consequences.

The scientific literature on colonial irrigation is scarce and so this study fills that gap. In my research I made use of unpublished information preserved in archives alongside published sources and literature, often in Dutch. I also utilized interview material pertaining to encounters with engineers and other experts. Part of the data was collected in Indonesia during two field trips undertaken in the 1990s (in August and September 1993 and then in February, March and April 1995 in what were, respectively, the dry and wet seasons). For the listing and explanation of my primary and secondary sources, see the **Sources**. But there is more to rectify than deficiency since the writings on colonial irrigation that do exist reflect the already mentioned traditional biases (further explained in **Chapter 2**), as well as the new kinds of misconceptions discussed above.

Four main themes inform and organize this book: the development of modern irrigation, the process of colonial state formation, the rise of irrigation engineers and the accompanying ideological beliefs. Irrigation development is especially highlighted in the four case studies. In conjunction with colonial state formation I shall examine, amongst other things, colonial policy and the development of the administrative organisation. The "formation" of Public Works and the developing of the technological knowledge of the engineers are the points particularly reviewed in my examination of the rise of engineers. Ideological factors will be outlined in relation to state formation and the emerging engineering profession.

Parts I, II and III correspond with three phases distinguished in the colonial state formation process (1830-1885, 1885-1920 and 1920-1942), explained in **Chapter 2**. Each consecutive pair of chapters has a fixed structure: a technological chapter with a case study and a "contextualising" chapter that focuses on the state (administration and policy), engineers (Public Works and the technological approach) and contains a concluding discussion in which the facts surrounding irrigation, the state and engineers in relation to each other are evaluated. The four cases form the backbone of the book, the contextualising chapters give the conditions and the final discussions are of a summarising and analytical nature (also providing supplementary information on results, knowledge and the professionalization of the engineers). In **Part II**, on modern irrigation activities in the transition period between the early colonial and the modern colonial state, two cases are presented and discussed. This part also has two contextualising chapters. The above-mentioned main questions are returned to in **Chapter 11**, that is, the **Conclusion**.

The first two chapters discuss irrigation from colonial, post-colonial and technological-historical perspectives and they sketch the main arguments of this study. **Chapter 1** gives the colonial view but it also questions this ode to modern irrigation. **Chapter 2** introduces Science, Technology and Society in the broad perspective of this book. Subsequently, it contextualizes the colonial view of irrigation, especially the ideology, showing how the sporadic modern studies partly confirm and partly differ from this view. After having noted how distorted and incomplete earlier images are, this chapter sets the stage for the present study. The **Conclusion** gives the answers to my research questions as formulated in the final section of **Chapter 2**, with special attention to the ideological overtones of the irrigation efforts. The **Epilogue** explains what happened in the irrigation areas of the four cases examined after independence while clarifying the various relevant backgrounds.

1

'The Dutch have gone, their monuments have been left behind'

Introduction: the colonial image of irrigation engineering

> While the engineer must necessarily be a man of vision, yet at no time can he afford to be a visionary. Without vision the people perish, without the dreams of the engineers modern civilization would be impossible (F.H. Newell, quoted in Thal Larsen 1932: 22).

The dams in the Pemali and the Cisadane rivers (See **Figures 1, 2 and 4** in the **Prologue**) are impressive feats of engineering and evident vestiges of colonial irrigation technology. Together with other irrigation works that Indonesia has inherited from its colonial overlords, they somehow support the words of the former Director of the Dutch Indies Department of Civil Public Works (spoken in 1922 during a festive gathering on the occasion of the 75th anniversary of the Royal Institute of Engineers) thus making what he said seem somewhat prophetic. This engineer, P.J. Ott de Vries, realised early on that modern irrigation works would be destined to outlive the colonial state:

"Well, if for any reason our nation should be inadvertently forced to leave the Indies for good then the Dutch people will have to thank Dutch engineers for the fact that even the Indians will claim that even though the Dutch have gone, they have left behind them their monuments" (Ott de Vries 1922: 744, compare Van Doorn 1994a: 121-122).

In this chapter I will begin by examining the impressions formed concerning irrigation in the Dutch period which should also serve as an introduction to colonial irrigation intervention. On the basis of certain literature produced by writers of that period I shall trace the outcome of irrigation activities, the matters to which results were attributed and show how these things were presented. Many of the elements touched on will be returned to more extensively later on in this study.

Colonial praise for modern irrigation

"Something Great Was Achieved There"

In a speech given on the occasion of the fourteenth anniversary of the Agricultural College in Wageningen, in 1932, J.H. Thal Larsen who was then the College's vice-chancellor painted a glorious picture of the state of affairs in the field of irrigation in the Dutch East Indies. While alluding to the situation in Demak where the above-mentioned dam at Glapan constituted an important improvement he commented (1932: 21) that famines were indeed a thing of the past:

"Famines of the sort seen in the *Demak* region in 1848 and 1872 are a thing of the past and that is, not least, due to the fact that agriculture has been protected from drought and flooding. All that has been achieved in this area will – coupled with the many other good structural works – constitute a durable and favourable impression of Dutch dominion in these regions, regardless of what those who do not wish to judge the deeds of their forefathers according to the spirit of the times might think: they will rather reflect the elevated beliefs of one's own times".

Figure 1.1: Indonesia superimposed onto a map of Europe (from: De Vries 1928)

Thal Larsen's speech was no exception. In the final decades of Dutch rule in the extensive archipelago (see **Figure 1.1**) fancifully known as "the emerald isles" and many proud stories were told of what had been achieved under colonial administration. The best known of these being the collection that appeared in 1941, just before the time of the Japanese invasion entitled *Daar wèrd wat groots verricht* ("Something Great Was Achieved There", edited by the lawyer, W.H. van Helsdingen – former chairman of the Indies People's Council and the lawyer Dr. H. Hoogenberk). In that publication there were almost 40 experts who contemplated the consequences of "the great endeavours made by the Netherlands to bring peace and prosperity to its Empire overseas" (p. VI). Indeed, that turned out to be favourable because, according to these contributors, the Netherlands had fully realised the expectations voiced by Jan Pietersz. Coen during the early phases of Dutch hegemony in the archipelago ("Great things may be achieved in the Indies") and thus had every reason to be proud. In the book appropriate attention was devoted to "Western technology". The engineer H.C.P. de Vos, the first Professor of Hydraulic Engineering at the College of Technology in Bandung wrote in that connection a section on irrigation intervention.

Rice (which is termed *padi* in the fields) requires large quantities of water which means that it can only be grown in wet climates. In Java the winds of the west monsoon blow from November until April. These northwesterly winds bring with them the rains (also known, after the winds, as the west monsoon) thus ensuring that during that period there is water in abundance. In the colonial era the farmers grew rice – also then the main food crop – on ordinary dry ground and in fields surrounded by a dike so that in that way the rain water could be retained as well as in areas supplied with water by means of irrigation (known respectively as *tegalans* or *tegals*, rain-dependent *sawas* and irrigated *sawas*). What was most common was rice cultivation in irrigated fields (see **Figures 2.1, 2.2 and 2.7**, see also **Figures 8.3, 8.4, 8.6 and 8.7**). The population made sure that sufficient water was supplied. The farmers tapped the water from streams or springs, from wells and (artificial) water reservoirs and from rivers. They made use of such things as bamboo, stone and other natural materials to force the water upwards. They created channels to guide the water to the desired destinations and arrangements were made to ensure that the water be distributed as fairly as possible over all the land. When it came to irrigation, the people were not reliant upon the rain that fell at any given time because they drew on water from a larger river area. While certain water sources dried up in the dry season (during the east monsoon time when those winds blew) others retained water. In that way the farmers were thus able to also grow rice outside of the wet season.

Javanese irrigation systems were small-scale, simply structured and not very durable (see **Figure 1.2**). In connection with the latter point, when water levels were high dams would be washed away and channels would collapse. That was something that chiefly occurred as a result of the *banjirs*, in other words, the floods that suddenly arose in the rainy season. With the help of Western technology Dutch irrigation engineers were able to improve the existing systems and create new ones.

De Vos's description of *De strijd om en tegen het water* ("The Battle for and against Water") was triumphant but not devoid of factual details. He concluded that of the more than 3.3 million hectares of agricultural land in use for rice cultivation in Java there was "complete technological irrigation works" provision for 1.3 million hectares, a surface area equivalent to two-fifths of the Netherlands (De Vos 1941: 284[1]). What was important in this connection was the different types of dams, such as fixed weirs or thresholds (see **Figures 1.3 and 1.4**) and dams with openings that could be closed off or sluices (also known as movable weirs, see the **Prologue**, **Figure 4** and **Figure 10.1**). On top of that there were also large reservoirs or basins that had been built with high dams. Those basins were designed to collect water in the west monsoon season which would subsequently be used in the east monsoon season. According to De Vos the reservoirs constructed in 1941 had a collective capacity of around 400 million cubic metres of water! For those who did not find that impressive enough De Vos had something else in store. He asserted that the work of the engineers had led to a situation in which "all the water available in Java fell under technological water management" (De Vos 1941: 277). As far as the financial efforts of the administration in the Indies went De Vos reported that between 1900 and 1940 the sums expended on irrigation activities (the preparation and execution of works as well as their maintenance) had amounted to a total sum of 270 million guilders.

---

[1] Modern irrigation works created by engineers were termed "technical" or "technological" in colonial times; people therefore also alluded to "technical" or "technological" watering or irrigation systems. I shall return to this terminology later.

Figure 1.2: Javanese dam (photo WR)

The picture sketched by De Vos becomes extra colourful in the light of other information contained in the same book. During the colonial era the population saw a period of rapid growth as is reflected in the contribution written by the well-known economist, J.H. Boeke. Just the title of this section is revealing enough: *Van vier tot vierenveertig millioen zielen op Java* ("From Four to Forty-Four Million Souls in Java"). Modern irrigation works served to help the growing population, which was dependent upon rice cultivation, to support itself and evidently this was a success because elsewhere in the book we are told that localised agriculture in Java was sufficient "to virtually completely feed" the entire population (Vink 1941: 358).[2]

[2] A publication that came out just after Indonesia's independence reported that in 1941 a situation had been achieved in which "despite the sharp growth in the Javanese population there was a rice surplus rather than, as had often been the case in the past, a rice shortage" (Berkhout 1956: 34). Even though colonial treatises tended to emphasise that less sugar culture also benefited from modern irrigation. That will be returned to later in this section. See for a post-war weighing up of the colonial policy, notably by people formerly involved, Baudet and Brugmans (1961). Cf. Baudet and Fennema (1983).

Many other colonial writers, especially the engineers, were pleased to boast about achievements in the irrigation areas. In various of the contributions such claims are supported by extensive statistics. An article published by the engineer P.L.E. Happé, who worked for the Provincial Public Works Department in Semarang, is a good example of this. In 1939 the picture that Happé sketched for Java, including the neighbouring island of Madura, was one of progress. His conclusions were in the first place based on the amount of land provided with modern irrigation facilities. He furthermore pointed out that this was something that had considerably increased over the course of time, going from 50,000 hectares in 1895 to 1.2 million hectares by 1936. That represented a rise from 2% to 40% of the total *sawa* acreage that fell under the authority of the Indies state. In fact during that period the total *sawa* surface area had not remained constant. It had risen from around two million hectares in 1880 to two and a half million hectares in 1895 and finally, to three million hectares by 1936. This increase was (partly) attributable to the expansion of modern irrigation. (See **Appendix B**).

Happé then went on to indicate that the amount of money spent by the colonial administration on the preparation, construction and maintenance of modern irrigation works, despite the fluctuations, continued to increase. In the 1895-1936 period these spendings went from a good half to almost eleven million guilders per annum. From 1908 onwards the sums revealed a rising trend finally reaching a high point in the years 1920 and 1921 of at least ten million guilders. After that a decline set in which was then followed by another rise. This final rise was to culminate in a record sum of almost eleven million guilders in the crisis year of 1929. In 1935 the total government spendings fell to an all-time low when, at around 3.4 million guilders, they were almost equivalent to the level of spending in 1910. On top of that there were also the private contributions made by the sugar industry which, from 1919 on, was obliged to contribute financially to irrigation activities, as sugar cane is grown in the same fields as rice (see **Figure 2.8**, see also **Figure 8.5**). These contributions amounted to sums which varied from 35,000 guilders in 1934 to two and a half million in 1926. All in all, by 1936 the total government spendings in the field of irrigation had risen to about 220 million guilders. (See **Appendices C and E**).

We are able to deduce certain supplementary details from an English language publication generated by another engineer by the name of Van der Meulen in 1940 (obviously the success of the engineers in the Indies was expected to reach beyond the country's borders). W.A. van der Meulen provided explicit details of the yearly government spendings in the whole of the Indies when it came to the construction of what he termed "technological" or "scientific" irrigation works. What emerged was that after 1935 the spendings had started to rise again. The money expended in the Outlying Regions of Sumatra and Celebes (now Sulawesi) was separately accounted for. What became evident was that the money spent in Java and Madura constituted the greater portion. It was not until around 1910 that the Indies government began spending money on irrigation works in the Outer Islands but, at first, the sums remained low (below the two million guilders a year). It was only in the years of recovery, after 1934 that the money spent on irrigation works outside of Java and Madura was to constitute a substantial portion of the total government spending level (in 1938 that was over 30%). (See **Appendix D**). As far as the total spendings for the construction of irrigation facilities in Java and Madura were concerned this had risen to around 228 million guilders by the end of 1938 according to Van der Meulen.

Modern irrigation led to bigger rice yields because the *sawa* acreage and the production level per hectare had increased and because the opportunities to produce more than a crop a year had improved. In turn production increases led to a rise in the land rent income. The balance between the costs and benefits of modern irrigation was summed up in the term "rentability". This system indicated whether investments in the contraction of irrigation works could be earned back. Happé compared the increase in the land rent level in terms of percentage to the average rate of interest for fixed Indies debts and concluded that the rentability of the constructed irrigation works was low. It was particularly in the period when big sums were being expended (1916-1933) that the increased income taxes fell below this interest rate. However, Happé demonstrated that if the indirect increase in the land income (from all other kinds of taxing other than land rent) resulting from the improved irrigation situation were included the rentability would look favourable alongside of the rent from state debts (also in fact to a lesser degree in the case of high spendings). The economic result of the irrigation works was thus one that was very satisfying to the writer. (See **Appendix E**).

Engineers made much of the success of the work carried out in the field of irrigation but non-engineers managed to make their contribution too, people like for instance A.D.A de Kat Angelino, chronicle writer, pioneer and defender of colonial policy in the Indies. In his monumental *Staatkundig beleid en bestuurszorg in Nederlandsch-Indië* ("State Policy and Administration Concern in the Dutch Indies") of 1929/1930 he weighed up the results of all the efforts that had been made:

"Many large water works, weirs, reservoirs (waduks), including impressive samples of technological and organisational ability have particularly emerged since 1900 and the work is still continuing and all kinds of large and small waduks with large, secondary and tertiary channels are being created as bringers of harvest certainty and public welfare".

"In addition in Java this [i.e. the technological knowledge, WR] dominated the whole irrigation organisation, a virtually living organism of the finest intricacy while the population only has to take care of the very small channels which have no technological aspects" (1930: 336-337).

De Kat Angelino (1930: 337) further indicated that in connection with the distribution of water a "regulated water control" situation had been created where engineers and civil servants were in charge but where users also had the opportunity "to help to defend their own interests themselves".[3]

Colonial writers presented the intervention of engineers in irrigation in Java as a "success story". What was that success due to? Irrigation engineers were rather inclined to pat themselves on the back.

[3] Another non-technologist writer who sang the praises of the results of modern irrigation activities was the well-known colonial economist, G. Gonggrijp. In his *Schets eener geschiedenis van Nederlandsch-Indië* ("Sketch of the Economic History of the Dutch Indies", 1928: 181) he wrote that in this area "great work" had been accomplished during the last decades of the nineteenth century. The picture that he sketched was generally one of progress (cf. the revised edition of Gonggrijp's book of 1957, p. 129; elsewhere I shall refer to the most recent edition). Cf. Furnivall (1939).

The heroism of the engineers

In all the descriptions given by colonial engineers of the creation of modern irrigation facilities there is always something of a taste of heroism. Engineers were heroic in their endeavours to control the unruly tropical flows of water and that was something they had to do far away from home in an exhausting climate and in circumstances that were generally difficult. It was especially the pioneers among the monument constructors who were, in the eyes of later generations of engineers, the true heroes. In his *Honderd jaar irrigatie* ("A Hundred Years of Irrigation") speech of 18th October 1949 (just before the transfer of sovereignty!) given on the occasion of the 25th anniversary of the Technical College in Bandung the engineer and Professor, H. Vlugter indicated that for the engineers who had been there at the beginning so much had been lacking, they had not had technological information or any good road connections. He then went on to add:

"Neither was there drinking water, electric power, good building materials like reinforced concrete, schooled employees, examples of how to construct irrigation works; there were no details about the crop water requirements and not even a Public Works Department let alone an Institute for Road and Public Works Research to which they could turn for expert advice – in short, there was simply nothing" (p.I. 100).

However, there was one thing that engineers did have and that was "real Dutch bricks transported as ballast by ships sailing on their outward journeys to these regions" (ibid.) as well as their knowledge of dikes, polders, shipping canals and sluices gained from the Delft Royal Academy for the Training of Civil Engineers both in the Country's Service and for Industry and for Trade Apprentices, founded in 1842. Both means were only helpful to a limited degree as Vlugter made clear to his audience in the following provocative way:

"If indeed one of your people, sirs, would wish to go tomorrow to New Guinea to build there in the interior a dam I would be glad to give him a load of bricks and my blessing and should he succeed in building there a dam that still stands in a hundred year's time then he will earn my respect" (ibid.).

The engineer R.A. van Sandick, the well-known chief editor of the weekly magazine *De Ingenieur* ("The Engineer"), who had also been Chief Editor of *De Indische Gids* ("The Indies Guide"), a "national and literary" monthly publication, and editor of the weekly magazine *Insulinde* (stands for the Indonesian Archipelago), began his career with the Indies Public Works Organisation but was forced to return to the Netherlands for health reasons. However, his heart remained in the Indies (Ott de Vries 1933:83). Van Sandick devoted much attention in many articles to the work being done by the engineers in the Indies. He also presented the pioneers as technological heroes. In 1929 he outlined in a publication the differences between the work of that time and the work done 50 years before. Just like Vlugter he pointed to the defective means available and to the difficult circumstances of the past. It was especially in the inland areas that things were difficult for the engineers because there they were

"lonely and isolated; in the wilderness (jungle) they were completely out of touch with European civilisation and even with the civilisation of the big Indies cities which often had a dreadful effect upon people's morale and their nerves" (1929: 269).

Van Sandick had great admiration for the pioneers:

"It is remarkable that in quietly fulfilling the tasks assigned to them so many of them have managed to do excellent work thanks to their feelings of obligation, industriousness, energy and devotion. The structural works created in the Indies, particularly in the field of irrigation remain quiet, permanent monuments to their untiring diligence and competence" (ibid.).

In the eyes of Dutch engineers the irrigation techniques of the local population were not high standard, not only were the farmers unable to find ways of utilising the rivers in the flat coastal regions (like, for instance, the referred to Pemali plains) but, to their minds, the Javanese irrigation systems in mountainous areas were also rather poor (see **Figures 1.2 and 2.1**). The engineers with their extensive knowledge of all things Western more or less saw themselves as saviours of irrigated rice cultivation. In an older contribution Van Sandick (1901a: 418) managed to effectively speak for many engineers when he claimed:

"Every ... inland irrigation system embodies in itself the seeds of decline. Here it is the too deep drop created by the channels that leads to their collapse while elsewhere the channels become silted up. Every year the temporary works consume considerable materials and manpower and ultimately fail to meet the desired goals. Water is wasted. Sometimes the branches of larger rivers are simply dammed up in order to obtain water which means that where much water falls in the river area the banjir water finds its way into the various channels. The recurrent annual damage is simply regarded as an occupational hazard rectified by the perennial enlistment of large-scale statutory labour. After several years all the irrigation systems constructed by the inlanders fail to meet the required demands. It is therefore necessary to intervene with European technology".

From the publications produced by Van Sandick one gains the impression that the development of modern irrigation systems was an inevitable and inescapable process. Before the introduction of modern facilities Javanese irrigation methods dominated. Van Sandick (1912b) called this the age of "inland or wild irrigation". During that period, under colonialism, there was intervention, on the part of the Dutch, with irrigation activity. Those who intervened in Javanese irrigation were not engineers but rather Civil Service employees active in the various regions or Residencies. According to Van Sandick (1912b: 917) using traditional techniques they traversed the "boldest of human geography", they submitted themselves to "orgies of wild irrigation". Things could not continue like that: "The logic of the facts which was stronger than all reason was finally to bring that era to an end. Irrigation activities got completely out of hand" (Van Sandick 1912b: 918).

As far as Van Sandick was concerned it was the defective Javanese technology and the failing intervention in irrigation on the part of civil servants that gave rise to the development of modern irrigation. This occurred in several logical consecutive stages. Ultimately, in order to put an end to all that muddling on, the colonial administration called in the help of engineers. The intervention was actually limited to the creation of several structural works but, although the Indies government would not immediately admit it, more was required:

"It was only under pressure that the Government came to realise that just building individual structural works and creating a main canal was not sufficient but that solid surveys and the producing of a complete design, also as far as water distribution was concerned, were things that should precede all irrigation activities" (Van Sandick 1912b: 919).

Because there was no choice in the matter the government decided at a certain point that engineers should be given the opportunity to design and construct entire irrigation systems (see **Figures 2.3-2.6**). This was to herald the phase of the "technological surveying and constructing of irrigation works". Irrigation works also needed to be managed and that was something that was, at first, also the responsibility of civil servants but here again they fell short:

"To the great dissatisfaction of the Government it emerged that the Civil Service was not capable of managing such an extremely fragile and complicated irrigation machine. The officials were continually confronted by irresolvable questions which was why, for the second time, the engineers were called in" (Van Sandick 1912b: 919-920).

The involvement of engineers in the matter of management heralded the period of "technological water control" (see **Figures 2.9-2.12**). According to Van Sandick it was still the case that the sugar industry profited more from this than Javanese agriculture. Hence the reason that the author advocated that a fourth stage should be moved to: the age of the "agricultural control of irrigation" (this will be pursued in **Chapter 6**).

In yet other contributions it was the role of technologically-scientifically schooled engineers in the development of modern irrigation that was just as highly acclaimed. In the earlier referred to jubilee speech of Vlugter irrigation history was presented as a progressive developmental thing in which pioneers made way for engineers who then built to their hearts' content. Subsequently, around 1925, there was a period that was characterised by the breaking away from fixed forms and by a striving towards perfectionism. Even in this latter phase the deeds of the engineers were not utterly devoid of heroism: they were "big in small things" (Vlugter 1949: I. 102, see **Chapter 8**).

In short, according to the engineers, it was particularly great men – notably the pioneers and the founder Lamminga – who were to be thanked for the positive results of all the colonial irrigation activities and the success was also down to the implementation of Western technology and knowledge. However, the engineers did not manage it alone. They were working for the Indies government but why was the government interested in the construction of modern irrigation works? Why did it continue to spend large and even greater sums of money on this?[4]

The great political weight of irrigation works

In 1926 De Vos, who we came across earlier as one of the authors of "Something Great Was Achieved There", gave a speech on the occasion of the sixth anniversary of the Technical College in Bandung. Using numerous historic examples he demonstrated how "irrigation, welfare and culture" (as his speech was also entitled) are interrelated. He asserted (1926: 183) that the role of irrigation technology in the developmental history of mankind is "of overriding importance". Towards the end of his speech he told his public that "the beautiful task" reserved for irrigation engineers "[is] that of providing, collecting and distributing life-giving water" (p. 190). He placed the engineers within the framework of "a thousands-year-

[4] And, why did the administration set up and expand an irrigation service? (In the 1880s there was even such a thing as an "Irrigation Brigade" for a number of years, see **Chapter 4**). In all the colonial literature on irrigation that I draw on here there were no statistics to be found on the extent of the irrigation service but there were, of course, figures. In 1878 there were 60 engineers who were employed by Indies Public Works Organisation, this reached a peak in 1930 with 263 and the level finally dropped to 202 in 1934 (Limburg 1936: 428-429, see **Appendix F**).

long" tradition and finally ended his speech with several sentences taken from the (approximately 4300 year-old) inscription of Hamurabi: "I have turned desert expanses into well-irrigated fields; I have made them fertile and plentiful and converted them into regions of happiness" (ibid., see also p. 186). The message was clear: nothing was more important than irrigation. What remained implicit in De Vos' words was the political importance of irrigation activities (after all, Hamurabi was no irrigation engineer). Other engineers, however, pointed more explicitly to this aspect as was evidenced from the very beginnings of modern irrigation.

The engineer H. de Bruyn (see **Figure 4.1**) who was one of the pioneers and twice Director of Public Works in the Indies, was convinced of the significance of modern irrigation facilities for the colonial order. In 1858, when compelled by the coloniser the Javanese were forced to cultivate certain crops such as sugar (i.e. the "cultivation system", see **Chapter 4**), he wrote that "a masterly network of cultures" had been devised but that people "had failed" to consider transport means and "the irrigation works with which such a culture system is so closely related" (p. 119). Later De Bruyn also presented other advantages. In 1869 (just before the Cultivation System was abolished) he proposed that the outcome of his suggested irrigation programme "would bring fame and fortune for the Netherlands but in the first place it would stimulate everywhere peace and rest and welfare and be of use to the Javanese" (1870: 52). In his optimism De Bruyn therefore envisaged no obstacles for irrigation activities: "Only enthusiasm for that no matter which party people belonged and – since everyone was convinced of the great importance of such works – that was indeed no wonder" (1870: 5).

In 1910 at the time of the assuming of his position as Professor of Indies Hydraulic Engineering at the Technical College in Delft the founding father Lamminga asserted that with modern irrigation the rationale lie with colonial rule:

"If, as a colonising nation, we are to successfully fulfil our obligation then the interest in public works in which concern for irrigation plays such an important part, will have to be fully accepted. Therein shall also dwell our chief rights to the property of these wealthy countries. Our main resistance to the greed of other nations will have to be found in the good control of the Colonies as demonstrated, for one thing, in the perpetual interest in improvement – also concerning the material welfare of the native inhabitants" (1920: 27).

Another example is provided by the engineer H.H. van Kol (see **Figure 4.4**). In 1901, in his capacity as a retired irrigation engineer and active member of the Dutch parliament (for the socialists of the *SDAP* party), he launched a general irrigation plan. He also presented that same plan during a general meeting held by the Royal Institute of Engineers. Van Kol pointed to the "deplorable situation of the Javanese population" and suggested that if one wished to improve this

"it would in the first place be necessary to find a solution to what was perhaps not the only but rather the main secret underlying the provision of welfare for all those millions of people: the provision of a decent irrigation system" (1901: 341).

Engineers were enthusiastic about the political weight of modern irrigation facilities but to what extent did non-irrigation engineers and, more importantly, the colonial powers share this enthusiasm?

Figure 1.3: The weir in the *kali* Waluh, 1926 (photo UBL KITLV 7782)

Figure 1.4: The weir in the Rambut, 1920 (photo UBL KITLV 18382)

In 1899 the lawyer C.T. van Deventer questioned the whole matter of Dutch colonialism in the Indies in his famous *De Gids* ("The Guide") article entitled *Een eereschuld* ("A Debt of Honour"). Van Deventer himself had been in the service of the Indies state (in a legal capacity) and was later to become a member of their Dutch parliament (for the liberals). One of the things advocated by Van Deventer was a welfare policy involving governmental activity in the three fields of education, emigration (from the densely populated island of Java to the Outlying Regions) and irrigation. His ideas were successful because he became the founder of the new movement in colonial policy that emerged after 1900, that of the Ethical Policy (see **Chapters 6 and 8**). The fact that irrigation efforts were important was something that was also agreed upon by the welfare commission established by the Indies government in 1902 under the new political system in order to research the causes of the then "lessened welfare" of the Indies population. It was a Civil Service commission chaired by H.E. Steinmetz who was then head of the Pekalongan department. As far as irrigation was concerned the commission decided in 1914 (it was a thorough investigation!) that the following fact should be brought to the government's attention which was that "one of the most powerful ways of stimulating public welfare in Java must surely lie in improving irrigation" (*Mindere Welvaartscommissie* ["Lesser Welfare Commission"] 1914: 29). The Ethical Policy was not without its results. In 1929 De Kat Angelino (pp. 335-336) was able to intimate, in writing, that since the early days of the welfare policy "Van Deventer's wildest dreams had indeed been fulfilled or were at least well on the way to being fulfilled".

The poor welfare position of the population that sometimes took on dramatic forms (as with, for instance, the famine in Demak referred to by Thal Larsen above) emerges in colonial literature as an important reason why the colonial administration found it important to finance the creation of modern irrigation works but there were other reasons as well. These other reasons had to do with sugar cultivation and political stability as may be illustrated by several examples.

In "Something Great Was Achieved There" De Vos saw that there was a relationship between the development of modern irrigation systems and the population growth. This latter development was reason enough for the Indies government "to get its engineers to create irrigation works" (De Vos 1941: 276). Apart from the matter of food provision for an ever-growing population there was, according to this author, an "economic factor" at work (p. 283). In the first place this had to do with sugar cane, a commercial crop requiring irrigation. Rice was grown in the rainy season (west monsoon) at a time when the quantities of water (the debits) were great. Sugar cane was by contrast an east monsoon crop. Before the depression of the nineteen thirties hit, at a time when even the "wonder cane" introduced in 1925 by the East Javan experimental station offered no solace the sugar industry had been (according to another chapter in the book) "for a long time the pride and glory" of the Indies (Weijer 1941: 311). The colonial authorities profited from this directly at the time of the Cultivation System when sugar cane was being cultivated "on high authority" and later on indirectly through the profit taxes imposed upon the sugar industry (see **Chapters 4 and 6**).

The entry *Bevloeiingen* ("Irrigation") in the *Encyclopaedie van Nederlandsch-Indië* (the "Dutch East Indies Encyclopaedia", abbreviated to *Encyclopedie*, Vol. I 1917) linked the early days of modern irrigation to compulsory sugar cultivation. As far as later efforts in the field of irrigation were concerned the author discovered that the cause was to be found in the welfare policy:

"As the ideas relating to the Governmental task and the plans for the revenue derived from colonial income gradually began to change and the conviction grew that all available means should be channelled into promoting public welfare, so interest in irrigation grew until, especially around 1885, ever more activity started to accompany irrigation issues" (p. 294[5]).

Happé (1939) was also someone who had an eye for the political aspect of modern irrigation. As has been illustrated above, it is clear that he sketched irrigation development in terms of irrigated fields, government spending and rentability. In so doing he indicated that irrigation works were only ever really undertaken if it could be proved that they were profitable. At the same time, though, he emphasised the importance of "ideal" motives in the decision-making process surrounding irrigation works activities. Apart from the general promotion of public welfare there was also the satisfaction of the population to be considered. According to him this latter factor was of importance in areas where the population was "restless". A third ideal underlined by Happé was the "supporting of authority". He reported that the Indies administration sometimes believed "that the proper technological improving of primitive irrigation works leads to great appreciation of Western capabilities and so results in a highly desirable supporting of authority" (1939: II. 22).

Happé maintained that these "constitutional" motives were especially of importance in regions where authority was new. He furthermore saw the economic advantages of this "in the form of lower expenses being incurred for food provision and for the legal, police and prison authorities" (ibid., see also p. II. 13, compare Van Doorn 1994a: 229-230)[6].

Questioning the colonial view

If we summarise all the lyrical considerations pertaining to modern irrigation in Java already outlined by colonial authors then what they add up to is the conclusion that the introduction and expansion of modern irrigation facilities was a great success that buoyed society on in a process of progress. It was asserted that all of this was made possible by the fact that Western technology was superior to Javanese technology, that the work was done by heroic and brilliant irrigation engineers and that the colonial administration adhered to a favourable policy in which the political importance of modern irrigation was emphasised.

To put it rather more precisely, we might further specify that: in the prevailing views on the development of modern irrigation there were two main components to be identified. Some of the notions relate to irrigation itself comprising what (still) remain visible technological monuments and all kinds of statistical material: the *sawa* area under modern irrigation could be considerably increased. It was (partly) through the creation of modern irrigation works that the entire agricultural area was able to increase while the Indies government continued to pump more and more money into this area. The suggestion made by colonial authors was that the intervention of engineers in the traditional existing irrigation systems of the Javanese was a great success. Another aspect had to do with the relationship between irrigation and society in terms of the social consequences of modern irrigation. Under this aspect I would include the realisation that thanks to the creation of modern

[5] I am not certain who exactly wrote the relevant article in the "Dutch East Indies Encyclopaedia" but the list of compilers for that particular section does contain the name Lamminga.

[6] The contributions made by engineers supplying historic information on modern irrigation in Java that are not discussed here are those of Weijs (1913) and the accompanying entry *Waterstaat* ("Public Works Organisation") in the "Dutch East Indies Encyclopaedia" (Vol. IV 1921, first written by De Meyier). Metzelaar (1946) provides certain historic details on irrigation from the agricultural viewpoint.

irrigation works the growing population was able to continue to support itself and sugar cultivation also benefited from this. What is also encapsulated in this realisation is the view that Western technology facilitated a process of technological, social and economic progress that was all part of a wider process of progress within Indies society.

On the matter of the factors that made all this development possible according to colonial views – that is to say the developmental conditions for modern irrigation – we may find the following assertions in the literature discussed:

1. Modern irrigation works were necessary because Javanese systems were inadequate; they were defective, wasteful and doomed to failure. The intervention of civil servants who were, in a technological sense, unschooled, only served to make matters worse.
2. The developing of a modern irrigation system was a technological process with a momentum of its own. The developmental process simply had to be as it was with the various developmental stages merging, as it were, into each other. The engineers who possessed their own technological-scientific knowledge were the main players and the leading roles were left for the pioneers and for Lamminga, the founder.
3. Political factors were important. The colonial administration had its interests in the creation of modern irrigation works: it profited from the land rents because the works were economically sound. On top of everything else, sugar culture constituted a source of income. The Indies government furthermore went along with all the irrigation activities because that was something that fitted in with its policy of welfare promotion and its desire to maintain "peace and order" (a typically Indies concept of the role of government, see below). The developing of an irrigation system was a technological process in which the administration dictated the ultimate constraints.

All of this gave rise to many questions, all of which could be reinforced by "counter arguments" highlighted in the same writings – that is to say – thoughts that did not fit in with the prevailing views. Was the development of modern irrigation in Java really in all respects, as late-colonial writers would have us believe, a success story? And do these writers present any indications to the contrary? Happé (1939) reported in the figures he produced that he had not taken into account the Solo Valley Works expenses. Not only had this been the greatest irrigation project undertaking of all time in the Indies but it had also been the biggest project disaster of all time. Indeed, it was referred to by various of the above-mentioned authors like, for instance, Vlugter (1949) who termed it an educational experience. However, the attention paid to this disaster pales into insignificance when compared to the attention given to the achievements of the engineers.

The notions put forward on the factors underlying the development of modern irrigation really give rise to the following questions:

1. Were the modern works really all that superior to the original Javanese structures? Traditional irrigation had an extensive past and people knew that but somehow the old technology was only visible to the colonial engineers in archaeological remains (as reported in *Encyclopaedie* Vol. I 1917: *Bevloeiingen*) and that was not something they included in their assessment of existing irrigation systems. In their eyes what they saw were small-scale village irrigation systems that were defective. However, if we take Happé's (1939) figures then we can see that in 1936 60% of the entire *sawa* acreage was still being watered by means of Javanese systems. De Vos (1941: 281) commented in conjunction with traditional irrigation systems in the hill and mountain areas that such intervention often amounted to "curbing measures" rather than to improvement works. In passing he (ibid.) mentioned that the regional systems were "good enough and sometimes too good"! (This related to works in the upper reaches areas of rivers that were disadvantageous to certain lower reaches situations).

2. Was the rise of modern irrigation truly a development process with its own dynamics in which engineers had a leading part to play and where there was a colonial administration that gave them the opportunity to create and follow their own technological-scientific laws? As we have seen there were other parties involved, like for instance the Civil Service people and those involved in the sugar industry. What precisely was the part they played in the creation of modern irrigation works? Were the civil servants shunted away when the Indies government brought in engineers?
3. Were the Indies administrators limited to creating policy conditions? The colonial government clearly had interests in modern irrigation works being created but could it allow engineers to simply do as they pleased without this having an effect on modern irrigation development? We saw in any case with Van Sandick (1912b) that the government was somewhat reserved about involving engineers. Clearly it was no foregone conclusion, at least for the government, that engineers should automatically be allowed to intervene in irrigation matters.

In the case of questions 2 and 3 above it is really the nature of the relationship between irrigation and society that has to be examined, but notably between irrigation and the state. Engineers and civil servants were part of the colonial state just as was, for that matter, the Indies government. As we have also seen, governmental policy varied over the course of time and irrigation tasks gradually fell into the hands of engineers. The question is, how were the changes in policy and operational organisation linked together and how were developments in modern irrigation in turn linked to that. We shall return to all of these questions and specify the leading ones for this study after we have first considered a number of theoretical aspects of irrigation and technological development.

2

'Minimal openness, unfair assessment'

Theoretical framework: modern perspectives on irrigation development

> Each present has the past it asks for (Beerling 1962: 53)

> As soon as one – with the whole modern science of philosophy – recognizes that all observational knowledge is "theory loaded", a direct appeal to the "facts" becomes meaningless (Lorenz 1990: 282)

In the colonial past it had been suggested by the engineer Lamminga that efforts should be made to record the history of modern irrigation in Java. In fact in a letter of 13th March 1909 addressed to the Director of the Department of Civil Public Works Lamminga wrote the following:

"I have always regretted that so little has been mentioned [concerning the important irrigation works executed in Java, WR] and that, with the exception of several independent activities ... it is only in the Technological Annual Reports issued by the Department of Civil Public Works that publications are to be found on irrigation works.
Almost without exception all these reports reveal very little about the economic and financial sides of the works and are determined by the technological considerations. However, in the departmental reports that aspect is also treated in a dismissive way, which is extremely difficult for Indies engineers and virtually incomprehensible for others because of the lack of maps and drawings. ... it is therefore difficult to study the reports which only provide a dull listing of figures lacking any inspiration ...
The consequence of such minimal openness concerning the larger works undertaken by the Department of Civil Public Works is, on the one hand, that there is a lack of appreciation and an underestimation of the significance and the results of the works and, on the other hand, an unfair assessment of the Department's activities because they are given too little publicity.
I therefore intend to help to rectify this situation by compiling descriptions of the larger irrigation works ..." (Voorduin 1914: 1).

The Director agreed with Lamminga, as did the Indies government. The Governor-General took it up with the Minister of the Colonies in the Netherlands who delegated the task of pursuing the matter to the engineer J.C. Voorduin. Lamminga himself was unable to help because he was too busy. Voorduin began by dealing with the Pemali Works (1914), the works of the "master" himself. However, that was as far as it got so nothing actually came of the recording and reporting of the history of modern irrigation in the Indies which was what Lamminga's suggestion might have led to.

In the colonial era the development of modern irrigation in Java therefore largely remained a closed book. Apart from separate project descriptions all that we have from that period are the brief overview articles of engineers and the superficial discussions in colonial writings about other aspects of Dutch colonial activities on that island passed on by non-engineers. Most of these contributions have been discussed in **Chapter 1**. As we shall see, in the post-colonial literature on Indonesia there is also only diversified information on the development of modern irrigation in colonial Java. In this respect Boomgaard (1987: 71) pointed out that historiography was "a task long overdue" (compare De Vries 1961: 271).

With all the necessary modesty in this study I shall follow in Lamminga's footsteps and give a contribution to filling this gap in colonial history. This chapter shows my approach, based on the field of Science, Technology and Society (STS) and the History of Technology, as an integrated discipline, in particular, which serve as the frames of reference of this book. First, I will show how the colonial impressions of modern irrigation and its rise were given an ideological slant. In that connection I shall also focus on post-colonial Indonesian studies in which aspects of colonial irrigation activities will be highlighted. Any recent research that may in any other way be of relevance to my subject of study will be also be considered in the theoretical background to this study subsequently dealt with in this chapter. I shall discuss the insight derived from recent research into technological developments before going on to reveal the underlying basis of this study. In the final section I shall address the main questions posed by this book. There I shall highlight some of the important limitations while at the same time explaining the method adopted in this study.

The ideology of colonial irrigation

Progress and professionalization

It was not so strange to see that it was precisely in the final decades of colonial administration that many writers decided to extensively highlight all the achievements relating to modern irrigation in the Dutch East Indies. That was something that had to do with the spirit of the times. Nationalism among the Indies population was something that had been awakened under the welfare policy that had been adhered to since the beginning of the twentieth century and which started to take on serious proportions during the nineteen twenties and thirties. It seemed that the era of unchallenged power had passed. Indeed that was something that became clearly evident when, after the Second World War and the Japanese occupation of the Indies, the struggle for Indonesian independence commenced. On top of everything else the depression of the thirties and all the economising policies were to put a definite end to the heyday of the Ethical Policy. All in all, this weakened the position of the Netherlands. The colonial overlords did all they could to find ways of legalising and justifying their presence and they did that with the necessary verve as evidenced, for example, in the in **Chapter 1** referred to publication entitled "Something Great Was Achieved There". It was thought that under the inspired leadership of the Netherlands "our Indies" would be swept up in the march of nations. The motherland had given the country peace and welfare as well as progress and civilisation. In all of that a special place had been reserved for irrigation which was seen as one of the terrains in which Western technology was clearly able to manifest itself (another terrain being that of communication means).

We could increase and specify our understanding of the ideological nature of the colonial views surrounding all the activities undertaken in the field of irrigation and the developmental conditions revealed for modern irrigation by examining the "spirit of the day" and the specific interests of the various groups involved, using insight and data from Science, Technology and Society. This field of academic research and activity does not only bring technology researchers from different backgrounds together, but also their views on technological development. This has led to an understanding of differences and similarities and cross-pollination (because researchers adopt viewpoints from other disciplines), but also to the development of new "interdisciplinary" approach. The latter reflect the ideas in the art as a whole.

Excursus 2.1 Science, Technology and Society

The multi-disciplinary domain of Science, Technology and Society was created after the Second World War. Science and technology played an important role in this war. That was not so strange given the image of science and technology as subservient to the advancement and modernization of society, which prevailed at that time in much of the Western and the colonial world; it persisted from the end of the eighteenth century and continued until the nineteen sixties. Lakoff (1977: 357) described this "social image" in the following way: "the progress of science and technology has been seen as the basis of all social progress and of the faith of rational humanists in the indefinite perfectibility of the human species" (compare Nelkin 1977: 407).

The war experiences (for example the atomic bomb) problematized the relationships between science and technology, on the one hand, and society (at that time mainly politics), on the other hand. The result was a science and technology policy in which the government left the scientists and technologists free: they could give form and content to their work themselves. This "laissez faire" policy went together with great (financial) support: there was trust in science and technology. This policy favoured (or confirmed) a "positivistic" view of science and technology, with an emphasis on the social and political neutrality (and autonomy) of both. In the sixties, this changed under the influence of, among others, environmental issues and the arms race. In general, science and technology as a means to progress came under fire, and a need emerged for (democratic) control and direction.

In the mid-1960s Ellul for example, in his The Technological Society *severely criticized the dominant role of science and technology in the modern industrial society (the book was published in 1954 in French! See also Ellul 1980). A tradition developed of technology and science criticism (and even an "anti" attitude), in which the researchers, among others, denounced the (presumed) neutrality and autonomy of science and technology. It was not all criticism alone. Thus, there was a more or less practical follow-up in the so-called Appropriate Technology (AT) movement. This especially affected the field of development cooperation. However, it was not limited in its attention to the non-Western world. Schumacher's* Small is Beautiful *(1973) dealt with the "inappropriate" technological system of the West in most of its chapters. AT acted on an ideological basis[1]. Yet she had as an important merit a contribution to the realization of a vision of technology as a social and steerable phenomenon. In an otherwise sharp criticism of the alternative technology Hollick wrote (1982: 226) thus:*

[1] Ideologically this movement slightly missed its mark (i.e. the idealisation of decentralised and small-scale technology) thus making it redundant as an alternative analysis framework for modernisation theories. A nonetheless interesting suggestion made by those adept in Appropriate Technology was that Western technology might include a certain "code", namely "the genetic code of Western culture" (see Riedijk 1982: 4 and 1986b: 18). This notion, which is analytically hard to uphold, supports the significance of ideological factors in technological development. Other important contributions in the field of AT are Riedijk (1986a), critical Rybczynski (1980), in industrial countries Boes et al. (1989), applied to irrigation Schoemaker and Figee (1982), in the Indies Telkamp (1981). At seems to have disappeared from the scene, but the issues are not and some authors remain relevant (see e.g. Adas 1989:16).

"Perhaps the greatest contribution of the appropriate technology movement to date has been the awakening of a widespread realization that technology is a controllable force for human betterment, rather than an autonomous juggernaut".

The views of Dickson (1981) provide an example. He emphasized the political nature of technology:

"In an attempt to guarantee the maintenance of this hegemony as a prerequisite to its material prosperity, and sometimes its very survival, the dominant class in any society – whether feudal, aristocratic or capitalist – will attempt to ensure that wherever possible technological innovation remains subordinate to these requirements" (Dickson 1981: 180-181).

"Technological innovation does not spring directly from a laboratory bench. The application of abstract knowledge to practical tasks ... is already a politically-determined process. The legitimation of this is provided by the apparently neutral interpretative scheme of positivist science, rather than collective practical experience. It is this legitimation that science provides, as much as the potentially-useful knowledge that it produces, that is important for an understanding of the social role of contemporary technology" (Dickson 1981: 186).

Around all studies of the relationships between science, technology and society, the new field developed in the nineteen seventies. There is a wide variety of topics, including science and technology in less developed countries ("technology transfer") and the relations between science, technology and the modern state, studied by researchers from diverging disciplines and backgrounds, including the History of Technology. Connecting theoretical principles are a "critical" perspective (critical of the idea that technology and science would be neutral and independent, critical also against "technocratic", i.e. in favour of democratic accountability and control) and, related to this, a "contextualistic" approach to science and technology (much emphasis on the importance of the social context).[2]

Science, Technology and Society studies, especially regarding the History of Technology, show that the belief in technological progress is something that we first see among the professionals involved in modern technology, in other words, the engineers. For a number of decades they truly believed in the general ethic that technology was a kind of salvation (Lintsen 1985: 193 onwards). Traditional discussions in the field of the History of Technology, one of the scientific disciplines devoted to the development of technology, bear evidence to this. Up until recently such discussions were chiefly the terrain of engineers. Their descriptions only focused upon inventions, discoveries and the successful applications that are conducive to promoting technology and society. In a standard work on the history of technology in the Netherlands Van Lente et al. (1992: 24) formulated it as follows: "In the eyes of the authors, the history of technology constitutes the epic of the subjection of nature to human ingenuity, an epic in which inventors fulfil the role of heroes" (compare Layton 1977: 208).

---

[2] See for the development and content of Science, Technology and Society (or Science and Technology Studies) Spiegel-Rösing (1977: 7-8) and Edge (1995), and in general the two consecutive STS "handbooks" in which these and other referred to articles are to be found: Spiegel-Rösing and De Solla Price (1977) and Jasanoff et al. (1995). See for a Dutch contribution Van der Graaf (1984). See for a recent handbook Kleinman and Moore (2014).

The technological chronicle writers presented the relationship between technology and society somewhat simply in the following way: "The relationship between technology and society could be summarised in one word as: progress" (ibid). The examination of the development of modern irrigation in Java discussed above is something that fits into this traditional view of the History of Technology. The accounts were written by engineers. They emphasised the role of modern irrigation technology and, together, they formed an epic of heroes who prevailed over nature and who, in so doing, did society a favour.

The older History of Technology studies reflect the views of technology alive at the period in question and the professional ideology adhered to by engineers but, in addition, they indicate the importance of technology to society while promoting the status and position of engineers and that too added up to a prejudiced view (Van Lente et al. 1992: 24). In the nineteenth century Dutch engineers underwent a process of professionalisation. This was something that went hand in hand with a general process of modernisation continuing within Dutch society that embraced infrastructural improvement (railways and canals for instance) and industrialisation. In their endeavours to gain recognition and power the engineers emphasised the contribution made by them to economic development and to the population's welfare. One way of doing this was by praising "great works". In conjunction with the "social question" that became relevant towards the end of the nineteenth century (the dismal living conditions of industrial labourers) they affiliated themselves to the ethic of improving social welfare. (Lintsen 1985: 39 onwards, see also Lintsen 1980).

The hagiographic tales of irrigation engineers about their illustrious predecessors and the enthusiasm they showed when it came to their field of study and its implications for politics may also be viewed in this perspective (even though they were not all of a historic nature!) Just as in the Netherlands the engineers in the Indies (the Indies engineers) constituted part of an up and coming professional group striving to gain social appreciation and influence (Lintsen 1980: 202-204). De Bruyn, the pioneer of modern irrigation of the nineteenth century referred to in **Chapter 1** was certainly also swayed by considerations of status in his plea for irrigation activities. Later the social question in the Netherlands also had colonial repercussions in the form of "lessened welfare" (giving rise to the "colonial question") and, in their desire to do something about this, the Indies engineers followed the example of their colleagues in the mother country. This was how Van Kol (1901) arrived, as we have seen, at the idea of creating a great plan. After the turn of the century the professionalisation of Indies engineers continued unabated. Van Sandick (1912b), whose views were dealt with in **Chapter 1** at length, sketched the development of modern irrigation as being in fact a process of professional formation: irrigation intervention became a matter for engineers. His overt goal was not to further the cause of engineers even though by describing the historical significance of the role of engineers that was something that he implicitly did do. He was rather concerned with transferring responsibility for water management from engineers to agricultural experts. In his eyes that would lead to a better situation for the population. The promoting of the interests of the professional group is also something that is reflected in Lamminga's views. We saw earlier how this founder of modern irrigation technology in the Indies (as confirmed by Dirkzwager 1977: 60) promoted his profession by linking it to the colonial order. His proposal to create a (kind of) history of modern irrigation is another example of this. It emerged that he had in mind a clear objective which was to make known the construction of irrigation works and to in that way praise the work of the engineers employed by the Civil Public Works Department.[3]

[3] As we shall see later (in **Chapters 5 and 6**) there was also another very special reason for wanting to improve the image of engineers at that time which had to do with the Solo Valley project failure and all the consequences which that had.

Figure 2.1: Rice terraces, 1939 (photo UBL KITLV 54330)

Figure 2.2: Flat rice fields, 1900 (photo UBL KITLV 3745)

Within the colonial context there was also another ideological background to the impressions surrounding modern irrigation. The belief in progress that was based upon science and technology was given substance in the shape of the civilisation mission ("mission civilisatrice"), also sometimes termed "the white man's burden". The West saw itself as better developed than the east and therefore morally obliged to share its achievements with its unfortunate contemporaries. It was a mission that developed in relation to Western expansion in the area of colonialism and imperialism.[4]

On the basis of several studies on "global research into technological development" that serve to highlight the Western civilisation mission and its roots we can further explain the effects which that mission had on the colonial views of irrigation development in the Indies. Alvares (1980) provides us with a stimulating analysis of the technological aspects of Western expansion. He takes as his starting point the world in about 1500. By that time the history of mankind had reached a stage when there was a mosaic of peoples, each with its own technology and culture. Alvares calls these "paradigms of technology and culture". These are the concrete manifestations of his model of "technology and culture". He calls it the model of "homo faber", the creating individual influenced by the nature around him and by the culture of which he is a part. The author deals with three such paradigms: the Western (originally English), the Indian and the Chinese. He indicates how, over the course of time, the range of paradigms of technology and culture diminished to the extent that at one point there was even a real danger that only the Western model would remain. Indeed, all kinds of means were employed to expand this one paradigm, including the trivialising of others and the praising of the own paradigm which was (and still is) presented as the only option.

The colonial image of the rise of modern irrigation, an integral part of which was the negative esteem for Javanese technology, certainly fits in well with the Western vision of global technological development described by Alvares. With some of the stories, like for instance those of the pioneers, one would almost be led to forget that irrigation was not a Dutch discovery and that it had been implemented in Java since time immemorial. The view of irrigation in general was also a coloured one in colonial times. Much was then known about "historic" irrigation including the fact that irrigated agriculture of small farmers was something prevalent among many ancient peoples in a diversity of continents, among which the Incas in what is now Peru. In that connection it was no exception for large works to be constructed at the instigation of those in power and for large numbers of workers to be deployed. In colonial literature large-scale irrigation was associated with the starting point of all "civilisation" beginning with the land between the Euphrates and the Tigris in Egypt. Simultaneously the superiority of modern irrigation was always emphasised. (See, for instance, De Vos 1926 and Thal Larsen 1932).

[4] The colonial relationship between the Netherlands and the Indies which began in 1596 with the signing of the first treaty between Cornelis de Houtman with an Indies monarch and ended 350 years later when, in 1945, Sukarno claimed independence for the Republic of Indonesia was something that developed within the stage of worldwide processes of change resulting from European expansion. After the time of the "voyages of discovery" trade between European and non-European countries started to flourish. Trading posts were established that sometimes expanded to population settlements. Trade, originally in tropical agricultural products, and later also in raw materials for the mining industries was unfair: it occurred under threat or the use of arms and later under the supervision of authoritarian regimes. The aftermath of the colonial era, which ended after the Second World War, still persists today. See for details of Western expansion history in general Lemaire (1976), Wallerstein (1974, 1980), Hobsbawm (1989), Wolf (1982) and Wesseling (1988).

How did post-colonial writers perceive the Dutch irrigation interference? Did the colonial imagery remain intact or was it adjusted? Unfortunately, there are no (substantial) post-colonial studies on the development of modern irrigation in the Indies[5]. There are studies, though, on other aspects of the Dutch colonial approach in the Indies archipelago with attention for irrigation. These studies reflect colonial attitudes towards the development of modern irrigation but in different respects they provide important supplementary information. Some of the most important of these studies will be examined below.

Sugar or rice?

One study that directly has its roots in the world of colonial experience is that of a former Civil Servant employee by the name of Burger (1975). He describes the history of Indonesia in terms of an opening up of the interior, notably of the village economy, to the international market and evolution. Because of this a process of de-feudalisation was set in motion in the nineteenth century and a process of modernisation in the twentieth century. Both these processes were the result of what Burger called emancipation politics. In conjunction with all this progress he briefly sketched an image of the rise of modern irrigation in terms of an increase in *sawa* acreage and government spendings.[6]

Other post-colonial studies that focus on colonial irrigation efforts tend to temper the impression of glory and success. One question that particularly arises is whether the irrigation works were particularly intended to promote the population's rice cultivation activities or to promote sugar cane cultivation on the part of European entrepreneurs (see for rice cultivation **Figures 2.1, 2.2, 2.7, 8.3, 8.4, 8.6 and 8.7** and for sugar harvesting **Figures 2.8 and 8.5**). From the colonial standpoint the onus was upon improving the general welfare of the Javan population but recent studies have queried these motives. One classical study on the development of agriculture in Java is Geertz' *Agricultural Involution* (1963). Geertz, who is an anthropologist, did historical research into the relationship between increased agricultural production and population growth and the part played by modern irrigation. In view of the fact that both crops were cultivated alternately on the same pieces of land the relationship between sugar cane and rice was for him a "mutual" one: both profited from improved irrigation. To his mind modern irrigation supported colonial exploitation because it encouraged sugar production that was destined for foreign sugar refiners without being too detrimental to the population's food production. Sugar culture expansion did, however, encroach upon the acreage available for rice cultivation but modern irrigation raised productivity thus cancelling out the negative effects of sugar production. Due to the situation of sharp population growth and because rice harvests were improving, in particular, as a result

[5] Apart from: the Dutch predecessor of this book (Ravesteijn 1997, see also 2002a, b, 2006, 2007a, b, 2010) and a follow-up study (Ertsen 2005, see also Ertsen and Ravesteijn 2004, 2008). There is a small Indonesian study on colonial irrigation intervention in Indonesia written by Angoedi (1984). He describes the rise of modern irrigation at a time when government policy was changing. Various engineers at the Agricultural University of Wageningen have graduated with theses on irrigation management in colonial Java (e.g. Ter Hofstede and Van Santbrink 1979 and Ertsen 1993). The beginnings of a historical study of irrigation development in Java have been produced by Schokkenbroek (1988). Various details on the development of Indies hydraulic engineering from the civil engineering angle are also given by Dirkzwager (1977). Mrázek (2002) writes about Indies engineering in relation to nationalism. The history of civil engineering and the Public Works Organisation in a broad sense in colonial and post-colonial Indonesia can be found in Ravesteijn and Kop (2008). See for historiographic details on the Indies e.g. Lindblad (1992), Buiter (1993) and De Jong (1998).

[6] Burger's approach was not unlike that of the colonial figure, Gonggrijp (1957, see **Chapter 1**, **Note 3**). His PhD thesis on *De ontsluiting van Java's binnenland voor het wereldverkeer* ("The Opening up of the Javan Interior to World Traffic") dates from 1939. See also Creutzberg (1974: VII-XIII).

of agricultural intensification a process of "involution" or of "inward development" was set in motion which led to economic stagnation and to poverty amongst the population.

Geertz' view of modern irrigation links up a bit with colonial ideas in this respect, especially where he indicates what is the influence of the interests of the population. With his involution concept, however, he really departs from the aspect of optimistic progress. What was also new was the emphasis placed upon colonial exploitation, a phenomenon served in two ways by modern irrigation works: directly by encouraging the cultivation of sugar cane and indirectly by raising the food production levels (more produced from smaller areas) of the population (compare here, however, De Vogel 1924). Geertz' "involution theory" and his statistical support of this have been heavily criticised (for instance by Van Schaik 1986 and White 1983; see for a good overview of the discussion Hüsken 1988: 22-29). Geertz' notion that modern irrigation was a pillar of colonial exploitation remained intact and was followed up in studies that placed the creation of modern irrigation works in the colonial era in the light of the sugar industry (see, for example, Alexander and Alexander 1978, Hüsken 1988 and Van Schaik 1986 and see for an Indonesian study Loekman Soetrisno 1980).

The irrigation-for-rice view was also supported, for instance by Booth, who has produced various studies on post-colonial irrigation and agriculture in Indonesia. When she summarises the activities of Indies administration in the way quoted below, Booth (1977 part I: 46) is really adhering to the colonial view of modern irrigation, notably as sketched by Van der Meulen (1940) in his English-language publication:

"Massive expenditure on irrigation by the colonial government in the first three decades of the century expanded the area of "technically" or government-operated irrigated land in Java and Madura to about 1.2 million hectares by 1938. The total expenditure on irrigation both in Java and the Outer Islands was estimated to have reached 228 million guilders".

Booth (idem.) also demonstrates that she is aware of the less successful aspects of colonial irrigation intervention when she questions some of the results of such intervention:

"In addition to the land under government irrigation schemes, there was approximately 1.5 million hectares of "locally irrigated" land under village organised irrigation schemes, and a further 665.000 hectares depending solely on rainfall. Outside Java and Madura there were extensive amounts of land under village-based irrigation schemes and yields of *padi* per hectare from these lands appeared to be higher than on Java. Yields of dry-stalk *padi* per hectare in Java appeared to have stayed constant at a little over two tons per hectare for the entire period during which irrigation facilities were being expanded".

"Whatever else it had achieved, colonial government expenditures on irrigation had not appreciably improved levels of food consumption. At best their measures had only averted further deterioration in living standards for the bulk of the population".

Booth (1977 part I: 45, see also part II) was furthermore critical about the organisation of water management in the colonial period (according to her there was an "institutional vacuum" at village level: much was left to farmers and village authorities) and in that connection she doubted whether many entire irrigation systems (including so-called "tertiary" canals for the *sawas*) would have been created. In conjunction with that latter point she drew a parallel with the sugar industry:

Figure 2.3: Inlet sluice for primary canal at Notok weir (photo WR)

Figure 2.4: Inlet sluice for secondary canal in the Pemali area (photo WR)

Figure 2.5: Structure for dividing the water from the primary to secondary canals in the Pemali area (photo WR)

Figure 2.6: Division structure for tertiary canals in the Pemal area (photo WR)

"Certainly in those areas where the sugar companies were leasing land, government irrigation service and local officials would have been under pressure to complete the tertiary network (with unpaid labour if necessary). But often the rice fields were simply flooded during the wet season directly from the main and feeder canals, with little attention being paid to the construction and maintenance of a tertiary network which would have allowed regulation of water to each field. This meant that those fields nearest the outlet received most water (not always an advantage as they could be swamped when draining was inadequate)".

In view of the limited amount of land watered by modern irrigation means that was utilised for sugar culture (in 1925 that was, for instance, 17%) she really maintained (ibid.) that: "it clearly would not be correct to argue that all government irrigation infrastructure was being used by foreign estates".

Booth then goes on to provide many statistics which do serve to significantly supplement and refine views of colonial irrigation efforts. For instance, she compares the money expended on irrigation provision by the Indies government to the total government expenditure. In that way it becomes evident that in 1871 the government spent less than 10% of its annual income on irrigation and other public works and that in the twentieth century that portion increased to 18½% in 1905, 37.7% in 1913 and to 39.2% in 1921 (while the government money spent on railways was respectively: 8.9%, 11.3% and 16.4%) (Booth 1988, 1990, see **Appendix G**)[7]. Despite all the additions made and adjustments Booth remains optimistic about colonial irrigation activities. For example, in her 1988 study she linked Indonesian successes in the area of food production to colonial agricultural policies (by 1986 the country had become self-sufficient as far as rice production was concerned) and therefore also to irrigation improvements (see, for example, p. VI).

In his study of "the greatest adventure of the Netherlands" Van Doorn (1994a: 11) gives a detailed description and analysis of the rise of irrigation engineers in the Indies. At the beginning of the chapter "The Triumph of Technology" he quotes Van Sandick who surmised, in 1900, that "in Java irrigation politics is just as weighty, urgent and necessary as social politics in the Netherlands" (p. 105). He demonstrates how the striving of engineers to achieve a better position for themselves was something that was especially evident within the framework of the competitive battle between the Indies Public Works Organisation and the Civil Service. In that connection the engineers showed that they cared about the lot of the population, though their ideas were truly "technocratic". After all the necessary ups and downs the engineers finally managed, towards the end of the nineteenth century, to turn this conflict to their advantage. Van Doorn also emphasises how important irrigation care was to local agriculturists (compare Van Doorn 1982, see also Moon 2004)[8].

In view of the fact that here above we have just touched on the ideological moment of colonial image-forming in conjunction with irrigation we cannot avoid beginning a similar discussion on post-colonial literature. We saw that colonial powers, such as the Netherlands, tended to mask their colonial and imperialistic behaviour with ideologies of dominance and superiority and notions of giving shape and form to the civilising mission. After the Second

[7] From this it may be concluded that when irrigation activities were at their height in 1921 the relative share of the Indies government's contribution had dropped somewhat since more was being expended on railway infrastructure but the discrepancy remained marginal. For details on government spending corrected in conjunction with Indies public works the reader is referred to **Appendix H**.

[8] This latter point made by Van Doorn will be returned to in **Chapter 6** when I shall discuss the matter of Ethical Policy. Van Doorn (1994a) also touches on the subject of the rise of railway engineers and he sketches the atmosphere of competition between both groups of engineers. The conflict will be dealt with in **Chapter 8**. The views of Van Doorn will also be further examined later in the present chapter.

World War many colonies became independent. The old ideologies continued, though, to make themselves felt and were made concrete in the modernisation programmes of the post-colonial governments supported by the former holders of power. These programmes aimed at "development" which was to be effected by implementing the Western paradigm of technology and culture. Once again, modern technology was to play a central part (Adas 1988, Alvares 1980). In this connection the contributions of scientists consisted of studies in which the processes of change in the third world were described and analysed in terms of the Western experience or the existing perceptions of that. These modernisation studies led – or were at least based upon – unilinear phase theories (with modern Western society as the goal) that served as beacons or gauges for concrete development processes in non-Western countries. An early example of one such modernisation study is that of Burger (1975).

Invariably the modernisation programmes did not have the desired effect which meant that in the nineteen sixties the underlying modernisation theories were heavily attacked. What this also resulted from was the social problems that were then emerging in Western society, such as the environmental problems. In other words, the ultimate goal had lost its allure (see **Excursus 2.1**). As has been explained, Alvares (1980) unmasked the Western paradigm of technology and culture and showed it to be one of the many variations of his model. Adas (1989) also criticises the value-laden nature of modernisation. Alvares (1980) stressed the value of "indigenous" technology and culture. In the cases of India and China he refers in this connection to the high developmental level of irrigation facilities[9]. The fact that in pre-colonial times Java had also had a refined irrigation system was borne out by Van Setten van der Meer (1979, compare Christie 2001). According to Alvares such a native knowledge system can constitute a better basis for development than all kinds of Western notions. In that connection he also emphasised the need for Appropriate Technology (his closing chapter was aptly headed "The Logic of Appropriate Technology"). In the field of development cooperation new possibilities were being sought and the Appropriate Technology movement (discussed in **Excursus 2.1 and Note 1)** that had emerged earlier under the influence of Schumacher's "small is beautiful" slogan (1973) fitted in nicely with all of this. The arrival of technical projects that were adapted well to local circumstances and cultural factors was a welcome alternative. (See also Adas 1989: 15).

There were other, more critical, approaches that emerged in reaction to the modernisation theories, one of which (in the Netherlands) was Wertheim's (1973, 1983, compare Wertheim 1956) "dialectic evolutionism" in which "emancipation" (the liberating of nature and of repressed social structures as driving forces in the history of mankind) was a central concept, together with the "dependency theory" that stressed the inequality between countries (imperialism as an existing and historic phenomenon being a central concept, see, for instance, Frank 1971). At the same time a tradition of empirical investigation was developing. Geertz' study which, as we have seen, also had a critical undertone was of essential importance in this connection and it was to inspire a whole new generation of researchers (some of whom were Dutch) to conduct historical research and do field work. As mentioned, in the process they tore to pieces the work of their instigator.[10]

---

[9] His views are endorsed by Pacey (1990). He points out (p. 18, 31) that it was in Asia that irrigated rice cultivation was first developed. He made it clear that in some areas, like e.g. in China and India, this was accompanied by large dam and canal construction and, in China, even by large works designed to control flooding. See for the Americas Weatherford (1988).

[10] See for modernisation theories in the field of the Dutch social sciences and the reactions to those theories Van den Muijzenberg and Wolters (1988), for an international overview of development theories e.g. Shrum and Shenhav (1995) and for imperialism – notably concerning the Netherlands – e.g. Kuitenbrouwer (1994) and Locher-Scholten (1994, 2004).

In the meantime, modernisation as a descriptive concept for the technological, organisational and other changes in Western and non-Western societies continued to exist and to furthermore give rise to new modernisation studies that were less complimentary than the older studies. What was also different about these studies was that they had a strong empirical basis as is exemplified by the studies of Booth (see above) who examined the modernisation of irrigation and agriculture in Indonesia (attention is given to her findings in the **Epilogue**). The question as to whether the modern irrigation works created in the colonial era were predominantly intended for the local farmers or for sugar crop cultivation can be linked to the discussion on "critical" researchers and "modernisation" researchers. Subsequently it can be concluded that the empirical material now available supports the irrigation-for-rice view (to be returned to later in this chapter and to be further explored in the remainder of this study).

The post-colonial studies carried out by Booth, Geertz and Van Doorn would encourage one to adopt a more balanced view of colonial irrigation development. In addition to that Van Setten van der Meer prompts one to re-evaluate Javanese irrigation. In turn, all these studies support my questions on colonial image creation. The earlier post-colonial studies emphasise the importance of sugar culture in connection with the creation of modern works but the studies of Booth and Van Doorn contest that[11]. All the studies (including that of Burger) examine particularly the relationship between the irrigation efforts and government policy in relation to agriculture or more generally. In that way irrigation development itself remains something of a closed book.

In the previous section I sketched the ideological nature of the colonial conception of the rise of modern irrigation. It was progress-oriented thought focussed on modern technology that gave rise to the main misrepresentations. Engineers supported this line, not least in conjunction with their professional aspirations. Within the colonial context there was also a civilising mission. What I have shown in this section is that there is a sequel to the colonial views but that they are also elaborated and corrected in post-colonial studies. These studies could be similarly placed within an ideological framework but here they stand out because of their empirical character. Modern technology development studies likewise endeavour to avoid ideological "bias". Here below I shall consider the tools offered by these studies.

A historical-technological view of irrigation development

Technological development as a social process

Technological development is something that is studied by engineers and historians but also by researchers affiliated to other scientific disciplines like, for instance, sociologists (Social History of Technology), economists (innovation research), philosophers and cultural anthropologists (see, for example, Bijker 1984: 48 onwards and 1995: 230; see for anthropology Pfaffenberger 1988). Each of these disciplines has its own specific approaches, though the STS-field provides a common umbrella identity.

Studies on technology development may be distinguished from each other on the grounds of their views of technology in relation to science and society. To do that one must acknowledge the development which is perceptible in terms of time and the new approaches that arose in reaction to the older approaches. However, the older types of approaches are still to be seen in present-day writings (see Bijker 1995). Before going into these approaches it

[11] From the point of view of differences of emphasis the two views are also reflected in the academic technological world, at least till recently: at the University of Technology in Delft P. Ankum adhered to the irrigation-for-rice view while at the Agricultural University of Wageningen L. Horst stressed more the part played by the sugar industry (P. Ankum, personal communication, May 1992; both are now retired).

will be useful to first clarify several concepts. In the various definitions and descriptions of engineering and technology (also in every-day usage) the following four significant recognisable components are to be found:

1. material artefacts and infrastructure (technique [adjective: technical], technics; for the modern technical systems based upon science the term "technology" is used [adjective: technological]; the "hardware"),
2. the management of material technique or technology (social technique, social technology; the "orgware"),
3. the knowledge and skills required (the "know how" as reflected in the term "technology" in the sense of "the theory of technique"; the "software") (compare Bijker 1925: 231, Van Bentum 1995: 13, Van Lente et al. 1992: 24 and Pieterson 1993: 14-15),
4. the human activities and actions related to the bringing about of material technology and management (the construction activity and the building up of control systems).

The developing of technique (or technology) often has to do with the changing of material aspects (the introduction of new artefacts or techniques) but it might also relate to changes in knowledge or other issues or to all those things put together.

In some studies of technical development an approach may be recognisable which encapsulates the motor of the development of technology itself. In this way technical development is seen as an autonomous process and social development as a consequence of new techniques. It is a view that is for example propounded in older technique historiographies that presented engineers as heroes and furthermore presented the view that discoveries and progress were the trump cards (see above, one example being Forbes 1959). In yet other studies on the development of techniques we see reflected an approach in which society (including the economy and also, for example, the state) sets the pace. In such cases technical development is seen as deriving from social development (see, for example, Noble 1984). The two approaches are termed "internalist" (or internal) and "externalist" (or external) in accordance with a similar differentiation in terms of the history of science. It is a differentiation that implies criticism. In this connection it is often a metaphor that is applied in which technique is compared to a black box. With the internalist approach the onus is upon what happens within that box which thus excludes social factors. By contrast, externalist researchers do not consider the contents of the black box: that is something excluded from their view of matters.[12]

The approaches, albeit with nuances, are reflected in the above-discussed colonial publications on the development of modern irrigation. Some authors emphasise the technical factors while others stress the influence of the colonial administration. Van Sandick (1912b) saw an internal need: the Indies government had no alternative but to accept the irrigation engineer and his technical-scientific way of doing things. The "logic of the facts" produced a process that followed its own laws. He also saw a logical development in the area of water management in the direction of agricultural control, though for him that was more a(n attractive) possibility than a necessity. Vlugter (1949) also gave an overview in technical terms in which pioneers, builders and perfectionists were the logical consecutive groups of technologists. However, nonetheless with Van Sandick (1912b) the influence of the Indies administration is visible as an initiating and pioneering if not always enthusiastic body. With him it had to conform to the possibilities of technology. Vlugter (1949) equally recognised the initiating role of the government, though more implicitly. Other colonial authors were

[12] The external approach is sometimes also called the "contextual" approach or "social shaping". See for the debate on the internalist and externalist approaches in the history of science ("content" versus "context", intellectual versus contextual factors) MacLeod (1977). See for the debate within History of Technology Pieterson (1993: 17) and Bijker et al. (1987: 19).

inclined to attribute a much greater role to the government. In "Irrigation" (*Encyclopaedie* Vol. I 1917) the motor behind the development of modern irrigation is the policy for the stimulation of rice cultivation. The information on colonial irrigation development provided in post-colonial literature on Indonesia is mainly of an "externalist" nature (there were no other intentions). In these studies written by non-engineers modern technology in general is seen as a fact of life and as a manipulable variable: as an instrument of various policies for the stimulation of rice or sugar cultivation, or both[13].

With the internalist approach there is a second differentiation to be made. There are views that emphasise the role of knowledge and yet other views that abide by the internal dynamics of the (material) technical side itself which are respectively termed by Bijker (1995: 237 onwards) the "cognitivist" and the "materialistic" approaches. In the case of knowledge what is often involved is "technical science"[14].

All the different views of technological development discussed here are of a deterministic nature and (ultimately) the motor of development is sought in techniques themselves, society or science. However, technology is really the work of mankind and technicians, who in practice are occupied with the developing of (a) technique and are guided by diverse considerations possibly linked to knowledge, the techniques themselves and society. What also goes with this is their striving for recognition and influence. Conversely, all kinds of groups and bodies which exercise influence upon the technicians are involved in these technical developments. In this connection new approaches to technical development use the metaphor of a "seamless web" (Bijker et al. 1987: 9, see also Bijker 1995) to indicate that technical things are themselves seamlessly interwoven in society. Such a social-technical complex is something that develops gradually (Bijker 1995 refers to "sociotechnical ensembles"). Inventions have a pre and post history which is what makes technical development an evolutionary rather than a revolutionary determined process (leading on from heroic technical breakthroughs). The new approaches distinguish themselves from the older ones through their extensive empirical research. For all kinds of thinkable discrepancies (internal/external, technical/social, science/technology as purely and applied science respectively) an empirical approach is also recommended. In order to indicate the presumed integral nature of technique and society and to also unravel it, several different approaches involving a number of "general concepts" have been developed which together are known as "social constructivism".[15]

---

[13] An exception to this is the work of Alexander and Alexander (1978). They pointed out that from the point of view of design and construction colonial irrigation works lent themselves more to sugar cane cultivation than to rice growing. Ultimately the view presented by the Alexanders is one of an "interactive" image of technology and of technology and policy (cf. Van Schaik 1986: 139-140, where thought concerning the creation of large reservoirs is lacking, see **Chapter 10**). Van Doorn (1994a) has an eye for the development of technology when he discusses the failed Solo Valley Works. Adas (1989) gives an exemplary description and analysis of the development of the Western view of technology but remains "externalist" in the process. Alvares (1980) devotes much attention to technology and Leidelmeijer (1992) to technical development in relation to the sugar industry in Java.

[14] In this connection science and technology (or technical science) are distinguished and what is intended with the latter is purely applied science (see **Note 18**). We can therefore see that the differences in approach to technical development are thus partly derived from the fact that different meaningful elements of techniques are differently evaluated.

[15] See for the social-constructivist approach SCOT (i.e. the social construction of technology), the system and the actor network approach Bijker (1995: 249-252) and Bijker et al. (1987). Compare with Kuhn (1971) who, unlike Popper who emphasised the role of major discoveries in the history of science, pointed out that scientific revolutions are rare and that most scientists are occupied with "normal science" within an established "paradigm". Apart from that Kuhn found that technology and science are different as is borne out by what he once casually remarked about technology to the effect that "the principle *raison d'être* is an external social need"

In comparison with the deterministic approaches Bijker maintains that the social-constructivist way of viewing matters makes a more adequate description of the development of technology possible because it possesses "better instruments to analyze the development of technology *in relation to society*" (1995: 237-238). These tools comprise a number of insights together with the relevant concepts which may be summarised and linked together as follows. Various people and groups are always involved in the development of an artefact (engineers, entrepreneurs, consumers, government bodies). These people who may or may not be united in "relevant social groups" (like-minded individuals involved in an artefact) are linked together with the artefact concerned in a "network" which may, moreover, include yet other elements (for instance regulations) to form a "system". Any network or system needs to be built up and that requires technical and non-technical (including sociological) qualities. Sometimes that goes wrong and the technical development fails. If, however, it goes well then a socio-technical system will arise that will "automatically" further develop – all the "actors" involved take care of that.

Social constructivism has not gone totally without criticism. The facet "relevant group" does, for instance, present a problem. There are therefore also non-relevant groups. Precisely which groups are or are not involved in technical development all depends on the power relations within society. Since social constructivism does not take this into account Winner (1970:370) terms it elitist. There is no thought for social structures nor, according to the same author, for culture. Winner (ibid.) claims that social constriuctivism:

"disregards the possibility that there may be dynamics evident in technological change beyond those revealed by studying the immediate needs, interests, problems and solutions of specific groups and social actors".

Winner (1970: 370-371) was thinking there of "deeply seated processes in society" which are for instance expressed in "structural relationships between classes" and "the attitude of mastery and domination that characterizes modern technics". He furthermore criticised the lack of an "evaluating" perspective: "an evaluative stance or any particular moral or political principles that might help people judge the possibilities that technologies present" (1979: 371)[16].

The applying of social constructivist ideas to the History of Technology has helped people to distance themselves from the old traditional approach discussed above and to develop a new one. In the referred to work on the history of technology in the Netherlands the authors see the history of technology as, for instance, a continuous process so that

---

(1971: 19). Social constructivism is heavily influenced by the history of science and sociology. The theory of the "heroic inventor" seems to be a variation of the "great man theory" apparent in other variant forms in other scientific disciplines, like e.g. in sociology, when it comes to organisation culture (the founder of a company presented as a hero, see e.g. Deal and Kennedy, see also **Note 24**).

[16] What Winner also criticises is the fact that not enough attention is given to the social consequences of technical choices, like e.g. the consequences undergone by "irrelevant" groups and the association between autonomous technology and technological determinism. Another critic of social constructivism is Radder (1992). What is also interesting is Bijker's (1995) recent revelation. After having completed a fruitful career in the field of development models he concluded that an adequate theoretical framework for the analysis of his "ensembles" was still lacking and he lobbied for a return to the old question of the consequences that technology has for society since: "The toll of academic respectability threatens to produce politico-cultural irrelevance" (p. 255).

"the role of the great inventor is placed in perspective and attention is demanded for the numerous, at first sight less spectacular, innovations and for those responsible for them" (Van Lente et al. 1992: 24)[17].

Social constructivism with its view of technological development as evolutionary and as a social process is a source of inspiration for me, but not the only one as emerges from the foundations of this study formulated here below.

Points of departure

Just like the social constructivists I am fascinated by "the mystery of the whole" (Bijker et al. 1987: 9). I share their view that everything is related to everything else and when it comes to possibly distinguishing things I am inspired by the empirical material. What accompanies that is a broad understanding of irrigation techniques or technology (for me there is no principal difference between technique and technology). Just like techniques in general irrigation techniques have four distinguishing facets:

1. irrigation works (such as weirs, canals and sluices) and infrastructure (irrigation works, collected together in systems and altogether forming a complete irrigation network)
2. the managing of irrigation works and systems (the controlling and organising of water distribution and also maintenance)
3. the activities and actions linked to the development of irrigation and management facilities (the preparing and constructing of works and the setting up of control arrangements and structures)
4. the required knowledge and skills (the technical or technological approach to irrigation works and irrigation science) (compare Van Bentum 1995: 13, 234-235 and also Diemer 1990).

In the case of irrigation technology one may therefore think of irrigation works, entire irrigation systems, the managing of that, the developing of all these infrastructural and control facilities as well as the system as a whole and the knowledge involved. Just like technology development as a whole, the developing of irrigation techniques can relate to all these aspects. When it comes to the development of irrigation techniques or, in short, the irrigation development, this may be understood to mean the creation of works and the setting up of management facilities directed at the evolving (or changing) of an entire irrigation system and its accompanying management (manifested in the expansion of the irrigated and controlled area), the changing approach to the construction and exploitation of works and the growth in knowledge. (Compare Van Bentum 1995: 13).

---

[17] The older approach is also still alive (according to Bijker 1995: 239) in Basalla (1988). Compare also with Pieterson (1993: 14) and colleagues who instead of envisaging technological development as a continual process are inclined to rather defend the "discontinuity thesis".

Figure 2.7: Transplanting of rice seedlings, Jratunseluna area (photo WR)

Figure 2.8: Harvesting sugar cane, Pemali area (photo WR)

All the referred to aspects of irrigation techniques and irrigation development will be examined in this study but for analytical (and practical) reasons I would just like to refine some of the concepts beforehand. In conformity with the social constructivist movement (but also in slight deviation from it) I follow the approach to (irrigation) technological development, which looks for divergent factors that made these developments possible or for the conditions under which the development took place. In this connection I draw on the older (deterministic) approaches insofar as I distinguish between the various factors presented as explanations for technical development: technical factors in the narrower sense of material-technical factors (irrigation facilities and management and the establishment of that), cognitive factors (knowledge of irrigation) and social factors (the colonial context). Having distinguished thus it is best to look for the conditions for (irrigation) technique development. By focusing attention on a certain aspect of technical development it becomes possible to examine in the other facets of that the extent to which this made the development possible; the other aspects may therefore be considered as qualifications for conditions. Here I am predominantly preoccupied with the development of irrigation techniques in the narrowest sense of the word (the material side) and I shall research the conditions of a cognitive and social nature that were important in all of this.[18]

The development that I focus on in this treatise does not have to do with the construction of a completely new system but rather with the changing and expanding of an existing one, namely the Javanese irrigation system (known in short as Javanese irrigation) that existed long before the Dutch set foot on Indies soil. Subsequently the system was developed with the help of Western knowledge and materials under the guidance of irrigation engineers. In that connection the term "modernisation" is used as a framework. As I see it the modernisation of a colonial society embraces all technical, social, economic, political and cultural changes that may be seen as issuing from colonial intervention. Such an all-embracing process of change was indeed continuing in the Indies. My attention will focus particularly on the relevant technical aspects, that is to say, on the introduction and expansion of Western irrigation technology. To my mind modern irrigation techniques is therefore something that is synonymous with Western irrigation techniques and what primarily interests me is the subject of modern works and infrastructure and also of a modern system in general (in short: modern irrigation).[19] In the colonial period the irrigation works that had been

[18] Knowledge can pertain to technical science but it can also include craftsmanship or non-Western knowledge. I recognise that all knowledge systems need to be dealt with "on an equal methodological footing" (Watson-Verran and Turnbull 1995: 111). However, I think that differentiating between techniques and knowledge is particularly useful in the context of modern techniques (which is what I focus on in this study) in view of the fact that there knowledge has created independence for itself in the technical sciences, which e.g. have been and are influenced by other sciences. Modern technology thus becomes "scientifically supported techniques" (Pieterson 1993: 15). When one unlinks the knowledge aspect it becomes possible to research the influence that technical science has upon technological development (and conversely to study the effect of technology upon scientific development). With regard to the differentiation between science and technical science I shall adhere here to the notion that the latter does not only relate to applied science but that it represents an independent knowledge encompassment and that the two are "intermixed" (Layton 1977: 208-210, Bijker 1995: 240-241). The search for conditions for technological development is reflected e.g. by Mumford (1967) who sees that socio-cultural conditions precede the flowering of techniques (see also Layton 1977, cf. Andriessen 1991). Van den Ende (1995) also sees with technological development a differentiation between knowledge and society. Unlike this researcher (of computer technology) I do not use any particular "model" to "explain" the development in question. While this study emphasizes the "hardware" and the "orgware" of irrigation technology, in his follow-up study Ertsen (2005) focusses on the "software" (cf. Ravesteijn 2002a, see also Ertsen and Ravesteijn 2004, 2008).

[19] See for a descriptive modernisation concept e.g. E. Weber (1976) even though his study has to do with the "modernisation of rural France". He shows that "undeveloped France was integrated into the modern world and the official culture – of Paris, of the cities" which was effected "through roads, railroads, and a money economy"

created by engineers were termed "technical" while the Javanese systems were termed "wild" (i.e. there was technical versus wild irrigation; see above). They are terms that resound in modern irrigation science. Brouwer (1991: 2) consciously uses a description from the nineteenth century when he defines "irrigation" as:

"the artificial conveying of water for the purposes of agriculture, a systematic distributing of water over the area to be irrigated and a draining away of that same water to the natural outlet routes after the water has been put to best possible use"[20].

What is perhaps most striking of all is the term "systematic". Brouwer (ibid.) means by this "a systematically created civil-technical water management system". The reference here is to what he terms "technical irrigation systems (1991: 48). Brouwer (ibid.) furthermore distinguishes two other sorts of irrigation systems known as wild and semi-technical systems. Wild systems are those that have evolved without the intervention of engineers. Semi-technical systems are ones in which some components have been replaced by engineers.[21] In view of the concept of modernisation I prefer to speak here of "modern" (rather than technical) and of "Javanese" or "traditional" (rather than wild). The accompanying term "semi-modern" is not used in this study (I shall come back to this in the **Conclusion**). The structures contemplated here are all irrigation works created by engineers (using Western methods) and in all cases I call them "modern", even where separate works are concerned that form part of what are otherwise traditional systems.[22] In the case of modern works it is not automatically presumed that they are by definition superior to traditional works. Indeed, if that were the case they would have to prove their superiority[23].

(p. xii). See for a similar description of a village in Germany Weatherford (1988) and in the Netherlands and the Indies Van den Eerenbeemt (1989). Lintsen (1992-1995) and colleagues similarly make use of the term "modernisation" in this sense when tracing Dutch technological history (Van Lente et al. 1992: 21-22).

[20] This is De Meyier's definition (1891: 1), also reiterated by Van Maanen (1924: 1).

[21] See Booth (1977) who sometimes also refers to "technical irrigation".

[22] In later colonial history it was also the term "modern" that tended to be used in connection with irrigation. In the colonial era (and even today) modern works were also referred to as permanent works in contrast to the temporary nature of Javanese works. These are terms that will be occasionally used. The term "system" was already being used by colonial engineers. I use this term to denote separate systems and also to describe the Javanese network in general. For me "system" represents a totality of material provisions. Colonial engineers also referred to "irrigation areas" which were or were not provided with permanent irrigation works and occasionally I adopt the same terminology. In that connection, however, I make more frequent use of the term "project". This familiar but somewhat anachronistic term is used in relation to plans that are to be executed or are being carried out. It is a term that reveals something about the way in which irrigation works come into being and it is the rise of this plan-wise approach that forms subject of study here. Essentially projects are of a temporary nature but with irrigation projects that temporary aspect sometimes becomes rather blurred because they tend to last a long time and are, after completion, invariably followed by other structural activities other than just the maintenance work, so that work on them never really finishes. Obviously this makes the difference between projects and "irrigation areas with permanent works" rather vague. By "irrigation works" I mean completed works or ones that are in the process of construction and this may refer to one structure (e.g. a weir) or to a whole collection of structures (i.e. an irrigation system). (See for "project" Van Doorn 1994a, see for "permanent projects" Ankum 1988 who discusses the post-colonial rehabilitation projects in Indonesia. These latter projects will be returned to in the **Epilogue**). In the case of Javanese irrigation I avoid the terms "inland" and "native" because of the possible colonial and preservational associations of these terms.

[23] Similarly, we can distinguish traditional technology history from modern technology history and colonial studies from modern studies. From what has been stated above it emerges that modern History of Technology and technology studies are less ideological which therefore makes them "better".

I shall basically support the social constructivist view of society (and will, in some respects, constrain this view) by producing insight gained from the social sciences which is particularly derived from "transactionalism" and discussions on "state formation" processes. Various groups were ultimately involved in all the colonial irrigation efforts. In the colonial writings discussed above not only engineers came into the picture but also civil servants and sugar refiners. It was pointed out that the engineers were in pursuit of power and recognition which is a normal enough phenomenon for an up and coming professional group but also, simultaneously, nothing other than a variation on the theme of the struggle of all groups to protect and advance their own interests (a kind of struggle that can be equally expected of other groups which we shall come across in the saga of colonial irrigation activities). It is something that is commonplace in the social sciences. In the field of political anthropology for example, but also within organisational sociology, much attention is given to all the groups that compete in the "arena" for the various outcomes of decision-making processes. Transactionalism, which is a social-anthropological movement offers here a useful point of departure. Boissevain (1974) gives shape and clarity to this approach.

Boissevain (1974: 231) defines the interests always pursued by people in the area of social interaction as "scarce and valued ends" pointing out that prestige and power are all part and parcel of that (p. 232). With their "self-interested action" (p. 231) people proceed to compete with each other and to seek out allies: "everywhere people compete with each other and search for allies to help them achieve their goals" (p. 232). That is how people conduct politics "for they compete directly, via friends and friends-of-friends for valued scarce resources, for prizes which form the important goals of their lives" (ibid.). Boissevain links individual action to the evolution of social order. While striving and competing people form alliances, coalitions, groups, organisations, classes and other social cooperations and all these associations put together form the fabric of society:

"Coalitions, groups, classes and institutions are composed of people who, in different ways, are bound to each other. Together they form the constantly shifting network of social relations that we call society" (1974: 233).

The (trans)action is something which, according to Boissevain, goes in a certain direction. The striving of individuals is directed towards emancipation which leads to a conflict of interests in which the status quo is at stake:

"Man, in order to emancipate himself from the constraints of his social, cultural and physical environment, attempts to bring about changes in the balances of power. Other persons, who benefit from the *status quo*, try to prevent such changes. Change and resistance to it are thus inherently related" (1974: 232-233).

The ideas of Boissevain give us more insight into the character of "groups" and "networks" thus making a (social) description and analysis of technological development easier. I shall continue to use the word "group" as a general term for social units while distinguishing "institutions" where organisations are explicitly involved. The term "institution" may, for instance, be applied when one is talking of the state and its various bodies (see below).[24]

[24] The term "coalition" is used several times in this book to denote loose associations. In line with Boissevain's ideas (and common language usage) I confine the terms "actors" and "network" to people, groups and the products of interaction. Boissevain developed his dynamic "network view" of society in reaction to the static view of the structural functionalists who conceived of society as "a system of enduring groups" (1974: 9). With technological development the network approach also seems to be more dynamic than the system approach, though in the early phases of its development the latter deviates little from the former. See for a discussion of

With Boissevain it is the term "emancipation" that comes to the fore, the notion of people freeing themselves from constricting ties. I attach to this a general and evaluating perspective in the sense intended by Wertheim (of being freed from natural and social forces, see above). That is something that fits in well with the critical tradition of Science, Technology and Society. As a theoretical concept (emancipation as a necessary tendency in history) this term has, like "modernisation", lost its impact (see, for instance, Van den Muijzenberg and Wolters 1988). There is emancipation and repression meaning, in other words, that the liberating of one group can lead to the suppression of another. Yet, the emancipation concept adopted by Wertheim can, to a limited extent, be applied here. Emancipation is, for instance, recognisable in the process of professionalisation experienced by colonial engineers (and instantly one group that had to pay the price: that of the administrators).[25]

In the earlier discussion of the colonial views of modern irrigation it was the Indies state that was considered. What was pointed out was that the role and the interests of the colonial government in the development of modern irrigation were not absolutely clear and that those were things that moreover changed over the course of time. Precisely how important technological development was to the colonial state is indicated by Headrick (1981, 1988). He shows (1981, for example on pp. 3-20) that colonialism and imperialism were partly made possible by technological innovations. When it came to the matter of exploring areas outside Europe steam ships and quinine were of central importance. It was unthinkable that these regions could ever possibly be brought under European rule without the aid of quick-firing weapons. If colonial administration was to be consolidated it would be necessary to develop communication and transport networks: navigation routes, telegraph lines and railway connections. Such infrastructural works were also created in the interests of colonial exploitation. Headrick (1988, especially on pp. 171-205) showed that free trade imperialism developed in conjunction with industrialisation and the rise of modern science and techniques. He suggests that British imperialism in India and Egypt was made possible because of the creation of modern irrigation systems. Two of the prerequisites of these projects were modern

---

Boissevain's work Verrips (1995). One of the criticisms levelled against transactionalism resides in the concentration upon "big men". Unlike the theory of the "heroic inventor" in History of Technology the "strong men paradigm" of Boissevain (and others) devotes much attention to the "disciples". I make use of the social constructivist system concept though the term "system" is chiefly used in conjunction with irrigation. Van Lente et al. (1992: 25-26) use the term "actor" in a similar way to that used here. They are alert to the position of power of an actor and to his interests but views on power formation are lacking just as are views on state formation: they conceive of the government as a sort of group. The authors also use the term "system" in the broader sense. According to them the advantage of this is that possible rivalry between techniques can in that way be better understood: social embedding lends stability to techniques. They maintain that with this system concept the differentiation between cause and effect disappears. In order to be able to properly map out technical development they furthermore use the terms "variation" (thanks to inventors), "selection" (which occurs in an environment of users, central government, physical factors and competing technology) and "diffusion" (the spreading of techniques) (Van Lente et al. 1992: 26-28).

[25] Compare with Basalla (1988) who makes sparse use of the concept of progress in conjunction with technological development. A descriptive modernisation concept is useless as an evaluating perspective. Modernisation and emancipation are things that can well be at odds, as e.g. with the various views on the whys and wherefores of modern irrigation works (sugar or rice; see in general Breman 1976). One point of departure for a new theoretical modernisation concept that could well be used in the assessing of technological development is to be found in Lemaire (1976). He points out that in cultural anthropology the "Europe centrism" that once prevailed had to make way for "cultural relativism". According to him, post-colonial westernising made the latter ideology untenable. Lemaire believes that what is needed is a new "cultural philosophy" and he presents the building blocks for that in the form of a strengths and weaknesses analysis of both Western and non-Western society. Compare also with Kothari (1980) who supplemented Alvares' notions of local development with a plea to form a new perspective of unity and uniformity at global level.

technology (in the sense of knowledge) and the development of a solid state ("inspired despotism").[26]

Any state consists of a (central) administration or a government and an administrative body which usually comprises various special services alongside of an administrative service. This entirety of institutions develops and changes within a process known as state formation. Broadly speaking, a state embraces the people (citizens) that fall under its responsibility and the relevant inhabited area (the land). The first duty of a state-in-incubation is that of demarcating its territories in relation to other peoples or countries and guarding its borders. Generally an army is required for such "external" state formation. What is first and foremost of importance for the citizen is that a monopoly be established for the exercising of violence. Rival groups cannot be tolerated. In such "internal" state formation processes a police force fulfils a useful function (as does an army in many cases). What this is all about, politically and administratively, is building up a system for the effective issuing of orders and for ensuring that this system permeates through to the right areas, to the country's citizens. Another important area of attention is economic production. When all is said and done the state is responsible for caring for its citizens which includes adopting policies to combat poverty and to "elevate" its people. Roads and other kinds of infrastructural facilities are needed and/or desired in the light of the different state tasks and creating such infrastructure is often also a task in itself.

State formation processes have been predominantly studied in Europe (see, for instance, Tilly 1975, E. Weber 1976, Elias 1972, and Boissevain and Friedl 1980). The state form that ultimately emerged from this was that of the "national state" which, according to Tilly, is characterised in the following ways: it controls a demarcated area, has a relatively centralised administration, is independent of other organisations and retains a monopoly on the exercising of violence[27]. Equally, the non-Western world was also a stage for state formation processes and one of those processes was colonial state formation[28]. The concept

---

[26] In this way Headrick (1988) supports the earlier-mentioned irrigation-for-sugar view. With his two development conditions for modern irrigation he, too, stays close to the colonial view. From the analytical stance he provides an internal factor (knowledge) and an external factor (the state). However, he stresses the importance of the role of the state. Headrick (1988: 5) lobbies for a "contextual history of technology" (in which technology is the context). The drive on the part of engineers to achieve emancipation and (the development of technology in relation to) state formation are things he fails to discuss. See for a critical discussion of Headrick's ideas A Campo (1992: 34-35, 629). There are not all that many studies available on colonial technological development in relation to state formation or other social variables. Apart from the studies referred to by Alvares, Adas and Headrick there are also the general studies of Pacey (1990 and 1992). Pacey (1992) devotes attention to the state in relation to technical progress in seventeenth and eighteenth century Europe. Compare with Etemad (2007) who modifies the role of modern technology in the European expansion following upon the Industrial Revolution.

[27] Tilly used the term "state formation" as a neutral alternative for the loaded terms "political development" or "political modernisation" (modernisation as an ideological concept!) He avoided the term "building" which also betrayed the fact that one was considering retrospectively from an end situation. Later he had difficulty with the term "national state" since this masked the differences in the developmental processes of the various European states. His alternative was therefore "consolidated state". Apart from anything else, "national" implies homogeneity and homogeneous states are by no means the rule. In that way Tilly detached himself from the "unilinear" character of state formation: there are many types of states and many ways for them to be formed. He therefore found that it would be better to speak in that connection of "transformation" rather than "formation" (Tilly 1994: 4-6). In line with all the other publications on this subject I shall retain the term "state formation".

[28] Here a little needs to be said about pre-colonial state formation. Van Setten van der Meer (1979) emphasised in his analysis of Indo-Javanese states the harmonious and rather static character of the relationship between villages (*desas*) and state administration (*kraton*). The *kraton* and the *desa* needed each other. Food and labour were supplied in exchange for protection and large-scale public works. The consequence of this was that villages remained relatively independent and retained their own irrigation techniques and control. Other authors,

"colonial state" sounds like something of a contradictio in terminis, in view of the fact that such states are – by definition – subordinate to their mother countries. Yet there are a number of authors who demonstrate that the term can be implemented and that the relationship with the colonising country is precisely one of the important characteristics. I shall limit myself here to the Indies. One of the first people to bring up the question of Indies state formation was Van Baal (1976) who was himself a former civil servant but since then a number of researchers have followed in his footsteps.

In his book on the *Koninklijke Pakketvaart Maatschappij. Stoomvaart en staatsvorming in de Indonesische archipel 1888-1914* ("Royal Package Shipping Company. Steamshipping and State Formation in the Indonesian Archipelago 1888-1914" (1992; see also A Campo 2005) A Campo describes and analyses the expansion of steam shipping in the Indies in terms of state formation. He (1992: 27) defines colonial state formation in the following way:

"- the establishing and reinforcing of real sovereignty and the actual governing of a clearly defined area of land by a foreign power;
- the striving for ultimate independence which is certainly temporarily accompanied by the retention of a political bond with the motherland;
- the striving, in the longer term, for a greater degree of legal and political equality without nevertheless wanting to, within the foreseeable future, affect the existing privileges of the foreign upper echelon and the actual social divisions".

Broadly speaking the period between 1870 and 1920 was of decisive significance for Indies state formation. The Netherlands managed to extend its political authority, which previously had been chiefly limited to Java, to cover the entire archipelago. In the process, J.B. van Heutsz made a name for himself as the "completer of the Dutch Indies" (Stapel 1941: 40). For one thing he was able to (temporarily) settle the protracted Aceh (Atjeh) war (Van 't Veer 1980). A Campo showed that steam shipping played an important part in Indies state formation. It was through the building up of its network of shipping lines that the Netherlands was able to make its power and influence extend to cover the entire archipelago.[29]

however, maintain that it was conflict and change that typified the old Javanese state and other such states (Slamet 1968, Adas 1981, H. Schulte Nordholt 1988). The kind of pre-colonial state of the type seen in South-East Asia might, according to Adas (1981), be classified as a "contest state". H. Schulte Nordholt (1988: 8-9) explains that this was what applied to the situation in Bali. In so doing, he distances himself from the "theatre state" concept introduced by Geertz to describe Bali because of its cultural wealth of ritual. We might want to ask ourselves whether the Indo-Javanese states were exponents of the "hydraulic society" model presented by Wittfogel (1957) (in which large-scale irrigation provision formed the basis for dictatorial power). Slamet (1968: 87) maintains (with the necessary reservations) that this was so but Booth (1977: 34-35) disagrees. See for an overview of the discussion on the pre-colonial state Locher-Scholten (1994 [2004]: 18-20). See for the building of new nation states Fukuyama (2005).

[29] See for further information on this process of external state expansion Van Goor (1986) and also Clemens and Lindblad (1989). See also A Campo (1986) who discusses the rise of the Royal Package Shipping Company in relation to the development of the capitalistic world economy.

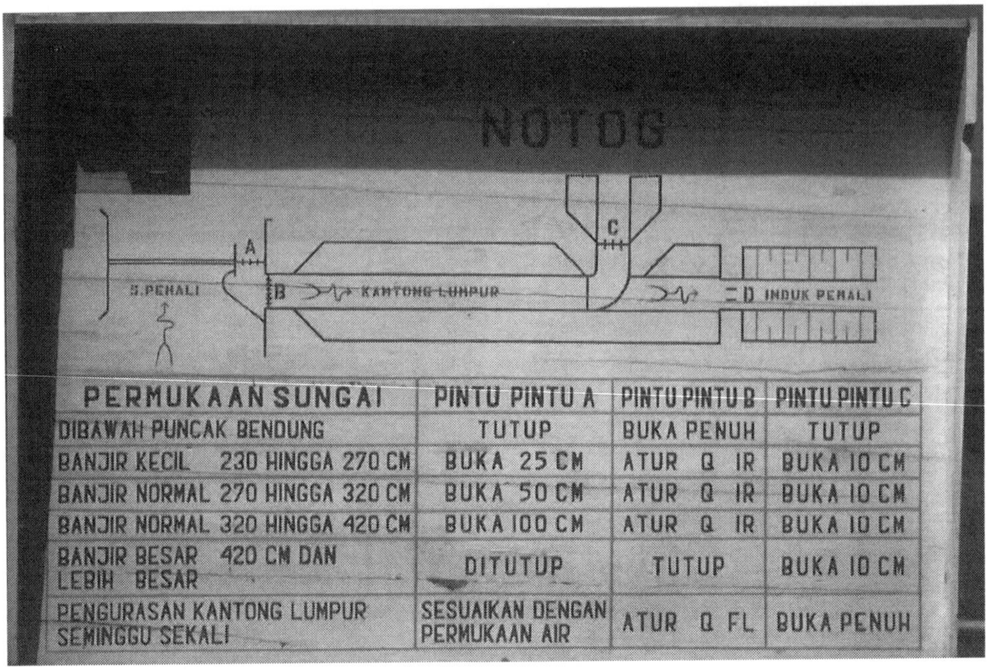

Figure 2.9: Information board showing the structure of the Pemali headworks and instructions for operation (photo WR)

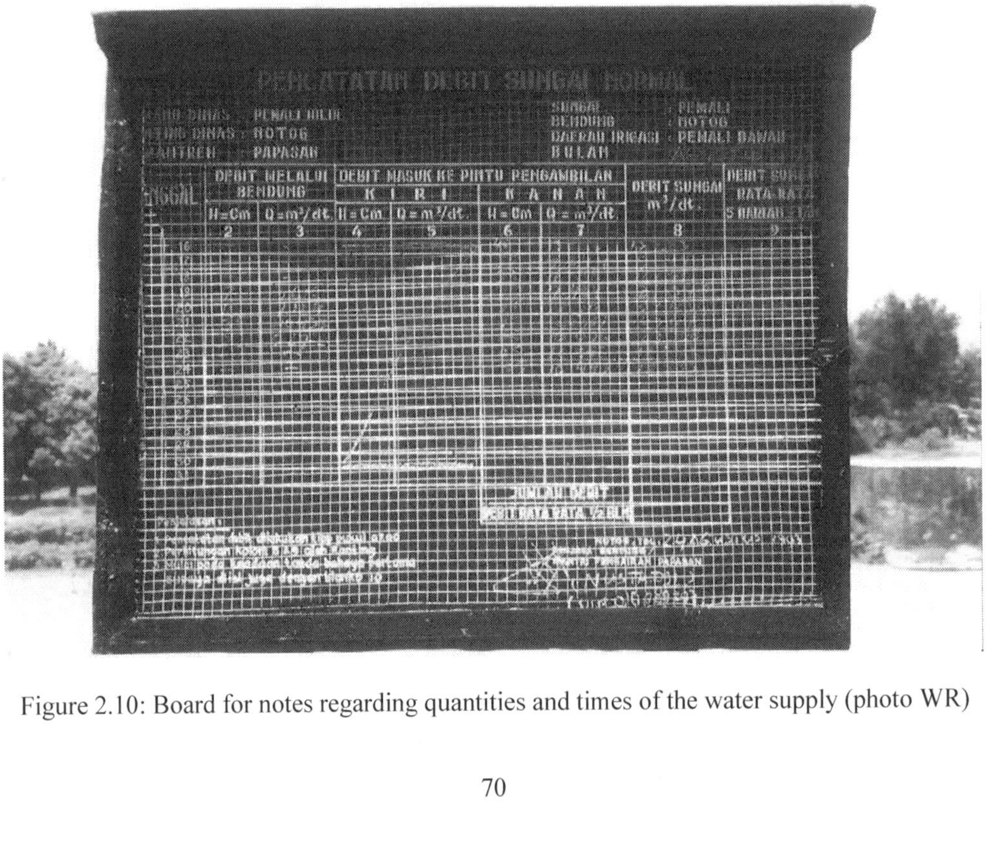

Figure 2.10: Board for notes regarding quantities and times of the water supply (photo WR)

Figure 2.11: Signs showing information about crop plan and water supply, Pemali area (photo WR)

Figure 2.12: Lockkeeper (*Mantri*) with family and neighbours, Pemali area (photo WR)

Indies state formation furthermore involved the organisation of the administration (the internal side of the process). The person who headed the colonial administration was the Governor-General. He it was who led the colonial government, known as the *gouvernement*, and he operated upon the orders of and in collaboration with the Dutch ruling power including the Minister of the Colonies (in passing we shall see that the coloniser had its own state formation which thus altered the organisation of the ultimate responsibility). The Governor-General was also in charge of the Civil Service in which the Residents were key figures. The tasks of this administrative service changed over the course of time and that applied also to its position. Later new tasks and specialised services were introduced, one of which was the irrigation service. Van den Doel (1994) describes and analyses the development of the Civil Service, which he related to the process of state formation. In his publication *De stille macht* ("The Silent Power", pp. 445-446) he outlines four different phases[30]:

a. The first phase is that of the early colonial state. The state has a monopoly of power and it exploits the "indigenous" society in the interests of the mother country. The administrative body developed in this connection is of a simple character.
b. Subsequently a process of modernisation emerges. The state passes on the baton of exploitation to private entrepreneurs. On the basis of idealistic considerations and in the interests of these entrepreneurs the state makes an effort to inform and school the population and to provide infrastructure. An extensive and specialised administrative bureaucracy is created.
c. The third phase is characterised by a striving for joint involvement in administrative matters, both on the part of the European and the indigenous population and by the state taking advantage of this.
d. Finally an independent state is established which just becomes another in a series of modern nation states.

Two of the groups that were involved in the state formation process were the engineers and the civil servants but they both had different interests. The extending of the intervention of engineers was something that had its consequences for the work of the civil servants. Further information on this is provided by Van Doorn (1994a) who was referred to earlier. He draws a picture of the modernising of the colonial state in which civil servants and engineers found themselves forfeiting and gaining power respectively. This led to the development of a (limited) technocracy.

The administrative structure changed and so too did the policy. The Cultivation System and the Ethical Policy, both of importance to irrigation in different ways, have already been discussed. Other forms of policy were the free trade politics and the crisis policy (see **Chapters 6 and 10**). There was, in fact, one goal of administration and policy that never changed and that was the "tranquil quiet" of Multatuli. Hüsken (1988: 255) formulated this sentiment in the following way:

"During the course of its history Java has been exposed to a mixed medley of rulers who, apart from being interested in rice production, seemed to be obsessed with questions of order and safety, from the King of Wengker referred to at the beginning of this chapter at the moment when he commanded his subjects "to be orderly" to the colonial regime with its fascination for "peace and order". Indeed, it seemed that the ultimate ideal of each

[30] In so doing he based his ideas on Rokkan (1975: 570-573) who differentiated four phases in the development process of European nation states which were characterised respectively by: 1. the establishing of a power monopoly, 2. a process of identification designed to melt the population to a national whole, 3. the striving of the population for equality and participation in the political process, 4. the redistribution of power.

administrator was to be able to report that "the peace ... in this region has not been disturbed".

In this connection it was intimated above by Happé (1939) that one of the driving forces behind the emergence of irrigation works was "peace and order".

State formation is something that also goes hand in hand with ideologies so that the state is able to rationalise and legitimise its existence. The civilising mission expressed in the Indies through, for instance, the Ethical Policy was just one such ideology. In this connection Adas (1989: 203) had the following to say:

"The small numbers of Europeans who actually governed colonized peoples relied on their superior technology not only for communications and military clout that made the ongoing administration of vast areas possible but also for the assurance that they had the 'right', even the 'duty', to police, arbitrate disputes, demand tribute, and insist on deference".

One specific predominant ideology within the Javanese context was the ideology of wet rice cultivation. Dove (1985) argues that this was not better, that is to say, more productive, than dry rice cultivation. The fact that there was a transition to irrigated agriculture was down to the fact that traditional Javanese rulers had a preference for that because it raised production levels. Wet rice cultivation was more intensive which meant that people lived in denser concentrations. Checks were thus easier to carry out than when the population was more dispersed. The image that fitted this was that wet rice cultivation, as opposed to dry cultivation, made more rational use of labour and land. According to Dove this latter assumption was wrong. The colonial administrators took on board the old Javanese prejudices. The dry method of farming was labelled "overcropping". Consequently, the Cultivation System was applied to the areas where irrigated rice cultivation already existed. Sugar became an important cash crop but rubber was not. Dove (1985: 21) underlines that the difference between both crops was:

"due not to the agronomic requirements of one crop versus another, nor to the greater marketability of one crop versus another, but rather to greater susceptibility to more intensive, larger scale, and more profitable (for the government) systems of cultivation".

The idealisation of wet rice cultivation was not something that was linked to modern techniques but it did, also because of the decision to make sugar cane a cash crop, bring it to the attention of the state[31]. As has been mentioned, the colonial state not only had ideological ideas about rice growing (and the *desa*) but also about modern irrigation. The difference, however, was that the object of that idealisation was not a Javanese phenomenon. Even though the Javanese perhaps had good rice production levels and close-knit village

[31] Another dominance ideology, also not founded upon modern technology, is to be found in Breman (1980). Just like Dove he reveals that colonial rule leads to a rift in the conceptions of the state between law and reality. He views the notion of the *desa* (1980: 42, 3) as being an "isolated, self-sufficient, tightly-integrated and homogeneous system", as being an example of "invention of tradition" in the framework of "an expanding system of control from the top of society". Breman (1980: 42) goes a step further when he asserts: "Once it had been created and used as a cornerstone for policy execution by the colonial state, the desa system subsequently received ideological affirmation, especially the support of the Adat Law school during the Ethical period at the beginning of the 20th century". Compare this with Hüsken (1988) who shows that the social differentiation of the town that he studied differed over the course of time but that there was never a situation of homogeneity. Scott (1996) indicated that the state also developed "simplifications" and presented e.g. the view that a forest consists of *Normalbaüme* ("normal trees") which makes modern, economically answerable forestry possible.

communities their irrigation techniques were, in the eyes of the ruling power, defective. Modern techniques were designed to correct this weak point bringing with them progress and civilisation.

The technical aspects and the role of (irrigation) engineers in the colonial state formation process have so far been given little attention. Headrick (1981, 1988) reveals an interesting pattern of knowledge, techniques and the colonial state but he does not discuss the emancipation of engineers and state formation (see **Note 26**). Van den Doel (1994: 234) devotes just one paragraph to the rise of the Indies Public Works Organisation in his extensive study of the history of the Civil Service – a history that he more or less equates with the process of state formation. A Campo (1992) does indicate a clear relationship between technique and the state. However, his study dwells particularly on the history of a company, the Royal Package Shipping Company, that is able to thank the introduction of one innovation (the steam ship) for its existence. It would appear that steam navigation and state formation were closely and interactively intertwined. Van Doorn (1994a) devotes attention to the rise of the engineers in relation to civil servants and state formation but there is no big role in all of that for technology. Other groups that he gives attention are railway engineers and sugar producers.[32]

In short, there are various points of overlap between state formation and (irrigation)-technological development in general and in Indies society in particular while little is known about the connection between the two. This offers a good point of departure and a fruitful perspective for the study of the development of modern irrigation in Java in relation to the process of Indies state formation.[33]

From epic to research

Questions arising from the colonial and post-colonial views

The colonial conceptualisation of modern irrigation development is one of technological triumph and social progress. Aided by technological science and the Indies government, hard-working engineers were seen as being enormously successful in the modernising of what were viewed as defective Javanese irrigation systems. As we have seen, this was an image that fitted in with traditional technological history in which engineers, goaded on by their thirst for power and recognition, produced an ideologically tinted presentation of things which matched the past prevailing view of a technology based progress ethic. There was also the accompanying uncritical and disparaging way in which non-Western technology and culture was viewed.

---

[32] Ample attention to engineering and state formation, of course, in my 1997 dissertation. In addition, Ravesteijn and Kop (2008) extensively discuss the interaction between the development of civil engineering and state formation, both in the Indies as in Indonesia.

[33] Although that is not strictly necessary the government was according to Brouwer (1991) involved by definition in the creation and control of "technical irrigation systems" thus also in my "modern irrigation". A state formation perspective is, in the colonial context, especially when it comes to the matter of irrigation, more fruitful than other perspectives like a "class perspective" (see the criticism discussed on Winner's social constructivism). Such a perspective is e.g. presented by Dickson (1983). A technological-historical approach with plenty of thought for structure and culture is given by Pieterson (1993). In their *Maatschappijgeschiedenis van drie industriële revoluties* ("Social History of Three Industrial Revolutions") the authors of this study contemplate technological developments in relation to social problems, social relations and legitimising. This study builds on the viewpoint presented by Bertels (1973) who connected the social sciences and history (including History of Technology) by distinguishing between "structure" and "events". See for a critique of this Lintsen (1982), cf. Van den Ende (1994).

As we have seen in **Chapter 1**, the colonial view of modern irrigation and its emergence gives rise to a series of questions concerning the failures, Javanese irrigation, the role of other non-technical parties and the relationship between irrigation and the state. Post-colonial Indonesia writing does not offer adequate answers to these questions. Though modern Indonesia studies do provide us with a certain amount of supplementary information they partly echo colonial views while partly at the same time introducing new types of one-sidedness. Generally speaking these studies reinforce the questions we have in relation to colonial conceptions but they also give rise to new questions like: what was modern irrigation chiefly intended to support, was it for sugar or for rice cultivation?

If all these questions are to be answered then research needs to be done into the development of modern irrigation in colonial Java and attention needs to be paid to the successes and failures attached to the creation of modern irrigation works, also in relation to society, and to the negative and positive sides of Javanese irrigation, to irrigation engineers and other involved parties and finally also to the possible guiding influences of colonial administration and, in general, to the relationship which existed between (irrigation-)technical and political developments. Such research should lead to a view of colonial irrigation development that not only consists of a consecutive row of technological triumphs and social progress and which is not exclusively Western-oriented and engineer-directed and which does not ultimately present a too simplified view of the role of the government. Furthermore such research should provide clarity on the way in which irrigation development and the development of the state (state formation) were interwoven.

This study reports on precisely that kind of research. My endeavour will be to remove the rise of modern irrigation from the atmosphere of bombastic rhetoric so familiar to colonial discourse and to present it in a more realistic light. Just to dampen expectations it should be emphasised that not all the questions raised above will be extensively answered. I shall, in fact, focus on three main questions. Though focussed on the first two themes formulated in the **Prologue** (irrigation and state development), they give rise to discussions of the other themes (rising engineers and ideology) as well.

The three main questions

1. How precisely did modern irrigation develop in colonial Java?

What is involved here is a description of the development of modern irrigation in Java, by far the main scene of the Dutch colonial irrigation efforts in the Indies, in the broader sense. The matters I shall focus on will be the creation of works and the construction of modern irrigation infrastructure in general, the structure of modern irrigation control forms, the changes appearing in all of this and the growing body of knowledge on irrigation. All these facets will be dealt with but not to the same degree and extent. I will look especially at the construction of works and at the modern systems created as well as at the way in which irrigation engineers tackled all of this. The evolving of control provisions is something that will come in second place. The way in which knowledge grew is also something that will not be dwelt on extensively. There I shall examine the salient elements (and not the intricacies of irrigation science and engineering education) including the (scientific) approach. Thus a first (clear) defining constraint of this study is given[34]. When it comes to the matter of modernisation in

[34] As far as the development of knowledge goes (and therefore also irrigation as a technological science or as a sub-discipline of civil engineering) it would be interesting to study the old manuals (like those of De Meyier 1891 and Van Maanen 1924, 1931) as well as the lecture notes (or readers) produced by colonial Professors in irrigation engineering (or Indies Hydraulic Engineering) of the day both at the Technical College in Delft and at the Technical College in Bandung. Furthermore there are the lecture notes of C.A. Begemann, J. Haringhuizen,

the field of irrigation I shall go on the figures produced in this chapter but these statistics will be supplemented and specified in a number of ways. Furthermore, certain of the effects that modern irrigation had on socio-economic developments will be discussed but not in any great depth.

2. What were the conditions underlying the development of modern irrigation in colonial Java?

This is a general question of an analytical nature aimed at mapping out just what was needed to modernise Javanese irrigation and at tracing the factors that made irrigation development possible. In answering this question I shall make the modernising of irrigation infrastructure and the way in which that went the central focus. In order to limit the myriad factors I shall concentrate on the conditions that come to the fore or the matters that are at least suggested in the various literature on the social development of technology, that is to say, conditions in the area of science, technology and society (predominantly knowledge and society). The indications of this discussed in the colonial literature looked at in **Chapter 1** were: failing Javanese systems, engineers and their technological science and the political significance of irrigation works. Suggestions are also made in relevant post-colonial studies, one of which being that the engineering profession was coming into its own and another being the ideologies that underlined the importance of technology. The explicit conditions mentioned by Headrick (1988) are, a strong state and modern technological knowledge which moreover emphasises the role of imperialism (as revealed, in the case of the Indies, in the sugar industry). Colonial state formation turned out to have different facets – apart from the establishing of colonial rule it also had to do with the creating of a state (and it included the formation of the Public Works Organisation) as well as policy and again ideology – each of which could have been of importance in its own right. I shall research all these (possible) conditions and, in so doing, I shall adhere to a specific development perspective: I shall see how the conditions developed (by for instance concentrating upon the processes of professionalisation, knowledge acquisition and state formation). With this question comes a second constraint of this study which means that I shall focus mainly on modern irrigation and that I shall only consider Javanese irrigation in relation to Western methods.[35]

3. How did the development of modern irrigation in Java and the development of the Indies state influence each other?

What is of importance here is the interaction between state formation and irrigation development. I am not just interested in the condition-creating nature of the state for irrigation development and how that changed over the course of time but also conversely in the question: was the development of modern irrigation decisive for the process of change seen in the state? In this question attention is directed particularly towards the engineers and towards their contribution to the state formation process. There is a third constraint that emanates from this point. As far as the groups involved in irrigation activities go I shall only examine those that were of importance in this connection, in other words, the Public Works engineers and the Civil Service employees. Other actors, like for example the sugar producers and the actual

---

H.C.P. de Vos and C.W. Weijs to be examined, all of which are kept in the Haringhuizen-Schoemaker Collection in the National Archives of the Netherlands in The Hague. Much of this has been done by Ertsen (2005).

[35] For more details on traditional irrigation the reader is once again referred to Van Setten van der Meer (1979) and Christie (2001).

population, will only be considered insofar as their influence is reflected by engineers, civil servants and the government itself: in other words, these actors will not be given separate attention[36]. Ideology is also discussed in this connection, especially the part played by ideological factors in irrigation development in relation to colonial state formation.

The approach

One way of tackling this study is by viewing technological development as a continuous and evolutionary process with heroes and pioneers and gods of a lower order as well. It is a process with a cognitive aspect in the form of knowledge accumulation. Moreover, there is one very important social aspect, which is that engineers create technology which is how networks or socio-technical systems with other relevant groups come into being. In all of this we see people and groups as actors in pursuit of their own interests who thus become entangled in power struggles. In irrigation development civil servants formed one such other group. Historical technological development might be viewed in terms of modernisation. In the case of irrigation development in Java that had to do with the technological aspect of the emergence of modern Indies society. What is important in a colonial context is to see how a modern (colonial) state developed. In the Indies this took the form of a central administration that also had a welfare policy and so made use of a specialised administrative organisation which included an irrigation service. In the process of Indies state formation Civil Service employees formed a very important participating group, just as did Public Works engineers. It was the *gouvernement* which, in its capacity as the highest administrative body, gave form and direction to this process.

In this study most attention is devoted to the irrigation engineers who were the first people involved in the irrigation efforts. There are two processes that are of importance in this connection: the process of expertise formation in the technical-scientific sense (since engineers acquired ever-more knowledge) and professionalisation (the rise of the engineering profession; the first process is that of professionalisation in the narrowest sense). As far as knowledge-acquisition goes I remain, as indicated, global in my approach. With professionalisation I will chiefly look at the way in which the irrigation service developed, especially, from 1866, the Department of Civil Public Works. This service was occupied with the creation of irrigation works but it was also the organisation through which the engineers sought to defend their interests (for more attention to professionalisation and all other kinds of interesting facts on civil engineers, like for example their backgrounds, the reader is again referred to Van Doorn 1994a).

The Tangerang Works with its massive weir in the Cisadane river forms one of the four cases examined here in order to give a picture of irrigation development in Java. The second case study derives from the activities of the founder, Lamminga, in the form of the Pemali Works. I shall also be looking at a project that turned into a big blunder: the already referred to Solo Valley Works. Finally, the pioneers will be mentioned in connection with the building of the weir in the Sampean, which is the oldest situation examined here and which constitutes the first of the Sampean Works. These four cases were selected on the basis of the following criteria:

[36] In connection with his comments on the need to write about the history of irrigation in the Indies (see above) Boomgaard wrote (1987: 71) that if that was to happen "a large number of pages will have to be dedicated to the clashing interests of peasants and estate companies". In the present study that is not what is of uppermost importance. Those who devote attention to the sugar producers are Ter Hofstede and Santbrink (1979), Van Doorn (1994a) and Van Schaik (1986).

a. The works had to, of course, typify the development of modern irrigation as a whole and for a certain period within that era in particular. In order to find such cases I looked first at the works that the engineers in question found important or, to put it more neutrally, at works that were given much publicity by engineers. I wanted to have "monuments of colonial technology" but I was not only interested in major feats. I was also interested in works which might be termed less successful but which had nevertheless drawn much attention. As far as the monumental character of works was concerned I allowed myself to be influenced by my own travel experiences. In these respects the cases selected could be said to have scored higher than others. The importance of three of these works has really already emerged from what has been explained earlier in this and the previous chapter. Only the Sampean weir remained undiscussed but in view of the fact that it was the "oldest" modern work – as will emerge later – it drew the necessary attention.
b. The first criterion automatically led to large works, immediately bringing with it one particular limitation. Before these works came into use a decade had usually very soon passed by. The amount of research work per case was therefore great which was why only a limited number of situations could be examined. Hence the reason that I arrived at the number of four.
c. In order to be able to say something about the whole of Java the works also had to be geographically distributed over the whole area. That was why I stuck to the rather obvious East, Central and West Java divisions (the most important places being, respectively, Batavia (presently, Jakarta), Semarang and Surabaya).[37]
d. To facilitate a link with state formation the cases all had to fit into a broad periodisation of colonial history. In that connection I first stuck to a popular division based on colonial policy (the Cultivation System, 1830-1870; free trade imperialism, 1870-1900; the Ethical Policy, 1900-1942 [actually till approximately 1930]; and the crisis policy [following the 1929 Wall Street Crash] of the 1930s), but I later replaced that by a more rough distinction on the basis of the above literature on state formation (early colonial state, 1816-1870/90; transition period, 1870/90-±1920; the modern colonial state, ±1920-1942)[38]. With the new division I was also able to meet the history of the cases. The works were furthermore used to segregate the various phases. Further information on these four cases and the criteria abided by is given in **Table 2.1**.

When it comes to the matter of the selecting of the various cases, various points can be made. The most important question is undoubtedly whether it is possible to clearly sketch the development of modern irrigation in Java (and to relate that to state formation) on the bases of the four – that is to say, precisely these four – particular cases. In this study I hope to make that plausible[39].

---

[37] Just like the way in which the works were chosen, the option to examine Java was influenced by the material available: that was where modern irrigation began, the Outlying Regions were only considered later on. The works constructed on the other islands actually received little attention from engineers (except in the case of Van der Meulen 1940). A second geographical limitation, the choice to focus on what was termed "government lands", issued from the material available for a similar sort of reason. Therefore, except for a few references, no attention will be devoted to the Principalities of Yogyakarta and Surakarta. A third limitation – also emanating from the material – was the fact that private estates had to be excluded (except for where they happened to become state-owned areas such as in the Tangerang plain).

[38] Discussion can especially be focused on the question of when the state turned towards modernisation. Depending on their various angles of approach, authors take a point somewhere between 1850 and 1890 (see e.g. Van den Doel 1994: 21 and A Campo 1992: 28-29, cf. Locher-Scholten 1994 [2004]: 5 ff.).

[39] The limited nature of the material will lend the conclusions a somewhat "orientational" character (see Blok 1977: 73 ff. and for an example, Wolf 1969). See for a justification of the four case choices **Appendix I**. Works other than the four referred to works will be focused on in boxes.

Table 2.1 The four cases[40]

State formation	Period	Case
Early colonial state *Cultivation System	1816-1870/90 1830-1870	Sampean Works *10,500 hectares *East Java *1832-1887
Transition period *Free trade imperialism *Ethical Policy	1870/90-±1920 1870-1901 1901-1930	Pemali Works *30,800 hectares *Central Java *1889-1910 Solo Valley Works *156,100 hectares *East Java *1881-1917
Modern colonial state *Crisis policy	±1920-1942 1930-1942	Tangerang Works *54,600 hectares *West Java *1916-1942

This monograph provides empirical material on the development of modern irrigation in colonial Java which thus means that it contributes to a more balanced view of matters. The current study does not have a pure technological-historic objective; it also seeks to contribute to the studying of technological development in general. It will first aim to achieve this by presenting material on a theme which, up until now, had not been thoroughly examined (colonial technological development) from an original angle (state formation). In the second place current technological development insights will be backed up with new theoretical views (derived from transactionalism and state formation theories) and the practicality of this combined approach will be tested by analysing irrigation development in Java. Thirdly and following upon the ideological contextualisation of the colonial view, this study will indicate and argue how the ideologies of technological optimism and faith of progress permeated colonial irrigation engineering. Finally, this book will provide historical background information to present-day issues in the field of irrigation in Indonesia, which means that it will also have practical implications.

[40] The indicated works duration relates to the period of main activity. In that connection it is not only the construction period that is referred to but also other activities such as project preparation. Exact information on this is given in the case descriptions. See for a fifth case Ravesteijn (2000).

I

INGENUITY AND AUTHORITY

1830 – 1885

3

'Despite failures, congratulations to the pioneers'

The weir in the Sampean

> Whenever we encounter an artifact, no matter what its age or provenance, we can be certain that it was modeled on one or more preexisting artifacts (Basalla 1988: 209).

The history of the weir in the Sampean takes us back in time to the first half of the nineteenth century. At that time the engineer C. van Thiel had been sent out there by the Indies government to build a dam in the river. According to the available historical data this was the first piece of irrigation-related engineering in Java. It was thus also the first irrigation work to be able to lay claim to the predicate "modern". In the general irrigation works overviews regularly published by the Indies Department of Civil Public Works in its annual report (see, for instance, *Verslag BOW* ["Civil Public Works Report", 1910: 2-5 and 1925: 2-7) mention was made of two works that had been constructed with the help of Dutch technological know-how and which had preceded the Sampean weir construction. The two works were the *Oosterslokkan* and the *Westerslokkan* canals constructed under the auspices of Buitenzorg in the eighteenth century (see, for example, Thal Larsen 1932: 18, Rietveld 1932: 278, *Encyclopaedie* ["Encyclopedia"] Vol. I 1917: 290-291). The first canal connected the river Ciliwung with the Batavia, the heart of the Indies possessions of the *Vereenigde Oostindische Compagnie* ("United East Indies Company" or "Dutch East Indies Company", abbreviated to *VOC*). The Javanese head of Kampong Baru – a community that constituted part of the Buitenzorg estate – started the construction work in 1739. With the support of the Governor-General, Van Imhoff, these interested landowners managed to complete this canal between 1749 and 1753.

The canal was in the first place designed to serve as a waterway for the conveyance of products. It was only in the second place that it was seen as an irrigation source for the surrounding land. The great difference in ground levels created insurmountable problems for navigation which was why irrigation became the sole objective. The authorities drew up rules and regulations for the tapping of water and in 1777 an engineer was put in charge of the works. That engineer was Siven Johan Wimmercrantsz. It was the council of *Heemraden der Bataviasche Ommelanden* ("Water Reeves of the Batavian Possessions") of the day that had ultimate responsibility for the works. Because of the waterworks the Ciliwung had too little water to circulate in the canals of Batavia in the dry season and keep them navigable. This state of affairs was what gave rise to the creation of the *Westerslokkan* which connected the Ciliwung with another river, the Cisadane. Wimmercrantsz put forward his plan and began to execute it in 1776. This canal was also designed for irrigation purposes. Over the course of time, though, the original objective was forgotten and the number of subsidiary canals created increased. Because of this, the *Oosterslokkan* became one of the most important irrigation thoroughfares in the Residency of Batavia.

Neither canal was, in the first place, intended for irrigation purposes[1]. The weir in the Sampean was, however, created for irrigation purposes. In line with the favourable tone of other articles of the day on modern irrigation (see **Chapter 1**) this was a fact that Rietveld (1932: 278) was proud to present in his "A hundred years of the Sampean Weir":

"the sending out of the engineer known as Van Thiel in 1932 [may] be viewed as the first step made by the government along a path which, within the space of a hundred years, would lead to an entire extensive irrigation network throughout Java" (cf. Thal Larsen 1932: 18).

The dam created by van Thiel was the first in a whole series of structures to be built by colonial engineers in the Sampean for usefully implementing water as well as for controlling the river (see **Figure 3.2**). It was not always plain sailing, though. Wisdom was something that fluctuated. If we study the history of this the underlying drama becomes all too clear, certainly in the light of the simple solution that was later to follow all the trials and tribulations: that of a natural rock threshold in the river. A report of this is given below[2].

Figure 3.1: The weir in the Sampean with drainage sluice
(photo A. Hillebrand, from: Rietveld 1932)

[1] Another canal that linked the Cisadane with Batavia was the *Mookervaart* ("Mooker channel"). That canal was dug in 1681. See for all these canals **Chapter 9**.

[2] Sources: *Verslag BOW* (1895), Rietveld (1932) and *Bladzijden* ("Pages") (1914 and 1915). Just like Rietveld, the editors of the *Waterstaats-Ingenieur* ("Public Works Engineer") referred triumphantly in "Pages" to the Sampean weir developments. From a glorious present (plenty of funds to draw on, the quick approval of designs) people looked back to the "enormous effort and care that had previously been put into the creation of irrigation works of significance" (*Bladzijden* 1914: 151). The fact that over the course of time much had gone wrong only underlined the tenacity of the pioneers. The development of the Sampean weir was something that was also fully explored by Vlugter (1946) (on the basis of Rietveld 1932). Reports on the activities may be found in the *Koloniaal Verslag* ("Colonial Report").

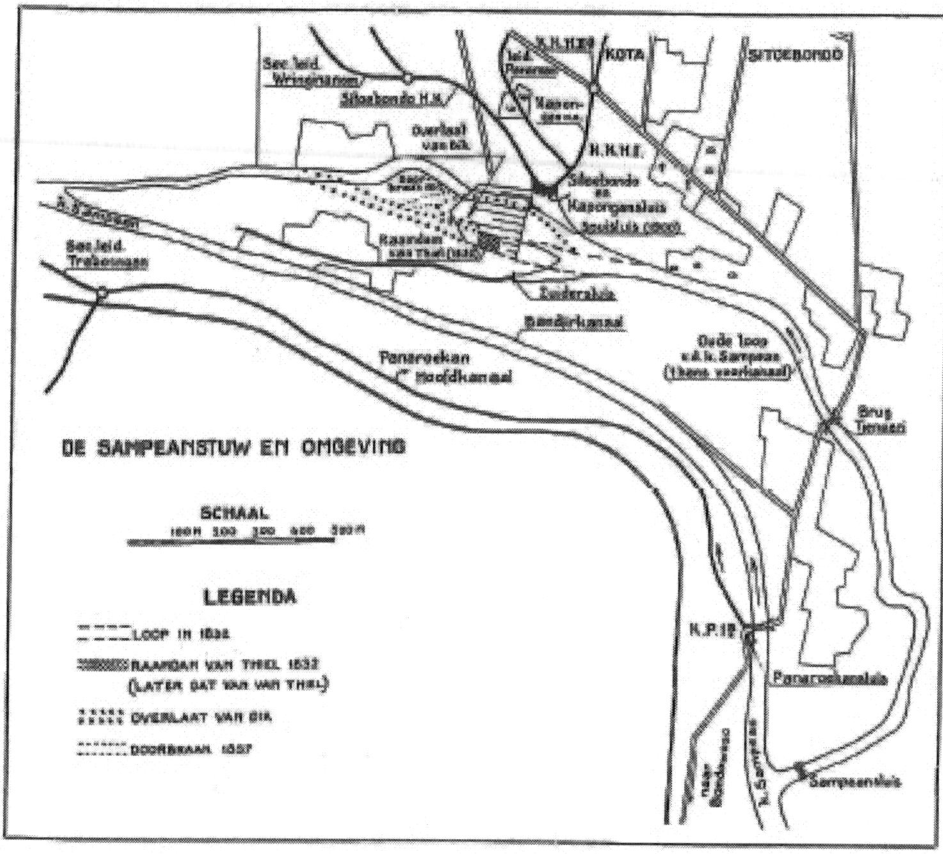

Figure 3.2: Map of the work area in the Sampean delta (from: Rietveld 1932)

The first dams

Van Thiel's framework dam

The Sampean is a river that flows through the former Residency of Besuki. It flows northwards ending in the Straits of Madura. Besuki was the most eastern Residency of Java. In colonial times the area was known as the "Javanese back of beyond" and, to a large extent, it belonged to what were known as the "newly reclaimed areas" (*Bladzijden* 1914: 151). It was an area characterised by explosive population growth. By the end of 1905 it had some 970,000 inhabitants, many of whom originated from the island of the same name across the Straits of Madura. The chief source of income in the region was agriculture, an industry that was not unfamiliar in Java at that time. Apart from cultivating rice, the farmers also grew maize and tobacco plants. These products were grown for own consumption. The ground was fertile and also suitable for the cultivation of sugar cane. The first sugar refineries, which were constructed by Dutch entrepreneurs, date from the first half of the nineteenth century. By the end of 1914 there were 10 such refineries. The other marketable crops being produced at that time were tobacco (34 companies), coffee and rubber. (*Encyclopaedie* Vol. I 1917: 278-9)[3].

[3] Compared with other crops the sugar industry remained modest in Besuki (see Booth 1988: 76, 79 table). The

The Sampean basin covers around 1200 square kilometres (De Meyier 1920: 80). Not very far from the estuary, some two to three kilometres to the south of the place Situbondo dams had already been created in the river before 1820. With the water that was forced upwards it became possible to supply the surrounding plains with water. The area supplied was probably around 13,600 *bouws*[4]. Later the point was redirected to a place near to Situbondo. The dams were Javanese made and presumably of the sort described in a later account as being made of branch bundles "held together and pressed together by palm trunks" (De Meyier 1891: 228). These dams kept being washed away and so had to be reconstructed.

In 1832 engineer Van Thiel built a more permanent dam at the place where the traditional one had once stood. The plaque decorating a section of the surrounding wall of the present weir reminds us of this glorious fact. The text makes mention of the "interim civil engineer" and conveys also that it was J.F. de Bruyn Prince, Resident of Besuki and Banyuwangi[5], who laid the first stone. Van Thiel's dam was made up of a framework of heavy *jati* wood beams[6] filled with river stones, hence the name "framework dam" for this particular type of dam. The dam was 45 metres long, eight metres high, 23 metres wide at its base and nine metres wide at the top. The amount of *jati* wood that went into making the dam was possibly around 400 cubic metres. As far as finding all the necessary material and required labour was concerned, Van Thiel could rely on the support of the Resident who instructed the population to provide both these things free of charge by providing what was known as statutory or forced labour, a form of corvée service[7]. (See **Figures 3.3 and 3.4**).

Sampean delta is still a sugar growing area where sugar trains, dating from the colonial era, transport the cane from the fields to the refineries. While I was in the area I heard of the existence of some four such refineries and I also visited several of them, one of which dated from 1820.

[4] 13,600 *Bouws* represents the size of the later irrigation area, excluding the extension made possible by the extensive irrigation works created around the turn of the century (see below in this same chapter). One *bouw* = 0.7 hectare.

[5] Banyuwangi was really a separate Residency. In 1881 it was made a Regency of Besuki. (*Encyclopaedie* Vol. I 1917: 144).

[6] *Jati* wood, alternatively known as teak. "Jati wood which, particularly because of its prevalence in Java has become a popular wood sort can, because of its qualities, be used in very versatile ways in the ship-building industry, for public works and rail construction, in house-building and for many other purposes. In Java it is also the commonest sort of furniture wood. Few other wood sorts can beat jati wood for its firmness, strength and durability and, provided suitable tools are used, it is easy to work" (*Encyclopaedie* Vol. I 1917: 616).

[7] It was necessary to resort to forced labour because the phenomenon of contractors was (virtually) unheard of in those days. People simply followed the instructions given by Van Thiel who, apart from being the weir's designer, was also the director of works.

Excursus 3.1 Constructing a framework dam

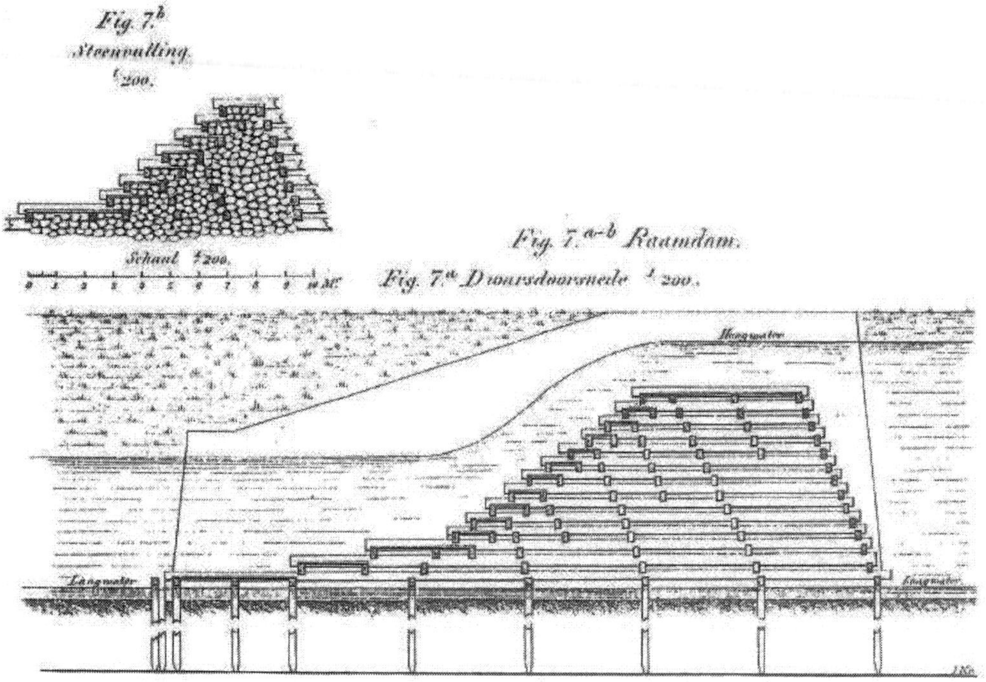

Figure 3.3: A framework dam (from: De Meyier 1891)

Exactly how such a framework dam was made is explained by the irrigation expert De Meyier (1891: 231-233; see ***Figure 3.3****). It was not necessary to divert or dam up the river. What was a prerequisite was the low water of the dry period, at least for the establishing of the foundations. The building commenced with the making of cemented land-abutments between which "post lines were hammered into the river" (p. 231).*

"The post rows in which the posts are placed side by side for 2 to 2.5 metres are positioned at 4 metre distances, middle to middle, and are a little closer at the bottom end. They are so dispersed that the end posts are in line with the land-abutment edges" (ibid.)

The posts formed a level surface upon which further building could be based. This was done with the use of foundation beams (i.e. traves). These traves were positioned in the direction of the dam, in other words in a direct line with the flow of the river where they were attached to the posts by means of tongue and groove connections and plunged as deep as possible into the water. If the water flow remained minimal then it would be possible to immediately sink a row of vertical dam planks into the riverbed but if the flow was too great this would create too much upward pressure. In such cases the plank placing would be delayed and in the meantime work would continue on the first framework dam section.
The framework was constructed as follows. Crossbeams would be placed on top of the traves (in the water flow direction). These would be "notched over the traves and fastened with jag bolts" (p. 232). The distance between these beams would vary (depending on the "water pressure") between 0.60 and 2.50 metres. On the crossbeams further beams would be placed in the direction

of the traves and a second layer of crossbeams would be introduced. The work would progress in this fashion until the required framework height was reached. Until such a time dam planks could be sunk after several layers had been constructed. As work progressed on building the framework and making it ever higher so the space in the middle would be filled with stones from the river or with rubble.
As the framework grew higher the beams that were consistently placed in the direction of the dam were not piled directly on top of each other but were instead staggered to ensure that the bolt connections were not completely aligned. This meant that as the dam got higher it also became narrower. The downstream slope was made more gentle than the upstream slope. The holes formed in the process were filled with planks. In this connection De Meyier reported the following:

"The slope facing downstream is steeper and because the stone filling cannot at that point be directly exposed to the effect of the water, the consecutive receding traves between the crossbeams have solid planks nailed into them, the far end of which are buried in the body of the dam and held in place by the largest pieces of stone. The water thus gradually trickles down a series of steps which effectively reduces much of its force while the silt carried by the river slowly serves to close all the spaces between the stones" (p. 232).

According to J.A. Krajenbrink, the engineer who was an authority in the field of framework dams, this gradual waterfall process made it unnecessary to create a fascine work layer (i.e. to reinforce the riverbed against water impact). It was thought that a second row of dam planks placed at a four to five metre distance from the dam with, once again, in the space in between a pile of stones, would suffice[8].

There were three watercourses that tapped off the impounded Sampean water and they all had open inlets. There were two watercourses in the right bank of the Sampean, the Northern canal and the Kapongan canal. The Panarukan canal branched out from the left bank. The dam pushed up the water too little to supply the Kapongan channel sufficiently, which was why a second dam was created. That second dam was a temporary one. It raised the top of the framework dam by 60 centimetres. As a consequence, both the other watercourses began to be bothered by *banjirs* to a greater extent than previously. This was why provision was made in the Northern canal for, in the event of emergency, water to be able to flow out to the river (via what was known as an overflow). Due to the water pressure the watercourses required high levels of maintenance.

The problem that started to manifest itself with the dam was that water was beginning to pass beneath it through the soil (bed seepage) and the riverbed behind and under the dam where water flowed over fell was beginning to disintegrate. Moreover, the wood used to build the dam began to rot over the course of time. Surprisingly, the dam remained in tact until 1850. Six years earlier, though, it had become clear that in view of the state of the woodwork another solution would have to be found.

---

[8] De Meyier used for his description of the constructing of a framework dam a publication of J.A. Krajenbrink's from 1851 (*de l'Irrigation*). As far as the fascine layer was concerned he had his reservations and further Sampean weir developments would prove that these reservations were indeed well-founded. Further information on the framework dam in the Sampean is also provided by Van Lakerveld and Brocx (1864: 703-704). The quantity of *jati* wood used (400 cubic metres) reported in the "Civil Public Works Report" was estimated on the basis of the drawing accompanying this description (*Verslag BOW* 1895: 296, cf. Rietveld 1932: 279).

Dik's overflow system

It was the engineer S. Dik who came up with a new technique for pushing the water upwards. *Jati* wood had in the meantime become a scarce commodity (probably because of all the dam-building activities) and people thought it would be unwise to again use such vast quantities of it. There were therefore no immediate plans to build another framework dam[9]. Instead Dik proposed constructing a cemented overflow to thus change the riverbed. This construction would not cut across the river's flow as had been the case with the framework dam, instead it would run parallel to it. The water would pour over the dam in a sideways direction. Among Javanese dams this was a common type of overflow and Dik was evidently inspired by this style of *awiran*[10]. With this overflow system the Kapongan watercourse could remain in position but the other two channels would have to be altered.

In 1847 people set to work and four years later the construction was completed. The top of the "Dik overflow" stood around 1.20 meter higher than the framework dam had stood. To either side of the overflow sluicing walls (walls to sluice water in a given direction) had been built that were 77.50 metres long. After passing over the dam the water fell twenty metres and so a long deluge plain was created. Much of this area (49 metres of it) was cemented. For this purpose use was made of what was known as "local brick in ordinary cement". The Panarukan channel was given a new opening where a sluice known as the Southern sluice was constructed. This meant that the old opening had to be closed. The sluice was given two openings, one that was 3.40 metres wide and one that was 1.80 metres wide. Both openings were 6.80 metres high. The upper section of the opening was closed off for 4.70 metres with barrier beams. The larger opening was given a wooden sliding panel so that the remaining 2.10 metres could be closed off while the small opening below remained open. The Northern canal opening was also moved and the new opening was likewise given a sluice, the Northern sluice. This sluice had five openings that were 3.20 meters wide and 5.02 meters high. Barrier beams closed off the openings to two metres above the bottom and the rest was controlled with sliding gates. This watercourse was given the new name: the Situbondo channel. Altogether the works cost *f* 130,244 and the money required was made available by the Indies government. (See **Figure 3.5**).

As it turned out, the overflows' deluge plain could not take the force of the water and the concrete base soon became damaged. In 1855 the layer was replaced with what was known as reinforced stone. By governmental decree *f* 9627 was put aside for this purpose. There were also problems with the Dawuan channel, a side canal of the Situbondo watercourse. The water supply to this canal was regulated by means of a temporary dam in the Situbondo channel. This dam negatively affected the inlet sluice capacity which was why, in 1856, the Dawuan channel was given its own inlet for *f* 1200 and this, again, was funded by the government. The complaint to the effect that the Kapongan channel was being supplied with too little water persisted. Endeavours were made to repress these objections by providing temporary dams.

---

[9] It was generally "the unsystematic felling of forests" which, in those times led to *jati* wood shortages. This problem came to an end when the forests were placed under the regulatory control of forest rangers. (De Meyier 1891: 231, *Indisch Staatsblad* ["Indies Gazette"] 1866, see for the depletion of *jati* woods *Encyclopaedie* Vol. I 1917: 617).

[10] An overflow is in effect created by lowering the river dyke through which water is able to flow away at high-water periods. In the nineteenth century, overflows were common along the Maas (a Dutch river) and other large rivers (M. ten Horn-Van Nispen, personal communication, July 1996).

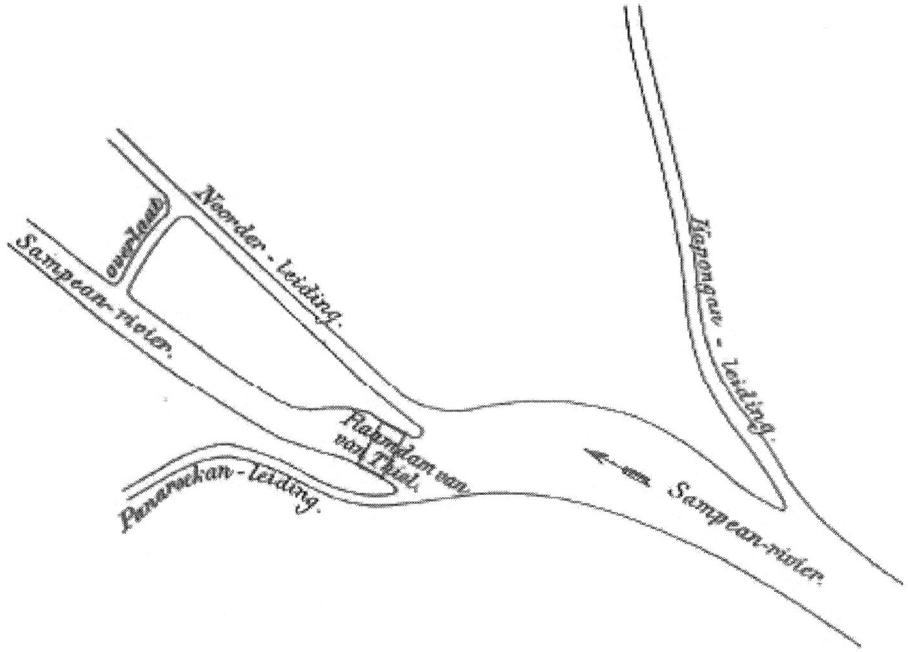

Figure 3.4: The Sampean headworks situation in 1832 (from: *Verslag BOW* 1895)

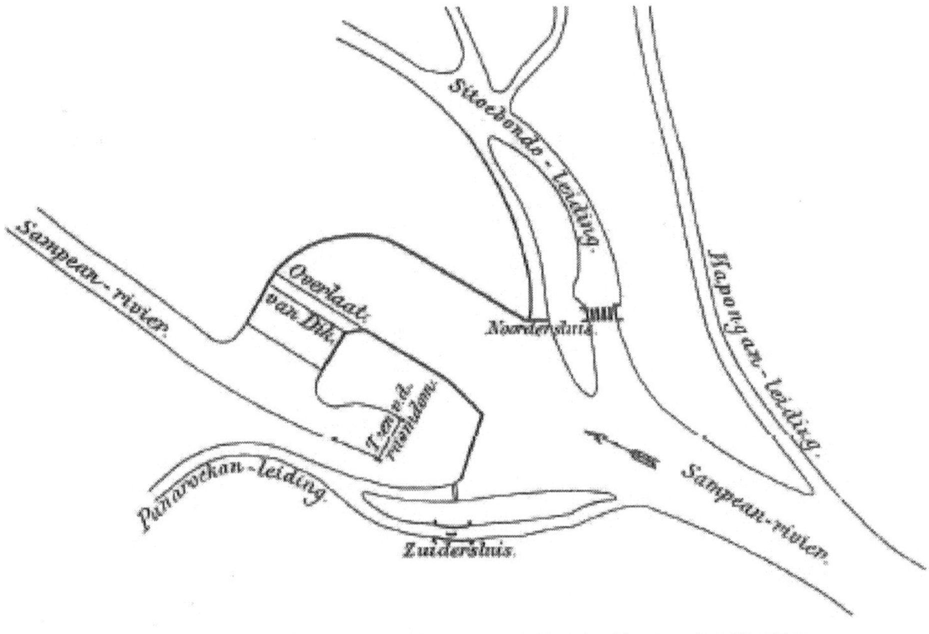

Figure 3.5: The Sampean headworks situation in 1851 (from: *Verslag BOW* 1895)

The later Public Works Director, H. de Bruyn, then Chief Engineer within the Public Works Organisation, paid a visit to the works in 1856. He was able to confirm that the works were in a poor state of repair. The dams in the old canal openings were too low beneath the highest *banjir* levels. The sluices could not be worked in the intended way. The sliding gates that were held in wooden grooves had to be manned with wooden windlasses and sheer manpower. This was not effective though and so a rammer was used to close the sluice gates. The new Dawuan channel opening was dangerous and it was feared that it would flow into the Situbondo channel. The masonry of the overflow deluge plain had once again become damaged. Gullies had furthermore sprung up in the riverbed beneath the overflow. The Resident made *f* 1500 available for the raising of the old canal dams. Other suggestions on ways of improving the situation were being contemplated when, in 1857, a high *banjir* considerably worsened matters. The right-hand sluice wall was washed away for a length of 52 metres and behind it the water had made a new route to the river. At other points, soil had been eroded behind the sluice wall works. The old dam in the Panarukan channel had been washed away altogether and the Dawuan channel had been badly damaged. Dik's overflow system had not been very successful. In the report written by P.J.G. Beyerinck in 1858 for the Director of Public Works, the engineer's remarks were not completely devoid of irony when he wrote the following about the situation:

"What may in truth be said of this permanent weir is that it is capable of ensuring that by raising the banjir level the water of the Sampeang sees to it that these waterworks are destroyed while the same weir lacks the capacity to push the water of this river up high enough at low water-level times for it to be useful for the watering of the fields" (in: Rietveld 1932: 279, cf. C. 1873).

Temporary dams

In order to safeguard the irrigating of fields the Resident decided, immediately after the devastating *banjir* of 1857, that a temporary dam should be constructed (see **Figure 3.6**). This dam was constructed in Javanese style, from wood and river stones and without the intervention of engineers. Under the supervision of local civil servants the population banded together to voluntarily construct the dam. The Resident paid out a sum of *f* 2000 to subsidise this forced labour. That money went towards food; each labourer received "ten farthings" (around six cents) per day. In order to repair the wall that had been destroyed the Indies government made available a sum of *f* 78,000, also in the year 1857. First of all, though, a suitable design had to be produced. In the years that followed, little really happened. At the instigation of the Public Works Director engineer Beyerinck wrote a report (see above) but the order to draw up a plan did not come until 1864. The Public Works Organisation was plagued by personnel shortages but at least a number of smaller works were completed. The Dawuan watercourse was closed off from the river and connected to the Kapongan channel. In conjunction with water provision a temporary dam was erected in the latter canal (the Paraman dam). For these and other works as well as for the collecting of materials for the repairing of the damaged sluicing wall, a sum of *f* 39,661 was spent in 1866[11].

In the end, the temporary dam was to remain in tact until 1875 and, insofar as it was not completely washed away, it was perpetually subjected to damage. For this reason dam upkeep and rebuilding became a recurrent annual commitment. Because the water damaged the banks and eroded the riverbed the dam became ever bigger and heavier and therefore also more costly over the course of time. In many places the riverbed was eroded as far as the stone area (the

[11] Quite where that money came from is not exactly clear. Presumably much of the funding derived from the Indies government treasury.

padas section) which, in turn, made it difficult for poles to be driven into the bed. Because of this erosion the connection between the dam and the riverbed – that was supposed to be watertight – left much to be desired. By 1866 dam maintenance had cost *f* 62,823 and in the 1866-1875 period the expenses totalled *f* 102,494. Much of this money was presumably spent on reimbursing the people who had been forced to offer their services for this work. In view of the fact that corvée labourers received minimal pay these sums would indicate that thousands and thousands of man-days must have gone into building the dam. The actual costs were, however, even higher. It was also the case that a certain amount of unpaid forced labour was enlisted. The population was, moreover, required to supply materials free of charge as well. All in all, there were a number of decisions that had to be taken before the Resident and the government could get funds authorised for the dam building activities and obtain the required manpower for the job in hand.[12]

In a number of respects the dam took its toll and brought with it more disadvantages than advantages. Rietveld (1932: 280) summarised the disastrous nature of the temporary dam as follows:

"One can safely assert that these temporary dams have ultimately exhausted the whole area. In the period leading up to 1872 an average of 25000 man labour days per year was being consumed (i.e. that, on average, there were 300 men working each day - day in, day out!) and that the labourers were drawn from a region of 18 poles (i.e. extending to roughly the Bondowoso and Besuki regions). The dam consumed entire forests of natural growth and bamboo (jati had long been almost used up) so that in the 5 to 6 Districts of the Panarukan area there were only about 125000 bamboo plants left.
The Inland civil servants had little choice but to continue working for and on the dam. Had the resultant irrigation system been satisfactory then all the trouble might have been somewhat repaid, however, that was not in any way the case and the region's welfare was visibly deteriorating".

In 1866 the Chief Engineer Beyerinck came up with a plan in which it was proposed that Dik's overflow be renovated so that the upper limit be lowered, the sluicing walls built higher and the sloping side restored and again plastered (with trass mixture cement). Another component was the overflow in the gully that had come into being in 1857. The most striking component was the "needle weir" in the Sampean that was 79 metres wide and had ten openings. This weir was semi-automatic which meant that when water levels were high an opening would be created in the weir by means of a float. Beyerinck estimated that all the works would cost some *f* 648,000. In view of the high cost level the Indies government did not automatically agree to Beyerinck's plan. It first sought advice from the Resident whose views were positive. The Indies government then put the proposals before the Dutch administrators. The Minister of the Colonies questioned whether there were not other more urgent irrigation matters. He was thinking in that connection

[12] On the matter of how the funds were spent, how many resolutions were required to obtain this funding, and what administrative levels were involved, sources are not exactly unequivocal. It is from the "Civil Public Works Report" that I conclude that the money was needed to pay for manual labour: in this connection decisions were called for from the Resident and the government "on a number of occasions" (*Verslag BOW* 1895: 298). According to Rietveld (1932: 280) "the annals make mention of innumerable Governmental, Directors [of Public Works, WR] and Residents's resolutions" pertaining to money and forced labour for the maintenance and repair of the temporary dam. Rietveld thus implies that Public Works was involved in the project. From other similar cases I only know that an "accord" was required from the Director of Public Works for work to be able to go ahead on a temporary dam (see **Chapter 4**). (In general I noticed that the various government decisions were not published in the official "Indies Gazette". In the "Colonial Report" only incidental reports on repair work appear, e.g. in the report on the events of 1864, p. 692 and on 1869, p. 376).

about the works in Grobogan, one of the regions that ten years previously had been hit by famine (see **Chapter 4**). That was as far as the plan got[13].

Permanent structures

The fixed weir

The situation in the Sampean delta remained unsatisfactory and the temporary dam continued to absorb funds. When, in 1870, the Resident again called for help the Director of the Department of Civil Public Works finally took action. He found that Beyerinck's plan needed to be revised (i.e. made cheaper) and so he passed it on to the engineer J.C. Schumm who in 1871 produced an interim plan and a final plan in 1872. He maintained that silt, driftwood and loose stones might be problematic in the case of a movable weir and so abandoned that particular plan. The plan produced by Schumm contained the following components:

1. to clear up the overflow and the framework dam remnants,
2. to create a fixed dam made of stone that would be around 162 metres long and 1084 metres wide (!) with a deluge bed of 50.36 metres,
3. to raise the northern sluicing wall and lengthen this wall to make it join up with the Northern sluice,
4. to construct a new southern sluicing wall adjacent to the Southern sluice,
5. to raise and improve the two inlet sluices.

The weir would consist of two walls, an upper wall (up-stream) and a lower wall (down-stream). These walls would serve to link together the cross walls. The spaces created in the process would be filled with "stone". The entire thing would be covered with a thick masonry layer (a metre deep). This masonry would be given an "olive-shaped" (half hollow, half rounded) form. The upper area of the covering layer would consist of a "roll layer" composed of stone that would be one stone deep. These stones would be Dutch Waal (river) bricks. The cement used to plaster the layer would be Portland cement (i.e. cement made of lime and loam). The top of the dam would be finished with "freestone blocks". Schumm also wanted to divide the deluge bed into sections, fill the sections up with stone and plaster the whole thing with Portland cement. Using voluntary labour the whole plan would cost some *f* 532,292.

The Director approved Schumm's plan and the Indies government was likewise approving and made the necessary sum of money available. After being put out to public tender it was the contractor C. Maarschalk from Probolinggo that was given the job. His estimate of *f* 509,870 slightly undercut the budgeted amount. Meanwhile Schumm had returned to the Netherlands because of illness and so responsibility passed to the engineer A.M.S. Hoogerwaard. During construction it soon became clear, in 1873, that certain adaptations would be required. One thing that the planners wanted to do was to move the structure ten metres upstream in conjunction with the riverbed level. For the same reason it was proposed that the foot of the deluge bed might be lowered. A base wall was also required on the northern sluicing wall side. The government granted permission for all these changes and made available the extra *f* 5597 requested for the wall base. (See **Figure 3.7**).

[13] The Indies budget of 1868 did put aside a large sum of money for the purpose of "replacing works with works that were better constructed than the dam at Situbondo ... and the connected sluices: works that were already demanding much renovation every year without sufficiently meeting the relevant needs" (*Koloniaal Verslag* 1869: 376), but that money had not yet been put to use. Later needle weirs were built in Europe (Rietveld 1932: 281), even in the Netherlands (in the nineteenth century; Arends 1994).

Further alterations were, however, prohibited. Below the old framework dam the water had created a deep hole that had come to be known as "the Van Thiel hole". Because of this the dam sides required stronger foundations and so in 1874 measures were taken to rectify this but that was not the only problem. One major difficulty lay in the connection between the deluge bed and the hole. In 1875 the entire situation was made worse by two successive *banjirs* which not only destroyed the temporary dam that was still there but also damaged the works then being constructed. The sheer force of the water even changed the existing natural situation. In the open middle section of the dam that was being constructed a deep gully had been created in the riverbed, which extended a distance downstream.

The Chief Engineers, H. van Ketwich and G.A. Pet, were sent to Situbondo to find a solution to the problem, together with Hoogerwaard. A proposition made by Hoogerwaard in 1874 was updated and approved by the Indies government and extra costs of *f* 215,224 were involved. The measures taken were these:

- The Van Thiel hole was filled and partially cemented over. To ensure that the water could not seep in, a sluice dyke was erected with, as a continuation, a sluice wall. The wall had as its foundation the foot of Dik's overflow.
- In order to reinforce the deluge bed a "half stone roll layer" of Waal bricks was added to the structure. The layer was then finished off with Portland cement.
- The gully at the base of the deluge bed was filled with rubble, river stones and gravel for a distance of 100 metres and the whole thing was cemented in with "inland" brick. At the extremities and at two points in the middle "casing walls" were constructed. The sides were similarly finished. To ensure that erosion could not occur the bed to the left and right of the gully was levelled out. Where the gully again commenced measures were taken to prevent bed soil erosion. This was done by depositing stone and bamboo corves filled with river stones.

Because of the eroded gully the repairing of the gaping weir section – extending over some twenty metres – required special measures. There the upper wall of the weir was given a concrete box foundation between the dam post sides. The sluices were improved in the following way. They were provided with 3.90-metre-long arched passages that were 2.40 metres high in the middle. The tunnels were given sliding panels that were 3.05 metres high and were secured in iron runners. The winding systems on top of the sluices were provided with two booms secured in sheds and covered in galvanised iron. A further *f* 5757 was required to improve the sluice bases. Again the government was compliant and, by 1876, the works were completed. The "Colonial Report" of 1877 (p. 143) proudly reported that the work had been completed within the scheduled period and that the works furthermore "fully met the requirements". That was a rather optimistic claim. Some ten years would pass before the situation could be called satisfactory.

The deluge bed

It was during the first west monsoon season after the weir's completion that the greatest damage was incurred. The gully precautions taken turned out to be inadequate. The gully only eroded further thus endangering the dam wall and the concrete deluge bed floor. In addition, some 7400 square metres of the plasterwork of the temporary dam was damaged. In reaction to this a temporary dam composed of river stones was built in the gully at a distance of around 80 metres from the threatened deluge bed. Compulsory labour was used and the Resident made available a sum of *f* 4008. The renewing of the plaster work cost *f* 6772 and it was the Director of the Civil Public Works Department who gave approval for this amount to be expended.

During the 1877-1878 west monsoon season trouble again arose. It was notably the *banjir* of 11th March that created havoc. The floodwater rose extremely high because the passage under a bridge upstream (the Cipuri bridge) had become blocked. Later the same bridge was washed away. The water rose to 2.70 metres above the top of the dam. H.H. van Kol, the engineer to later become the SDAP representative in parliament calculated that the flood had moved at a rate of 1788 cubic metres per second . The plasterwork of the dam was again damaged, this time over an area of 12,000 square metres. The roll layer floor of the deluge bed was damaged in places and had completely disappeared in certain spots. The temporary dam in the gully was swept away and the gully eroded further, also in the width. Finally, the base beneath the deluge bed was worn out everywhere and all over it dents and holes could be detected. The engineer Van Kol got down to work. He drew up a reconstruction plan to be executed with compulsory labourers. The Indies government ploughed *f* 52,113 ("*f*" stands for Dutch guilders) into the project. The results, however, including the construction of a second temporary dam in the gully, were anything but satisfactory.

In 1875 when Pet had visited the site in conjunction with the water damage he had drawn a disturbing conclusion. All the works in Situbondo were built on *padas* which was thought to be a solid type of stone. Pet now concluded that in view of all the erosion this was not at all true. The subsoil layer in fact contained much loose stone and revealed many faults. The *padas* area did not therefore exactly constitute a stable riverbed. What also became apparent was that the layer was only some six to ten metres deep. When Pet carried out his inspection the gully already extended from the end of the *padas* layer to the lower edge. As a result of this, the *padas* layer had become undermined and had started to crumble. If the gully were to become wider and deeper the weir would ultimately be in danger. Pet maintained that in the end this would necessitate the construction of a new (extra) weir. He thought, however, that quite some time would pass before that stage would be reached and so he maintained that temporary measures would be good enough. This turned out to be an optimistic view! The future came quicker than Pet had anticipated and by 1878 the situation had become very serious. The height difference between the base of the deluge bed and the downstream riverbed was already nine metres by then. The area between those two points was an unprotected sloping plain. The deluge bed could not, moreover, stand up to the *banjir* force. It could be anticipated that the annual repair expenses would be high. The alternative option was to cover the bed with granite or some other hard type of stone but this was not a cheap solution (that would cost one to two million guilders!)

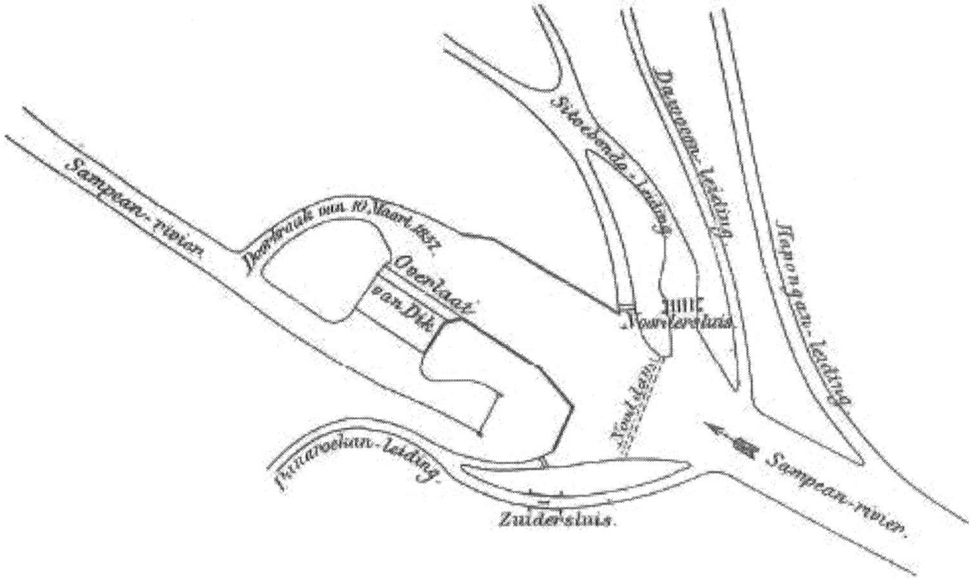

Figure 3.6: The Sampean headworks situation in 1857 (from: *Verslag BOW* 1895)

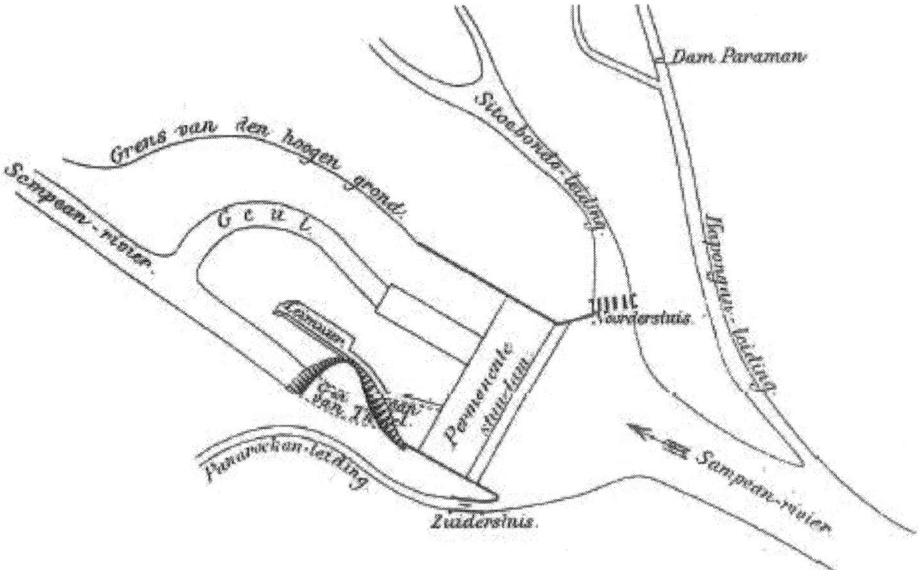

Figure 3.7 The Sampean headworks situation in 1876 (from: *Verslag BOW* 1895)

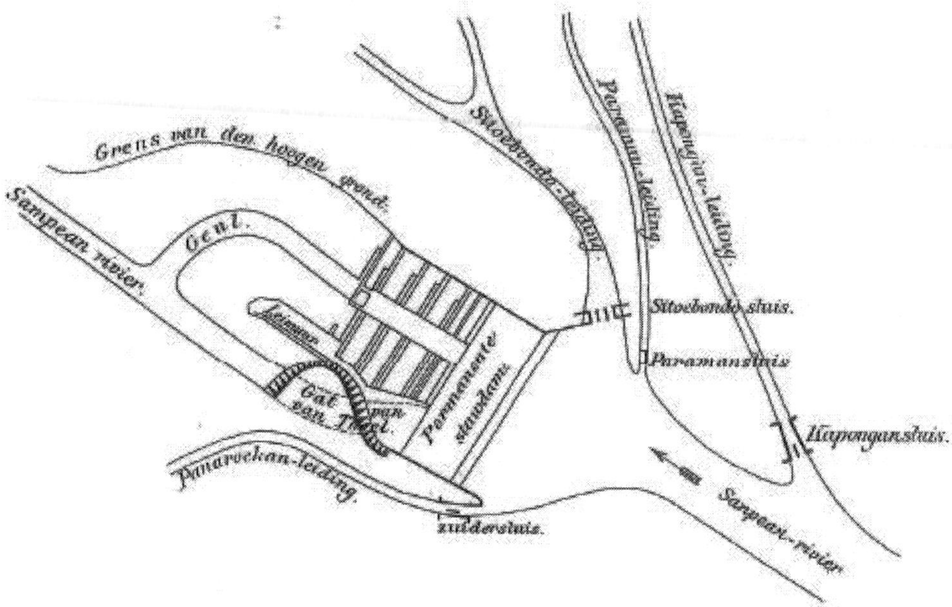

Figure 3.8: The Sampean headworks situation in 1882 (from: *Verslag BOW* 1895)

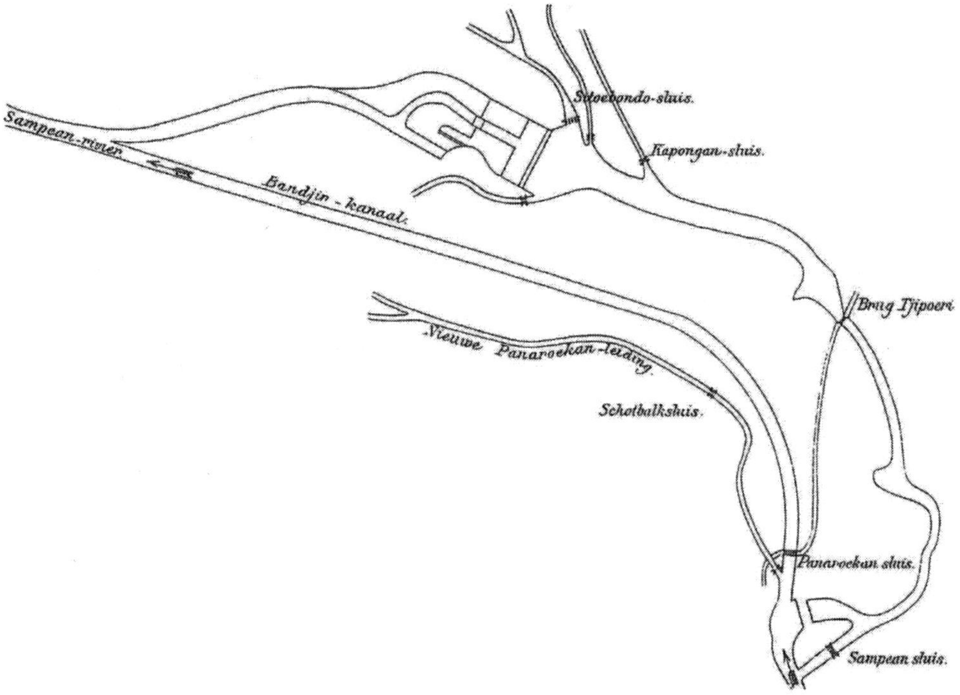

Figure 3.9: The Sampean headworks situation in 1886/87 (from: *Verslag BOW* 1895)

The riverbed beneath the deluge bed which was composed of *padas* became even more damaged in the west monsoon season of 1878-1879. The temporary dams in the gullies were also washed away and the structures placed at the beginning of the gully, which formed a second (temporary) deluge bed, were also seriously damaged. Because of this the base of the deluge bed was also undermined. Everything was repaired and a sill (threshold or cross-dam) with an ogee-shaped deluge plain was cemented between the gully and the northern sluice wall. During the following west monsoon period the repaired dam was again washed away and a new one was immediately constructed. In order to protect the cemented floor of the deluge bed in a more permanent sort of way a cemented deluge chute was created at the beginning of the gully. The Resident allocated a sum of *f* 7878. The deluge chute was connected to the threshold that had been created the previous year. The *padas* bed continued, however, to erode. After the 1879-1880 west monsoon season the Resident made *f* 14,659.30 available for new provisions in the form of an ogee-shaped floor along the foot of the deluge bed, an extension of the masonry floor along the sluice wall and for the construction of two new cross dams. In 1881, six new sills, costing *f* 26,065 were built at the Indies government's expense. In 1882 the government made a further *f* 27,150.75 available for the extension of the concrete floor and for the creation of new ogee-shaped floors. (See **Figure 3.8**).

In 1878 the watercourse situation altered. Because of the Paraman dam the Kapongan watercourse became completely silted up in March of that year. The dam was therefore cleared away. At the Resident's expense a new dam was then created which was connected with the Sampean via an inlet sluice in the form of a culvert. With the help of compulsory labour the job cost *f* 1976. The new channel was named after the old dam even though, in actual fact, the old Dawuan channel had again been made serviceable. The problem now was that in times of *banjirs* too much water flowed into the Kapongan watercourse. In 1880 the government therefore reserved *f* 35,811 for the construction of a sluice. The labourers responsible for the job were paid 12½ cents per day. The sluice had two openings of the same dimensions as those in the Situbondo sluice. In the case of this latter sluice, however, two of the five openings were superfluous and so they were cemented in. The redundant sliding panels and winding systems were made available for the new sluice. Later on, in 1882, further work was carried out on the Situbondo sluice in connection with the floor and sluice walls. The government spent *f* 17,999 on this project.

The banjir canal

In 1878 it became clear that the deluge bed beneath the weir was not going to hold out. At the time it was therefore decided that the dam should only be used as a weir and that it should no longer serve as a spillway for the *banjir* water. By digging a canal through the higher lying harder soil it would be possible to divert this water. The Resident put *f* 1797 towards research into the feasibility of this plan. In 1879 the Senior Engineer H.P. Gutteling and engineer Van Kol submitted a plan for a *banjir* canal. The Director of the Civil Public Works Department turned to Hoogerwaard, the Chief Engineer, for advice. It subsequently became apparent that the Director had objections to this plan. Gutteling and Van Kol had proposed that a sturdy earthen dam be built alongside of the permanent weir so that the Sampean could be dammed off. The problem was that this earth dam would have to be very high which meant that the existing inlet sluices would have to be raised. It was expected that the dammed off branch of the river would become very silted up and that the water supply to the sluices would then become insufficient. The Director expressed a preference for a dam in the river near to the mouth of the *banjir* canal. He suggested beginning with a narrower and shallower gully. The digging of this canal would provide more insight into the type of soil needing to be excavated and it would furthermore alleviate pressure on the weir.

In 1880 the Indies government made a sum of *f* 170,278 available for this temporary gully. This sum was based on an estimate of 12½ cents per day for manpower. Meanwhile work on the project commenced under the supervision of Van Kol. The work that had to be done in the narrow gully was inhuman or, as expressed in the Indies "Civil Public Works Report" (*Verslag BOW* 1895: 307), it was "extremely difficult" because of "the great heat and because it was so hard for people to pass the hacked out stone up the steep sides" (ibid.). If the whole canal were to be excavated more use could be made of machinery and soil could be transported away by train. This was just one of the reasons why people wanted to start as quickly as possible with the digging of the whole canal. When work on the gully finally convinced the Director of the Public Works Department that the soil would be suitable for canal excavation work he gave orders, in 1881, for a final plan to be drawn up. The final plan was ready within a matter of months. Once again, the standard remuneration was 12½ cents per day. By government resolution a further *f* 150,044 was made available for the canal. The work was delayed though for various reasons. A cholera epidemic broke out at the end of 1881 among the labourers and later there was a dynamite shortage. Apart from the cholera epidemic there was a general problem with workers because of a labour shortage. In September 1882 the Resident calculated that 390,000 man-work-days would be required if the work was to be completed by 1st November of that year and that was 50,000 man-work-days more than was available to them. The Resident therefore resolved to bring in 50,000 free coolies who would be paid 50 cents a day. The government agreed to this plan and made available an extra *f* 18,750.

By the end of 1883 the canal was ready enough to be used for the conveyance of much *banjir* water and by mid-1884 it was completely finished. (See **Figure 3.9**). The canal was 2386 metres long (the length given in the first plan). At the beginning of the canal its bed breadth was 30 metres tapering gradually to twenty metres at the end. It was designed to transport 1000 cubic metres of water per second and a total 643,000 cubic metres of ground had been excavated. For the excavation of the rocky areas 24,000 kilos of dynamite had been used.

The lock in the Sampean was of the same design as the Situbondo lock. The sluice was given five openings, each of which was 3.16 metres wide and 2.30 metres high. The length of the tubular opening was 6.40 metres. The sliding panels and winding systems were virtually identical to those of the previously mentioned sluice. The Sampean sluice was completed in 1884. The sluice was dry constructed, that is to say, built on dry land before the river was diverted to it. The construction site was near to a bend which was cut off after the dam's completion. Both the lock and the dam were the result of forced labour at a rate of 12½ cents a day. The works cost the Indies government *f* 160,955. The Panarukan channel was given a new inlet at the beginning of the *banjir* canal. The inlet was provided with a new sluice with an opening that was 2.20 metres high and 3.30 metres wide. The panel from the large shaft in the Panarukan lock was fitted into this sluice. The channels and sluice were completed by 1883. This job cost the government *f* 38,165. Once again, the type of manpower used was forced labour at the standard tariff of 12½ cents per day. In the old Panarukan lock the small cylinder was kept open. In this way several acres of *sawa* that had been cut off from the Panarukan area by the *banjir* canal could remain supplied with water. When work had started on the digging of the canal a temporary aqueduct should have been created for the Panarukan canal over the works in question. In 1881 the Resident had put aside *f* 8546 for this very purpose. A temporary bridge over the canal was also required so in the same year the Resident made *f* 9492 available for this purpose. This bridge, the Kapuran bridge, was later extended and improved. Both the government and the Director of Civil Public Works made available respective sums of *f* 8457 in 1893 and *f* 1588 in 1884 for this project.

The canal was, however, immediately damaged in the first west monsoon period following its completion. The canal bed eroded and the banks collapsed. Widening the canal brought with it the danger of a breakthrough between the canal and the Panarukan channel that flowed parallel to it. At the bridge land-abutment points there was the danger that these structures might become washed away. The Indies government contributed a further *f* 15,655 for various purposes including for the cementing, in places, of the canal bed and banks and the creation of a sluice (with partition beams) in the channel for in case both watercourses started to merge. A year later the central government contributed a further *f* 2095 for other jobs, partly precipitated by the west monsoon of 1885-1886.

In the night of 19th and 20th April, 1887 there was a gigantic *banjir*, even greater than that of 1878. At that time the biggest channel was able to deal with 2075 cubic metres per second. The flood was partly caused by a blockage at a bridge over the Sampean, upstream from the *banjir* canal (the Weduri bridge). The water flowed over the Sampean lock and the dam in the old river bend. The water level even rose above the weir but it was notably the dam that suffered. It cost the government some *f* 20,596 to rebuild and raise the dam and use was made of unpaid labour. The entire job was completed in 1887. At the Sampean sluice the wind works were placed at a lower level. What had become apparent was that the long rod beams tended to bend during *banjirs* so that the panels wobbled loose. All of this cost *f* 1310 and once again the bill was for the government. In 1889 and 1890 the government expended a further *f* 61,239 on a new bridge over the Sampean[14]. This bridge was to replace the old one that had been giving problems. At the same time the Sampean was widened at the point where the old bridge had stood which was where it flowed through a narrow chasm. The bridge even had a gully for irrigation water. In 1894 a second gully was created for *f* 3247 and this time the bill went to the Civil Public Works Department.

The *banjir* canal made the weir virtually superfluous. The stone threshold at the head of the dam served as a new dam and the Sampean and Panarukan locks operated as descending step locks.

Finally

The sequel

The report brought out by the Civil Public Works Department (*Verslag BOW* 1895: 310) asserted that since the completion of the dam in 1887 "no difficulties ... had been experienced" with the various works. That was perhaps true but the phase of making alterations to works was certainly not over. Towards the end of the century great problems arose due to silting up. A new structure was required, also in conjunction with other works then under construction.

By 1887 the engineers were not, in fact, finished. The irrigation network for which the weir had been constructed still needed to be perfected. After the completion of the *banjir* canal estimations started being made for an entire canal system. The engineer responsible for this was M. Ypelaar and it was under his supervision that the *banjir* canal was also rounded off. Already in 1878 the Resident had been pushing for such developments but the Public Works engineers first wanted some reassurance about the permanence of the headworks. Surveys continued until 1891 and from 1889 onwards design plans were also being made. This was to lead to different sub-plans. The works actually commenced in 1891. It was discovered that the main channels of the canal system were badly silted up and the Situbondo and Kapongan locks also contained silt banks. This was this reason why a plan for an outlet sluice in the permanent weir emerged in 1898. The plan was passed by the authorities and the sluice which had four openings, each of roughly two metres, was completed in 1900 (see **Figure 3.1**). The entire job cost the Indies

[14] This included a sum of *f* 12,374 for the cost of importing wrought iron works from the Netherlands (the "Civil Public Works Report" of 1895: 311 referred to "wrought iron stone works").

government *f* 20,555. By 1906 everything was finished which meant that "complete technical" irrigation provision could be claimed to have been achieved for an area of 15,200 *bouws*. The whole irrigation network had cost *f* 906,347 and it had taken 973,450 man-working days to complete.[15]

The works suffered badly from floodwater. Early in 1916, for instance, there were *banjirs* of roughly 2700 cubic metres per second on two successive nights. The water rose above the dam and lock, damaged a main irrigation network canal and caused flooding Panarukan. Because of these *banjirs* the wall of the Sampean lock was raised and, to protect Panarukan from further flooding, the bed of the Sampean was widened. The new outlet sluice continued to give problems: the gully that had perpetually ruptured in the past when *banjirs* had hit displayed, in its role as outlet gully, the same problem and so required continual renewal. Finally, there were also difficulties with the irrigation network system including the erosion, anew, of canals. Maintenance and repair was a major issue! (I shall return to various other aspects of the Sampean Works, including the irrigation network aspect, in later chapters).

Costs

As one traces the history of the Sampean Works it becomes clear that – for engineers – creating irrigation works in Java was certainly not something that could be called problem free. After getting off to a promising start (with Van Thiel's framework dam) and a rather less promising continuation (with van Dik's overflow) a period followed in which Javanese-style dams became responsible for the pushing up of water levels. After some twenty years, the engineers came back in force and built a permanent weir. At the time "Van Thiel's hole" became a problem. It became apparent that the permanent weir could not, unfortunately, stand up to flood water pressures. Finally people in this area gave up the fight and the water was diverted via a *banjir* canal. The new weir was a stone hump in the river! According to Rietveld (1932: 286) all the efforts were, "for three-quarters, a catalogue of failures and disappointments". These failures and disappointments also turned the whole thing into a very expensive series of events.

In 1887, a provisional stop was put to the Sampean weir activities. By then approximately two million guilders has been spent on the weir (see **Table 3.1**). That included a sum of roughly *f* 105,000 for the 840,000 paid man-days of forced labour for a reward of, on average, eight cents per day. Between 1876 and 1887 200,000 man-days were worked. The number of unpaid days of forced labour in the 1832-1876 period is unknown but estimates put it at probably more than a million (Rietveld 1932: 286). If all the works (up until 1887) had been completed with voluntary labour (at 50 cents per day) then the Sampean weir would have cost almost three million guilders to construct. Fifty-five years of water provision for over 15,000 *bouws* had therefore cost the state millions of guilders. Judging by the results the costs were, according to the experts, high. The "Civil Public Works Report" (*Verslag BOW* 1895: 310) had the following to say about this:

"The costs are extremely high if one realises that in actual fact nothing has been created apart from one prise d'eau with various inlet locks. The channels have, for the most part, been dug by the local people themselves and permanent division works are lacking".

[15] The channel mouth situation in the weir was later altered. The two openings in the Situbondo lock that had been cemented closed were opened up again and came to form the new Kapong weir. The Paraman channel once again became a branch of the Kapong channel. (See **Figure 3.2**).

The report attributed the high costs to the inefficient way of tackling the job and, ultimately, to the fact that people had carried on working in the wrong place:

"One may assert that the outcomes might have been considerably more favourable had extensive surveys preceded the drawing up of designs. In the past that was not the custom but for a number of years now it has been the practice to do that.
The engineer Van Thiel designed his weir to be constructed at the spot where he had found an inland dam. The engineer Dik, however, adhered to the place where the various channels had started off from.
At the time nothing much was known about the way the Sampean river flowed; there were no topographical maps, all that people did know was in which mountains the rivers had their sources.
In 1866 and 1872 the engineers Beyerinck and Schumm stuck once again, as though it was a foregone conclusion, to the old prise d'eau spot because the mouths of 2 of the 3 channels were already provided with permanent inlet sluices.
So it was that, forced by circumstances, people persisted in pursuing avenues which, in retrospect, proved to be the wrong ones and which they would not have chosen either had they been able to oversee the situation from the very beginning" (pp. 310-311).

Van Kol who had himself worked on the Sampean works wrote in 1901 (p. 343) about the Sampean weir:

"Year after year the dam was washed away and every time it was replaced by new dams the only result being that in an area with a radius of 300 metres more than 2 million guilders was spent and – officially – more than 2 million man-days of labour was got through but one can be sure that beyond the auspices of the Native and Civil Service more than 2 million man-days were used".[16]

Van Kol confirmed the conclusion drawn in the Civil Public Works Report: "Those were the fatal consequences of maintaining the spot selected by the inlander [native, WR] for draining off water" (Van Kol 1901: 343-344).

Rietveld also pointed to the difficult working conditions (no essential necessary details, primitive tools). He therefore commemorated the Sampean weir's hundred year existence with "respect and praise for the Sampean delta pioneers who, under difficult circumstances, had managed to engineer much" (1932: 287).

---

[16] Van Kol also referred to the *Verslag BOW* (1895) but his numbers remained higher than the numbers reported there. Later Van Kol was to look back nostalgically on his Sampean weir days: "Often we engineers anxiously kept watch at night together with the site engineer, terrified that within a couple of hours the product of years of work would be destroyed and that, with the washing away of the dam, a densely populated region would be robbed of its fertile-making water" (cited by Van Goor 1899: 127, Van Goor who had doubts about the need for the *banjir* canal, see **Chapter 7**).

Table 3.1 The Sampean Works expenditures

Year	Job	Sum (in guilders)	Funds from Government (GVT), Resident (RES) or Public Works (PW)
1832	Van Thiel's framework dam	-	-
1851	Van Dik's overflow	130,244	GVT
1855	Repair work	9,627	GVT
1856	The Duwan channel inlet	1,200	GVT
1856	Raising dam canals	150	RES
1857	Temporary dam	2,000	RES
1857-1866	Repair of the emergency dam	62,823	RES/GVT/(PW?)
1866-1975	Idem	102,494	RES/GVT/(PW?)
1857-1866	Gathering of materials	39,661	GVT
1872	Permanent weir	509,870	GVT
1873	Foot wall	5,597	GVT
1875	Hole, deluge bed and gully	215,224	GVT
1876	Weir bases	5,757	GVT
1877	Dam in gully	4,008	RES
1877	Repair	6,772	PW
1878	Idem	52,113	GVT
1878	Paraman lock	1,976	RES
1878	Banjir canal research	1,797	RES
1880	Deluge pit	7,878	RES
1880	Gully	14,659.50	RES
1880	Sills	26,065	GVT
1880	Kapongan weir	35,811	GVT
1880	Banjir canal	170,278	GVT
1881	Idem	154,044	GVT
1881	Sampean weir and dam	160,955	GVT
1881	Panarukan channel	38,165	GVT
1881	Aquaduct over the gully	8,546	RES
1881	Bridge over the gully	9,492	RES
1883	Bridge extensions	8,457	GVT
1884	Bridge covering	1,588	PW
1882	Floors	27,150.75	GVT
1882	Repair of Situbondo weir	17,999	GVT
1882	Banjir canal	18,750	GVT
1885	Repair of canal and weir	15,655	GVT
1886	Idem	2,095	GVT
1887	The Sampean weir winding systems	1,310	GVT
1887	Dam repairs	20,596	GVT
1889-1890	Bridge over the Sampean	61,239	GVT
1894	Bridge groove	3,247	PW
Entire Sampean weir		1,955,293.25	
1891-1906	Irrigation network	906,347	
1899	Outlet weir	20,555	GVT
Entire Sampean Works		2,882,195.25	

* On the basis of the *Verslag BOW* (1895). The sums given are those that were allocated and used. On the odd occasions that money was left over those amounts have been deducted.

A nature-technology spiral

One might view the emergence of the "curious water supply" project in the Sampean river as a battle with nature. From that point of view the intervention with irrigation precipitated unexpected natural consequences which, in turn, led to new types of involvement. The net result was that in a spiral of activities a process of technical development was unfolded[17]. What directly gave rise to Van Thiel's framework dam was the fact that Javanese dams had been a failure. The new dam exhausted the supplies of *jati* wood in the area and ultimately caused a deep hole to be hollowed out. The breakthrough of 1857 and the creation of a deep channel appeared to have been brought about by van Dik's overflow. All the emergency dams further undermined the subsoil. Generally the dams had to be made bigger and sturdier because the river undermined so much. The Sampean continued to widen so that ultimately a weir had to be constructed which was more that a kilometre wide! As it turned out, the 1875 weir was not strong enough to stand the water pressure. While the dam was still under construction, the water had scooped out a deep gully in the riverbed. Once in use, the dam only perpetuated this damage to the riverbed. The temporary solution thus became to construct a canal of some 2½ kilometres around the entire complex.

The ever-increasing force of successive *banjirs* became a tale in itself with nature revealing itself in all its unruliness. When designing the *banjir* canal it had been presumed that the Sampean's maximum water transport capacity was 1000 cubic metre per second, just slightly higher than the maximum calculated by Melchior[18]. The biggest throughput volume so far experienced had been that of 1878, of 1788 cubic metres per second. Other than that, no volume higher than 700 cubic metre per second had been monitored since 1876. In 1887 it was more like 2075 cubic metre per second that flowed past and by 1916 that had risen to around 2700 cubic metre per second! Evidently there could be great fluctuations in the amount of water transported by the rivers and the monitoring of such volumes was very time-bound. The increased pressure on the Sampean was probably not so much a consequence of the dam as of human intervention in the form of the deforestation process going on in the river's upper reaches. This deforestation was, in turn, probably a consequence of the growing population and the increasing drive to exploit nature that went with such population growth.[19]

This way of viewing matters; of seeing nature and technology as being interrelated was not completely absurd. It would, however, be a misconception to think that the modern Sampean Works was completely developed in such an "autonomous" way. The original Javanese dams kept being washed away. The temporary dams constructed by administrators in the 1857-1875 period turned out to be no better. They were traditional dams constructed on the Resident's orders, which made use of many hours of forced labour. Having to rebuild a dam on a yearly basis is perhaps something that in the end becomes trying and perhaps even impossible to sustain

---

[17] Compare this with Casimir's (1984) "scientific-technological spiral".

[18] See for Melchior's calculations **Chapter 5, Note 7**. See for an overview and discussion of methods and formulas for determining river discharges Ertsen (2005).

[19] Already in the nineteenth century the engineer De Bruyn had pointed out that Java needed to have its forests replenished. He drew attention to the connection between deforestation on the one hand and flooding in the west monsoon season and water shortage in the east monsoon season on the other hand. He saw deforestation as the result of "badly thought out agricultural expansion, as lack of supervision over rivers and forests and as a shortage of laws based on science and findings" (1863: 105). Governor-General Rochussen surmised that rainfall levels might have dropped because of the disappearance of forests. This point will be returned to in **Chapter 4**. Changing water transport levels and the accompanying water works problems was something that was not unknown in the Netherlands either (see Ten Horn-van Nispen et al. 1994 and Van de Ven 1993).

but it was one of the possibilities, certainly at first. This immediately begs the question of why engineers had to become so involved.

Van Thiel's decision to construct a dam in the Sampean had a policy background. Rietveld (1932: 277) clarified this as follows:

"A hundred years ago it was just like today: economising was what counted. This did not, however, reduce involvement on the part of government in irrigation affairs, as in the past, it was sooner endeavours to stimulate financial recovery that prompted the Government of the day to explore that so far unexplored terrain".

Since 1832 irrigation engineers had been active in the Sampean delta but in the 1857-1875 period technical help was not available and so administrators bridged the gap. After that engineers were once again available but the Civil Service definitely played a prominent part in the history of the Sampean's irrigation development. Apart from local civil servants, the Resident and the government, the Dutch Minister of the Colonies also became involved.

The next chapter explores the building of the Sampean weir in its wider context. In this connection we shall examine modern irrigation development in general in the 1830-1885 period and that will be discussed in the context of early colonial state development. The kind of questions that will arise are the following. To what extent were the Sampean delta works typical of the period? Were the kinds of failures and disappointments experienced with the Sampean Works also characteristic for other irrigation projects? Could the process of "professionalising" government involvement in irrigation, as evidenced in the Sampean weir project, be termed a more general occurrence? What was the relationship between the creating of modern irrigation installations and governmental policy? What was the relationship between Public Works engineers and the Civil Service and how did this develop?

4

'The Javanese can make water flow uphill'

The power struggle between Public Works and the Civil Service

> ... entire generations, in Asia, Africa, and Latin America, have been taught to believe that they had no technical past or history to speak of. A piece of propaganda, which if taken to its rigourous conclusion, would imply that for the hundreds of years that these societies have survived (before Western contact) they have existed purely on sunshine or some form of manna that fell religiously from the heavens.
> ... it is more than necessary that we begin to see that *homo faber* is not to be identified merely with Western *homo faber*: with the Western productive and cultural system. ... we think that any technological problem can only be solved in the Western way. What indeed did the Southern nations and their peoples do to solve their technical problems before contact with the West in 1500? (Alvares 1980: 35-36).

Irrigation is no matter of opinion but of calculation. C.L.F. Post, engineer at the Indies Department of Civil Public Works, made this clear in a sharp and notorious book that was published in 1879. When he wrote this book, a battle raged between Civil Service administrators and Public Works engineers. The engineers lobbied furiously for the creation of modern works but, as Post showed with numerous examples, the all-powerful civil servants were not keen to renounce their influence in the field of irrigation. Ultimately, though, the "clerks" were to taste defeat in 1885 which meant that engineers were free to go their own way, so marking a new phase in the development of modern irrigation in the Dutch East Indies. Let us not, however, race ahead but begin at the beginning.

1

2

3

4

Figures 4.1-4.4: Colonial irrigation engineers:

1. H. de Bruyn (from: Kielstra 1887)
2. A.G. Lamminga (photo J.J. de Haan, from: Weijs 1921)
3. J.E. de Meyier (photo Ad. Zimmermans, from: Melchior 1914)
4. H.H. van Kol (to a painting by C.A. Feldmann, from: Van Sandick 1926)

The state as entrepreneur

Liberal or traditional[1]

The period of Interim British Rule (1811-1816) constituted a temporary break in Dutch power over the Indies archipelago. In 1814 the colony was returned to the Netherlands following the Convention of London and so the task of establishing rule in the area began. When the *Vereenigde Oostindische Compagnie* (the "United East Indies Company" or "Dutch East Indies Company", shortened to *VOC*) had gone bankrupt in 1798 and its possessions had been taken over by the Batavian Republic there had already been discussion on the way in which the colonial administration should be given form and content. Some maintained that the United East India Company administration, which was feudal and indirect, should be continued. The Resident, responsible for the administration of one given region (the Residency), played a major part in all of this. He operated through Javanese leaders. Others were more in favour of a "rational-bureaucratic" style of administration directly exercised over the population. We might say that together these views constituted the "traditional" and "liberal" models (compare Van den Doel 1994: 102).

Differences were reflected in ideas about policy. The traditional model envisaged a system of exploitation in which the state remained in charge of the population's resources: land and labour. The policy characteristics of the liberal model were: land in hereditary tenure for the population, free labour, the establishment of private industry and state incomes derived from renting out land (see, for example, *Encyclopaedie* ["Encyclopedia"] Vol. II 1918: 415).

The Governor-General, Daendels (1808-1811), and the English Governor, Raffles (1811-1816), had adopted a liberal stance. One of Daendel's important deeds had been to construct the "Grote Postweg" (Great Mail Road) along Java's northern coast. This reduced travelling times in Java and therefore fitted in well with "free-thinking" administrative reforms. Raffles introduced land rents. The farmers were therefore no longer required to cultivate crops ("allotments"), as in the *VOC* period, but they did have to pay tax for the land they rented. When the Indies reverted to Dutch rule the systems that had been adopted were at first continued.

During the first years after the power switch one Commissioner-General – appointed by King William I in 1814 (who, by virtue of the 1814 constitution, was responsible for colonial rule) – began to regulate affairs in the Indies. In 1815 they were given, for that specific purpose, the governmental statute (a state ruling especially created for the Indies). On this basis they were able to restore the old governmental system which looked like this (see, for instance, *Encyclopaedie* Vol. I 1917: 280 onwards). The highest Indies authority (the Indies administration) was in the hands of the Governor-General. The first such incumbent was the Commissioner-General Van der Capellen who, in 1814, was also immediately made Governor-General (he held that position from 1816 until 1826). The Governor-General governed in conjunction with the Indies Council, a body comprising several individuals (for example five around 1900). Together they comprised the *gouvernement* or Indies government. The Indies Council once again became effective in 1819 when the commissioners completed their work (see, for instance, *Encyclopaedie* Vol. III 1919: 524). Furthermore, there were local administrators (the Civil Service) which, in Java, was divided into seventeen regions or

[1] Besides Van den Doel (1994) and Hüsken (1988) I have used general literature for this subsection, including several articles in the *Encyclopaedie van Nederlandsch-Indië* ("Dutch East Indies Encyclopedia"), e.g. *Cultuurstelsel* ("Cultivation System", Vol. I 1917: 545-552), *Bestuur* ("Administration", Vol. I 1917: 279-288), *Departementen van algemeen bestuur* ("Departments of general administration", Vol. I 1917: 585-588) and *Koloniaal beleid* ("Colonial policy", Vol. II 1918: 411-420). Where I felt this sense, I have included a reference in the text.

Residencies. Alongside of the heads of regional administrations, the Residents, there were also Assistant-Residents or Controllers. The Javanese heads or Regents did not at that time form part of the Civil Service (though later they did). They worked together with the Assistant-Residents and were regarded as the Dutch administrator's "baby brothers".

The Governor-General was supported by his civil servants assembled in the General Secretariat. The regional heads had their Residential offices at the Civil Service. Alongside of this, the Indies State also recognised a central (civil) governmental system. The Commissioners-General restored this office and extended it (see, for example, *Encyclopaedie* Vol. I 1917: 585). They revived the General Auditor's Office and then installed the Financial Council. Following the governmental statute of 1818, created and decreed by the Commissioners, this Council was re-named; it was dubbed a Head Directorate with one Director and four Councils. This Directorate made itself responsible for the general administration of the domains, goods, incomes and spendings. The Councils were in charge of a further unspecified aspect of the responsibilities.

The financial state of affairs in both the mother country and the colony was in poor shape (see, for example, *Encyclopaedie* Vol. I 1917: 545 and Hüsken 1988: 13). The Dutch state had also saddled itself with the *VOC* debt which amounted to a sum of 120 million guilders. The colony itself was in permanent debt. That had been the case under Daendels and Raffles and things did not improve when Dutch rule was reinstated. Van der Capellen's spendings were high (notably because of various wars) and his sources of income minimal. His application for a large loan was viewed in a dim light by King William I. In 1825 he sent Viscount Du Bus de Gisignies to the Indies to revitalise the economy. Du Bus economised where possible. In 1826 this economy drive led to the shrinking of the central administrative body. Henceforward there was one financial Director-General and two (Vice) Directors: one for Means and Domains and one for Products and Civil Stores.

The Commissioners-General had upheld liberal views but, during his time as Governor-General, Van der Capellen had quickly switched to the other approach. Du Bus was instructed to discover which system was the most effective one and this, of course, refuelled the directional debate (see, for instance, Hüsken 1988: 13-16). In 1827 Du Bus brought out a report in which he lobbied for the development of European companies and free labour. One of the King's advisors was general Van den Bosch. Though he was at first in agreement with Du Bus he came, in 1829, with recommendations for a completely different policy which amounted to a "revamping" of the *VOC* system of compulsory cultures (Hüsken 1988: 15). It had here to do with crops which, unlike rice, could be sold on the international market. The King who was having to deal with, amongst other things, the financial burden of the Javanese war (1825-1839) decided to go along with Van den Bosch's plans.

In 1830 a new governmental statute was introduced in which what was known as Van den Bosch's Cultivation System (*Cultuurstelsel*) formed the basic policy. As Governor-General (1830-1832), as Commissioner-General (1832-1834) and as Minister of the Colonies (1834-1839), the policy's creator also remained its chief innovator. In 1832, when Van den Bosch took the step of approaching the Residencies beforehand in connection with the supplying of quantities and types of products the policy caught on throughout Java. At first it met with opposition from administrators, private parties and even from the Indies Council (*Volksraad*) (see, for instance, *Encyclopaedie* Vol. I 1917: 548). This finally came to an end when Van den Bosch became Commissioner-General, thus gaining dictatorial power. Because of the new system or policy the central state organ was extended in 1832 with the introduction of a Director of Cultures. To ensure that the Cultivation System functioned properly a further governmental statute was introduced in 1836. The main change which this brought was that of the demotion of the Indies Council to an advisory board.

The Cultivation System[2]

The chief principles of the system were the following:

1. The population had to give up a portion of its agricultural land (rice fields) for the purpose of crops to be cultivated for the European market. This would involve the further drawing up of agreements.
2. The portion to be relinquished would amount to a fifth of the total agricultural area of a *desa*.
3. The cultivation of cash-crops for export should not be more labour-intensive than rice growing.
4. No land rent should be levied for the land that had been given up.
5. The crops grown for export should be given to the Indies government. The difference between the estimated value of that and the land rent that would have been due for the relevant land was paid out to the farmers.
6. Crop losses caused by natural disasters would be financed by the government.
7. The Javanese heads were basically in charge, the supervision exercised by European civil servants would be marginal.

The Cultivation System was in the first place directed at sugar and indigo. The raw sugar cane was to be converted into a marketable product in refineries and to this end contracts were signed with private refinery owners (usually of Dutch or Chinese origin). Other crops, such as tea, tobacco, cinnamon and pepper soon followed, these latter crops constituting what were known as "small cultures". Another crop to be rapidly included in the programme was coffee. Unlike with the other crops, new uncultivated land, was used for the growing of coffee crops.

By the time Van den Bosch left the Indies in 1834 he had transferred nine to ten million guilders to the Dutch state. The Cultivation System was at its zenith in the 1840-1860 period when large profits were made. Hundreds of millions of guilders found their way to the Dutch treasury. On average, the profits amounted to some twenty million guilders per annum. The contribution made by Indies takings to the Dutch state's profits as a whole totalled 19% in the 1832-1850 period and 32% in the 1851-1860 period (Fasseur 1975: 204). Coffee, sugar and indigo were the crops that produced the biggest returns. The "small cultures" were a failure; it was only pepper that made a little money.

The Cultivation System also marked the beginning of the era of the Exploitation Policy (*Batig-Slotpolitiek*) where the objective was to secure low export tariffs for colonial products destined for the Netherlands. The exploitation principle continued until 1877, but the relevant policy remained in tact until 1901. In the mother country the profits made from colonial trade were ploughed into, for instance, railway construction work and canal infrastructures. The *Nederlandsche Handel-Maatschappij* ("Dutch Trading Company", abbreviated to *NHM*) took responsibility for the transport and sale of products emanating from the Cultivation System. The *NHM* was established in 1824 by King William I for the purpose of stimulating trade, navigation and industry in the Netherlands. In a certain respect it was a resurrection of the *VOC* era: only that company could sell the products. The trading company received the products from the Indies government on order. Unlike with the *VOC*, though, the profits went to the government. The *NHM* received transport and commission payment. The company put the products on the market in Amsterdam which thus, just as with the *VOC*, became a storage place for colonial products.[3]

[2] I refer particularly to the following literature: Van den Bosch (1834), Van Deventer (1865), Van den Eerenbeemt (1989), Elson (1984), Geertz (1963), Fasseur (1975), Gonggrijp (1957), *Indische Staatsblad* ("Indies Gazette", 1834), Van Niel (1981), Van Schaik (1986), Van Soest (1869-1871) and *Encyclopaedie* ("Encyclopaedia") (Vol. I 1917: 545-552, Vol. II 1918: 415-418). Here and there I have included a reference to these (and other) literature in the text.

[3] Because they arranged transport, *NHM* also stimulated shipbuilding. With its export of cotton to India, they encouraged the textile industry (see Verbong 1988).

In practice the Cultivation System worked differently from the way that had been envisaged (except, no doubt, in the case of the last-mentioned stipulation; see, for instance, Gonggrijp 1928: 123 and also Geertz 1963 and Van Schaik 1986). Though this had not been the intention, a degree of force was clearly involved. It emerged that a fifth of people's land was not always enough, often a third and sometimes half or even more than half of a farmer's land was commandeered. Sugar cane and indigo cultivation was much more labour-intensive than rice cultivation. Land rents were not lowered and there was no making up of the difference between the valued price of the product cultivated and the land rent. When crops failed it was the agriculturist who had to pay for this. The reason why theory and practice had come to lie so far apart was largely because civil servants wanted to make the very most of the profits. This was in their interests too because they received what was termed a "culture commission".

The successes of the Cultivation System were overshadowed by the rising poverty and the increasing number of disasters that were hitting the population and the Cultivation System (all its abuses included) was not the only factor in all of this. "Cultural services" were not the only demands put upon the population. There were other types of compulsory personal services: forced labour for the government, services rendered to Javanese heads, and desa service. When waterworks structures had to be built and maintained the government frequently made use of forced labour. The burden created by all these other services increased considerably in the 1830-1850 period. It was in the Residency of Cirebon where, as a test case, rice had been added to the Cultivation System that things finally came to a head. In 1844 the rice harvest was dismal in many places and in Cirebon that led, in combination with the high rice prices, to famine. A couple of years later things went wrong again, but this time it was worse. The failed harvests led in two Regencies of the Residency of Semarang, namely Demak and Grobogan, to widespread famine (1848-1850). In his overly dramatic description of the situation Van Soest (1871: 220) said the following:

"Whole groups of emaciated, sunken-eyed people, clearly reflecting the dreadful agonies of hunger stumbled along the roads like ghosts. There were those who tried *eating grass and leaves* and who gazed at the cattle with inflamed stares, enraged because those animals could satisfy their hunger with such fodder. Others laid themselves down on the edges of bridges or on the banks of rivers in the hope that, *in sleep they might fall into the water* thus escaping consciousness and their problems"[4].

According to colonial sources, the population of Demak and Grobogan fell from, respectively, 336,000 and 98,500 souls in 1848 to 120,000 and 9000 people by 1850. More than 100,000 of them had died of hunger while the rest had moved into the hinterland. Elsewhere in Central Java population numbers had also dropped by hundreds of thousands for the same reason.[5]

[4] Italics by Van Kol (1901: 342) who quotes in support of his plea for a comprehensive irrigation plan (see **Chapter 8**) Van Soest. Van Kol attributed these words to an "official report". Van Soest, however, relied on supposedly private messages (cf. De Meyier 1891/92: XII-XIII and The Meyier 1902: 177-178). See also Van Bosse (1893).

[5] Van Soest (1971: 221-2), cf. Fasseur (1975: 52-53). Fasseur (1975: 202) considers the Cultivation System "only partly directly to blame" for the famines.

The Governor-General J.J. Rochussen (1845-1851) was quick to limit the forced growing of any crops, including the indigo plant. At the same time he endeavoured to improve the water engineering situations in the badly hit areas. He encouraged an improvement plan for Demak which led, for instance, to the construction of the weir in *desa* Glapan (see **Box 4.1**), mentioned in Chapter 1.

Reforms[6]

The famine in Demak, Grobogan and elsewhere not only prompted technological steps to be taken but it also precipitated a political debate about the Cultivation System in general. In effect, the directional debate initiated at the beginning of the century was revived. But the political arena had changed. From 1840 onwards liberalism had become ever stronger in the Netherlands. This culminated in the constitutional reform of 1848 which gave way to a form of parliamentary democracy thus putting an end to the absolute power of the King which extended to colonial areas. The parliament or the States-General (consisting of the First and the Second Chamber) began to wield its influence upon colonial policy: both the general policy regulations of the Indies government and its financial policy would in future have to be established by the States-General.

This led, in 1854, to yet another new governmental decree for the Indies. The idea behind this was to improve the people's economic situation (which was to include abolishing slavery!) It amounted to a compromise between the advocates and opponents of the Cultivation System[7]. The situation experienced with the system made a liberal line of politics unavoidable but the financial advantages stood in the way of complete abolition from an economic angle. The Cultivation System was thus retained within the new statutes. Regulations were also drawn up which aimed at protecting the population. The new regulations also offered the prospect of free agriculture and free labour and amendments were furthermore made to the central administrative body. The dominant position of Finance was done away with and the control of the various branches of general administration that fell under the overall supervision of the governor-general was placed in the hands of Directors. The King determined the numbers of Directors according to the tasks in hand. Five were appointed, for: Finance, Means and Domains, Products and Civil Supplies, Cultures and for Civil Public Works.

---

[6] In addition to the sources in **Note 2** reference can be made to Van Welderen (1905-1907). Again, I will confine myself to a single reference.

[7] A well-known opponent was W.R. Baron Hoëvell. He inspired Van Soest (1869-1871) to his critical study of the Cultivation System.

Box 4.1 The weir at Glapan

The problem in the area related chiefly to drainage in the wet season. Up until the beginning of the nineteenth century the region was still a marshland area (or inland sea). The *Prauwvaartkanaal* ("Proa traffic channel") constituted the only drainage canal in the area and it made the region dry enough for rice to be cultivated there. Drainage and (in the dry season) water provision remained problematic. In the circumstances, crop failure was a perennial occurrence. The improvement plan presented by the engineer Van Thiel (including plans for a weir in the Tuntang) did not reach fruition. There was neither money nor personnel for this. Immediately after the period of famine steps were taken to change things on the basis of this same plan; the first plan was to expand the drainage canals.

Going on new surveys, an engineer by the name of Dik elaborated the plan for a weir in the Tuntang river. The construction of the weir at Glapan materialised in the 1852-1859 period. The dam forced the water up thirteen metres. There were two inlet locks. The irrigated surface area was approximately 12,000 *bouws* big which was less than had been estimated.

Neither the weir nor the improved drainage system provided an adequate solution to the problems in the region. In 1872 the threat of famine once again loomed large. Because of this, preparations started being made for what would come to be known as the first irrigation project (for an entire irrigation area) based on technical-scientific methods. This project did not start until 1881 and it did not reach completion until 1894. (Slinkers 1891/92, compare *Encyclopaedie* Vol. I 1917: 582-583)[8].

The novel *Max Havelaar,* which appeared in 1860, made public and openly questioned the state of affairs in Java, notably the way in which the population was abused by the Javanese heads[9]. Though its author, Multatuli, was not opposed to the Cultivation System as such he did indirectly contribute to its slow but certain fall from popularity. In this respect it was the actions of Fransen van de Putte, Minister of the Colonies (1863-1866) that had effect. He could be seen as one of the founders of the new liberal colonial policy. In 1860 he had published a paper entitled: *De regeling der suikercontracten op Java* ("The Regulating of Sugar Contracts in Java") in which he argued in favour of abolishing the Cultivation System. Under his regime indigo, tea and cinnamon were removed from the agreement in 1862 and tobacco in 1866. Pepper had already been dropped in 1862. Sugar cultivation remained a part of the Cultivation System but Fransen van de Putte made improvements to this in 1863. He determined that in the future contracts with sugar refiners should be publicly drawn up. This constituted a first step on the road to free enterprise. He also involved himself in the population's irrigation interests (Gonggrijp 1927: 161). The compulsory growing of sugar was ultimately to be gradually abolished as well in the 1870-1891 period. The coffee culture situation to which Douwes Dekker (pseudonym for Multatuli) had already drawn attention persisted – though to a decreasing degree – until 1914. It was the most profitable of all the ventures and also the one that was least detrimental to the population. Van de Putte also put an end to the culture profit shares.

---

[8] See for more details on the project **Chapter 6**.

[9] Translator's note: "In the book *Max Havelaar* (1860) the protagonist, Max Havelaar, a civil servant in Java protests about the way in which the Javanese population is being exploited by the Dutch coloniser but his protest is ignored by his superiors. Multatuli, pseudonym for Eduard Douwes Dekker (1820-1887), not only used his own experience as a civil servant in Java but also the literary form to make the political point that he was opposed the Dutch colonial political stance of the day". The famous Van Sandick (see **Chapter 1**), who in the early eighties of the last century worked in Bantam, concluded (in his *Lief en leed uit Bantam* ["Love and Sorrow from Bantam"], published in 1892) on the basis of local research that other than Multatuli alleged Assistant Resident of Lebak has not been unjustly treated in 1856 and that this case was no disgrace for the Netherlands (see Ott de Vries 1933: 82).

Fransen van de Putte was furthermore responsible for the introduction of what was known as the Accountability Law which was adopted in 1864 and became effective in 1866 (and was later to be amended and updated many times, see *Encyclopaedie* Vol. I 1917: 517 onwards). The Law emanated from the constitution of 1848, especially as far as its financial policy was concerned. The Accountability Law actually required that the Indies budget be established anew each year by the States-General, by law. It was also stipulated that the budget should be specified for every section of the general administration (see below). As a result, the Accountability Law made the budget the basis for the entire colonial policy which was then placed under the control of the States-General.

Van de Putte's Cultural Law was not a success. The point of this Law was to organise the distribution of land to individual private parties and to determine the land rights of the original population. Private industry was slowly developing and the main problem was that of securing land for such enterprise without this being too much at the expense of the original population. Earlier on one of the Ministers for the Colonies, G.H. Uhlenbeck (1862-1863) had submitted a parliamentary bill that would make it possible for the people to rent land on the basis of "communal contracts" (see *Encyclopaedie* Vol. III 1919: 218). His proposal also stated the circumstances under which "inlanders" might be hired as labourers. This bill was not passed. Van de Putte produced a new proposal. He wanted to make people owners of the land to which they had hereditarily determined access. Such a change around was not politically feasible.

The whole question was not resolved until 1870 when the Minister of the Colonies, E. de Waal (1868-1870), another well-known innovator came along. His Agrarian Law supported the population's legal rights. The Law stated that land could be distributed to private parties as property or held in hereditary tenure but only where no possession rights existed. Any form of transfer of legal rights from "inlanders" to "non-inlanders" was prohibited. It was, however, possible to rent land to private parties. Even the Sugar Law that was to put an end to compulsory sugar production was effected during de Waal's term of office. In view of the introduction of both these Laws, 1870 came to be seen as the year when Dutch free trade imperialism started up.

The Accountability Law precipitated a general reorganisation of the central administrative body. In 1866 "general administration departments" were set up, each of which was headed by a Director. The division into departments clearly reflected the changed insight into government tasks. Means and Domains became the terrain of the Department of Finance. Products and Civil Supplies, together with Cultures, was placed under the Civil Service Department. Civil Public Works became a separate department. Another department was the Department of Education, Honorary Services and Industry. In 1870 the Department of Justice was created. It was now the case that within the state organisation there were three bodies that were directly involved in the exercising of colonial administration: the Governor-General's secretariat, the Civil Service (including the Residential office) and the Civil Service Department, the central body for regional administration. The people employed within these organisations were all known as "civil servants" but it was especially those who worked for the Civil Service who carried weight. The inter-relationships were not always clear and so they gave rise to conflict. There was also lack of clarity and conflict between the "administrative " officials, the civil servants, and their technical colleagues, the engineers, in other words between the Civil Service and Civil Public Works.

A public works service

Water and the state[10]

When Dutch rule was reinstated in 1815 the Commissioners-General had focused their attention on "governmental responsibility in relation to the state of the land with regard to water", as the definition for "public works" (*waterstaat*) reads in the Dutch East Indies Encyclopedia (*Encyclopaedie* Vol. IV 1921: 700). In 1818 they drew up a control regulation which stated that "the daily control" of rivers, canals, harbours, seaheads, locks, dams, bridges and roads was the concern of the Resident. This did not apply to Batavia: there the day-to-day supervision was the responsibility of a Chief Inspector who was also in charge of the public works affairs within other Residencies. The Chief Inspector was assisted by three Inspectors, each of whom was responsible for a particular area (similar Public Works Inspections existed in the Netherlands). Civil buildings did not, however, fall under public works. Separate regulations were drawn up for that sector.

In view of the financial problems of the time, King William I decreed, in 1825, that all public works and civil buildings services should be subject to economic measures. In 1827, under the Commissioner-General Du Bus, this led to the cessation of Public Works as an organisational entity (*Encyclopaedie* Vol. III 1919: 708-709 refers to an *administratie* ["administration"]). Public Works was amalgamated with Civil Buildings (also an administration) and both came to fall under the Director for Products and Civil Stores. The consequence for Public Works (and also for Civil Buildings) was that both thus came to lack expert supervision (previously there had been Chief Inspectors). The new regulation saw to it that "engineers" were appointed in Batavia, Surabaya and in Semarang. It was the first time that the term "engineer" was given to someone with a civil function (*Encyclopaedie* Vol. IV 1921: 709). These employees fell "under the direct command" of the relevant Resident. The regulation was of an interim nature. The permanent agreement – which differed from the interim one on a number of points – was drawn up in 1829. The engineer in Batavia was promoted to the position of independent Chief Engineer. The first of these incumbents was J. Tromp, an important individual in the early history of the Public Works Organisation in the Indies. Already in government service since 1816, he became the Batavian Chief Engineer from 1828 until 1854.

In those days engineers did not have an important part to play in the field of irrigation. Except for in Batavia, Public Works Regulations placed responsibility for the upkeep and construction of irrigation works with the Resident. That meant that at local level it was often civil servants who took it upon themselves to have dams and channels created. The actual work was carried out by the local population, on a forced labour basis, of course. Overall responsibility for the work was in the hands of the relevant civil servants and/or of the Javanese administrative chiefs. Large works required the help of many thousands of people deployed in forced labour. Technically, this work was approached in a Javanese way. For instance, massive earthen dams were created from washed-up soil and from a small percentage of transported soil. The framework was made of branches bundled together. It could take more than a year to construct such a dam. The number of workers employed was sometimes more than 1000 a day. Irrigation works that were made in this way were not very durable. Any random *banjir* could ruin such dams. At any rate, they never lasted more than five or six years. (Van Gendt 1868).

[10] Much information can be found in the article *Waterstaat* ("Public Works", *Encyclopaedie* Vol. III 1919: 700-731), co-written by the Meyier. Melchior (1914: 90) wrote about (an earlier version of) this article that it contains a "treasure of historic particularities", whose collection must have cost "a lot of work and study". See also Bosse (1893).

The vast sums of money made available at that time for public works just gives one an indication of the hugeness of the scale of such projects. The workers recruited by the Civil Service received some kind of payment even if it was minimal. The *f* 622,000 expended on public works in the 1845-1849 period which was "no mean sum for that time" was probably largely spent on paying labourers for their efforts (*Verslag BOW* 1892: 170)[11]. In special circumstances the Civil Service did call upon engineers to help them construct various works. This led to activities in the Sampean Delta and to the construction of the dam at Glapan. The number of engineers remained limited: three or four until 1829, five between 1829 and 1844 and 10 in the period up until 1854 (*Verslag BOW* 1892: 170). Since they were also expected to carry out other duties as well (see below) that naturally restricted the possibilities. The rise in the numbers of engineers would indicate that they were becoming increasingly involved in irrigation works activities.

One engineer who stood out in the early days of modern irrigation technology in the Indies was H. de Bruyn (familiar from the Sampean Works), a former military engineering officer (trained at the Royal Military Academy in Breda) who, after an unsuccessful career as a coffee plant grower, once again began to serve the country in 1847 and ended up in the Products and Civil Supplies Directorate. From 1852 until 1858 he was the Public Works Division engineer stationed in Surabaya. De Bruyn came to be associated with the Solo river estuary diversion, but that was not his main achievement. The Public Works Division situation in the Surabaya area – which had become the most important Division – was bad around 1850. One of the problems was that the Surabaya river (one of the two branches of the gigantic Brantas river) was transporting ever less water. Apart from anything else, the sugar refineries in the Brantas delta were suffering because of this. De Bruyn therefore ensured that water was better distributed between the two river branches. One of the works undertaken in this connection was the building of the movable Lengkong weir (see **Box 4.2** and **Figure 4.5**).

The emergence of the Civil Public Works Department

Governor-General Rochussen who had witnessed the disasters in the Demak and Grobogan areas while he was in charge there and who had done all in his power to ease the situation had previously revealed that he was in favour of irrigation works being created by engineers. In 1847 he wrote a letter to the Minister of the Colonies, J.C. Baud (1840-1848), in which he requested that the engineer numbers be increased. He emphasised the importance of "artificial irrigation" and also drew attention to the worsening ecological conditions:

"It is thanks to artificial irrigation that the Indies soil is so fertile, indeed, without such conditions it would be impossible to *guarantee* the expansion of rice cultivation.
I emphasise here the word *guaranteed* because the matter of relying on any regularity in the changing of the seasons, upon which rice culture originally depended, seems more and more to be founded on a weak basis because the rains are not so frequent and in central Java they are not so abundant as in the past. (Naturalists ascribe this to the disappearance of wooded land which has gradually had to make way for different types of cultures and which has been used to provide construction material and fuel for our defence works, civil buildings, for sugar refineries and indigo factories, for tobacco sheds and for so many other agricultural and industrial needs).
We must therefore no longer allow rice cultivation to be dependent on rainfall; it should, in fact, be based on the above-mentioned guaranteed basis of *artificial irrigation*" (Rochussen 1853: 209, compare *Encyclopaedie* Vol. IV 1921: 714).

---

[11] A modern irrigation work in this period was a lock in the Melirip rivier (see **Box 4.2**).

Box 4.2 The movable weir at Lengkong

When, in 1843, a dam in the Melirip river, constructed by the Javanese looked as if it was about to collapse it was decided that this should be replaced by a cemented weir (a dam-like barrage with doors in it). This weir would spare the thousands "of human hands involved in the upkeep and monitoring of the dam" (*Nota* ["Memorandum"] 1857: 59). It was designed by H.A. Tromp who, in the 1834-1843 period, was the engineer with the highest status in the Surabaya Public Works Division. The job was completed in 1847.

In its lower reaches the Brantas branched out to form two rivers known as the Porrong and the Surabaya. The Melirip linked together these two branches and supplied the Surabaya river with water from the Porrong. Javanese and Dutch intervention in the water engineering situation gradually gave rise to a situation in the whole Brantas delta area which, in the early fifties, became intolerable. The poor location and the poor traditional maintenance of the weir in the Melirip only amplified the problem. In the east monsoon season there was a shortage of water and in the west monsoon period there was the danger of flooding. This was detrimental to rice and sugar cane cultivation of the area. The sugar industry was important. There were eleven sugar refineries in the area. Water was needed in the first place for the growing of sugar cane but at that time the refineries also required running water to power their water wheels.

De Bruyn put forward an improvement programme which included the suggestion of building a movable weir (or weir sluice: a weir with locks) at Lengkong. All in all, it involved a whole new system of water distribution. The works, which included several irrigation sluices (inlet sluices) at Lengkong, a number of canals and four overflow sluices were completed by 1857. The entire project formed what was at that time the biggest network of waterworks in the Indies. It provided irrigation for an area equivalent to 40,000 *bouws*. Five and a half year's work went into it. The total cost amounted to over 2.6 million guilders. The sugar industry expressed its thanks in the form of a silver dinner service. De Bruyn himself thanked the Governor-General Duymaer van Twist (1851-1856): "He, in fact, had complete and utter confidence in the designer from the point of view that he gave him free rein to do as he pleased; he made available the required funds – a sum of 24 tons of gold – without consulting the Chief Administrator and no limits were put on the annually expended sums" (De Bruyn 1870: 25).

(Sources: *Bericht* 1854, *Nota* 1857, Kielstra 1887: 1144-116)[12].

The necessary "artificial irrigating" of agricultural land was a task that Rochussen believed to be the specific domain of engineers. He had little confidence in the "residents and their inferior type of management", which at that time was chiefly focused on the creating of irrigation works. Despite all the good intentions "[they] will, in practice, come up against the lack of specialist knowledge of the engineer and in their many other activities they will not be able to compensate for that" (Rochussen 1853: 209). The Civil Service employees knew little about irrigation and that led to a waste of manpower. Rochussen (ibid.) also found it "no wonder"

[12] The movable weir at Lengkong of De Bruyn was in service over a hundred years. In 1973 he was replaced by a new one. A part of the wind works of the old weir has been saved and is exhibited on the spot. When working in the Brantas delta in the beginning a similar chain of events occurred as the "nature-technology spiral" in the Sampean Works described in the previous chapter.

Figure 4.5: Door of the movable weir in the Brantas river at Lengkong, 1910
(photo UBL KITLV 27547)

"... that in most of the works activities undertaken by civil servants a degree of wasted manpower was to be detected which could be converted into figures if one were to add up the expenses of all the costs in terms of days worked and all the building materials provided by forced labour. This, in turn, would create amazement because of the expenses involved in deploying such so-called cost-free labour".

Rochussen stood up for expert involvement in irrigation. For him this meant "that no major irrigation works should be constructed which had not been surveyed and designed by experts" (p. 210) and further "that the maintenance of existing works be supervised by experts" and "that an irrigation system be adopted for the entire island, after expert investigation" (ibid.) Rochussen also wanted the Royal Decree of 1825 to be withdrawn so that an own organization for Public Works could be reinstated (pp. 140-141).

Meanwhile civil engineers had come under attack. The amalgamation of the Public Works and Civil Structures Administrations had led to problems. Public Works engineers were now also involved in the construction of other than water engineering works. This led to poor results, notably in the field of civil constructions. There was, moreover, a shortage of personnel and it was always the public works projects that were neglected.[13]

Rochussen's plea was acknowledged in 1854. A year earlier the later Minister of the Colonies, Uhlenbeck, had been given the order to put forward suggestions on a better way of managing public works. This immediately led to the creation of a new, but interim, service. Uhlenbeck was a military engineers' major and thus someone from outside the "corps". Because of these proposals King William III was prompted to extend the central state machinery in 1854 by appointing a "public works director". The resolution led to the establishment of a "bureau of public works" which had as its objective "to exercise control and supervision over public works and the country's civil public works organisations" (*Indisch Staatsblad* 1954: 1). Civil buildings and public works thus remained combined. The service's first Director was Uhlenbeck who remained in office until 1861.

The Bureau consisted of 82 technical employees, 35 of whom were engineers: an Inspector and Head, a Chief Engineer, three First Class Engineers, six Second Class Engineers, ten Third Class Engineers and fourteen Trainee (or Aspiring) Engineers. There were 47 Supervisors in four classes. The Bureau also had six Chief Clerks. There were also Coolie Chiefs (*Mandurs*), Clerks and Office Juniors (for these people no numbers were given, just sums of money). For all these employees and for the other costs a fixed allowance existed within the Indies budget of *f* 289,000. The resolution also indicated that engineers should preferably be recruited from the Royal Academy in Delft and should have their civil engineer's diploma. In special cases it was possible to sit an engineer's exam in the Indies under a commission of civil engineers who had studied in Delft (*Indisch Staatsblad* 1854: 1-2).

Further stipulations followed in 1855. The Governor-General, Duymaer Van Twist, then decided to establish eight Public Works Divisions (alternatively known as Inspectorates). Java had four such Divisions: Batavia, Tegal (later: Cirebon), Semarang and Surabaya. The resolution determined how personnel was divided between the Divisions and the Bureau in Batavia. In the Divisions the concern was to have guide numbers. Only the Fourth Division (Surabaya) was

[13] See De Leon (1851). For this critic (p. 15) buildings and water management structures are works "that can hardly be brought to one branch of government, as the experience, in the Indies, has already shown so many years without harming the parts themselves mutually". De Leon suggested to place civil buildings elsewhere, notably under the military engineering corps. Despite the fact that much went wrong in irrigation works, he limited himself in his critical review of the operations of the "civil engineering corps" to examples in other areas. By the way, the aforementioned J. Tromp, Chief Engineer in Batavia, was heavily criticized in the publication of De Leon. Public Works engineers were at that time in the Netherlands involved in the construction of civil buildings as well (see Ten Horn-van Nispen et al. 1994).

given a Chief Engineer (De Bruyn). At that juncture the head office in Batavia was divided into two Divisions: a First or Technical Bureau and a Second or Administrative Bureau. The Technical Division had three engineers (the Director included) and two Supervisors. Four of the six Chief Clerks worked in the Administrative Division (*Indisch Staatsblad* 1855: 1-2, 4; for details of the way in which the personnel members were divided up see the included "numerical state division"). The balance of power between Public Works and the Civil Service was unclear. As far as Public Works personnel in the regions was concerned the regulation announced different arrangements:

"The relationship between the engineers and supervisors to the heads of regional administration and the division chiefs will be further stipulated in separate ordinances (*Indisch Staatsblad* 1855: 4)".

As we shall see that was to take some time! The Public Works Bureau marked the beginning of an independent public works service. During the state reforms of 1866, when departments with general administrations were set up, the Public Works Bureau was converted into the Department of Civil Public Works.

Director De Bruyn

After the Bureau of Public Works had been established De Bruyn, the Chief Engineer, wrote a memorandum in which he lobbied for expansion but especially also for Public Works to be organised in a completely different way (De Bruyn 1858[14]). He based his views on the irrigation situation in Java which he did not see as favourable. Unlike other observers[15], he was not impressed by the skills of Indies farmers when it came to the matter of erecting irrigation works:

"The Dutch, coming as they did from their flat and marshy country, were surprised to see how each year the Javanese provided their rice fields with water that came down from the mountains. Every defective weir, every defective lock, every little dyke alongside of rice fields seemed to them like a feat of engineering" (De Bruyn 1858: 120).

Elsewhere in the memorandum De Bruyn used even stronger wording: "And the uninitiated stared in amazement at the products of inland water engineering, all of which was put down to instinct!" In passing he also criticises the idea alive at the time that the Javanese possessed natural talents where water engineering was concerned.

De Bruyn maintained that it did not take much to realise that Javanese irrigation engineering was nothing special as is evidenced by what he intimated in another connection:

"a civilised layman [need] only use his eyes ... to see how badly the inlanders deal with water; to see how it is wasted in the most irresponsible of ways; to see how little each man thinks about his neighbour; how randomly the water is dealt with that could be controlled" (cited in: Kielstra 1887: 128).

---

[14] The report is partially published in Kielstra (1885: 118-121, it was a brief description here) and partly in De Bruyn (1863: 61-65, the part about "rivers and waterworks"). The references concern the page numbers in these publications.

[15] An early example was Mr. H.W. Muntinghe, who held high administrative functions among both the Dutch and English governments. He wrote in a report in 1817 about the Javanese among others: "along hills and valleys he leads his waters" (quoted in Gonggrijp 1957). Van Sandick (1912b: 918) spoke of "the tale of the beaver instinct of the Javanese".

In his memorandum of 1858 De Bruyn decries Javanese water works point by point. When it came to building dykes, for example, "the Javanese did not have the faintest notion", the irrigating of fields was "extremely primitive" and the weirs

"are too numerous, cannot stand up to sudden water surges or to overflows and they lack protection against undermining. In every rainy season most of these works are swept away by the force of the flow, only to be erected again with similar lack of skill" (p. 121).

According to De Bruyn it was high time for the irrigation situation in Java to be improved. He referred in that connection to the Cultivation System. He called it "a brilliant system" but argued that people had not thought about the required transport means and irrigation works (1858: 119, see also **Chapter 1**). He found that "the marvellous results that had been promised" could only be realised with "those works which in all civilised countries could only be created with the help of the knowledge of civil engineers" (ibid.)[16].

In his account De Bruyn gave an overview of the requirements and established that in this respect Public Works did not or was not able to provide enough for these requirements. He then went on to plan an organisation that would be more fitted to the task. It consisted of a general and a regional service. The general organisation would have to comprise seven public works divisions (or districts) in Java. De Bruyn related the borders of those regions to the basins of the rivers. All the division heads would have to come directly under the service's Director. These heads would only be responsible for supervising. The execution of work would not be their responsibility but the responsibility of the Director. The regional service would consist of local engineers who would be subordinate to the Resident of the relevant area. De Bruyn wanted to create "a rich, well formed and well tested corps of public works engineers" (1858: 119). He advocated also that the lower-level staff, both of European and Javanese origin, should be well schooled.

De Bruyn sent his memorandum to the Director, Uhlenbeck, who immediately returned it under the pretext that it was inopportune. While in the Netherlands for a while, for health reasons, De Bruyn showed his memorandum to Rochussen who was by then Minister of the Colonies (1858-1861) and to J. Loudon who was to succeed Rochussen as Minister of the Colonies (1861-1862) and who was later to become Governor-General (1872-1875). Both gave their approval and, insofar as circumstances permitted it, De Bruyn received their support.

In 1860 De Bruyn and the engineer S. Westerbaan Muurling, who was later to be his son-in-law, went on a study trip to France and Italy. Westerbaan Muurling had just completed his studies at the Academy in Delft and was planning to go to the Indies. Upon the advice of De Bruyn, who found practical forming important alongside of theoretical training, Rochussen decided to send the two on a trip. Later the travellers were joined by another pupil, the Architect A. van Lakerveld. In his travel report De Bruyn once again indicated what action he maintained should be taken in the Indies. He mentioned four points:

"The woods in the plains should be replanted and the mountains once again filled with trees.
Every residence should be given a water or a river and dyke administration.
The rivers and everything connected with them should come under technical supervision.
In Java a fixed water measurement should be established" (De Bruyn 1863: 177).

[16] As Rochussen De Bruyn thought that government officials could not help, because they lacked "both the time and the training for thorough investigation and satisfactory treatment" (De Bruyn 1858: 119).

De Bruyn maintained that before deforestation and reforestation occurred and administrations could be installed, local research should first be carried out. He recommended creating a commission for this purpose. Expert supervision and a fixed water measurement would only become feasible possibilities if Public Works was properly organised.

In 1861 De Bruyn was made Director of Public Works by the Indies government. De Bruyn tried to put his ideas into practice but that did not work very well. In 1865, under the Minister Fransen van der Putte, the Public Works staff was expanded. The number of engineers thus rose to 65 and included: one Director, two First Class Chief Engineers, two Second Class Chief Engineers, eight First Class Engineers, twelve Second Class Engineers, twenty Third Class Engineers and twenty Trainee Engineers. De Bruyn had in fact requested 181 engineers![17] In 1867 a new Public Works Regulation was drawn up (*Indisch Staatsblad* 1867). It reflected precious little of the ideas put forward by De Bruyn. The Regulation chiefly laid down how the relationship should be defined between the Director of Public Works, his staff and the Resident. According to this arrangement the balance of power clearly fell with the Resident:

"Each head of a regional administration is a superintendent for the land's civil public buildings and works in his particular region and so he is, as such, responsible for the appropriate management of this branch of service" (*Indisch Staatsblad* 1867: 1)[18].

With regard to the personnel of the Public Works Divisions (see above) the following points were laid down:

"The senior engineer has, in the district for which he is responsible, direct control over the area's civil constructions and works ...
The senior engineer and the other civil public works officials are directly answerable to the head of the regional administration" (*Indisch Staatsblad* 1867: 2).

De Bruyn had to contend with a shortage of funds, personnel and competence, which meant that he could do little to improve the irrigation situation. Sometimes he was forced to agree to propositions in which engineers had not been involved as was the case with the Javanese dams for the Menenteng channel (see **Box 4.3**) and in the Pemali river (see **Chapter 5**).

De Bruyn's far-reaching proposals and his unceasing battle to achieve these ends put him on a bad footing with the government. The introduction of the Accountability Law in 1867 did little to improve relations. De Bruyn found that as a result of this Law he really required more administrative personnel, but that wish was never honoured. In the end he returned to the Netherlands in 1868 on sick-leave.

---

[17] The technical staff of Public Works was further extended to the following composition: four Architects First Class, four Second Class, fifteen Overseers First Class, 30 Second Class and 30 Third Class. The administrative office was also reinforced and came to consist of a Head and twelve Clerks.

[18] The term "superintendent" was not defined, and gave rise to discussion. The engineers understood the term in the sense that the Resident had the power "to act on behalf of the government in cases of urgency" (Post 1889: 117). They found that the Resident should not use them for the purpose of achieving his own ideas in the technical field. In 1871 the concept received the content the engineers wished. (Ibid.).

De Bruyn the second time around

In 1869 De Bruyn gave a speech to the Utrecht division of the *Maatschappij tot nut van den Javaan* ("Company for the Benefit of the Javanese"). He once again showed how

"being informed by science and experience was the most effective and economical way of achieving a large-scale systematic improvement and expansion of Javanese irrigation networks which was something that, in turn, would give rise to such wealth" (De Bruyn 1870: 52[19]).

Box 4.3 The Menenteng channel

In Losari, a District in Cirebon, it was necessary to draw water from the Cisanggarung for small farming businesses and, above all else, for sugar cultivation. Apart from requiring water for the growing of sugar cane it was also needed to power the water wheels for two sugar refineries. It was decided that in order to obtain such quantities of water a dam should be erected in the Menenteng gorge. When traditional methods failed the engineer J.A. Krajenbrink drew up a plan in 1843 for the construction of a dam and a watercourse through a tunnel. The plan never materialised. Another plan of Krajenbrink's, which possibly came about because of Van Thiel's recommendations, envisaged constructing a framework dam beneath the gorge. The building of this dam commenced in 1844. Its executor, Krajenbrink, operated on behalf of the Cultures' Directorate. In 1849 when the dam was as good as finished it capsized as a consequence of a *banjir*.
Other solutions were put forward but ultimately the relevant Resident settled for a plan for a temporary Javanese dam above a gorge and a watercourse excavated in the rocks there. By then the situation had changed: both sugar refineries had switched to steam power. When, in 1863, De Bruyn decided to go along with the Resident's decision the administration executed the work. Each year the dam had to be rebuilt.
Several years later, the Javanese dam became the subject of critical discussion for a commission of engineers. The plan for reconstruction and improvement was not rounded off until 1878. It was a plan produced by the engineer De Meyier (see **Figure 4.3**) with alterations proposed by, amongst others, the engineer Pet. Work started in the same year and it was completed by means of forced labour. The engineer who had overall responsibility was W.F. Heskes. During the job, which took four years to complete, it became clear that various adaptations would have to be made. The area irrigated covered 10,000 *bouws*. The project's total cost was about 535 thousand guilders" (Menenteng 1888).

In his speech he was expressly concerned with "the material interests of the inland population" (p. 5). This speech, De Bruyn's previous writings and also his recommendations produced in response to a request made by the Minister, De Waal, on what should be done in the area for irrigation led, in 1871, to the creation of a commission that was given the task to submit "a fully worked out and elucidated proposal for the regulation of irrigation systems in *Java* and *Madura*" (De Bruyn et al. 1875: 1). Even though he was back in the Indies by 1871, de Bruyn was not invited by the Governor-General Loudon to join the committee until 1872. Loudon's predecessor, Governor-General Mijer (1866-1872) had kept De Bruyn on reduced pay in the interim period. The commission brought out its report in 1873 (De Bruyn et al. 1875[20]). The

[19] De Bruyn (1870: 523) made a connection with the "pending major Agrarian Law" adopted in 1870 (see above).

[20] De Bruyn was probably the principal author (see the Meyier 1921: 719).

report contained, amongst other things, a draft regulation plan for irrigation. It ascribed general water control to the Director of Civil Public Works. According to another stipulation, Java and Madura should be divided into irrigation districts "which would have as their borders the various river area divisions" (p. 38).

As the following articles show, the draft regulation left little doubt about who was in control:

"Art. 28. In each district a chief engineer or engineer supported by the required European and Inland personnel is entrusted with the task of water control, policing, distribution and irrigation. Art. 29. Everywhere in this regulation where there is mention of authorised power, what is meant is the chief engineer or engineer referred to in the previous article" (ibid.).

The ruling contained more stipulations relating, for example, to watercourse rights and to the transportation of water over another's land as well as to the distribution of water and the relevant water amounts. The report also gave an overview of the irrigation situation of the day in Java and Madura, notably from the "water rights" angle[21]. At the instigation of the commission Loudon instructed De Bruyn, in 1872, to carry out further research into the irrigation situation in Java.

In 1874 De Bruyn once again became Director of the Civil Public Works Department. Again this was Loudon's work. When, in 1875, he had to make way for Van Lansberge (1875-1881) De Bruyn no longer received support. Under the new Governor-General the climate changed as far as irrigation was concerned: "In the Indies it seemed that the Public Works Organisation was being seen more and more as a luxury commodity" (Kielstra 1887: 136). In the seventies circumstances were indeed unfavourable for enterprises that cost money: coffee prices fell and the Aceh war intensified. The report submitted by the above-mentioned commission was therefore not followed by action which meant that the draft ruling referred to was not pursued. During De Bruyn's second term as a Director the personnel numbers were again increased within Public Works, in 1874. This was a consequence of a proposal made by his predecessor, the engineer W.H.F.H. van Raders (1870-1874)[22]. The number of engineers rose to 75: five First Class engineers (three of whom were to operate as independent Inspectors), five Second Class Chief Engineers, fifteen First Class Engineers, 25 Second Class, fifteen Third Class and ten Trainee Engineers[23]. As far as irrigation works went, little again happened, construction-wise. Tired of all the conflict, De Bruyn handed in his resignation in 1877 and it was accepted.

[21] For technical data was referred to the writings of De Bruyn, including the publications of 1863 and 1870.

[22] In the period 1868-1870 engineer Beyerinck, who we encountered in the history of the Sampean weir, was Director of Civil Public Works (see for a list of directors **Appendix J**). Van Raders had been in the said committee.

[23] Background of the formation extension of Civil Public Works was the unfavourable rank ratio of the layout of the engineering corps of 1865. The new ratio gave more promotion opportunities. A short time later, the number of Chief Engineers was reduced with two and the number of First Class Engineers increased by two. (*Encyclopaedie* Vol. IV 1921: 718, 721-722). To the benefit of a regular complement of staff a scheme was introduced in 1874 involving the recruitment of future engineers studying at the Polytechnic School in Delft (the successor of the previously mentioned academy for the training of engineers, see Baudet and Makkink 1992) under favourable terms, including a scholarship and after graduation, before being sent to the Indies, a prospect of a year secondment to large projects in Europe. This arrangement has been in force for only four years, but among the 19 engineers who came to work by it were "eminent forces", including engineer Lamminga. (See Ott de Vries 1933: 82).

Reaction to the reaction

The Civil Service employees felt that De Bruyn's actions had gone against them and they were supported in this by Van Lansberge, the Governor-General. In view of the unrest he had a new Public Works Regulation drawn up outside Civil Public Works. The man Van Lansberge commissioned to do this was J.P. Sprenger van Eyk. He was the Director of Finance and, as such, responsible for the compilation of the Accountability Law. For the engineers, the regulations amounted to a retrogressive step. The Residents became (even more) involved in the management and control of public works affairs. These were the ruling's opening words: "The heads of regional administration are responsible for the management and control of the country's public works" (*Indisch Staatsblad* 1877: 1). The number of Public Works Divisions in Java was limited to three. Regarding the position of engineers within the Divisions, the ruling stated the following: "The civil public works civil servants working in any given region are obliged to follow the instructions of the head of the regional administration" (ibid.). With the introduction of this ruling Civil Public Works management passed into "administrative" hands. The choice fell with H.J. Bool who had made his reputation as "secretarial official" (he was Director of the Civil Public Works Department from 1877 until 1879).

The ruling precipitated sharp reactions from the engineers. One of the milestones was the book written by Post, *Over den waterstaat in Nederlandsch-Indië* ("About public works in the Dutch Indies") that was published in 1879. As was clearly publicised on the title page of his book, Post was a First Class Engineer within the Civil Public Works Department. His book constituted a sharp criticism of all administrative intervention in technical affairs. Post, like Rochussen and De Bruyn, was critical of the irrigation works that had been created by Javanese and administrative employees and he supported his argument with numerous examples[24]. Post found that the technological "hobbyism" of Civil Service administrators had led to the "useless squandering" of the population's labour and time. He thereby indicated that apart from involving ordinary forced labour it also sometimes involved "disguised" forced labour[25].

Post pointed out that the image that many civil servants had of Javanese irrigation efforts was a positive one. They saw irrigation as "a matter for which the inlanders, through their centuries-old experience had gained special knowledge" (p.90). This sometimes led to the view that it might be best not to interfere: "People worry that too much intervention on the part of the authorities might create confusion rather than be of any use" (ibid.). By supporting the actions of the civil servants this constituted a direct attack on the work of the engineers. Making use of the "special knowledge" of the Javanese and of their resources in the form of forced labour, Post whole-heartedly supported the construction of irrigation and other public works. Post's comments were blatantly clear:

[24] A "horrible example" of administrative intervention Post (1879: 33) found in the situation in Demak: "The fertility of this division, the former stock-barn of rice for the whole of Java, has been deteriorated by forty or fifty years ago carelessly constructed dams, such that this same region now received the nickname of "the classic land of famine"; while this landscape that used to be so fertile cannot now, other than at the expense of some millions in irrigation works, permanently be able to meet the need for sufficient food for its own people". Thus Post pinned the famine in Demak (1848-1850) on to the administrative officials. So the region had ever been a "stock-barn" of rice (see Van Bosse 1893: 80). The Panarukan Regency in the Sampean area was sometimes called the storehouse of Java as well (C. 1873). See also **Box 4.1**.

[25] In the nineteenth century one tried several times to curb the forced labour, but that remained without much result. Forced labour would continue to exist on Java until 1916. (See e.g. Gonggrijp 1957: 128-129).

"It should be mentioned that the way in which the Javanese and, in their wake, administrative civil servants, learning from their example, build dykes might well be seen as an answer to the question of how a dyke should *not* be constructed (pp. 33-34, note 1).

The measures taken in recent years in Batavia in matters related to public works can only be explained by proposing that it must be a fallacy that the Javanese are excellent irrigation engineers" (p. 89).

Post maintained that civil servants were not "business-like". One of his remarks (p. 125) on the civil servant, Bool's, succeeding of De Bruyn as Director of Civil Public Works was this: "Where are Mr. Bool's qualifications, what are the skills that give him the authority and competence to in any way judge the engineers?"

One particularly good example of the lack of knowledge of civil servants emerges from a conversation that Post had (in company) with O. van Rees, the man who was later to become Governor-General (1884-1888). This man believed that the Javanese were such good irrigation engineers that when irrigating their rice fields they were even able to make water flow uphill in open channels. Van Rees was convinced that this was no optical illusion. The secret supposedly resided in the fact

"that the Javanese are so good at selecting terrain that the water first flows downhill for several kilometres to then, after having passed the lowest watercourse point, continue several kilometres up a sloping channel until the sawas that have to be irrigated are reached" (p. 88)[26].

Post believed that as a result of the Accountability Law there was a tendency for public works and other service areas to be made subservient to the "Batavian secretariat" (p. 149). According to him, it was because of the 1877 Regulation that engineers had been involved. Post maintained that several other earlier resolutions anticipated this. He pointed, in this connection, to the resolution of 1876 which claimed that a large number of works including dykes, watercourses and dams were – as regards design and construction – in the hands of civil servants. As far as the Regulation itself was concerned, Post (p. 121) showed that he was offended when it came to the matter of being "put to work" by engineers:

"Such being set to work is reminiscent of the `putting to work' of prisoners which does, as indicated in the first article, have certain connotations in administrative language. In other words, objections on the part of engineers against orders made by you, the Resident, relating to technical matters may not be heard or tolerated by you. Your orders have to be followed in silence and without the slightest protest".

Post's book was even discussed in parliament. Bureaucratic reactions were inevitable and a pamphlet written by Van Gijn ensued. He wrote his *De verwaandheid van de technici contra de kommiezerij* ("The Conceitedness of Technologists towards Administrators") from his perspective as a clerk. His opinion was as follows:

[26] Van Rees later claimed that he had only said this in order to make Post, ever to promote respect for the subordinate engineers, angry (Van Sandick 1912b: 918).

"The entire contents of the book amount to nothing less than a series of incorrect presentations of the facts and, in the rare instances where the truth is told, part of the truth is concealed so that a document of accusations is compiled against the 'Secretariat-Clerks' ..., which invents certain facts, half tells others and takes yet others so completely out of context that no unbiased researcher can adhere to the opinion presented by the writer" (pp. 3-4).

Van Gijn suggested that many engineers deeply disdained anything "that smacked of *administration, rules, order* and *law*" and that they "*forced* the government, *urging it most urgently* to create stipulations that gave technology a subordinate role" (p. 5).[27]

The resistance put up by the civil servants did nothing to help. The protest mounted by the engineers compelled the organization of Public Works, its relationship to the Civil Service included, to again be forced to come to a head. This occurred with a regulation that appeared in 1885 (*Indisch Staatsblad* 1885b). The gist of this was that Public Works was subdivided into a General and a Regional Service. As has been demonstrated, this had already been lobbied for by De Bruyn. Within the important General Service the engineers were ultimately subordinate to their own Director and thus independent of the Resident. The 1885 regulations placed engineers in such a position in relation to the civil servants that nothing more would have to be relinquished on their part.

Irrigation and the state

Headworks

The construction of Van Thiel's framework dam in 1832 marked the beginning of the intervention of engineers in the Sampean delta and in Indies irrigation affairs. At Situbondo it was not until the eighties that the efforts of engineers resulted in a satisfactory final situation. At long last a weir had been constructed that could be called permanent and which owed much of its permanence to the creation of an encircling *banjir* canal. The permanent weir in the Sampean constructed in the 1830-1885 period serves as an example of modern irrigation engineering. Other such works were the weir at Glapan in the Tuntang, the Surabaya delta works (including the movable weir in the Lengkong), the Menenteng channel and the works in Bagelen (see **Box 4.4**)[28].

[27] See for the discussion, among others, De Bordes (1880) and *De Indische Gids* (1880 2 I: 288-292, 893-899, II: 266-269).

[28] Furthermore, in the period 1830-1885 some (small) works were performed in Galuh (Cirebon), Bantam and Krawang (Batavia). Reviews of works from the period to broadly 1890 among others in Van Kol (1901) and Van Bosse (1893). Important works in the Netherlands in the last century, whose construction was made possible by the surpluses in the Indies were: the North Sea Canal (1865-1876) and the New Waterway (1866-1872). (The North Holland Canal was dug earlier, namely in the period 1819-1824). The first serious plans for the *Zuiderzee* ("South Sea") Works date from mid-nineteenth century, the plan of engineer C. Lely 1891, was only in 1918 decided to implement. (See Ringers 1938, Ten Horn-van Nispen et al. 1994, Van de Ven 1993).

Box 4.4 Irrigation works in Bagelen

In the old region of Bagelen (amalgamated with Kedu since 1901) the work of the engineer G.A. Pet led, in the sixties of the nineteenth century, to this region being known as "the classical technical irrigation area" in Java (Weijs 1913: 14).
One example was to be found in the Rebuk watercourse improvements. This channel was one of two that led away from the Bedono river. There were no man-made structures and each year much manual labour was required to repair and maintain the channels. The *prise d'eau* or inlet was renewed by cutting away rocks that jutted out into the river. The inlet was given a lock. In order to direct the water to the old channel a tunnel was excavated in the rocks. The channel was deepened and linked with a second channel via a second tunnel that passed right through a series of hills and which thus also no longer required a separate inlet. Other tasks involved constructing two deluge dams, two overflows and a culvert. By 1867 the work was completed. The watercourse provided 2260 *bouws* with irrigation water. A total of 164,880 working days of forced labour had been used up and a further *f* 7485. Pet estimated that the returns on improvement work amounted to *f* 40,000 per year. He arrived at this conclusion because he anticipated that there would be a rise of *f* 20 per *bouw* in the land rent value. Thanks to all the expert guidance the job was quickly completed: "The fact that this work has, from the very beginning, progressed steadily and successfully may be ascribed to the fact that from start to finish there has been the uninterrupted and good expert supervision (of the engineer I.F. van Lakerveld)". (Pet, cited in: De Bruyn 1870: 32; all the information on the Rebuk channel derives from an account written by Pet in 1869, largely reported by De Bruyn 1870)[29].

The dam in the Sampean and other irrigation works, too, were created to encourage the cultivation of sugar cane which meant that they served the interests of the state and of private industry. Sugar cane was a crop that farmers cultivated for "higher authorities". In the days of the *VOC* there was a thriving sugar cultivation industry in Batavia while sugar growing elsewhere was of little significance. This had partly to do with the climate: in West Java it was more humid. It was only when, at the beginning of the nineteenth century, a variety of cane was discovered (at the East Javan experimental station in Pasaruan) that was suited to the drier East Javan climate, that the whole sugar industry could really take off. From Pasaruan the industry quickly caught on, also in the Sampean area. (Go 1966: 52-64, compare Leidelmeijer 1992). The process of improving irrigation systems was also in the interests of the small farming rice cultivation industry. The weir in Glapan was constructed after the area had been struck by famine. Again, though this irrigation structure was chiefly constructed for the sugar industry the rice growers were also able to benefit from it. After all, the same *sawas* were used for rice and sugar cane because the crops were grown in rotation. The other function of the irrigation works was to provide a drainage system: all part and parcel of irrigation provision and also, at first, to provide the power required for the sugar refineries. With the introduction of steam power, water wheels became redundant.

The Sampean weir replaced a Javanese dam. The traditional irrigation system for separate land allotments thus remained in tact. The same happened elsewhere. Sometimes new weirs were built but there, too, the initiatives were limited to separate works that linked up with existing systems. Dam building constituted the main engineering area of intervention in irrigation matters and Van Kol (see **Figure 4.4**) observed that, up until 1885, it was "chiefly only Inland dams that were replaced by permanent works". It did not stop at dams, though. Engineers also created other

[29] See also Weijs (1913: 13-14). According to him (p. 13) the "uncommon activity in irrigation area Bagelen" was no direct result of the activities of De Bruyn. He considered this "to have arisen naturally".

structural works such as inlet locks, overflows, deluge dams and canals. These, too, only amounted to partial improvements. In the Sampean region it would take until the nineties for improvements in irrigation networks to materialise. One exception to this was the Demak Works which commenced in 1881 and which was to constitute an entire irrigation project. This project was not finished until 1894, long after the period discussed here. The modern headworks built by engineers up until 1885 could cope with the irrigating of some 100,000 *bouws* of agricultural land, but this was merely a drop in the ocean. In 1885 the total agricultural acreage was 3,570,416 *bouws* and the irrigated area was 1,677,717 *bouws* (from the *Koloniaal Verslag* ["Colonial Report"] of 1886/87, see **Appendix K**).

What applied to the Sampean weir also applied in general. It was found that a traditional dam (or a traditional system elsewhere) was not good enough which was why the help of Western technology was sought. When the first facilities constructed by engineers in the Sampean area began to give way and Javanese constructions were fallen back on it became evident that history was starting to repeat itself: again the traditional structure (the "temporary dam") was inadequate and so engineers were brought in to build the permanent Sampean weir. The annual report produced by the Civil Public Works Department (*Verslag BOW* ["Civil Public Works Report"] 1892: 171) described the general sequence of events as follows:

"The reason for constructing these works was often to be sought in the difficulties encountered by the population and by management in maintaining existing irrigation works without involving the construction department or in the repeated failed endeavours to somewhere create new irrigation works. Technical officials would only be called in to help when, for example, it proved impossible to maintain a weir in its existing form with the available means in order to avoid repeated washing away of the dam, subsequent threatening of the rice harvest and simultaneous heavy pressures on the population (repairwork often relied on unpaid forced labour)".

Van Thiel's framework dam was a success but that was not always the case with framework dams as the history of the Menenteng watercourse was to prove. The framework dam built by Krajenbrink in the forties in the Menenteng gorge collapsed before it was completed. The involvement of engineers in the Sampean delta could not generally be termed a success story. As Rietveld reported, the history of the Sampean Works was rather a tale of misfortunes and disappointments. Things also went badly wrong with other works as well; take for example the dam in the Tuntang:

"The Glapan weir about which in Colonial reports continued optimistic signals were produced was subjected, just as other works of the day, to all sorts of discontentment. Shortly after its completion in 1859 the roll layer of the deluge surface was almost completely destroyed. At one point the entire job was nearly abandoned in favour of building in another place. It was only because of Director De Bruyn's persuasive action that this did not happen and Dik's work was renovated in such a way as to meet the desired end" (De Meyier 1921: 715, compare De Meyier 1891/92).

What was the reason for all these technological mishaps? As has been illustrated, the laborious development of the Sampean weir was attributed to the decision to choose the Javanese tapping place as a construction point. The decision of Van Thiel and engineers after him to build there was not so much steered by wisdom as by necessity (and perhaps even by the desire to operate carefully). There were no exact maps of the area to be irrigated and all kinds of essential details were missing as Van Kol (1901: 343) was able to report from personal experience:

"When I arrived at the dam in 1887 there was no single map of the river, no single record of the situation above the weir. Nothing of the irrigation area had been mapped out and it was the inland draining-off system that was relied on".

In the case of the Sampean Works: the "works without a plan", this did indeed lead to "discontentment" (ibid.). The working method adopted with the Sampean Works did not stand up on its own. The engineers created irrigation work designs that were based on very sketchy details. They made use of large-scale maps (1 : 10,000 to 20,000) and were content with just a few altitude levels. This was reflected in the designs produced, which consisted of nothing more than an indication on the map and several drawn in outlines and structures (Van Ilcken 1893: 413). At an old mooring point, for example, the engineers built a permanent dam. Such unplanned works lacking good maps and based on few surveys amounted again, in itself, to a consequence of the limited means available. There was a shortage of personnel and funds. Engineers were in "ambulatory service", that is to say, they were deployed when help was urgently needed. Weijs (1913: 8) sketched the consequences in dramatic terms:

"Too hastily setting to work without previously making studies of water levels and drainage systems, not to mention other important hydrographic features, had almost become the rule. As a result, works that had hardly finished being constructed, and which had often been designed with a shameful underestimation of the banjir force of the rivers, were frequently washed away. Yet other works – executed without a knowledge of the smaller flow rates – generated disappointing water levels".

There were positive results as well, though. For instance, the irrigation works constructed in the Brantas delta did stand the test of time[30]. According to Weijs, successful works demonstrated that much can be achieved provided that the means are sufficient. He posited that the fact that much did go wrong could not therefore be attributed to lack of knowledge but should rather be seen as a result of the "deficiencies in the network within which that knowledge was tapped and imparted" (1913:9). Without belittling the brilliant work of an individualist by dismissing it as being founded on pure luck it would also seem somewhat exaggerated to conclude, from the one or two success stories, that there was sufficient know-how available. The history of the Sampean weir clearly proves that it was a process of learning by trial and error that had been set in motion and that slowly but surely people were learning how to deal with the forces of nature (water forces, the soil). In all of this nature was not a constant but rather a changeable factor, made fluid also by human intervention (not only in the form of the weir construction but also, undoubtedly, because of activities elsewhere in the river area). Subsequently the *banjir* pressure in the Sampean delta intensified.[31]

The increased knowledge gained from constructing the Sampean weir was something that was of general interest. After having pointed to the high costs of the weir Rietveld (1932: 286) went on to highlight the following:

---

[30] See Weijs (1913: 8-9, 11-12) and Vlugter (1949: 103). The irrigation works in Bagelen were successful, but found themselves twenty years later, due to lack of maintenance, for 60% in disrepair (*Encyclopaedie* Vol. I, 1917: 297).

[31] The experiences of other works were not different. This process was not unique to the Indies: elsewhere engineers worked on this empirical basis as well. (See for India e.g. Headrick 1988, for the Netherlands Ten Horn-van Nispen et al. 1994). The engineers who accomplished something in this way, like De Bruyn and Pet, were true "ingenuous men" (cf. Dirkzwager 1977: 15 ff.).

"But also, and that is not the least of the achievements of the engineers who worked in Situbondo, ... invaluable experience had been gained. Often the premium for knowledge is high but here one may definitely question whether the knowledge gained was so expensive. Let us just focus on two issues: the large part played by Sampean observations in Melchior's study on maximum river transport capacities and furthermore the scepticism that has grown surrounding the *padas* 'soil type', a collective name used to describe a number of more or less good or unfavourable notions. Who could estimate the monetary value of the two aspects?"

All the experience gained from the first irrigation works, positive and negative, culminated in the publication of a first "handbook" on irrigation matters towards the end of the nineteenth century: De Meyier (1891)[32].

Javanese dams were poorly constructed and claimed many lives. This view, popular among engineers, did not quite paint a complete picture about traditional dams. Some kinds were good, one example being the one known as the Japara dam. It was made of coconut palm wood and bamboo and, structure-wise, it was not unlike the sort of dam built by beavers. This sort of dam was perfectly suited to smaller rivers. The engineer Pet who provided Bagelen with many modern irrigation works, was enthusiastic about the "beaver dams" (De Meyier 1891: 229-230). Javanese irrigation engineering could also be a source of inspiration at times, as was borne out by Dik's overflow which, ultimately, was not a great success. Also, as far as the drawing off points were concerned, not everybody was negative about the local population's choices of places. Weijs (1913: 6) later wrote of traditional irrigation that it was based on "experience passed on from generation to generation". He showed that he took this experience very seriously:

"That experience represented no mean force because with what he was able to achieve in the field of irrigation, the inlander was able to make himself be seen as a born irrigation expert. Should the professionals find something to criticise in that even they will be compelled to realise that the inland irrigation works often succeed due to the correct choice of place for dams and drawing off points, through authoritative channel laying and through the efficient, though sometimes meagre adaptation, of building material and so on, indeed, sometimes through their sheer courage these people even command one's respect" (ibid.).

In the Sampean delta and elsewhere the Resident and the civil servants under him did not see any problem in letting the population create dams. They took the initiative and led things. They made use of materials and labour obtained as a result of forced labour. The techniques employed to create these works were Javanese (see **Figure 4.6**).

Creating modern irrigation works constituted an alternative to such intervention in irrigation on the part of civil servants. Krajenbrink's framework dam in the Menenteng gorge, for example, was just as quickly destroyed as any traditional dam created at the request of the Civil Service. The engineers got a bad reputation because of this work and later the choice fell with a Javanese solution (approved by De Bruyn!) The projects supervised by civil servants in the field of irrigation also had one important advantage: "when it came to the art of realising irrigation works at no expense ... it was ... the Inland Administration rather than the Public Works Organisation that was by far the best at doing this" (Weijs 1913: 9). But cheap solutions could

[32] It is a part in a multi-volume work on *Waterbouwkunde* ("Hydraulic Engineering") edited by Henket, Schols and Telders. Previously A. Lakerveld and Brocx (1863-1871) appeared. In their *Handleiding voor bouwkundigen en industrieeelen* ("Guide for Planners and Industrialists") irrigation works (construction work in the field of irrigation) are a less essential component.

eventually become expensive solutions as was demonstrated by the dams in the Sampean and elsewhere. Because of a lack of funds, engineers started producing poor results but this was not a reason for switching to modern irrigation. Weijs (1913: 8) thus also concluded that:

"The early days of technological intervention were characterised ... by so much adversity that it was difficult to establish confidence in engineers in this area and many contended that it would thus be best to let the inlander go his own way".

Modern irrigation, Javanese irrigation and "administrative irrigation" were rival forms of irrigation in which various systems of knowledge and skills were at stake. It was only very gradually that the modern approach gained ground. This vicious circle of limited means and results was not unfounded: it was a function of the context of the colonial state. In general terms Weijs was right, the system that engineers were forced to work within restricted their results. What kind of system was that then?

Change and resistance

The beginnings of modern irrigation in the Sampean region was rooted in the time of the introduction of the Cultivation System. That was no coincidence. The construction of the framework dam was a direct consequence of this. Sugar was one of the chief products during the time of the Cultivation System and the Sampean delta was one of the regions where sugar cane was cultivated. Other irrigation works erected by engineers, like for instance the movable weir in Lengkong, had a similar background. The state was able to benefit from irrigated crops but that was not something that automatically led to modern irrigation expansion. The Cultivation System was based on a form of colonial policy that was modelled on state exploitation and what gave rise to this was the bad financial situation in the Netherlands and in the Indies. As a consequence, the Indies government only made means available if there was absolutely no other choice and if the envisaged goal was being served. In the run up to the exploitative state, Public Works had collapsed in its role as a relatively independent organisation (that is, as a separate administration). The policy originally adopted by the government in the area of irrigation was therefore undeveloped and allowed little space for creating irrigation works of a technical-scientific nature. Up until 1854 the number of engineers thus remained limited to ten.

Apart from the limited means there was another important limiting factor standing in the way of engineering intervention in irrigation. Because the state had been established along traditional lines there were many irrigation activities that engineers were not very involved in. The Resident was an important figure in all of this. Up until 1854 the Civil Service was entirely responsible for the construction of irrigation works and it operated accordingly. If the Civil Service saw that its approach provided no good solution it would call in the engineers and they would be requested to build a separate structure. Because there were so few of them the engineers could not meet all the demands. In the case of the Sampean region the requests for technical help of 1857, and later, could not be answered and so the only solution was to be found in constructing dams without the help of Public Works. When the engineers were called out they were beset by disaster. The vicious circle of limited means and results in which they were trapped thus gained an extra dimension. The engineers were subordinate to the administrators but because they had no results to show there was little they could do to change their position.

After 1854 the position did change a little. The outbreak of famine turned small farming into a significant irrigation objective. The weir at Glapan was built as a direct result of all the famine and disaster in the Demak area. The disasters also precipitated the creation of a separate public works service, in 1854. Having a separate organisation for public works was something that fitted in well with the process of state formation then going on in the colony. Liberalisation in the Netherlands caught on in the colony. Gradually the colonial state started to lose its purely exploitative character and slowly the interests of the population became more and more important. Famine certainly speeded up this process. The result was that in a process of expansion and differentiation the colonial state changed from being a state with limited interests and means (a "nightwatch state") to being a welfare state in which the Public Works Organisation heralded the arrival of a series of welfare services (I will return to this in **Chapter 6**).

The changes really came very slowly. De Bruyn had a lot of good ideas but the way he operated as the Director of the Public Works had little effect. Under his influence personnel numbers within Public Works were considerably expanded (going up to 75 by the year 1874). This increase did not, however, bring with it a sharp growth in modern irrigation. Works that did materialise, like the permanent Sampean weir, in 1876, remained more the exception than the rule. In Demak, Tegal, Grobogan and elsewhere engineers started doing surveys (*Verslag BOW* 1892: 171-172). Many plans were not developed. One might assert that it was the plans that were not executed which, despite all the reasons and plans for this, better typified the state of affairs in the field of irrigation than the works that were executed (Van Kol 1901: 343-344). This not only applied to the De Bruyn era at Public Works but also to the whole ensuing period, up until about 1885.

De Bruyn wanted to do things but could not. The government remained frugal in its provision of means[33]. The exploitative past remained ingrained in people's memories. De Bruyn's biographer formulated it thus:

"Those in power who remembered the days when no Public Works Organisation, as such, existed were not inclined to listen to De Bruyn's ideas. There was money enough – we were living in the golden age of exploitation policy which had, in 1862 for example, brought in a revenue of 38 million guilders – but Indies Public Works remained the poor step-child. While in the Netherlands a network of State railway lines was being laid on the basis of financial resources gained from Indies funds, a deaf ear was turned to the wishes of those who wanted Indies Public Works, which related so closely to the interests of the population and thus indirectly with the treasury, to be done justice" (Kielstra 1887: 129).

The rivalry between the various dominating forms of irrigation and approaches to irrigation had a social-political component. Civil servants and civil engineers were embroiled in a struggle for control over irrigation affairs. Obtaining the favour of political persons in power was an important part of all of this. Rochussen, Loudon and De Waal were advocates of modern irrigation facilities but van Lansberge and Mijer opposed this.

---

[33] The history of Sampeanwerken taught us that any large sums came from the government. The Accountability Law, which required making an itemized annual budget, did not alter this conclusion. The Resident and later the Director of Public Works gave only small amounts (and also on a more occasional basis). They had but a limited budget at their disposal.

Figure 4.6: Javanese dam, 1920 (photo UBL KITLV 18375)

At first the Civil Service employees were relatively powerful and could only be kept in line by the government seated in Batavia. The heads of regional administrations determined what happened in the Residencies and whether or not engineers would be deployed in the creation of irrigation works. For their part, the engineers tried to break free from the grip of the Civil Service. They contested what were, to their mind, the wasteful irrigation activities of the administrators which were, they believed, based upon the defective Javanese approach to irrigation. They stressed the importance of expertise and endeavoured to make irrigation works exclusively their terrain. Reinforced by famine and liberalisation, their struggle led to the creation of the public works service. This constituted an important step forwards for the engineers. In the area of irrigation, though, the rivalry which existed between engineers and civil servants was certainly not reduced, it was merely given a stronger institutional bent. Through the Public Works Bureau the engineers were given a firm basis at the heart of power: Batavia. A power struggle then started to develop between independent bodies which were later to become general administration departments.[34]

The engineers wanted money, personnel, modern irrigation expansion, power and influence and ultimately, they wanted change. The conflict which existed between engineers and civil servants was basically that of an opposition group to the established order (compare Boissevain 1974, see **Chapter 2**). The intervention of engineers in irrigation affairs was something that had been induced by the Cultivation System. In no way had it been the intention of central and regional administration to simply let the engineers do as they pleased but the genie had been let out of the bottle and engineers were prepared to fight for their cause. At first De Bruyn sought support by pointing to the usefulness of engineering works for the purposes of the Cultivation System. The ambitions of the Public Works Organisation met with opposition from the Civil Service. Later, when circumstances changed, De Bruyn started to use the plight of small farmers as his argument. Public Works was still opposed to the Civil Service but now it also wanted to contribute to changing the established order. The engineers had started out as an interest group striving for upward mobility but later they came to manifest themselves more emphatically as an opposition group directed towards social change. The standpoint should not, of course, be exaggerated. In its striving for power and influence Public Works attached itself to the liberalisation cause. The engineers contributed to this liberalisation but also rode on the waves of its success. This road was successful for Public Works as was also evidenced by the counteraction of the seventies and the sharp debate that this unleashed. Van Gijn substantiated his attack upon the engineers by, amongst other things, referring to the works in the Sampean delta: "Just go to the *Panarukan* if you want to see what sums of money technologists have literally thrown into the river Sampean for absolutely no practical purpose"[35].

---

[34] I present the establishment of the Civil Public Works Department as a step in the process of liberalization in the Indies. This was no uncontroversial view for contemporaries, though the process itself was known. We saw that De Bruyn was not happy with the Accountability Law, which entailed more administrative work. We also saw that Post found that the Law induced the "Batavian secretariat" to expand its power. He saw something quite different than liberalization: since the introduction of the Law "the attention of the Indies government and her bureaux is, instead of the public interest and the people's welfare, increasingly drawn to the Plaza and the Courtyard of the Hague (i.e. the Dutch government, WR)"(ibid.). By the way, I understand that Post with the "Batavian secretariat" not only referred to the general secretary of the Governor-General, but also to other parts of the central state apparatus, including the Department of Civil Service. Post also spoke of "secretariat-clerks", meaning the senior non-technical government officials in Batavia (see one of the quotes of Van Gijn [n.d: 3-4] and Van Gijn n.d.: 3, note 1).

[35] Van Gijn also referred to the plan for the Kabuh canal. This involved irrigation of approximately 12,500 *bouws*. In 1873 it was decided to implement it. The following year, the performance of the work, however, was discontinued. (Van Gijn n.d.: 17-18).

The conflict surrounding intervention in irrigation also had an ideological side to it. Engineers had to prove that irrigation based on techno-scientific principles was, in that respect, superior to traditional methods and to the works created by the Civil Service. Here, De Bruyn was very instrumental. To his mind Javanese structures were botched-up jobs (compare De Bruyn 1858: 118). Instead of adhering to the theory that the Javanese were naturals when it came water matters he presented the view that traditional irrigation methods led, by definition, to decline and that intervention on the part of engineers was therefore inevitable. He related modern irrigation to science and civilisation. Among the civil servants who still staunchly supported the Javanese approach there was the positive image that traditional irrigation had remained in tact for a long time. This image was also slow to disappear in engineering circles. As was seen with Weijs (1913), the positive image created by Javanese irrigation reverberated in the twentieth century. His outline of the developments surrounding engineering intervention in irrigation in the Indies left everyone in no doubt of the fact that he found modern irrigation methods superior to those of the past. On the whole it was the negative image that dominated.[36]

By 1887 things were ready: the works designed to draw water from the Sampean were completed. The professionalisation of irrigation intervention that this displayed was also a general trend. In 1885 a new Public Works Regulation was phased in for public works which worsened the conflict between Public Works and the Civil Service and operated in favour of the engineers. In future the construction of irrigation works was to be the prerogative of engineers.

Despite the fact that De Bruyn succeeded in achieving little he was, according to the engineers who came after him, an important figure for Public Works in the Indies. Weijs (1913) attributed the success of Rochussen's battle to two occurrences: the famine in Demak and Grobogan and, to "the brilliant action within the Indies Public Works Organization of one of the greatest men that the branch of service has known, the engineer H. de Bruyn" (p. 11). Many of De Bruyn's ideas were not introduced until later like, for instance, his proposal to divide Public Works into a general and a regional service (De Bruyn 1870: 19). The first time that De Bruyn formulated this idea was in 1858 (Kielstra 1887: 123). De Bruyn was also ahead of his time with other ideas like, for instance, the notion that Java should be divided into small public works divisions, a plan that materialised in the form of Irrigation Divsions, first introduced in 1888 and in his instigation to introduce legal water rights, something that did not come in until 1936! Finally, De Bruyn smoothed the way for Van Bosse's General Irrigation Plan of 1890 while in his proposal for a new general irrigation plan in the form of an inventory of the problems and requirements in the field of irrigation, Van Kol (1901) reverted to the ideas first voiced by De Bruyn. These points will be variously returned to in later chapters.

An independent public works service

The traditional and liberal models of colonial government and policy (derived from the directional struggle) determined the boundaries within which the Indies state developed in the nineteenth century. Until the second half of the nineteenth century the state was based on the traditional model. The Indies government had a feudal side to it (reminiscent of the way in which things were arranged in the time of the *VOC*) and it was indirect with the Resident in the central position (like a sort of viceroy). The state's objective was to exploit; its means was the Cultivation System. Gradually liberalisation crept in. This came about because of the rise of liberalism in the mother country and the famines in the colony. The state lost its exploitative directionality and began to think more of the population's interests. The central administrative

[36] After the failure of Solo Works (see **Chapter 7**), at the beginning of the twentieth century a revaluation of the Javanese irrigation took place. The quote Weijs conveys this. The positive image was popular among the emerging agronomists. (See **Chapter 8**).

organisation of the early colonial state became heavier and more diversified. The Cultivation System era first saw a Director of Cultures and later a Director of Public Works. When general government departments were set up, the Civil Public Works Department was one of them.

When it came to the intervention of the state in irrigation affairs, two distinct approaches could be distinguished: the engineers' approach and the way in which civil servants dealt with matters. In the early colonial state the Civil Service was dominant. This also manifested itself in the field of irrigation. The Cultivation System and famine that accompanied it were to give rise to the construction of a number of important modern irrigation works, separate structures designed to support existing irrigation networks. Irrigation affairs was the responsibility of the Civil Service which intervened as and when it pleased. Liberalisation in general and the endeavour of engineers to expand modern irrigation and improve their position transported them into a new era.

The 1870-1890 period saw a change in the state formation process. The early colonial state disappeared from the stage and the modern colonial state was waiting in the wings. The Public Works emancipation process was completed and the engineers were given the green light. The chapters in the following section explore these developments in more detail and also reveal that there were repercussions for the engineers.

II

TECHNOLOGISTS AND TECHNOCRATS

1885 – 1920

5

'The creation of a flourishing plain'

The Pemali Works

> To construct a technology is not merely to deploy materials and techniques; it is also to construct social and economic alliances, to invent new legal principles for social relations, and to provide powerful new vehicles for culturally-provided myths (Pfaffenberger 1988: 249).

As was illustrated in the **Prologue**, it was around the turn of the century that the engineer A.G. Lamminga set up modern irrigation systems in large areas of the Pemali-Comal plain along the northern coastline of Central Java. In so doing, he laid the foundations for modern irrigation technology in the Indies. I also mentioned the fact that Lamminga's innovative and pioneering work was commemorated when, in 1930, a monument was erected in his honour at Tegal, the place where he had lived and worked. Lamminga thus became the first and, in fact, the only irrigation engineer in the Indies to have a monument erected in his honour. In this chapter we shall discuss Lamminga's work.

The Pemali-Comal region extends over an area of over 80 kilometres. When Lamminga appeared on the scene in February 1895 a start had already been made on the series of irrigation works to emerge in this area. After his departure in May 1903 these activities continued for several decades. Here I want to focus on the Pemali Works which was Lamminga's chief project in the area (see **Figure 5.1**). During the 1930 ceremony the chairman of the committee responsible for the memorial initiative reminded those gathered together for the occasion that the "once barren, bare and desolate" Pemali plain had been transformed "by the creative genius of Lamminga into a flourishing region" (*Lamminga monument* ["Lamminga monument"]1930: 121). For the Pemali Works Lamminga drew up a general plan which foresaw the construction of an entire irrigation system from a weir in the river to the final sections where the farmers tilled the earth. He did so only after the main works were in progress, though, consequently, these works had to be swiftly changed during construction. Unforeseen circumstances also necessitated various adaptations. In the description given here below of the realisation of the Pemali Works what will clearly emerge is that Lamminga's strength did not only lie in the field of material technology.[1]

---

[1] Chief sources: *Verslag BOW* ("Civil Public Works Report" 1892: 175-181, 1893: 168-172), Voorduin (1914) (Voorduin had been involved in the irrigation project set up in the Sampean region). I also consulted: *Verslag BOW* (from 1894 until 1910 and 1925); the National Archives, notably the Haringhuizen-Schoemaker Collection, nos. 76 and 124, and nos. 165 and 167 of the Groothoff Collection; Van Marle (1894), Lamminga (1902), *D.* (1902). Progress reports are to be found in the *Koloniaal Verslag* ("Colonial Report"). See also Ter Hofstede and Van Santbrink (1979) who took the Pemali Works as a case in their study of colonial water management.

Figure 5.1: Inlet sluice at the weir in the Pemali river (from: *Verslag BOW* 1909)

The works

Planning for 50 years

The Pemali has its source in the hills of Central Java at the spot where three springs form a lake. The river's basin covers an area of some 890 square kilometres (De Meyier 1920: 80). From the point where it leaves the hills, the Pemali flows through an extensive plain. To the north of Brebes, the main town in the local department (or Regency) of the same name in the Residency of Pekalongan (previously known as Tegal), the river flows into the Java Sea. In the colonial period the coastal area was marshy. By 1900 the forests that had once covered this area had been largely destroyed. Each year the river burst its banks which was something that created much inconvenience for the town of Brebes. Rice cultivation in the plain was also affected by this.

The plain extending behind the left-bank reaches as far as the Babakan river. In the 1888-1890 period, the normalisation and damming up of this river put an end to the perpetual floods in the northwestern section of this area. The region was covered with rice fields encompassing an area in excess of 20,000 *bouws*. There was, however, no structural irrigation system: the population drew irrigation water from small streams but the water supplies in these streams were minimal and erratic. Consequently, the prospects in the area were not exactly rosy from an agricultural point of view. Voorduin (1914: 16) summed up the situation as follows:

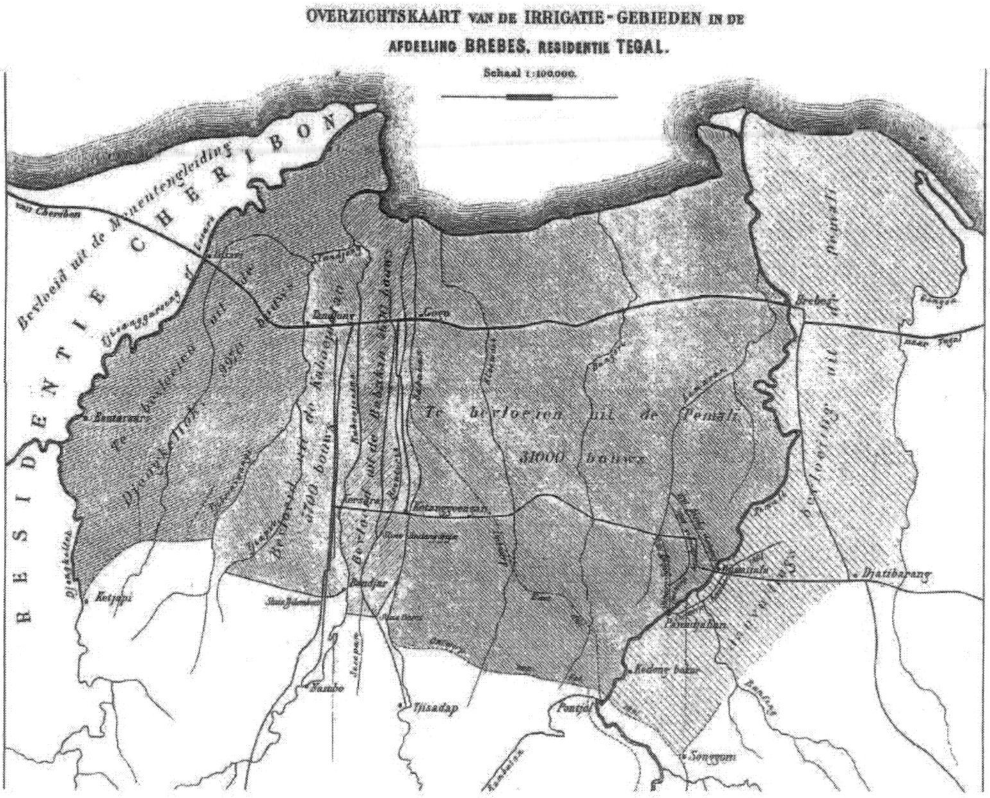

Figure 5.2: Map of the irrigation areas in the Brebes area, showing the final design of the Pemali irrigation system (from: *Verslag BOW* 1892)

"The consequences of this situation do not need to be described in such detail: rice cultivation was variable and precarious and in the years of little rain the harvest failure rate was high. Just like the upkeep of the fields, the cultivation of the soil left much to be desired. The young plants were seldom transplanted in time, poor rice varieties were grown which could be rapidly harvested. Second-crop cultivation hardly ever occurred, in the East Monsoon season there was no water for bathing in and drinking water had to be obtained from wells but it remained in short supply and of poor quality. The population density was low and, notably in the South, the population included many bad elements".

At the time there was, however, little poverty among the population, the reason for this being that the per capita land ownership level was high. The same did not, however, apply to the northern plains region (the District of Tanjung). While the people of the south were housed in stone dwellings with tiled roofs, the *kampongs* (Javanese settlements) in the coastal region created a "sad" impression (Voorduin 1914: 16-17).

The right-bank which bordered on the Gangsa river was more prosperous. The area of land irrigated there was 8600 *bouws*, though not all of that area was always well watered. There were various watercourses the most important one being the Krupak watercourse. In that region 3700 *bouws* of land depended entirely on rainfall levels. Flooding was a major hazard in the area, notably in the north-east. The flood water issued from the Pemali but the Gangsa also created problems. Though there was more second-crop cultivation here than on the left-bank, the yield remained minimal. During the west monsoon season much of the ground served as pasture land but cattle numbers dwindled. On the right-bank there was the important cultivation of sugar cane which supplied a couple of refineries. One of the refineries, Jatibarang, was established in the chief town of the Sub-District of the same name which was the second most important place in the area after Brebes (the other refinery, Adiwerna, was situated in the District of the same name in the Regency of Tegal). The cane fields covered a total area of 900 *bouws*. The ground was rented from the population for *f* 22,50 to *f* 30,00 per *bouw*.[2]

It was believed that the economic situation in the region could be improved with irrigation water drawn from the Pemali. In about 1840 the engineer J.A. Krajenbrink was commissioned to draw up a plan but, possibly because of lack of time, this request was never honoured. At this time the Indies Civil Public Works Department did not yet exist and there was only a handful of engineers. In 1851 the Controller R.A. Sijthof proposed drawing off water at the Wanacala *desa*. He maintained that in this way some 20,000 *bouws* on the left-bank could be supplied with water (see **Figure 5.2**). Sijthof estimated that the costs would amount to some *f* 16,927. The proposal was not accepted. When asked to give advice, Krajenbrink discovered an important mistake in the height calculations. A year later Sijthof submitted an amended plan but because of the shortage of technical staff it was impossible for the plan to be implemented.

---

[2] For his sketch of the situation before the creation of the Pemali irrigation works Voorduin made use of the report on the Pemali Works produced by the Rentability Commission in 1900. The people in the Commission were A.G. Lamminga, J.W. van der Valk (interim Chief Inspector of Cultures) and A.J. Wijnmalen (Assistant-Resident of Brebes). In that report the situation was viewed especially from the angle of improving the agricultural situation (or of maximising agronomy). The small population's circumstances did not seem to be all that bad (except, no doubt, in the unfavourable years, in the left-bank area, see also *Verslag BOW* 1892: 168) and it was probably the relatively high proportion of land per head of the population that gave little cause for intensive farming. The population of the Pemali plain (which included the Districts of Brebes, Banjaharjo and Tanjung) totalled more than 400,000 in 1920 (in the Residency of Pekalongan as a whole that was almost 2.3 million and in 1890 over 1.6 million), the population density in 1920 was some 450 persons to the square kilometre (in the Residency: aro. 400 and 291 in 1890). In 1920 the number of *bouws* of *sawa* owned per head of population was aro. 0.18 (0.12 in the Residency) and the rice production was aro. 4.62 *pikols* per head (in the Residency 3.12, a *pikol* being 61.76 kilo) (*Landbouwatlas* ["Agricultural Atlas"] 1926, tables: 10-11, 52, Hasselman 1914: Annex P; see for details of the population size, the *sawa* area and the rice production per head of population in the three Districts of the Pemali plain, also in comparison to the same proportions in the Brebes Regency and the Pekalongan Residency **Note 18**).

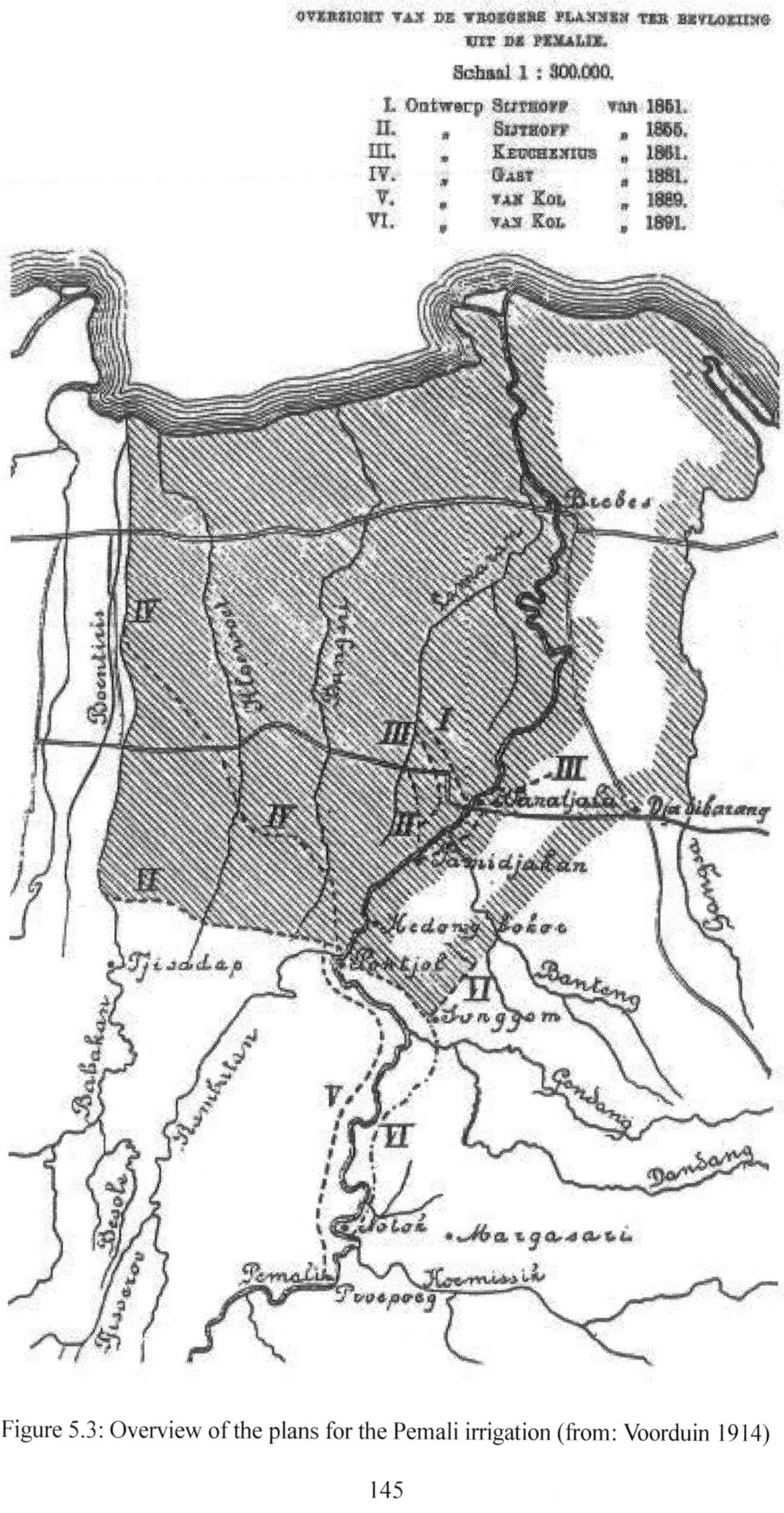

Figure 5.3: Overview of the plans for the Pemali irrigation (from: Voorduin 1914)

Sijthof was not one to give up easily, though: in 1855 he produced a more detailed design. This design included plans for a channel at the Pamijahan desa. The idea was that by means of a framework dam the river would be forced upwards so that water could pass into the *kali* (river) Lamaran via a main canal with a stone inlet weir. In time, it would be possible to in this way obtain irrigation water for 22,400 *bouws* of land. Sijthof estimated that the costs would be around *f* 46,000. These calculations presumed that use would be made of forced labour at a rate of fifteen "farthings" (a good nine cents) per man, per day. At the instigation of Uhlenbeck, the Director of Bureau of Public Works, the Indies government expressed to Sijthof its "great satisfaction" for this (*Verslag BOW* 1892: 176). In practice this plan was not executed, Uhlenbeck really maintained that it required certain modifications. He believed, for instance, that the weir should be made higher and stronger. The Director asked the Head of the Second Public Works Division (based in Tegal) to create a plan that would fulfil these requirements. The "Civil Public Works Report" (*Verslag BOW* 1892: 176) included the following comments on Uhlenbeck's instructions:

"It is rather astonishing that no reference is made to the entirely incorrect reasoning that actually gave rise to the assumption that even in the case of the lowest east monsoon water levels, there would be water enough in the rivers to irrigate 4000 *bouws* of land, a fact which has been completely disreputed in practice".

Because of the pressure of time the new plans did not reach the Director of Public Works until 1858. Instead of containing plans for a wooden framework dam it had been proposed that a concrete weir should be built. The anticipated expense was three times as high as before: *f* 151,640 (including 12½ cents per day for the coolies). The proposal was then sent back because more elucidation was required.

After another few years had passed by without anything happening, L.W.C. Keuchenius, the Resident of Tegal, proposed in 1861 that a temporary weir be constructed at Pamijahan. This would involve creating canals on both the left and right banks. The work could be completed on the basis of unpaid forced labour and would therefore cost a mere *f* 1,000. The Director of Public Works was happy with this solution and so this was followed by a governmental implementation order. The government decided that the coolies should be awarded a sum of 12½ cents per day for their efforts and so *f* 9,000 was made available for this purpose. At the point when most of this money had been used up the dam capsized because it had been built too high in the hope of limiting the earth-moving for the canal on the left-bank. An extra sum of *f* 30,000 was therefore required to construct a lower dam and a deeper canal. This money was granted by the government in 1862. In 1865, after hundreds of thousands of days of man-hours of forced labour had been put into the project, the (new) Resident of Tegal decided to halt the project. His decision was based on the recommendations of S. Verburgh, the Senior Engineer, who maintained that a permanent dam should be created and that a study should be made to determine where the *prise d'eau* (water supply point) should be located. He believed that it should be located further upstream thus necessitating an elongation of the already excavated canal. Though it was decided in 1866 that this plan should be investigated nothing happened for ten years.

The proposed surveys were finally begun in 1876, under the supervision of the engineer C. Gast. The reason why that happened then was because the Resident of Tegal had once again raised the question of irrigation using water from the Pemali. Two years of surveys finally led to the creation of a plan that was finalised in 1881. A trainee engineer was appointed to help Gast with the project and by the time the plans were submitted Gast had been made Chief Engineer. The findings had, indeed, indicated that the water supply should be situated further upstream at the Poncol *desa*. The plan included ideas for a weir in combination with a sluice or drainage weir and an inlet sluice on the left-bank that would be connected to a main canal and a network of secondary and smaller channels. This project would make it possible to irrigate 21,000 *bouws* of land. It was proposed that the weir should be made of stone and that it should be 70 metres long and six metres high. Provision was made for a tunnel that would connect the two banks. The partially sloping weir and fascine work would be 120 metres wide and it was estimated that the entire job would cost *f* 2,283,819. These calculations were based on the presumption that everything would be done with normal workers who, unlike forced labourers, would receive normal pay. If just the weir and the main canal had been constructed on the basis of normal labour terms and forced labour had been used for the other works then the expenses would have amounted to *f* 1,764,979. It would thus take six years to complete the works. The land rent, where the amount due would correspond to a portion of the harvest, would go up by *f* 6 per *bouw*.

These plans gave rise to some discussion. T.C.J. Kroesen, the Director of the Department of Civil Public Works had his reservations. He suggested designing the fascine work differently (with an upright water overflow structure divided into two steps) so that the breadth of the whole structure would be reduced from 120 to 55 metres. Gast agreed with this proposal but not with Kroesen's suggestion that the weir should be made higher (and thus also longer) in order to supply a larger irrigation area. Kroesen also asked the Resident to give his views on the matter of rentability. In 1883 the Resident intimated that he viewed this in a positive light. In 1885 the Director of Civil Public Works, J.H. Janssen van Raay (1884-1889) found it necessary to seek further advice on the matter of the works' rentability from Dr. J.H.F. Sollewijn Gelpke, Chief Inspector of Cultures. He believed that "no advantages worth mentioning might be expected from these works" (*Verslag BOW* 1892: 179). Without being more specific, he furthermore claimed that "the completion of certain other works ... might be seen as more urgent" (ibid.). The Director of Civil Public Works did not agree with Sollewijn Gelpke's recommendations. Bearing in mind the Public Works Regulations of 1885 – to the effect that irrigation works could be given top priority in few populated regions (see **Chapter 6**) – he advised the government, in 1886, to seriously consider the notion of temporarily dropping the idea of obtaining irrigation water from the Pemali. That, then, was what happened.

The Van Kol plan

In 1889 the engineer H.H. van Kol produced a memorandum in which he toyed with the idea of drawing irrigation water from the Pemali river. Van Kol, who had been working in the region since 1887, had made exploratory investigations and had drawn certain conclusions. He proposed that the point at which water might be channelled off from the Pemali should be fixed even further upstream, at Prupug. That would involve constructing an aqueduct over the Rambatan river and the main canal would have to be dug through very undulating terrain. The area to be irrigated would be 31,000 *bouws* big and a lower weir would suffice. Van Kol estimated that such a project would cost *f* 660,000 his estimations being based on employing for the job normal paid labourers.

In 1890 Tydeman, the Resident of Tegal, asked the Indies government to implement Van Kol's plan. The Resident had calculated that the works would bring in 15% interest (from the outlay capital) and so on these grounds he found that other possible works ideas should be abandoned. The Director of Civil Public Works, M.J. van Bosse (1889-1892), had, it is true, given instructions in 1889 for investigations to be carried out at Prupug in order to determine the river's capacity, but he was less optimistic than the Resident. Unlike the Resident, he did not wish to interfere with the other work that was in progress. He also maintained that the expenses would turn out to be considerably higher than Van Kol had estimated and upon which Tydeman had founded his favourable rentability verdict. In this connection the "Civil Public Works Report" (*Verslag BOW* 1892: 179-180) reported the following:

"That figure was not based on a plan but rather on little more than an estimation arrived at after a certain amount of terrain inspection had been carried out. Furthermore, it only related to the construction of a prise d'eau with a main canal while the creation of secondary and smaller channels would be left to the local population. The Director maintained that this ideology was wrong because in this way best possible use would not be made of the works created by the government: only the fields in the direct vicinity of the canal would benefit and indiscriminate drawing off of water would lead to the canals' ultimate destruction, especially where one is dealing with such large quantities of water as is the case here".

The Director of Civil Public Works included the Pemali Works in his General Irrigation Plan (see **Chapter 6**) and put aside *f* 2,250,000 for this purpose. He ordered Van Kol to carry out the necessary surveys and to come up with a suitable design. Van Kol produced a preliminary plan in 1891. In this plan the *prise d'eau* was located at Notok, not far from the previously chosen spot. He decided that the main canal should be situated on the right-bank. This offered important advantages: shallower excavations into the ground could be made and, on the right-bank, irrigation could be effected without the need for a second inlet sluice. The area irrigated could thus be extended by some 600 *bouws* (to a total area of 37,000 *bouws*). Van Kol had based these calculations on a requirement of 0.8 litres of water per *bouw*, per second. As far as the water supply was concerned, he had estimated that the flow rate of the Pemali would be about 30 cubic metres per second. The weir was to be 2.70 metres high and 70 metres long. One component was to be a drainage sluice. The main canal that was to commence at the weir was given an inlet sluice. At Songgom *desa* the main canal would be divided up into the *Oosterleiding* ("the Eastern channel") and a canal which, via an aqueduct at Poncol would be led over the Pemali). This main canal would then branch off into the *Noorderleiding* ("the Northern channel") and the *Westerleiding* ("the Western channel"). Van Kol budgeted the expenses at *f* 1,116,000 (everything to be done with paid labour and without "subsidiary channels"). The job would take eight years to complete.

Van Bosse's reactions led to several alterations. It was decided that the weir should be raised by a metre to make the main canal deeper, narrower and thus, also, cheaper. The Director then ordered people to draw up the final designs for the various sections. The first final design to be submitted, in 1892, was for the *prise d'eau.* The Inspector of Cultures, F.A. Liefrinck, was asked to provide his views on that design. The conclusions he arrived at in 1893 were positive. Liefrinck's views were based on the following points:

"that in the East Monsoon season, as well as in the West Monsoon season, an important water source could thus be accessed;
it would not necessitate particularly expensive or complex works;
the nature of the soil which, for a large part, had been converted into sawahs that depended on rainfall;
the proximity, to the East and to the West, of densely populated areas;
the closeness to the kotta *Brebes* which constituted a not unimportant trade centre and the reasonably good communication means so that it will undoubtedly be easy to transport rice away from the area" (*Verslag BOW* 1893: 168).

In 1893 the government made a sum of *f* 195,042 available for the construction of a weir with an outlet sluice and an inlet sluice.

The water supply point[3]

The work commenced with the necessary preparations which included creating an access road, building storage places and creating night-stay facilities and a Director's dwelling. The dwelling was built for J.W. van Marle who had succeeded Van Kol in August 1892. In June 1893, though, van Marle was replaced by the engineer T.W.C. Herckenrath who supervised the works until February 1895. The work really started with the construction of the inlet sluice and this was followed by the creation of the outlet sluice. By 1894 both works were as good as completed.

The weir was constructed between 1896 and 1897 and the job was supervised by Lamminga (see **Figure 5.4**, see also the **Prologue, Figures 1 and 2**). The (*padas*) earth was too hard for poles and planks to be sunk into it. That had been attempted (in 1895) but when, in 1896, the "foundation pit" was revealed it was discovered that no dam wall had been formed. The alternative was a foundation made of concrete blocks. The weir level was also raised by 33 centimetres, the reason for this being that when preparing other works it had been discovered that there were more possibilities for improving and extending the irrigation facilities on the right-bank and that people also found it desirable to make good use of those possibilities.[4] During the construction of the weir, and partly because of that, the left-bank started to crumble. This made it necessary to lengthen the dam by fifteen metres. Another advantage attached to this decision was that the maximum possible water conveyance capacity was expanded. Bearing in mind the observed maximum water volumes witnessed elsewhere in the Residency that was, it seemed, no mere luxury either. In 1896 the structure was put to the test when, in the Pemali river, the water volume rose to 1015 cubic metres, 55 cubic metres more than had been anticipated.

After the water supply system had been completed, a sandbank developed along the river's right-bank. The sandbank extended to in front of the opening to the inlet sluice. Attempts were made to prevent the build-up of sand by perpetually flushing out water, but to no avail. The next step taken was to create groynes in the river. This was more effective. From 1901 onwards, when the inlet sluice as a whole was opened, there was still the problem of great silting-up in the main canal. The outlet sluice capacity thus had to be increased and that was something that was accomplished in the 1903-1904 period.

---

[3] See **Figure 5.3**.

[4] The importance of modern irrigation on the right-bank was possibly linked to the sugar industry. That was, at any rate, where the cane fields were.

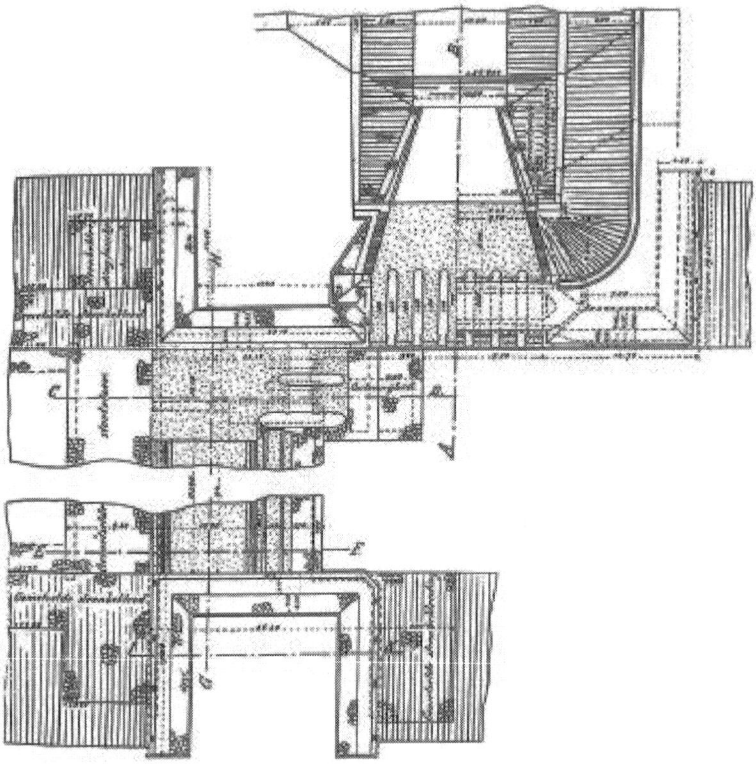

Figure 5.4: Plan of the weir in the Pemali river at Notok (from: Voorduin 1914)

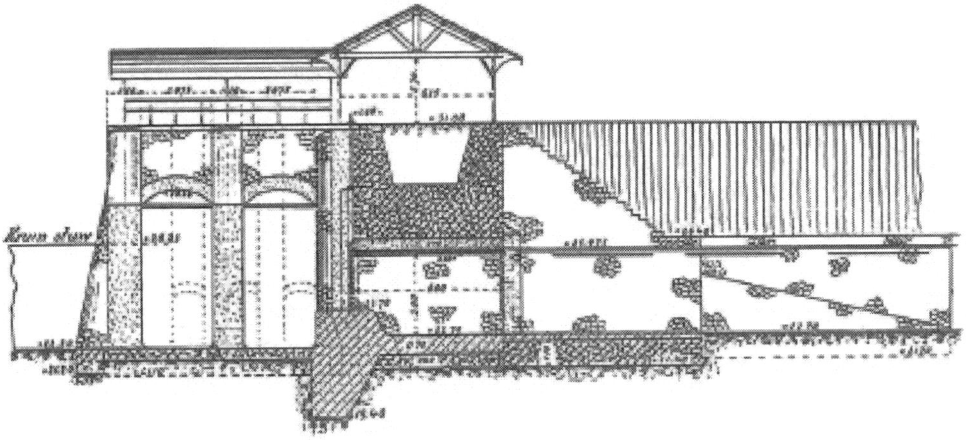

Figure 5.5: View of the discharge sluice and cross section of the inlet sluice at Notok (from: Voorduin 1914)

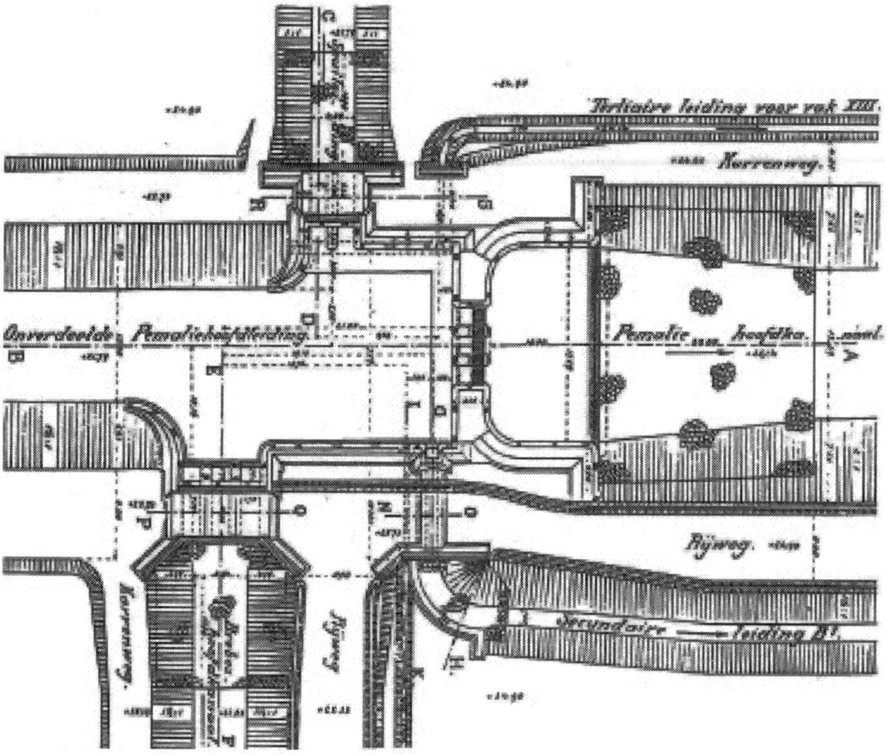

Figure 5.6: Main division work in the Pemali irrigation system at Songgom
(from: *Verslag BOW* 1909)

Pigure 5.7: Division work at Songgom (from: *Verslag BOW* 1909)

Excursus 5.1 The Pemali weir sluices
The inlet sluice had seven openings, each of which was 1.80 metres wide and 2.30 metres high and they were spaced one metre away from each other. The pipes were six metres long and wooden doors and barrier beams had been introduced to close them off. There were winding mechanisms to operate the doors. Because of the alterations in the height of the weir and the depth and breadth of the main canal the Director decided that the first part of the floor of the opening should be raised by a metre. It thus rose to one and a half metres above the floor level of the outlet sluice. Later this also proved to be favourable in connection with silting-up problems in the main canal.
The outlet sluice consisted of three pipes that were 1.25 metres in diameter, two metres high, four metres long and placed at one metre distances from each other. The openings had wooden sliding doors. A heavy trapezium-shaped pile that was 4.10 metres wide at the base and 2.14 metres wide at the top, separated the outlet sluice from the weir. A downward sloping canal situated behind the sluice transported water to the level of the water pool behind the weir. A dividing wall separated the canal from the pool.
When the outlet sluice was renovated, two openings were created instead of three and these new openings were considerably larger. They were 2.875 metres wide and 6.16 metres high (see ***Figure 5.5****). Because of the deep gully created along the left-bank by the spouting out of water, the dividing wall created to separate the outlet water from the pool, had already been removed. By also shortening the dividing pile that had been placed downstream, even more outlet water flowed into the pool. The openings were given wooden doors composed of two parts; both sections could be raised independently. The sliding doors were given protective iron coverings but, in 1911, bronze covering material was used instead. In this way there was less friction which meant that four instead of six men could operate the winding mechanisms.*
Despite the alterations made to the weir in conjunction with structural problems discovered during construction, the prise d'eau *costs turned out to be lower than had been estimated by the Indies government (ƒ 185,580.82). The reconstruction of the outlet sluice cost an extra ƒ 18,975.50 (including the creation of three deluge beds in the main canal). This was also turned out to be lower than the amount of ƒ 19,100 made available by the government. The total cost of these headworks thus amounted to ƒ 204,600*

The undivided main canal

In 1893 the Director known as Van Marle submitted the final plan for the first section of the main canal. The "undivided main canal" was to be 8.5 kilometres long. In that same year the Indies government put aside a sum of ƒ 631,289 for the completion of this work using paid employees so the work could be speedily begun. The extending of the irrigation area on the right-bank meant that the canal should be able to transport more water (36.6 instead of 29.6 cubic metres) which was why it was made slightly deeper. Because of its very position the canal interfered with the natural flow of the Pemali river. To rectify this problem, it would be necessary to divert the river water under the canal in three different places. Each of the three siphons consisted of three concrete pipes that were one and a half metres in diameter. The water flowed into the pipes from a pool. In this way the water could be spouted out of the canal.[5]

[5] The outlet construction consisted of three openings in the canal dyke, each of which could be closed off. Just a little further on from each outlet the main canal would be given a stop log sluice with five openings, each 2.80 metres wide. It became apparent that the outlet facilities were not sufficient to save the main canal from silting up. After a major blockage resulting from the high *banjirs* of 1910 an extra outlet sluice was constructed in the 1911-1912 period. This new sluice had four openings, each two metres wide. The new sluice had a capacity of 75 cubic metres per second while the old sluices could only cope with 28 cubic metres of water per second. The main canal was later

Here and there it was necessary to make the inclines less steep or to give them extra protection but apart from that the constructing of the canal went quite smoothly. As far as finding labour was concerned, this was difficult because of the area's thin population and because, especially with canal construction, much labour was required. This led, in 1894, to the step of introducing convicts for the excavation work. Labour was required for the digging work but also for the transportation of soil. With regard to this latter point, Voorduin had the following to say (1914: 40):

"Ground transport was partly carried out with locomotive-drawn or hand-drawn tippers and partly in the traditional East Indies way of getting coolies to transport the soil away by carrying it in baskets".

By 1897 the main canal was completed. The first canal section ended at the Songgom *desa* where it branched into two main canals: one for the left-bank and one for the right-bank. A water distribution structure, completed in 1898, made all of this possible (see **Figures 5.6 and 5.7**). The inlet sluice in front of the right main canal – the Brebes main canal – had three openings, each 1.70 metres wide and two metres high. The left main canal – the extended Pemali main channel – would flow over the Pemali through an aqueduct. The distribution structure also included the mouths of three other channels: a secondary one and two sub-channels. The width of the sluice of the secondary canal was one metre and it was 0.45 high. The sub-canals were supplied with water via concrete pipes of 50 and 35 centimetres in diameter. For the rest, the distribution system had an outlet sluice with two openings that were each one and a half metres wide and two metres high.[6]

The general Lamminga plan

It was only after the detailed maps of the Pemali area had been completed that it became apparent that the land to be irrigated was different from what people had first imagined it to be like. The area concerned was around 16,153 *bouws* on the right-bank and 30,220 *bouws* on the left-bank. This had already (partly) given rise to alterations in the canal and the dam. At that stage, there was no general plan for irrigating with water from the Pemali and

"it was feared that in continuing without any general preliminary plan even greater difficulties would appear on the horizon which would only be resolvable at great financial expense" (Voorduin 1914: 49).

In the second half of 1896 Lamminga produced such a general plan. The plan gave an overview of the various sections of the Pemali Works: the main channels (the Pemali and the Brebes canal), the secondary feed-in channels, the secondary irrigation sections, the drainage channels and all the structural works. The various elements of the design were coded according to a certain system. For example, the structural works were labelled "K1P" which stood for the *prise d'eau* (i.e. structural work [*kunstwerk*] number one in the Pemali area) and "K32B" which stood for structural work number 32 in the Brebes main channel area. The plan formed the basis for all further activities. On that basis final designs were drawn up for all the projects that needed to be

given an inlet sluice for an area of 237 *bouws*. This consisted of a concrete pipe that was 0.60 in diameter and 23 metres long that led into a water distribution point to which two subsidiary pipes were connected.

[6] In connection with the desired height of the aqueduct, the water level in the distribution structure had to drop by 1.85 metres. This was achieved by constructing a stop log sluice with three openings, each 1.60 metres wide.

completed. When drawing up his plans, Lamminga based his ideas on the extensive preliminary investigations that had been made into the available and required water quantities and into the composition and state of the terrain. What was, for instance, important was the precipitation gauges. When it came to executing the general plan, the collecting of details and the making of calculations simply continued.[7]

The irrigation plan was based on the existing situation. Streams and ravines were sought out for water conveyance. The dividing up of the secondary sections issued forth from the way in which the conveyance channels were created. Later, two more such channels were added. The largest section covered 13,054 *bouws*. The Brebes area contained eight sections and it was an area that was much troubled by flooding. The area with the biggest section was frequently flooded and it was with a view to this that it was proposed that the *kali* Klikiran, into which the Krupak canal fed, should be connected with a side branch of the Pemali. The existing channels would not be adequate, even if they were expanded.

It was the dividing up into sections that made it possible to design secondary channels. On the left-bank the designing of irrigation facilities gave rise to no problems; on the right-bank, however, such provision was impossible because of the flooding that took place there. The route of the secondary channel in the largest section of the Brebes area was in the flood zone, just like the actual section itself, which meant that it could not be precisely determined. It was on the basis of the established irrigation sections that the capacity of the secondary channels was determined. The secondary channel network was again linked to the final main canal design. In the case of the various irrigation sections, definite plans were also made: the exact areas to be irrigated and not to be irrigated in each section were clearly established. From the net surface area, followed the first indications of what the required channel capacity would be.

The channel capacity also depended on the water requirements. There were different factors that played a part in determining this. The nature of the subsoil was important, as too was the soil cultivation pattern. Less water was needed for sugar cane cultivation because the crop did not require irrigation water in the wet period. Presuming that 20% of the cultivated land was devoted to sugar cane and that 0.8 litres of water per *bouw*, per second was available, the normal water consumption for rice could be increased to one litre of water per *bouw*, per second. In addition, the size of the section supplied with water from the channel was significant for the capacity of the channel: the smaller the final sections, the larger the capacity would have to be in terms of litres per *bouw* and per second. When growing sugar cane a small section would sometimes be missed out while with the larger sections it would be probable that 20% of the area would be put aside for sugar cane cultivation. Moreover, water supply disruptions created fewer problems in a large section. Research into the design capacity of canals produced a graphic projection of the required amount of water per *bouw* and per second for the various areas in which a continuous curving line indicated the capacity (known commonly as the Tegalan Capacity Line, see **Chapter 6**). The graph showed that with smaller land areas the capacity

[7] The importance of rain gauging was evident from the reports made afterwards: in his article on the Pemali Works, Voorduin made use of a study produced by Van Bemmelen (1908) on rainfall levels in Java. What was particularly striking was to see how many calculations had been made in connection with the Pemali Works and that many formulas had been used in the process. That was already evident in the design of the dam. When establishing the maximum number of horses required, Lamminga and his colleagues used measurement data derived from Lauterberg and Iskowski's formulas. Voorduin also referred in his article to Melchior's discussion on determining the largest water tapping off systems from Javan rivers. When establishing the capacity of the weir it was Dubuat's formula that was used. Voorduin used a newer formula, one of Bazin's formulas, to calculate the capacity of the weir. Melchior's article is printed in the *Tijdschrift van het Koninklijk Instituut van Ingenieurs (Verh.)* ("Journal of the Royal Institute of Engineers" [Proceedings] 1901/1902, p. 46. For Bazin's formulas Voorduin referred to: Van Kooten, "Formulas for the Drainage of Tumbling Bays and Sluices", *Tijdschrift voor Nederlandsch-Indië* ("The Dutch East Indies Journal") 1904/1905, p. 40.

increased in a more than proportional way, varying from 0.8 times with normal usage and areas bigger than 1000 *bouws* to three times as much in the case of no *bouws*. (See **Figure 5.8**).

The main canals

The main Pemali canal grew to a length of 21,950 metres, measuring from the weir at Notok to the last distribution sluice for the last two sections. The section from Songgom measured 13,425 metres. This second section of the main canal displayed fourteen structural works including an aqueduct and six inlet sluices.

The aqueduct was constructed in a straight stretch of the river that was about 76 metres wide (see **Figure 5.10**). When the aqueduct was constructed the river was widened. The structure settled for in 1896 was one in which the supporting section comprised three spanning structures, each of 30 metres. These rested on two cemented land-abutments and two piles in the river. On the bridge arch there were two iron troughs that were 3.25 metres wide and placed one and a half metres high. On top of that was a road: the aqueduct was also a 140-metre-long bridge. During construction, there were several problems that arose. More stone was required than the river could provide which meant that hard limestone had to be brought in from the surrounding area. The sinking of planks for the pile foundations was, here too, a difficult task. In the end, the sinking was simplified by digging a pit. Finally, because of a fire, the construction of the upper structure was delayed.

The first inlet sluice was also the most important sluice: it was the draining off point for five (secondary) sections. At first it was decided that two inlet sluices should be created in this area but later it was decided that they should be combined. In fact, in the very first place three sections had been planned. Ultimately, though, five channels were needed: two secondary ones and three sub-channels. Altogether the sections measured 22,408 *bouws*. The other structural works linked to the Pemali main canal were siphons (one with a spouting mechanism and several with a bridge) and one bridge. In the interests of the population, yet other structures were required. In the dry season the streams that criss-crossed the area were completely dry which was why at the main channel eight "bathing places for people and cattle" were dug (Voorduin 1914: 75).

When the Brebes main canal was being constructed there were two possible routes to choose between. The important question there was whether the Jatibarang sugar refinery should be included in the Brebes region. If so, then it would be necessary to create a more northerly route. If connection with the new canal was not necessary, then a more southerly route could be chosen. The latter route would be less expensive, partly because there fewer structural works would be required. Up until that time the refinery had drawn the water it required for the refining of sugar from two other rivers: the Gung and the Kumissik. These two rivers had less water than the Pemali and in places where that was possible, the drawing of irrigation water was shifted to the Brebes canal. The average level of the Pemali could drop a long way in years of drought, probably even below the levels of the Gung and Kumissik. This led to the decision not to change the water supply situation for the sugar refinery. For the Brebes area the southern route was sufficient. (See for an overview of all the Pemali Works, including those discussed below, **Figure 5.9**).

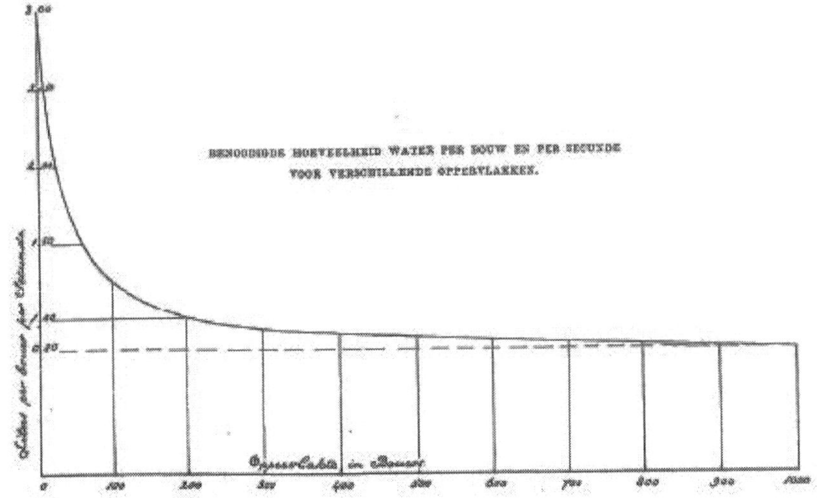

Figure 5.8: The Tegalan Capacity Line showing the required quantity of water per *bouw* and per second (vertical axis) for various surfaces (horizontal axis; from: Voorduin 1914)

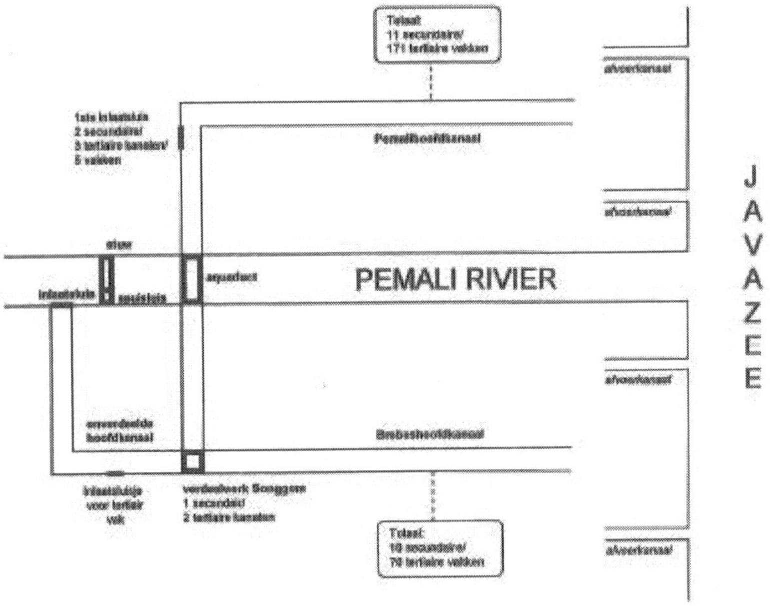

Figure 5.9: Schematic overview of the Pemali irrigation showing the canal system and the irrigation sections. Explanation: *rivier*=river, *stuw*=weir, *inlaatsluis*=inlet sluice, *spuisluis*=drainage sluice, *onverdeelde hoofdkanaal*=undivided main canal (or channel), *hoofdkanaal*=main (or head) canal, *verdeelwerk*=distribution work, *secundaire/tertiaire kanalen*= secondary/tertiary canal, *aquaduct*=aqueduct, *secundaire/tertiaire vakken*=secondary/tertiary sections, *afvoerkanaal*=drainage canal.

Figure 5.10: Aqueduct in the Pemali irrigation system, 1902 (photo UBL KITLV 27711)

Figure 5.11: Secondary canal in the Pemali-Comal area, 1927 (photo UBL KITLV 18383)

The irrigation works network

When it came to dividing secondary sections into tertiary sections or final irrigation stretches the following factors were of importance: a. natural barriers (drainage channels!), b. *desa* boundaries, c. the section shape (no small sections), d. roads and such like, e. the infrastructure of tertiary channels, f. the desirable size (around 200 *bouws*). When there were six secondary sections, further splitting up was not necessary: these sections were also simultaneously end sections. The relevant secondary waterways did not, as was usually the case, supply a group of tertiary sections. There were also occasions when the secondary channels were branched, in one section that happened as many as seven times. In the end, 11 secondary sections were created on the left-bank and ten on the right-bank. These were respectively sub-divided into 171 and 70 tertiary sections. From the section division the ultimate surface area to be irrigated could be worked out. In this case that was 46,553 *bouws*. Of this area 30,939 *bouws* was in the Pemali region and 15,377 *bouws* in the Brebes region. The remaining 237 *bouws* obtained water directly from the main canal that had no branches. (See **Figure 5.9**).

The routes of the secondary channels were established in conjunction with the section divisions. The technicians drew up the routes on the terrain but the local population had to construct the pipelines in what was known as *desa* service. With the secondary connections height differences often had to be negotiated. This was done with the help of waterfall dams (see **Figure 5.11**). In all, some 122 of these were constructed and the drops varied from ten to 118 centimetres. There was a differentiation between waterfall dams that were located in the middle of a structure and those situated just below a dividing sluice. They were given square and trapezium-shaped openings, respectively. The shape of the opening was important in conjunction with fluctuating water volumes (more or less water passing through the channels). If the opening had the correct trapezium shape then the water level above the dam would remain the same as in the channel.

The water flowed from secondary to tertiary channels via division sluices equipped with doors and winding mechanisms. The agreed to objective was that water should be distributed in proportion to the size of the sections. This was achieved by introducing pipes of different diameters at the sluices. Voorduin (1914: 86) referred in this context to "proportional water distribution" and he saw this as "a matter of great significance for good, simple and as practical as possible water distribution". To this he added the following:

"In the months of November and December, when water supplies fluctuate a lot, the fair distribution of water would be completely impossible if this demand were not met in broad outline; in the mornings and evenings the water levels often vary considerably and, moreover, the levels change as well during the course of the day. One would need to employ an incredible number of people to regularly adjust the sluice gates only to achieve an insufficiently proportional distribution of water if this process could not be, to a certain extent, automatically regulated" (ibid.).

There were other technological solutions to the problem of evenly distributing water such as constructing waste weirs that were trapezium-shaped in cross-section.

When the water being drawn off fell 50% below the maximum level, the system of even distribution would be dropped. Supplies were most often depleted in the east monsoon season and the drop in water level crept in slowly. At those times people were not averse to regulating water supplies by using doors and water raising methods. If there was little water, perpetual water provision then became less attractive and distribution was preferably achieved "in response to the differing demands" (ibid.).

When the water amounts drawn off reached exactly 50% even distribution was still just about possible, but not without extra supervision. Voorduin (1914: 89-90) elucidated it thus:

"In such cases, the water level in the tertiary pipes is hardly above, indeed, in many cases it is even below surface level. This was a problem that could be surmounted but only if the water level in all the secondary and tertiary pipes was raised even higher. When levels dropped to 50% the fields closest to the dividing sluices would have little or absolutely no water at all while the fields that were further away would be able to receive their proportional amount of water. What one might now expect to see is that the owners of sawas located nearest to the distribution sluice will try to raise the water levels in the tertiary pipes wherever possible (but at the cost, of course, of the general water level) because the level in the secondary channels is higher. No further explanation is needed to point out that then the situation of fair distribution will be seriously disturbed. To minimise this problem as much as possible it was decided that in cultivating the land attention should be paid to the fields just referred to which should be dug and cultivated last of all".[8]

The branching off of a secondary canal was something that was initiated with the aid of an inlet sluice. The other types of structural works involved in networks of secondary water supplies were siphons and bridges. A number of strategic points in the irrigation area would also be linked together by means of telephone line connections. As far as the supply and drainage pipe lines in tertiary sections went, it was the population that played an important part. It was in co-operation with the *desa* population that the irrigation personnel established the various routes. The work was carried out in *desa* service under the supervision of a *Mandur* (see Numans 1916: 338-339).

Drainage

When it came to draining away water use was made of existing streams. Sometimes it was necessary to improve or widen such streams. The Klikiran (see above) would be diverted. A connection would then be made with a stream that would serve as a drainage channel and with a secondary channel that would thus be supplied with more water. This kind of suppletion was particularly welcome in the dry season. Dykes were constructed sparingly because good conveyance required channels without dykes. The measures taken in conjunction with drainage served to sharply reduce the numbers and the severity of the floods, though floods issuing from the Pemali itself continued to occur.

The upper river reaches

As far as the Pemali region was concerned, the execution of works projected in the general irrigation plan, was not yet a reality. In the nineties of the century before last, the east monsoon caused levels in the Pemali to drop very low. This gave rise to an inquiry and in 1901 the Indies government even appointed a special commission for this very purpose. The Pemali Commission drew on representatives from all areas and included:

---

[8] See for a (detailed) criticism of Voorduin's views of even water distribution (with a reply from Voorduin) Kloppenburg (1914: 1018). Water distribution was more than anything a question of management. In the Pemali region the water management system that was ultimately developed did not see proportionalism as the most important norm (see the following section). See for a discussion on "proportional" as opposed to "absolute" water distribution **Chapter 6**.

1. H.J.W. van Lawick van Pabst, Chief Inspector of Cultures (chairman),
2. A.G. Lamminga, Director of the Irrigation Works in North Tegal (vice chairman),
3. J.W. de Bruijn Kops, Public Works engineer (secretary),
4. the Regent of Brebes,
5. the Deputy-Advisor for the Coffee Cultivation,
6. the Assistant-Resident of Brebes,
7. the Forester from the Tegal-Cirebon forest area.

This Commission brought out its report in 1903. In the findings, the conclusion was that the fall in the east monsoon water levels in the Pemali region could mainly be put down to rice cultivation expansion and to the shrinking of the wooded area in the upper river reaches.

The people of the mountainous inland area created their own little dams in order to irrigate their rice fields. On the whole, these dams served that purpose adequately and made year-round rice cultivation possible. In certain places there was no west monsoon irrigation at all because the population was unable to control the high water levels. There people thus had to rely entirely on the supplies of the dry season. The Congkar dam served to exemplify the situation well. Each year, at the start of the west monsoon season it was washed away. This dam had a negative effect on the east monsoon water levels in the Pemali as well as on year-round rice cultivation elsewhere in the area.

The *huma* ("shifting cultivation") method common in the region only promoted deforestation. The Commission called this type of agricultural practice "scandalous" and further went on to say

"it is a barbaric way of carrying out agriculture, only permissible in poorly developed societies where, apart from having a thin population large tracts of agricultural land are available and where forests cover such vast areas that large-scale felling cannot have negative climatological and hydrological effects. This is not, however, fitting in Java where there is already talk of overpopulation and a shortage of agricultural land" (cited in: Voorduin 1914: 12).[9]

The Commission proposed that in order to improve the water situation the following measures should be taken:

a. Rice cultivation should not be allowed to be extended in the dry period.
b. A permanent *prise d'eau* should be constructed at the place where the Congkar dam was situated in order to supplement irrigation supplies in the east monsoon season with water collected in the west monsoon season.
c. East monsoon irrigation should be reduced in a large area where people cultivated rice the whole year through.
d. East monsoon irrigation should replace west monsoon irrigation in other areas.
e. Water distribution in the upper reaches of the Pemali should be managed by the service responsible for the exploitation of irrigation works in the plains.

The Commission furthermore recommended that, for example, the forest areas should be replenished.

The government took the Commission's proposals to heart. In 1904 it made *f* 50,480 available for the *prise d'eau* that was to replace the Congkar dam.

[9] Compare with Dove (1985) who maintains that the traditional shifting cultivation method was more productive than wet rice cultivation (see **Chapter 2**).

Excursus 5.2 The Congkar dam

The new dam was 1.60 metre high and 30½ metres long and it was equipped with an outlet sluice that had two openings, each three metres wide. There was also an inlet sluice that connected with a canal which, after crossing a side river was linked up with the old Congkar channel. While the old dam had provided water for about 600 bouws *of land, the new system could water 980* bouws. *The greater part of the irrigated land was to the east of the Pemali (606* bouws *including 64* bouws *which, in the old situation, had obtained water from another temporary dam). The irrigation possibilities to the west of the river could really be considerably increased (going from 58 to 374* bouws*). This did, however, require a new aqueduct over the Pemali. The* kali *Keruh, in which the Congkar dam was situated, was in fact a mountain stream. When* banjirs *came, loose boulders could cause great damage. Though this was taken into account during the construction of the dam it was still necessary to, in 1910, line the floor behind the dam with "dressed" river stone.*

A more general policy that was in line with the proposals made by the Pemali Commission was to follow in 1907. The Indies government had first invited the Directors of Civil Public Works, the Civil Service and Agriculture to provide their recommendations on the proposals. After that in a letter addressed to the Civil Service Director the government made clear what was its viewpoint. The government wanted to get rid of restrictive regulations as far as planting rice and supplying water was concerned. It did however urge people to put a stop to *huma* agricultural practices and to extend the wooded land area. This was to be done cautiously bearing in mind that as far as ownership rights linked to *huma* cultivation were concerned "one was confronted with situations arising from peculiar ideas held by the population which, because of years of passive by-standing on the part of the Administrators, had somehow been sanctioned" (missive from the first Governmental Secretary, dd. 5th November 1907, no. 3021, cited in: Voorduin 1914: 15). Subsequently, technical people were sent out to the area to oversee water control affairs by improving the existing irrigation facilities and by introducing water regulations. Special attention was given to the *kali* Erang irrigation area because that was where most water wastage was thought to take place.[10]

Management

The beginning

Although the Pemali irrigation project was not completed until 1903, it was possible to make partial use of the works by 1899. The question, though, was how? In other words, how should the water be allocated? It had been presumed that 0.8 litres of water per *bouw* and per second would be made available. This was only in the west monsoon season though. During the remainder of the year, water would remain a scarce commodity in the Pemali region. Moreover, the population usually wanted to start cultivating rice as early as possible in the rainy season. In such circumstances

[10] In 1909 two inlet sluices were constructed in the *kali* Erang consisting of a barrier wall with an opening provided with a sliding door. A sum of *f* 1810 was put aside for this. Three years later another eight sluices were built.

"little further explanation is required to emphasize that to avoid ending up with a situation in which man merely starts to care for himself without considering his neighbour's interests: a situation which would moreover only increase the wastage of precious water, precisely at the beginning of the West Monsoon season, it is in the first place necessary to lay down and to enforce fixed rules so that the available water is dispersed justly and fairly and agriculture can benefit from this" (Voorduin 1914: 108).

To make water distribution as efficient as possible Lamminga divided the irrigation area into five groups of tertiary sections ("*golongans*"). The idea was to allow the rice crops in each *golongan* to start growing at another stage so that the water resources available could be distributed time-wise as well. The amount of water available varied: in the west monsoon season the water levels rose, only to fall later and to reach a complete low point in the east monsoon season. The second advantage of dividing the water into *golongans* was that water provision could be linked to the fluctuating availability of water. The dates when water provision from the various *golongans* commenced were: 16th October, 1st and 16th November and 1st and 16th December. Later, the final date came to be dropped when the management regulation of 1910 dictated that the water supply of the fifth *golongan* should coincide with that of the fourth. The time when water started being supplied from the different *golongans* varied from year to year.

As far as possible the *golongans* were created in such a way that the surface levels remained equal and so that the ownership of the inhabitants of the same *desa* was spread over different *golongans* in order to stimulate mutual co-operation. There was one further stipulation which was that two subsidiary sections irrigated from the final separation sluice of a secondary channel should belong to *golongans* that were not consecutive to each other where water provision was concerned. If three sections were involved then the smallest two could be situated in consecutive *golongans* but the biggest section would have to be at least one *golongan* away from them. These regulations were designed to ensure that everywhere the maximum amount of water was utilised.

Water controlling commenced in the 1899/1900 harvest period and expanded as new works came into operation. When it came to the matter of introducing the actual exploitation method, there was extensive collaboration between the Director of the irrigation works (Lamminga), the Assistant-Resident of Brebes, the Regent and the relevant Controller. Subsequently, in every area where works were completed, meetings were held between administrators and *desa* elders. Those who at least had to be present were the Regent, the Controller and the Director of the Irrigation Works. The Regent would outline the intentions. The population was permitted to air its views, although according to Voorduin (1914: 109) this did not happen much in practice: "Invariably the only request made was for the number of *golongans* to be limited to three and that was impossible because the river water available did not permit that". Endeavours were made to encourage the population to share their nursery fields and to preferably situate them in the commencement area of tertiary channels, but all in vain:

"The objections to the last-mentioned measure had firstly to do with the inconvenience of having to transport the young plants too far when planting them out in the fields, and secondly with the fact that the yield of a field that had previously been used for nursery stock was generally lower than that of other sawahs so that the land owners were not generally keen to relinquish their fields to later be used as nursery areas for others" (ibid).

Stipulations

When creating the *golongans*, Lamminga at first adhered to the system previously applied in the Pekalen region of East Java, the irrigation area where his career had begun. In the 1882-1893 period he had created an irrigation system for the watering of more than 10,000 *bouws* of land (Lamminga 1895). In this network the *golongans* were laid out in a village-oriented way. Each *golongan* covered a fifth of the land of every village. That meant that the *sawas* in tertiary sections often fell into different *golongans*. In the Pemali region it became apparent that it was absolutely impossible to abide by such boundaries when allocating water. Hence the decision to view the tertiary final sections as irrigation units and to thus group these in *golongans*.

The "Regulations on the use of and distribution of water in the Pemali region", laid down by the Resident of Tegal in 1910, defined a *golongan* as follows:

"a collection of final sections in an established number of sections involved in an irrigation network which, when it comes to distributing irrigation water in the West Monsoon season for the purposes of the various paddy field crop phases, are made equally full" (cited in: Voorduin 1914: 108).[11]

The regulations placed day-to-day management and supervision relating to the irrigation works and to the use of the works with the Head of the Pemali-Comal Irrigation Division (see below) and its personnel. They were responsible for seeing that water reached the various channels and end sections. The officials involved were Dutch Supervisors, Javanese Supervisors (*Mantris*) and Coolie Chiefs (*Mandurs*).

The important variables related to water provision were, the state of the terrain, the size of the sections and the agricultural phase of the *golongan.* The regulations differentiated between west and east monsoon irrigation. The former was basically oriented towards rice cultivation and the latter to the cultivation of other (second) crops. The general water requirements for rice in the different growth phases were laid down as follows:

- preparing of nursery beds: 0.3 litres per *bouw* and per second for 14 days
- preparing for planting out: one litre per *bouw*, per second for 42 days
- further, until harvest time: 0.8 litre per *bouw*, per second and gradually less.[12]

The regulations also stipulated the general water requirements of crops in the dry period and it differentiated between two categories, giving maize and sugar cane as the "normal types". The west monsoon irrigation situation was regulated by the *golongan* system but east monsoon irrigation was organised on a demand basis. For the small-farmers group it was an irrigation official (the *"ulu-ulu golongan"*, see below) who supervised this. In the case of sugar cane, water was basically supplied in a market-garden fashion. This meant that accepted and thus measured quantities were used. The tapping points were therefore equipped with gauge dividers. Temporary personnel was employed to take care of the supervision required for this sort of water allocating.

The regulations also anticipated various reactions to water shortage: water supply delay, proportional quantitative reductions and the enforcement of neighbourhood regulations. With a view to the importance of stimulating co-operation between irrigation personnel and the local

[11] In main outline, the regulation adhered to was the management regulation laid down by the engineer J.P. Kruimel, described in a memorandum in 1905. He succeeded Lamminga and was project director until September 1905. The regulation can be found in the Dutch General State Archive, the Groothoff Collection, no. 167.

[12] These water amounts required for the different growth phases of rice were integrated into what was known as the Pemali Consumption Guideline (see Brouwer 1991: 14-15, cf. Ter Hofstede and Van Santbrink 1979: 33 ff.)

civil servants, the Javanese ones included, the ruling stipulated that irrigation personnel representatives should attend management meetings. One of these meetings was a monthly conference of administrators with the Assistant-Resident (of the Brebes Regency). It was stated that the (Dutch) Irrigation Division Supervisors should also attend this meeting. Other meetings took place at District and Sub-District level (see below).

Within the final sections what was important was the supplying of water to the *sawas*. This was more a question of "water provision" than of water distribution (Voorduin 1914: 112). The (specific) crop requirements was the main criterion. The water ruling of 1910 placed the responsibility for water distribution in the final sections with the *Ulu-Ulu Golongans*. This was a new water master function but it linked up with the function of *Ulu-Ulu* that already existed in some areas. The *Ulu-Ulu* was responsible for irrigation affairs and was, as such, part of village administration, falling under the authority of the Village Chief. The ruling made in the Pemali region was different; there the water master was detached from local administration bodies.

By 1907 a ruling had already been made in relation to the position of the *Ulu-Ulu Golongan* in which the task was described as follows

"to distribute irrigation water within the final section, to supervise the continuation and directional maintenance of tertiary 'to and from' supply systems and to check the crop situation" (cited in: Voorduin 1914: 113).

The *sawa* owners elected the *Ulu-Ulu Golongan* but the Regent had to sanction this choice. To do this he would first seek advice with regional administrators, including the District Chief (the *Wedono*) and from the engineer in charge of supervising water distribution. (See **Figure 5.12**). The interested parties were also responsible for paying the *Ulu-Ulu Golongan*. The amount owed depended on the size of the area concerned. For land that was rented out for the sugar industry it was those business people who had to pay the contribution.[13] The *Ulu-Ulu Golongan* was to be viewed as a local authority delegate (or as a delegate for a number of local authorities) but that was not where he belonged. His power derived from the colonial administration. In short, the *Ulu-Ulu Golongan* was "to be seen as a representative of his fellow inlanders who forms a link between irrigation personnel, a link which it is asserted, is indispensable" (ibid.). The Village Chiefs had meanwhile lost their formerly powerful position in the matter of allocating water. This seemed like a moot point but, in the regulations, it was made clear that ultimately people did not regret this:

"They [the Village Chiefs, WR] have thus, in this respect, been prevented from abusing their power within the desa. Simultaneously their influence has been somewhat diminished which might be seen as a problem but, according to the explicit reassurance of the Administration, water management has in no way suffered because of this. In fact, it has been better guaranteed than before" (ibid.).

[13] Sugar cane cultivation increased substantially in the irrigated area, going from 900 *bouws* before the time of the project to 3800 after that time (I shall return to this matter). As far as water distribution was concerned, just like elsewhere in Java, what was known as the "day and night ruling" (of feeding the sugar crops in the daytime and rice crops by night) had probably also applied in these parts (see **Chapter 6**).

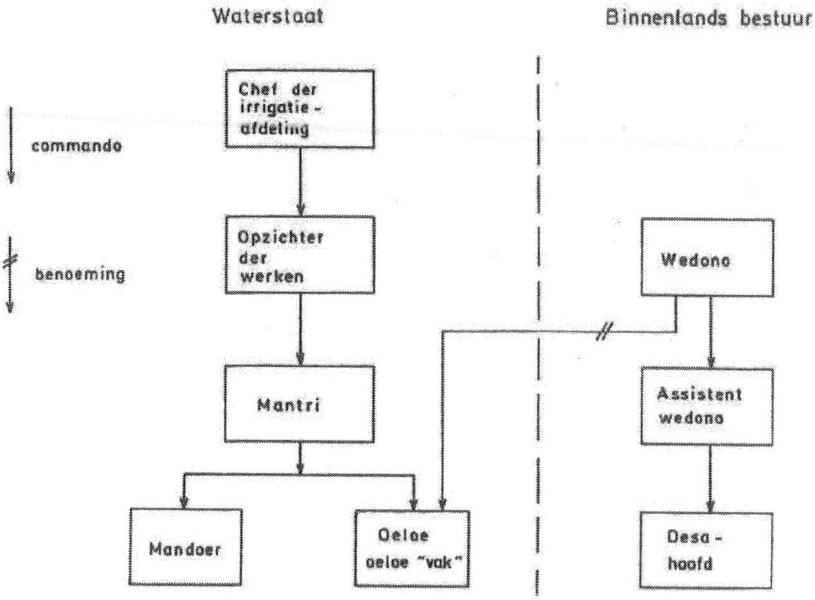

Figure 5.12: Organisation plan for the management of the Pemali Works
(from: Ter Hofstede and Van Santbrink 1979). A *Wedono* is a District Chief, an Assistant-*Wedono* is a Sub-District Chief. The *Wedono* would be consulted by the Regent who confirmed the appointment of the *Ulu-Ulu Golongan* (see the text).

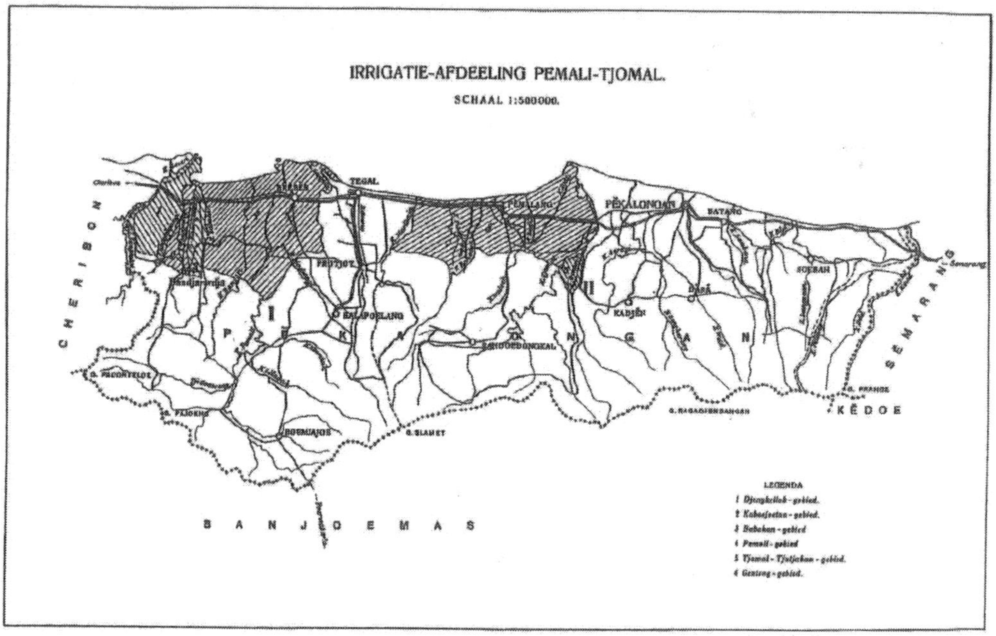

Figure 5.13: The Pemali-Comal Irrigation Division (from: *Verslag BOW* 1910)

The *Ulu-Ulu Golongan*'s work areas ended on the borders of the tertiary sections. Responsibility for conveying water to the final sections was with other officials: the *Mantris* and *Mandurs*. They were in charge of supervision and water distribution (under the authority of Dutch overseers). The *Mantri* was a special official. He was in charge of taking care of the operation, surveillance and maintenance (see below) of a work (or works). He also had to supervise the *Mandurs* and the *Ulu-Ulu Golongans*. The *Mantris* had to attend management meetings at District level (at least once in the three months) and at Sub-District level (at least once a month) and their task was

"to report on their water distribution activities, to make proposals in that connection and ... to carry out enquiries with the desa chiefs whenever possible complaints or objections arose" (Voorduin 1914: 114).

Just as the water master functioned as a link between farmers and irrigation personnel, so the *Mantri* served as a link between irrigation personnel and the managers (ibid.).

When it came to maintaining main and secondary canals and structural works the irrigation personnel had merely a supervisory role. The work partly relied on forced labour and partly on free and paid labour.[14] Those responsible for these jobs were the *Mantris* and *Mandurs*.

How the upkeep of the tertiary inward and outward water supplies was to be organised was stated in the "Orders for the maintenance of tertiary channels in the regulated irrigation areas of the Pemali, the Babakan, the Kabuyutan and the Jengkellok rivers in the Pekalongan residency" laid down by the Resident in 1905. It obliged the *sawa* owners to do the practical work. The way in which the work was divided and organised was planned by irrigation personnel in consultation with civil servants. The order was followed by a whole host of rules stipulating exactly who had to do what, and when. This was quite an improvement compared to the way things had been in the past if one notes what Voorduin (1914: 115-116) had to say about the matter:

"Since the implementation of this order the upkeep of tertiary supply channels has been perfect. In the past that was different: notably in the case of drainage connections, too little was done which meant that not infrequently the Administration had to intervene. Furthermore, those ordered to work sometimes did not turn up which made things difficult for the ulu-ulu. It was especially the sawa owners who did not live on the spot who could sometimes be awkward. The rule for them was that they should appoint a substitute who lived in the desa who would then be responsible for maintenance".

The engineer J.G. Numans had few good words for the state in which he found the tertiary channels when he took up office as Director of the Pemali Works in March 1907.[15] To his mind the population had made a mess of things:

"The findings have shown that the upkeep of the tertiary channels can no longer be left to the population. When the undersigned was made responsible for the management of the Pemali Works it became clear that the network of tertiary channels was in an extreme state of neglect;

---

[14] Over the course of time, unpaid forced labour started to give way to paid labour. In the Pemali area such forced labour debts were paid off. In 1912 e.g. 50,781 service hours were compensated with *f* 7,617.15 (Voorduin 1914: 115).

[15] In the period between the time when Kruimel departed and Numans took over office the following engineers had been made directors of the Pemali Works: O.E. Rappart, September 1905 till April 1906, P.J. Bertel, April 1906 until September 1906, P. van der Kaaden, September 1906 till March 1907.

this was particularly the case in the western District of the Pemali region with a surface area of 30000 *bouws* which before the irrigation works were created was devoid of irrigation water.
...
Many channel sections could not even be found on the terrain because after the paddy harvest the channel dykes had been destroyed by grazing water-buffalo. Other channel sections had been diverted and made to run in zigzag fashion which meant that there was no longer sufficient cohesion between the channels. The changes had been made by the sawah owners who felt that it was better if the waterways ran along the borders of their sawahs. What also sometimes emerged was that the downstream regions of the channels had been completely filled in.
In the West Monsoon season, when water was needed for the nursery beds and for the tilling of sawahs, the most urgent repair work would be done to the channels.
The watering of the stock for second crops and for sugar beet was therefore accompanied by enormous water loss" (Numans 1916: 339).

The Pemali-Comal Irrigation Division

The water distributing and the maintenance of the Pemali Works was finally to be consolidated by the Irrigation Division that was established in 1908 for the entire Pemali-Comal region (see **Figure 5.13**). Irrigation Divisions were special management organisations (see **Chapter 6**). The Pemali-Comal Irrigation Division also included the upper reaches of the river and thus met one of the propositions made by the Pemali Commission (see above). The Division was led by a Head who, as "section engineer", was also in charge of the area in which the Pemali Works were situated (the Division's main Section). He was stationed in Tegal. (*Verslag BOW* 1910: 202-204, see also National Archives, the Haringhuizen-Schoemaker Collection, no. 124 and *Mindere Welvaartscommissie* ["Lesser Welfare Commission"] 1910: 156-163).

For the Pemali Works there were two Dutch Overseers stationed in Brebes and Songgom. They were responsible for the control of a part of the Section (the "lower section"). The technical personnel (including those in the river's upper reaches) was further made up of seven *Mantris* and 21 *Mandurs* including four Sluice *Mandurs*. See for an overview of the various officials, their tasks and relationships to each other and to the Irrigation Division managers of the Pemali Section **Table 5.1** (and **Figure 5.12**).

Table 5.1 Managerial organisation for the Pemali Works

Office holders (hierarchical line)	Tasks	Relation to management / population
Section Engineer (also Irrigation Division Head in Pemali-Comal)	management of Pemali (first Section of the Pemali-Comal Irrigation Division)	convene with management of the Pekalongan Residency
Supervisors (Brebes/Songgom)	Sub-Section control	consult with Regent-level managers (Assistant- Resident and Regent)
Mantris (assisted by Mandurs)	to oversee distribution of water/primary and secondary system upkeep	deliberate with management at (Sub-)District level
Ulu-Ulu Golongan	water allocation in tertiary sections	elected from sawa owners (independent of village administration)

Finally

The Pemali-Comal Works

Another important project in the Pemali-Comal region was the Comal-Cacaban project comprising three smaller projects that were completed in the 1896-1906 period. Lamminga drew up the provisional plan for this as well as the final design for the various project sections. It was under his supervision that the headworks were completed which included the dam in the Comal at the place Sukowati which could supply 13,272 *bouws* of land with irrigation water.[16] The works in which Lamminga was involved encompassed almost 154,000 *bouws*. Even when all these works were completed the creation of irrigation facilities still continued. The Sengkarang Works were completed in 1925, thus providing the entire coastal region with modern irrigation systems. By that year the Pemali-Comal Works extended over almost 170,000 *bouws*. **Table 5.2** gives an overview of all the works (from west to east), of the area covered, the period of execution and of Lamminga's contribution to the projects. (See **Figure 5.13**)

With a number of the works, notably the Jengkellok, Kabuyutan and Babakan Works (in West Brebes) and the Waluh Works improving the drainage system (i.e. the conveying away of water) was an important facet. With regard to the works in West Brebes, Weijs (1921: 374) had the following to say:

"The annual inundations were of such magnitude that even the great post road connecting Tanjung and Losari was frequently flooded over for long periods during the west monsoon season which meant that the community there had to be supported by a proa raft stationed in Tanjung and they were, just as one might well expect, thus almost completely washed away".[17]

At the end of the colonial period came the building of the reservoir at Penjalin. This lake which had a capacity of around 2.4 million cubic metres was completed in 1934. By serving to supplete the Pemali water shortage this reservoir opened up new possibilities for the planting of young stock, sugar beet included, during the east monsoon season. (Polderman 1935, Polderman et al. 1935). After a while, it was also important to carry out major repair work in the region. An example of such necessity was the Kaliwadas weir in the *kali* Genteng, a side river of the Comal. The construction, in 1932, of a bar put an end to the havoc continually being wreaked in this dam by the ravages of water. (Verschoor 1935).

---

[16] See e.g. "Preliminary design for the improvement of drainage and irrigation between Comal and Cacaban (Regency Pamalang and district Maribaya) 1895-1897" (1896), from the Haringhuizen-Schoemaker Collection in the National Archives, no. 62, and also in the same archive, the Groothoff Collection, no. 165.

[17] See for details on the works in West Brebes *Verbetering* ["Improvement"] (1899). An overview of the history of these works may be found in Van Sandick (1898). He contested comments made by the Van Kol couple to the effect that these works were executed "as a result of the shock that seized our government on the occasion of the Bantam revolt" (a murder in 1888; p. 150).

Table 5.2 Overview of the Pemali-Comal Works (1890-1925)

Works	Size (in *bouws*)	Construction dates	Lamminga's part
1 Jengkellok Works	10,409	1904-1910	preliminary design, final plans, prise d'eau and main canal
2 Kabuyutan Works	5,625	1890-1902	completed, put into operation
3 Babakan Works	3,891	1890-1894	completed, put into operation
4 Pemali Works	46,553*	1893-1903	preliminary design, all final plans, executed, brought into operation
5 Gung and Kumissik Works	35,436	1909-1925	research, preparations
a Gung Works	25,735	1909-1925	
b Kumissik Works	9,701	1909-1919	
6 Comal-Cacaban Works	37,402	1896-1906	preliminary design, final plan, execution of headworks
a Rambut Works	12,266	1900-1906	
b Waluh Works	11,864	1896-1906	
c Comal Works	13,272	1900-1906	
7 Genteng-Sragi Works	17,233	1892-1919	improvement and execution of works
Total Lamminga's Works	153,750		
8 Sengkarang Works	15,709	1914-1925	
Total Pemali-Comal Works	169,459		

* Over the course of time irrigation areas varied in size. The *Verslag BOW* (1910) gave, for the Pemali Irrigation radius 44,370 *bouws* and the 1925 report 43,745 *bouws*. I use here the figure given by Voorduin (1914: 130) derived from the 1908 report.

Sources: *Verslag BOW* (1925), Weijs (1921: 374), Voorduin (1914)

Costs and benefits

Round about 1910 the total costs of the Pemali Works had risen to *f* 2,309,300 (Voorduin 1914: 106). This sum also included the costs of all the works which, after the year 1903, the year in which the Pemali irrigation network was more or less finished, were undertaken. The expenses may be broken down in the way given in **Table 5.3**.

Table 5.3 The Pemali Works expenses

Activities*	Cost (in guilders)
Surveying and project work	159,000
Execution	2,140,500
Transport at the state's expense	9,800
Total	2,309,300

* The entire job was carried out under the supervision of the Civil Public Works Department.

The final sum corresponded roughly to the sum total of all the expenses which the Indies government had, over the course of time, approved. The final total was in fact slightly lower. The amount of money made available had been *f* 2,311,851. Some 1,248,900 hours of forced labour had been used up (at least that was the officially permitted number of man-hours). By completing some of the works with such labour instead of having workmen on a payroll about *f* 201,000 had been saved. There was little difference between the actual expenses and the 2.25 million guilders which had been estimated necessary for the Pemali Works in the general irrigation plan of 1890. At this point it should be noted that the cost of the Brebes main canal and the works in the upper river reaches had not been included in that last sum. The works had cost *f* 52,- per *bouw* and that was not much. An opinion that was dated even then (because of the Solo Valley Works, see **Chapter 7**) was that irrigation works should not cost more than *f* 100,- per *bouw* (see Weijs 1913: 19).

In its 1900 report the Rentability Commission estimated (see **Note 2**) that the net income from the Pemali Works would be *f* 93,140. There was, however, on the benefits side also the increased land rent yield to be accounted for of *f* 128,515 and the company tax of *f* 8,593. On the negative side there were the costs of exploitation (maintenance included) budgeted at *f* 43,968 per annum. Going on a projection of *f* 2,100,000 for the entire works the Commission calculated that the net returns would be around 4.4% of the budgeted expenses (known as the outlay capital). In those days such a percentage was viewed as reasonable (the minimum rent level was 4%, see **Chapter 6**). The Commission furthermore saw possibilities for expansion, for increasing sugar cane acreage by 8500 *bouws*, which would give the sugar industry a boost. The population, for whom increased rice harvests could be beneficial, would also profit from this sugar industry growth because wages would rise, more materials could be supplied, more transport would be needed and such like. Altogether, according to the Commission, this would make the population at least six times as wealthy as growing second crops. All in all, the Rentability Commission's conclusions were very positive:

"From the foregoing details it is evident that the creation of works designed to irrigate the Pemalie, combined with due attention to water drainage, will be a good thing for a large part of the regency of Brebes; that because of this a previously generally poorly developed area will be able to become a prosperous region in which many will be able to earn a decent living; that alongside of the inland agriculture the European agricultural industry in the Pemali region will be able to pursue its development; that the expected benefits directly payable to the treasury will promise a good rent level on the capital outlay; that from the capital invested already more than half has been expended; that for all the reasons mentioned it must be seen as highly important for all parties concerned that the works are energetically pursued and completed as soon as possible" (cited in: Voorduin 1914: 121).

Were these expectations realised? There were, indeed, signs that the economic situation from 1904 onwards, the year when the works became fully operational, did improve. The irrigated *sawa* area grew from approximately 28,600 *bouws* before the project was begun to 46,553 after its completion (the 1908 figure). The rice harvest per *bouw* also rose proportionally. Alongside of the 1898 yields the production level rose in the 1904-1912 period by, on average, more than twelve *pikols* per *bouw* to 37 *pikols* per *bouw*.[18] Other improvements were that the annual land rent debits due to failed harvests and uncultivated *sawas* in the 1899-1909 period reflected a falling trend and that the planting of second crops increased sharply (going from around 4050 in 1898 to 25,669 *bouws* in 1912!) (Compare Van Schaik 1986: 138-139).

Rentability in the narrower sense of the word, as examined by the Rentability Commission and as explained above, only affected the cash flow of the government and did not take into consideration the population's higher agricultural incomes, was a disappointment. The operational costs were lower than estimated but the profit from land rent added up to only a fraction of that estimated amount. **Table 5.4** gives the sums and the estimates. As mentioned, the total Pemali Works costs were *f* 2,309,300. We can thus calculate that the rent was 0.7% of the outlay capital, a poor result in view of the expectations![19]

[18] The assessments concerned "paddy experimental crops" (Voorduin 1914: 124, 131). The Brebes District had between the years 1916 and 1920 an average rice production level of 35.36 *pikols* per (successful) *bouw*. In the Districts of Tanjung and Banjaharjo that was 29.40 and 29.85 *pikols* per *bouw* respectively. The average in the Regency of Brebes was 31.98 *pikols* rice per *bouw*, in the whole Residency of Pekalongan 27.42 *pikols*. The population in the Brebes, Tanjung and Banjaharjo Districts was, in 1920, respectively 151,071, 125,041 and 124,653 souls, in the Regency of Brebes 573,841 and in the Residency of Pekalongan 2,268,571 souls. The number of *bouws* of *sawa* per head of population was, in the three Districts, in 1920, 0.15, 0.21 and 0.18 respectively and in the Regency and Residency 0.16 and 0.12 respectively. In the three Districts the rice production per head of population was, in 1919/20, 5.12, 3.86 and 4.88 *pikols* respectively. In the Regency as a whole it was 4.20 and in the Residency 3.12 *pikols*. (*Landbouwatlas* 1926, tables: 10-11, 52, see for the development of rice production in Pekalongan and Java in general Booth 1988, see for general production figures in the 1870-1910 period also **Appendix L**).

[19] Voorduin (1914: 126) noted in this connection that the land rent had not yet been increased and "it is only for that reason that the work has not yet brought advantages for the country which may reasonably be expected and which the population has been enjoying for some time". A revision of the land rents was being held up by the introduction of a new land rent ordinance established by the government in 1907. (See **Chapter 6**). See also, for the rentability of the Pemali Works, Lamminga (1910: 25-26). Compare Happé's rentability calculations (1939), see **Appendix E**.

Table 5.4 The Rentability of the Pemali Works (in guilders)

	The 1900 rentability company estimates	The actual sums around 1910
Increased land rent yields	28,515	
Increased company tax returns		8,600**
Total	137,108	43,900
Exploitation costs	43,968	27,500 ***
Net earnings	93,140	16,400

* In the years 1898-1910.
** Taking the budgeted figure. Voorduin (1914: 125) had no other figures available but did notice that the company tax increase was just a tiny aspect of all the indirect advantages of the works, and that was a consequence of the fact that the population had significantly more to spend.
*** In 1912. The sugar companies contributed *f* 2052.61 in 1912 to the exploitation costs. This money was expended on appointing "assistant *mandurs*" for water distribution, and for placing water measurement gauges, and so forth. The sum is not included in the mentioned exploitation costs.

The sugar industry was able to expand considerably. The amount of land devoted to sugar cane rose from 900 (over 3% of the irrigated area) to 3800 *bouws* (over 8%) of which 2400 *bouws* was on the left-bank of the Pemali where previously there had been no sugar cultivation. In the western part of the Pemali region a new refinery, Bandajaratma, was established while another existing refinery, Ketanggungan-West, became active in that area. The number of sugar refineries and cane crops in the area thus doubled. It was an increase that was less than had been expected. The reason for this was that bearing in mind the (irrigation) interests of the population, the government had been rather reluctant to provide refineries with licences to increase sugar cultivation (on land to be rented from the population).[20]

[20] Brebes, Tanjung and Banjaharjo were the three "cut cane Districts" in the Brebes Regency. In 1922 there were 22,215 *bouws* of *sawa* in the Brebes District, 2866 *bouws* of which, or 12.9%, was used for sugar cane. In Tanjung there were 26,283 *bouws* of *sawa*, 734 of which, or 2.79%, were for sugar cane. In Banjaharjo there were 22,239 *bouws* of *sawa*, 1369 *bouws* of which, or 6.16% was for sugar cane. The average for the three Districts was 7.02% and for the entire Pekalongan Residency, 13.12% (*Landbouwatlas* 1926, Tables 78 and 29). For information on the growth of the sugar industry in the Pekalongan Residency see Van Schaik (1986) and Knight (1993), and for the social consequences of this in the Pemalang Regency see Lucas (1977), see for the expansion of the sugar industry in Pekalongan and in the whole of Java Booth (1988). According to Schaik (1986: 139) there was no increase in the number of sugar refineries after the completion of the Pemali Works (see also in his account figure 7.1 on p. 129).

The Pemali ruling

Improvements in the situation in the Pemali region resulted not only from the irrigation works but also from the way in which those works were managed. The Pemali Ruling had many advantages. A commission that studied the water situation in the Demak area listed the following:

1. Each grower knows a long time in advance when he is going to have access to water.
2. Work in the *sawas* can be evenly divided up.
3. Javanese agriculture is orderly and systematic; it is no longer necessary to rush the soil tilling process.
4. The production costs and paddy prices have been more evened out.
5. The usefulness of having introduced the *Ulu-Ulu* system is recognised by all. (Voorduin 1914: 117).[21]

The Demak Commission's opinions about this ruling were positive:

"In the Pemali region, apart from maintaining and developing, there is still much to be done, yet for the future, because of the organisation of irrigation exploitation as in the way sketched above, a solid foundation has been laid and it has, as has proved useful and necessary, been realised in a way unique to the region, utilising the strengths of the population and also the available resources" (cited in: Voorduin 1914: 117).

Lamminga's biographer added weight to this argument thus:

"Under those successful regulations his works succeeded in recreating what had, up until then, been in many respects an extremely neglected region in one of the most prosperous parts of Java thus making the available agricultural land much more productive by converting tens of thousands of bouws of uncultivated land into fertile sawas" (Weijs 1921: 374-375).

After its introduction, the Pemali Ruling was developed and modified. In 1917 the *Ulu-Ulu* regulation of 1907 was revised. At first there were various ways of paying, including paying in kind. Under the new regulations, however, payment could only be financial and, even though the obligation to pay rested with the interested parties, it was enforced by the intervention of the irrigation service. What did not change was the fact that in connection with the land they rented the sugar concerns had to contribute to the salaries of the *Ulu-Ulus*, even if these water masters were not directly involved in the irrigation of their cane crops. In 1924 the number of *golongans* was increased to six. That was done with a view to the growing sugar industry. In order to be able to start preparing the land for cultivation in good time the sugar cane growers had to look to the first *golongan*. With five *golongans* it was virtually impossible for them to have sufficient ground in the first *golongan*. After 1930 it was the introduction of new cane varieties that had to be planted earlier and the poor economic climate that caused cane cultivation to die out which gave people reason to innovate change in water management in the Pemali-Comal region (see **Chapter 10**). (Graadt van Roggen 1932 and 1935).

The Pemali Ruling was also criticised. Theoretically the *Ulu-Ulu Golongan* was an independent incumbent but in practice he was dependent on the Irrigation Division (the *Mantri*!) and the administration which, in conjunction with the relevant engineer, had to ratify his re-election. The changes in his salary structure further reduced the autonomy of the water master. Some engineers, who were more interested in having kinds of water boards, regretted this degree

[21] The report brought out by the Demak Commission dates from 1908. Its authors were Lamminga and two Agricultural Inspectors. This issue will be returned to (in **Box 8.2**).

of dependence (for instance Happé 1936a: VI. 142-143). The debate on the Pemali Ruling also had a broader context in which the pros and cons of the various water regulations were discussed. Here it was especially the population's influence that counted.[22]

A paragon of construction and management

When one thinks of modern irrigation expansion round the turn of the previous century in the Residency of Pekalongan, it is the person known as Lamminga who springs to mind as being inextricably intertwined in all of this. His works were seen as exemplary. The Pemali Works constituted an irrigation project that had become "a standard work serving as an example for numerous other irrigation works in the Dutch East Indies that have been and are still being realised" (*Lamminga monument* 1930: 121). As far as technology was concerned Lamminga earned his spurs by creating what amounted to complete and integrated irrigation systems. His plans were founded on thorough research and on a general design in which the system was worked out to the very last detail. Lamminga was not, however, the first irrigation engineer in the Pemali region. When he arrived in the region the headworks were already being constructed according to a plan laid down by Van Kol. Lamminga had no alternative but to accept this. His plans, though, were based on all the most recent data and insight into the land areas possibly to be irrigated. For the dam and the first section of the main canal that meant that gradually the execution of these activities would have to be somewhat altered.

Creating an entire irrigation system automatically led to the following step; that of having to create a managerial basis for the whole network. Indeed, irrigation works could only be beneficial (to all parties!) if the aspects of water distribution and maintenance were well organised. Lamminga was someone who appreciated that and who thought beforehand about what might be the best management system and then integrated that into his general scheme of things. In the next chapter we shall see that it was particularly in this respect that Lamminga was innovative. What we shall also discover is that as regards political and governmental policies he did not in any way operate in a vacuum but that irrigation was rather, in his day, a hot issue on the political agenda and that a massive programme existed for the expansion of modern irrigation facilities. In short, the following chapter will place the work of Lamminga in its rightful broader technical and political context.

---

[22] This issue will be returned to in ensuing chapters, but first in **Chapter 6**. See for a critical examination of the Pemali Ruling Ter Hofstede and Van Santbrink (1979: 141 ff.) They viewed the growing dependence of the *Ulu-Ulu Golongans* upon the irrigation service (and the colonial administration) as a reinforcement of governmental influence in favour of the sugar industry and they maintained that the "de-feudalising of water management" (the detaching of the water master from village administration), in turn, became a new repressive force for the population. Citing Slamet (1968), they simultaneously equate this detachment of the *Ulu-Ulus* from village rule with the illegal affecting of village autonomy.

6

'Towards the complete irrigation of all government land'

The mandate of the Civil Public Works Department

> Technology does not just provide, in its individual machines, the physical means by which a society supports and promotes its power structure; it also reflects, as a social institution, this social structure in its design. A society's technology can never be isolated from its power structure, and technology can thus never be considered politically neutral (Dickson 1981: 180).

The engineer H. van Brakel, the main character in a Dutch novel published in 1890, was not a happy employee of the Indies Department of Civil Public Works[1]. Contemplating his low salary he resented the lot that had befallen him "as engineer within Civil Public Works leaving him in the grasp of the Dutch Indies Government" (p. 13). Van Brakel was somebody who needed a lot of money because he enjoyed gambling and thus had high debts. After having become impossible to get on with within Civil Public Works he threw himself into the small business construction industry. His father-in-law who owned a coffee plantation warned him against the business life but Van Brakel believed that he, a "qualified engineer" with "scientific knowledge that no one could steal from him" (p. 148), was untouchable. In the end, the engineer fell on hard times. Ultimately he found work with an enterprising shoemaker. By nicknaming him "*mandur*" (leader of the coolies) this employer verified his downfall. Daum first published the book in 1886 in serial form in the *Bataviaasch Nieuwsblad* ("Batavian Newspaper"), the journal that he had established. Paradoxically this was, in general, a good period for civil engineers. The backdrop to Van Brakel's downfall was one of emancipation and growing independence for the Public Works Organisation. Opposed to the human drama described by Daum there was the social success of the service. That success will be elucidated in this chapter[2].

As far as the actual execution of public works went we learnt in **Chapter 4** that the Civil Public Works Department and the Civil Service were basic rivals and that in 1885 the Indies government resolved that dispute by coming out in favour of Public Works. Here again we resume where we left off by indicating how the government turned the organisation that Van Brakel had abhorred and blamed as being the root of all his problems into a powerful body, thus giving engineers the opportunity to embark on a large-scale construction programme which, as will be chiefly seen in the ensuing chapters of this section, was not completely positive. We begin here by explaining the changing role of the state.

---

[1] Maurits (pseudonym of P.A. Daum), *Ingenieur B.O.W.*("Engineer Civil Public Works"). I refer here to the second edition of 1976. The writer Rob Nieuwenhuys wrote in his foreword that all of Daum's books "end in disillusionment, on a lonely note and invariably with utter decline" (p. 8). Cf. Van 't Veer (1980b: 20).

[2] Van Brakel's superior at the Department of Civil Public Works the Chief Engineer Willert also came to a bad end. Despite his "many years of faithful service" he was "cast out onto the sidelines because of his unscrupulous nepotism" (pp. 152-153).

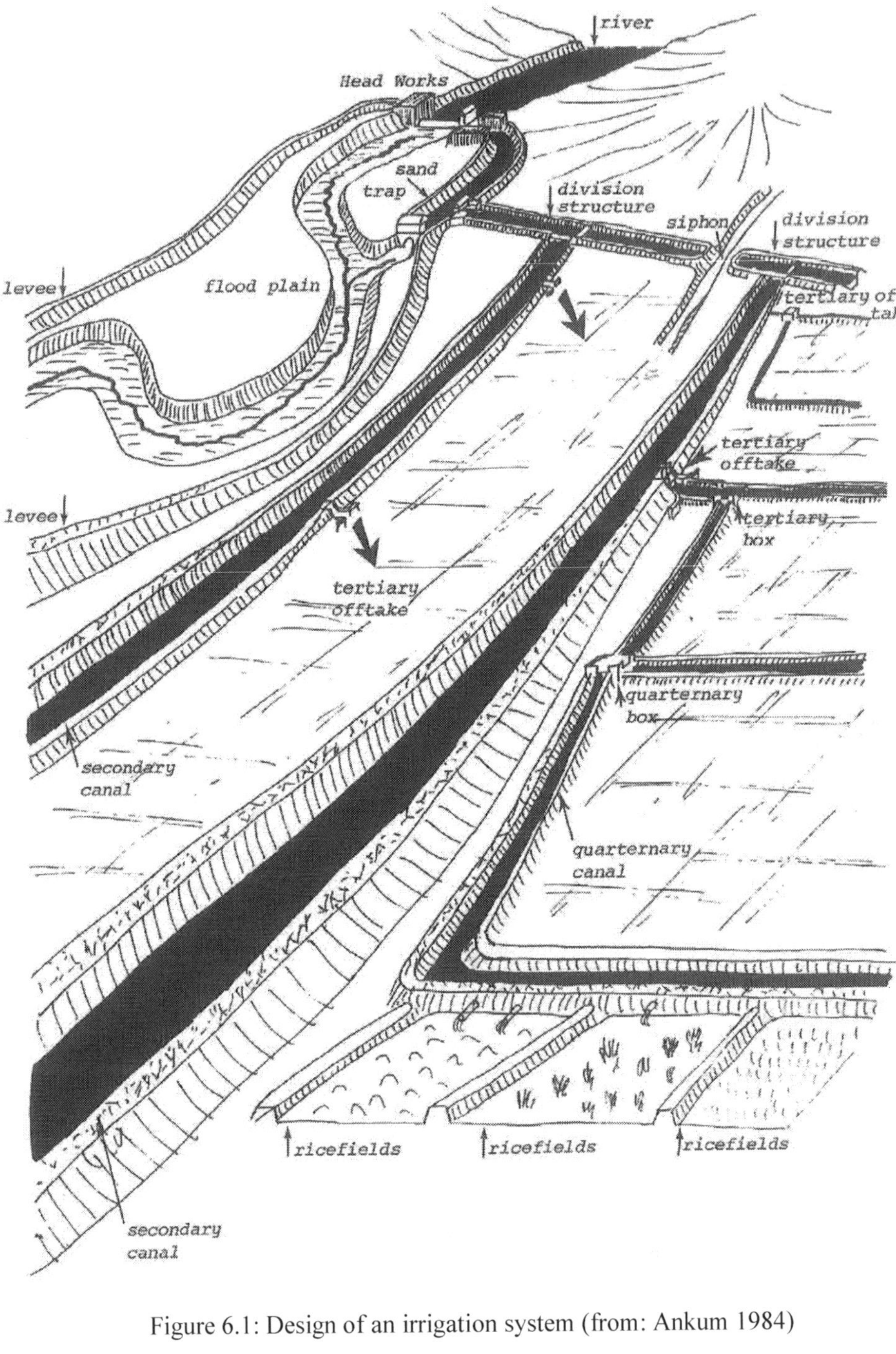

Figure 6.1: Design of an irrigation system (from: Ankum 1984)

Between exploiting and caring

Liberal policy

In **Chapter 4** we saw how, influenced by liberal reform, the early colonial state changed. At first it was the Indies government that was the exploiter but gradually, over the course of the nineteenth century, it relinquished this role. This led to the situation that, in 1870, with the introduction of the Agrarian Law and the Sugar Law, "free trade imperialism" was initiated. Protecting the land rights of the Javanese population, the former law made the free establishment of enterprise possible while the latter law saw to it that over the course of time compulsory sugar cultivation was abolished. Agriculture thus became the setting for private initiative and the Dutch (and other Europeans) established a series of new agricultural businesses (culture companies) that occupied themselves with the production and processing of sugar cane, tea and other crops. (See, for instance, Baudet and Fennema 1983: 30)[3].

In the case of sugar cultivation, an important source of income for the Indies government, the transition from state-run to private enterprise was not completed over night. It first started with the government gradually withdrawing from its involvement in sugar cane production. The cane, which the population had been forced to cultivate, was still sold for a fixed price to the sugar refiners who had been around for a long time but these farmers otherwise remained independent. Ultimately, in the 1879-1891 period, the government ended its direct involvement in the cultivation of sugar cane. (*Encyclopaedie* ["Encyclopedia"] Vol. IV 1921: 178). Generally things were not easy for the sugar industry. The protection of the sugar beet industry in Europe led to overproduction and to a drop in the sugar price on the world market. In 1884 this turned into a crisis. At the same time the sugar industry was assailed by something known as the "*sereh* disease"[4]. The government reacted by decreasing taxes. Because of the *sereh* disease outbreak the sugar industrialists decided to set up (more) experimental stations. Gradually these stations started to concern themselves with all aspects of the sugar industry. Because of this, and also because of their co-operation in the socio-economic field (involving the taking over, by banks, of many private sector businesses) the sugar refineries were able to cope with all the problems facing them. It was only after the turn of the century that the situation improved. In 1903 there was a new sugar crisis and, because of this, the Brussels Convention put a stop to the protection of the sugar beet industry. The sugar market subsequently recovered. Reinforced by research and co-operation the Javanese industry was ready to take advantage of this situation. (See, for example, Gonggrijp 1957: 127, 132, 140 and also Bakker 1989).

The new economic order gave birth to a new task for Indies government, namely that of supporting free enterprise by providing infrastructural works such as roads, bridges and irrigation works. In 1875 money was thus made available for the creation of railway lines and a modern harbour for Batavia (Tanjung Priok) (Gonggrijp 1957: 131, 134; see for increased governmental investment in infrastructural works **Appendices G and H**).

---

[3] Apart from the political background factors (notably liberalisation) it was also economic aspects that stimulated the rise of free trade imperialism: in the second half of the nineteenth century the Netherlands became involved in a process of industrialisation (see De Jonge 1978 and Lintsen 1992-1995). Other favourable circumstances were the improvements made in navigation (fast clippers and steam ships) and the opening, in 1869, of the Suez Canal (constructed by Ferdinand de Lesseps) (Gonggrijp 1957: 113).

[4] This name was coined because the disease in sugar cane so much resembled that of the grass of this same name (A. Nardus L. or A. Schoenanthus L. from the genus Gramineae, Andropogon Linn., *Encyclopaedie* Vol. III 1919: 753-754).

Ethical Policy

In **Chapter 4** I also made it clear that, more than in the past, the Indies government was beginning to focus more on the interests of the Javanese population, partly by force of circumstance. To use the popular jargon of the day, the government became "milder" in its attitude towards the population. It was a tendency that was to be perpetuated also after the initiation of free trade imperialism. Admittedly, while free enterprise was primarily intended to provide the population with advantages (see, for instance, Gonggrijp 1957: 120) it also stimulated the government to ensure that the people were not abused. Another reason why government intervention increased was because the Javanese and Maduran population had risen so sharply, going from twenty to thirty million in the 1880-1905 period (Gonggrijp 1957: 125, compare Creutzberg 1972: 734 and Boomgaard 1980). In this connection it became important to develop a political stance aimed at encouraging Javanese agriculture, in other words, to develop a food policy. Infrastructural works, notably irrigation works, fitted well into such an ideology. (See, for example, De Vos 1941: 276).

As has already been indicated, the endeavours to turn things to financial benefit remained, as did the drive to perpetuate the Exploitation Policy. We also saw that after 1877 there were no more economical (export) balances. The main reason for this was the Aceh war (begun in 1873, see Van 't Veer 1980a) but there were also other contributing factors, one of which was the falling coffee culture yields (*Encyclopaedie* Vol. II 1918: 417-418). Apart from anything else, this meant that activities in the field of public works remained limited. Infrastructural works were always a heavy burden because the Indies government did not borrow money for that. The works had to be financed from ordinary resources while the population was expected to provide unpaid labour. (Gonggrijp 1957: 127-128). In the nineties, however, the view that money could be lent for infrastructural works somehow took root but only under the important condition that it should be possible to raise interest and repayment funds from the returns. As we shall discover this rentability led to various inevitable problems. Indeed, it was not until the second decade of the twentieth century that it would become customary to borrow money for public works (Gonggrijp 1957: 129).

Under these circumstances the prospects for the population were not particularly favourable by the end of the nineteenth century. Population growth was threatening the standard of living. The government embarked on a welfare policy but the Exploitation Policy prevented this from taking on substantial proportions. Furthermore, because the sugar market was at a low ebb few people could be employed in that corner of industry.

As has been indicated above, things were to change within the sugar industry after the turn of the century. A similar thing applied to government policy. In her speech given on the occasion of the Dutch opening of parliament of 1901 Queen Wilhelmina announced the dawn of the Ethical Policy. It was a "moral obligation" towards the Indies population that had prompted the Netherlands to formulate this Policy which was described as an "honest administrative policy, devoid of self-interest that had been drawn up by the mother country and was in the interests of the land and people of the colony" (*Encyclopaedie* Vol. II 1918: 419, see also Brooshooft 1901: 4 ff.). Subsequently the financial footing between the colony and the mother country changed. The Exploitation Policy was abolished and all the money that the government earned from taxation could be entirely expended in the Indies itself. In fact it was even the case that finances started flowing into the colony because the Ethical Policy brought with it an extensive welfare programme. None of this was sheer coincidence. The ethicist Brooshooft (1901: 5) even went as far as to claim that this "forceful penetration of ethical sunshine through clouds of darkest egoism" had a 150-year history! (Compare Brooshooft 1887). Van Doorn (1994: 149) gave the Public Works Organisation a pioneering role in all of this: "What can be said of the irrigation service is that it was dozens of years before its time in its pursuit of the ethical direction" (compare Fasseur 1995: 28 ff.; the matter of the Ethical Policy will be further expanded in **Chapter 8**).

A state within the state

The Public Works Regulation of 1885

Lamminga journeyed to the far away Indies in 1881 in the company of a number of other engineers such as C.W. Weijs and P.T.L. Grinwis Plaat. All three engineers had been taken on by the Indies Civil Public Works Department by virtue of the favourable arrangement of 1874 (see **Chapter 4, Note 23**). The engineers were familiar with Post's book (1879) which painted a somewhat sombre picture of the circumstances under which engineers were expected to work in the Indies (see again **Chapter 4**) and clearly this was a subject of discussion during the voyage. According to one of them Post had done little to deter them:

"We were too convinced of the fact that should the Indies public works engineers so desire, their service would only increase in importance and as far as the accompanying prestige was concerned" (Weijs 1921: 373).

This optimism proved to be not completely unfounded because in 1885 the Indies government established a new Public Works Regulation that was favourable as far as the engineers were concerned. The government maintained that it was desirable to give the engineers a working environment that corresponded more to their capacities. In that respect the protest launched by Post and other engineers following the Regulation of 1879 could be termed successful. The government had a second objective which was to make cuts in its budget. This drive to economise was born of necessity, after all, there was no longer a politics of exploitation to profit from[5].

The honour of developing proposals in the light of both objectives fell to the engineer J.A. de Gelder, member of the Indies Council[6]. He maintained that if personnel numbers were cut back it would be possible to make savings. The number of engineers would be reduced to 39, thus almost halving the workforce! In anticipation of the new ruling the government agreed to this proposal (*Indisch Staatsblad* ["Indies Gazette"] 1885a). The Regulation, drawn up by De Gelder and accepted by the government, really brought with it improvements for engineers. It somehow managed to convey that irrigation activities were vital to the population. What it basically proposed was that the Public Works Organisation should be divided into a general and a regional service. This was a set up which, as has already been mentioned, had been previously lobbied for by De Bruyn. The General Service was the most important branch and it comprised:

- the Technical Division
- the Irrigation Brigade
- the Public Works Divisions.

[5] Another factor that undoubtedly prompted the Indies government to consider reviewing this Regulation was the need to support the sugar industry, especially since it was, at that time, in dire straits. Moreover, Van Rees - who was at the time governor-general (1884-1888) - was not particularly a supporter of the drive to construct modern irrigation facilities (see **Chapter 4**).

[6] De Gelder, who had previously rendered services through his "heroic exploits in combat with pirates" (Van Sandick 1912: 786), had distinguished himself within the Public Works Organisation by creating the harbour at Tanjung Priok in Batavia for which money was made available in 1875. When the harbour was almost completed in 1883 the Krakatau erupted. De Gelder's works withstood the enormous tidal wave that the eruption brought with it which brought him even greater glory. (Van Bosse 1912: 789).

The Technical Division already existed, just like the institution of the Public Works Divisions. The number of Divisions was expanded from three to seven and included two new Divisions for the Outlying Regions.

It was the Irrigation Brigade, though, that drew most attention. It was the task of this branch to "fully prepare for irrigation all the government land that came into consideration for rice cultivation" (*Indisch Staatsblad* 1885b: 1). The regulations (1885b: 1-2) added to this the following priority:

"To this end the Brigade will first of all tackle the matter of improving on existing defective water channels; it will then deal with the irrigation of suitable terrains in heavily populated areas and finally it will turn to dealing with the watering of uncultivated land or wasteland in low or unpopulated areas".

The Regulation (p. 2) continued as follows: "All the surveys and projects required for that objective are to be conducted and compiled by the Brigade's staff". The Brigade was thus expected to collect data and integrate it into its project proposals. These proposals would then have to be directly submitted to the Director of Civil Public Works. If the resolution was positive the work would not be then carried out by the Brigade. The realisation of projects was the work of the General Service in co-operation with the Public Works Divisions. For major projects special services would be set up.

According to the Public Works Regulation of 1879 the engineers were subordinate to the Resident but when the new ruling came in the relationship was clearly different. Within the General Service the engineers were independent of the Civil Service people. They were only answerable to their immediate superior and ultimately to the Civil Public Works Director. The regional heads were only responsible for the respective and much smaller Regional Service[7].

Over the course of time, amendments were made to the 1885 regulations but nothing was done to diminish the status of the engineers. For instance, the Irrigation Brigade, headed by W.F. Heskes was disbanded in 1889 (*Indisch Staatsblad* 1889) but this was only as far as its existence as a separate service was concerned. The Brigade was incorporated into the E Technical Division which fell immediately under the Civil Public Works Director. In fact, this was a move that was somewhat regretted by the engineers[8]. The hierarchy of activities, with the improving of existing

---

[7] It is possible to debate the internal consistence of the Regulation as far as the influence upon the engineers is concerned (see National Archives, Ministry of the Colonies, Resolutions 1886). Criticism was directed towards the 1885 stipulations, notably to the aspect of personnel size, in e.g. the *Soerabaiasch Handelsblad* ("Surabayan Newspaper") which as a result of and in the spirit of the congress of the *Nederlandsche Maatschappij ter bevordering van Nijverheid* ("Dutch Society for the Stimulation of Industry"), held that year in Purmerend, lobbied for the expansion of modern irrigation facilities in the Indies. It was calculated that with its ten engineers of the day it would take the Irrigation Brigade 375 years to develop a minimal irrigation programme. (*Irrigatie* ["Irrigation"]1988, cf. Verburgh 1884 and Saltet 1896). There were similarities between the organization of the Indies Public Works Department and its counterpart, the Dutch State Public Works Organisation (*Rijkswaterstaat*). The latter organisation also had a central service and a sort of regional service made up of the various provincial services. The traditionally important components of the Dutch organisation were the water boards and the public legal bodies for the maintenance of dykes etc. (See Lammers 1929 and Ten Horn-van Nispen et al. 1994). The introducing of water boards was also important in the Indies (see the remainder of this chapter and **Chapter 10**). In the Indies, Provinces with their own Public Works Departments did not emerge until the very end of the colonial period (see **Chapter 10**).

[8] Lamminga (1900) stated that because the Irrigation Brigade had been disbanded the Public Works Organisation could no longer be said to have any central leadership. Weijs (1913: 16) pointed out that the reason for taking these steps was "never really made clear". Boomgaard (1987: 70) suggested that in 1889 the irrigation service was a "separate entity" within Civil Public Works. That was not correct, the "separate entity" which had existed up until that time (the Irrigation Brigade) had just been disbanded! What was also inaccurate was the claim made by Metzelaar who, in a three-part authoritative work on agriculture in the Indies written by Van Hall and Van de

works at the top of the list, was also discarded at the request of the Civil Public Works Director, M.J. van Bosse (*Indisch Staatsblad* 1890b). His reason for changing this was that this stipulation stood in the way of the development of some five designs for major projects emanating from surveys carried out in the pre-1885 era (Van Bosse 1901: 358). After T.C.J. Kroesen (1879-1884) and H.L. Janssen van Raay (1884-1889) the Civil Public Works Department once again had, in Van Bosse, a technical man at the helm. This was another sign that in the eighties engineers were prevailing over civil servants. From 1889 onwards the Directors continued to be recruited from Public Works circles[9]. As far as engineer numbers were concerned the decline envisaged by De Gelder was never materialised. In 1888 the group was at its lowest with 53 engineers (according to Saltet 1896: 1, see also **Appendix F**, in which the number of engineers quoted for 1888 was 71, *Encyclopaedie* Vol. IV 1921: 727 and Van Sandick 1912: 786). In 1890 the government determined that the number of engineers should be fixed at 60 (*Indisch Staatsblad* 1890a). By 1900 there were 96 engineers (Thal Larsen 1912: 930)[10].

A scientific approach

The 1885 Regulation confirmed the notion supported and propagated by engineers to the effect that irrigation works should be based on scientific findings. Apart from anything else, that meant that extensive field research should take place beforehand. A second facet of the new approach was the fact that irrigation works and entire irrigation systems had to be thoroughly designed.

In **Chapter 4** we saw, for instance, that preparatory research in the period leading up to 1885 was either not done at all or hardly took place. The means for such research were simply lacking. There I also remarked that the general level of knowledge possessed was insufficient. Apart from lacking practical and theoretical knowledge about maximum transport volumes and soil types very important insight was lacking at that time, namely that simply establishing headworks was not enough. Lamminga (1910) emphasised this point when he gave a brief overview of what had been done in the past in the field of modern irrigation. Because of lack of research and also because everything had to be done quickly things did, according to Lamminga (1910: 5), go wrong in two main respects with a number of the irrigation works:

"It was not only so that these permanent works themselves were badly damaged thus necessitating repair work and invariably bringing inconvenience for agriculture but it was also the case that the construction thereof did not meet the exaggerated expectations that had generally been expressed because nothing was done to change the actual irrigation system as a whole".

Koppel asserted: "The Department of Civil Public Works was established in 1854 but it was only later, in 1889, when a separate Irrigation Division was set up that the question of the creation of irrigation works was systematically promoted" (1946: 204).

9 Up until 1920 Van Bosse's successors were: G. van Houten, J.E. de Meyier, H.P. Mensinga, A.P. Melchior, W.B. van Goor, J. Homan van der Heide and P.J. Ott de Vries. We shall come across these important engineers in this chapter and in subsequent chapters. (See **Appendix J**).

10 Even though all the stipulations of 1885 and afterwards heralded better times for engineers civil servants still remained critical, see e.g. Liefrinck (1896/97). This Civil Service employee (he had been Controller and Inspector of Cultures) thought positively about Javanese irrigation and was a fervent supporter of the fact that state intervention should be kept to the minimum. Here and there I shall, where relevant, allude to Liefrinck's views (see for a reaction to his article Melchior 1897). Apart from anything else, engineers remained dissatisfied because of the poor promotion prospects (see e.g. Saltet 1896).

Figure 6.2: Inlet sluice, East Java, 1920 (photo UBL KITLV 2580)

Figure 6.3: Inlet sluice at tertiary canal, Java, 1915 (photo UBL KITLV 33959)

According to Lamminga the Irrigation Brigade had been chiefly established in response to this last factor, to the knowledge

"That it was necessary to treat the irrigation system as a whole as a cohesive organism unable to operate properly unless all the correct functioning of all its parts was taken into consideration" (ibid., compare Lamminga 1885/86 and Liefrinck 1896: 1187).

When it came to the creation and operation of the Demak Works it was the engineer G. van Houten who was the inspirational source behind the new work method. It was for the first time in the history of engineering intervention in irrigation matters in Java that – with these works – a plan for a complete irrigation system was drawn up and carried through on the basis of extensive preliminary research. (See **Box 6.1**)

Box 6.1 The Demak Works

In sequel to the weir built at Glapan in 1859 that was described in **Chapter 4**, the engineer Van Houten began in 1872 to collect data for the purposes of a fully thought through irrigation plan. In so doing he was the first engineer to make use of the methods of triangulation and altitude measurements. The project design was ready by 1878 and the work started being executed in 1881. By 1889 an important part of the works had been completed and the entire job was not finished until 1894. The area of land irrigated was 61,900 *bouws*. (Slinkers 1891/92, *Verslag BOW* 1910 ["Civil Public Works Report"], compare De Meyier 1891: 133-137 and Weijs 1913: 14-15)[11].

The Irrigation Brigade was given the task of collecting data and creating irrigation maps so that on that basis it would, in the long-term, be possible to establish a stable and as good as possible irrigation situation. The 1885 Regulation (*Indisch Staatsblad* 1885b: 2) produced the following overview of the data to be collected:

"The brigade collects and orders ... the data produced by rainfall observations in *Java* which are of interest to irrigation. With all the chief rivers they determine what are the basis and the water levels, they calculate the water flow rates and, with the help of maps based on topographic and statistic details, they draw up irrigation maps clearly indicating the river basins and the existing water channels and irrigated fields which also show exactly how the relevant fields are irrigated as well as indicating what are the degrees of irrigation in relation to the volume of water required for one entire irrigation period.
Through experimentation they determine how much flowing water is required for one full irrigation round of various fields and they become familiar with the construction and effectiveness of the structures created both by Europeans and Inlanders in the Dutch Indies for the purposes of irrigation".

It was hoped that the surveys, observations and tests would lead to feasible designs for irrigation facilities (irrigation projects). The plans would, it was hoped, become blueprints for complete irrigation systems with both headworks and works for the designation of water supplies. An

[11] According to Weijs (1913: 13) De Bruyn played no part in the preparation of the Demak Works. Just like the irrigation activities of Pet in Bagelen, Van Houten's work was "of his own doing" (see **Chapter 4**). Van Houten was described as "one of the greatest Dutch hydraulic engineers of the 19th century" (by J. Nuhout van der Veen, cited by Van Sandick 1918b: 660).

irrigation system comprised networks of different types of canals and channels:

- a main supply canal, serving to collect water from rivers and to convey it to the next type of canal, in other words
- the secondary canals designed to transport water to the secondary irrigation sections and to then pass it on to
- the tertiary channels designed to distribute the water over the *sawas* or to take it to the tertiary end sections after which it arrives in the
- drainage canals which take the water back to the river or to other water expanses.

In addition to that all irrigation systems included many constructions or structural works. I shall just mention here the most important ones. The main canal received its water from an inlet that would often be provided with a sluice (an inlet sluice). This would be part of all the various works constructed in a river at a water drawing point which, collectively, were known as a *prise d'eau* (or water catchment). There would be a weir (or barrage) that might or might not be movable (and may or may not have flood-gates). The weir would be standardly equipped with a sluice or draining sluice and/or a draining off canal with sluices. The system would furthermore contain one or more large distribution works in the main canal (with more sluices, in reality inlet sluices) and larger or smaller inlet sluices at the secondary or tertiary channels. Other (possible) components were damming up or outlet systems in channels, deluge dams (or sloping gullies) in watercourses or culverts (leading the water under a road or dyke). The complex might also comprise one or more aqueducts, siphons (leading the water under another canal), roads and bridges. When constructing (permanent) structural works as much as possible use would be made of durable materials such as stone and cement. (See in this conjunction the explanation given by Melchior in 1897, for instance on pages 1288 and 1289, see **Figure 6.1** and see for inlet sluices **Figures 6.2 and 6.3**).

The 1885 ruling gave engineers the opportunity to set about their work in the way that they had proposed of preparing and executing irrigation projects for entire irrigation areas. It was just a general plan of campaign that was still lacking. In 1890 Van Bosse managed to rectify this. His General Irrigation Plan was added to the Indies budget for 1891. It amounted to a combination of all the projects that had been prepared and were feasible and it included an estimation of the costs. Originally the plan included nineteen projects which, altogether, covered an area of 577,300 *bouws*. Van Bosse estimated the costs at *f* 35,525,000 which included the wages for the labourers to be hired[12]. Van Bosse maintained that the entire plan could be realised within a space of ten years. (*Verslag BOW* 1892: 171-173, Van Bosse 1893, see **Table 6.1**). The way in which the projects were selected was fairly random. Van Bosse (1901: 359) said of this:

"As a rule the proposals were usually based on rice shortage (a euphemistic way of referring to imminent famine) or poverty amongst the population, either because of the evident impossibility of maintaining existing inland works or because of a desire to consolidate or expand such works".

Poverty and desperation were invariably what instigated irrigation works plans. Generally the background would be a situation in which population density was high and water availability scarce. Another important factor was the presence of Dutch plantations, notably for sugar cane. (See Van Kol 1901: 344 and also Gerst 1901: 416, Liefrinck 1896: 1183 and Melchior 1897: 1303-1314[13]). After 1890 further new projects were added to the plan.

[12] The engineers saw more disadvantages than advantages behind the use of obligatory labour which was why they (gradually) began to replace this in their budgets with outlays for paid labour.

[13] The correlation between modern irrigation and sugar cultivation will be underlined later on in this chapter when we come to discuss the organising of the control of irrigation areas. For more information on the services of Van

Table 6.1 The General Irrigation Plan of 1890

Irrigation projects*	Residency	Area**	Construction period
1 Demak Works	Semarang	47.554	1853-1894
2 Kening Works	Rembang	3.440	1889-1890
3 Pateguan Works	Pasuruan	2.853	1887-1891
4 Pekalen Works	Pasuruan	9.709	1883-1893
5 Manggis Works	Kedu	6.110	1850-1908
6 Cihea Works	Preanger	6.900	1891-1901
7 Babakan Works	Pekalongan	3.891	1890-1894
8 Kabuyutan Works	Pekalongan	5.625	1890-1902
9 Pemali Works	Pekalongan	43.745	1893-1903
10 Comal-Cacaban Works	Pekalongan	37.402	1896-1906
11 Sampean Works	Besuki	15.387	1875-1901
12 Indramayu Works***	Cirebon	48.671	1857-1917
13 Genteng-Sragi Works***	Pekalongan	17.233	1892-1919
14 Magetan and Ngawi Works***	Madiun	35.457	1891-1922
15 Zuid-Bagelen Works	Kedu	35.540	1864-1906
16 Serayu Works***	Banyumas and Kedu	18.711	1880-1919
17 Solo Valley Works	Rembang and Surabaya	223.000	Stopped in 1898
18 Lusi Works	Rembang	21.000	Not executed
19 Sindangpitu Works	Yogyakarta	36.000	Not executed
20 Tangsi Works***	Kedu	2.875	-1909
21 Molek Works	Pasuruan	5.669	1901-1904
22 Kedungkandang Works	Pasuruan	6.935	1904-1915
23 Ciujung Works***	Bantam	31.947	1905-
24 Jengkellok Works	Pekalongan	10.409	1904-1910
25 Kertosono and Warujayeng Works***	Kediri	20.315	1903-1911
26 South-Jember Works	Besuki	70.000	1908-

* Projects 20 to 26 were added later.
** In *bouws*. Different sources give different figures. In each case the most recently available figures were used, usually estimates given after the works had been completed. Certain of the works projects were later split up and thus appear under different headings in the sources (compare, for instance, the Pemali-Comal Works overview given in **Chapter 5**).
*** Included in the General Work Plan 1907-1911 as non-rent providing.

Sources: *Verslag BOW* (1892: 171-173, 1900: 137-142, 1909: 309-314, 1910: 2-10, 1925: 2-12). See also Lamminga (1910: 6-11) and Van Sandick (1912: 915-916).

Bosse, see Van Sandick (1918a).

The execution of irrigation projects was something that cost a lot of money. In this connection the Indies government insisted that projects must be remunerative (i.e. for the state). For quite some time the matter of rentability had been a work aspect that had gained attention but suddenly it became an important condition. Rentability was especially based on the estimated land rent rises deriving from improved irrigation. The minimum required increase amounted to 4% of the outlay capital. The government set up the Rentability (or Profitability) Commission in 1897. It was responsible for testing all project designs. Various relevant bodies were involved in the Commission. The Departments of Civil Public Works and the Civil Service produced two permanent members. The permanent member for the Public Works Organisation was Lamminga and the Civil Service was always represented by the local administrative head. In the years after 1907 the levying of land rent was improved with the arrival of the new Land Rent ordinance. *Sawas* were divided into "productivity groups". The new law promised an increment in the land rent profits but whether or not this actually happened is not quite clear[14].

After the turn of the century money was made available for non-profitable irrigation projects. The Indies budget for 1903 differentiated between works that were "directly productive" and works for which "productivity was uncertain". After 1905 money was made available for the latter-mentioned types of works. Non rent-producing works were clearly differentiated from rent giving projects within the General Work Plan for irrigation activities which, in 1907, was to succeed Van Bosse's General Irrigation Plan and was to remain in force until 1911. Some four non-profitable projects derived from the previous plan were included in the new plans. (*Verslag BOW* 1909: 309-315[15], see **Table 6.1**).

Technical water management

After irrigation works had been created they then had to be made operational. This concerned especially the distribution of water but also the necessary maintenance. The managing of water areas was in any case an important matter, also in areas provided exclusively with Javanese irrigation. Following the stipulations laid down in conjunction with the creation of works the Indies government decided to also base control on modern principles. It was to this end that the "irrigation divisions" were created (see, for example, Weijs 1900). This comprised the river catchment areas of one or more rivers.

The Divisions were responsible for the following tasks:

- the maintenance of irrigation works and notably the distribution of water;
- upkeep, repair and the renewal of irrigation facilities;
- the possible designing and creating of smaller works.

The Irrigation Divisions were a part of Civil Public Works and were manned by technical personnel headed by an engineer. The engineer had under him a staff of engineers and foremen. Even though engineers were "at the helm" the supervision of the Divisions was the responsibility of the Resident. The first Irrigation Division to be created was Serayu. It was formed in 1888 as a kind of test case and definitely established in 1892.

The population geared the exploitation of irrigation works to the rice cultivation cycle (see, for instance, Van den Broek d'Obrenan 1918: 33-34). The farmers sowed the nursery plots in October. The tilling of the fields and the sowing of the rice took about two weeks. After that the

---

[14] See Happé (1939). *Sawas* were also divided up before 1907 into groups and sorts, see for an example of this Voorduin (1914: 119). I shall return to the subject of land rent in **Chapter 8**.

[15] See for the discussion on the financing of irrigation at the beginning of that century between A.W.F. Idenburg, the Minister of the Colonies, W. Rooseboom, the governor-general, and the Indies Council, Creutzberg (1972: 38 ff. and also p. 178 ff.).

large field would be prepared. The entire process, including the transplanting of the nursery plants, would take about one and a half months. After three months the rice would be ready for harvesting. Irrigation water was therefore required from October to March. In the ripening period the rice required less water. Indeed, less water was desirable because the soil had to "dry out": the full ear could not be allowed to collapse. At the harvesting time the ground needed to be completely dry. In conjunction with the availability of labourers and ploughs the population did not plant and harvest at the same time. Water use therefore gradually rose to a maximum and also slowly (even more gradually) diminished.

During the time of technical water management the fields were grouped together into final sections or tertiary sections with an area of some 200 *bouws*[16]. The rule was that the population's agricultural activities within such a *sawa* section must be the same. This type of co-ordination applied equally to the activities taking place within the final sections that were gathered into one group (see below). When it came to the water distribution (or allocation) within a final section people's individual demands could be taken into account and there were various possibilities. One could allow the irrigation personnel to organise water distribution according to the demands of those involved. Another option was to pass on the responsibility for distribution to the interested parties. Here there were two prevalent views of water management: the "liberal" and the "centralistic" angles. According to the first view the water could be put to best use in situations where water distribution relied on the working of free forces. The state only dictated the main rules. According to the second view it was the role of the state that prevailed, it would intervene on the basis of planning.

In order to determine what was the best exploitation method the government decided to carry out an experiment with two of the General Irrigation Plan projects that were about to be completed: the Pekalen Works and the Pateguan Works. The first irrigation works, which provided some 10,000 *bouws* of land with water, were completed by Lamminga in the 1882-1893 period. One facet of this project had to do with the reconstruction of a weir that had been built previously but which was not very reliable. (Lamminga 1885/1886 and 1894/95). Lamminga immediately made himself responsible for control. In so doing he contributed to the design of the centralistic Pekalen Management Regulation that came into force in 1894 and which, after the necessary amendments had been made, was officially sanctioned in 1901. Lamminga designed the Regulation together with a Civil Service representative, the Controller H.D.A. Obertop. (Lamminga 1905)[17]. The Pateguan Works, extending over some 3000 *bouws*, were created by Weijs and reached completion in 1893. (See Weijs 1900). One year after the Pekalen water regulation system came into force the liberal Pateguan Management Regulation was introduced in a section of the irrigation area. This Regulation had been thought out by Weijs in conjunction with the relevant Assistant-Resident J.H.F. ter Meulen.

In the case of the Pekalen Works the water distribution was "absolute", in other words, entirely based upon the water requirements of the crops (see **Figure 6.4**). The irrigation personnel organised water supplies right up to the final section. The irrigation overview given in the extensive welfare research (see **Chapter 8**) described the Management Regulation as follows (*Mindere Welvaartscommissie* ["Lesser Welfare Commission"] 1910: 95-96):

[16] It was in circular no. 20717/E of 30th December 1898 that the Director of Civil Public Works had dictated this statutory size.

[17] Others who were involved in the creation of the Regulation were C.J. de Jaager, then the local Assistant-Resident, and the engineer M. Ypelaar who completed the Pekalen Works (Lamminga 1905).

"In broad outline the situation is that a system introduced for an area covering ten thousand bouws of sawahs has been introduced on the basis of a cultivation plan for inland agriculture and for the providing of irrigation water to that agricultural land in accordance with that plan ...
...
It divides the irrigation area according to the time when padi has to be planted and into six sections known as golongans. The fields belonging to the first golongan must be planted between 1 and 15 December, those in the second between 15 December and 1 January, etc. until the last golongan is finally planted out with padi between 15 and end of February.
...
Water distribution is now organised entirely according to this cultivation plan, i.e. the soil is watered according to the times when, as stipulated in this cultivation plan, that needs to be done for the nursery beds, the tilling and the transplanting. Apart from at those times no more water is given than is strictly necessary for the maintenance of the crops.
...
The cultivation plan which is precisely stipulated in the desa states and on one map and which is thus intended for every part of the irrigation area has to be established beforehand so that exactly where irrigation water needs to be provided and will be supplied for the tilling and planting is known".

When it came to designing and creating the Pekalen Works this method had already been anticipated: the irrigation area was sub-divided into secondary and tertiary sections through which the water passed via a network comprising a main canal and secondary canals.

The Pateguan water regulation system was "proportional", water distribution was based on the size of the area to be irrigated (see **Figure 6.5**). This was put into practice by introducing a network of circuits. In the area to be irrigated the water in the main circuit would branch off to supply the various circuits within which it would be similarly dispersed over the various final sections. With the Pateguan water regulations the dispersal within the final sections was left to the interested parties. The system was described in the welfare study (*Mindere Welvaartscommissie* 1910: 98-99) as follows:

"According to the principle that parties interested in the same tertiary channel and therefore the various fields irrigated by the different branching off, may be combined to form one water circuit, that the water circuits emerging from the same secondary channel are brought together to form one sub-water district and that the sub-water districts receiving water from the same main channel form one water district. Thus, in connection with their collective irrigation interests, irrigated terrains may be transformed into larger or smaller organic units. Except for the apparently necessary deviations due to the actual situation, the relevant irrigation area was divided into water circuits *(golongan ajer)* of approximately 200 bouws each in surface cross-section and each, totally or partly embracing a sawah area of the greater part of four or five and sometimes even a greater number of desas. Whilst now the distribution of water between the various water circuits is now largely determined by irrigation personnel according to rules drawn up by the Administrators, it is so that neither the Administrators nor the irrigation personnel has anything to do with the way water is distributed within the water circuits, unless when settling differences.
...
Bearing this in mind there is a so-called ulu ulu appointed to every desa who is a member of the town council who is thus close to the machinations of that body and the activities of the desa chief.

The ulu ulu of the different desas who have sawahs in the same water circuit form together for that circuit one committee of water distributors, which is known as a *circuit administration*."[18]

Unlike with the Pekalen Works, the circle system was not something that had been foreseen at the time of the creation of the Pateguan Works. Originally the same Management Regulation applied in the area as with the Pekalen Works. It was only after complaints were received from the population that the proportional method was introduced. In the first part of the area where that was introduced that went well but not so well in subsequent areas.

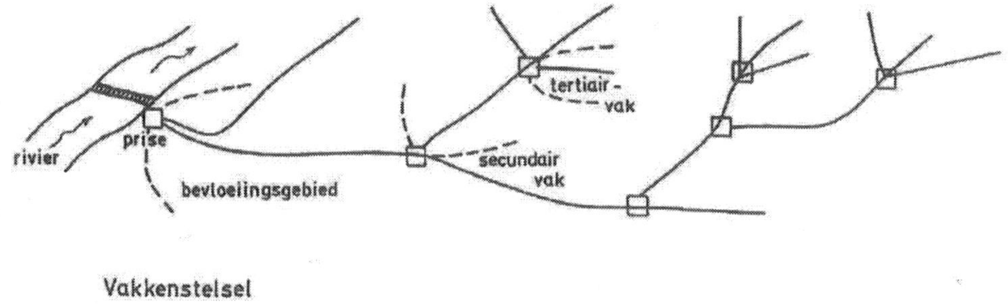

Figure 6.4: System of absolute water distribution (from: Ter Hofstede and van Santbrink 1979)

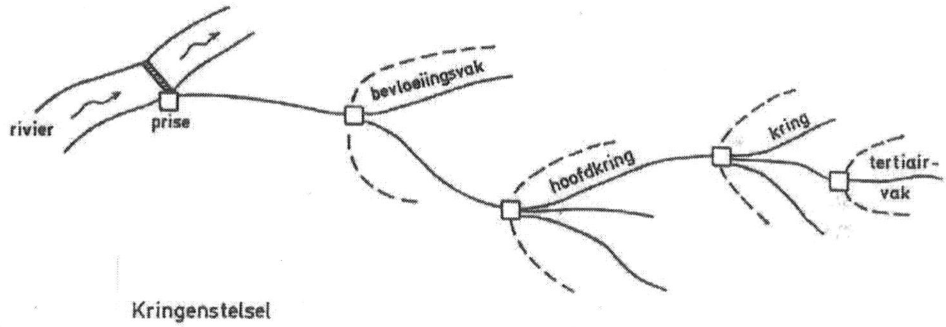

Figure 6.5: System of proportional water distribution (from: Ter Hofstede and van Santbrink 1979). Explanation of 6.4 and 6.5: *vakkenstelsel*=system of sections (absolute water distribution), *kringenstelsel*=system of circuits (proportional water distribution).

Most of the engineers were supporters of the Pekalen Management Regulation. Most of the support for the Pateguan regulation system, which was indeed liberal, came from the Civil Service. Despite the disappointing Pateguan outcomes the Indies government decided in 1899

[18] Javanese water distribution had (probably) been traditionally proportional. The circuits resembled, as emerges from the quotation, Dutch water boards. Another source of inspiration was the Balinese *subaks* which were also types of water boards (see Liefrinck 1887). The Balinese *subak* will be discussed in **Chapter 10**.

that this was in fact the most appropriate way of dispersing water. Yet it was the Pekalen regulation system as described in the law of 1901 that was to form the basis for later water regulation systems elsewhere.[19]

What was important when it came to managing irrigation areas was the aspect of the distributing of water between local agricultural activities and centralised sugar cane cultivation. Sugar cane was an east monsoon crop. It was planted in mid May at the earliest, though in connection with the preparing of the fields the ground had to be ready much earlier. Water was of crucial importance to sugar cane. Because of the Cultivation System a situation had arisen in which the sugar planters were lord and master over the available water. Fields that contained sugar cane were given priority over rice fields. That was something that was, for instance, evidenced in the day and night ruling which dictated that *sawas* would be watered at night and cane plots in the day time. With the later circumstances that situation which undoubtedly went back to the time of the Cultivation System was not ideal. Van den Broek d'Obrenan (1918: 35-36) formulated the situation as follows:

"However the sugar refiner soon realised that if matters were to be well organised it would be better to insure his company. In spite of bribery and arbitrary measures he often saw that at the critical moment the supply of water to his crops would dry up which meant that, day and night, he needed to be on the alert. This meant that he could rapidly be persuaded to make money available to place officials, civil servants and Public Works employees in the position of being able to appoint personnel in order to organise water distribution".

The various water agreements corresponded as far as supplying water for the purpose of sugar culture was concerned where it was distributed on demand. The sugar refiner would submit a request to the manager of the relevant irrigation works and this request would then be integrated into the work plan drawn up by the technicians for water distribution. While the population was expected to finance the irrigation water through the land rents something different had been thought up for the sugar refiners. In order to meet the costs they were expected to reimburse the personnel encumbered with the task of distributing the water. By way of preparation for this move the government decided to set up a Permanent Irrigation Commission in 1906. (Van den Broek d'Obrenan 1918: 34, 36)[20].

The expectations surrounding the new approach to the construction and control of irrigation works were high (see, for instance, Ilcken 1891). What exactly the results of this were will be discussed in the following section.

[19] See also Lamminga (1905: 761-766) in conjunction with the Pekalen regulation system and for the Pateguan method, Weijs (1900). It was De Meyier (1902: 186) who gave Weijs support from the technological angle. Liefrinck (1896) was a supporter of the Balinese-style water boards and thus of circuit water distribution. See for a discussion on both types of systems Ertsen (1993) and also Ter Hofstede and Van Santbrink (1979). The unattractiveness of the Pateguan method resided, according to Saltet (1912: 70), in the fact that it required a circuit administration, a circuit head and circuit meetings, indeed "that ballast had made the water regulation so complicated that people had become apprehensive about introducing it". See also Cramer (1920).

[20] Homan van der Heide (1899) and Sibinga Mulder (1912) emphasised the importance of sugar cultivation in the whole water management scenario. Technical control was expensive for the sugar refiners but "their previous system of controlling, fighting and bribing was even more expensive" (Van den Broek d'Obrenan 1901: 415). Later the sugar refiners were also required to contribute to the water network construction costs (Happé [1939: II. 25] reports on this after 1919, see **Appendix C**).

Irrigation and the state

Projects

The Pemali Works constituted an instance of a complete irrigation project. In the history of the works the old partial approach to matters is clearly recognisable: the preparations related only to the headworks and in the first place to the weir. It was only later that Lamminga drew up a general plan for the remainder of the works. In that later plan, main and other canals, the section divisions and also the various structural works were attuned to each other and drawn together to form one integrated whole. When it came to nominating the various components a new system was adhered to. Lamminga's plan was based on extensive preliminary research, notably into water supplies and requirements. While the plan was being executed data continued to be collected. For example it was necessary to determine the maximum debit of the channels. In this connection, it was important to know what was the average water requirement. The study gave cause for a graph to be drawn up reflecting the required water volumes in relation to the size of the areas to be irrigated (a capacity line).

Before satisfactorily rounding off the Pemali Works, Lamminga had already adapted his work method to the Pekalen Works (Lamminga 1894/95). He followed the example of the pioneer Van Houten. Weijs (1921: 374) wrote in this respect:

"Through his skilled and accurate way of preparing and designing irrigation plans the engineer G. van Houten had made a name for himself as a great Indies Public Works engineer. His works in the Demak were widely seen as a fine example of engineering. It was an example that was to serve as a norm on a great scale, as mentioned above, for irrigation and drainage works elsewhere. Indeed, with his Pekalen Works Lamminga was one of the first to confirm the truth of this".

With the Pemali Works Lamminga made use of the experience gained in the Pekalen area. There he had also constructed an aqueduct. The shrink and stretch installation used there for connecting together the troughs and the plaster work had worked well and therefore also served as an example when creating the Poncol aqueduct. Much the same went for the deluge dams and the distribution sluices. Lamminga improved the main deluge dams by making the openings trapezium-shaped. It was a constructional shape that was later implemented with the distribution sluices which in connection with the even distribution of water also underwent improvements in other ways. The Pemali Works contributed clearly to the process of collecting knowledge, for instance in the field of drainage canal provision. In comparison with other weirs, such as those in the Sampean and the Tuntang, the Pekalen weir constituted an important step forwards. By having chosen a good spot to erect it but also by making the weir wider than the river, Van Kol and Lamminga made sure that in this way damage could be prevented. The weir's great width did, however, encourage silt-bank formation which meant that later, just as with the weir of Lamminga himself in the Comal, this solution was abandoned. Silt formation could not however be avoided altogether and so attempts were made to disperse such build-ups by flushing water. The experience gained with the Pemali weir where it had turned out to be necessary to expand the capacity of the drainage sluice was extremely useful. All that knowledge could be applied in the building of new weirs such as the one in the Comal. (Lamminga 1911).

The work method adopted with the Pemali Works found its basis and repercussions in the 1885 ruling that introduced the Irrigation Brigade which, in 1889, was incorporated into one of the Civil Public Works Department's Technical Divisions. The objective of the brigade was to collect all the information required for the new works. A second task was the development of irrigation projects. In the case of the Pemail Works research and design were not in the hands of the brigade. There it was local engineers who did the work which was originally only directed towards headworks. The project commenced with just the weir. Important preliminary work was done by Van Kol in the service of the Second Public Works Division. The actual job operations side was in the hands of the General Service. For large projects, like the Pemali Works, separate Services were set up.

The Pemali Works constituted one of the nineteen projects of the General Irrigation Plan drawn up by Van Bosse in 1890. The plan also embraced other projects in the Pemali-Comal area: the Kabuyutan Works completed in 1902 and the Comal-Cacaban Works completed in 1906 (see **Table 6.1**). The Jengkellok Works added to the plan later on reached completion in 1910. The Genteng-Sragi Works, also constituting part of the plan, were not completed until 1919. In the meantime other projects had been started up in the Pemali-Comal area. All in all, the activities continued until far into the twenties.

In other areas the engineers also had good results. By 1900 the following General Irrigation Plan projects had been completed: the Demak Works, the Kening Works, the Pateguan Works, the Pekalen Works and the Manggis Works. Altogether they provided irrigation water for 67,447 *bouws* of land. They were important pioneering projects. With the Demak Works Van Houten had introduced the new systematic approach. The Pekalen Works was Lamminga's achievement and the Pateguan Works Weijs's achievement. The Kening Works (for the irrigation of 3440 *bouws*) constituted the first project to be realised entirely according to the principles of the Irrigation Brigade (see Van Bosse 1893: 69). The engineers involved were De Val and Pierson. Later on the latter was to apply the experience gained with the Kening Works to the Solo Valley project which was a far bigger project (the Kening was a tributary of the Solo). In 1903 when the Pemali Works finally reached completion three other projects were also completed. By 1910 the number of projects executed had risen to twelve. The collective area irrigated by these modern works projects was 218,156 *bouws*. One of the projects realised in that period was the Sampean irrigation project (see **Box 6.2**).

Box 6.2 The details of the Sampean delta irrigation system

Towards the end of the eighties the engineer M. Ypelaar started making assessments and plans for the channel network in the Sampean Delta. By 1891 plans were far enough for the work to begin. The work commenced in the Panarukan area with the construction of the south main canal which was later to change its name to the Panarukan main canal (the original Panarukan canal became the north main canal). The canal was situated at the foot of the hills. That meant that many of the drainage canals had to be laid under the existing channels so that culverts were required. They were designed to be too small which meant that most of them later had to be enlarged. With the new canal 1400 *bouws* of irrigated area was gained. The canal and the necessary secondary and tertiary channels were completed in 1896.

By then work had also begun on the northern section of the irrigation area. In 1896 the improving of the existing main canals reached completion. Those were the Kapongan main canal and the Situbondo main canal including the eastern and western branches. By 1900 the remainder of the work had been completed, that was: the secondary and the tertiary channels and the drainage canals.

In 1901 the activities linked to the improving of the drainage channels in the first area commenced and that was completed in 1906. By then an area of 15,387 *bouws* had been provided with modern irrigation systems. The costs (excluding the drainage sluice in the weir): *f* 906,347. After the completion of the works the Sampean-Pekalen Irrigation Division was created in 1907 so that the area received technical management. (Rietveld 1932, see also **Chapter 3**).

Control

Once the Pemali Works were completed the control of the works had to be organised and that was something to which Lamminga paid great attention. Indeed, he had already done much the same with the Pekalen Works. Weijs (1921: 374) commented of the Pekalen Works that they:

"were the first in the long line of so-called 'regulated irrigation works', which would soon provide the Indies Public Works engineers more generally with such an important, their full skills requiring task, which involved the issue of taking care of the execution of fair water dispersal between the sugar culture and the cultures of the inland population. Lamminga met the requirements of this issue by giving full attention both to the creating of the works and to the preparing in a purposeful way and the exploitation of the works".

Just as in the Pekalen area, Lamminga already began considering the matter of control when designing the Pemali Works.

The Pekalen regulations which had also been drawn up by Lamminga differed from the Pateguan regulations which Weijs had been involved in. With the former Management Regulation it was the water requirements of the crop that was central whereas with the latter Regulation it was the size of the irrigation area that was decisive. The water distribution system was respectively absolute and proportional. The Pekalen regulations gave cause to sub-divide the irrigation area into sections while with the Pateguan regulations the dividing was into circuits. What differed greatly with both systems was the level of involvement of the local population. With the Pekalen system it was the irrigation personnel who organised everything to the last detail while with the Pateguan system water distribution in the irrigation *sawa* area was left to the population to arrange. It was with the Pekalen system that the aspect of technical control was most advanced. Admittedly the Indies government found the Pateguan method the best but in practice it was the other system that was copied[21].

When developing control in the Pemali area the Pekalen Management Regulation was taken as the basic starting point. It was not surprising to see that it was only under Lamminga that the exploitation was finally realised. However the Pateguan Management Regulation had its merits the strong point of that being the *Ulu-Ulu*. In the discussion surrounding the Pateguan regulations it emerged that his position remained difficult. He was subordinate to the Village Chief and also to the *Mandur* within the Irrigation Division which made his manoeuvring space minimal. (*Mindere Welvaartscommissie* 1910: 108-114, compare Ertsen 1993). The *Ulu-Ulu* was introduced to the water regulating process in the Pemali area but his position changed. There he was detached from the village administration. The Pemali Management Regulation, established in 1910, thus constituted a sort of compromise with what had previously been rival regulations. The Regulation which was also known as the Tegal Golongan Regulation was to become a model for later regulations.[22] That did not alter the fact that over the course of time the Pemali

[21] The fact that the discussion surrounding both systems was to continue for a long time is evident amongst other things from some four letters written about the Pateguan regulations in the 1908-1909 period which are included in the irrigation overview compiled in connection with the welfare study (*Mindere Welvaartscommissie* 1910: 108-114). One of those letters was from Weijs. What these letters show is that on the one hand the Civil Public Works Department and the Civil Service were diametrically opposed to each other while on the other hand the inefficient co-operation of irrigation personnel had come to form a main stumbling block when it came to innovating the Pateguan regulations. (Cf. Ertsen 1993). The Pateguan ruling was later defended by Ter Meulen (1918).

[22] See for water regulations, besides *Mindere Welvaartscommissie* (1910) also the *Verslag BOW* (1911, B. Appendix II). In fact it was not until 1936 that the water regulation was given a legal foundation in the General Water Regulation (see **Chapter 10**).

Management Regulation did change. The *Ulu-Ulu Golongan* found himself in a more dependent position with regard to the irrigation service when, as of 1917, his payment issued from this service. The number of *golongans* was extended in 1924 to six[23].

What was important was the way in which water was divided between the agricultural activities of the local population and the sugar cane growing industry. The different water regulations did not deviate on this point and it was certainly not easy to give equal weight to both interests. Weijs (1921: 374) had the following to say about Lamminga's efforts in this field:

"The fact that there he was able to turn what had originally been an attitude of hostility to the sugar refineries into an attitude of utter trust in the uprightness of his intentions and insights – that was coupled with great respect for him as a person – certainly indicates that even then he was on the right road in his judgements concerning this far from simple question. He was also able to exercise great tact when dealing with such matters".

The water regulations were able to soften the hard edges of the day and night ruling which saw to it that water went to the sugar industry in the daytime and to the local population's rice fields at night. Under the new regulations it was possible for the water to become available to the population in the afternoon. However, that was not sufficient and the day and night regulatory measures remained a thorn in the side for the population. The alternative was to create small reservoirs (*waduks*) near to the fields so that water for the local population could be collected at night and distributed in the daytime. These so-called night *waduks* were not yet present on a significant scale (see **Chapter 8**).

In 1908 the Pemali-Comal Irrigation Division finally came into being. Other irrigation Divisions were: Brantas 1901 (introduced as an experiment in 1892), Serang 1908 (tested out in 1892), Madiun 1909 and Cimanuk 1910. The government would later extend this number to fourteen and Madiun would be extended with the catchment area of the Solo (because of the events in the Solo area described in **Chapter 7** this final plan was not carried out). All the Irrigation Divisions were established in areas where there was an important sugar industry (Van Sandick 1912: 920). These Irrigation Divisions all covered considerable areas. The Irrigation Division Brantas was a good example of this (see **Box 6.3**). The creation of the Pemali-Comal Irrigation Division came about after the Pemali Works had been completed, just as was the case with some other works in the region. These works entered into use and, just as with the maintenance of the works, a new organisation structure was required. Elsewhere it was also the case that once works had been completed an Irrigation Division would be set up like in the Pekalen-Sampean area where the government created an Irrigation Division in 1907. This sequence was not absolute. Sometimes the creation of an Irrigation Division would precede the construction of new works (see **Chapter 8**).

---

[23] See Van Maanen (1924: 24) for a calculation of the number of *golongans*.

Box 6.3 The Brantas Irrigation Division

The Brantas Irrigation Division was half the size of the Netherlands. After the completion of his Pateguan Works in 1893, the engineer Weijs was made Head of this Division and he remained in that position until 1899. It was an area with a population of four million, a sixth of the total Javanese population. That made the population density there twice as high as in the Dutch motherland. The agricultural acreage was some 500,000 *bouws*, 325,000 of which was irrigated (globally this was respectively an eighth of the total agricultural area and a fifth of the total irrigated area: figures from 1900; see **Appendix K**).
There were 600 plantations, 90 sugar refineries and some twenty indigo factories: half the size of European agricultural enterprises. There were eight engineers, 22 foremen and 1100 lower-level personnel members (including those responsible for water distribution, assessors, drawers, writers, *Mandurs* and guards). There was a 1200 kilometre-long telephone network with 165 telephones. (Weijs 1900, compare Van Sandick 1912: 922).

Rentability

The Pemali plains project could be termed a technical success but generally the objectives set in conjunction with the General Irrigation plan were too ambitious. All in all, the nineteen projects, which together covered some 577 thousand *bouws* of land, were to take ten years. By 1900 only five projects had been realised (67,447 *bouws*). Apart from the Demak Works they constituted smaller projects. Two of the works in the plan were abandoned and one project was stopped. By 1910 four of the projects in the plan had still not been completed (120,072 *bouws*). Of the seven works added to the list over the course of time, only three had been completed by 1910 (18,953 *bouws*). (See **Table 6.1**).

The reason why the results were overall so disappointing needed to be sought in the financial area. With the Pemali project the costs had roughly worked out as budgeted at 2.3 and 2.25 million guilders respectively. This successful state of affairs was certainly not representative for the general situation. Despite the poor results of 1900, a large amount of the sum of 35½ million guilders budgeted for the irrigation plan, approximately 26½ million guilders, was expended in that year. Ten years later, of the 22 projects in hand, fourteen had been completed while eight were still on-going and some 50 million guilders had been expended (Lamminga 1910: 12, Weijs 1913: 18).

The General Irrigation Plan therefore drew considerably on the available financial means. The Indies government was not inclined to instantly pour out funds in the way that the engineers expected it to. When the government considered the possibility of financing projects with borrowed money that was in itself a positive development since it would provide more scope for activities. The problem really was that projects would have to reflect a positive cost-benefit relationship in advance as established by the Rentability Commission. The Pemali Works scored high in that respect but with other projects the rentability aspect was much harder to prove. The recommendations made by the committee in the time that Lamminga was in it did to a large extent undoubtedly emanate from him (Weijs 1921: 375). His active participation was, however, unable to stop the considerations relating to the financial works often being negative. Paradoxically, in view of the original intentions, the rentability demand turned out to be an important reason for the minimal results when it came to the implementation of the General Irrigation Plan. In his discussion of the outcomes Van Bosse (1901: 361) cited the rentability question as "the main cause of the disappointing state of affairs". He furthermore remarked that:

"Those who first linked the word rentability to irrigation works have given me many sleepless nights. Apart from the land rents there are various other factors that are related to rentability and it was certainly no easy matter to decide upon. In a sarcastic mood I did once inquire after a similar calculation of the rentability of the sluice at IJmuiden and of the Merwede canal just to give me a guideline when it came to what people were trying to construe in connection with irrigation works" (ibid).

Under the Ethical Policy the execution of non-profitable works was also considered but it was still the rentability requirement that was to determine how modern irrigation was to develop. In the period leading up to 1910 this in fact continued in much the same way as had been the practice before 1900. During the first decade of the new colonial policy period there was no discernible boom in the creation of irrigation works. The four unprofitable projects stemming from the General Irrigation Plan that were included in the General Work Plan of 1907 were the same ones as those listed above as not having been completed by 1910; in 1911, when the new work plan expired, they still had not been completed. It was not until some ten years later that the work was rounded off. Of the seven projects added to the General Irrigation Plan at a later date, three found their way into the work plan. Things went better with these projects though and two of them were completed by 1911. (See **Table 6.1**). In the end, the engineers turned their problems to good advantage by making rentability an integrated part of their approach. De Vos (1926: 185) wrote the following on this matter:

"In general, one may ... assert that technology only becomes scientific when economy is displayed. ... No saying is therefore less true than the one which claims that it is economy that threatens wisdom. This may be incidentally true but what is generally true is that it is economy that leads to wisdom and which only sometimes, with respect to its own still growing and imperfect creation, may be blamed for carelessness".[24]

The success of the engineers

Daum's fictional character, Van Brakel, who worked for the Indies Public Works Organisation, was occupied with such jobs as "the hardening of roads, the painting of government buildings and the whitening and tarring of post depots" (Daum 1896: 10). When Lamminga arrived at Public Works in 1881 things were not very different. There was always a lot of routine maintenance work to be done. Weijs (1921: 373) reported that this was often jestingly called "whitening and tarring". Paperwork required much attention and little research was done. The situation that Lamminga found at Public Works was not unlike that sketched by Post (1879). What was of great importance in all of this was the subordinate position of the Civil Public Works Department in comparison to the position of superiority of the Civil Service. The ruling of 1885 put an end to that situation. The Civil Service continued to exercise a degree of influence in the small Regional Services, but generally engineers were the ones in control. The ruling made it possible for them to pursue their technical-scientific approach. What particularly characterised this kind of irrigation work was the fact that the designing and constructing of complete irrigation systems was preceded by thorough field research. The executing of works according to a general plan that was applicable in the whole of Java was something that was later developed. Engineers were able to start working with the result that this automatically led to the extension of modern irrigation facilities.

---

[24] In the discussion on rentability engineers looked across their own borders, see e.g. Van Sandick (1905) who discussed this issue in conjunction with irrigation works in the west of America.

The execution of (the projects of) the General Irrigation Plan did not go as desired. The costs of the works turned out to be higher than estimated and the actual work took longer than planned. Because costs kept on rising this led to the preliminary financial-economic examining of projects. If projects proved to be unprofitable they would not be approved. This did not make the irrigation plan easier to execute and it led to delays. Later, with the rise of the Ethical Policy, money was made available for non-profitable projects. Indeed, rentability became a permanent aspect of the technical-scientific approach and so the foundations for modern irrigation science were laid.

Apart from implementing a modern work approach when it came to the construction of irrigation works, there was also the aspect that engineers began to become involved in the social organisation of irrigation systems which constituted an important new step in the intervention of colonial administration in irrigation affairs. For a long time the Indies government had been convinced that water management was something that was too important to just be left to the local population to organise, especially when it came to the distribution between rice and sugar crops which was why government officials had been put in charge of this. After 1885 such management constituted the final stronghold of the Civil Service. In this area the engineers managed to win just as much important terrain. The introduction of technical control together with Irrigation Divisions and water regulations was what put an end to the dominant influence of the administration. The engineers completely changed water management: it was given a much more systematic character and the population was given a lot more involvement. The best way of distributing water then became the topic of a discussion that had many marks of a background dispute between the Civil Public Works Department and the Civil Service. Weijs's liberal Pateguan Management Regulation which proposed that water should be proportionally allocated, was the one that proved best in an experiment that was done. Lamminga's centralistic Pekalen Management Regulation that claimed that water distribution should be absolute was the one to be most broadly adopted to the disadvantage of the Civil Service which had a preference for the Pateguan regulation method. Ultimately the Pemali Management Regulation, which was the one to be finally seen as exemplary, represented a combination of both methods. The *Ulu-Ulu Golongan* selected from the *sawa* owners had to ensure the co-operation of the population. Furthermore, in defence of the Civil Service, it should be noted that the relevant civil servants had co-operated in the creation of both regulations and that the Civil Service continued to remain involved in the management of irrigation works. In following chapters we shall see that this involvement tended to become greater rather than less and that irrigation control moreover remained a topic of discussion until the end of the colonial period[25].

The circumstances surrounding policy, state and Public Works were therefore favourable for the construction of irrigation works as of 1885. How did Lamminga fit into the picture? His work was trend-setting. With the Pemali Works – and the other works in the Pemali-Comal region in which he was involved – Lamminga put into practice a new approach in a way that was to prove exemplary for later engineers. It was really with the smaller Pekalen Works that he found things out, both with respect to the infrastructure of the works and as regards water distribution and maintenance. With the Pemali Works Lamminga linked knowledge gained from experience to scientific insight so that his innovations also constituted an impetus in the field of irrigation engineering. Apart from designing and thinking out entire irrigation systems he managed to achieve advancements in knowledge on the building of weirs. Through his activities

[25] Apart from the emancipatory aspect concerning the battle for water and apart from the notions about what might be best, the discussion also revolved around money: involving the population on a large scale was cheap but keeping the matter entirely in one's own hands was the expensive option.

in the Rentability Commission and as a practising engineer he was able to further contribute to making rentability a part of the scientific approach[26].

On the stage of modern irrigation activities Lamminga was certainly no deus ex machina. He built on the work of others, of pioneers in the Sampean Delta and elsewhere (also in the Pemali area!) who commenced with the construction of headworks. Even the notion that the construction of entire irrigation systems should be based on sound research was not purely Lamminga's idea, it was rather an idea taken from a predecessor of his, the engineer Van Houten. While in a technical respect the works of Lamminga were perhaps not particularly innovative his involvement with water management was. He was one of the first engineers to devote attention to the exploitation of irrigation works and to think out good regulations. In view of the co-operation with the Civil Service the "great engineer" was not alone in this respect either. In the field of irrigation control it is Weijs who is seen as the second founder of modern irrigation technology (or of "the modern irrigation system") in the Indies (Ott de Vries 1936: A 269). He became well known in conjunction with the Pateguan Management Regulation but really made his name as the Head of the Brantas Irrigation Division. At that time, after having been extremely involved in construction, the Civil Service gradually lost what had amounted to its dominating influence in the area of management though its assistance was still sought in the drawing up and introducing of new water regulations. It was a situation that made contact with the Civil Service difficult. Alluding to the tact and policy employed by Weijs in this connection and to his "special powers of persuasion" Ott de Vries (1936: A. 267-270) described Weijs as a "diplomat" when comparing him to Lamminga whom he termed an "old war-horse". He elucidated this (p. 270-271) as follows:

"As far as the management of irrigation works goes one should not forget that this, just like the construction of most of the relevant works was first in the hands of the almighty Civil Service. With the increasing levels of specialisation and differentiation within the Indies administrative system the Civil Service administrators are perpetually being compelled to settle for less than they had bargained for but half a century ago irrigation control was still the feather in the cap for many an employee within the Civil Service.
For tactful men such as Weijs it was possible to also remove that feather from the tail perfectly imperceptibly and painlessly".

Lamminga and Weijs made their knowledge and experience available to others both within and outside the Public Works Organisation. Lamminga held high positions both within the Third and the Fourth Public Works Divisions (of Surabaya and Semarang). Weijs was made Head of the Irrigation (E) Division within Civil Public Works (1905-1908). Both were made Extraordinary Professors in Indies Hydraulic Engineering (especially irrigation) at the Technical College in Delft: Lamminga in 1910 and Weijs in 1913. In his inaugural speech Lamminga emphasised the significance of the field. He (1910: 4) maintained that the "study of the art of irrigation" was not just the domain of future Indies engineers but of every civil engineering student who "should know just as much about this field of hydraulic engineering as about land drainage, polders etc." For Lamminga working in the interests of irrigation was nothing less than a mission if one reads his following remark:

"Can there be any greater satisfaction for the engineer than to recreate dry, thinly populated, poor regions with very limited means for the cultivation of crops in richly endowed areas where everything then grows in abundance thanks to the life-giving force of water which, due to the

[26] Once operational, the Pemali Works demonstrated the precise problematic nature of rentability. This possibly contributed to making policy less stringent in this respect.

engineer's skill, energy and devotion is drawn from the rivers which previously simply flowed into the sea, their resources untapped? Is it not a beautiful conquest to be able to tame all kinds of feared torrents of water, to protect land from the floods which ruin the crops in the fields and cause widespread damage? He who has had the good fortune of being able to create such irrigation and flood control works will have received satisfaction from his work which, after all, remains more important than the material side of things" (Lamminga in the *Weekblad van Nederlandsch Indië* ["Dutch Indies Weekly Journal"], 19 April 1914, cited by Weijs, 1921: 377).

These fine words were not, however, to change the fact that a few years later Lamminga was to renounce his position at the Technical College because of the "less than miserly ... salary" (Weijs 1921: 377)[27].

The Pemali Management Regulation has remained in force right up until the present. In post-colonial rehabilitation projects this type of water control system with an independent *Ulu-Ulu Golongan* was reverted to (Ankum 1989: 350, 356, see the **Epilogue**). Certain knowledge and insight gained through the Pemali Works has also remained visible to the present day. That applies in the first place to the Pemali Consumption Line drawn up for rice water requirements. In conjunction with this and other use lines Brouwer (1991: 12) writes the following:

"These consumption or water use lines based on experience gained from practice have had a great deal of influence upon the way in which people think about water consumption but are becoming more and more replaced by a combination of water requirement estimates calculated on the basis of evapo transpiration and practical experience.
When it comes to calculating the water requirements for rice fields in Indonesia much use is made of the model created by Van Goor and Zijlstra. It is a calculation model that combines the evapo transpiration estimates relating to the crop in the growth season and to water requirement figures obtained during land preparation periods".[28]

The Pemali water requirement line subject constitutes compulsory lecture material for irrigation engineers in training at the Delft University of Technology. Much the same goes for the Tegalan Capacity Line in relation to the designing of supply canals (represented in **Figure 5.8**, see Brouwer 1991: 18-19).

The limits of emancipation

Liberated and contented the Public Works engineers embarked on a massive irrigation programme in the post-1885 era. When the costs (to be incurred) threatened to rise very high the Indies government set up the Rentability Commission. In that way the government was able to at least throw a spanner in the works and slow down the progress of the work being carried out. The rentability issue also had consequences for the position of the engineers. Through a

---

[27] Lamminga did, however, demonstrate his continued enthusiasm for his field by creating the Lamminga Fund willed in his last will and testament in which a significant portion of his capital was made available for Indies hydraulic engineering activities (Haringhuizen 1920). The fact that Lamminga is known as a founder or, more generally, that his name is still known today, may even be due in part to this very same fund! (R. Brouwer, personal communication, October 1994). Lamminga and Weijs were two skilled engineers but there were, of course, many others. One such person was the earlier-mentioned Grinwis Plaat who was also made Professor of irrigation engineering at the Technical College in Delft. He became particularly well-known through his study trips made to Northern Italy and Spain (1895).

[28] In the three month period when the rice grain actually ripens Brouwer (1991: 14) reported that the water requirement was 0.7 litres per second rather than the 0.8 litres quoted in the Pemali ruling (Voorduin 1914: 111).

Departmental representative in the Rentability Commission the government gave the Civil Service again a prominent role in the decision-making process on irrigation works. But it was not to stop at that. Rentability paved the way for small holding agriculture which meant that irrigation works had to be measurably useful. After 1900, in the era of the Ethical Policy, a department set up for small farmers became involved in modern irrigation activities. In other words, rentability put an end to the autonomy of the engineers. This matter will be discussed in more detail in **Chapter 8** but first we shall examine the high-profile Solo Valley Works project.

With this the largest project of the entire 1890 General Irrigation Plan costs simply soared with the result that in 1903, the year in which the Pemali Works reached completion, the Dutch government decided to halt the entire project. The Pemali Works were to serve as a model for later similar irrigation projects but the Solo Valley Works were equally central to the further development of modern irrigation in Java. The disappointing experiences with the Solo Valley project certainly affected the discussions on rentability and the importance of irrigation works to small agricultural activities. The experiences also went a long way towards contributing to the fact that the Public Works Organisation lost its mandate and to influencing irrigation activities such as those taking shape in the early days of the Ethical Policy in both the financial and technical sense. In **Chapter 8** we shall see how the Solo Works did not only give rise to a turnabout in the intervention with irrigation. Round about 1900 things were going badly with the Javanese population; there was evidence of "diminished prosperity" as poverty was euphemistically labelled in colonial terminology, even in the areas where engineers had provided irrigation works! This general problem was to have an equally great impact on the further developments surrounding modern irrigation.

In 1903 the Solo Valley failure really overshadowed the success in the Pemali plains. The Solo Valley Works put a damper on the development of modern irrigation systems in Java. Paradoxically, however, it would appear that up to a point it was that disaster that partly established Lamminga's reputation as the founder of modern irrigation systems. There was no doubt that Lamminga was a competent engineer but his name as a founding-father was to come later. It was in 1930 that he was first viewed as such when a monument was unveiled in his honour. The fact that it was not until 27 years after the completion of his main project that this recognition came might perhaps be put down to the fact that it was not until later that the success of that work and of other projects of Lamminga's was appreciated once people realised how badly things could also go wrong. When Weijs (1913: 21) remarked that the Pemali Works had become "the best considered, the most seriously executed and in all respects the most successful exponent of technical irrigation intervention in the Indies" he also added that Lamminga had in that way been of service "in rebuilding confidence in that intervention". He was referring to the Solo Valley Works. The following chapters will examine the ups and downs of the Solo project and the effects that the project was to have on irrigation policy and on the position of the Civil Public Works Department.

7

'Faith arrives on foot but leaves on horseback'

The Solo Valley Works

> Greater than the mystery of natural growth is the mystery of the natural cessation of growth. There is measure in all natural things – in their size, speed, or violence. As a result, the system of nature, of which man is a part, tends to be self-balancing, self-adjusting, self-cleansing. Not so with technology, or perhaps should I say: not so with man dominated by technology and specialisation. Technology recognises no self-limiting principle - in terms, for instance, of size, speed, or violence. It therefore does not possess the virtues of being self-balancing, self-adjusting, and self-cleansing (Schumacher 1978: 122).
>
> I have no doubt that it is possible to give a new direction to technological development, a direction that shall lead it back to the real needs of man, and that also means: *to the actual size of man*. Man is small, and, therefore, small is beautiful. To go for giantism is to go for self-destruction (Schumacher 1978: 133).

In a letter of 29th October 1887 addressed to Janssen van Raay, Director of the Civil Public Works Department, C.H.A. van der Wijck, the Resident of Surabaya, wrote that conditions in the Bengawan Jero District were so miserable that for part of the year people were forced to live on bamboo rafts. These rafts were indoors attached to the posts of the houses. They contained what was known as a *balé-balé*, a resting couch made of bamboo. Sometimes, in order to escape the rising water, these couches were simply raised. The Resident wrote:

"It is not uncommon for families to spend several months living on such balé-balés, day and night, and in great discomfort. That is where people eat and sleep, where the woman cooks and works, where children play and where people are born and die while many dessas provide no dry areas for burying corpses so that these have to be transported elsewhere" (letter of 29th October 1887, no. 11366/A from Van der Wijck, Resident of Surabaya, cited by Telders et al. 1900: 32).

This message was one of the factors that was to give rise, in 1893, to the biggest irrigation (and drainage) project in the history of the presence of the Dutch in the Indies.

Five years later the Minister of the Colonies, J.T. Cremer, temporarily halted the entire project. Amongst other things his telegraph message (of 7th November 1898) addressed to the Governor-General of Batavia stated the following:

"Further research and clear work plan with reliable estimates relating to Solo Valley Works required before further credit can be provided. Inevitable consequence: suspension of activities" (National Archive, Ministry of the Colonies, Resolutions 1898, 4).

Figure 7.1: The Solo river, 1872 (photo UBL KITLV 47 D 9)

This marked the beginning of the end for the project: in 1903 the Minister of the Colonies, A.W.F. Idenburg, decided to stop it altogether. In this way the affair took a surprising turn. It seemed that expenses were going to be significantly higher than had originally been budgeted and so Cremer intervened. He then set up a solid commission composed of experts who, in a hefty and thorough report, recommended that the works be continued (Telders et al. 1900[1]). In deviating from this plan, Idenburg not only contested the opinion of the Solo Commission but also the wide support that it received from engineers. He moreover opposed the views of trend-setting Ethical Policy upholders, such as Van Deventer. In meeting the needs of the Bengawan Jero region the project did, in fact, fit in very nicely with this particular policy that had been introduced in 1901.

[1] The report by Telders, Leemans, Kraus and De Meyier was so comprehensive and detailed that it serves as an exemplary example of colonial irrigation science (see e.g. Ankum 1984: 10). See for fisheries and irrigation in the wet area Gruyter (1934).

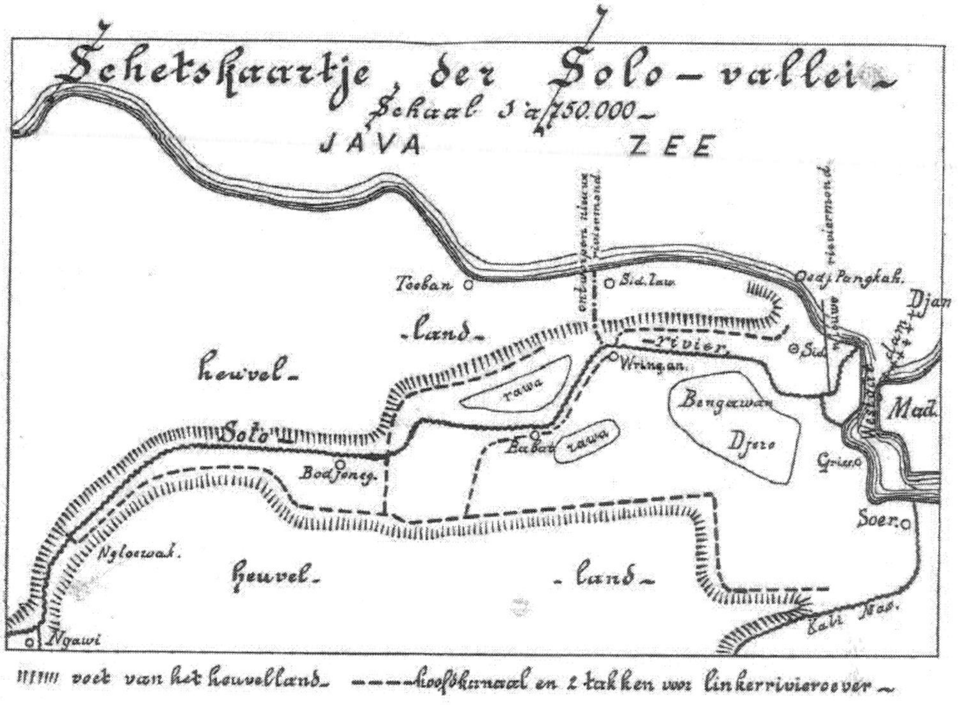

Figure 7.2: Map of the Solo Valley (Quant 1899)

The deferment and the abandonment of the Solo Works indeed created considerable consternation in engineering circles. It was variously referred to as a drama, a debacle and a disaster (see, for instance, Weijs 1913: 18-19). The engineers were not, however, prepared to be beaten. On a number of occasions they tried to revive the project. The plan was to preoccupy people until the end of the colonial period but the project would never again be resumed (see the **Prologue**, **Figure 5**)[2]. In retrospect the Solo Valley project was to gain "legendary" status among its proponents (see De Meyier 1910) but generally it came to be remembered as a "black page" in the history of modern irrigation engineering in Indonesia (Vlugter 1949: I. 101). This chapter sets out to highlight that black page. Particular attention is paid to the decision that was taken to halt the project. I shall try to find an explanation for this and it will be a quest that will be continued in the next chapter. While much has been written about the project as a whole, what is lacking is a summary of the works' progress and a clear account explaining why the project was stopped. The existing literature on the subject amounts to a collection of tracts contributing to the

[2] Even after independence, the discussions on the Solo Valley project have continued. The report by the 1900 Solo Commission is now still on the table, literally: when I visited the *DHV* (now: Royal HaskoningDHV) engineering bureau in Jakarta in 1993, it was working on it. The Indonesian government had consulted *DHV* on the report. After returning home I gave the firm at their request information about the project. In the 1980s, the project was taken out of the closet, especially the part of the dig through to Sidayu Lawas. When I later came into the Solo Valley, I heard that, outside Public works or other public bodies concerned, the project was brought up in different ways. So had an occupant in a letter to the local government advocated the once discontinued Dutch work to start again. After independence, several other plans were developed for the Solo Valley. Pending a comprehensive plan, one is currently working on separate measures, while the canal to the Java Sea has been completed. See for postcolonial work and plans for the Solo Valley the **Epilogue**.

arguments put by the project's supporters and opponents, tracts which thus serve as sources for the debate given below[3].

Apart from constituting an intriguing story we shall see that tracing the history of the Solo Works gives us interesting insight into the way in which engineers operated, notably with regard to their political dealing strategies. It would seem that what was just as important as being in possession of technical qualities was the ability to bluff, be persuasive and to establish good contacts!

The big plan

The auspicious Lord of the Waters

"Bengawan" is the Javanese nickname for the Solo river which, when translated, means: "big river" or, more lyrically, "the auspicious Lord of the Waters" (see **Figure 7.1**). Some 540 kilometres long, the Bengawan Solo is the longest river in Java.[4] The Solo has a catchment area of no less than 15,000 square kilometres (De Meyier 1920: 80), covering the four Residencies of: Surakarta, Madiun, Rembang and Surabaya.

When alluding to the Solo Valley it is notably the area surrounding the lower reaches of the river that is being referred to[5] (see **Figure 7.2**). According to a low estimate made at the end of the century before last, the region was then inhabited by some 720,000 people. At that time the population put most of the land in the area to agricultural use. Rice was the main crop. An irrigation system based on running water was lacking. Generally the *sawas* were dependent on the rain that fell during the west monsoon season. The local people retained the rain water in numerous small reservoirs (*waduks*) and conserved it until the dry period[6]. Because of the shortage of "live" water, agricultural production levels were quite low. The summer monsoon season also led to floods that swept the area plaguing people and land alike: that was another problem in the Solo Valley. Extremely little water flowed in the Solo during the dry period but in the wet season there was an excess of water. The Bengawan Jero region close to the estuary was

---

[3] Engineer J. Homan van der Heide, who later became director of Public Works, in 1899 wrote a book about the irrigation on Java and paid much attention to the Solo Works. In another book (1901), he expanded on the Solo Commission report. Further many articles were published about the works, including in *De Ingenieur* ("The Engineer") and *De Indische Gids* ("The Indies Guide", see, for example, the register of 1896-1905 of "The Engineer" and generally Hartman et al. 1901, 1906). In addition to these and other publications, which will be referred to in the text, my main sources are the said report by Telders et al. (1900) and the *Verslag BOW* ("Civil Public Works Report"; for design, implementation and stoppage 1895: 327-346, 1896: 194-197 , 1897: 135-138, 1898: 141, 163-165, 1900: 137-138; for work in the Bengawan Jero and elsewhere in the Solo Valley the reports from 1902, for the "revival" of the project in the 1920s the reports 1925-1927 – more precise indications in follow-up notes). Furthermore, *Het Verslag van de Handelingen der Staten-Generaal* ("The Report on the Proceedings of the States-General"; in particular, 1898/99 and 1903/1904) have been used as well as archival material from the National and *BOW* Archives.

[4] The Solo has over time acquired the *Bengawan* title of the Brantas, the second longest river in Java (Naerssen 1938 A. 65). In the basin of the Solo, especially in upstream area, and in that of the Brantas Indo-Javanese kingdoms flourished in the period 500-1500, including the kingdom of Majapahit (see Van Setten van der Meer 1979 and Slamet 1968).

[5] In the Solo Valley, near the village Trinil (at Ngawi), in the late nineteenth century Dubois found the skull of a human ancestor called Java Man, later classified as Homo Erectus (Leakey 1981: 113-114, see also Telders et al. 1900: 12).

[6] Thousands of such reservoirs were present in the Solo Valley according to Van Kol (1901: 346). Cf. Kroesen (1871). See **Figure 10.2**.

always particularly hard hit by the heavy rains. The region was very low-lying (part of it being below sea-level) and every year it became flooded. On the face of it, this silty water created fertile soil but the excessive amounts of water also caused much damage (De Meyier 1902: 187). The 60,000 people living in the region – as part-time raft inhabitants or not – were described in one qualification of the day as "destitute".

The Solo flows into the Western Narrows which is a continuation of the Straits of Surabaya. It was through these waters that sea-going vessels were able to reach the harbour of Surabaya. This harbour, the second biggest in Java after Tanjung Priok in Batavia, was an important one, for instance, for sugar export. The vast amounts of silt transported by the river did, however, come to threaten navigational movements in the river.

Irrigation plans and other other plans

The first ideas for modern irrigation in the Solo Valley date from 1852. The plans were drawn up by A.A.V. Ledeboer who was, at the time, a Trainee Engineer at the Public Works Organisation. He thought of digging a canal that would start at Padangan and would serve to transport the water of the Solo river some 60 kilometres further, to the Babat District. The water would flow into the canal through a free inlet and at Babat there would be a parting of the ways. One branch would follow the southern bank of the river while the other branch would be led along the base of the northern hills. This canal system would supply 60,000 *bouws* with irrigation water. Another idea that Ledeboer had was to tap water from a tributary of the Solo, the *kali* Pacal. This plan would require a three-metre-high weir but the area irrigated would be larger, namely 75,000 *bouws*. Neither of these plans was to reach fruition: the deep lie of the river in combination with the low lie, notably of the eastern valley section, would create insurmountable problems.

Using the water of the Solo for irrigation purposes became an issue once again in the seventies, particularly in the late seventies[7]. It was not so much agricultural production or water hindrance that gave rise to this issue as the risks caused to shipping by silt deposits in the Surabaya area. Research showed that the deposits were so great that they constituted a navigational hazard[8]. In 1877 Walter, the first engineer appointed to the Surabaya Residency, proposed that the Solo estuary should be redirected to flow into the Java Sea by excavating through the northern hills starting somewhere between Tuban and Sidayu Lawas. This would mean that the Solo would be led 80 kilometres away from its natural estuary. As a result, the river's old course would become silted up. Subsequently it would be necessary to take precautions to protect drinking water supplies in the region and this would necessitate a canal which, in turn, would provide the solution to another problem. The closing off of the Solo was something that also provided a threat to inland (prau) shipping between Surabaya and the city's hinterland. In constructing a canal this threat would be dispelled. The idea was that the canal might also be used for irrigation purposes.[9] The engineer J. Dijkstra, who from 1877 onwards carried out surveys for an irrigation plan, revised Walter's design[10]. Dijkstra suggested going

---

[7] According to a letter to "The Indies Guide" research for an irrigation scheme in the Lamongan Regency has been done in the early 1870s, such "at the direction of a European industrial". However, it did not come to a plan (*Herinnering* ["Reminder"] 1892).

[8] The silt discharge of the Solo was 23 million cubic meters per year, with a drainage of 11.3 billion cubic meters. For the Upper Rhine these figures were 2.75 million and 80 billion cubic meters respectively. So as the Rhine drains seven times as much water than Solo, the last river brings more than eight times as much silt to sea. (Telders et al 1900: 9-10).

[9] This is presumably the channel scheduled from Kalitidu, see **Figure 7.3**.

[10] Dijkstra's proposal can be found in the report of the Dijkstra-Nijgh committee. This committee, established in

more to the east to connect the Solo with the Java Sea by creating a canal through the hills between Wringin Anom and Sidayu Lawas. This proposal did not diminish the need for a second canal and irrigation provision remained an option. In a later plan it was proposed that the Solo might be redirected even further eastwards, to near where the estuary then was. Water would be taken to Ujung Pangkah by means of a canal. That canal would start from a point beyond the *kali* Miring, a branch of the Solo that flowed into the Surabaya Straits. As this branch would also be cut off it would still be necessary to have a canal for shipping. The notion that this canal could simultaneously be used for irrigation purposes was retained in the new plan.

In 1881 engineer J.L. Pierson who had taken over Dijkstra's work came up with a new irrigation plan (see **Figure 7.3**). His was a preliminary design. Pierson proposed that a movable weir be constructed in the Solo river at Ngablak. This would also be the point where two canals would intersect the river, one in a northerly direction and one in a southerly direction. This would make it possible to irrigate 120,000 *bouws* of land. The southern branch would also be suitable for shipping. Pierson estimated that the construction work would cost some 7,620,000 guilders and that it would take some five years to complete.[11]

Indeed, the estuary of the Solo was diverted to Ujung Pangkah in the 1882-1885 period. Experts maintained that it would not be necessary to close off the *kali* Miring. Instead it was decided that a lock should be constructed. This lock was completed in 1888. When the need for a shipping canal was abandoned the incentive to set up an irrigation plan also dwindled. Ground inspections and other surveys aimed at creating a practicable plan continued until 1885 when these activities were aborted on the advice of the engineer J.A. de Gelder. He maintained (see **Chapter 6**) that the treasury could not afford to finance another such expensive irrigation project alongside of the Demak Works. Plans to irrigate the Solo Valley did not fit in with the Public Works Regulation that came into effect in 1885 either. These regulations, drawn up by the same de Gelder, ultimately gave priority to "improving existing defective pipes" (see again **Chapter 6**). When it came to drawing irrigation water from the Solo this was not a consideration. The anticipated profits did not seem to justify the execution of an irrigation plan either.[12]

Small works projects were therefore carried out in the hope that the situation in the Solo Valley might improve. Weirs and sluices were constructed in tributaries together with a number of small reservoirs. Ultimately the improvements were of marginal significance. In reality, matters only worsened for the population: changing the course of the Solo's estuary had only led to more flooding in the Bengawan Jero region[13].

1878, studied the silt deposition in Surabaya and made proposals for the diversion of the Solo (see Telders et al. 1900: 18-19).

[11] This plan is also known as the plan Dijkstra, see Creutzberg (1972: 180). We will see that this plan emerges again later.

[12] A report from the Chief Inspector of Cultures, Dr. J.H.F. Sollewijn Gelpke, pointed this out. Herein, the expected yield increase was criticized. Following this report, and also referring to the cost of the Demak Works and the Regulation of 1885 the government rejected an irrigation plan for the Solo Valley in 1886. (National Archives, Ministry of the Colonies, Mail report 1886).

[13] Telders et al. (1900: 286). See also Van Kol (1903: 6), which indicated that the diversion of the Solo had increased the *banjir* level in the Bengawan Jero by half a meter. Compare with Van Kol during the treatment of the Indies budget for 1904 (in *De Ingenieur* 1903: 867).

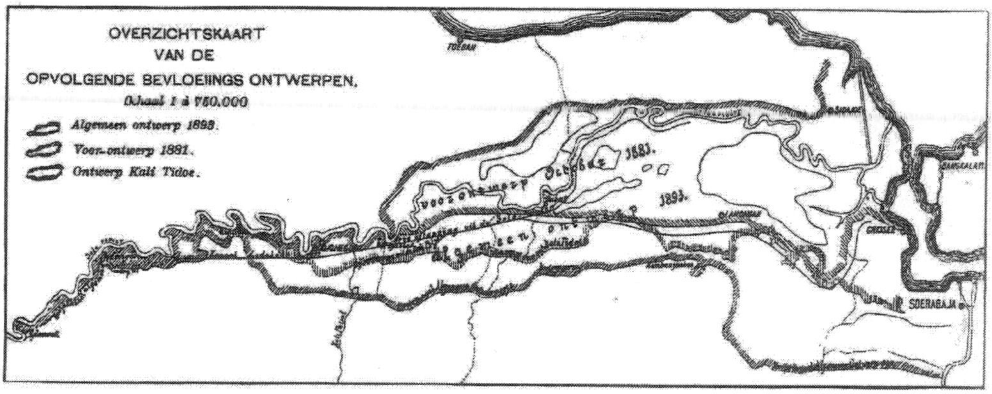

Figure 7.3: Overview of the irrigation plans for the Solo Valley (from: Telders et al. 1900)

The Pierson plan

In anticipation of the abolition of the prioritisation stipulated in the 1885 regulations, in conjunction with the irrigation works still to be constructed, (see above and **Chapter 6**) surveys carried out in connection with an irrigation plan for the Solo Valley were resumed in 1889. Going on his 1881 design and surveys conducted after that time, Pierson set about preparing a definitive project. His report came out in 1891. In that report the movable weir at Ngablak had made way for a permanent weir situated further upstream, at Ngluwak. The report also contained Dijkstra's proposal to excavate a canal leading to Sidayu Lawas. Earlier on Pierson had emphasised the importance of this canal and he had argued that the canal leading to Ujung Pangkah could only provide a temporary solution to the silt problem in Surabaya. He furthermore believed that the canal would improve drainage in the Solo Valley and that this would subsequently help to dry out the Bengawan Jero (Pierson 1891).

At the request of the Minister of the Colonies, W.K. Baron van Dedem, the Director of the Department of Civil Public Works, Van Bosse, provided further information. Preliminary canal and weir designs were ready. Van Bosse drew up a preliminary budget to the tune of eighteen million guilders. In that budget it was presumed that the unit price would be 80 guilders per *bouw* and that the area to be watered was some 223,000 *bouws*. When estimating the unit price Pierson, who had provided the information, based his estimates on his experiences of 1889-1890 with the small Kening Works (see **Chapter 6**). Minister Van Dedem went on to demand a detailed budget based on research and more information pertaining to the economic side of things (i.e. rentability). This led to a detailing of the technical, budgetary and economic aspects and thus to a fully worked out plan. Total cost projections rose to 18,930,000 guilders (see **Table 7.1**) and the project's completion period was put at six to seven years.

Table 7.1 The 1892 Solo Works budget estimates (in guilders)

Land purchase	907,000.00
Inlet structures	1,341,002.97
Soil excavation in the main canal	4,323,630.84
Soil excavation in the secondary canals	658,334.37
Irrigation sluices in the main canal	114,858.81
Irrigation sluices in the secondary canals	24,984.80
Embankments etc.	439,325.47
Siphons beneath the main canal	2,714,571.53
Siphons and aqueducts for the secondary canals	149,855.26
Bridges	177,619.89
Weirs and blow-out constructions	226,405.47
Excavating towards Sidayu Lawas	4,373,665.00
Drainage in Rembang (left bank of the Solo)	252,454.80
Verge ditches, divers etc.	188,105.20
Dwellings, offices etc.	291,410.00
Personnel	1,759,906.00
Unforeseen expenses and miscellaneous costs (5½%)	986,869.59
Total	18,930,000.00

Source: Telders et al. (1900: 35)

Apart from being authorised by the Civil Public Works' Technical Division (E) the plan was described as "very favourable" by Van Bosse as far as its technical aspects were concerned. When it came to the plan's economic aspects, advice was sought from various of the officials involved. Most of the opinions, including those of the Residents of Rembang and Surabaya, were favourable. It was only F.A. Liefrinck, the Inspector of Cultures, who was more cautious (*BOW* Archives E II-92, 2). He was not worried about the calculated profit rise but he did have doubts about the expenditure estimates. In general he saw only the Bengawan Jero as a problem area and he thought that in executing a plan that far exceeded the requirements of this region the population of the Solo Valley as a whole would rise. In his recommendations Van Bosse counteracted Liefrinck's financial doubts by pointing out that they were based on out-of-date figures. The new and detailed cost estimates would serve to dispel such doubts.

Meanwhile Pierson had been on leave in the Netherlands since the end of 1892. He had thus been able to personally lobby for his cause with Minister Van Dedem. Apparently he had done this with "great persuasive powers" (Von Essen 1910: 254, see also De Meyier 1910: 823). This speeded up matters and in 1893 the Dutch government presented the plan to its parliament in the form of a bill. The bill contained the following technical proposals:

1. to redirect the Solo river to Sidayu Lawas and the Java Sea by means of a canal leading through the northern hills,
2. to create a weir with sluices at Ngluwak designed to raise the water level by about eight metres,
3. to have a primary canal that would be at least 165 kilometres long,
4. to create secondary canals with a collective length of 900 kilometres,
5. to establish a series of sluices, siphons and bridges (for the complete overview see **Table 7.1**).

More than five times as big as the Pemali Works and at least four and a half times as big as the Demak Works it was to constitute the biggest irrigation project ever undertaken in Java (see the General Irrigation Plan, **Table 6.1**). The chief components were likewise large-scale by Javanese standards and even by world standards (De Meyier 1898: 23)[14].

While the plan was being debated in the Second Chamber (Lower House) one of the questions that arose was whether the moving of the Solo's estuary might not be detached from the irrigation works project. Since the construction of a canal leading to Ujung Pangkah would not serve to improve the quality of the navigational waters in the Straits of Surabaya it had been decided, in 1892, that a dam should be built in the Western Narrows extending from the western point of the island of Madura (Ujung Piring) and going as far as what was known as the Jamuan reef. The commission, which had approved these plans, now thought it wise to see what would be the effects of this construction before going ahead with the new canal. The Minister adhered strictly to the idea of the unity of the works plan. Finally, with a 55 to 16 vote majority, the plan was approved.[15]

Even before the plan was passed by parliament Van Dedem had asked Pierson, whom he in any case wished to be the project's incumbent, to begin with the necessary preliminaries. Pierson started up the procedure of looking for contractors for the excavation work. Despite his optimism reactions were not forthcoming. When the box in which contractors had been invited to deposit their quotes was opened it turned out to be empty. This meant that the government would have to excavate the canal itself. Early in 1894 Pierson returned to Java. The work of the Solo Valley Works Service, which had meanwhile been set up, could commence.

Operations are halted

During the earth-moving operations it became apparent that the sums of money that had been reserved for this job were too low. The wages offered had enlisted interest from too few labourers which meant that the pay would have to go up and this put Pierson in a financial predicament. He tried to keep expenses down by doing large-scale excavation work with big machinery.

During the course of 1896 the Director of the Civil Public Works Department, Van Houten (1892-1898; formerly involved in the Demak Works) grew skeptical. Going on the total cost levels budgeted for sections of the project he began to fear that the estimated final sums were indeed far too low. Van Houten asked Pierson for an explanation and early in 1897 the latter produced a report.[16] In this report Pierson estimated that the excavation work for the main canal would cost nine million guilders instead of the previously calculated amount of 4.3 million. In all, he estimated that the project would require an extra nine million guilders. When the

---

[14] The flow rate of the main channel was similar to that of the "infamous" Ganges Canal in India (De Meyier 1898: 23), infamous because the high flow rate in the hundreds of kilometers long channel induced erosion (see Headrick 1988: 177 ff.). Still some general information for comparison: the main channel of the Solo Works was at the weir on the ground about 70 meters wide, wider than the North Sea Canal that in 1899 in a "large scale improvement" was widened from 36 to 50 meters (Ringers 1938: 255); in length the main channel was similar to the Suez Canal which was much narrower (Poirier 1957).

[15] In the debate J.F.W. Conrad, a member of the said commission, pleaded to ensure that henceforth more expertise would be called in in such large works. He quoted a French proverb: du choc des opinions jaillit la vérité. (See Van Sandick 1898b: 8). Attention to the bill for the Solo irrigation and the treatment in parliament in *De Ingenieur* and *De Indische Gids* from 1893.

[16] In 1896 the first criticism appeared in the press, namely in the newspaper *De Locomotief* ("The Locomotive"). Van Sandick (1898a: 5) wrote this and further indicated that the financially disappointing state of affairs "already for years ... was an open secret for many technicians" (p. 6).

Governor-General heard of this he decided to set up an investigation. He appointed, to this end, a commission composed of two Chief Engineers of Civil Public Works, L.H. Slinkers and H.P. Mensinga. In its report (National Archives, Ministry of the Colonies, Resolutions 1898, 1) the commission concluded that Pierson had only done a small proportion of all the excavation work and that virtually none of the construction work had been realised. Slinkers and Mensinga were, however, of the opinion that he had made a good job of preparing the actual project and organising it as a whole. They had not found any technical blunders. The two engineers did find, though, that Pierson had devoted too little attention to the way in which the project should be executed (to the work plan). One of the problems to be pinpointed was that the irrigation design merely consisted of the main canal and other important canal routes plotted on a topographical map. Slinkers and Mensinga estimated that the total costs would amount to 38 million guilders which was a further ten million guilders more. They did, however, see ways in which savings could be made and costs brought down to 25½ million guilders. In their opinion the works would take seven to eight years to complete. Despite everything their recommendations were positive.[17]

In 1898 the engineer De Meyier (1898-1901), also the author of the first manual on irrigation affairs (see **Chapter 4**), became the new Director of Civil Public Works. He, too, produced a report on the project (National Archives, Ministry of the Colonies, Resolutions 1898, 2). He maintained that the overall plan needed to be drastically revised and carefully thought through. One of the things he opposed was the building of the weir which was an issue he had tackled before (De Meyier 1898). All the same, the Civil Public Works Director did think that the plan should be executed.

The new Minister of the Colonies, Cremer, heard only in the latter half of 1897 that the budget would probably be exceeded. He made this known in parliament and the following year he decided that the project should be suspended. At that time spendings amounting to a total sum of 15.7 million guilders had been authorised (all authorisation resolutions were withdrawn at the end of 1898 by which time the funds had almost been exhausted; see **Table 7.2**).

Table 7.2 The authorised Solo Works spendings (in guilders)

1893	1,324,000
1894	5,535,532
1895	1,683,088
1896	7,158,900
1897	61,700
Total	15,763,220

Source: Telders et al. (1900: 52-53)

The recommendations were indeed positive but they did create a great deal of disruption. The experts who had been brought in pointed out that the preparations had been inadequate; they proposed amendments and they called for further research. What was evident was that the recommendations were contradictory in certain important respects like, for instance, on the point of combining the river diversions and the irrigation plan: Slinkers and Mensinga agreed to this but De Meyier did not[18].

[17] Slinkers later claimed that when Van Dedem asked for more information (see above), the answer should have been "that the information was not available for such estimate, and that many years should elapse before it could be submitted" (in an article in the *Java Bode* ("Java Herald"), quoted in *De Ingenieur* 1899: 29). Everything was based on the specified unit.

[18] There was also an advice of Van Houten, in fact, on the report of Slinkers and Mensinga. Van Houten found the

In the Second Chamber one of the ways in which Cremer justified his decision was as follows (*Handelingen* ["Proceedings"] 1898/99: 242):

"In the Indies there is talk of *hoping, believing* and *thinking* ... but, Mr. Speaker! at the end of the day, such exclamations are not enough for me; doing things in an ad hoc sort of way, as has been the case up until now, can no longer be tolerated".

The Minister also added to this a sociological remark; the fact that De Meyier and other advisors were in favour of pursuing the project while he was against it was, he believed, a matter of formulation and responsibility. The advisors had focused on the question: where do we go from here? That was a matter of responsibility for them. After all, it had to do with a "judicially dictated" project. Cremer found, though, that in his position his responsibility lay elsewhere: he had to ensure that the money was well spent and where the Solo Works was concerned this remained debatable (*Handelingen* 1898/99: 241-242).

Apportioning blame

The halting of the Solo Works project gave way to discussion about the causes of the related (financial) problems. The main question being asked was who or what had failed. Had it been the responsibility of one or more persons including the designer/executor Pierson or was it the fault of the Indies Public Works Organisation as a whole?

In their report Slinkers and Mensinga placed responsibility with Pierson and the Civil Public Works Department Director, Van Houten but they did show a degree of understanding. The sharp criticism, though, came from de Gelder. As has been mentioned, already in 1885 the irrigation plan surveys in the Solo Valley had been stopped at his request. After that he had become entangled in a debate with the editorial staff of the *Nieuwe Rotterdamsche Courant* ("New Rotterdam Courant" [*NRC*], see *De Ingenieur* 1898: 587-589). He was critical also of the personal nature of the decision-making process (Pierson's understanding with Van Dedem). De Gelder also found it bad that preparations for the resolutions had been made in the Netherlands (in part at least and during the time when Pierson was on leave) and he found it absolutely unacceptable that the final decision had been arrived at the Netherlands[19]. De Gelder's views on the Public Works engineering corps were decidedly positive: "this corps is not involved in the matter at all" (ibid., further criticism levelled at the *NRC* editorial staff came from Slinkers, see *De Ingenieur* 1899: 29-30).

Van Sandick (1898b) became involved in this discussion as well. He rejected the views of De Gelder but was similarly at odds with the *NRC* editors. The Public Works Organisation would, to his way of thinking, be left with both credit and debt items. Van Sandick was not so disturbed by the overspending. The New Waterway in the Netherlands (excavated between 1866 and 1872) had been a "resounding success", even though it had cost 30 million guilders instead of the budgeted six million. Elsewhere (1898a) he suggested it was simply impossible for people to take absolutely everything into consideration. He was reminded of the reply once given to a Minister by a "world famous engineer" upon being accused of having overstepped his budget: "Did you think, then, that I was God!" (1898a: 1)[20]. Referring to the criticism that had already

design of the weir properly, De Meyier did not, as at second sight Pierson himself! Another disagreement concerned the capacity of the main channel: Slinkers and Mensinga found that it could less, Van Houten did not think so, De Meyier agreed with Van Houten. There was even a fourth opinion on the table: the report of Liefrinck 1892 (*BOW* Archives E II-92). See for treatment of the various advices Van Sandick (1898a).

[19] Van Kol (1901: 344) even went so far that he called the Solo Works later for this reason a special case.

[20] Van Sandick (1898a: 1) still called the National Museum in Amsterdam, the Palace of Justice in Brussels and the

appeared in the press in 1896 (see **Note 16**) he wondered on that occasion why it had in fact taken so long for the project to be abandoned (1898a: 6).

The fact that preparations had not been thorough, that there was no good work plan and that Pierson had thus fallen short was quite apparent from a report drawn up by a Public Works delegate who had been to have a look at the project shortly before it was halted:

"Matters have not been well enough thought through; 110 steam machines have been brought in. Everything is being done by trial and error. Work has not started on any of the structures, equipment still has to be assembled, expensive installations still have to be set up. There is a transport cable with a 9000 M3 per month capacity while at the final point only 200 M3 of stone can be collected; huge limestone warehouses are to be stocked by Decauville rail and only now has it been discovered that the warehouses are not required. Very good quality stone is being fired in field kilns to construct new European-style brick kilns that will supply even better bricks. A 100 km. long railway line with a 60 cm. gauge track with a regulated two-way train service to transport a handful of pieceworkers, wood for burning and mailbags. A number of dwellings, offices etc. all on a much too opulent scale, blindly obedient personnel used to all kinds of premiums and gratuities, but no sign of any intellectual input on the part of engineers".[21]

Pierson came in for heavy criticism but did receive some support. The man who later became the Director of Civil Public Works, Homan van der Heide, maintained that if there was evidence of a Solo Works scandal,

"then it related to the way in which the name of the leader of the project had been dragged through the mud in the Netherlands on the basis of unfounded pretexts and accusations that did not hold water" (1899: 257-258).

For Homan van der Heide, Pierson remained "a man who had provided exceptional services" (1899: 259) and someone who was a credit to the Public Works Organisation. According to Homan van der Heide the blame for the suspension of the project could not be pinned on Pierson or on anyone else or, for that matter, on Public Works. He believed that the cause of the problem was the tight budget policy that had been adopted and this led him to view the (alleged) "one-two" game between Pierson and Van Dedem in a very different light:

"The usefulness, the desirability, even the necessity to improve and extend the irrigation system are things that are not questioned, yet people are as careful as possible to take every opportunity not to spend any money on this. That is the political standpoint that has persuaded, or perhaps lured, engineer Pierson and the Indies authorities to grab with both hands any opportunities where chance parliamentary and personal circumstances made it possible to get something done,

---

Opera in Paris as examples of works whose "genius designers" are known as "heroes of science and art", despite the fact that their works had "cost an amazing number of millions more" than they thought. Also in the construction North Sea Canal in the Netherlands, the estimates were exceeded many times (according to De Gelder in *De Ingenieur* 1898: 588). De Gelder (ibid.) further found that the history of the New Waterway indicated that the most eminent engineers may disagree with technical matters. See for budget overruns also Homan van der Heide (1899). I bring here in remembrance also the Panama Canal that experienced a false start in the 1880s: the company of Ferdinand de Lesseps went bankrupt with a deficit of 200 million guilders! The canal was completed by America in the period 1907-1914. (Poirier 1957). See also **Chapter 6, Note 3**.

[21] Passage from a letter from 1898, cited by Van Bosse in his biography of De Gelder (1912: 787-788). Van Bosse set the affairs of the Solo Valley project alongside the approach of the Gelder in the construction of the port in Tanjung Priok. Here it was all gone much better.

as in 1893 with the Solo Works because, as far as the Indies was concerned, the project had not been well enough prepared" (Homan van der Heide 1899: 258).[22]

In an internal memo Minister Cremer's attention was drawn to Pierson's "unsuitability", to the failure of Van Houten and to the poor relations between the two men (National Archives, Ministry of the Colonies, Resolutions 1898, 3[23]). In the Second Chamber he made it quite clear that he had not looked into the matter of answerability in such great depth. He was thus cautious with his remarks. The Minister did however criticise Van Houten for having, in 1897, held on to Pierson's new estimates for six months before sending the information on. By commenting that the detailed plan had passed through "all the advisory phases" (*Handelingen* 1898/99: 242) within Civil Public Works Cremer thus cleared the name of Van Dedem, his predecessor. On the matter of the Public Works Organization in general he commented (ibid.):

"This whole unfortunate business, Mr. Speaker, does not reflect badly on the entire Indies public works engineering corps. If that were so things would be extremely dismal within that corps but that, I am persuaded, is not the case. Neither can all the responsibility be placed on one person. In drawing up and assessing the plan and in putting forward relevant proposals the usual procedure has not been changed: the hierarchical structure has been respected and no covering up or cheating has taken place between parties either in the Indies or in the Netherlands".

A divided commission

After having stopped the works' activities Minister Cremer set up, at the end of 1898, an "Advisory Commission for the Solo Valley Works". The Commission was instructed to: "bring out written recommendations on the way in which the suspended Solo Valley Works activities in Java might further be dealt with" (Telders et al. 1900: I). The Commission consisted of four members:

- J.M. Telders, Professor and Dean at the Polytechnic in Delft,
- W.F. Leemans, Inspector of the Dutch Public Works Organisation,
- J. Kraus, Professor at the Polytechnic in Delft,
- J.E. de Meyier, Director of the Indies Civil Public Works Department.

After having carried out careful research into the matter this group published its report in 1900 (Telders et al. 1900). The Solo Commission viewed the plan in a positive light. They maintained that the "main components of this large-scale irrigation project, namely the inlet at Ngluwak and the main and sub-canal plans ..." were "... purposeful" (Telders et al.: V). The Commission only disagreed with the plans for the canals intended to supply the Bengawan Jero with water because they thought that a different route should be followed. They therefore proposed an alternative route.

---

[22] See for aid to Pierson, who was dismissed at his own request in 1899, an article in *De Ingenieur* (1899: 28-29) taken from *De Locomotief.* It called the Solo Works, analogous to a "model farm" for agriculture, "model works". See also Von Essen (1910: 254), which pointed to Pierson's ambition to create a "model work". In the article in *De Ingenieur*, following upon the objections of De Meyier (1898a) against the weir, we find the wisdom that "a technical project has not one certain solution as a mathematical problem; so one should understand that the idea of the old dam has as much right to exist as the idea of the director".

[23] In the memorandum we find a note that Pierson apparently was not a persona grata with the Director of Civil Public Works. Van Houten would have struggled that Pierson had been put in charge of the project in the Netherlands. This elicited to Minister Cremer the note: "Truly Indies!" Cremer showed thereby that he considered this contradicted by a letter from Van Houten.

The Commission had calculated that only half the originally estimated volumes of water would be required for irrigation purposes so they put forward suggestions to accordingly save on water. Alongside of the original plan the gentlemen also saw possibilities for summer monsoon irrigating so that the population could obtain water supplies for the cultivation of second annual crops. This would also make it possible for them to grow sugar cane on a scale that would, so the Commission believed, make the establishment of 25 sugar refineries a viable option. As far as the proposal to change the course of the Solo river was concerned they maintained that research into water movements and silt transportation in the navigational waters of Surabaya was first warranted[24].

The Commission budgeted the project's total costs at around 49.4 million guilders. This estimate included expenses for excavating a canal to the Java Sea put at some 10.6 million guilders. Of the estimated final sum approximately 15.4 million guilders had already been expended (compare this with the authorised cost sum total given above). With these new calculations the cost per field had risen to 174 guilders. According to the Commission it would take about fifteen years for the job to reach completion. They furthermore commented (1900: VI):

"The incredible exceeding of the originally estimated cost levels stemmed mainly from the fact that the soil excavation and general expenses had simply been vastly underestimated, together with the amount of time estimated for the job as a whole. By and large, all the other cost areas were also budgeted on the low side".

The members of the Commission who lived in the Netherlands (i.e. everyone except for De Meyier) were impressed by the "hugeness of the dimensions and by the number of ground excavations and structures" (ibid.). They believed that the great financial miscalculations might be put down to the fact "that people might not have realised the true magnitude of the project" (ibid.). They believed that Pierson would otherwise not have based his calculations on the statistics derived from a smaller works project (the Kening Works). The Commission also observed that people might likewise not have assumed that, per unit, irrigation costs for a larger area work out cheaper than for a smaller area.

Most of the Commission members foresaw the direct and indirect advantages that the project would bring with it, like a rise in the yield of rice and other crops and greater crop success guarantees for staple crops as well as the emergence of a blooming sugar industry. One member saw things differently. De Meyier (Telders et al. 1900: 286-289) emphasised that for at least fourteen to fifteen years the project would drain around two million guilders from the Public Works Organisation's annual budget. A further one million could be added to that for operations, maintenance and for rent and repayment. That was a lot of money, especially when one considered that the immediate profits to be gained from the works came to the same amount. The Civil Public Works Director made it crystal clear that it was only 10% of the project area, the Bengawan Jero, that actually suffered from flooding. Because of the silt formation the flooding only gave rise to a gradual raising of the soil surface level. In the long-term De Meyier found this to be the best solution[25].

The Civil Public Works Director warned against building up expectations for modern irrigation that might be too high: lack of water was merely one reason – not even the main one – for poor crop results. De Meyier argued that up until that time the providing of irrigation works

---

24 Under Pierson the dam to the Jamuan reef was completed in 1896 and this seemed to have a beneficial effect (see also Quant 1899: 418).

25 See for a similar position but then with regard to the Demak Works on the part of the Civil Service Post (1879), referred to in the introduction to **Chapter 4**.

had not, or had hardly at all, done anything to improve the population's affluence. Insofar as crop yields had risen, economic or social structures had always prevented the people from directly benefiting from such increases. He found it absurd to hint at food shortages. He maintained that nature regulated the balance between food supplies and the population. Java as a whole did not suffer from rice shortages. There was enough rice but it was the shortage of transport means and the way in which the price mechanism worked that made distribution uneven. De Meyier also suggested that rice need not be the only main source of sustenance. He went on to point out that Java constituted part of the world of trade and industry and that the population should therefore have money. The sugar refineries would be a good source of income but he believed that it would only be possible to have ten refineries. He warned of the inherent disadvantage of sugar cultivation, namely that it would lead to falls in rice crop yields. Since land had to be available early in the year for sugar crops the Javanese would be forced to switch to shorter cultivation cycles and thus to inferior varieties of rice.

On the technical side De Meyier maintained, in line with previous recommendations made to the Minister (see above), that the project remained feasible. He even made little of the doubts he had once had concerning the weir design (compare De Meyier 1898a, and Van Goor's 1898 comments on this, and De Meyier 1902: 191). In other respects, though, he had not come to view technical matters in a more favourable light. On the contrary, more so than the other Commission members, he was inclined to see major risk areas. On the matter of the diverting of the river he also diverged widely from his colleagues. While the others were inclined to go along with the suggestion, De Meyier believed that the best solution to the problem of the silting up of the navigational lanes in Surabaya was to be found in returning to the old situation of allowing the Solo to reach the sea through the *kali* Miring. This was something he had mentioned in his previous recommendations in 1898. The decision to further research the matter was one that really united the Commission making it able to produce technical recommendations "on which all were unanimous" (Telders et al. 1900: VII). In (financial-)economic terms they were not united though which meant that De Meyier remained in the minority with his views. He lobbied to halt the project altogether and, in so doing, deviated from the stance taken in 1898.

On the matter of responsibility, the Commission seriously attacked Pierson but otherwise it did, on the whole, support the views expressed by the Minister. In seeking to explain why things had gone wrong the Commission pointed to the "impatient" and "hasty" character of the decision-making process as well as to the exceptional nature of the project. Van Dedem was let off the hook because he had "so earnestly pushed for an accurate assessment of the work to be done" (Telders et al. 1900: VI). With regard to the functioning of the Public Works corps the Commission was full of praise:

"On a number of occasions over the last few years the Solo matter has elicited harsh words in conjunction with the policies and the services provided by our engineers in the Dutch Indies. The Commission is, however, pleased to be able to report that its entire investigation has convinced it that, in technical and moral terms, the Public Works Corps has come out on top, that it comprises outstanding elements who because of their expertise and application to the tasks in hand may be viewed as top professionals among Dutch engineers" (p. II.)[26].

[26] Pierson's biographer did later an attempt at defending the declining engineer. He pointed out that Pierson was relatively young when he was charged with the execution of the Solo Works (42) and also poorly paid, because not appointed to a high rank. He also argued that the decision-making based on global and summary data differed entirely from the ordinary affairs of Public Works. (Von Essen 1910: 254).

Discussions on the solutions

In engineering circles it was not just the matter of apportioning blame that was important. As time went on the discussion focused increasingly on the matter of how things should develop in the Solo Valley in the future. The Solo Commission had clear views on this issue: the project should be resumed. At an earlier date Homan van der Heide (1899) had lobbied to continue the project and most of the engineers involved in the debate agreed with him and with the Commission that the project should be completed[27]. Van Sandick was, for instance, one such supporter. At the end of his series of discussions on the Solo report he placed himself clearly on the side of the majority view within the Commission (1900: 527)[28].

Meanwhile engineers were also thinking of ways to solve what were specific Bengawan Jero problems. The main idea was to combat periodic flooding in the area by improving drainage and averting flooding in the Solo river. One of the engineers to come forward with ideas was W. Elenbaas who was employed in the Solo Valley. In 1902 he proposed creating two massive reservoirs, one of which would be filled with water from the rivers Kerjo and Cawak and one of which would be situated in the *kali* Gondang. The collective capacity of these two reservoirs would amount to some 190 million cubic metres. They would thus be able to supply irrigation water the whole year round. Just like the measures put forward to combat flooding, Elenbaas believed that this proposal might supplement existing plans for irrigation in the Solo Valley. He thought that such supplementary plans might help to simplify the entire project. The financial savings that these plans would facilitate would weigh up against the extra expenses incurred by such additional construction work. The big advantage of this plan was that it could be quickly realised – within a five to seven year period – Elenbaas estimated. In an article on the subject Elenbaas furthermore called for agricultural research into the situation in the Kening Works area because there, after brief initial production increases, falls in rice yield levels had been recorded (see below). Research would have to explain why this had been the case.

In the debate on the resumption of the Solo Works Van Kol, who was by now a member of the Second Chamber, seized on the plans proposed by Elenbaas as a suitable alternative option. In a meeting arranged by the Royal Institute of Engineers he immediately became engaged in discussion with Van Sandick. He suggested that the original project be dropped altogether and that instead the "little reservoir plan" be introduced together with moves to improve drainage in the Begawan Jero region (*Stand* ["Status"] 1903: 824, see also Van Kol 1903).

On a previous occasion Van Kol had been very critical in the Second Chamber about plans for the Solo Works weir (compare De Meyier 1898a). His views were based on his own experiences in Java, chiefly in conjunction with the Sampean weir:

"Presuming that the position is right, the construction of the weir should be firmly condemned by everyone with weir construction experience in the Indies.

...

For 8 years I was witness to the well-known problems surrounding the construction of the huge weir at Situbondo in the Sampean river. It was a project that continued for 30 years. Each year huge sums of money were spent on Portland cement, sometimes more than 20,000 guilders.

[27] Apart from that, Homan van der Heide disagreed with the Solo Commission in the sense that he did not agree with the proposed reduction of the capacity of the work (1899: 266). He worked that out later (Homan van der Heide 1901). See for a detailed discussion of his book from 1899 Koster (1899), see also Wong Tanie (1900).

[28] See also Driesen (1900). Tubergen (1901, 1902) afforded some critical observations on the report and the works. Positive discussion of the Solo report also in "The Indies Guide" from 1900 (by Van Sandick [1900c] who was then editor of this magazine).

Together with the foreman we engineers often sat up all night terrified that within a matter of hours the results of years of labour might be destroyed and that, with the sweeping away of the weir, a densely populated area might be robbed of all its fertile-making water. In those days if anyone had asked me, as an engineer, to work on a project like the Ngluwak weir – even though I had never had anything to do with the Solo Works – I would rather have immediately handed in my notice than start working on a 21 metre high weir in such circumstances" (cited in: Van Goor 1899: 127).

Van Goor who had designed the Ngluwak weir (see Van Goor 1898) employed this criticism in two ways. In the first place he pointed out that the Sampean is a mountain river which makes it very different from the Solo. In the second place he said that he believed that the big mistake that had been made with the Sampean weir was that the works had been made to "as it were, hang in mid-air" (Van Goor 1899: 127 because the foot of the structure was situated at least nine metres – Van Goor based his calculations on what was then the most recent height of six metres – above the bed of the lower river, see **Chapter 3**) but with the planned Solo weir this problem had been carefully avoided. That had been achieved by allowing the cemented slope of the weir to extend some four metres below the river bed. He continued his attack by positing that Van Kol (and his colleagues) had rather too quickly given up work on the old Sampean weir with the excavation of the *banjir* canal. There it would have been possible to change the angle of the weir's slope which, in turn, might have made it unnecessary to dig a canal.

Meanwhile De Meyier had not been idle. In his capacity as Director of Civil Public Works (up until 1901) he had been involved with all of Elenbaas's plans. Later he reinforced his point of view in an article on "irrigation fanaticism" (1902). There he criticised, amongst others, the Solo project's supporters. He again objected to aspects of the project on technical grounds. He pointed (1902: 191-192) particularly to the risks attached to creating a 165-kilometre-long main canal. De Meyier (1902: 192) moreover restated his views on the matter of repositioning the Solo's estuary. During two meetings convened by the Royal Institute of Engineers in 1902, in which the river's redirecting was discussed, it became apparent that a majority was in favour of the plan. (See, for instance, Cohen Stuart 1930: B. 21). De Meyier, who was present at the first meeting, afterwards turned down an offer to join the institute (Melchior 1912: 90). De Meyier (1902) also elaborated on his economic views in relation to the Solo Works by pointing out how important the silt transported with the water was for fertilising the fields. Already once before De Meyier had underlined the importance of silt in agriculture (see, for example, De Meyier 1891: 11), and this notion was also relevant to the economic views he aired within the Solo Commission. He argued (1902: 182-183) that in the case of longer canals the water in them contains hardly any silt towards the end of the canal so that vital increased production yields in such areas is thwarted. Because of the low silt content of irrigation water it might be possible that after a number of years of good harvests the ground could even become infertile. De Meyier (1902: 183) thought that this might explain why production levels were falling in the Kening region (reference is made to this problem in conjunction with the Solo Valley Works on p.192).[29]

[29] The fall in production in the Kening Area was established by the Inspector A.H.J.G. Walbeehm (1901a), who thus interfered in the debate on the Solo Works. Homan van der Heide went straight into discussion with him (see e.g. Walbeehm 1901b). The Solo Commission found the long channels in this regard no point (Telders et al. 1900: 283-5), and furthermore considered that the silt could settle best in the channels, although that gave a different problem (from silting, see Homan van der Heide 1901: 295 ff.).

Halting the project

In 1903 Idenburg, the Minister of the Colonies, finally arrived at a decision – albeit an interim one – in conjunction with the Indies budget for 1904 for the Solo Valley Works. When it came to plans to divert the Solo river he made it clear that such a decision could only be taken after research initiated by the inspection service – set up in 1901 – for the navigational waters of Surabaya, had been completed. He was guided by the recommendations made by the Solo Commission which had called for further research. Regarding the main point, that of possibly resuming the irrigation works, he was inclined to follow De Meyier's recommendations to stop the project. In order to alleviate problems in the Bengawan Jero region the Minister decided to, after all, go for the reservoir option. The Minister was convinced that:

"If the creation of small reservoirs within the area through which the Cawak, Kerjo and Gondang rivers flowed could do anything to relieve the situation in the Bengawan Jero then plans to execute the big irrigation project should be temporarily shelved" (*Handelingen* 1903/04, Appendix B: 17).

Before any decisions could be made to go ahead with creating reservoirs it would be necessary to have a fully elaborated proposition. This would emerge from a plan on how to combat flooding in the region: a plan that had been approved by the Minister a year earlier.

During the relevant parliamentary debate ("Proceedings of the States-General", see *De Ingenieur* 1903: 851, 865-868) it became apparent that an important reason for the Minister's opposition to the works rested in the belief that in extensive irrigation areas the fertilising silt would not reach the more remote fields. He also maintained that in such a huge area it would be difficult to plan rice cultivation according to a rigid planting schedule while that was something that was necessary if irrigation water was to be optimally utilised everywhere. The Minister's decision elicited agreement from Van Kol, but also criticism from others, for instance, from the engineer J.M. Pijnacker Hordijk. In 1893 he had been a supporter of the works and in 1898 he had regretted that these activities had been suspended. On that latter occasion he had stated that he was convinced that the States-General would share his view if they, like him, were to pay a visit to the region (see Pijnacker Hordijk 1901: 363). Again he showed disappointment claiming, with a degree of resignation: "What's it to me whether or not I once again outline how unsatisfactory things really are for the population?" ("Proceedings of the States-General", quoted in *De Ingenieur* 1903: 866). Pijnacker Hordijk did not, however, agree with the silt problem outlined by the Minister. He maintained that irrigation water was just as important without its silt content. In the debate what also emerged was that the recommendations of the Indies government were not positive. Although this was not made public:

"enough had been leaked to gather that the Minister had not received the support he needed in the Indies to pursue the project" (Pijnacker Hordijk, "Proceedings of the States-General", quoted in *De Ingenieur* 1903: 866).

Previously – in 1900! – someone had asserted in a letter from the Indies, that the government had shown that – partly as could be seen by the fact that preparations were being made to go ahead with a project in the Bengawan Jero area – it was anticipating that the Solo Works project would not be resumed (Van Sandick 1900b: 790, see also van Sandick 1900c: 1334, compare Driessen 1901)[30].

[30] The service of the Solo Valley Works was abolished in 1901 (*Verslag BOW* 1901: 137-138). In an annex to a note from Governor-General Rooseboom to Minister of the Colonies Cremer dated July 26, 1901, a continuation of the Solo Works is still a clear option, even though the criticism of De Meyier from the Solo report conveys here; an

The Inspectorate for the navigational waters of Surabaya, which was disbanded in 1904, brought out its final report in 1905. The report's findings particularly supported De Meyier's point of view. The conclusion was that the existing position of the Solo's estuary could not be detrimental. The proposition to re-route the river was thus dropped (Ribbers and Van Gelderen 1906, for example p. 136, Snell 1928: 36, compare Cohen Stuart 1930: B. 21-23). This led to the parliamentary decision to cease the Solo Works project altogether (*Verslag BOW* 1905: 135).

Its sequel

Keep it small

From 1902 onwards the Civil Public Works Department embarked on various works, all of which were designed to alleviate the problem in the Bengawan Jero region. The right Solo dyke was renovated, sluices were constructed (for instance the Kuro sluice in the *kali* Blawi) and drainage canals were widened. Other measures were simultaneously undertaken, also in the management area. In certain higher lying parts of the region numerous small reservoirs and marshes (*rawas*) were improved and technologically controlled. The Bengawan Jero commission was set up in order to obtain yields that would be as high as possible. The commission consisted of Javanese administrators, irrigation service representatives (*Mantris*) and the relevant farmers. The commission decided what should be planted and where and when this should be done. Elsewhere in the Solo Valley the quality of *waduks* and their management was also improved and new small reservoirs were created as well. Existing irrigation sources were extended too and the managing of this also fell into the hands of engineers (Pareau Dumont 1940)[31].

The establishing of larger reservoirs did not go so quickly. Alongside of his original suggestions Elenbaas made further plans for his two small reservoirs and altered plans for one of the reservoirs. With the reservoir in the basin of the Kerjo and Cawak he included a third river, the Lamong. He did this because observations had shown that in the drier west monsoon season the reservoir would otherwise not be filled (*Verslag BOW* 1903: 171, 1904: 153). The plans did not, however, materialise. There were delays on the Dutch side because in 1904 Minister Idenburg was still interested in Pierson's original 1881 plan in which Dijkstra (by then a retired Chief Engineer) had had an important part to play. Instead of the approximately 22,000 *bouws* that could be irrigated with the current plan, the older plan would provide some 120,000 *bouws* with water. The Minister looked to Rooseboom, the Governor-General, for advice but he was in favour of the reservoir plan. That was not to say that people were extremely enthusiastic about the second plan. The high excavation costs (the Kerjo, Cawak and Lamong waduk amounted to 4½ million guilders), also in relation to the anticipated returns, was a drawback. Elenbaas's proposals were therefore not executed. His successor, the engineer A.H. Saltet, found the reservoirs too big and he was moreover afraid of silting problems. He therefore suggested that the capacity of the reservoirs should be limited. That idea appealed to Civil Public Works. What emerged from this proposal was the Prijetan *waduk* design with a nine million cubic metre

advice of the Indies Council dated March 20, 1903, and a letter of Minister Idenburg to Governor-General Rooseboom dated August 7, 1903, speak of the reservoir plan (see Creutzberg 1972: 52, 73 and 89).

[31] See also Van der Does de Bije (1919), to whom I return below. See further for all the (small) improvement works the "Civil Public Works Reports"; for the works in the Bengawan Jero e.g. *Verslag BOW* (1903: 171, 1904: 152, 1905: 135 ff., 1906: 137 ff.); for source irrigation elsewhere in the Solo Valley e.g. *Verslag BOW* (1912: 9-10). From 1905 to 1907 the works in the Bengawan Jero were discussed separately in the "Civil Public Works Reports" (separate from the discontinued Solo Valley Works) in the General Considerations, from 1908 under its own title. Possibly the staple food in the Solo Valley changed from rice to maize. Pareau Dumont (1940: A. 75) mentioned at least that corn was main food crop.

capacity (Creutzberg 1972: 180-181, 193-194, Robbers 1913, see also the 1903 *Verslag BOW*: 171, 1904: 153). The Prijetan reservoir was finally completed in 1917. With this new reservoir it was possible to grow five rice crops every two years, also thanks to good drainage and smooth management (Pareau Dumont 1940: A. 76, see also Snell 1928).

The Ministerial resolution to halt Solo Works activities seemed to open up the way to other alternatives but it did not in any way imply that the project's resumption would be ruled out (see the quotation above). The resolution provided space for new considerations. Elenbaas (1902) bore in mind the possibility that the Solo Works project might well go ahead: he saw his reservoir plan as supplementary to the larger project (see above). Despite the "definite" halting of the project in 1905, Saltet did not think differently about matters (Robbers 1913: 450). But, with all the improvements, was such a huge irrigation plan necessary?

The big dream

As far as the engineers were concerned the Solo Works file had not exactly been closed. Most of the engineers had supported the Solo Commission's report. For them halting the project amounted to a disaster. It was therefore not surprising that engineers such as Lamminga kept pressing for the work to be resumed. Lamminga (1910: 6-7) wrote in his inaugural address: "As far as I am able to see no complete or adequate answer has, at any stage, been given to the question of why the Solo Valley commission's recommendations have not been followed up". His conclusion was therefore this: "The Solo Works project is still on the agenda" (ibid.).

Homan van der Heide had been a constant project resumption supporter. For instance, in the report brought out on the welfare study he stood by his views (*Mindere Welvaartscommissie* ["Lesser Welfare Commission"] 1910: 181). In 1911 Homan van der Heide was made Civil Public Works Director for three and a half years. He could not have been given a better opportunity for pursuing the Solo Works project with renewed verve. When, in 1912, a newspaper report appeared containing comments along those lines (in the *Soerabajasch Handelsblad* ["Surabayan Newspaper"]), De Meyier (1912a: 663-664) got up and opposed it. In his criticism of desires to apparently still execute the Solo project plans the former Civil Public Works Director focused attention on the improved situation in the Bengawan Jero. But that was not his only counter-argument. He once again drew attention to the negative experiences with the Kening Works in order to demonstrate that the problem of falling agricultural returns was something that had been evident since 1893 (see above). At that time the population had apparently asked the Controller to wind up the works (completed in 1900). He furthermore questioned the importance of the financing role apparently to be played by the sugar industry (ten million guilders for concessions) and the matter of the profit to be made for the population. As far as this latter point was concerned he commented:

"When one carefully considers this notion there is nothing that has so far been worked out on such a scale when it comes to the matter of exploiting the population in the interests of big capital" (De Meyier 1912a: 664).

In his article De Meyier alluded to an earlier published article of his (1910). There he had underlined what were the technical objections to the works, to the weir and to the main canal and he had expressed it thus:

"It is our sincere opinion that, had the project been a success, the construction that was to be employed for raising the level of the water of the Solo river would, in the process of damming off the branch of the river to be cut off, have been seriously in danger of being burst through with the first given banjir. The 165-kilometre-long and, at its starting point, 80-metre-wide main canal must negotiate numerous side rivers with a number of dangerous structures. Had the headworks already been constructed so that this canal could have been fed into then each of those works would, in turn, have been susceptible to seepage, annual subsidence and breakthroughs that could not be rectified in one rainy season while, almost on a yearly basis, the lower levels of buildings would be flooded and serious crop failure would be commonplace" (De Meyier 1910: 823).

De Meyier contended that the works would therefore be doomed to "almost certain" failure[32].

Figure 7.4: Lock Mlirep, draining the Bengawan Jero on the Solo river, 1930 (photo UBL KITLV 4333)

Support from the engineering world for Homan van der Heide's enterprise was inevitable. Thal Larsen (1912) reacted vehemently to De Meyier's articles. In the case of the Kening Works he pointed out that the fall in rice yields was the fault of the population itself because they had so badly and systematically neglected the water conveyance networks. He reminded everyone that De Meyier had at one time gone along with the Commission's technical recommendations. Thal Larsen also made it clear that he saw little potential in small-scale irrigation projects (see **Chapter 8**)[33]. In the end, the irrigation plans for the Solo Valley were dropped again but, once again, not really for good.[34]

---

[32] This article also found a way to the report on the welfare investigation (*Mindere Welvaartscommissie* 1910: 244).

[33] I will return in **Chapter 8** to the last point of Thal Larsen and also to the Kening works. An "engineer" and the Regent of Bojonegoro mingled in the discussion, both were pro resumption. De Meyier (1912b and 1913) made short work of their responses.

[34] Not picking up the Solo Works made itself felt significantly in the reporting by Civil Public Works. Thus the

The ongoing debate

The engineer Van der Does de Bije (1919) was also of the opinion that things had changed for the better in the Bengawan Jero region. One of the matters he highlighted was the fact that because of all the measures that had been taken it was now possible to harvest two crops a year, either by having a double rice harvest or by having a rice harvest and a harvest of another crop. Despite this, he still maintained that there was good reason for once again questioning the matter of irrigation in the Solo Valley. One of the main issues was that the rapidly rising population level was giving rise to food shortages. Van der Does de Bije argued that it would not be necessary to change the course of the Solo but that the irrigation situation for the valley as a whole should be reviewed. Going on the data then available he then went about amending the Solo Commission's plan. Reverting to old ideas he once more argued in favour of a movable weir at Kalitidu . Van der Does de Bije's proposition was not immediately taken on board but it did serve to keep the Solo plan discussion going. One of the plan's advocates was, for instance, Otto de Vries, the former Civil Public Works Director. He maintained (1922: 741) that the project should definitely be pursued: population expansion made "intensive utilisation of the water derived from the Solo river, that largely flowed out to sea unused, unavoidable". To his mind the reason why the project had not been continued was because of a shortage of personnel.[35]

On 8th July 1924 the engineer E.J.L. Führi argued in favour of resuming the Solo Works project during a sitting of the People's Council, a representative body for the Indies population (see **Chapter 8**). This produced results. Civil Public Works again decided to examine the plan and also to again set up a Service for the works. In 1925 the engineer D.C.W. Snell was made Director of this Service by the government and upon appointment he was asked to look into the possibilities of resuming the Solo Works project. (*Verslag BOW* 1925: 133-138, see also the "Civil Public Works Report" of 1926: 152-156, 1927: 108-111, Creutzberg 1974: 39)[36].

In 1928 Snell produced a report. The Chief Engineer proposed halting the project for once and for all and just carrying on as they always had done in the past. In this way he revealed that he was a proponent of big reservoir facilities such as the Prijetan *waduk*. Snell was cautiously optimistic about the *waduk* irrigation possibilities in the Prijetan area and lobbied for the creation of a second big reservoir, the Pacal *waduk*. He further discussed plans for the integrated Kerjo-Cawak-Lamong *waduk*. Unlike the plans for the other two reservoirs this one was oriented towards the proposals made by Elenbaas. Snell maintained that they should not take things too quickly. Before making firm decisions on this proposal the results produced by the Pacal irrigation scheme should be awaited, indeed:

---

following statement was published in the report on 1915 (p. 117): "Contrary to previous years, henceforth these works will no longer be included in a separate section, for reasons [that, WR] the actually discontinued works are no longer in the first place of interest". From 1908 the works had its own section, after 1915 it became a subsection. Homan van der Heide argued his case in 1914 again in the Welfare Commission and without any result (*Mindere Welvaartscommissie 1914*: 28, see **Chapter 8**).

[35] Meanwhile floods continued to ravage the area: just in 1922 there was one that brought a lot of damage (see National Archives, Ministry of the Colonies, Mail report 1922, no. 841). Elenbaas (1923) found a pretext in this period to once again draw attention to his proposal for a combined Kerjo, Cawak and Lamong reservoir.

[36] At the same time, there were initiatives by the concerned Resident and the Minister of the Colonies to, regardless of the possible resumption of the Solo Works and in anticipation of the decision about this which was not expected soon, establish small irrigation works and create a plan for "economic uplifting" of the region like the improvement plan for the backward parts of Batavia (i.e. the Tangerang area, see **Chapter 9**) (Creutzberg 1974: 37-39). There are several mail reports on these issues to the resumption of the Solo Works and the improvement of the situation in the Solo Valley, see among others National Archives, Ministry of the Colonies, Mail report 1924, no. 2686.

"The great disappointments that have so far characterised the initiation of irrigation projects in the Solo Valley should serve to warn us to exercise the greatest of caution" (Snell 1928: 85-86).

Snell primarily saw the creation of irrigation works in the Solo Valley as "complicated agricultural questions" (p. 86) and so he believed that the agricultural research that had been taking place should be continued. At the end of his speech he reminded everyone of the importance of proper informing, agriculture-wise and of good co-operation between Public Works and the agricultural information service. Finally, he noted that all sorts of small works projects aimed at improving the water situation should be pursued. One of the things he mentioned in this connection was source irrigation. In 1929 the government accepted Snell's proposals (*Encyclopaedie* ["Encyclopedia"] Vol. VIII 1935: 405, Pareau Dumont 1940: A. 76[37]). One of the things this led to was the construction of the Pacal *waduk* that was completed in 1933 (see Lieneman 1931). For the main routes to this reservoir use could be made of "parts of the once dug and still existing main canal remaining from the former 'Solo Valley Works' abandoned in 1898" (*BOW* Archives E VI-27).

Over the course of time the situation in the Solo Valley and also in the Bengawan Jero improved considerably although the drainage of the latter region did remain a problem (see **Figure 7.4**). This was the reason why, towards the end of the colonial period, the Solo plan again became a topic of debate. At a meeting chaired by the Governor of Eastern Java and attended by delegates from the world of agriculture, Public Works, economic affairs and the government which was convened to discuss the improving of irrigation and drainage in the Bengawan Jero region there was at least one important question that was again raised: the matter of digging through to the Java Sea (Pareau Dumont 1940: A. 76, see also Creutzberg 1974: 460).

Finally

The postponed strike

After it had been worked on for five years Cremer, the Minister of the Colonies, put a stop to the irrigation project in the Solo Valley because of the financial miscalculations that had been made. Though the works were not anywhere near completion much of the budgeted sum had been spent (15.4 of the 18.9 million guilders). The indications were that the expenses would far exceed expectations. On top of this, though the available recommendations all indicated that the job should be continued, there was much uncertainty to contend with (further research required!) and many implicit contradictions.

On the face of it, Cremer's decision to put a halt to the project was understandable. He was confronted by what promised to be a considerable overstepping of the budgetary limits and he saw it as his task to prevent this from happening, also because the spendings were not clearly specified. The only question that we, like Van Sandick (1898), can ask here is: why did it take so long to decide to stop? Apart from personal factors (Pierson, Van Houten and their attitude), it would seem to have been, above all else, a question of organisation. Apparently the Civil Public Works Department was incapable of reacting quickly. It is conceivable that it was its hierarchical character that slowed down effective communication: what the lower ranks had known for a long time was not quickly conveyed to the upper echelons (compare De Gelder in *De Ingenieur* 1898: 588-599). The Solo report indicated that procedures had not gone perfectly smoothly but it did not attach any negative conclusions to this concerning the Public Works Organisation, but this was not to be the end of the story (see below).

---

[37] Creutzberg (1972: 89, note 74) reports incorrectly that the irrigation project has been resumed in the Solo Valley in 1926. However, compare Creutzberg (1972: 280-281, note 232).

The terminating of the Solo Works project or, more to the point, the failure to attain the project's objectives, was an important reason why that the objectives of Van Bosse's General Irrigation Plan of 1890 (to see that 577 million *bouws* was supplied with water by means of modern irrigation at a cost of 35½ million guilders) were not achieved. With its 223,000 *bouws* target the Solo project was by far the biggest one of the entire programme (more than four and a half times as big as the second largest project, the Demak Works project). As far as costs were concerned, it was the most expensive project yet: 18.9 million guilders as opposed to the 35½ million for the plan as a whole. The 15.4 million guilders that had been expended in 1898 had not brought the acreage objective a single acre closer and so this could be regarded as wasted money.

In the previous chapter we saw how, after ten years of construction work, the results of the General Irrigation Plan had, for the rest, been disappointing. One of the reasons given for this was the fact that under the Exploitation Politics regime means provision had been sparse. A similar thing could naturally be said of the Solo Works. In a situation where the financial resources for irrigation activities were not endless the Minister obviously felt disinclined to make great extra sums available. Homan van der Heide clearly indicated this when he exonerated Pierson and Public Works of blame for the fiasco in the Solo Valley. To his mind the cause of all the trouble was "the peculiar political inclination to make many plans and to do little or nothing in practice and that, in the case of irrigation works, has been the policy more than ever in the past 6 to 8 years" (1899: 258).[38]

Another reason why irrigation plan outcomes had been disappointing was rentability. The Solo Works had played an important part in such discussions. The matter of rentability had been raised in the past and the Rentability Commission had also existed when the predicted Solo Works overspending problem had been made known to the relevant Indies and Dutch authorities (officially at least). Experience with this project ensured, however, that the financial aspect of projects received extra attention and it made the rentability question extra acute. Paradoxically, though, the disaster in the Solo Valley led to a relaxing of the rentability demands. In the Indies budget of 1901 Minister Cremer based part of his differentiation between productive and non-productive irrigation works on "the gloomy findings made while working on the Solo Valley project" (cited in Van Kol 1901: 365).[39]

---

[38] See also above on the question of responsibility. Homan van der Heide (1899: 256-257) saw behind the cessation an austerity wish: stoppage yielded for 1899 three million guilders. He thought that they had already begun in 1897 by cutting back on the Solo Works by reducing the amount to be processed annually. He saw parallels with other works, among others the Waluh- and Genteng Works in the Pemali-Comal area.

[39] We will see in **Chapter 8** that the Solo works would still affect the profitability issue in another way, namely in the redefinition of this problem in agricultural sense.

Mysteries surrounding the stopping of the project

One of the stated objectives of the Solo Valley Works project had been to improve the lot of the populace. It was notably the inhabitants of the Bengawan Jero region that were in a difficult position. Above all else, the Ethical Policy intended to improve people's welfare which was why a continuation of the project had been defended by trend-setting ethicists such as C.T. van Deventer. In his *Een eereschuld* ("A Debt of Honour") of 1899 he judged the project positively. Even though it would not be instantly effective, because of the high costs, he all the same maintained that the wish to improve "the pitiful existence of thousands of people perpetually threatened by illness and famine" by "re-creating" an "extensive district alternately plagued by drought and floods" and turning it into a "flourishing province" was reason enough to justify the continuation of the project. He furthermore added (1899: 212):

"If a river bursts its banks do we, in our country, allow God's water to flow over God's fields as long as it cannot be proven that the costs of dyke enclosure and drainage will be covered by the tax paid by the inhabitants of the river banks?"

Van Deventer calculated that the debt of honour owed by the Netherlands to the Indies amounted to 200 million guilders[40]. In an election speech he outlined how this sum should be spent. He wanted to spend around 47½ million on a couple of big works, of which:

"27½ million would go on completing the Solo Valley Works (the suspension of which had again exposed innumerable desas and arable land, to which hope had finally been promised after years of desperation, to periodic flooding and periodic drought and which had robbed thousands of local inhabitants and Indo-European individuals of employment) while around 20 million would be spent on building a harbour for Surabaya (Java's second trading city)" (Brooshooft 1901: 126).

Was the Solo project really a humanitarian project? Despite the evocative pretext (raft inhabitants!) it was not purely that. As the history of the plan makes clear, improving the navigational waters of Surabaya was a major factor. When, in the end, the Solo's estuary was only redirected to Ujung Pangkah and it was further decided that the *kali* Miring should be kept open, the basis for the irrigation plan collapsed and the whole thing became indeterminate and vague. The Solo plan did not fit in either with the 1885 stipulations that particularly aimed at improving existing irrigation systems. The altering of the Solo's estuary did not seem to be very successful and it even added to the problems in the Bengawan Jero. This instigated renewed interest in the big project, made possible by the abandoning of priorities with regard to the irrigation efforts of 1885. When the project had started up in 1893 there had been at least two main objectives: to improve the situation in the Solo Valley, notably in the Bengawan Jero region, and to improve access to the harbour of Surabaya. The project did therefore have a humanitarian background which was partly to be addressed by altering the course of the Solo but there were also other, economic, interests as well. [41]

[40] The amount claimed by Brooshooft (1901: 125). Compare with Van Deventer (1899: 229) who mentioned 187 million guilders, but without any interest rates.

[41] Actually we saw in the quote from Van Deventer that he also wanted to make money available for a project to improve the port of Surabaya itself. As the second sale city this harbour also served an ethical concern for him.

As we have already seen, the Ethical Policy was executed along the lines laid down by Van Deventer and money was made available for non-profit-making irrigation works. This did not help to speed things up but ultimately almost all the projects emanating from the Van Bosse plan would reach completion around the year 1920 (see **Table 6.1**, see also, for example, Hasselman 1914: 59). The Solo Works project was, after all, abandoned. In this respect Van Deventer did not get his way (compare De Kat Angelino 1929: 335-336). Why not? Van Doorn (1994: 150) maintained that his views had weak foundations:

"Naturally Van Deventer, and after him Brooshooft, advocated that the suspended Solo Valley project should be continued but anyone who compares their noncommittal opinions with those voiced in the actual discussions in public works engineers' circles cannot but conclude that it was good intentions rather than knowledge of matters that dictated their positive point of view".

If we examine the "actual discussions in public works engineers' circles", however, then we can see that, like the ethicists, the people with the technical know-how were of the opinion that the project should be continued and not even for ethical reasons. The Solo Commission which a Minister appointed after the project had been suspended came, after thorough investigation, to a positive conclusion, also from an economics point of view. The Commission members were of the unanimous opinion that the works were technically sound and also, apart from in the case of one member, that rentability was guaranteed. Despite the importance of the project to the local population, its technological feasibility and the fact that it would earn back the money expended on it Minister Idenburg decided, in 1903, to put a definite stop to it all. The question is, why did he do this?

The Solo Commission had unanimously established what its technical recommendations would be but this "unity of votes" was a little false. The Commission was divided on the matter of the diverting of the Solo river and on other main issues. De Meyier wanted to use the *kali* Miring again for the Solo estuary while the others were in favour of digging as far as the Java Sea. The compromise was to call for further research. On other matters the unanimity gave only a random indication of views. De Meyier had previously had his doubts about designing a weir that would have to force water up eight metres. Within the Commission he temporarily held his tongue on this matter but he admitted to finding other ideas, like the creation of a 165-kilometre-long canal, risky. With him clear technical objections were also to arise later. However, unlike in 1898 when the Minister's recommendations revealed technical contradictions, the recommendations of the Commission were absolutely positive. That, then, could not have been the problem. One important point included in the (financial-)economic considerations of the dissident De Meyier had to do with the Bengawan Jero. The "desperate" nature of the lot of the people in this area had created a convincing case in favour of the project. De Meyier could not find any justification for setting up a project costing millions that would extend over the entire Solo Valley. Liefrinck, the Inspector of Cultures, had raised the same objection once before. Despite his financial misgivings he had actually had fewer problems with the anticipated yield increase, unlike De Meyier[42]. The Civil Public Works Director furthermore found that the works were too much of a drain on the budget. The engineering community supported the Commission's (majority) recommendations. De Meyier came to stand alone (also where his attitude towards the river diversion was concerned), the only ones who supported him were Elenbaas, who was his subordinate, and Van Kol. In the end, the Minister followed the minority view put forward by De Meyier, but not blindly. The arguments put by De Meyier definitely played a part in the considerations of Minister Idenburg but they did not constitute the entire reason for his deciding to drop the project.

[42] As mentioned, a previous Inspector of Cultures, Sollewijn Gelpke, following an earlier plan, also had problems with the estimated revenue increase.

It is conceivable that the lack of consensus was what led the government to postpone its decision. The time factor did at least contribute to the negative outcome[43]. After 1900 new objections to the works were raised. One stumbling block was, for instance, the diminishing rice harvest in the Kening area where Pierson had commenced irrigation activities. Apart from not helping the construction engineer's reputation this also fed all the pessimistic estimates relating to expected yield increases. Another (according to De Meyier [1902] related) objection was that the silt would not be able to reach the distant fields. A third problem was that regulating agricultural matters would be difficult. It was notably the last two doubts that were to play an important part in the decision-making process. These problems were branded "technical" (see, for example, *De Ingenieur* 1904: 867) but that only partly covered the issue. The problem of having too little silt was clearly one of an agricultural (or agricultural-economic) nature. De Meyier did not make this point all that clear in the Solo report (only implicitly in conjunction with the minimally increased yields for modern irrigation facilities) but he did underline it in his 1902 article. The second objection brought forward by the Minister in 1903 was likewise of an agricultural nature though it was, strictly speaking, a problem of control: that of how to plan and co-ordinate agricultural activities in such a huge area. It was De Meyier who then paved the way for yet another argument. Elenbaas who, up until 1901, had worked under him developed a small-scale improvement plan for the Bengawan Jero. In 1903 this seemed like a cheap and effective alternative to the big plan. It was an alternative that certainly would have corresponded with the ethical intentions of Minister Idenburg who was, after all, a confirmed ethicist (Van Doorn 1994: 149)!

In 1905 it became apparent that it would not be necessary to change the river's course. As has just been mentioned the irrigation programme derived – in historical terms – from the plan to re-route the river. In the year 1893 the Solo Valley project was presented as an integrated project. In its recommendations to resume the irrigation project the Solo Commission ventured to do the following: it differentiated between the irrigation side and the river re-coursing side of the job and only gave the first part of the job its approval![44] Nevertheless, with a view to the historical situation, it is not unthinkable that the wider irrigation plan was even more rapidly abandoned when the navigational waters of Surabaya no longer gave rise to the need for drastic measures.[45]

For the engineers things were not over in 1903, especially since the decision to halt plans had really seemed to leave matters open. Even though, by 1905, river diversion seemed to be superfluous the entire plan was revived by Homan van der Heide. But here also the adage 'tomorrow never comes' could be applied. The policy adopted of making small improvements, creating *waduks* and carrying out agricultural research was, at that moment, effective enough in order to play for time. A decade later the plan once again became topical, this time without the river re-coursing permutation. The rate of progress was, again, reason enough to allow things to

[43] For the postponement (and subsequently cancellation) personal factors can be identified as well: in 1901, T.A.J. van Asch van Wijk succeeded Cremer as Minister of the Colonies, but he died in 1902, after which Idenburg took office as Minister. Before his death Asch van Wijk had asked Leemans and Kraus if they were willing to make a bill to resume the Solo Works. Telders was already deceased. When the Minister also died, he still had not received a reply. Whether that answer has yet come, is not known, but under Minister Idenburg that was irrelevant anyway. (*Minister* 1902: 707; see for the enthusiasm of Van Asch van Wijk for a "substantial" approach to irrigation Creutzberg 1972: 280).

[44] By focusing only on the Bengawan Jero De Meyier went a step further in subdividing the works. The diversion of the Solo river took on, through the detachment from the entire project, like the irrigation part, an "independent existence" (Schalij 1903).

[45] We can even go a step further and, in accordance with the state of affairs before 1900, claim that the doubts over the river diversion already put into question the irrigation project (cf. Quant 1899: 418).

come to a standstill. The possible diversion of the Solo was something that was finally to be raised again at the end of the colonial period!

We may thus conclude that De Meyier had had an important part to play in the whole Solo Valley Works decision-making process. In word and deed he had mounted a true crusade against the Solo Works. Even after his retirement from the position of Civil Public Works Director, in 1901, he waged an unending battle against the works as is evidenced by his numerous publications on the issue. In this connection his biographer wrote the following:

"With respect to the irrigation works De Meyier's point of view remained perpetually enigmatic. ... From his numerous publications on the matter one is forced to conclude that, for him, these works constituted a favourite topic of study. When it came to the relevant executing of the tasks his satisfaction was, however, generally much less.
... De Meyier felt little for constructing major irrigation works ... Regarding the economic viability of the works in a country like Java, with such high rainfall levels, he was ... rather skeptical" (Melchior 1914: 89)[46].

What one may question is why the Minister was prepared to take De Meyier's (deviant) views so seriously. What should also be questioned is why new agricultural objections had been raised. These are issues that will be examined in the next chapter.

A crisis situation

In his inaugural lecture, given in Delft, Lamminga sought an explanation for the minimal progress in the field of irrigation. The structural explanations he gave were: lack of funds, poor weather conditions and a shortage of manual labourers. On the other hand, though, he maintained that the Public Works Organisation had too few employees and that it was badly organised. To his mind what caused the bottleneck problem was the labour-intensive design work for which too few people were available. Regarding the relevant organisation he wrote (1910: 13):

"A section-engineer draughts a design that is first of all assessed by a division manager. After that it is passed on to the Civil Public Works Department in Batavia where it is assessed anew and often criticised. The consequence is: back to the drawing board and, sometimes, to the same results".

Ten years previously Lamminga (1900) had brought before the Public Works Organisation his suggestions for improvements. Apart from being responsible for irrigation projects Public Works was also in charge of various other sorts of jobs like the constructing of roads, bridges and buildings. The Divisions for all such activities fell under the supervision of the Civil Public Works Director. What Lamminga really wanted to do was to set up a central body within the Civil Public Works Department that would be responsible for irrigation matters. What came to mind was the Irrigation Brigade of the day (see **Chapter 6, Note 8**). Lamminga also proposed that the Public Works Divisions should be reinforced.

The slow preparation process that characterised most projects did not apply in the case of the Solo Works. Since Pierson was on good terms with the Minister resolutions could be pushed through quickly.[47] Yet, despite this, the project reflected organisational deficiencies, notably

[46] De Meyier was of an older generation than many engineers, like Homan van der Heide, who were for the resumption of the Solo Works. Possible that this "generation gap" played a role in the forming of opinion. (G. de Jager, personal communication, September 1996).

[47] Compare the conduct of De Bruyn and the political support from Rochussen and Loudon this produced (see

when it came to acting quickly and efficiently. The speed of progress and the functioning of the Public Works Organisation were issues that were raised in the discussion on responsibility for why the Solo Works project had got so out of hand financially. The conflict was only worsened by the Solo Commission which dealt out a few stealthy blows to various individuals (notably Pierson) but which further glossed over everything. In the final assessment Public Works was freed of blame. The corps was, on the contrary, held in high esteem both technically and morally. This issue was, however, to have a sequel.

In spite of all the Commission's claims, confidence in Public Works had been seriously shaken. In retrospect Ott de Vries (1936: A. 270) summed up the situation with the familiar utterance: faith arrives on foot but leaves by horseback. Weijs (1913: 19) spoke of a heavy blow for Public Works: "Heavily weighed down by it all mechanical interference in irrigation matters continued for a while but confidence in its ability was deeply shaken". Van Sandick (1898a: 5) finally expressed similar sentiments and spoke of the "worrying wound" inflicted on irrigation affairs by the Solo Works, a wound that "might even bleed it to death". The consequences were also felt. In spite of its overall positive assessment of the activities of Public Works, the Minister, Cremer, ordered the Commission to put forward proposals to reorganise the Department. This advice did not become public knowledge. On various occasions Van Sandick pressed for views to be made public, especially because in a couple of the suggestions he saw signs that the pre-1885 situation might be returned to (Van Sandick 1901: 537). How would it all end? Technology could not escape from shaken confidence either. According to Weijs (1913: 18-19) the Solo Works cast a "dark shadow" over the success of the involvement of engineers in irrigation activities. This required reorientation. More of the same thing in the form of a resumption of the project was out of the question. So, what should then be done? While the tackling of irrigation works was in a state of crisis, the Ethical Policy was making ample funds available: this was an acute problem. These questions (and also the matter of Lamminga's reorganisation proposals) will be returned to in **Chapter 8**.

Where Lamminga had been successful Pierson had failed. Had Pierson succeeded in his mission he would undoubtedly have been *the* founder of modern irrigation technology in the Indies. However, as it was, he was unable to control spending and, according to some critics, made a thorough mess of things. This did not exactly guarantee him a position in the hall of fame. On the contrary, Pierson was to create a black page in history. All the Solo Commission's work had been to no avail: the project was reinstated but the designer/contractor was not. The question that remains is, why was it that the project was not continued even after it had be thoroughly investigated, improved upon and economically justified by the Commission? De Meyier saw his efforts rewarded even though in 1903 agricultural arguments predominated. Whether or not the right decisions had been made remained a moot point but the project was stopped for good, despite continuing discussions about it.

In 1885 the irrigation engineers had set about work enthusiastically under what was, for them, a favourable ruling. In the wake of the rentability question their power had been somewhat reduced. This slowed them down but it did nothing more than that. By absolutely damping the high expectations of engineers the Solo Valley Works gave rise to change. While rentability had somehow helped engineers to get their feet back firmly on the ground the Solo Works had swept the ground from under their feet. Their inability to satisfactorily round off this project had shaken their confidence. For the outside world these events were a sign that the attention paid to rentability had been justified and also that the steps that had been taken to slightly tone down the ambitions of engineers had been insufficient. Among engineers this freedom had led to giantism and megalomania (see in this connection the opening quotation of **Chapter 8**). After the prestige

Chapter 4). The so-called coolie deficit, which Lamminga turned down as a structural explanation, was, however, a substantial problem in the Solo Works: it drove the cost up.

gained by engineers in previous years a relapse was now occurring. This could well have consequences for the balance of power between Civil Service and Civil Public Works. The rentability question had given the administrators some reprieve but now all the conditions were right for them to gain the upper hand. Even though it seemed to be an obvious corollary, the ripple effect in the power game would only be partly felt. The emancipation process of the engineers in relation to that of the administrators could not be reversed or, to put it another way, the decline of the administrators was inevitable. Other relationships developed, however, in which the curtailing of engineers was just as prevalent.

To understand exactly why the Solo Works project was halted one needs to look more closely at Ethical Policy. That will be done in the following chapter. What will also become clear will be the effect that the engineers' Solo activities had on their position as a whole and how irrigation matters in fact further developed.

8

'An inseparable companion of agriculture, welfare and progress'

Involvement in irrigation as teamwork

> If technics is to be brought back into the service of human culture, the path of advance will lead, not to the further expansion of the Megamachine, but to the development of all those parts of the organic environment and the human personality that have been suppressed in order to magnify the offices of pure intelligence alone and therewith to maximize its coercive collective enterprise and quantitative productivity (Mumford 1972: 213-214).

In 1903, at the highpoint of the Solo drama, the civil servant C.E. Bodemeijer stood up for the sake of engineering involvement in irrigation (Bodemeijer 1903). It had not always been that way! Between 1896 and 1898 Bodemeijer had been Controller in Geding (Kraksaan), the area within which the Pekalen Works fell and from 1900 until the end of 1901 he had been the Assistant-Resident of Tuban where the Kening Works were situated. He found it important to express his opinions on both these works

"especially now that in recent times it is becoming fashionable to cast aspersions on the usefulness of irrigation works created by experts, though – I am given to understand – everywhere else in the civilised world such usefulness is not doubted for a minute" (p. 204.).

He indicated that because of the professional supervision the Pemali Works had not given rise to problems. This was, he maintained, "a blessing that cannot be valued enough" (1903: 205).[1]

Bodemeijer gave the irrigation engineers encouragement and, in 1903, that was something they badly needed because, as we saw in the previous chapter, 1903 was nothing less than a disaster year for them. It was the year when the decision was taken to abandon the Solo Valley project, thus confirming its failure. Subsequently everything: the relevant technology, the organization of Public Works and the irrigation policy was disrupted. What had played an important part in the discussion was the matter of the declining paddy harvests in the Kening area which had received a modern irrigation system – made by Pierson – before the Solo Works had been started on. It was good to hear from Bodemeijer, precisely because he was a civil servant, that part of the blame for that could be placed on the local population. The only thing

[1] Neglect of the drains as cause of the declining rice harvest was earlier suggested by Van Sandick in an article in the newspaper *De Locomotief* ("The Locomotive"; dated November 6, 1903). Bodemeijer could confirm that from personal experience and, consequently, found that Van Sandick hit "the nail on the head" (1903: 204). We have seen that Thal Larsen rebutted De Meyier similarly. He thereby also cited Bodemeijer (1903).

that the engineers could be criticised for was for not having paid more attention to technical control. In the Kening area where there was water in excess water regulation, unlike in the Pekalen area where every drop counted, was not the obvious solution. But this was a mistake that could be rectified.[2]

Bodemeijer's "irrigation talk" went down well with engineers but it also fitted in well with current discussions in engineering and other circles where, around 1900, a general debate on modern irrigation was raging, partly because of the Solo Works issue. The central question was: what should be done? Clearly a new approach was needed. This chapter will reveal exactly what did happen. We shall see that the new policy contained elements that had been introduced by Bodemeijer, namely that much attention should be paid to control and to adopting agriculturally sound approaches.

As we saw in **Chapter 6**, round the turn of the century the rentability question had reduced the independence of engineers and given back the Civil Service a certain degree of power. We also saw that the administration had retained an important say in the management side even though this influence was of a technical nature. The new era brought with it a third category of people involved in irrigation activities: agriculturalists. This chapter will examine this facet and look into the implications that this had for irrigation policy. Considerations relating to the Solo Works will also be pursued. Ultimately we shall try to understand better why things were as they were. In the previous chapter it became apparent that the project itself offered too few leads for such considerations as did the Ethical Policy insofar as that was discussed. Many people who knew what they were talking about found the project technically, economically and ethically sound. In conjunction with the decision not to resume the project one factor was hinted at, namely, agricultural objections but why this should have been such a major factor did not become clear. This chapter will take a closer look at state formation developments in the Indies after 1900 in an endeavour to provide a more plausible explanation. We shall also study the repercussions of the trauma of stopping the project, for irrigation in general and for the state, and we shall examine the consequences attached to this.

---

[2] *De Ingenieur* ("The Engineer") had taken over the article by Bodemeijer from the *Tijdschrift voor het Binnenlandsch Bestuur* ("Magazine for the Civil Service", 26: 24-30). The problems in the Kening area were solved by improving maintenance and management, the latter by introducing the Pemali scheme (*Verslag BOW* ["Civil Public Works Report"] 1905: 162-164, see also *Verslag BOW* 1906: 165, 1907: 169-170). But that was obviously not sufficient, witness De Meyier (1912) (see **Chapter 7**).

Figure 8.1: The Technical College in Delft, around 1900 (photo National Archives)

Figure 8.2: The Technical College in Bandung, 1929 (photo Collection Museum of the Tropics)

The (lesser) welfare state

Striking an irrigation policy balance

In his speech given to the Utrecht division of the *Maatschappij tot nut van den Javaan* ("Company for the Benefit of the Javanese"; see **Chapter 4**) De Bruyn, the second Civil Public Works Department Director, was absolutely confident about the future where the intervention of engineers in irrigation was concerned:

"I hope ... that I have succeeded in ... demonstrating to you ... in broad outline the road that has to be followed if, in conjunction with the important relevant Agricultural law [of De Waal, WR] and illuminated by science and experience which is, in other words, the most appropriate and economic road to follow, any systematic large-scale improving and expanding of irrigation in Java which can lead to such rewards of wealth is to be achieved.
The outcome will only augment Dutch fame and fortune but, first and foremost it will: stimulate everywhere peace and calm and welfare and be of benefit to the Javanese" (1870: 52).

Around 1900 the outcome was in actual fact different from that predicted, or hoped for, by De Bruyn. The building of new works had in fact come to be associated with disappointment, disaster and shaken confidence. That was because of the Solo Valley but not only because of that. Around the year 1900 there were other setbacks that the engineers had to contend with.

In the first place what became evident was that little had been achieved: 67½ thousand *bouws* which, by 1900, had been provided with modern irrigation facilities in conjunction with the General Irrigation Plan was not a very impressive result. In that year the total agricultural area was 4.2 million *bouws* of which 1.8 million were irrigated, chiefly by means of Javanese methods (according to Happé (1939), by 1900 100 thousand *bouws* had modern irrigation systems). In the second place, modern irrigation was not always a guarantee for improved welfare. In the Pemali Plains the engineers had laid the foundations for a flourishing economy but that was not the case everywhere. It was not the case in the Kening area, for instance. But things could get even worse. Around 1900 famine again broke out in the Demak and Grobogan regions, despite the fact that a weir had been built in Glapan and the Demak Works had been created!

If we view modern irrigation in its wider perspective, taking into account the agricultural and population developments of the time, then we can gain a better grasp of its significance[3]. Between 1870 and 1900 the area of agricultural land irrigated expanded enormously, in fact it increased by nearly half a million *bouws* (going from 1.4 to 1.8 million *bouws*). This was a trend that remained apparent throughout that period. Before 1885 such expansion could almost only be the result of efforts undertaken by the local population because it was only after that date that the engineers really came into the picture. The results of their efforts were, however, limited: by 1900 only a couple of projects had been completed. That meant that in the post-1885 period the process of extending the irrigated acreage was something that likewise must have been achieved chiefly by Javanese means. A portion of the modern irrigation systems actually replaced the Javanese systems. It could therefore only be claimed that a contribution was being made to raising productivity. As far as improvement was concerned, taking into account irrigated and non-irrigated land, this was minimal and it could just as well have been put down to agricultural

---

[3] I base myself on some research into the colonial records, the results of which can be found in **Appendices K and L**. My data reach to 1910, but for my argument here I use them only for the period until 1900. I am well aware that a more detailed study would be possible, e.g. based on the reports of the welfare investigation (*Mindere Welvaartscommissie* ["Lesser Welfare Commission"]1905-14).

intensification – including increased labour levels. In the relevant period rice production rose by 70% (going from over 46 to over 78 million *pikols*). Apart from the fact that the area irrigated had increased and productivity had risen, this increase was largely due to the cultivation of non-irrigated land areas. The influence of modern irrigation could therefore also be said to have been of little significance, in fact it was more minimal than extending of the irrigated area!

Consequently, it is possible to deduce from data on land cultivation development and harvest improvement that right across the board irrigation efforts did little to influence the agricultural situation between 1870 and 1900. Together with statistics on population growth[4] this does not give us a particularly rosy picture of the population's economic development.

Sugar versus rice

Despite the sugar crisis of 1884 and the *sereh* illness outbreak, things did not go all that badly in the 1870-1900 period as far as sugar production was concerned. From Gonggrijp's 1957 figures it is evident that there was a big increase in acreage and in the production level per *bouw* (see **Appendix M**). Considering how minimal the expansion in modern irrigation facilities had been the rise in sugar production, notably as far as the average yield per *bouw* was concerned, was rather surprising. The rise in production derived chiefly from the improved cultivation methods achieved thanks to the experimental stations.

The effect that the sugar industry was having on small farming was becoming a point of concern (see **Figures 8.3-8.7**). As we have seen, irrigation works were being introduced to regions where the sugar industry had been established (like in the Sampean and Pemali areas) but that was not the only thing that was happening: Van Bosse's General Irrigation Plan also provided works that were solely designed for the local population (like, for instance, in Demak). Moreover it was never only the sugar industry that benefited from irrigation: sugar cane and rice crops were grown in rotation on the same *sawas*. But there were problems.

The claims made by the sugar refineries to land rented from local inhabitants were greater than official figures indicated. The land area devoted to sugar cane cultivation was several times greater than was deducible from the figures, partly because cane crops extended over more than a year and partly because of the three year rotation system (see *Encyclopaedie* ["Encyclopedia"] Vol. IV 1921: 180, and also Alexander and Alexander 1978). There was furthermore evidence that because of the long sugar cane cycles the population was having to resort to cultivating shorter growth period, inferior varieties of rice (as emphasized by De Meyier in the Solo report, see **Chapter** 7). As was pointed out in **Chapter 6**, another problem surrounding the sugar industry was that of management. The various water regulations (the Pateguan, the Pekalen and the Pemali rulings) did not vary as far as allocating water to sugar cane or rice crop cultivation was concerned which did not mean to say that there was no discrepancy between the two. When it came to receiving water the sugar industry often took priority. As has already been pointed out, unlike with the construction of irrigation works, when it came to creating irrigation sectors there was a clear bias in favour of the sugar industry. Another common practice was the day and night arrangement ensuring that sugar cane received water supplies in the daytime and rice crops at night-time. Even though the new regulations modified the day and night ruling this still remained a point of contention.

[4] In the period 1880-1905 the population grew by 54% (from 19,794,505 to 30,360,667 souls) (Gonggrijp 1957: 125). Spread over 30 years (as the period from 1870 to 1900), this amounts to 64%, slightly less than the increase in rice yield. However, the increase in production in the period 1880-1905 was only 21%! Production per capita thereby fell from 3.12 to 2.46 *pikols*. More demographics for Java in Boomgaard (1991 and 1980).

Diminished affluence

Towards the end of the nineteenth century people began to realise that standards of living were worsening for the Javanese. Colonial exploitation came in for heavy criticism and pleas were heard for restitution. Van Deventer's 1899 *Een eereschuld* ("A Debt of Honour") became the most famous plea. The impact of this tract on colonial policy was comparable to that of the *Max Havelaar* lobby of the writer Multatuli (1860, see **Chapter 4**, **Note 9**). The matter of refunding was something that had already been championed by Domela Nieuwenhuis in 1888 and again, ten years later, by Van Kol (Gonggrijp 1957: 185). Due to the famine in Demak, the general drop in living standards and the various pleas for policy changes in favour of the population, from the protective political measures introduced by the state when it withdrew from economic life to make way for the private sector, something known as the Ethical Policy was able to develop.

As far as the Dutch government was concerned (according to *Encyclopaedie* Vol. I 1917: 581) the fall in living standards and, not least, renewed famine in Demak was reason enough to initiate a new investigation into "diminished welfare" among the people of Java and Madura. These plans were announced by Queen Wilhelmina in 1901 in her opening of parliament speech, together with plans to amend colonial policy. The welfare investigation was to continue until 1914 when it was rounded off with a report produced by the responsible commission. The report contained information on welfare standards in Java and Madura, it put forward the Welfare Commission's proposals and resolutions and, finally, it expressed what it believed had led to the fall in standards of living. The report consisted of twelve sections (or volumes) broken down into 45 sub-reports. Apart from the findings already mentioned there were findings on fisheries and fishing, poultry farming, cattle farming, transport, agriculture, trade and industry, irrigation, law-enforcement and the police and on the economy of the *desa*. In conjunction with irrigation three reports came out in the 1907-1910 period, one of which provided an overview (*Mindere Welvaartscommissie* ["Lesser Welfare Commission"] 1905-1914, 1910). The relationship between the sugar industry and small farming was discussed in the overview and also in the report section on agriculture (*Mindere Welvaartscommissie* 1908).[5]

The reasons for diminished wealth or, for the economic predicament of the Javanese which was bad when compared to that of other groups such as the Europeans and "Strange Peoples from the East" (*Vreemde Oosterlingen*), like the Chinese, was generally sought in areas such as climate, the character of the people and colonial policy. The worsened standard of living was put down to population expansion, to the Exploitation Policy and to the sugar industry crisis but also, for instance, to the advance pay system, to lack of co-operation between labourers and those who rented land and to the siphoning off of profits in the private industry sector. (Gonggrijp 1957: 177-180; see for an overview of the outcomes Hasselman 1914). In terms of policy advice the welfare investigation only reinforced the path that had been followed since 1900. What was that policy? We have seen that the Ethical Policy brought with it financial changes: the abolition of the Exploitation Policy, but there was more.

[5] The sugar culture, esp. in relation to the agricultural population, also was topic of study outside the welfare research, see Van Rees and De Graaff (1900 and 1907).

The promotion of small farming

After a career in government, including a period within the Means and Domains Directorate, K.F. Holle decided, in 1856, to go into the tea business. He first became administrator in a tea company but later he started up his own company. He was seriously concerned about the lot of the Javanese and so, in an endeavour to improve matters, he started doing agricultural experiments. He carried out tests with rice and thus developed improved cultivation methods. He also did tests with other unfamiliar crops. The government saw something in the work of Holle and so it supported him and, in return, Holle proved himself as an "honorary advisor" to the government. From 1875 onwards local civil servants were involved in the task of helping to improve rice growing in Java. Much experimentation continued and seed was even used from the Buitenzorg Plant Centre established in 1817. In 1896 the government decided to cultivate some eight experimental fields under the auspices of the Plant Centre. (Van Deventer 1904: 225-227, see also Van Kesteren 1896).[6]

In 1905 these developments led to the establishment of the Department of Agriculture, Trade and Industry which was established for the express purpose of promoting agriculture in Java. Its main task was: "to devise plans which would lead to permanent more satisfactory results for inland agriculture" (Explanatory Memorandum accompanying the bill relating to the introduction of the agricultural department, cited in *Mededeelingen* ["Announcements"] 1924: 288).

The Department's first Director was Dr. M. Treub (1905-1909). The Plant Centre was a part of the Department. Just as had been the case in the past, for sugar, an experimental station was set up, in 1908, this time for rice and second crops. In 1911, at the instigation of the Department's second Director, Dr. H.J. Lovink (1909-1918) the *Voorlichtingdienst van den Inlandschen Landbouw* ("Information Service Centre for Inland Agriculture") was set up. Agricultural education developed as a corollary. (See, for example, De Vries 1961: 273-276).

The Ethical Policy was oriented towards the interests of the Javanese people. But how was that to be realised? Van Deventer, the Ethical Policy pioneer, proposed that a financial reimbursement of 200 million guilders should be made. Half of that sum would be sufficient to clear the Indies of two loans. The remainder could be put towards improving the country's prosperity. As was pointed out in the previous chapter, he had in mind two projects, one of which was the Solo project. It was proposed that the remaining 50 million guilders should be spent on:

"establishing state agricultural credit banks and financing irrigation works, insofar as that cannot be financed from loans or through the usual channels, continuing with the cadastral estimates for the levying of land rent, extending the telegraph network for the outer parts – and, as soon as such measures lead to economic improvement or the direct benefits increase: organising coffee-growing so that labourers can receive better wages for their work (as far as I can see this is one of the *most urgent* matters), lowering the postal and telegraph tariffs, in a word, pursuing the reform work by ploughing back into it the money obtained from it" (Brooshooft 1901: 126).

Although there was no question of refunding, financial support did flow into the colony. That occurred within the framework of an extensive welfare promotion programme launched in the Indies by the Dutch government. Van Deventer was the chief architect of this programme. As was evident from his restitution proposal, he gave high priority to irrigation works. He also maintained that in view of the fact that the population was rapidly increasing, it would be important to encourage Javanese migration to the Outlying Regions. A third idea he had was to stimulate education so that the population would ultimately be more equipped to protect its own

[6] One of the fields was in the Pemali area (Voorduin 1914: 117).

interests. This threesome: irrigation, migration and education was to form the basis of the welfare policy. (De Kat Angelino 1929: 335 onwards). In all of this there was one factor that remained unmentioned and that was agriculture although, from the above quotation and from other passages, (see, for instance, 1904: 219) it is obvious that Van Deventer was aware of the importance of this. (See also for the ethical direction followed Brooshooft 1901).

In view of the fact that the people had become less prosperous, stimulating agriculture was the most important issue. The central welfare programme points enumerated by Van Doorn (1994a: 149) were general education, providing agricultural information and education, issuing credit and forming co-operatives and irrigation. He furthermore (1994a: 163) maintained that the Agricultural Department symbolised the Ethical Policy.

Emancipation

Apart from abolishing the Exploitation Policy and setting up an extensive welfare programme there was a third central aspect to The Ethical Policy: the emancipation of the Javanese population. Here, education was of central importance. Through wider access to education the population would be able to play a greater part in governmental affairs for instance in the fields of administration, justice and technological employment. Alongside of such "administrative emancipation", people's participation in general affairs would be increased. (*Encyclopaedie* Vol. II 1918: 418). What came to be known as emancipation politics was something that had emerged after dozens of years of discussions (see, for instance, Post 1879: 149). The main concern was to find ways of filling the administrative vacuum that had been created between Javanese villages and the state by establishing bodies rather like Provinces in the Netherlands. All of this was finally to be settled in the indies through what was known as decentralization. In 1903 the government ruling pertaining to this had a further three articles added to it. Starting in 1905, local and regional boards were created which gave local inhabitants (the Javanese included) a certain degree of access to local authorities. This related to local councils and other local jurisdictions and regions. Contrary to what had been intended, self-government did not get off the ground: government duties remained in the hands of civil servants. (*Encyclopaedie* Vol. I 1917: 574-576)[7].

Ultimately the Ethical Policy and the political aspirations of the Indies population which had evolved because of this new policy, led to the installation of the *Volksraad* (People's Council), in 1916. The relevant government ruling was accordingly amended. The People's Council would uphold the interests of the Indies. Initially it was suggested that the old Indies Council (see **Chapter 4**) could be expanded by introducing "private parties", later "inhabitants" (Dutch people, "Strangers from the East" and Natives). In the end it was decided that a separate representative body should be established. The Governor-General was able to consult this body and, indeed, he was obliged to do so when determining the Indies budget and other important financial affairs. There had to be at least 39 members, a quarter of whom had to be Javanese while the remainder were European or strange easterners. The chairman was appointed by the Crown, half of the remaining members were appointed by the Governor-General and the other half were appointed by the local and regional councils referred to above. The Council convened once every two years. (*Encyclopaedie* Vol. IV 1921: 612-623, see also *Mededeelingen* 1924: 47-70).

[7] There were also other forms of decentralization, such as the passing of power from higher to lower levels within the administrative apparatus (including Javanese municipalities) and the education of "self-governing regions" and "region funds" (see *Encyclopaedie* Vol. I, 1917: 574-576).

Modern imperialism

The Ethical Policy put an end to the Exploitation Policy and therefore also to state exploitation. Unlike the people's standard of living which had suffered under the new conditions, it seemed that the free enterprise approach to production – possible from 1870 onwards – flourished. As was indicated in **Chapter 6**, the government had resolved to be supportive of this drive to develop private initiative, also in the sugar industry and, under The Ethical Policy, that is what happened. Apart from anything else, this meant that the government remained active in the field of infrastructural works.

The Department for Government Companies, established in 1907, was devoted to the cause of improving infrastructure. This Department occupied itself with post, telegraph and telephone matters and, in 1909, rail and tram transport was added to the list. Before that, though, transport had been a Civil Public Works Department policy area catered for by a more or less independent division. In setting up the Department for Government Companies the state was again taking economic tasks upon itself and, according to Van Doorn (1994a: 163), the formation of this Department did indeed stand for "regained belief in the importance of state exploitation". On the whole, the state stuck to the imperialist course first established in 1870 and followed since then. All of this was borne out in the drive to improve infrastructure and typical "ethical" measures, such as the resolution to stimulate education, in no way conflicted with this. Education for the populace was something that facilitated emancipation but, as well as that, it constituted a conscious policy to "westernise" in conjunction with further state and economic developments. The Ethical Policy was a double-edged sword: a welfare development instrument but also an instrument of modern imperialism. (Van 't Veer 1980a, see also Van 't Veer 1980b: 20-21).[8]

A service amongst services

Van Kol's general irrigation plan

"There is ... no alternative", asserted Van Kol (1901: 342) in his plea for a new general irrigation plan, "decisive action must be taken where irrigation advancement is concerned if growing problems are to be halted". Van Kol was an inspired man. When he was prevented from further pursuing his career as an engineer in the Indies (he had, for instance, been involved in the Sampean and the Pemali Works, see **Chapters 3 and 5**) he went into politics. Between 1897 and 1909 he served as a member of parliament in the Dutch Social Democratic Workers' Party. During that period he became heavily involved in irrigation affairs, partly by advocating that a new general irrigation plan should be introduced. (See for details of Van Kol's life Van Sandick 1926)[9].

[8] The rise of the Ethical Policy was accompanied by a process of "external" state formation (see **Chapter 2**), esp. by the "conquest" of Aceh by Van Heutsz (1898-1904). Van Heutsz became in 1904 Governor-General. He stood for order and security in the belief that these were conditions for development and prosperity increase. In his thinking the "imperialist" Van Heutsz was close to the notorious "ethicist" Dr. C. Snouck, Islam scholar and adviser to the government. (See Gonggrijp 1957: 197, Van 't Veer 1980a: 186 ff.; see for the Ethical Policy still De Jong 1989).

[9] Van Kol studied at the Polytechnic College in Delft (1871-1876) at the time of the famous "red" Professor B.H.. Pekelharing. The latter immediately became honorary president of the Student Debating Club after his appointment in 1874. In the same year Van Kol became chairman of this dispute, "in which at that time ideas described as subversive were proclaimed" (Van Sandick 1926: 1025, Van Sandick was secretary of the club). Because of his socialist ideas Van Kol missed out on an Indies scholarship (not Van Sandick, see Ott de Vries 1933: 82; see for the scheme **Chapter 4**, **Note 23**). A controversial aspect of Van Kol's reputation is the fact that "to make money for a good cause" (Charité et al. 1989: 347) he bought a coffee plantation in East Java with money he borrowed from Domela Nieuwenhuis, a founder of the socialist movement in the Netherlands. Van

Van Kol presented his plan to an assembly of the Dutch Institute of Engineers (on 9th April 1901). His standpoint was "the pitiful situation of the Javanese population" and he asserted that if this state of affairs was going to be improved then it would in the first place be necessary to pay attention to "resolving what was surely the biggest secret, if not the only one, in order to provide those millions with prosperity" namely "by providing that country with a decent irrigation system" (1901: 341). That was something that had not been achieved with Van Bosse's General Irrigation Plan. Van Kol pointed out that only a fifth of those plans had been completed (p. 346)[10]. As well as wishing to improve the lot of the Javanese there was one other reason why Van Kol wanted to create an irrigation plan. He also did it

"in order to dispel a kind of limited confidence – so that there would not be evidence of the lack of confidence – which had arisen in conjunction with irrigation works since the time of the Solo Works disaster" (p. 341).

Though this was quite unnecessary, Van Kol once again listed all the advantages of having good irrigation facilities. The assets for the Javanese were: production increases, reducing the failed harvest level, decreasing illnesses, enabling people to choose the best time to grow and the best varieties to plant, creating space for second crops in the east monsoon season (sugar!) and finally "ensuring that the problems that inevitably await him [the native] unless there is some kind of intervention, are avoided" (p.341). The advantages for the government were: higher land rent incomes, less debit in connection with crop failure, less fallow land, higher returns because of the various taxes levied, more profits from other sources like, for example, the railways (because of increased purchasing power on the part of the population) and furthermore "what was otherwise to become unavoidable in the early years – saving on 'relief works' spending in emergency situations" (p. 342).

What, then, did he want? In the first place he wanted research, research into what was required in terms of large works, small works and reservoirs and also into the required quantities of water. The overview emerging from this for "the entire irrigation requirements" (p. 347) was what formed the plan. It would furthermore be necessary to discover how much water was actually available. Such an inquiry would hopefully lead to an overview map of the irrigation situation in Java. All this research could best be carried out in and by the various Irrigation Divisions which was why Van Kol advised that everywhere where this had not yet been done such Divisions should be set up (at that time there were only three and Van Kol had in mind fifteen, see **Chapter 6**). Van Kol's ultimate plan was to produce a list of works categorised in various ways, according to rentability or whatever. Van Kol estimated that this would cost some 900,000 guilders.

Kol "defended the 'exploitation' of the Javanese in the fight against the 'exploited' European worker by referring to the good treatment that the Javanese received in his business" (ibid.). Van Kol kept himself also busy in a different way with water, i.e. by a commitment to the dowsers (Van Sandick 1926b: 1028).

[10] Compare the contribution by Van Bosse to the debate at the Royal Institute of Engineers (1901). For an evaluation of the General Irrigation Plan: see above and **Chapter 6**. Van Kol (1901: 346) drew a comparison with British India and called it a "shameful example", that is to say, for the Indies. According to him there was spent 295 million guilders for the irrigation of ten million *bouws* in 1897/98 (compare the 26½ million guilders which was issued in 1900 for the General Irrigation Plan, see **Chapter 6**). The total length of major and minor channels in British India was, according to Van Kol, equal to the circumference of the earth. India is considered the birthplace of modern irrigation technology. Important was R.C. Kennedy's formula for a "stable regime-canal" (a channel that does not become eroded but also not being deposited, due to too low a flow rate), developed in the late nineteenth century. This formula was later taken over by Dutch engineers, including Homan van der Heide (1905). See Headrick (1988: 171-208), cf. Reddy (1990).

Before any of the works could be started on it would first be necessary to carry out further technical inspections. Van Kol maintained that while doing plan-related research it might already be possible to start improving and extending existing irrigation networks. In the words of Van Kol (p. 346):

"There are hundreds of small weirs which, after brief, on the spot inspection, may well be improved upon in the interests of irrigation.
There are also thousands of small canals which have been created by the natives for which engineers could, after several hours of inspection, provide suggestions for substantial improvement".

In the Solo Valley there are

"thousands of reservoirs where it has been proven that, generally, the reservoir surface area ratio to the sawah surface area ratio is 1 : 1.2. Furthermore, in those places, high dams made of faggots have been created but these dams gradually rot away and are not protected against alluvial deposits which, in turn, leads to much waste of manpower. If one wishes to supervise this process in an expert way it will not be possible to provide quite enough water for irrigation by creating reservoirs as the natives do but it will at least be possible to prevent harvest failure and to meet the most urgent requirements for water supplies" (ibid., compare Kroesen 1871).

We shall take a closer look here below at the discussions on the repercussions of Van Kol's ideas. Simultaneously the (technical) side of the irrigation activities will be covered, as will the organisational side of matters.

Irrigation versus railways

In 1899 Homan van der Heide predicted that if nothing whatsoever was done then there would be famine and unrest in the Indies. He maintained that seeing to it that irrigation was improved was the only way of staving off pending disaster. He pointed out that if the current situation were allowed to continue Dutch interests could also be jeopardised (1899: 295) but as well as that he believed that there was a moral obligation

"on the side of the Netherlands to at least endeavour to do everything in its power to save the Javanese from imminent starvation, especially in view of the fact that a way of achieving that goal had been found: now it was only the financial means to that end that needed to be resolved"[11].

Homan van der Heide certainly did not stand alone in his plea to improve irrigation. Everywhere the importance of good irrigation was recognised. Within the Civil Service, for instance, we see that Bodemeijer who was mentioned and cited earlier also lets us know that the "unmistakable advantages" of modern irrigation "are really so obvious" that we can hardly doubt its usefulness (1903: 205; however, compare Walbeehm 1901a and b). The significance of (modern) irrigation furthermore came to the fore in conjunction with the agricultural point of view (see, for example, *Mindere Welvaartscommissie* 1908: 175).

[11] Homan van der Heide also stressed the importance of irrigation for sugar industry (see e.g. 1901: 379 ff.).

Even though the great importance of irrigation activities was universally recognised the matter of its importance as a welfare means was not totally free of doubt or beyond debate. As far as the intervention of engineers was concerned there was at least one area of competition: the railways. The conflict of interests between transport means and irrigation works arose, for instance, in Solo Valley project discussions. De Meyier who was opposed to continuing with the works project pointed to the importance of transport (Telders et al. 1900: 288). This fundamental question also cropped up when the Royal Institute of Engineers met to discuss the "general irrigation plan for Java". In his reply to Gerlings who showed himself to be in favour of allowing both facets to develop simultaneously (1901: 363) Van Kol proposed the following (1901: 366):

"When compared to irrigation, the railways has been unfairly favoured; already, for various reasons, four times more money has been spent on rail infrastructure. What is undoubtedtly one of the reasons for this is the fact rail construction serves the interests of Europeans while irrigation works solely serve the interests of the native population".

In the Second Chamber Van Kol and Pijnacker Hordijk debated the pros and cons of irrigation works versus railway infrastructure on a number of occasions, for instance during the various budget debates around 1900 (Van Kol 1911: 183, 303, see also Idema 1924: 137).[12] Transport matters were originally the concern of Civil Public Works which meant that competition with irrigation provision was an internal feud. When, in 1909, transport became the responsibility of the newly formed Department for Government Companies competition between irrigation and the railways became a weightier, more institutional issue[13].

[12] Gerlings was a board member of the *Indisch Genootschap* ("Indies Society"). Pijnacker Hordijk was, however, an advocate of the Solo Works (see **Chapter 7**), and he was not ashamed of "irrigation fanaticism" (see below). He (1901: 362) even agreed with with Van Kol's plea for a new irrigation plan, but not with his preference for small works. In the debate about the cessation of the Solo Works, he said: "Why Mr. Van Kol only wants to help the people whose lands can be irrigated by small works and wants to leave another part to their miserable fate remains a mystery to me" ("Proceedings of the States-General", see *De Ingenieur* 1903: 866). Regarding the early Solo Works Pijnacker Hordijk (ibid.) asked whether first a famine should happen there, as in Demak, before the government would take action.

[13] For the competition of the irrigation versus the railroad engineers, see Van Doorn (1994a: 123-145). For the development of the railways, see also Van Doorn (1994b). Interesting from the viewpoint of professionalization is that irrigation and railways had been in the same boat: as part of the process of state formation both areas of public concern went through a similar emancipation in the nineteenth century (see also Post 1979: 16-19). See **Appendices G and H**.

Figure 8.3: Harrowing of rice-fields with water-buffalos, 1910 (photo UBL KITLV 2481)

Figure 8.4: Planting out of rice seedlings, 1900 (photo UBL KITLV 12186)

Large versus small works

Although the matter of improving the irrigation situation in Java may not have been the sole issue focused on, it certainly received a great deal of attention. The point was, what sort of attention did it receive? In presenting his general irrigation plan Van Kol had made an important suggestion. The criticism, however, was heavy. Gerst (1901: 417) referred in the discussion carried out during the meeting of the Royal Institute of Engineers to Cremer, the Minister of the Colonies who was alleged to have said of Van Kol's plan: "Let us not turn such a general irrigation plan as this into a peg on which other plans can be hung up" and he concluded by saying:

"So far there have been two main hang-ups surrounding every irrigation works plan: the first of those two is rentability and the second is the fear of miscalculation in conjunction with the Solo Valley disappointment. Now, with his general irrigation plan, Mr. Van Kol wants to add a third hang-up. Before we know it we shall have an entire cloakroom in which to safely hang up all the irrigation plans".[14]

Another criticism came from De Meyier (1902) who, in his article with a similar name, tackled the matter of irrigation fanaticism. The advantages presented by Van Kol (1902: 187-190) had not convinced him. De Meyier raised the matter of events in the Kening area where, as is known, agricultural production first rose before falling after modern irrigation had been introduced. He furthermore showed little enthusiasm for the consequences for the population of (expanding) the sugar industry which was something that was partly precipitated by falling rice production levels[15]. De Meyier (p. 185) also found that in creating such a plan Van Kol would also ultimately delay the construction of irrigation works.

What the minister had to say clearly influenced the engineers but, conversely, the minister was also interested in their reactions. While the 1903 budget for the Indies was being debated Van Kol brought up the matter of his plan in the Second Chamber for the fourth time. The relevant minister, Idenburg, referred to the discussion carried out within the Royal Institute of Engineers in 1901 and did not go into the matter any further ("Proceedings of the States-General", see *De Ingenieur* 1902: 824).

Van Kol's idea of concentrating on smaller irrigation works in order to improve on and expand existing irrigation systems was better received. Such works had been previously lobbied for (for instance by van Ilcken, 1891: 423-424) and in the 1885-1890 period priority had even been given to such ideas. However, with the General Irrigation Plan the development of irrigation intervention had been pushed in another direction, in the direction of larger works. The technical-scientific method, or the way in which the engineers implemented this method, promoted "theoretical" work such as the extensive gathering of all kinds of data on the subject. This, in turn, only reinforced the preoccupation with big projects. In his day Van Bosse had done away with the irrigation activity hierarchy because that only hindered the execution of a number

[14] Gerst worked on a part of the Indramayu (or Sindopraja-Dutamati) Works, which was put into operation in 1899 (the whole work was completed in 1917). The discussion at the Royal Institute of Engineers on the plan of Van Kol continued in the absence of the spiritual father in a future meeting (dated June 11, 1901).

[15] De Meyier was referring to De Jaager (1901). The Resident (of Kediri) wrote in response to a letter from 1899 from the Chief Inspector of Cultures, H.J.W. Lawick van der Pabst, a note about the profitability of the waterworks at the request of Kraus of the Solo Commission. De Jaager deemed irrigation improvement necessary for the agricultural population, while he also saw big benefits for the sugar industry. Kraus found the memorandum of such importance that he did not hesitate "to take advantage of the permission granted by the author to me to give it publicity" (Kraus in his preface to the published note, see also Telders 1900 et al.).

of larger projects which relied on the gathering of data (see **Chapter 6**, see also *Encyclopaedie* Vol. IV 1921: 727). For many engineers, such as Homan van der Heide, this was the route they would have preferred to follow. In the book where he writes an apology on the Solo Works (1899), he also emerged as a supporter of large-scale irrigation activities (see also Van Sandick 1912b). Because the results were, however, disappointing certain doubts existed around 1900 (also in Van Sandick's mind 1912b, see below) and engineers started to seriously entertain the possibility of constructing smaller works. In this respect De Meyier was on Van Kol's side: he too was an advocate of the small-scale approach (1902: for example p. 185, compare pp. 194-195).

The small-scale idea bore fruit. In the first place it was beneficial where the improvement and creation of small but modern irrigation works was concerned. The Director of the Civil Public Works, H.P. Mensinga (1901-1905), took steps in that direction in 1904 (see Creutzberg 1972: 310). In the second place, attention was given to the matter of improving Javanese irrigation. In 1905 the man who was then the Director of Civil Public Works, A.P. Melchior (1905-1908), distributed a circular in which he came out in support of village irrigation. In this way the Residents and the Heads of the Public Works and Irrigation Divisions were informed that the government was

"with the help of some of the funds made available by the Netherlands for the purposes of economic development in the East Indies, both prepared and able to extend its aid and to, more than in the past, offer its support to works dedicated to serving inland irrigation" (in: *Mindere Welvaartscommissie* 1910, Annex 8).

Already the minister, Idenburg, had pressed for such support by turning to Van Heutsz, the Governor-General, for instance in a letter of 12th January 1905 (see Creutzberg 1972: 310 onwards). In that letter he was critical of the reserve shown by the Civil Public Works Director Mensinga in this respect. He was afraid that the population would start putting down watercourse "that were just for local use" at the government's expense. The minister did not find this a problem. The objective, that of improving the economic situation, justified the means "even if those improvements were only relevant to a small group and even if, under normal circumstances, such responsibilities were normally left to the desa itself" (Creutzberg 1972: 311).[16] In this connection it was not strange to see that Javanese irrigation, with which since the time of De Bruyn engineers had wiped the floor, underwent a re-evaluation. For instance Weijs (1913: 6) suggested that with their experience the Javanese had "conquered the call" to be "born irrigation engineers"[17].

The attention paid to agriculture on the part of the Javanese population only served to reinforce the preference for small irrigation projects. With the Ethical Policy concern for irrigation was made secondary to encouraging small farming. As far as the intervention of

[16] In 1909, the Director of Civil Public Works, W.B. van Goor (1908-1911), issued a follow-up circular. In it the role of the concerned population was expanded. Under the circular of 1905, it was only approachable for excavating. That was now "as much as possible the coolie labour to be carried out" (1910, Annex 9). The circular of 1905 was partly due to the ideas of Civil Public Works Director De Meyier (see Thal Larsen in 1912: 929). See for the promotion and improvement of small and Javanese works also Creutzberg 1972: 180-181 (in a memo of Minister Idenburg to Governor-General Rooseboom) and 194-195 (Rooseboom's answer).

[17] See for a full view of the corresponding quote **Chapter 4**. Moreover, Weijs (1913) showed, however, no doubt that he considered modern irrigation superior to Javanese. A positive assessment of the Javanese irrigation we find also in De Meyier (1902: 181-182). Traditional irrigation had a good reputation among government officials, but that seems over around 1900. Bodemeijer did not like it anyway. He (1903: 205) referred to this irrigation in terms of "messing and spilling" and called the state in which this was possible "to one's heart's content" a "paradise for any right-minded Javanese farmer".

engineers in irrigation was concerned, improving this particular agricultural sector has always been an important objective (Van Ilcken [1891] had lobbied for the provision of simple irrigation works together with steps to improve Javanese agriculture). In this respect the bigger projects had not had sufficient impact. This was the reason why in agricultural circles people were not so enthusiastic about bigger works while Javanese irrigation was precisely what was highly valued (*Mindere Welvaartscommissie* 1908: 175 onwards). The plea launched by engineers in favour of small-scale works was thus well received by agriculturists. As has been explained, work on the execution of (major) projects emanating from the 1890 General Irrigation Plan in the meantime continued including, for instance, activities in the Pemali-Comal area. Certain of the unremunerative works received extra support within the framework of the General Work Plan of 1907. That, though, was as far as things went: new large works projects were not yet embarked upon, that was something that would happen later (see below).

Technical control versus agricultural control

There was another idea of Van Kol's that found its way into the policy and that was the notion of improving control. As we have seen, during the course of the nineteenth century the intervention of engineers in irrigation affairs had gradually extended to tertiary realms. It was notably Lamminga who saw to it that this development was completed through his Pekalen and Pemali Works. A logical next step was for control to become more centrally directed. To this end Irrigation Divisions were set up. In effect Van Kol was now pushing for an expansion of these Divisions, even without the emergence of large works projects. The Divisions could busy themselves doing the preparatory work for (small) works.

The Department of Agriculture, generally recognised among engineers as a department capable of providing good irrigation services, was locked in conflict with the Civil Public Works Department as far as irrigation system control was concerned. Engineers of standing argued that irrigation work exploitation should be made the province of Agriculture. With the arrival of the Irrigation Divisions (begun in 1888) irrigation control had fallen into the hands of engineers. Compared to the previous situation, when civil servants had taken charge of control matters, this represented a big step forwards. Together construction activities in the field of irrigation and the introduction of technical control led to noticeable rises in sugar production levels. Apart from being attributed to the availability of sufficient water and to the certainty of its being supplied these rises could also be put down to the research into sugar cultivation being carried out at agricultural experimental stations. Rice and second crop cultivation activities produced no positive results. Putting irrigation water to good use required rational action on the part of the farmer. However, the agricultural know-how required for this was not something he possessed and the engineers, charged with the task of controlling the works, lacked such knowledge as well. Irrigation control organised by agriculturalists would (once again) represent an improvement. Van Sandick who had argued in favour of all of this (1911: 947, 1912b: 920) contended that a complete new era would thus be heralded, the era of agricultural control over irrigation:

"Because irrigation has to remain a means, not an end. The objective has to be to uphold the interests of local agriculture and learning how to do that and taking charge of that is only something that can be done by agriculturalists" (Van Sandick 1912b: 923, see also **Chapter 1**).[18]

[18] The figures I gave earlier, gave less reason for such a positive assessment of the contribution of modern irrigation works to the sugar industry. See for the character of Javanese agriculture and the importance of irrigation before Smits (1929: 122-137 and 58-62).

Van Sandick discovered that in 1912, due to a change in regulations (see below) other public works areas had become a part of the terrain of the Irrigation Divisions. He suggested that because of that Irrigation Divisions had begun to more closely resemble Public Works Divisions. Van Sandick concluded that because of this the exploitation of irrigation works might be at risk. He was convinced that through these changes the way was being paved for control to be switched to Agriculture. Van Sandick (1912b: 923) possessed indications that there were "invisible forces working in that direction".[19]

There were other views, though, such as that of Numans who was involved in the Pemali Works from 1907 onwards. He believed (1916: 342) that

"wishing, as some do, to make the agricultural department – which lacks the necessary expertise – entirely responsible for irrigation affairs which are almost entirely of a technical nature reflects ignorance on the part of those proposing such an idea.
The activities of the agricultural department should lie in tertiary areas.
It is pointless for the agricultural department to involve itself in water distribution affairs since such matters are totally controlled by tertiary water distribution mechanisms and can better be entrusted to technical civil servants".[20]

Ultimately responsibility for irrigation works' control did not go to the Agricultural Department. In practice, what happened instead of that was that co-operation between representatives from both Departments and from the Civil Service sector was developed. (I shall return to this point in the final section of this chapter)[21].

---

[19] Van Sandick (1912b: 921-922) called as allies engineers J.C. Heijning (former Head of the first Irrigation Division of Serayu and also that of Serang, with the Demak Works), M. Ypelaar (contributed to the creation of the Pekalen regime and was Head of the Division of Brantas, see for him Van Sandick 1926a), J. Nuhout van der Veen (former Head of the Technical Section E, cranked up the discussion with a publication from 1907), E.A.C.F. von Essen (successor of Pierson at the Solo Works), as well as Dr. M. Treub (Director of Agriculture). Voices even rose to move the whole irrigation service to the Agricultural Department and abolish Civil Public Works! (See *Mindere Welvaartscommissie* 1908: 189).

[20] Other opponents (mentioned in Van Sandick 1912: 922) were Lamminga (see 1910: 20-22), Homan van der Heide and De Meyier. Weijs also was an opponent as Cramer (1914: 18-19) and Civil Public Works Director Melchior. See for a discussion between the latter Director and his colleague of Agriculture Treub (and their successors Van Goor and Lovink) Creutzberg (1972: 327-341, 351). Attention to the issue also in Mindere *Welvaartscommissie* 1908: 52-53 and 189). Finally, on the Civil Service position, I can say that it was satisfied with the existing situation, the Director of the Civil Service S. de Graaff was that anyway (Creutzberg 1972: 372).

[21] Van Goor and Lovink, the successors of Melchior and Treub at Civil Public Works and Agriculture respectively (see **Note 20**) wanted to take a test (Creutzberg 1972: 340). Sibinga J. Mulder, who succeeded Lovink, was against the transfer of the Irrigation Divisions to his Department! (Sibinga Mulder 1912: 190-193, including discussion with among others Van Sandick). See on this issue still Saltet (1912), who discusses a brochure of proponent Nuhout van der Veen ("Again irrigation and agriculture on Java"). Saltet stressed that water management was entrusted to the Resident and welcomed the cooperation of administration and irrigation staff. He saw potential for a fruitful involvement of agronomists, but believed that these just as engineers should not act as "commanding". Worth noting from a professionalization perspective is Saltet's opinion that the engineer must comply with his duties and not "dabble in agricultural sphere" (1912: 71, the same criticism engineers had had on administrators in the previous century), nor directly or indirectly must strive to authority (by claiming authority). Illustrative in this respect is also the way he commented on agronomy. This would not be "an exact science", "but rests largely on perception" and "an agricultural training is not a necessary requirement for receptivity to impressions of perception" (p. 71). This kind of derogatory opinions had once befallen the engineers (see **Chapter 4**). See for the rise and influence of the Department of Agriculture Moon (2007).

Rent and silt

It was particularly through the agricultural information service's advisors that the Department of Agriculture remained active in the area of irrigation. One of their most important tasks was to estimate the anticipated benefits of works in relation to cost, in other words, the rentability. When policy changed in ethical terms non-productive works were given a chance but the rentability criterion still held. In fact it was intensified because local farmers had to benefit. That was why, in 1903, the Rentability Commission was extended and a representative from the new agricultural service – known from 1905 onwards as the Department of Agriculture – was brought in. Just as with the representatives from the Civil Public Works Department and the Civil Service, the agricultural expert (an Inspector) was made a permanent member. The involvement of agricultural advisors in irrigation thus included dealing with irrigation project proposals and making recommendations relating to water distribution and plant regulation. Alongside of that they also carried out crop experiments. One of the important aspects of such tests was to determine how much water each of the various crops, including of course rice, required. Another thing looked at was fertilisation which meant that the silt content of water became an important factor. (*Mededeelingen* 1924: 317-319, 314, see also Metzelaar 1946: 208).

Around the turn of the century interest in the silt factor increased because it had often been noticed that crop increases remained disappointing despite the advent of modern irrigation systems. As was mentioned in **Chapter** 7, De Meyier (1902) did point out that when transported long distances in canals water did tend to become less rich in silt. In this respect he differed from the Solo Commission which chiefly saw silt as a problem (see **Chapter 7**, **Note 29**). According to De Meyier Javanese irrigation worked well in this respect: much silt was allowed to reach the fields partly also because *banjirs* that were rich in silt (*banjir* silt!) was allowed into the watercourses. On the other hand this did cause a degree of damage which was why in previous modern facilities (for instance the Pekalen Works) efforts had been made to keep silt out altogether. In 1900 Homan van der Heide investigated the fertilising effect of irrigation water and argued that it was too often the case that the entire irrigation question was seen too much as a hydro-technical matter (getting water to the fields) and too little as an agricultural and economic issue. On the basis of all kinds of studies he indicated that silt was vital to fertilisation and that irrigation water should therefore have a high silt content. Homan van der Heide (1901) was critical of the Solo Commission's view that silt might be allowed into the watercourses but nothing more than that (at least this was an improvement on the old view which held that silt should be kept out of the watercourses altogether). He maintained that it was best to allow only floating silt particles into the canals which would then be transported into the pipes in fast water flows and released onto the fields. (See also Homan van der Heide 1905).

Silt fertilisation was a pre-eminently agricultural affair which was why the agricultural review section of the welfare investigation went into the matters referred to above in detail (*Mindere Welvaartscommissie* 1908: 175-180). Apart from doing crop experimentation in conjunction with irrigation projects the Agricultural Department also carried out general research into the silt content of irrigation water. In so doing people were perpetually curious to know why silt was so important. In connection with this latter point the conclusion was that silt was essential but that it was not the only ingredient. As far as fertilisation was concerned there were other substances dissolved in the water that were just as important to the soil, if not more important! (*Mindere Welvaartscommissie* 1908: 180, compare the remarks of Treub made to Creutzberg 1972: 327, 351, see further Metzelaar 1946: 207-208, Smits 1929: 52-57 and also Berger 1915. Other agricultural research will be discussed below).

A further important question also raised in connection with rentability was the matter of the financial contributions to be made by sugar refineries to irrigation control. It was in this connection that the Permanent Irrigation Commission was established in 1906 which is referred to in **Chapter 6**. In 1916 this Commission and the Rentability Commission were amalgamated to form the Commission for the interests of Irrigation Affairs in Java and Madura.[22]

The subsequent policy

Up to a point, the welfare investigation reinforced the policy course being followed which, influenced by ethical views on irrigation affairs, was adhered to from the beginning of the twentieth century and which was: to create small works, to improve Javanese facilities and to encourage technical water control. According to the irrigation overview volume there were only two (very) large projects that were seriously considered as viable: the Solo Valley Works (thus indicating that the report had not completely dropped the idea!) and the Krawang Works. Other large works were mentioned but the conclusion was that "endeavours should chiefly be made to improve existing irrigation networks" (*Mindere Welvaartscommissie* 1910: 214). The toning down of the rentability demand (regarding the application area, not the criterion itself, see above) that had been integrated into the General Work Plan was confirmed in the report, notably where smaller works were concerned (*Mindere Welvaartscommissie* 1910: 214[23]).

As far as control was concerned the outcome was that the biggest improvements in the field of irrigation to be made since 1885 were those that had been made by the Irrigation Divisions. For the future this meant

"that priority should be given to the retention, improvement and expert management of existing systems rather than to creating completely new works. Furthermore, it would certainly not be advisable to expend huge sums of money on this latter aspect, especially if such funds are to be raised at the expense of existing systems" (*Mindere Welvaartscommissie* 1910: 238-239).

Homan van der Heide agreed that the Irrigation Divisions had indeed been most instrumental in achieving the results attained, though this was something he was sorry to have to admit. The idea that priority should be given to control was, to his mind, "utterly wrong". He maintained that expanding irrigation facilities was more important than raising production levels and making economic progress and it was, moreover, cheaper. (*Mindere Welvaartscommissie* 1910: 239, notes 1 and 2). Just as the small-scale approach to irrigation had stagnated at the time of the big projects so also had Homan van der Heide's "more of the same" scenario somehow remained in the background.

Homan van der Heide travelled to Thailand which, at that time, did seem to offer opportunities for the creation of major irrigation networks[24]. On later returning to the Indies he was made Director of Civil Public Works (1911-1914). In his capacity as Director he tried to revive the Solo project and give the Krawang Works, a new big irrigation project, extra impetus.

---

[22] Van Rees and De Graaff (1900 and 1907). The Permanent Irrigation Commission had to do without an agricultural representative (see Metzelaar 1946: 206). Apart from a contribution to the cost of construction and management, the discussion was also about other contributions to be paid by the sugar industry, e.g. a tax per *bouw* (see De Jaager 1901). See for a discussion of irrigation in relation to the sugar industry Sibinga Mulder (1912), in which he received agricultural responses from among others Lamminga and Ypelaar. All the problems of the sugar industry for the population passed in review, in which attention was also paid to the so-called cane fires. These occurred in different regions, among others in Besuki (Sampean area). See Van Kol (1911: 190), Van Goor (1986: 60) and Elson (1984 and 1979).

[23] Van Kol was referred to by the small works (*Mindere Welvaartscommissie* 1910: 214).

[24] Homan van der Heide did so at the request of the King of Thailand, who with modern irrigation wanted to push up his country in the march of civilization. Due to various circumstances, these works were only carried out after the Second World War. (Ten Brummelhuis 1996).

Homan van der Heide's Solo Works initiative was supported by Thal Larsen (1912). At the instigation of Homan van der Heide Larsen turned against the criticism of De Meyier (1912a) attacking the view that constructing small works was a better idea. Commenting on Melchior's circular of 1905 Thal Larsen noted that those proposals had led to the development of the most expensive and least urgent works.

Ultimately the lobby for large irrigation works did bear fruit: such projects again became possible around the year 1915. The Welfare Commission's proposals and resolutions, published in 1914, contained the following government recommendations:

"One of the best ways of improving public welfare in Java is by improving upon irrigation, in the first place by providing new irrigation systems and in the second place by improving upon the existing systems while ensuring that existing systems do not fade too much into the background" (*Mindere Welvaartscommissie* 1914: 29).

This judgement of Solomon again innovated change: first it had been proclaimed that works should be large, now they had to be small! As far as technical control was concerned the same report indicated that this particular facet should be expanded but that priority should be given to large works projects.[25]

As far as the relationship between the sugar industry and small farming was concerned, the Welfare Commission had taken a decision that seemed to amount to running with the hare and hunting with the hounds: in regulating water supplies the "irrigation privilege", like the day and night regulation, was permitted to an "unlimited" degree except where this might be "too" detrimental to Javanese agriculture (*Mindere Welvaartscommissie* 1914: 38). The alternative to the day and night regulatory measures, adhered to in sugar growing areas, was the *waduk* system whereby water was collected in small reservoirs at night (in night *waduks*) so that it could be conveyed to paddy fields in the daytime. After numerous investigations – the first of which was in 1893 and the last of which was in 1915-1916 – after many debates and after several years of experimentation with night *waduks* the government decided, in 1919, upon the recommendations of the aforementioned Commission for the interests of Irrigation Affairs that, in the interests of the irrigation system as a whole, the *waduk* system should be adopted and the day and night ruling abolished.[26]

---

[25] It was decided to "introduce irrigation management in a general way" (*Mindere Welvaartscommissie* 1914: 21). "General" meant that much was left to the Javanese administration. The meeting concerned of the Welfare Commission was attended by Civil Public Works Director Homan van der Heide. Agricultural management was absolutely out of the question. On that occasion, there was again some support for the Solo Works, namely from K.A.R. Bosscha, Principal Administrator of the company of Malabar (Bandung) (*Mindere Welvaartscommissie* 1914: 28).

[26] *Encyclopaedie* (Vol. V 1927: 461-466), Van der Marel et al. (1919). See for a discussion the reporting of the welfare investigation (e.g. *Mindere Welvaartscommissie* 1914: 29-38, see above) and further Ypelaar (1914), Ramaer (1914) and *De Waterstaats-Ingenieur* ("The Public Works Engineer", 1915, pp. 73-82: articles by among others Master of Laws Ramaer, J. Sibinga Mulder and Ypelaar; pp. 184-187: article by the engineer G.J. Dijkerman and pp. 255-261: articles by Dijkerman and the engineer J.O. de Kat). Attention to the treatment of the day and night regulation in parliament in *De Waterstaats-Ingenieur* (1915: 82-86). A report of tests can be found in Cramer (1919 and 1921). The latter was the great promoter of the *waduk* system.

Changes within the Department of Civil Public Works

All in all, the mediocre results of the General Irrigation Plan and the events surrounding the Solo Valley project had seriously shaken the confidence of engineers. The upshot of this was that round the turn of the century many were in favour of reorganising the Civil Public Works Department. As has been mentioned, Lamminga was one of the people to offer suggestions but, not surprisingly, his improvement proposals were not adopted. What Lamminga (1900 and 1910) wanted was to return to the golden age; to the time when the engineers and their irrigation brigade ruled supreme (or, at least, to some ideal close to that). He was aiming, in other words, at power expansion but, certainly after the Solo Works, that was no longer an option. What, then, did happen?

Mention has already been made of the secret proposals made by the Solo Commission and of Van Sandick's subsequent curiosity (he thought that things would be just as they were in 1885). While the Indies budget for 1903 was being debated the minister intimated that according to the views of the Solo Commission, Public Works reorganisations could only commence once all the decision-making relating to the decentralisation of the administration in the Indies had been completed ("Proceedings of the States-General", see *De Ingenieur* 1902: 874). When, in 1903, the Dutch government decided to go ahead with decentralisation the consequences for the Public Works Organisation remained limited. It was only the construction and the maintenance of local and regional works that was delegated to local councils which, in the end, recruited their own personnel for such purposes. Since all of this only related to modest duties it was not really possible to cut down on central Public Works personnel numbers. Ultimately decentralisation led to an overall increase in the numbers of technical personnel and, partly because of this, to rises in irrigation works costs. (*Encyclopaedie* Vol. IV 1921: 729).

After 1900 the Public Works Organisation extended its scope. Within the new political set up the Outlying Regions, to which people according to van Deventer were to migrate from Java, became the centre of attention for irrigation. The responsibilities of Civil Public Works increased. This led to the establishment of new Technical Divisions which meant that by 1915 there were five such Divisions: Irrigation and Drainage, Bridges and Roads, Buildings, Harbours and Sanitation Works[27]. Because of all of this, personnel expansion became inevitable. By 1907 this had led to the resolution that each year the personnel composition was determined at the time of the Indies budget. (*Encyclopaedie* Vol. IV 1921: 729).

Decentralisation, the increase in the number of Irrigation Divisions (see **Chapter 6**) and the increased activities of Civil Public Works culminated, in 1910, in the introduction of a new Public Works Regulation (*Indisch Staatsblad* 1910). Already, commencing in 1912, the new regulation began to be amended, partly in conjunction with personnel shortages. Eventually the organisation was changed as follows. Three Public Works Divisions were created, but only in Java and Madura. The headquarters were in Batavia, Semarang and Surabaya. The Outlying Regions which had previously fallen into two Public Works Divisions were subdivided into three Inspectorates. The relevant Inspectors were situated in Medan, Palembang and Makassar. Another alteration was that the Irrigation Divisions were made to fall directly under the supervision of Civil Public Works (thus ruling out the Resident). All the large irrigation and harbour works likewise fell directly under Civil Public Works' authority while other public works (including the smaller irrigation works) were directly supervised by the various Public

[27] See also the "Civil Public Works Reports" that follow this format.

Works Divisions. The Irrigation Divisions were given more powers and other public works activities were controlled by them. The Public Works Divisions furthermore took on "an advisory role" as far as works controlled by the regional and local councils were concerned. (*Encyclopaedie* Vol. IV 1921: 729-730, see also Van Sandick 1912b: 922-923)[28].

Figure 8.5: Harvesting sugar cane at Pemalang, 1926 (photo UBL KITLV 7772)

[28] Due to staff shortages Danish and German engineers were attracted in this period! (Cramer 1914: 52). Personnel issues were already raised by Saltet (1896). After establishment of the Technical College in Bandung (see below) engineers trained in the Indies could meet the needs and the number of foreign engineers decreased (see **Appendix F**).

Irrigation and the state

Works

In 1893 Pierson made a start on the Solo Valley Works project which, briefly summarised, amounted to the following. It was hoped that by redirecting the silt-laden river in a northerly direction the harbour of Surabaya would be protected. What the works project also accounted for was a canal for navigational purposes, drinking water provision and an irrigation programme. Regarding the latter point, the Solo Works constituted the biggest irrigation project by a long way within the 1890 General Irrigation Plan as a whole. The weir and the main canal were extremely big, even by international standards. The works project turned out to be more expensive than had been budgeted, partly because of the high cost of labour. This was the reason why, five years into the project, the minister known as Cremer sent a telegraph message ordering that the project be halted. One of the project's objectives had been to create better living conditions for the local population, notably in the low-lying Bengawan Jero region. The Ethical Policy, initiated in 1901, aimed specifically at improving people's living standards and it was thought that, even though the works might turn out to be expensive or perhaps not even profitable the project would surely be continued. Moreover, the outcome of the extensive works investigation ordered by Cremer in 1900 had been positive. The Solo Commission's unanimous findings were that the works project was technically sound and most members agreed that it was also economically viable. The recommendation was thus to continue. Why, then, did minister Idenburg decide differently?

The objection to the plan raised by the minister in 1903 about silt not being able to reach distant fields was an objection of an agricultural (or agricultural-economic) nature. In the Solo report this was not a view that had been explicitly brought forward by De Meyier but his problems with rentability had pointed in this direction. In the end, the doubts he had voiced had related to the profit increases modern irrigation might lead to. Later (in 1902) he did in fact draw attention to the problem of silt content decreases in long canals, also in conjunction with the proposed Solo irrigation project. Around the turn of the century when the production increases brought by modern irrigation were disappointing the silt issue received much attention. Homan van der Heide maintained that the whole irrigation question was seen too much as a technical problem and too little as an agricultural-economic problem. The ethical politicians adhered to this by making small farming an important area of attention and irrigation matters subordinate to that. The newly created Agricultural Department carried out research into silt fertilisation and confirmed that indeed, together with other substances, silt was an important fertiliser. Note, thus, the solution found to the paradox of the Solo Works not being resumed under the Ethical Policy: the agricultural side of the project was weak (no evident rentability, no clear prospect of improving agriculture for the small population) at a time when promoting Javanese agriculture was really the central policy.[29]

Conversely, though, the Solo Works did influence policy. Round the turn of the century the rentability question had become an important issue. The focus was on increased production due to modern irrigation. Whether or not works were economically feasible was thus an agricultural problem and so it was that in 1903 an agricultural expert was added to the Rentability

[29] Governor-General Rooseboom substantiated the need for an Agricultural Department in a note to Minister of the Colonies Asch van Wijck dated April 14, 1902, inter alia, by referring to the Solo Works. He cited thereby the Civil Public Works Director Mensinga who wrote in a letter about the works: "One can say that the problem of irrigation is adequately resolved in Java from a purely technical standpoint, but repeatedly rising complaints about the experience acquired with works performed indicate that the demands of agriculture actually are not fully known" (Creutzberg 1972: 281; compare the corresponding position of Homan van der Heide 1900). See for other measures to encourage the Javanese agriculture than in the area of irrigation Smits (1929: 227-266).

Commission. Rentability therefore pointed the way to agricultural evaluation. At the same time, the whole Solo Works issue was also extremely topical. It was not only the case that this had a catalysing effect on the entire rentability discussion, it also contributed to giving agriculturists an important say in matters.

In the Solo Valley the bigger works project was not resumed, instead smaller works were concentrated on: dyke improvements, source irrigation and *waduks*. There were also plans to work on a number of bigger reservoirs and agricultural research was carried out. This was something that fitted in with the general irrigation concern ethos of the day. The disappointing results of the bigger projects, in terms of expansion and crop improvement, only increased the demand (also made by Van Kol) to focus on smaller projects. Concentrating on smaller works in order to improve and extend existing irrigation systems was thus the approach that was returned to. Embarking on small-scale irrigation activities in the interests of small farming was something that fitted in well with the Ethical Policy. Agriculturalists, the prime champions of the new policy, were, like certain engineers, cynical about big works and they emphasised the importance of Javanese irrigation systems. The Solo project did not fit in as well with the Ethical Policy as the alternative aid programme proposed by Elenbaas and other engineers. What Elenbaas proposed was something that fitted in well with the local situation. *Waduks* were, after all, a familiar Solo Valley phenomenon. The Solo Works was given a chance when small-scale irrigation activities were no longer the main policy objective but, with the revival of this other course of action, in conjunction with the Ethical Policy, there was no room for alternative action. Large-scale plans were thus temporarily out of the question. The projects proposed in the General Irrigation Plan were continued but nothing more than that was done. When Homan van der Heide wanted to revive all the big planning ideas during his time as Director of the Civil Public Works Department it was found that such ideas did not fit in with the current policies. In the meantime it had also been discovered that it was not necessary to change the course of the river and that the measures taken in the Bengawan Jero (and elsewhere) had been successful.

Homan van der Heide had produced one other argument in favour of resuming the Solo Works which was that the project would be very beneficial to the sugar industry. By making improvements to the original design in order to open up perspectives for the 25 sugar plantations and refineries the Solo Commission managed to make continuing seem attractive. Homan van der Heide took it all one step further: he maintained that the sugar refineries could also be asked to contribute to financing irrigation[30]. At the turn of the century the sugar market had been depressed and that had continued until 1903, the year when the decision to halt the project had been taken (compare Van Kol 1903: 18). After 1903 (and until 1916) the sugar industry flourished (*Encyclopaedie* Vol. IV 1921: 178). This occurred thanks to the execution of large irrigation projects, like for instance the Pemali-Comal Works.[31] From the point of view of the local population the advantages of the sugar industry were dubious. Whether this was so beneficial to the population was a moot point. In the Solo report De Meyier had warned that rice harvests could drop because sugar cane cultivation gave rise to the cultivation of inferior varieties of rice (compare in this connection *Mindere Welvaartscommissie* 1910: 68). Ten years later De Meyier was able to add to this another objection: that of the exploitation of the local population. At that time it was definitely the responsibility of the authorities to ensure that the population was not exploited.

[30] And not only they. Homan van der Heide also expected a significant financial contribution from the Dutch East Indian Railway Company, which would benefit from the increased transport (De Meyier 1912a: 663).

[31] Also in other areas it went well with the private agriculture and industry: Dutch entrepreneurs made fortunes with rubber plantations, oil and tin companies. Furthermore Dutch capital investors seized their chances, especially in the Outer Islands. Agriculture and mining companies were welcome investment objects. The big capital only began to render from the First World War. (Gonggrijp 1957).

When, at the time of Homan van der Heide, resuming the Solo Works became a serious proposition De Meyier again came with technical objections. In 1900 he had not raised such objections (though he had seen problems) but before that he had done (with the weir in 1898) and he did again later in 1910 (for example in connection with the 165-kilometre-long canal). On top of the differences of opinion on rentability it also became apparent that views were divided where techniques were concerned. In this respect it was a repetition of the 1898 situation. The contradictory nature of the recommendations had also been a factor in the stopping of the project. At the time of the opening of the Krawang Works, in 1925, Governor-General D. Fock who had been Minister of the Colonies between 1905 and 1908 had this to say about the Solo Valley Works:

"The fact that the works ... were not resumed or continued was not [like the halting, WR] a consequence of thriftiness or economising either; it was rather the differences of opinion between technical people that caused this" (*Feestelijke opening* [Celebratory opening] 1925: 12).[32]

Homan van de Heide who was forced to back down was able to realise his grand ambitions with another large-scale plan, namely the Krawang Works. This was the only new and large-scale irrigation project to get off the ground after the turn of the century. In his capacity as Director of Civil Public Works Homan van der Heide did his utmost to encourage preparations for these works. However, these works did not materialise until the 1919-1925 period (*Feestelijke opening* 1925: see **Chapter 10**)[33]. Around 1915 certain changes were made, which was undoubtedly partly prompted by Homan van der Heide. Irrigation activity spendings returned to the level of before the turn of the century and thereafter rose (see below). There was also evidence of a trend change in favour of large-scale irrigation facility provision: new big projects once again appeared on the agenda, one of which was the works in the Tangerang plains which will be discussed in the following chapter.

The Prijetan *waduk* constituted one of the Solo Valley improvements. It was an example of one project in a new category of large mountain reservoir works to confidently emerge after the turn of the century. Improving on existing reservoirs and creating new ones, all of which were designed for collecting water during the west monsoon season and releasing it during the east monsoon season, had been one of the ideas supported by Van Kol. Initially he had been interested in small reservoirs but ultimately he also came out in support of big reservoirs (Van Kol 1901: 346, 1903: 5-6, compare Van Kol 1911). On the whole there was not much enthusiasm for these reservoirs, partly because of the great expense they created (*Mindere Welvaartscommissie* 1910: 216). The expense aspect was also an argument in the case of the Solo Valley, in fact it was an important reason for why the Prijetan *waduk* was not completed until 1917. There were also agricultural objections attached to the creation of large reservoirs. Research had shown that storing water in river valleys in a limestone area (like that of the Solo Valley) did not particularly enhance the quality of the water (see, for example, Metzelaar 1946: 226, 207-208). In the Demak region, where famine had once again hit around the turn of the century, engineers launched what was known as the Great Rawa Pening Plan, in other words, what amounted to a gigantic reservoir. Since the advantages did not outweigh the disadvantages the plan was abandoned (see **Box 8.1**). All in all, as far as reservoir irrigation was concerned, the

[32] And then there was in the discussion about the Solo Works raised again by Homan van der Heide still a personal factor: the fact that Idenburg responsible for the abandonment decision was Governor-General during this period will not have done well to the cause.

[33] However, during his reign, Homan van der Heide has started a major maintenance plan for the Brantas Works (see *Encyclopaedie* Vol. VII ENI 1935: 116-117).

projects undertaken remained limited. (See for an early lobby for the creation of large reservoirs *Kunstmeren* ["Artificial lakes"] 1882).

Box 8.1 The Rawa Pening reservoir plan

For humanitarian reasons the laying of modern irrigation works in the Demak region commenced with the construction of the weir at Glapan (see **Chapter 4**); this was later pursued in the form of the Demak Works, the first project to be organised along technical lines (see **Chapter 6**). The events of around 1900 proved that all the trials and tribulations were not over.

In order to improve on the irrigation situation the Civil Public Works Department recommended creating a large, 225 million cubic metre capacity reservoir (just to compare, the Prijetan *waduk* had a nine million cubic metre capacity). The plan designer was engineer Varkevisser. During the east monsoon season the reservoir would be able to supply water enough for 30,000 *bouws* of rice. From an agricultural point of view the objective was found to be superfluous, there was water enough. Apart from anything else, in releasing water 4000 *bouws* of good *sawa* (two harvests a year) would be lost and 30,000 people would be forced to move house! The advantage would be that extra electricity could be produced and fish could be farmed. On the other hand, there were the enormous costs (of expropriating and moving huge numbers of people) that would be involved which would amount to twelve million guilders (400 guilders per *bouw*). All of that just to improve irrigation.

For the agriculturists the alternative was to wait and see what could be achieved with the existing irrigation and drainage facilities and those that were still to be created. That was what the administration decided to do. (Begemann 1935, *Mededeelingen* 1924: 320, Metzelaar 1946: 226-227).

Small-scale improvement measures, the creating of (small) reservoirs and the carrying out of agricultural tests were the central irrigation policy aims as far as the Solo Valley was concerned. That also remained the case when, in the twenties, renewed interest was shown in the Solo irrigation plan and (at the instigation of the people's council!) the government once again set up an investigation into the possibility of resuming the works project. An important factor at that time was the aspect of providing food. In view of the fact that the population level was growing rapidly this was a particular point of concern, also in view of the international situation. Ott de Vries (1922: 741) believed that it would be vital for the Indies to remain independent of the "limited" foreign market as far as obtaining rice sustenance supplies went. In passing, he also mentioned the "world disaster", in the form of the First World War that was just behind them.[34] It was certainly once again possible to think of embarking on major projects (see **Chapter 10**), but the agricultural survey (would this lead to higher yields?) was something that could not be ignored. The significance of the agricultural angle was apparent from the fact that Snell, the individual commissioned to research the viability of the Solo Works project, defined the irrigating of the Solo Valley as a complex agricultural issue. As a result of his investigation it was decided, in the late twenties, that the Solo Works project should be terminated once and for all. He did recommend, though, that the Pacal *waduk* be provided and that did come about. It was a period when other big reservoirs were being created elsewhere (see again **Chapter 10**). The small-scale replacement and other measures undertaken in the Bengawan Jero were good for alleviating the most acute problems but not for completely abolishing all the difficulties. This was why the Solo Valley project was never completely forgotten, not even after the colonial era (see the **Epilogue**).

[34] See for the food supplies of the Indies in general and the development of rice imports in particular Smits (1929: 85-103). See for the population growth Boomgaard (1980: 45, 50).

The Solo project was the upshot of a fixation on large works projects. Since 1877 information had been collected on details in the Solo Valley and this had led to the creation of a big plan. However, this long history of data collection was followed by faulty execution preparations. Later it even became apparent that the field research had also been deficient: new information was required (relating to the possible recoursing of the river). The alternative Solo Valley irrigation and drainage improvements were (apart from the Prijetan *waduk* project) the opposite to grand plans: they were all small-scale. As ever, it was a happy medium that was struck as may be learnt from making comparisons with the Pemali-Comal irrigation project where a series of smaller works had been created though, at 35, 37 and 44 thousand *bouws* these works were still of respectable dimensions (see **Chapter 6**). Though smaller than the Solo Works the series of irrigation projects in Pekalongan, covering almost 154 thousand *bouws* constituted what might be termed a sizeable irrigation area. Here the secret to success lay precisely in the piecemeal nature of the set up: the works were gradually constructed, bit by bit sections were built and subsequently put to immediate use. The disadvantage with the Solo plan was that it was so big and the works could only be put into use once the entire project had reached completion. The lesson to therefore be learnt from the Solo Works was not only that the project "had been too ambitious" (De Vos 1946: I. 101), but also that it lacked the component of a building up character (Soebandi, personal communication, February 1995, see also *Mindere Welvaartscommissie* 1910: 212[35]). The future would lie in planning medium-sized, easy to integrate projects (see **Chapter 10**)[36].

The preference for more modest-sized irrigation works that fitted in better with existing Javanese systems, was reflected in the government's spending[37]. Though the larger projects continued to require more funding there was, nonetheless, evidence in the 1902-1909 period of a drop in average expenses from at least one and a half million to around one million guilders per annum. The money spent on small works showed an increase both in absolute terms (from approximately 390,000 guilders to approximately 670,000 guilders in the same period) and in relative terms (from 19% to 39% of the total). (See **Appendix N**). The preference for small works really disappeared in the following decade and as of 1919 even the differentiation between both categories of works was no longer made: all types of works were treated the same (*Verslag BOW* 1919: 1, see also the overview of works given in the same report in comparison to the overview detailed in the "Civil Public Works Report" of 1910 which was considerably shorter!) Where was it all leading to? The amount of land with modern irrigation facilities doubled in the 1900-1910 period going from 100,000 *bouws* to 200,000. In the period leading up to 1920 the area of land provided with modern irrigation rose to 519,000 *bouws* which was an increase of 319,000 *bouws*. In terms of percentages the *sawa* acreage provided with modern irrigation went from 4.1% in 1900 to 7.9% in 1910 and 19½% in 1920. (See **Appendix B**)[38].

---

[35] The plan of Elenbaas did have this: his reservoirs were intended to complement the great plan. They could be built in less time than was needed for the entire project and were after completing ready to use.

[36] And of course also projects that were well prepared. While the Solo irrigation consisted of only a few indications on the map, the Pemali project e.g. was well thought from front to rear and back. See for a comparison of the Pemali-Comal and the Solo Works Weijs (1913: 20) and for the weir in the Pemali and the planned dam in the Solo De Meyier (1913).

[37] The small works involved in Javanese irrigation sometimes comprised many *bouws*. In the Irrigation Division Serang (Demak Works) e.g. there was a Javanese system of 27,500 *bouws* (*Mindere Welvaartscommissie* 1910: 266). So the criterion for "small" was financial. The states of Civil Public Works prove that it is (tens of) thousands of guilders instead of millions (see e.g. *Verslag BOW* 1910: 72 ff.). To give an indication of the average size: a line could be drawn at 1000 *bouws*.

[38] A few more data from the *Landbouwatlas van Java en Madoera* ("Agricultural Atlas of Java and Madura", 1926): The total area of land used for population agriculture in 1920 was 9,654,440 *bouws* (= 52.1% of the total

Versatile control

The second objection made my minister Idenburg to the resumption of the Solo plan had an agricultural side to it but it really related to control: the necessary gearing of agricultural activities to each other within the wider area was difficult. Whether agriculture stood to profit from irrigation works or not was ultimately a question of control. With the Ethical Policy, how works were controlled was an important point. Control had, in the first place, to do with how water was distributed. Various possible arrangements were thinkable (see **Chapter 6**). The regulations that were known were the Pateguan and Pekalen Management Regulations drawn up by Weijs and Lamminga respectively in conjunction with the Civil Service. The Pekalen regulation system was quite absolute. There water distribution was entirely in the hands of engineers. The Pateguan method was proportional leaving control of the peripheral areas to the population. The regulation developed in the Pemali region remained a compromise, thanks especially to the Javanese water master (the *Ulu-Ulu Golongan*). It was this regulation that became normative for regulations made elsewhere. Agricultural intervention, however, did thereby lead to local adaptations. This was how agreements for water regulation for the tormented Demak area were reached that were contributed to both by engineers and agriculturists (see **Box 8.2**). At that time the introducing and improving of water regulations was an everyday occurrence. Ultimately this would lead to the setting up of cultural plans which would have implications not only for water distribution but also for crop patterns (see **Chapter 10**).

Box 8.2 Management improvement in the Demak area

In an endeavour to combat the food problem manifested round 1900 the administration set up the Demak Commission some years later. The Commission consisted of Lamminga, then Head of the Third Public Works Division, H.C.H. de Bie, Deputy Inspector for Inland Agriculture, and P. de Roo de la Faille, Inspector for Agricultural Affairs. In its 1908 report the Commission showed great enthusiasm for the Pemali Management Regulation. (Voorduin 1914: 117). Previously Weijs had already lobbied to have this ruling introduced (*Verslag BOW* 1910: 260-269).

Unlike in the Pemali region it was not necessary in the Demak area to take into account the sugar cultivation interests: such interests were simply not relevant. This made it possible to allow west monsoon irrigation to commence at the best possible time for rice crops and what exactly the best possible time was depended on how damp it had been during the previous east monsoon season and when the west monsoon rains had begun. Since that was at a different time every year the agriculturalists recommended that this should be taken into account by establishing a new every year when irrigation should begin. Despite the opposition on the part of the engineers this proposition was effected in about 1920 (*Mededeelingen* 1924: 321).

The establishment of Irrigation Divisions was something that was beneficial to water distribution which was why so many were created after the turn of the century (fourteen in the end, see **Chapter 6**). As has been emphasized, the sugar industry played a big part in all of this: Irrigation Divisions were created in sugar growing areas. After the turn of the century these Divisions became even more interesting because they were also responsible for the operations of small

area of Java). The rice fields (with modern and Javanese irrigation and rainfed rice fields) covered in that year 4,397,598 *bouws* (Happé 1939 mentioned 2,670,700 hectares = 3,815,300 *bouws* for the government fields). The population numbered in 1920 34,976,419 souls (small difference with the figure of Gonggrijp 1957: 125). In 1924 the harvested area of *sawapadi* was 4,220,530 *bouws* and the harvested area of sugar cane 241,753 *bouws*. (Cf. **Appendices B, K and M**).

works and for maintenance. Small-scale irrigation work was something that definitely fitted in well with the Ethical Policy. Exactly how significant maintenance was emerged from the problems encountered with the various projects, such as the Kening Works. There rice production levels fell because people neglected their drainage systems. The solution was to improve maintenance and control (see **Note 2**). The neglecting of supply and drainage channels and particularly the disrupting of both these types of watercourses was something that was reported in conjunction with other works, like for example the Sampean Works (Thal Larsen 1912: 929). The solution remained the same as in the Kening area (see **Box 8.3**).

Box 8.3 The Sampean irrigation and the measures taken

In the case of the Sampean Works the entire irrigation network situation deteriorated (Rietveld 1932: 285-286). The measures taken were manifold. Around 1910 endeavours were made to prevent supply conduits from bursting by dumping rubble and planting vegetation (such as *kankung* and *canna*). It was the engineer C.G. Cramer, employed in the area between 1907 and 1913, who was particularly active on this front. He was working for the Pekalen-Sampean Irrigation Division established in 1907. The planting of vegetation was not a success because keeping it cut back and making sure that the waterways did not get blocked up was too much work. Notably "the canna grew so vigorously that the watercourse started to resemble an elongated Garden of Eden whenever the labourers stayed away for too long" (Rietveld 1932: 286). Where drainage systems were concerned people experimented with *Wildbachverbaung*, that is to say, the introduction of humps. These kept getting washed away. Ultimately, it seemed that the best solution lie in reforesting the upper reaches. (See, for instance, *Verslag BOW* 1908: 329-334, 1909: 509-513).

In this area agricultural intervention led to the adaptation of control and to the reducing the number of *gologans* from seven to four. Previously much rice was lost in the *gologans*, which received water at a late stage, due to disease (root rot). With the new system the loss level was definitely lower (*Medeelingen* 1924: 320-321).

Under the Ethical Policy, Irrigation Divisions were established before the completion of new works really justified such moves. When it came to setting up a new Irrigation Division people proceeded as follows (see, for instance, Van den Broek d'Obrenan 1918: 20-22). First of all the terrain would be investigated and all the river catchment basin borders mapped out. At the same time the personnel would undertake other activities relevant to the assessment of the water situation, like measuring rainfall levels. Afterwards attempts would be made to determine the flow levels of the separate river areas and within the region as a whole. All this information was important for the next step, that of making irrigation works preparations. The personnel also made a study of Javanese agriculture and irrigation. This research sometimes led to proposals relating to the maintaining and improving of irrigation systems and to the executing of such proposals. Totally in keeping with the Ethical Policy Van den Broek d'Obrenan (1918: 22) deemed "this to carry much weight and to be perhaps more important than the proposing of entirely new works". He elucidated as follows:

"Many inland works have, in the course of time, become ... so degenerated that they can no longer be of service; the upkeep of works will always place extremely heavy demands without providing any certainty that, when most badly required, i.e. in the midst of the rainy season, they can actually be of service. A large portion of the energy put into irrigation therefore relates to creating a situation of certainty for irrigation in any one area and to reducing the amount of labour required and the costs of maintenance" (ibid.).

Figure 8.6: Rice harvest, 1920 (photo UBL KITLV 19183)

Figure 8.7: Rice harvest with *ani-ani* knife, 1910 (photo UBL KITLV 2498)

Regardless of whether existing irrigation systems were improved to ensure that water distribution went smoothly, water regulation systems were in any case set up.

In the Bengawan Jero a special Irrigation Commission was installed which represented the various interests. More generally, local Irrigation Commissions (i.e. per administrational department) were developed which started being officially installed from 1920 onwards. The chairman was the head of the local administration (the Assistant-Resident). The relevant Section Engineer also had a seat on the Irrigation Commission (a Section being a part of an Irrigation Division Division) as did the agricultural advisor. At first the local population was not directly represented on this Commission, but later on it was, by higher Javanese administrators (like the Regent). (*Mededeelingen* 1924: 319, Metzelaar 1946: 206, Lammers 1942: 15, compare Van Doorn 1994a: 144). With these Irrigation Commissions it was as though the Irrigation Divisions, in which the technical element was reinforced because they were placed under the supervision of Civil Public Works, were somehow checked. In this way the Civil Service remained involved in control. The agricultural people were given a say in matters as well which was a meagre consolation for the advocates of "agricultural control" but always better than nothing.

Control was an important issue where the relationship between the sugar industry and small farming was concerned. Though decisions had been taken in favour of the *waduk* system round the year 1920 it would take very many years for the loathed day and night regulation to be phased out in practice, partly because it soon became apparent that the night *waduks* did not function properly which subsequently slowed down construction work (see *Encyclopaedie* Vol. V 1927: 216 and Metzelaar 1946: 218-220, 222; this matter will be returned to in **Chapter 10**).

Irrigation state

In 1900 De Meyier was opposed to proceeding with the Solo Works project because it would be too great a burden on the budget, because rentabilty was, to his mind, too uncertain and because the people of the Bengawan Jero could well be helped in a different way. His argument was well received, partly because it fitted in nicely with the welfare politics of the Ethical Policy and because the minister operated along the same lines as De Meyier. There is one other possible reason why this one Solo Commission member's influence was so great. One thing that had gained attention when the project had been dropped had been the part played by the Netherlands or, more precisely, events in the Netherlands in the project's decision-making process. In that respect the opinions of De Meyier, then Director of the Public Civil Works Department had weighed heavily because of his Indies connections. The aim of The Ethical Policy, which gave prominence to the Javanese population, was to give the Indies population a bigger say in the colonial decision-making process. What also fitted into this emancipatory political line was the notion the Netherlands might start to take the Indies more seriously. This represented, thus, a power shift from the mother country to the colony. It made De Meyier a prominent figure and, with him, the voice of the Indies government which had also brought out negative recommendations, became heard.[39]

What went hand in hand with the Ethical Policy was the move to increase governmental involvement and therefore also a process that lead to state expansion and differentiation. Alongside of the new services there were also two new departments that were created, the Department of Agriculture (1905) and the Government Companies Department (1907). Because of the success of the Civil Public Works Department's emancipation struggle in the nineteenth

[39] As Civil Public Works Director De Meyier naturally had a key role anyway: he was a consultant who was involved in the work, and moreover, he had the occasion to initiate works other than provided in the general plan. Even after his retirement De Meyier had an influential position in discussions on the Solo Works, namely as editor of the influential magazine "The Indies Guide" (until 1913).

century the Civil Service had already lost considerable influence. The new developments were to lead to a further dismantling of the Service (the relevant department included). For the Civil Service which was traditionally responsible for the people's interests, seeing that the Ethical Policy was predominantly being executed by other bodies was a bitter pill to swallow. Van Doorn who, like others, associated the Ethical Policy with the conservative and conservatory Civil Service (1994a: 151-152), spoke of the unfolding of a "fan of welfare services" to which he added the following (p.107):

"It was, above all else, this expansion in specialist services that posed a threat to the Civil Service. With the rise of pure technical services – like irrigation and the railways – things had remained reasonably amicable but now specialist fields were developing that affected the very core of the civil servant's job. The attractive and appealing 'development work' towards which the ethical philosophy coursed, was taken out of his hands".[40]

As was emphasised in **Chapter 6**, Van Doorn maintained that the irrigation service – the first to liberate itself from the administrative powers – was way ahead of The Ethical Policy. In another respect, too, the Civil Public Works Department was ahead of its time. Because of all its specialist services the Indies had soon become a technocracy "in the sense of having an order based on technical knowledge and achievements that ascribed strikingly important roles to technologists" (Van Doorn 1994a: 164). Together with Agriculture and Government Companies, Civil Public Works finally took over from the Civil Service that had once been the backbone of colonial administration. The great influence exercised by the specialist departments was not the only characteristic of the technocratic state. What also typified it was the amount of research carried out: into resuming the Solo Works, into agricultural research and, particularly, welfare research. That latter research project was monumental. Announced in 1901, the final report did not appear until 1914 at which time all the Welfare Commission's proposals still had to be elaborated (see *Encyclopaedie* Vol. IV 1921: 758). The state's technocratic character became clearly evident in the field of irrigation. With the Ethical Policy this terrain of governmental intervention virtually turned into an interdepartmental enterprise. The engineers remained dominant throughout, even though the confidence had been shaken by the Solo Works.[41]

Meanwhile, Indies hydraulic engineering had also become an established technological branch (or at least a disciplinary facet of the technological science of civil engineering). Preliminary study, entire systems design, the adopting of planned approaches to works' execution and technological control were the important aspects of the scientific approach to irrigation as it developed in the nineteenth century. Towards the end of the century rentability was added to this list and there was a new issue: agricultural surplus value, that emerged. With all these developments the "Indies hydraulic engineer" career began to take definite shape, also because

[40] This led in 1914 even to a protest movement under administration officials (Van Doorn 1994a: 106-107). The relative importance of the various government activities appears from expenditures. For "internal governance" these increased slightly from twelve to 12½ million guilders in the period 1904-1914. In the same period spending on "public works" grew from 11½ to 26 million and on "agriculture" from 0.8 to two million guilders. (For "education" the increase was five to thirteen million). (See *Overzicht* ["Overview"] 1916 and Van Doorn 1994a: 147, cf. **Appendix H**). See for an overview of the rise of the welfare services De Vries (1961).

[41] The number of engineers employed by Public Works (permanent staff) increased from 1900 to 1912 from 96 to 117. As of 1907, there were engineers in temporary employment as well; their number rose from four in 1907 to 12 in 1912. In the years 1902-1904 there was a dip. Then the number dropped below 90. The number of Architects and Supervisors grew in the period 1900 to 1912 from 235 to 314. (*Verslag BOW*, see Thal Larsen 1912: 930; cf. **Appendix F**). The total number of engineers in public service was 787 in 1930. These included 332 (42%) civil engineers and 257 (33%) agricultural engineers (these engineers acted after 1917, see **Note 43**). There were also mechanical, mining and electrical engineers. (See Van Doorn 1994a: 164).

engineers had organised themselves. A long time after the Indies Section within the Royal Institute of Engineers (*KIVI*) had been established in Surabaya, in 1851, and the Dutch-East Indies Section had been established in Batavia, in 1875, they set up their own society, in 1912, which was known as: The Dutch-East Indies Society of Public Works Engineers. Since 1876 the Dutch-East Indies Section of the *KIVI* had been publishing its own periodical known as the "Journal of the Dutch Indies Section". The new society also created a new own body: *De Waterstaats-Ingenieur* ("The Public Works Engineer").[42]

Through the appointing of Extraordinary Professors, from about 1903 on, Indies Hydraulic Engineering began to get attention from the Polytechnic College which, in 1905, was made the College of Technical Higher Education in Delft (see **Figure 8.1**). As has been mentioned, Lamminga put his name down for that position in 1910. Apart from Grinwis Plaat his predecessors were the engineer J.C. Heijning (hailed by Weijs [1913: 28] as "the instigator of success within the irrigation divisions") and, after him, there was Elenbaas (from the Solo Valley) before the time of Weijs. The field made it possible for Indies hydraulic engineers to specialise. In 1917 the Extraordinary Professorship was turned into an ordinary chair. Two years later the engineer J. Haringhuizen who had worked on irrigation affairs under Lamminga, succeeded Weijs (who had been the chair since 1913). When the College of Technical Higher Education was established in Bandung, in 1920, a similar type of course was set up in 1921, there it was De Vos who was the first Professor (see **Figure 8.2**).[43] In 1924 Indies irrigation received a new handbook, written by the Civil Public Department engineer T.D. van Maanen. It was a book in which all the experience and knowledge drawn from all the projects undertaken in the 1885-1920 period was comprehensively described and collated. The book contained what amounted to the fundamentals of modern irrigation science, including water control. Attention was given to the (minimal) rentability of irrigation works in a foreword written by J.E.A. de Vogel. Comparing this with De Meyier's publication (1891) it was evident that irrigation science had become a teachable field.[44]

What the Solo Works had proved was that engineers could not cope on their own. In his reflections Vlugter (1949: I. 101) remarked that what had been learnt from the Solo Works was that "before any irrigation works project could be embarked on it was imperative to obtain agricultural-economic advice". Naturally the disappointing results of other projects, such as the Demak Works and the Kening Works, only contributed to this. Furthermore, under the Ethical Policy irrigation activities were found to be too important to simply entrust to engineers. The Agricultural Department which had been made responsible for stimulating small farming

---

[42] In 1921 the Dutch Indies Section of the Royal Institute of Engineers became independent and created the Group of the Dutch Indies. *De Waterstaatsingenieur* and *De Mijningenieur* ("The Mining Engineer"), which came out from 1919, in 1934 went into *De Ingenieur in Nederlands-Indië* ("The Engineer in the Dutch East Indies") set up by the Group of the Dutch Indies (after independence: *De Ingenieur in Indonesië* ["The Engineer in Indonesia"]). (See e.g. Korving 1947).

[43] See for the history of the Technical College (now University) of Delft and the relationship with the "offshoot" in Bandung Baudet and Makkink (1992) and Baudet (1991). Berger obtained his doctorate with his above cited study *Landbouwkundige onderzoekingen omtrent de irrigatie op Java* ("Agricultural research on irrigation in Java", 1915) in Delft. The Agricultural College in Wageningen, founded in 1874, only received the status of university in 1917. See for the rise of the Wageningen training, in competition with the university biology Van der Schoor (1994). See for the scientific significance of agricultural research (by Treub) Van Berkel (1985: 215).

[44] In his review of significant technical literature in the field of irrigation from the colonial period Ankum (1984: 10) mentions together with Telders et al. (1901: the Solo report) also Van Maanen (1924). He mentions as the third and last work, the lecture notes by De Vos from 1925. In his view, the latter lecture notes and Van Maanen's textbook indicate to what knowledge they came in the "construction period" of the irrigation history. See for a handbook with purely technical data De Meyier (1920).

enterprises and which had thus become the government's most important instrument in conjunction with its welfare policy and progress politics, demanded its share. It emphasised the importance of fertilising (silt!) and, in general, it highlighted the economic advantages – for the population – of having irrigation facilities. Irrigation was presented as the "inseparable companion of remunerative agriculture, welfare and progress for the population" (De Kat Angelino 1929: 336). In the meantime, irrigation affairs continued to provide work for the Civil Service. Admittedly the engineers had managed to free themselves from the power of civil servants but it had not been a complete emancipation, certainly not as far as control was concerned. In the name of the people the Civil Service remained involved in irrigation affairs and, through rentability, it even managed to somewhat increase its influence.

The various departments involved in irrigation were caught up in a competitive battle relating to the degree of influence each had in irrigation matters. It was a battle staged within the Rentability Commission (later the Permanent Irrigation Commission) and within management organisation. In the new technocracy it was chiefly Civil Public Works and Agriculture that were at loggerheads with each other. Within the ranks of the engineers the main dispute related to large-scale versus small-scale works. Partly as a result of the influence of the Agricultural Department, which during the early decades of the last century was more openly supportive of the interests of small farmers than Civil Public Works and the Civil Service, the balance tipped in favour of small works. In the area of control the discussion focused on the position of the Irrigation Divisions: should these remain with Civil Public Works or should they be switched to Agriculture? In time it was also the case that irrigation practices had a reconciliatory effect: control demanded co-operation between Civil Public Works, the Civil Service and Agriculture. It was a co-operation that took shape in the local Irrigation Commissions where the population was also represented. This was where the technocracy came up against limits: in the Irrigation Commission meetings it was the regional head who wielded the chairman's hammer. In the matter of irrigation the Indies was not a fully-fledged technocracy[45]. With so much governmental intervention, however, the title "irrigation state" would have been quite an accurate one.[46]

Within the Indies irrigation state investments in modern irrigation were slow to catch on. As far as the annual expenditure on irrigation works was concerned, increases in conjunction with the Ethical Policy only became evident after 1910/15, that was when the spendings began to surpass those of the late nineties of the century before last – the period when the Solo Valley project was topical (1894-1898). After 1898 the annual investments fell from over four million guilders per year (in 1898 that was as much as 4.8 million, including what was expended on the Solo Works) to approximately two million per year (see **Chapter 7** and Thal Larsen 1912: 930). The Solo Works had been halted and, for the time being, the disappointment of that and other works projects gave people no incentive to again make high investments. By about 1910, though, all such frustrations had been forgotten and another convincing irrigation policy had been produced (compare Ott de Vries 1922: 741). In the 1910-1915 period spendings again increased going from 3.6 million to 5.6 million guilders before rising to a height of ten million guilders around 1920. (See **Appendix C**).

[45] Van Doorn also refused to commit himself: he (1994a:164) called the Indies an "unfinished technocracy", where the "power that the technicians had inherited from the government officials, ... [found] its borders where she met European business".

[46] I use this term only in a descriptive sense and not as a theoretical (or ideological) concept, as the term "hydraulic society" (with absolute state power) of Wittfogel (1957). The latter term has been applied to the ancient kingdoms of Java. Modern researchers emphasize, however, the conflictual nature of precolonial "hydraulic societies". (See **Chapter 2**).

What of the state's income? This derived from land rents. As was concluded in conjunction with the Pemali Works the administration had introduced a new land rent ordinance in 1907 which stated that *sawas* should be categorised according to various productivity groups. The new regulation was gradually introduced so that by 1914 it was being enforced everywhere. From 1919 onwards the land divisions were again revised.[47] On the income side, what was also important was the financial contribution made by the sugar refiners to the cost of operating and maintaining the irrigation works. This was not to become a regular source of income until 1919 (Happé 1939, see **Appendix C**).

Networks

Clearly the Solo Valley Works had gone "a bridge too far". Towards the end of the nineteenth century the irrigation engineers had great confidence in their own power but that was something that could not be substantiated in the shape of the Solo Valley project. Due to the success of the 1885 regulation the engineers became somewhat fuddled and complacent and they therefore lost their grasp on reality (partly because of their enormous enthusiasm) both in economic and political senses but also in a technical respect! They simply wanted to do too much. In the Solo Valley things finally caught up with them and the timing could not have been worse. The Solo Works pushed the involvement of engineers in irrigation into a crisis just when the Ethical Policy was foregrounding the interests of the population and making it seem that good irrigation possibilities were opening up for the engineers.

The Solo Works perfectly demonstrated what qualities, other than technical ones, were needed to start up a project. With regard to the works, the doubts and hesitations that had existed from the very beginning were countered by certain firm convictions and the utilisation of good contacts. The battle concerning the continuation of the works was fought out in the political (and social) arena. Because the budget had been exceeded the civil servants who in the past and in conjunction with their own interests had constantly held back (though in recent times to a lesser degree) were suddenly listened to in governmental circles. This applied in particular to the Inspectors of Culture who concerned themselves with the rentability of works. For the emancipated engineers a spanner was suddenly thrown in the works. They were forced to take a step backwards which later proved to be a good basis for making a new leap forwards. In actual fact, the dividing line between engineers and civil servants was not all that definite. In the discussions on modern irrigation De Meyier proved to be a critical engineer and various of the civil servants remained extremely positive in their outlook.

After the works had come to a standstill in 1903 the engineers had to repair their damaged image. They did that by producing good work and subsequently drawing attention to the results of their efforts, to such things as, for instance, the successful systems in the Pemali-Comal region. Because of this Lamminga was later put on a pedestal (engineers thus had to pay attention to "public relations" and to "impression management"). As far as presentation was concerned, Lamminga made himself useful by proposing, amongst other things, that certain large irrigation works projects be described (see **Chapter 2**). Civil servants (like Bodemeijer and De Jaager) who were convinced of the usefulness of modern irrigation were given all the leeway

[47] See for the land rent levy over the years Sollewijn Gelpke (1885), Happe (1939), Teng Sioe Tjhan (1933). See for an overview *Encyclopaedie* (Vol. I, 1917: 234-241). The levying of the land tax was in the hands of the Civil Service. The measurement of all land taxable grounds was the responsibility of technicians of the topographical service. The classification of the rice fields was also done by the administrators and not by agronomists, although this was possible because of the creation of the Department of Agriculture and for reason of the importance of agricultural research perhaps even obvious. Happé (1939: II. 13) could only mention one work that despite an expected low rentability had yet been implemented: the Pacal Works in the Solo Valley. See for a relativistic reflection on the profitability of irrigation works De Vogel (1924).

they needed from engineers to air their views. This also had to do with another strategy, namely that of (by means of coalitions) extending the networks that linked engineers to decision-makers.

In the end, the engineers emerged from the struggle relatively unscathed but they lost their autonomy and that was of course bitter. The process which had enabled them to emancipate themselves from working for the Civil Service and to become independent with their own public works service had been difficult enough. Irrigation involvement had gone from focusing on individual headworks to dealing with the setting up of entire systems involving everything from supplying water to dealing with the details of the tertiary services as well as from empirically learning from the mistakes of non-specialised engineers to the academic input of a schooled corps. They had also gone from constructing irrigation works to managing irrigation areas (department-wise). With the rentability question the government had previously ordered the engineers to stop and with the upcoming interest of small farming a new restriction had been imposed. The Solo Works functioned as a strong catalyst in all of this. New issues gave rise to new categories of experts: after the civil servants and the engineers it was the agricultural experts who became the third group to involve themselves with irrigation. In other words, irrigation involvement went from being a purely engineering-centred activity to being the communal terrain of engineers, civil servants and agriculturalists or, to being a shared state concern. Under these conditions much was achieved though around 1920 only a small portion of the *sawas* in Java were being irrigated in a modern way. The task ahead was a big one but the engineers and their associates were ready for it.

Irrigation concern became an important aspect of the state's welfare policy and, partly because of this, it gained around 1920 all the allure of a "modern colonial state". What that meant for the development of modern irrigation will be revealed in the third and final section of this study. What will also become apparent will be that the engineers and their employer were unexpectedly confronted with new challenges.

III

TECHNICAL PERFECTIONISM AND RATIONAL BUREAUCRACY

1920 – 1942

9

'Emerging from the economic and moral depression'

The Tangerang Works

> The scientific enterprise as a whole does from time to time prove useful, open up new territory, display order, and test long-accepted belief. Nevertheless, the *individual* engaged in a normal research problem *is almost never doing any one of these things.* Once engaged, his motivation is of a rather different sort. What then challenges him is the conviction that, if only he is skilful enough, he will succeed in solving a puzzle that no one before him has solved or solved as well. Many of the greatest scientific minds have devoted all of their professional attention to demanding puzzles of this sort. On most occasions any particular field of specialisation offers nothing else to do, a fact that makes it no less fascinating to the proper sort of addict (Kuhn 1971: 38).

The first ever Dutch waterworks to be constructed were in Jakarta, then known as Batavia. Long before the *Oosterslokkan* and the *Westerslokkan* canals were constructed in the eighteenth century the *Mookervaart* ("Mooker channel") had been excavated (see **Chapter 3**). This waterway was named after the bailiff, Vincent Van Moock, who owned land in that area. Together with "a company of certain special persons" (Jan Hooyman 1779, cited in Go 1966: 47) Van Moock created that canal in the 1677-1687 period. It formed a waterway between two rivers: the *kali* Angké, linked to the city canals of Batavia and the Cisadane. The canal was all part of a campaign designed to flush Batavia's waterways clean and to improve connections with the Tangerang, for instance for the purposes of transporting firewood. Van Moock did well out of the project because for some years he was able to receive toll money. (Posno 1936: VI. 107)[1].

Two hundred years were to pass by until 1926, the year when again this same area was to become the setting for the last major irrigation project in the Indies, that of the Tangerang Works. By then the creation of irrigation works had a long history in which much experience had been gained. Concern for irrigation matters was normal at that time which does not mean to say that technical know-how had stood still. Innovations continued to be made which were certainly not the least in irrigation history! However, that did not mean to say that the Tangerang Works constituted an easy project. The crisis was to complicate matters and, moreover, as a result of

---

[1] Going on a report published by the engineer Ingenegeren of the *Hollandsche Beton Maatschappij* ("Dutch Concrete Company") the contractor responsible for the sluice complex at Sewan (see below), Posno (1935: VI. 107) reported that work on the canal had started in 1682. The canal's estuary dated from the eighteenth century. The area around the Tangerang had a flourishing sugar industry in the *VOC* period, around 1700, in which the Chinese played an important part (Go 1966: 45 ff.).

administrative reforms operational organisation was also to change. All the routines and innovations in the field of irrigation will be further expounded on in the following chapter but first I shall give the details of the final casus in this study: the irrigation works in the Tangerang area[2].

Figure 9.1: Weir in the Cisadane, 1940 (photo UBL KITLV 27706)

[2] Sources: Van Breen et al. (1919), *Verslag BOW* ("Civil Public Works Report") 1926: 75-91), *Voorlopige cijfers* (" Provisional figures", 1924, 1926-1933), *Jaarverslag* ("Annual Report", 1928-1940), Dumas (1929 and 1933), Posno (1935), *Tangerangwerken* ("Tangerang Works", 1936) and the *BOW* Archives (E 1-28). Of the above-mentioned threesome it was Van Breen who then headed the works project. At that time Dumas was in charge of the irrigation works in the Regencies of Bantam, Batavia and Buitenzorg but later only in the Regencies of Bantam and Batavia. Posno worked for the Public Works Department in West Java. The description given in the "Civil Public Works Report" of 1926 was based on the "explanation of the general plan for the improvement of irrigation and drainage in the Tangerang plain" produced by the Chief Engineer D.C.W. Snell who we also encountered in conjunction with the Solo Works, from 1925.

Figure 9.2: Map of the Tangerang plain with the 1918 irrigation plan (from: Dumas 1929)

The works

The plans

At Tangerang, some eighteen kilometres to the west of Jakarta, is a region that is known as the Tangerang plain. That area has three rivers flowing through it, the Cidurian, the Cimanceuri and the Cisadane (see **Figure 9.2**). The area once comprised privately owned land areas which were:

"Extensive tracts of land both for agricultural and residential purposes that were allocated to private parties with special rights, either in the form of gifts or through purchase, rights that were fully owned by these private parties. The land was allocated by the United East Indian Company (the VOC), the English Interim Administration and the Dutch State Administration" (J. Heemstra 1940, cited in Go 1966: 75).

The landowner had special rights in relation to the "sitting tenants", notably in the field of tax levying, both in the form of demanding a portion of the harvest and in the form of exacting statutory labour (ibid.). The privately-owned landed property could rightfully be termed "states within states" (Heslinga 1923: 39).

The *padi* variety that constituted the main crop of the farming population in the Tangerang region was an inferior sort. It was an area that was plagued by poverty and frequent famine. The plains depended largely on the rainfall that was erratic and minimal. During the west monsoon season some 28,000 *bouws* would be watered. The general procedure was always as follows:

"As far as is possible and feasible the land owners utilise the vast quantities of precipitation that falls in the space of a few months which, collected from small waterways or, when banjirs come, tapped from large rivers, is kept in lakes and marshes. The main distribution of this water, by means of what generally amount to badly maintained and dilapidated weirs and inlet sluices, is in the hands of the land owner and his personnel while the remaining highly unregulated distribution is left to the population and its chiefs (mandurs)" (*Verslag BOW* ["Civil Public Works Report"] 1926: 78).

Because the existing irrigation systems were so defective, harvests would fail completely once every four or five years. Flooding, especially from the Cimanceuri, plagued the region. The flow of this particular river was most erratic because of the lack of wooded area in the river's source region. The felling of trees made the water supply in the other rivers very changeable as well. However, the problems in the area were not so much a result of natural as much as social circumstances. Just like elsewhere (see Go 1966: 76) the population suffered under the uncontrolled exploitation policies of the land owners. Dumas (1929: 200) generally attributed the "economic and moral depression" in the area to:

"the levying of taxes by the Land Owners in the Tangerang area on virtually all commercial activities undertaken by the tenants for the purposes of housing and maintaining their families while little or nothing is done to improve structural works, such as irrigation works and roadways, for the benefit of the population".

According to Dumas (ibid.) the most acute situation within the private agricultural areas was "the lack of properly technically organised irrigation systems and proper functioning drainage systems".

By 1911 the situation in the Tangerang plain was so drastic that the government decided to asphalt a number of (private) roads on a "relief-work" basis. That was the time when the preparations for an irrigation plan also commenced. In that connection it was therefore necessary to buy back private land. The government made an important step in this direction in 1914 when it determined that some 35 privately owned tracts of land in the Tangerang plain should be quickly put up for compulsory purchase. In 1916 the "Report concerning extensive local research set up for the existing general state of affairs and for the possible improvement of the irrigation and drainage of the Tangerang plain in the residency of Batavia" reached the offices of the Director of Civil Public Works. The report had been compiled by the engineers H. van Breen, who had headed the study, and L.J. Polderman. Other memorandums containing proposals on ways to improve the situation followed. The memorandum that appeared in 1919 was an important one, this "Memorandum concerning improvements to be made to irrigation and drainage situations in the Tangerang plain" was signed by the above-mentioned engineers and by H.W. Dumont (who, like Polderman was a Third Class Engineer).

Originally the intention had been to simply divide the plain into three irrigation areas that would be supplied from west to east by the Cidurian, the Cimanceuri and the Cisadane. The 1919 memorandum contained a proposal for the creation of just two irrigation areas, a northern area that would be irrigated with water from the Cisadane and a southern area that would be linked up to the Cidurian. These areas were respectively 57,000 and 17,000 *bouws* big. Plans to incorporate the Cimanceuri in the irrigation activities were dropped. Because of its irregular water supply, work in that river would be relatively expensive. Another factor to be considered was that the surplus issuing from the other rivers had proved to be sufficient for the whole irrigation area. There were also agricultural factors to be taken into account[3]. The water issuing from the Cimanceuri was of a poor quality. The Cisadane water was, by contrast, fertile and even better than the water of the Cidurian. The new irrigation plan thus maximised the benefits of the area to be irrigated from the Cisadane.

The 1919 memorandum provided a fully elaborated irrigation plan[4]. It was based on details relating to the quantities of water available and the volumes of water required. Such figures were obtained from rainfall measurements (records existed dating back to 1891) and from river water volumes and from field tests[5]. The data would then be processed on the basis of the mathematical knowledge of the day. The Cisadane had the most water: the minimum available flow rate was calculated to be approximately twenty cubic metres in the driest month and roughly 70 cubic metres per second in the wettest month (August and April respectively). The Cidurian offered much less: about five cubic meters is the driest month and some 22 cubic meters in the wettest month (the last being March!). As far as the water requirement was concerned, it was calculated that a maximum average of 1.1 litres per *bouw*, per second would be required for the predominantly low-lying Cisadane area and two litres for the hilly Cidurian region. The engineers also reviewed the *padi* yields. One thing they did was to create test fields or "experimental patches". For water supplies it was the Pemali regulation that was taken as a basis (see **Chapters 5 and 6**). The amount of water to be allocated per rice crop phase was adapted to the particular types of rice that it was thought would flourish best in the area. Four *golongans* were proposed for the two irrigation areas which also amounted to an agriculturally sound plan[6].

The plan contained the structure of the system for supply and drainage waterways and also a river improvement programme[7]. When sub-dividing the two areas into secondary and tertiary sections it was existing drainage routes that were followed as much as possible. The ideal artificial tertiary section construction size was conceived to be 250 to 300 *bouws*[8]. An overview of the required artificial structures, divided into main structural works (such as weirs), special structural works (like, for example, an aqueduct in a main channel) and normal structural works (inlets, deluge dams and such like in the irrigation channels) also constituted part of the grand design. The plan was also accompanied by an extensive detailed cost estimates. The General Total for all the project costs (excluding the purchasing back of private land) amounted to exactly ten million guilders.

[3] In this connection Dumas (1929: 201) referred to the research conducted by the agri-geologist, Dr. Julius Mohr.

[4] Another memorandum, dating from 1918, dwelt on the closing off and improving of the *Mookervaart*. It also contained proposals for two irrigation areas.

[5] The field tests were conducted by the engineers involved. The influence exercised from the agricultural side was limited to advising (Van Breen et al. 1919: 15 and 18).

[6] According to a report compiled by J.E. van der Stok in 1915 to which Van Breen et al. (1919: 23) referred.

[7] For drainage areas larger than ten square kilometres people used the Melchior method to determine maximum water flow levels. With smaller areas it was more the method of "known estimates" that was relied on. When determining channel profiles it was the graphs of the engineer J.M. Steevensz given in *De Waterstaats-Ingenieur* ("The Public Works Engineer") of 1918, no. 5 that were used.

[8] At that time the maximum customary size was 150 *bouws* (Dumas 1929: 204). With the Pemali Works that was 200 *bouws*. What is given here is the net size: just the *sawa*.

In 1918 and 1919 the first two land areas to once again be made land domains were: Pasilian and Kresek and other land areas were to follow. This made it difficult for the work to be started on. In the early twenties the country's finances were in a poor state which led to general irrigation work economy drives. This also affected the project in the Tangerang plain despite the fact that in 1920 the government had already given its approval for the first plans: the construction of the weir in the Cisadane and the widening of that same river. In 1925 the tides turned and the government's financial situation improved. To ensure that the funds were well spent the government installed a committee consisting of Directors from Civil Public Works, the Civil Service and Government Companies. The committee compiled a list of "special works", the aim being to improve the economic situation. One of the projects on this list was the Tangerang Works and the improving and extending of the road network (compare Creutzberg 1974: 37-39).

The first improvements

As far as the sequence of the works to be undertaken was concerned the project organisation first directed its attention (in line with Snell's 1925 report, see **Note 2**) towards the western part of the plain. That was where the Cidurian's catchment area was located and the first two land areas to be taken over by the state. Indeed, it was not to stop at those two tracts of land, according to the "Civil Public Works Report" (1926) some nine land areas had by then become state-owned.

The creation of dykes and the normalising of the river was part of the first work to be done and that included giving the Cidurian a new estuary to the sea. The colonial government authorised these projects in 1926 and made available respective sums of *f* 193,500 and *f* 169,700[9]. The basic assumption was that the maximum river flow rate would be 486 cubic metres a second (that was, during *banjirs*). This was determined on the basis of flow rate measurements and calculations according to the methods first developed by Melchior and Lauterburg. The river improvement works aimed at

"protecting, in the near future, the technically irrigated areas on both sides of the river against destructive banjirs which had led to repeated breaking down of the dyke systems that were generally too low and in a poor state and, almost annually, major damage was incurred to the crops which partly depended upon rain and which were partly irrigated by waduks" (*Verslag BOW* 1926: 84).

At the same time, the improving of the existing reservoir irrigation in the area of the two former land estates of Kresek and Pasilian was on the agenda, as was the plan to improve drainage. As far as the *waduks* were concerned this had to do with several marshes (*rawas*). Just as in 1926 the government gave permission for the following works to go ahead:

1. the cleaning and dyking-in of the channels that linked the Patrasana *rawa* with the Garugak *rawa* (*f* 8500),
2. the improving of the Patrasana *rawa* that was used as a reservoir, together with the tapping and throughput sluice (*f* 81,500),
3. the laying of the extensive irrigation works in the *sawa* area of 1665 *bouws* that was irrigated from the same *rawa* source (*f* 31,650),
4. the digging of a main channel (*f* 300,200).

[9] Due to work expansion the first-mentioned sum was later raised to *f* 1,005,000.

The Patrasana *rawa* (and via this the Garugak *rawa* and yet another marsh) obtained their water from the Cidurian provided that the water level in the river was high enough for that. For these purposes there was a construction known as a *banjir* inlet. When constructing the works for the purposes of the extensive irrigation network in the *rawa* area, use was made of the Pemali line to determine the capacity of the channels (see **Chapters 5 and 6**) and an average water requirement level would be given depending on the surface area to be irrigated. For a section 200 *bouws* big, that was one litre per *bouw* per second. In the case of larger sections no further reductions would be made since

"that involved existing sawa areas where only a minimal desa increase was to be expected and where ... the constitution of the soil is such that no growing of European crops, particularly sugar cane, would be conceivable" (*Verslag BOW* 1926: 88)[10].

The tertiary sections were made large (see **Note 8**). Even sections of 400 to 600 *bouws* were found to be acceptable. Since the soil was unsuitable for European crops (notably sugar) no efforts were made to divide the sections into smaller plots. In that way financial savings could be made. The implications of this approach were that much was left to the local population to sort out. This "simplified solution to the irrigation question" also "corresponded with the outlook of the Department of Agriculture" (Dumas 1929: 204). At a later stage, further sub-dividing of the sections would not constitute a problem.

Later works were executed in the interests of improving irrigation supplies drawn from the Garugak *rawa*. From this reservoir it was possible to irrigate a further 7400 *bouws* of land. In 1928 the government made available *f* 355,000 for these purposes. All these works gave a preview of the realisation of the drainage plan for the Tangerang plain. The Kresek and Pasilian plain would ultimately become a part of the Cisadane irrigation plan but until such a time the Cidurian remained in use for water provision. Whether or not the water level could be retained in the Patrasana *rawa* was uncertain and it was for that reason that people wanted the supply via the *banjir* inlet to be replaced by input from the main canal of the Cidurian works. The plan was to then pursue the normalisation of the Cidurian. The river meanders in the region of the *banjir* inlet provided the required upward pressure for the water. In the whole chronology of activities the construction of a weir in the Cidurian thus constituted a logical following step. The progress of the whole project depended on the repurchasing of new tracts of land but by then this process was so advanced (in 1926 there was still only one area to be bought back in the relevant region) that this was also possible.

The weirs

Van Breen, Polderman and Dumont presumed in their 1919 report that a movable weir would be constructed in the Cidurian at the Solear *desa*. Later, though, expenditure estimates were to indicate that placing a permanent weir further upstream would be a good deal cheaper, even though the main canal would then have to be lengthened and thus made more expensive. Another advantage was the fact that the soil in the Rancasumur *desa* area, where it was planned that a weir should be constructed in the bend of a river, was made up of solid material, what was known as Bantam tufa. "This tufa is so hard that the pickaxes used very soon become worn out" reported Dumas (1929: 205). It was, however, an excellent subsoil for the job in hand.

[10] The same applied to the Garugak *rawa*.

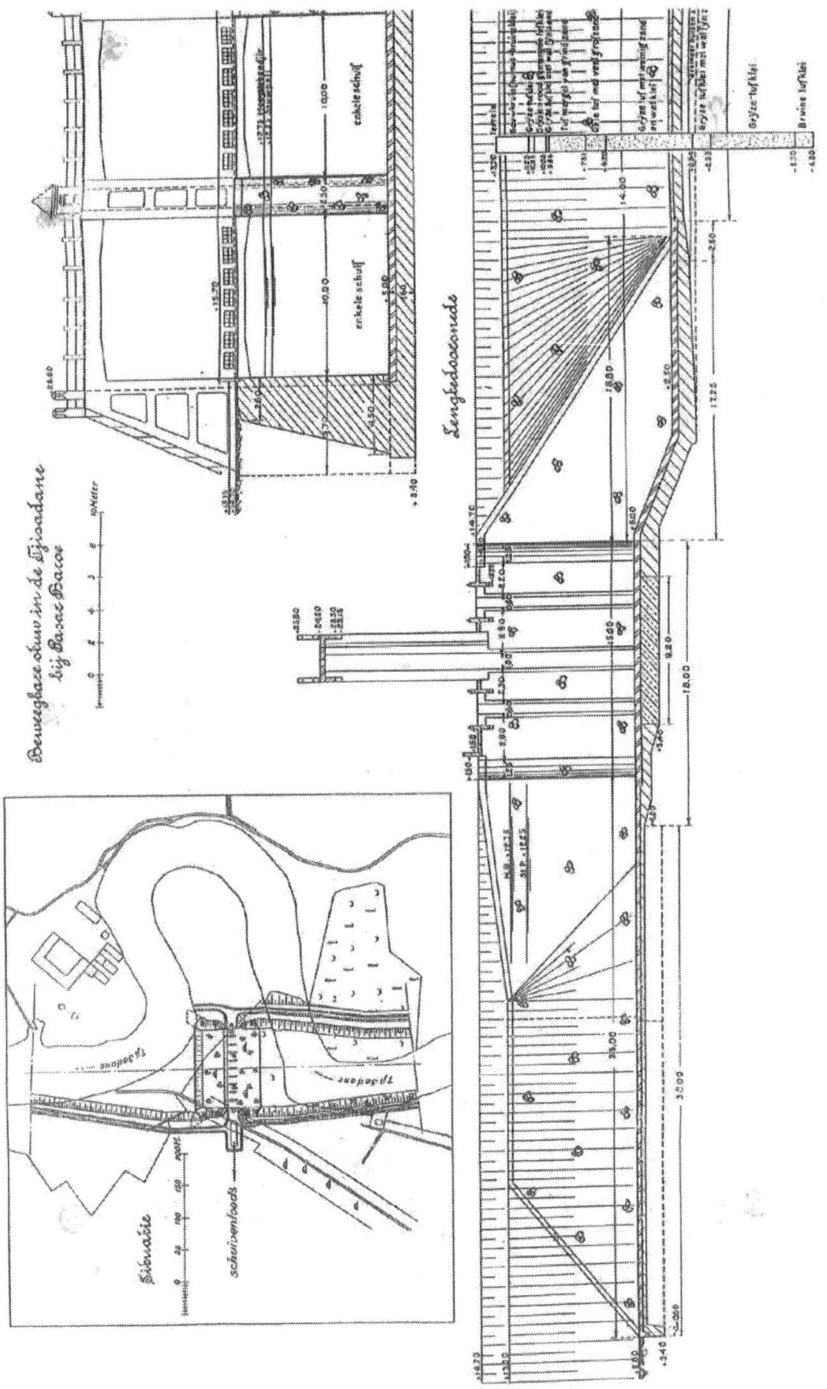

Figure 9.3: Situation, view and cross section of the weir in the Cisadane (from: Dumas 1929)

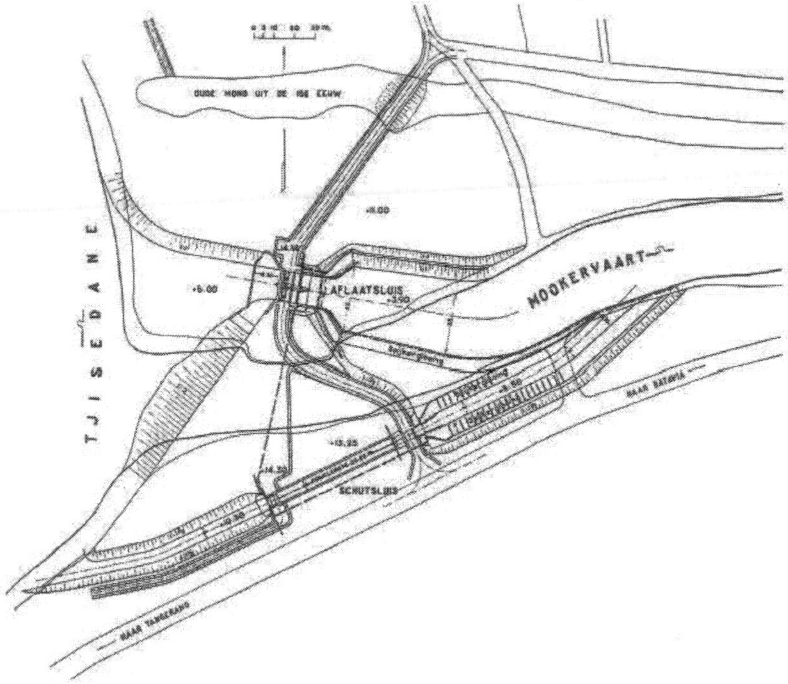

Figure 9.4: A situation sketch of the sluice complex at Sewan (from: Posno 1935)

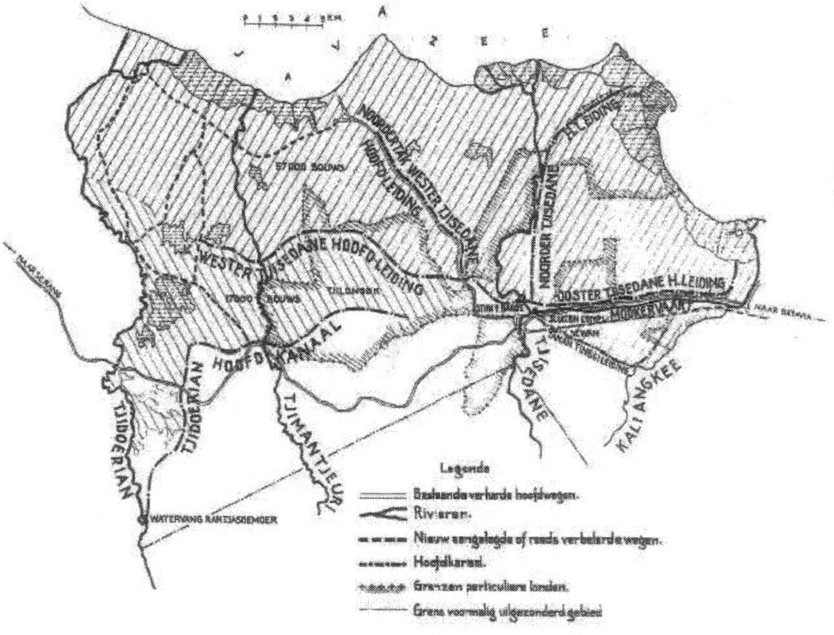

Figure 9.5: The waterway network of the Tangerang Works (from: Posno 1935)

Excursus 9.1 The weir in the Cidurian river

The maximum locally measured banjir *in the area was 465 cubic metres per second and this, of course, affected the dimensions of the weir. The weir was thus designed in such a way as to ensure that the "effective weir width" would be 37 metres. Of this width, seven metres was taken up by the two openings in the weir's outlet sluice. The remaining 30 metres was also divided in two: the weir was to be provided with a bridge but this required a pier in the middle. The forcing upwards of the water was estimated to amount to a level of 1.13 metres. At that point the river did not transport any pebbles or shingle, just sand and other lighter sink substances. That made it possible to create a weir that just consisted of a lining of the riverbed.*

The designed inlet sluice had five openings, each two metres wide that were situated 2.30 metres above the riverbed. In conjunction with the silt that flowed through the inlet sluice with the water it was decided that a second outlet should be made: an outlet trench 200 metres long that discharged into the river. This latter sluice had five openings, each 2.60 metres wide. The actual main canal was placed in front of the throughput sluice, thus ensuring that while spouting out water would not seep back from the canal. The main canal, which was calculated to have a maximum flow rate of 17 cubic metres per second, was 10.10 metres wide and two metres deep.

For the weir, the two and a half kilometres of main waterways and all the accompanying structural works, the government proposed making available, in 1928, a sum of *f* 573,000. The government made a further *f* 94,000 available for the construction of the approximately six kilometre-long rail line to the point where the weir was situated and for improving the connecting road. Civil Public Works took care of these activities itself and by 1930 the project had reached completion.

The headworks in the Cisadane constituted the biggest task. The location chosen for the weir was situated on what had formerly been the private estate of Pasar Baru, one of the land areas that had been made again a land domain in the pre-1926 era (see above). The maximum expected *banjir* level at the selected spot was 1600 cubic metres per second. The standard weir level was fixed at 12.25 metres above sea-level: 2.25 metres above the highest water level at that point. Tangerang was some two and a half kilometres upstream of the point where it was planned that the weir was going to be constructed. In normal circumstances the city would lie one and a half to two metres above the forced up water level. However, in the event of the maximum water level being reached Tangerang would certainly have become flooded. That was the reason why a movable weir was required. Indeed, it was known that *banjirs* developed rapidly in that area which was why a dam closing system that could be quickly operated was needed. That was the reason why Civil Public Works decided to drop the Stoney-gates idea proposed in the original plan developed by Van Breen, Polderman and Dumont in which "the partitions were rolled alongside of a loose trolley" (Bakhoven 1936: VI. 130[11]). Instead the choice fell with what were known as running wheel shutters of the style previously used for the weir in the Citarum in conjunction with the Krawang Works (see **Chapter 10**). The "gates run on wheels thus greatly reducing friction because of the roller bearings" (ibid.). The leverage height would be nine metres, which meant that with such gates the sluices could be opened up in fifteen minutes. The moving of the sluices would be electro-motor powered but it would also be possible to operate them manually[12].

[11] Stoney-gates were also planned for the weir in the Solo (Oostinjer 1898: 80-81).

[12] In the 1919 memorandum the critical query, "is this necessary?" was written alongside of the proposal to make the sluice doors electrically operable (Van Breen et al. 1919: 35). Still, the electrical installation came all the same which meant that a two-kilometre-long high-tension cable had to be laid. Evidently there was therefore electric power in Tangerang (compare the weir in the Citarum discussed in **Chapter 10**).

Excursus 9.2 The weir in the Cisadane river
The weir that was designed had ten openings, each of which was ten metres wide (see ***Figures 9.1 and 9.3,*** *see also the* ***Prologue, Figure 4****). Eight of the openings were provided with several sluices and two with the much more expensive double gates. The latter type of sluices made it easier to regulate the weir level in the event of smaller water volumes and to remove all kinds of floating debris. The construction required nine piles 9.70 metres high, two and a half metres wide and fifteen metres long. The piles would protrude about two metres above the highest water level. They were to be made of "potash mortar work" (Dumas 1929: 206). The upper part of the structural work was mounted on these piles. This was to be a "continuous construction in reinforced concrete" (Dumas 1929: 207). This was the point from which the sluice doors would be operated. The piles were placed on foundation bases that were partly constructed of reinforced concrete.*
In view of the turbulent water movements downstream of the weir it was decided that a 40-metre-long a two-and-a-half-metre-deep "tumble basin" should be created there. The base was closed off by a mortar-work box that was two metres deep. Over a distance of 17.50 metres the floor of the tumble basin had to be impermeable to water but not the rest of the basin because otherwise undesirable water pressure would build up. The solution found to this was to introduce drainage pipes. The entire floor would be at most one and a half metres deep. On the other side of the weir it was planned that a 35-metre-long and half-metre-thick floor should be created. The floor between the piles was made 1.20 metres thick and it had a 0.40 metre covering of natural stone.

The entire cost of the work was estimated at 1.4 to 1.5 million guilders (which included two inlet sluices on location in order to improve the water flow from the Cisadane, see below). The building of the lower section of the weir was contracted out to the "Dutch Concrete Company" for a sum of *f* 705,000 and work on that section commenced in 1929[13]. In 1929 and 1930 funds were made available for the sluice gates and the upper part of the structure, the sums being respectively *f* 400,000 and *f* 186,600. By 1933 the structural work had almost been completed with the finishing touch probably being put in 1934[14]. At any rate, the weir was not yet operational. The water channels were not yet ready and an important supplementary structure had to be built.

At this point let us just consider certain other works. Due to deforestation the source region of the Cimanceuri retained little water which was why the river often overflowed. Because of its high water levels the Cimanceuri moreover provided poor drainage possibilities for the rain water that fell in the lower-lying areas. What was required was normalisation and dyking-up of the river and one of the tributaries needed to be diverted. It was suggested that this tributary should be linked up with another river and thus directly to the sea. The costs of all these activities were estimated at *f* 782,000 and these funds were made available by the government in 1928 and 1929. The work was partly contracted out to a contractor. Furthermore there was work to be done

[13] Experience gained elsewhere had shown that one should not underestimate the water pressure build-up behind the weir (the Krawang Works weir had, in that respect, taught everyone a hard lesson, see again **Chapter 10**). As a result of that people wondered whether it might not be best to create a deeper box than planned or even to seal off the floor with a permanent dam wall. It was decided that they should first wait to see what (the excavations would reveal) the sub-soil was like. The result of this exploration is not known to me but the costs of the building of the lower section were lower than had been budgeted: *f* 687,100.

[14] The weir was scheduled to be completed in 1931 (Posno 1936: VI. 154, VI. 157), but that probably meant just the lower section. The activities linked to the doors and the upper part of the structure – which was admittedly less work than the lower section – were still continuing by the end of 1933 (see letter from Dumas dd. 11th December, 1933, *BOW* Archives E I-28, 2).

on the road network. A road plan was drawn up that was directed at improving existing inland roadways and constructing asphalt roads where the main arteries existed. The cost of the entire programme, involving 183 kilometres of road, was estimated at *f* 2,100,000. Half of this sum was to be obtained from irrigation funds (see a Snell memo made in 1925, National Archives, the Haringhuizen-Schoemaker Collection, no. 54). A start was made on improving the inland roads in 1926. The roads were constructed and at the same time the water channels were excavated alongside of them.

The Sewan sluice complex

"Mr. Van Moock would probably no longer recognise his 5-7 m wide little waterway", wrote Posno (1935: VI. 108), "since, over the course of time, it has taken on more the dimensions of a sizeable river"[15]. The *Mookervaart* which began a kilometre downstream of the weir in the Cisadane (at the Sewan *desa*) had, up until then, transported away a third of the water issuing from the Cisadane. Because of this the weir was unable to do its work properly and so the water was not forced up as high as it should have been. In view of the fact that the *Mookervaart* was linked to the city canals of Batavia, forcing water upwards at the time of *banjirs* would only have led to flooding in (the western area of) Batavia. Something therefore had to be done with the *Mookervaart*, but what? Meanwhile there was also a crisis going on so it should not at least cost too much.

Van Breen and Polderman wanted to close off the *Mookervaart* with a dam. Bearing in mind the shipping (proas and rafts) this would have to be accompanied by a lock. The canal itself also required locks. The implications of this plan were that the Cisadane would have to be able to accommodate all the future *banjir* water. For these purposes the river would have to be widened. Even though it was seen as desirable to allow this widening to occur in an as natural as possible way, in other words through the river itself, Civil Public Works found the necessary works to be too expensive ten years later. It was also believed that *banjir* water should still pass through the *Mookervaart* in order to keep the *kali* Angké estuary open. The idea that arose was thus to allow both the Cisadane and the *Mookervaart* to transport – at the most a sixth (200 cubic metres) – of the *banjir* water. This meant that separate irrigation channels would be required. At first it was thought that these could also serve as shipping canals. In the end, Public Works decided to retain the *Mookervaart* for shipping, without any locks. In conjunction with the *Mookervaart* there were three things that had to be done:

- the old estuary had to be closed off,
- a lock had to be constructed for proa and raft vessels,
- an outlet sluice had to be created for the Cisadane water (see **Figure 9.4**).

When it came to determining the sluice locations, particularly the lock's location, there was still much to be decided. Some wanted to use the mouth of the *Mookervaart* for the lock which had been dug in the eighteenth century and later replaced. That spot was more than a hundred metres to the north of the existing canal mouth which was to be closed off. Indeed, people wanted to construct the outlet sluice to the north of the existing river mouth but, in order to limit the ground transport requirements, at a point as near as possible to that mouth. This meant that any shipping destined for the canal would first have to pass by the drainage sluice. It was feared that in times of strong water currents the proas and rafts would simply be dragged along with the flow. For this reason Civil Public Works decided to place the lock elsewhere, to the south of the canal mouth. Because of the proximity of the provincial road there was not much space for the lock

[15] To the locals the *Mookervaart* was and is known as the Cisadane (Go 1966: 7). See in this connection the *banjir* canal near the Sampean which also took over the river's course (see **Chapter 3**).

which meant that it had to be elongated. Not far from the lock there was to be an inlet sluice for the secondary section, the Tanahtinggi. The cost of the entire project was budgeted at *f* 300,000 and the government was good enough to make the money available. Public Works contracted out much of the work to the "Dutch Concrete Company" and work began in 1934.

In connection with the design of the outlet sluice and the connecting of the sluice to the lock in the *Mookervaart*, tests were done with scale-models at the hydro-dynamic experimental station in Tanjung Priok. During the tests

"two things in particular were monitored, namely the water movements downstream of the structural work, to see that they were as gentle as possible and silt formation to ensure that it was avoided in the canal section between the lock and the Mookervaart" (*Tangerangwerken* 1936: VI. 155).

The outcome of the study was that a "power consumer in the form of a cog inhibitor " should be created and a certain form given to the confluence of the outlet canal and the lock (ibid.). Just as with the weir at Pasar Baru, the outlet sluice and the "upper sluice head" of the lock (the first sluice) were provided with electrically operated sliding doors on running wheels. The works were further equipped with modern communication means: a telephone connection was set up between, on the one hand, the weir and a point 20 kilometres upstream where a water-level gauge existed and, on the other hand, with the sluices at Sewan. In that way information could be quickly passed on in the event of *banjirs* arising. At the weir an automatic warning system was set up just for in case it was needed.

By 1936 the Sewan sluice complex was completed[16]. The festive opening of the Tangerang Works was organised on the sluice terrain. A year previous to that the central government had handed over the works to the new Provincial Public Works Department which meant that the opening of the works also marked an important moment for the Province of West Java which was, itself, also new. At the time, the Governor of West Java, L.G.C.A. van der Hoek commented, with a degree of pride: "It is the first time in the history of this province that particular attention has been devoted to the completion and inauguration of an important irrigation works complex" (*Tangerangwerken* 1936: VI. 153). The Director of the Department of Transport and Public Works (which was also new[17]), J.A.M. van Buuren (1934-1936) accepted the honours. At the request of the provincial administrators he conducted the opening ceremony on behalf of the government. He did that by pressing a button and so activating the upper sluice head of the lock. When the lock chamber had filled up "a decorated proa sailed in amid cheers from onlookers" (*Tangerangwerken* 1936: VI. 157). The next job was the opening of the Tanahtinggi channel by the Batavian Regent. The weir at Pasar Baru was finally operational and, during the festive opening, many people took the opportunity to at the same time view the weir. At that stage the irrigation provision remained limited to the secondary Tanahtinggi section that was some 3000 *bouws* big. In fact, the construction of the channel turned out to be something of a special task costing *f* 65,000. Three thousand *bouws* was not such a large area considering all the works (and celebrating) involved but the Cisadane irrigation waterway network was by no means complete.

[16] Details on the works written by Posno (1935). The lock gates for the structural works in the Tangerang were supplied by *Werkspoor* plant in Amsterdam and the *Constructiewerkplaats* ("Construction Workplace") *de Bromo* in Pasaruan while the moving parts were fabricated by the company *Figee* in Haarlem and the company *Gebr. van Swaay* in Batavia took responsibility for the electrical installations.

[17] All these administrative changes are highlighted in **Chapter 10**.

The water network

The water that had been forced up in the Cisadane was to be conveyed away by means of several canals. The calculations were based on a maximum flow rate of 48.50 cubic metres per second. As long as land was irrigated in turn this would provide sufficient water for the entire irrigation area. The draft canal network originally comprised the following four canals:

- the Northern Cisadane main supply canal (for around 14,000 *bouws*),
- the Western Cisadane main supply canal (for about 34,000 *bouws*),
- the Tanahtinggi canal (approximately 3000 *bouws*) and
- the *Mookervaart* (approximately 6000 *bouws*).

As has been indicated, it was decided that the *Mookervaart* would not be used as an irrigation canal. Instead of that it was agreed that a separate channel should be specially created: the Eastern Cisadane main supply channel (see **Figure 9.5**). Originally the plan had been to allow that channel to start near to the sluice complex in Sewan, just like the Northern Cisadane main channel. Later this idea was dropped and instead a tapping point near to the weir was chosen for both the waterways. That was also the spot that was chosen for an inlet sluice. In the original plan the mouth of the Western Cisadane main channel was situated approximately a kilometre down river of the Sewan complex. This too was later to be changed. The inlet to this channel also came to be situated close to the weir. That channel was given a northern branch and the whole channel itself was shortened. (Compare **Figures 9.2 and 9.5**). In the case of both inlet sluices (also with the outlet and throughput sluices, see above in connection with the Ciduran weir) the government made available a sum of *f* 360,000 in 1932.

The set up for the Cidurian irrigation network was somewhat simpler: a main channel was planned[18]. Originally this channel was designed to end at the Cimanceuri. The entire *sawa* complex between that river and the Cidurian, right as far as the Java Sea, would receive irrigation water from the canal. Later, though, when the Cisadane irrigation system was realised all of that was to change. The northern section of the area would then fall under the new works and the Cidurian system to the east was to be expanded. Ultimately the main canal was to be lengthened and, to that end, extended to the Cimanceuri.

As the buying back of private tracts of land progressed, so it became possible to pursue the works projects. After the weir in the Cidurian had been completed the project of completing the canal system was continued, starting with the main canal. As of 1930 money was made available for the completion of this latter canal. The construction of the secondary channels followed later (after 1934). It was possible to do that because by then all the land between the Cidurian and the Cimanceuri had become state-owned. In the case of the Cisadane irrigation situation matters were somewhat different. Since 1931 no further land areas had been purchased. A year before the opening of the headworks Posno (1935: VI. 105) claimed the following:

---

[18] This main canal was known as the Cidurian main supply canal. Later it came to be known as the Cidurian (main) supply canal. Evidently there was at the time the prospect of a main canal being created to the west. Irrigation to the west of the Cidurian, in the Ci Beureum plain (in the Residency of Bantam) was envisaged, from the very start, in the entire irrigation plan but precisely how that would take shape remained unclear. That plain on the right bank of the Ciujung was "awkward" to reach from that river according to the 1919 memorandum (p. 29). Later the Right Ciujung Irrigation was mentioned in the records which related to the Tangerang Works (that was 10,472 *bouws* big according to the 1925 "Civil Public Works Report"). As of 1929 this area was also taken in hand.

"During the buying back ... and because of the many ups and downs evidenced in the country's means situation of the past 20 years, a certain degree of stagnation has set in so that even extensive complexes have not yet been bought back. Because of this, irrigation improvements cannot yet be as extensive as had originally been envisaged".

The not yet repurchased land of Cilongkok was what stood in the way of the completion of the Cisadane irrigation project. It was in that area that an important section of the Western Cisadane main channel was to be situated. The completing of the projected Cidurian irrigation system was not possible either as long as that estate remained in tact. Beyond the Cimanceuri the relevant main channel was also scheduled to enter into that same area. Even though the Cidurian irrigation network could not therefore be completed the situation there was, however, better than with the Cisadane irrigation. The realisation of the irrigation works between the Cidurian and the Cinanceuri was within reach, albeit in a completely different way than had originally been intended. The *Javasche Particuliere Landerijen Maatschappij* ("Javan Private Estate Company") that had been established in the thirties, which had the government and the Province as shareholders, would have to provide a solution: they would be able to purchase land areas with money that did not issue directly from the treasury. In acquiring two large estates the company at least managed to justify its existence[19]. On these grounds and in the hope that a "certain amount" would emanate from the Dutch contribution for the purposes of welfare work in the Indies, the Governor of West Java remarked during the opening in 1936 that the "fairly high speed at which the works promise to be executed seems, at the moment, to be guaranteed" (*Tangerangwerken* 1936: VI. 154).

To conclude a remark about the extensive irrigation works. Insofar as there was the opportunity for this people installed the inlet sluices that had been newly developed in the thirties: the so-called Romijn gate. In that way water could be let through gradually and at the same time exactly measured (see **Chapter 10**).

Finally

The engineers involved had grand notions of the advantages of a modern irrigation system in the Tangerang plain for the population and the state. In the latter case, rentability calculations would prove that the capital to be ploughed into construction (of ten million guilders) would be earned back within fifteen to twenty years in two possible ways. Expropriating privately owned land involved introducing the land rent system and that constituted a source of state income. As the irrigation plan was realised so the land rent yield would rise considerably. It was also predicted that an "important sugar culture" industry would develop[20]. The "presence of the remains of previous small sugar refineries" dating moreover from a time when irrigation conditions were unfavourable, was just one indication of this (Dumas 1929: 209). The state became wiser to this from the profit taxation and the obligatory contributions to construction costs.

[19] Cilongkok was not included. That estate was valued at *f* 800,000, a high cost which, according to Posno (1935: VI. 107) made a speedy transaction impossible. Ultimately it was sold but precisely when is not certain. As far as I was able to establish it was not sold before 1940. It is possible that Cilongkok became state property in the Japanese period when expropriation became rigorous (M. Opperman, personal communication, November 1996).

[20] Though this would not happen everywhere, as has e.g. been illustrated, the Patrasana *rawa* was not suitable for sugar cultivation.

To what extent these expectations were justified is unknown for the simple reason that the irrigation works in the Tangarang plain did not reach completion during the colonial period[21]. It should be mentioned that there are no signs indicating that the areas that were completed gave cause for the establishment of an important sugar industry. There had been a flourishing sugar industry there in the past but by the beginning of the nineteenth century that was no longer the case. In the nineteenth century modern sugar growing had established itself in East Java and had rapidly spread from there (Go 1966: 63-64, see also **Chapter 4**). Go, who conducted anthropological field work in the area in the late fifties, made no mention of a sugar industry "revival". On the contrary, sugar mills "were nowhere more to be seen" (1966: 7). All he confirmed was the existence of reminders: "the remains of old sugar mills are still to be seen in the *desas* in the form of millstones which just serve as garden ornamentation nowadays or as a workbench for the bicycle repairer" (ibid.).[22]

It is therefore not possible to construct a costs and benefits analysis for the Tangerang Works. As far as the project itself is concerned what we can say is that the plan's set up and the actual execution of the works seem to have presented few technical problems for the engineers. As far as is known, the finished structural works also operated optimally. In the case of the Sewan sluice complex this could partly be attributed to the integrated outcomes of tests done with scale models. Such tests were an innovation. Much the same applied to the Romijn gate that was also implemented in that area.

The Public Works Department of West Java took over responsibility from the central Public Works Organization for the Tangerang Works in 1935. This marked an important change in the operational organisation. In the end, the Province only had ultimate responsibility for a few years but it still nevertheless shared in the successes of completion. In his opening speech Van Buuren, the Director of Transport and Public Works had the following to say:

"The confidence in the competence of the provincial organisation as evidenced in this handing over [of the Tangerang Works, WR] on the part of the government, is in no way put to shame" (*Tangerangwerken* 1936: VI. 157).

The Provincial Public Works Department had done good work, but they were not the only ones. The Tangerang Works constituted a successful co-production of provincial, central government and contracting parties. Van Buuren went on to say the following:

"During operations what has been convincingly demonstrated is the fact that the necessary co-operation between the Country and the Province can be both pleasant and fruitful.
Thanks to the professional directing of the Provincial Public Works Department where, apart from mentioning the head of Provincial Public Works, the engineer J.J. Jonker, I would also especially like to mention the chief engineer O. Werner Sörensen and also the engineer M.M.C. Posno as well as the good and well executed work of the contractor, the "Dutch Concrete Company" and – last but not least – the great support received from the Civil Service. Because of the help of all these people we have been able to achieve the result to be admired here" (ibid.).

---

[21] According to the information gleaned from engineers in the region the Cisadane irrigation system would not provide water for more than about 17,000 *bouws* (of the 57,000). In the case of the Cidurian irrigation works relatively more was achieved but the main canal was not extended; the aqueduct over the Cimanceuri was not constructed until the seventies! (See for more details the **Epilogue**).

[22] During my visits to the area I was not able to find any sugar growing activities of any consequence. As for the situation concerning the population, in a letter from Dumas written in 1934 (dd. 28th June) to the Head of the Provincial Public Works Department the "population's state of emergency" and "relief works" (*BOW* Archives E I-28, 2) were referred to.

Naturally Van Buuren had first of all started by praising the engineers involved, also adding that they had done their work in what had "often been difficult circumstances" (*Tangerangwerken* 1936: VI. 157). The problems which existed were in the financial sphere because the government's funds had been limited. That was in the first place manifested in the slow progression of the expropriation of private land but because of that construction activities had also suffered. Van Buuren (*Tangerangwerken* 1936: VI. 157) said in this connection:

"The era of serious financial concerns which had by then broken out and, indeed, in which we still find ourselves has led ... in relation to these works, to a certain slowing down of operations ..."

The crisis currently continuing formed the backdrop to the problems with the difficult financial circumstances around 1920 giving rise to all the delays. This slowing down had the possible useful side-effect of enabling plans to be improved. What is, however, interesting is the fact that the weir in the Cisadane constituted the first authorised structural work while six years later, with the Tangerang Works, small improvements were started upon elsewhere. Round about 1930 a whole debate started up about the *Mookervaart* which was no doubt induced by the economic situation of the day.

The Tangerang Works constituted one of the last colonial irrigation projects in the area where the Dutch had once excavated one of their first canals. After having constructed the *Mookervaart* the Dutch irrigation experts afterwards became active in all regions of Java. They commenced in the Besuki where Van Thiel's (1832) framework dam was to mark the beginnings of engineering intervention in the field of irrigation. When it came to the Tangerang Works, Dutch builders were back in Batavia and so things had thus come full circle. There are still certain matters that need to be explained, though, but that will be done in the following chapter where the further "scientification" and refining of irrigation technology, the decentralisation of the operational organisation and the consequences of the crisis will be further examined.

10

'Big in small achievements'

The modern irrigation system

> Technological systems, even after prolonged growth and consolidation, do not become very autonomous; they acquire momentum. They have a mass of technical and organizational components; they possess direction, or goals; and they display a rate of growth suggesting velocity. A high level of momentum often causes observers to assume that a technological system has become autonomous. Mature systems have a quality that is analogous therefore to inertia of motion. The large mass of a technological system arises especially from the organizations and people committed by various interests to the system (Hughes 1987: 76-77).

"Excellence. It is a privilege for me to witness the opening of this large-scale irrigation project" said Raden Toemenggoeng Soeriamihardja, the Regent of Krawang, spoken in 1925 on the occasion of the opening of the weir in the Citarum – and several other main sections of the Krawang Works (*Opening* ["Opening"]1925: 11) – at the Walahar *desa* (see **Figure 10.1**). He continued to express his feelings:

"A work such as this means that we are able to augment the welfare of local inhabitants in general and of the Krawang people in particular.
As everyone knows, much misery has been endured by the people because of the many failed harvests experienced here in the Regency of Krawang, specifically in the northern area. All of this is solely to blame on the lack of regulated and technically well controlled irrigation.
Furthermore, in the dry season, the Krawang plain is bare and dry while in the wet monsoon season there is the problem of an excess of water. Indeed, with the addition of the weir in the Citarum a new era will be dawning for North Krawang.
In the near future a hundred and ten thousand bouws of sawa will be regularly irrigated with water drawn from the Citarum which is very suitable for irrigation.
Excellence. I would like, if I may, to take this opportunity to respectfully thank the Government on behalf of the population for the creation of this important irrigation work.
Let us hope that before very long the bare and dry Krawang plain will be transformed into very fertile sawas for the well-being and blessing of the people.
That is my hope".

After a preliminary period of some 15 years an entry for the major project finally appeared on the budget plans in 1918. The completion of the weir represented nothing less than a milestone in the execution of the Ethical Policy. As D. Fock, the Governor-General, stated at the time of its entry into service (*Opening* 1925: 13): "Does this work not irrefutably demonstrate that for the Government the promotion of the population's welfare goes before all else?" (See **Box 10.1**)

It was particularly significant that the Regent of Krawang spoke on the occasion of the opening of the weir. The Governor-General, whom the Regent addressed in his speech as "Excellency", expressed this in the following way:

"The Government will pursue the road that it has set out for itself; it asks no thanks for what it has done because it was merely fulfilling its duty. However, it is gratifying to see that you sir, Regent of Krawang, have stood up today and spoken on behalf of the population. Indeed, this only shows that the population and the administrators who support the population, feel and understand how extremely important this work is" (*Opening* 1925: 13).

In 1925 sympathy for the population's side of things was no mere luxury. With its Ethical Policy the colonial government was able to involve the Javanese population more in the political decision-making process. In so doing, though, it conjured up forces that it was barely able to control. In its endeavour to attain independence the population presented the colonial state with a huge problem in the twenties and thirties which ultimately proved irresolvable within the existing order. It was a period when the state was been confronted with other major challenges too. The creation of the Krawang Works, just like the creation of the Tangerang Works, came at a time when the world's economic motor was displaying faults. It was a time when western capitalism and imperialism appeared to be declining in the face of the *Verelendung* (impoverishment) process predicted by Marxists. At first the problems could be coped with. The Tangerang plain project was halted in 1919 but the Krawang Works project – that had been planned somewhat earlier – was pursued. The biggest problems, though, were still to come!

This chapter traces the development of modern irrigation in the 1920-1942 period. In the final year of that period the Japanese for once and for all put an end to the dwindling dominion of the Dutch in the Indies. After a failed attempt to restore the situation after the Second World War the Netherlands finally submitted, in 1949, to the independence claimed by Sukarno and his followers in 1945. This chapter focuses on what happened in the field of irrigation in the twenties and thirties when the Indies was plagued by economic and political problems.

Figure 10.1: The weir in the Citarum (from: *Tien* ["Ten"] 1938)

Box 10.1 The weir in the Citarum river

Towards the end of the nineteenth century the idea of drawing of water from the Citarum for irrigation purposes was put forward and in 1895 the engineer Ypelaar embarked on the relevant research. The Rentability Committee, Lamminga included, were in support of this. In 1904 the engineer B.M. Blijdenstein submitted a first design proposal. After ten years Homan van der Heide, the Civil Public Works Director, recommended these plans to the government. The engineer J. Haringhuizen, later Professor in Delft but then Head of the Irrigation Division of Civil Public Works, made important contributions to these plans. Rentability became the basis of a discussion between Public Works (Homan van der Heide and his successor Ott de Vries) and Agriculture (Lovink) but it was the agricultural enquiries that were finally to lead to positive results. The entire project costs were estimated at fourteen million guilders but later this was pushed up to twenty million guilders and the work commenced in 1919. The weir was constructed as a fixed threshold in the river protruding two metres above the base. The structure was given four openings that were twenty metres wide and separated by five metre-thick piles. An eight-metre-wide discharge sluice was built on the left-hand side.

The slats of the movable weir were twenty metres long and ran on wheels. The whole thing was powered by a petrol combustion engine. The original choice for the actual shutters was for a German-style "rolling-weir" system (i.e. for Stoney gates). Since De Vos, later Professor at Bandung, was about to return to Europe on leave Public Works asked him to make a study of this. On the basis of his report it was gates on runners that were chosen. The German system was good but expensive. In conjunction with the high degree of friction a great deal of leverage was required and such leverage could only be achieved with electrical power. There was no electricity grid in that remote area which meant that a power station would have needed to be constructed especially for the weir. (*Opening* 1925, Bakhoven 1936, design of the weir in Van Maanen 1924; continued in **Box 10.2**).

Emancipation and ordeals

The political aspect

As was explained in **Chapter 7**, the Ethical Policy brought with it a process of emancipation and decentralisation. At regional, provincial and national levels that was to give the Indies population – the indigenous Indonesian component included – more of a say in matters. The People's Council, established in 1918, constituted a clear sign of the times. The 1922 revision of the Dutch constitution was just one of the things to happen. What was significant for the Indies was the fact that the term "colony" was removed from the constitution. Previously all controlling of and accounting for colonial financial means had to be approved by parliament (see **Chapter 4**). That even applied to the currency system. The new constitution turned this exception into a rule so that all Indies state administration-related matters had to be subsequently legally endorsed. It was generally recommended that the People's Council should also be consulted. The constitution also alluded to the way in which the Indies administration was structured: everything had to be legally laid down. The implementing of the new constitution was to lead to a process of administrational reform in the Indies. It was the creation, in 1925, of what was known as the Indies State Regulation that was to be significant. This law determined how the Indies government was to be set up. The position of the People's Council was ratified. The law also laid the foundation for the introduction of Provinces and Autonomous Regencies. Already, in 1924, ordinances had been promulgated to this end. As administrative bodies, the Provinces and Regencies received respective Provincial and Regency Councils. The idea was that the local population would be represented in these Councils. Executive matters were placed in the hands of separate bodies; in the Provinces that was the Board of Representatives. New political bodies replaced the local and regional councils and were set up after 1905 (see **Chapter 8**). Java was sub-divided into three Provinces. The Province of West Java was the first to be established in 1926 and East and Central Java followed in 1929 and 1930. (*Encyclopaedie* ["Encyclopedia"] Vol. V 1927: 78, Van den Eerenbeemt 1989: 182, Van den Doel 1989: 267 onwards).

With its educational and emancipation measures the Ethical Policy had quite inadvertently stimulated feelings of nationalism among the Indonesian population. The aim was to create an own state. The fact that political independence was, in itself, desirable was not something that was debated by the Dutch rulers; what they did dispute was the time-scale envisaged for effecting all of this. With all the political changes the Indonesian population gained more of a voice in the government's decision-making processes. For the Indonesians things could not change fast enough. In 1926, therefore, there were attempts to revolt – also in the Tangerang region – and a year later similar moves were made in Sumatra[1]. Once the government had recovered from the shock it reacted, not surprisingly, in a way that was diametrically opposed to everything the nationalists were trying to achieve. They not only halted the gradual democratisation process but also went as far as to turn back the clock by dividing up the tasks of the Dutch and "inland" administration in 1931. In its striving for consolidation the government continued to keep a firm hold on the reins of power throughout the thirties. As though goaded on by fate it thus raced towards its own doom. (Van den Eerenbeemt 1989: 182, Van den Doel 1994: 331 onwards).

The economic aspect

One of the presumed blessings of colonial administration was the inclusion of Indonesia in the developing world economy. Indeed, the world market was playing an ever bigger role in the production and consumption of commodities. By being incorporated into the international trade flow Indonesia also became automatically entangled in all the world economy's recessions and crises. Naturally the production of commercially grown crops with world-market-linked prices was the first thing to be hit. Although the population suffered losses in terms of financial income, subsistence farming was not in any way hit by the international situation but rather began to flourish. During the First World War the international market collapsed and so the archipelago had to draw on its own resources. After the war, world trade picked up and things started to go well in the Indies as well. That was followed, in the early twenties, by international economic recession which led, in turn, to financial problems within the colonial government which subsequently drew up economy measures. By about 1925 all the problems were over and the Ethical Policy could once again be fully pursued. (See, for instance, Gonggrijp 1957: 153 onwards and Creutzberg 1974: VIII-XIII).

The generous providing of means in order to "relieve" the population had only lasted a couple of years. The year 1929 saw the Wall Street Crash in New York which was to precipitate economic decline on an unprecedented world scale. This was to lead to a depression that was to persist until the mid-thirties. Perhaps the general malaise in the Indies may be characterised as follows:

1. between 1928 and 1935 the value of the entire export market fell to below a half of its normal level; Javanese sugar production fell by almost three million tons in 1929 to 500,000 tons in 1935 with the value dropping from 312 to 36 million guilders,

[1] Dominated by privately-owned states no administrative system comprising villages and village chiefs had been able to develop in the Tangerang plain as in most of the other areas of Java. That therefore made it possible for communism to spread rapidly in the region (Benda 1955, McVey 1965 and 1978).

2. the incomes of all groups of people involved in the monetorised economy (the Europeans, the Chinese, officials, workers in the sugar industry and the private sector) fell dramatically,
3. the government's taxes were halved in just a matter of years,
4. the prices of the main cash crops plummeted which was favourable for the population in general but not for the farmers,
5. many regions were hit by food shortage and the threat of starvation and underfeeding,
6. there was widespread unemployment among Europeans, Chinese inhabitants and Indonesians but, in the case of the latter group, this concerned hundreds of thousands of people (Van Doorn 1994a: 231-237[2]).

Unlike the decline in the early twenties the depression of the thirties amounted to more than a temporary situation. The tide of unlimited free trade and production had turned; at least, that was what contemporaries – irrigation engineers included – believed. For instance, A.M. Verschoor, an engineer employed at the Pemali-Comal Provincial Public Works Division had the following to say of the situation:

"More than once it has been asserted that the crisis that we are experiencing is of a *structural nature* which means to say that it is not just another periodic decline in the economic constellation of the production process. In fact, because of the situation, new forms will be created that will steer the process in completely new directions" (1934: VI. 87).

The government reacted to the problem in different ways. In order to combat unemployment it adopted a dualistic policy founded on the notion that European people who were unemployed needed to be taken care of while Indonesians did not because they probably owned some land and would have family or a *desa* to fall back on. The government also regarded the Indonesian population as one cohesive whole, as something collective, and so tackled the problem by adopting collective welfare measures (Van Doorn 1994a: 237-241). In one official document the situation was described thus:

"With regard to the Europeans the matter is, from a government point of view, related to one basic issue. With regard to the Indigenous population, the loss of jobs presents the government with a massive problem. Apart from in certain of the bigger cities one can hardly say of the Inlander that he is without employment in the strictest sense of the word. Even if he no longer has a sawah or any land or any permanent or temporary employment, he can always provide for his basic needs by doing casual work or making small negotiations while his family supports him where necessary. When, like him, there are hundreds who no longer have sufficient food so that in a given region the welfare level sinks too low – as was the case in 1930 – then this will be seen by the government as a collective phenomenon and instantly combated" (Indies Report 1931, part I: 412; cited by Van Doorn 1994a: 238-239).

Forced by the unfavourable financial circumstances by which it had been hit during the economic decline, the government decided to make drastic savings in all its sectors (see, for instance, Van Doorn 1994a: 232). Another dramatic consequence of the crisis was that it prompted the government to intervene more in the production process (see, for instance, Verschoor 1934: VI. 88-89).

2 See also Gonggrijp (1957: 172 ff.), Baudet and Fennema (1983: 37-47). More details are given by Creutzberg (1972 and 1974).

Decentralisation and rationalisation

Provincial Public Works

The inaugural ordinance for the Province of West Java read as follows:

"In the province of West Java – except in exceptional cases to be further stipulated by ordinance – *the control* of the streams, rivers, sources, brooks, lakes, canals and water channels within its dominion and which belong to the country will be handed over together with the power to, under its supervision, transfer *the control* of possible sections to other parties" (*Indisch Staatsblad* ["Indies Gazette"] 1925 no. 378, cited by Lammers 1929: 34).

What this meant was that the Irrigation Divisions, until then a part of Civil Public Works, were transferred to the provincial authorities. As far as the transferring of control tasks to "others" was concerned this had to do with lower "public judicial" bodies such as the Autonomous Regencies (*Indisch Staatsblad* 1925 no. 378, see Lammers 1929: 34). The exceptions that were mentioned were the water areas where Civil Public Works was working on major projects which were the Krawang, Tangerang and Bantam Works (*Indisch Staatsblad* 1926 no. 177, see Lammers 1929: 34). The works were completed by special Civil Public Works Irrigation Services. There was an Irrigation Service for the works in the Krawang Division and another Service for the works in the Divisions of Batavia and Bantam.[3]

The distribution and allocation of irrigation water was laid down in various regional and local water regulations which remained in force until such a time that they were superseded by provincial regulations approved by the Governor-General. The Regencies would also be able to establish regulations but these would obviously have to correspond to possible provincial regulations and the provincial Council of Representatives would have to be in agreement (Lammers 1929: 35).

There was "higher supervision" in the Province from the side of the Governor-General. In the case of the Regencies it was the above-mentioned Council that exercised this supervision. Higher supervision was sometimes important in conjunction with European agricultural enterprises that had quite a lot of influence but which also had to be allowed to be free to operate as they pleased. The Explanatory Statement attached to the founding ordinance for the Province of West Java (1st Ordinary sitting of the People's Council of 1925, part 3 item 191) reported the following in this connection:

"Such higher supervision can be especially urgent in the regions where the European agricultural industry is a prominent factor in economic life. Whilst on the one hand it is not unthinkable that its economic prowess, despite probably weak numerical representation, will nevertheless be reflected in the decisions of the managing councils one should, on the other hand, also ensure that no unnecessary impediments will be placed in the way of that industry" (cited by Lammers 1929: 36).

---

[3] The only other special Irrigation Service was one that was occupied with the works continuing in the Solo Valley (Lammers 1929: 34). As indicated in **Chapter 7** this service was re-established in 1924. The management of the so-called sluicing channels instantly fell to the Autonomous Regencies while waterways that were only of local importance remained, as in the past, the domain of the villages (*Encyclopaedie* ["Encyclopedia"] Vol. VIII 1939: 476). Lammers (1929) drew a parallel with the *Rijkswaterstaat* ("State Public Works Organisation") developments in the Netherlands.

Except for the exploitation of existing irrigation systems (including the "independent rounded off" aspects of works that were furthermore in progress) the Province was also made responsible for the creation of "works of minimal size" (Explanatory Statement 1925, see Lammers 1929: 36). Major projects remained "temporarily" the responsibility of central government "both from a financial and from a – closely related to the first point – technical point of view" (ibid.). It was really the idea that these works should gradually fall into the hands of the Province, with the exception of the largest projects. In connection with these larger works it remained necessary to retain a central public works service, i.e. (the Irrigation Division at) Civil Public Works (Explanatory Statement 1925, see Lammers 1929: 37). When constructing large and small works both the Civil Public Works Department and the Provincial Public Works Department would be able to help each other: "once organised at provincial level such matters will resolve themselves" (ibid.). Ultimately such co-ordination was, in practice, less spontaneous than predicted here. Moreover, there was also a degree of friction between the two government bodies.

One of the problems was with personnel numbers. The Provinces automatically received the personnel employed by the various local and regional councils that were disbanded. At first the Province of West Java also took on engineers from the Civil Public Works Department which led to the voicing of objections on the part of the Department. It was an expensive business (the engineers had to be bought into the local pension fund) which meant that the Director feared that his service might become disrupted. It was a move that was even to lead to a ban on the part of the government concerning the transference of Civil Public Works personnel to the Provinces. When the Province of West Java subsequently began recruiting its own personnel the government also put a stop to that declaring that such actions would lead to a "surplus of Provincial personnel". Naturally the Provinces were not happy about the situation (*Encyclopaedie* Vol. VIII 1939: 477).

As of 1930 the effects of the crisis started to be felt and the government was anxious to economise. It was in this connection that the Director of Civil Public Works, J.A.M. van Buuren (1930-1933; the same person who officially opened the Tangerang Works) was given the task, in 1931, to set up an investigation into "the efficient management of the provincial Public Works Departments" (letter from the Director of Transport and Public Works dated 10th July 1934 addressed to the Governor-General, *BOW* Archives E VIII-99, see also Q. 1932). The Provinces were not happy about this investigation and so were not particularly co-operative. Within their own circles they set up an (interprovincial) committee which took the wind out of the sails for the Director of Civil Public Works who was keen on rationalisation, simplification and retrenchment, but not at any cost. In the People's Council meeting of 11th August 1933 he said:

"The Government ... [finds] that the serious pressure of time is making it necessary to review past notions in order to ascertain whether they are still tenable while meanwhile learning to manage with simpler organisations and ensure that – in particular – administrative objections are made subordinate to any kind of retrenchment.

In so doing the Government must amend one particular matter, namely the notion that every merger and simplification will automatically lead to savings. Rationalisation, achieved by amalgamating, is limited on the one hand by the formation of complexes that are too large and which, due to carelessness, do not operate economically and, on the other hand, by the formation of heterogeneous complexes with differing objectives thus meaning that the unity achieved is merely a seeming unity that conceals numerous complications" (cited in the "Memo relating to a proposal for far-reaching moderations and reorganisations of the Public Works Department for the Province of Central Java", *BOW* Archives E VIII-99).

Ultimately all these developments were to lead to all kinds of proposals to economise including suggestions to reduce the numbers of administrative personnel (by simplifying regulations, transferring powers and restricting a number of bodies), by bringing together irrigation and general services and by contracting out more work. By 1934 certain of these proposals had already been implemented while others still had to follow. One example of administrative simplification was to be found in the disappearance of the Irrigation Divisions. Alongside of all these Divisions, District Services were originally set up in the Provinces which were made responsible for bridges, roads and buildings. Later they were merged with the Irrigation Divisions to form Provincial Public Works Divisions. These Divisions were therefore being reintroduced: with the establishment of the Provinces the three old Public Works Divisions had been given up. (Letter from the Director of Transport and Public Works dated 10th July 1934 addressed to the Governor-General, *BOW* Archives E VIII-99; *Encyclopaedie* Vol. VIII 1939; 476-477).

In 1935 large works lost their exceptional position. The relevant Irrigation Services (as well as the control of the water areas concerned) passed from Civil Public Works to the Province and, operational activities which were not as yet completed, became the responsibility of the Province but remained, it is true, government subsidised. The Tangerang Works and the other large works in Bantam and Batavia were entrusted to the Province of West Java.[4] The Provinces would not be capable of independently setting up further major works activities. The designs required government approval and also involved the Director of the Department of Transport and Public Works (see below) because he had to make recommendations to the government. (*Encyclopaedie* Vol. VIII 1939: 476-477, *Indisch Staatsblad* ["Indies Gazette"] 1934b and c, see also *Indisch Staatsblad* 1934a and Lammers 1929: 37).

The reorganisation of Civil Public Works

As will have become clear, with the development of the Provincial Public Works Department the work of the central Department of Civil Public Works had become less important, indeed not without some degree of protest from those involved. Apart from the irrigation works, bridges and roads also became the terrain of the Provinces. Civil Public Works lost its responsibility for buildings (the Public Buildings) which also became the domain of the Provinces, partly as soon as they were created and partly in 1935. Public Service (under Civil Public Works) really only remained to exist for what were known as the commercial ports, such as those in Batavia and Surabaya.

There were also other reorganisations that affected Civil Public Works. The Sanitation Works Division, the newest Civil Public Works branch disappeared though the involvement of the Department in the works, in the interests of improving public health – notably by creating domestic water supplies – had certainly not passed. In 1925 the Division was moved to the Public Health Service within the Department of Education and Services. There a special new Division was set up for works in the field of health technology, the Health Facilitation Works and Housing Division. The government was of the opinion that this would stimulate co-operation between technical and hygiene experts thus benefiting the creation of works for public health. For financial reasons the new Division did not get the required personnel. The responsibility for the execution and operation of works therefore remained in the hands of Civil Public Works insofar as such responsibility had not been passed on to the Provinces and Regencies. The Irrigation and Drainage Division remained occupied with the relevant activities and therefore became the Irrigation and Sanitation Division. The Health Facilitation Works Division was developing, however; if new personnel was required for various works then the requests were

[4] Responsiblity for the Solo Valley Works passed on to the Province of East Java.

passed on to this Division. In Surabaya, in 1929, an office was opened for the east of the Indies which amounted to a Sub-Division of the Health Facilitating Works. In the dark depression years, though, the office disappeared. (*Encyclopaedie* Vol. VIII 1939: 476).

Influenced by the economy drive politics in the wake of the depression the government brought about a merger between Civil Public Works and the Government Companies in 1934 which thus led to the creation of the Department of Transport and Public Works[5]. Branches of services that had once been divided were once again given new central administrations. Because of the amalgamation, the Irrigation Division was even expanded: it was also made responsible for the hydro-electric power stations. Various other measures followed. The Buildings Division and the Division for Bridges and Roads were amalgamated. The three Inspectorates of the Outlying Regions were given up and, generally speaking, Civil Public Works personnel numbers which had already been reduced in the early thirties were further cut back. All the reductions in personnel numbers ultimately led to an increase in the numbers of works being undertaken by contractors. (*Encyclopaedie* Vol. VIII 1939: 477, see also *Indisch Staatsblad* 1934d and e, see also **Appendix F**).

Irrigation policy

Under the Ethical Policy, irrigation had been a policy area in which spendings had increased rapidly since 1910 but it was not, of course, able to escape the economy measures imposed upon all its policy areas by the government in the thirties. In the twenties government spending on irrigation activities dropped to an average of seven million guilders per year marked at first by a slight fall only to be followed by a slight recovery. With spendings hitting almost eleven million guilders 1929 was a top year. In the thirties spendings fell to just above three million guilders with a recovery becoming noticeable after 1934. (See **Appendix C**).

The recession of the thirties obviously had major repercussions for the efforts being made in the field of irrigation. As far as the creation of works was concerned the recession did not fundamentally alter the character of those kinds of activities. Since about 1915 the priority had been to construct large irrigation works and that was the way things were to remain. The building of large water reservoirs in the mountains, an activity that got off to a hesitant start in the first decades of the twentieth century, was really to become established in the twenties and thirties (see **Figures 10.2-10.5**). River-derived irrigation systems were particularly successful in the east monsoon season when water was in plentiful supply. The reservoirs designated for accumulating water in the wet season made efficient irrigation possible in the east monsoon season. Generally speaking, the (fiscal) rentability of works remained the decisive factor when it came to the creation of works, though when finances became limited in the thirties, discussion was continued on possible ways of improving matters (see below). In view of the political unrest "ideal" (i.e. political) factors were important when it came to the construction of works. In all of this the "satisfaction of the population" and "buttressing the authority" were the goals while "the stimulation of welfare" by "improving irrigation" were the means. During the building of the Pacal reservoir in the Solo Valley (see **Chapter 7**) these considerations, especially seeking to stimulate "economic progress in an underdeveloped region" tended to dominate. (Happé 1939: II. 13, 22, compare Van Doorn 1994a: 229-230, see also **Chapter 1**). Shortage of funds did not in itself lead to significant changes in policy, like for instance moving the focus from large to small works, but together with all the other developments that were continuing irrigation concern did gradually take on a different form. That was particularly true of the exploitation of the works.

[5] The new Department was established in Bandung which meant that Civil Public Works, which had always had its offices in Batavia, had to move.

In conjunction with increasing intervention on the part of the government the (provincial) irrigation service became more active in the field of water management. The development of the sugar industry, the growth of the population (and therefore of agricultural activity) and increased intervention in administration in general made water management in general increasingly more important. The depression of the thirties and, because of that, the greater pressure on the available water resources gave this development an extra stimulus. Caught up in a world that was having to contend with sharply falling sales the sugar producers got together in a campaign that was to lead, in 1931, to the Brussels Convention and to the voluntary surmounting of production restrictions (*Encyclopaedie* Vol. VI 1932: 381). In Java the sugar cane acreage shrank between 1928 and 1935 by some 236,000 *bouws* (thus representing a reduction of some 83%!). The population therefore saw its income from sugar cultivation shrink in proportion to the diminishing cane acreage but, at the same time, this meant that agricultural land and irrigation water was made available. The expansion in the field of agriculture among the local inhabitants was therefore also a development that went hand in hand with falling sugar production levels. Employment in the agricultural sector thereby grew with some extra 350,000 jobs being created and the government stimulated agricultural expansion among inhabitants. (Swaan 1935: A. 410, Van Doorn 1994a: 241, Weijer 1941: 311, see also Graadt van Roggen 1935: VI 53[6]).

This development also led to problems. Sugar cane required irrigation in the east monsoon season but the falling crop levels meant that in that period there was soon a surplus of water. The local farmers resolved that problem by planting more rice, a crop which (compared to sugar cane) requires much more water. At the beginning of the dry period there might well have been plentiful supplies of water but not later on. Moreover at that time a certain amount of water still needed to be reserved for the population's second rice crops. The problems were not just limited to that season. In the rainy season cane did not usually require any water but the rice which replaced that crop did. The final upshot was of course that soon there was less water available for the cultivated acreage than required. (Swaan 1935: A. 410-411).

The irrigation service supported moves to expand agricultural initiatives amongst the local population by improving the distribution of the available water and by encouraging people to be as sparing as possible with water consumption. This was hardest in the dry season when the irrigation service was confronted with the task of

"estimating which local farming crops should be cultivated and in what quantities under the altered situation in the east monsoon season without running the risk of facing crop failure due to water shortage and while also keeping an eye on the optimal planting times in view of determining the fluctuating water requirements during the growth period" (Swaan 1935: A. 410)[7].

Everything was organised according to planting regimes which dictated when it was best to plant and which crops should be planted where. The planting regime first of all related to the cultivation scheme in the east monsoon season but it also provided indications for the west monsoon crops. (Gruyter 1933, Graadt van Roggen 1935: VI. 47-48, 53-54). Planting schemes were combined with water arrangements in the culture (or cultivation) plans which had been developed in conjunction with the water plans which therefore became more detailed. The idea

---

[6] Swaan and Graadt van Roggen were, respectively, the former Section Engineer for the Pemali Section of the Provincial Public Works Division Pemali-Comal and an engineer within the same Division and they were oriented particularly to the Gung and Kumissik area in the Pemali-Comal region and to that region in general.

[7] See also Graadt van Roggen (1935: VI. 53-54). Graadt van Roggen (1935: VI. 51-52) also discusses the changes in management resulting from the new cane varieties introduced (see also **Chapter 6**).

behind these plans was to maximise the water returns. The irrigation service also concentrated on improving water management by employing technical means, by using small water areas to improve irrigation systems and by only issuing water through measuring sluices (Swaan 1935: A. 410-411, Graadt van Roggen 1935: VI. 53-54). As we shall see, technology made that latter option possible in a simple way but before we come to that subject I would first like to devote some attention to several discussions that were being continued in the field of irrigation.

The Balinese subak

Around 1915, and at the request of the Resident of Bali, colonial intervention commenced in irrigation matters on that island (see **Figure 10.6**). The engineer P.L.E. Happé who was sent out to Bali was impressed by the high level of rice culture development there. He wrote an article about the irrigation works with valley closures and washed up earthen dams extending up to 40 metres high and tunnels that were sometimes more than a kilometres long (Happé 1916). Later when he was employed at the Provincial Public Works Department in Semarang (Central Java) he recalled his years in Bali:

"In view of the fact that rice culture there was fairly sophisticated, not only technically but also as regards management organisation, government intervention with irrigation ultimately resulted in weirs and sometimes also other works being constructed at the request of interested sawa owners. The cost of these works which, upon completion, became the property of the local population, was paid in advance by the state and then, I believe, paid back at a rate of *f* 4.00 per bouw, per year.
Before submitting a design I was first obliged to establish things contractually with the sawa owners.
Once a dam was completed the government's irrigation service afterwards had nothing more to do with it. Only in the area of maintenance would support still be provided. All the irrigation personnel, at that time at least, comprised only my people, a couple of surveyors and designers, a writer and furthermore a couple of foremen for the operating of the various flood-control dams" (Happé 1935: VI. 135).

Even though irrigation intervention was minimal "everything went perfectly, as far as rice culture was concerned" (ibid.). Happé also pointed out that Bali had a lower rainfall level than Java and was thus able to provide less water per *bouw*. "Nonetheless – and that is the crux of the matter – the harvest there is on average 2x as large as here" (ibid.). This demanded an explanation. Happé (1935: VI. 136) believed that a farmer's personal qualities were very important:

"If through these initiatives, one is able to stimulate a sense of responsibility and of community and if the farmer is able as far as his own padi culture goes to be self-supporting then he will be able to value the results of his own labours more and thus start to feel more independent and free, also towards his village chiefs. Undoubtedly such personal advances will also lead to improvements as far as the crop is concerned".

He went on to refer to the French writer Montesquieu who apparently pointed out "that more than its fertility the yield of the earth depends upon the freedom of its inhabitants" (1935: VI. 136). Bali, where the personal qualities of the farmers came to full fruition, was proof of this maxim. That was where, again according to Happé, the result of the "irrigation corporations" (*subaks*) that existed there "did as a result of this close co-operation, greatly support the feeling of independence" (ibid.).

A *subak* was an agricultural area that was irrigated from a channel. The *sawa* owners in a given area formed what was known as a *subak* association. Such an association or union occupied itself with rice culture in general and irrigation in particular. Just like the *desa* associations, which promoted general *desa* interests, these *subak* associations were:

"controlled by written regulations which contain directives relating to the ownership and transfer of fields, irrigation districts, the planting out of fields, the collecting of land rent, the tending of cattle, the settling of disputes between sawa owners, and so on. Just as in the desa associations the penalties for breaching regulations consisted of imposing fines and terminating membership or land possession. At the head of the subak is the pêkasih or klian-subak who, together with the chosen members, such as writers and messengers, forms the society's committee" (*Encyclopaedie* Vol. I 1917: 122).

Subak associations (or *subaks*) were very reminiscent of Dutch district water boards. Water boards were introduced in what were known as the Crown lands (Yogyakarta and Surakarta)[8]. Happé was in favour of introducing water boards elsewhere in Java that were organised along the lines of the *subaks* in Bali[9]. He maintained that in this way rice production per *bouw* could be increased so that the rapidly growing population might be cheaply provided for[10]. Happé pointed out that already some 200 million guilders had been spent on modern irrigation facilities and that none of that had led to an increase in the production level per *bouw*. The idea of introducing *subak*-like water boards thus presented a cheap and effective alternative option:

"As far as rice cultivation is concerned, are we able to raise the population to a higher plane thus leading to greater harvests per bouw, then, in that way, with few costs and effects, we shall be able to achieve what would otherwise cost millions in reclamation and irrigation works" (1935: VI. 136).

According to Happé the embeddedness of the *subak* in the Hinduism prevalent in Bali was no problem. There were also *subaks* that were either from or shared with Mohammedans and even with Chinese and Arabic *sawa* owners. Moreover, there were traces from the past to indicate that Java had known cultural situations that corresponded to those familiar in Bali. He furthermore maintained that it would be quite feasible to fit sugar culture into the agricultural picture. Factories would have to adopt entire water circles, or at least as much as possible ground there and so secure a fixed share of the water supply. Just like with the population, the industry would remain the boss of the show.[11]

---

[8] Originally the Crown Estates of Yogyakarta and Surakarta were independent of colonial rule. Over the course of time, however, their autonomy was gradually eroded and they became absorbed into the colonial administration structure. The water boards had existed there since 1907. Apart from anything else, the objective was to improve irrigation. In 1920 the Central Water Board Office, which fell under Civil Public Works, was established for the Crown Estates but, in conjunction with economy measures, it was closed down in 1936. (*Encyclopaedie* Vol. IV 1921: 730, Vol. VIII 1939: 477). See for irrigation in Bali H. Schulte Nordholt (1988). Dutch water boards were described by Lammers (1929: 28 ff.).

[9] Referring to *subaks* Happé spoke of water communities or water circles (equivalent to tertiary sections). He understood a water board district to embrace an irrigation area as a whole, with its own *prise d'eau* in a river. A water board could therefore contain various *subaks*. Happé was in favour of an adapted system: he found that "situations of the type in Bali could not be imitated" (1935: VI. 137).

[10] For figures concerning population growth the reader is referred again to Boomgaard (1980: 45, 50).

[11] As far as the agricultural activities of inhabitants went, the creation of a culture plan under the *subak* system would become the work of the farmers involved (Happé 1935: VI. 137).

Figure 10.2: Tradional reservoir (*waduk*), 1915 (photo UBL KITLV 3723)

Figure 10.3: Building a reservoir dam, 1929 (photo UBL KITLV 36769)

Figure 10.4: Reservoir, 1931 (photo UBL KITLV 25170)

Figure 10.5: Head canal of reservoir, 1931 (photo UBL KITLV 25171)

Happé got a discussion going on water management, water boards and the applicability of the Bali *subak* within the Javan context. His proposal concerning the introduction of *subak*-like water districts summoned up many dismissive reactions, but how could it be any other way?[12] Following the example of the traditional situation in Bali around 1915, was that now to be the result of a hundred years of experience with modern irrigation? Was this the destiny for irrigation after the world crisis?[13] The opponents had other solutions. The debate turned into a prolongation of earlier discussions about the various water arrangements (see **Chapter 6**). A reference to the "great pioneer of modern irrigation technology", Lamminga, could not be avoided (Van Witzenburg 1936a: VI. 30, 31-32). The proposal to the effect that *subak*-like water control should be innovated had something of the undertone of the proportional Pateguan Management Regulation which gave the farmers responsibility for water distribution. On the other hand, there was the absolutist Pekalen Management Regulation that was to develop into the Pemali Management Regulation. It was this final ruling, which incorporated the newly developed institute of the *Ulu-Ulu Golongan*, that was to predominate.[14] Happé's opponents supported the Pemali regulations: "the situation in the Pemali-Comal [may] certainly be seen as a good start and as something exemplary in Java" (Polderman and Graadt van Roggen 1936b: VI. 147). The *Ulu-Ulu Golongan* regulation (also sometimes termed the "*ulu2* regulation" and possibly qualified with the term "*pembagian*" or distribution) would fare well in the crisis:

"The unanimous verdict of all official bodies is ... that the population in the regencies of Tegal, Pemalang and Brebes where the ulu2 regulation has been in force for longest and has penetrated most deeply has dealt in an admirable way with the numerous and important welfare measures of the last 5 crisis years. [What is alluded to here is, for instance, the amending of the *golongan* regulation and the increasing of crop volumes in the east monsoon season and more intensive pest control, WR]. To a not insignificant degree this could be attributed to the close contact and natural co-operation developed here between the ulu2 pembagian and the population which is pleased to offer its annual contribution to its intermediaries which is something that cannot be said of all other levies" (ibid.).

Happé was not so impressed by the Pemali Management Regulation even though he did appreciate that this arrangement could be attractive to engineers:

"That ... the Pemali ruling in which the work of the tani [farmer, WR] is established according to formulas and figures is a system that is more suitable for controlling by engineers cannot be denied. Whether, in human terms, such a system of keeping the tani repressed is desirable is another question. Incidentally, this also kills the incentive to become self-activated which is not so great with them anyway" (Happé 1936a: VI. 140).

---

[12] Van Witzenburg (1936a), Polderman and Graadt van Roggen (1936a). There is furthermore a response from Happé (1936a), rejoinders from the first-mentioned authors (both 1936b) and final comment, again from Happé (1936b). Van Witzenburg worked as an engineer for the country's Public Works Organisation in Bandung. Polderman who we met in conjunction with the Tangerang Works was at that time Chief Engineer at the Provincial Public Works Pemali-Comal Division.

[13] Elsewhere Happé was more positive about the effects of the intervention of engineers in irrigation affairs (Happé 1939; see **Chapter 1**).

[14] See **Chapter 6**. The Balinese *subak* was often alluded to over the course of time in documents related to irrigation management; see, for instance, Grinwis Plaat (1895), the welfare reports (e.g. *Mindere Welvaartscommissie* ["Lesser Welfare Commssion"] 1910) and Van Rees and De Graaff (1900 and 1907) (see also Van Witzenburg 1936a: VI. 30).

Figure 10.6: Washing in an irrigation canal, Bali, 1923 (photo UBL KITLV 31090)

J.E.V.A. Slors, an Assistant-Resident (in Semarang) became involved in this discussion between engineers. He lobbied for the introduction of the Pateguan arrangement thus placing himself on the side of Happé. His line of argument was a striking one:

"In the case of matters of which it may be said that they cut deep into the soul of the Javanese people, we should not only allow those people to make their own views and insights heard but we should also give them the opportunity to be active in a practical way in their own community and according to their own habits and customs. The creating of water boards along the lines adopted in Bali must, for the time being, remain out of the question. What will become apparent in connection with the above proposed water distribution system [i.e. the Pateguan Management Regulation, WR] is that the tani will definitely be allowed to co-operate more in their own affairs which will invigorate the desa community and thus be a strengthening force" (Slors 1936: VI. 138, compare Stoppelaar 1930).

Such ideas as these were really not appreciated by most engineers nor by the administrators who bore ultimate responsibility. They were instead happiest to combat the needs of the day with more rather than less intervention, in other words with plans and ideas. That was clearly apparent from the General Water Regulation that will be discussed here below.

There was a further important aspect of water management that was (again) raised in the period in question and that was the notion of introducing night *waduks* or, storing water at night so that it could be released in the daytime. In **Chapter 8** we saw that Civil Public Works had been given the go-ahead by the government to create such field reservoirs. In that way people hoped that they would be freed of the hated day and night ruling. Agricultural investigation indicated, however, that these smaller reservoirs did not operate optimally. One of the problems was that through seepage and evaporation much of the water was lost. This led to the step of having the government initiate extensive research into the *waduk* system in 1926 and 1927. In that connection not only engineers were heard but also agriculturists, civil servants and the population. The final upshot of all of this was that preference was again given to an "alternating ruling" but then one with a whole range of possibilities: the so-called Hours and Twenty-Four Hours (or sometimes Days) Rulings. (Metzelaar 1946: 219-222[15]).

In the twenties and thirties it was not just irrigation management that was debated. Another point of dispute was the matter of the introduction of a water tax. In his plea for the Balinese-style *subak* to be introduced to Java Happé had mentioned in passing that there was a water tax in Bali and that such a tax should also have been introduced in Java. It was Clason (1936), an engineer at the country's Public Works Organisation, who made an emphatic and convincing plea for the introduction of water charges[16]. Water taxing would make exact rentability calculations possible. There would also be social-economic benefits including putting a stop to the practice of using water uneconomically. Another consequence would be "that it would make it possible for the Government to gain better insight into the advantages of exploitation and into the rationale of the business as a whole" (Clason 1936: VI. 25). Clason drew attention to India where there was a water charge system. In the Indies, though, things never got that far. Crisis or no crisis the view

[15] A day and night ruling therefore became possible once again. What emerged from the *subak* discussion was that this Ruling led a tough life, see for instance Happé (1936: VI. 144-145). The General Water Regulation could not surmount this problem either (see below). See for the (positive) point of view of the engineers on night *waduks* Haringhuizen (1931) and also Van Es (1931) and Swaan (1931). See also Van Schaik (1986: 139-140).

[16] (Together with Wijn) Clason had previously published details of the Tanggul-Bondoyudo Works in the Residency of Besuki (later: Jember) a project encompassing some 35,000 *bouws* (1935). By alluding to the depression the authors refer there (p. VI. 38) to the work provision aspect of irrigation works and, in that connection, they placed rentability in second place.

that that farmers should be made to pay for water use (as well as or instead of having to pay land rent) was not an idea that was to catch on. The Javanese farmer was dependent on the technical control that ruled his actions but he did not need to pay anything extra for that. (Meyers 1929: 269, Furnivall 1939: 323, see also De Vries 1933 and Koens 1934a)[17].

The General Water Regulation

The irrigation report that came out in 1875 (De Bruyn et al.) contained a proposal for a regulation that regulated water rights. The proposal was, however, never accepted. In 1923 a plea was received from the lawyer J.H. Heslinga, an interim country judge, for the legal regulation of water rights in *De Waterstaats-Ingenieur* ("The Public Works Engineer"). Heslinga (1923: 37, 41) explained why up until then the law had not been adopted: a ruling was difficult to establish (each ruling "virtually leads to unfairness") and there was no real reason for it: in short, the Indies government simply did as it pleased. Shortly afterwards, in 1925, a general water regulation design plan did appear but it would be another decade before the "General Water Regulation for the Government countries of Java and Madura" (*Indisch staatsblad* 1936) would be made known. After a history that went back to the pioneering days of modern irrigation, water control had finally been given a general legal basis.

The various water regulations which, since the end of the previous century had developed in conjunction with the emergence of irrigation works and Irrigation Divisions did, in effect, anticipate the General Water Regulation. The water regulations were to culminate in the Pemali Management Regulation that was widely applicable. The next step was to develop planting regulations. In practice, therefore, general water regulations developed in a bottom-up way. More pressure was required though and that was to come, but from a different direction. First came the process of administrative reform that was to lead to the establishment of the various Provinces. These area sections did indeed get to grips with water management but they also excluded certain irrigation areas. There was a need for a ruling that produced clarity. It was the economic crisis that was finally to give the general water arrangement developments a final push in the right direction. Influenced by this government intervention, as well as intervention on the part of the irrigation service, increased and there was a water rights ruling that fitted into all of that. (See, for instance, Graadt van Roggen 1935: VI. 48-48, Heslinga 1923, Lammers 1929: 28-29 and Metzelaar 1946: 212).

The ruling referred to "public waters" and provided the following definition:

"All sources, waterways and non-flowing waters which cannot be proved to be the exclusive domain of particular persons or bodies according to titles or tenure and which are not exclusively destined to be placed in the service of government institutions" (*Indisch Staatsblad* 1936: 6).

---

[17] The question of the levying of an "irrigation water service fee" was something that arose again in the Indonesian post-colonial period, also in the Tangerang Plain (notably the Cidurian area), but which turned out to be difficult to innovate (see the **Epilogue**). Water taxation was a new point in the discussion on the economic aspects of permanent irrigation works but it was also an issue that was given special attention in the period in question, not only because of the crisis but also because the KIVI and its Indies group had, during the 1929 world congress in Tokyo, been "instructed" to make a special study of this (see National Archives, Cool Collection, no. 93, see also Happé 1939). Happé was also a supporter of the small-scale improvement of existing irrigation systems. After referring to the simple irrigation service structure in Bali he (1935: VI. 135) left undecided the matter "of whether we had not been able to offer better help, namely not by providing expensive works along western lines but by repairing and improving existing inland works in a better way than the Balinese are able to do that. In this way we would definitely be able to adapt to the existing situation in a purer way". This was something that had been talked over various times before in irrigation history (see **Chapters 6 and 8**) but it was not something that was clearly followed up at the end of the colonial period (cf. Koens 1934b).

Public waterways could be freely used except for in cases where the use involved drawing water for irrigation and other purposes (e.g. the swilling out of villages). The Regulation stated that water use, also for irrigation purposes, should be organised by the qualified authority which was (ultimately) the Province. There were no exceptions to this. The Provinces had to draw up the provincial water regulations themselves though the General Water Regulation did stipulate precisely what needed to be regulated:

a. the allocation of areas where people could make claims for irrigation water,
b. the establishing of culture plans,
c. the planting of east monsoon season *padi*,
d. the establishing of times at which water distribution might commence,
e. the introduction of alternating use rulings,
f. the periodical emptying of channels and structural works in conjunction with maintenance.

Per irrigation area there was to be a provincial water ruling which would be established by the Provincial Council. The Governor-General had to give that ruling his approval.

The Regulation furthermore provided the necessary specific indications. In connection with the distributing of the scarce water supplies between the sugar cane crops and the rice crops the Regulation for instance proposed the following:

"1. If, in connection with the inaccessibility to the available volumes of irrigation water in an irrigation area rulings to take things in turn are introduced by which, both for the purposes of the cane refining cultivation as well as for the population's subsistence crops, water is provided for a number of hours a day (the hour ruling) and if there are no possibilities for storing water at night in order to issue it in the daytime then the irrigation water for the commercial cane crops will be provided in the daytime upon the understanding that such allocating to the other farmer's crops, except as in cases stated in the following section, will not commence any later than at three in the afternoon.
2. If, in the interests of other crops grown for local purposes, the growers are only entitled to water for less than six hours then the starting time mentioned in section one concerning water provision for these two crops may be delayed by two hours at the very most" (pp. 11-12).

If there was therefore no alternative then the day and night regulation was permitted.

The Regulation was clearly based upon "absolute" and not upon "proportional" water distribution:

"In an irrigation system the water conveyed in the irrigation channels is, as much as possible, divided up according to the requirements of all the crops planted in the respective area for irrigation water. The sorts of points which thereby need to be taken into consideration are the extensiveness of the land areas, the normal water loss from the channels and the water requirements for the various crops under the given circumstances such as the soil type, the type of terrain, the growing period, diseases, rainfall, etc." (p. 13).

Somewhat unnecessarily it was added in the regulations that:

"The establishing of the water requirements of the various crops under various circumstances as referred to in the previous article or the relationships between the water requirements of the respective crops will be based, as much as possible, on scientific data relating to optimum and minimum water usage" (ibid.).

As has been seen the regulations dictated also how the culture plans should be drawn up. This plan was described as follows:

"A plan established by a responsible authority pertaining to the use – for a stipulated period of time – of the soil in a given irrigation area or section of an irrigation area for the purposes of agriculture as well as for fish farming and fish propagation in ponds and sawahs" (p. 6).

A culture plan contains detailed information on the agriculture in the relevant area:

"A culture plan indicates for instance the points in time when and the nature of the crops (second crops, refining cane, padi, etc.) to be grown, the certain indicated sections of the area to be cultivated, the crops concerned, whether the land is to be cultivated or prepared for cultivation and the times when crops requiring water will not be planted in given areas" (p. 10).

The regulations furthermore determined that culture plans constituted the basis for all water supplying. What this really involved was planting organisation and water arrangement both in the east and the west monsoon seasons. The irrigation service drew up the plans. That service was responsible for good water control and culture plans were an important control instrument. It was, however, obliged to consult the irrigation committee(s) concerned (see **Chapter 8**). In this way administrators and agricultural officials were also able to influence the formation of culture plans. (Lammers 1942: 6-7, see also Metzelaar 1946: 212-213).

Culture plans also satisfied another need. The depression of the thirties made clear in a very dramatic way just how reliant the Javanese farmer had become on the international market. The government could not get around this. Verschoor (1934: VI. 89) suggested that the malaise not only gave reason for more intensive intervention of the irrigation service in irrigation matters

"but that it also prompted a change of course in that intervention which was more oriented towards the economic problems which a tani, released from his isolation and producing for a wider market, was likely to tackle".

Culture plans made it possible to uphold a market-oriented policy.

Laboratories

Shortly after its completion in 1925 the moveable weir in the Cidurian gave cause for concern. Downstream of the weir and some 30 to 40 metres away from the cemented chamber that met up with the floor of the structural work a huge hole had appeared. By 1928 that hole was eight metres deep. The cause was a hollowing out process due to the "insufficient diffusing of the force of the water that flowed over the weir and, particularly, of the water bursting out from underneath when the doors were partly opened" (Eijsvoogel 1929: 191). This started to threaten the entire structure. Although there was no immediate danger the engineers involved still believed that it was necessary to take speedy action. The idea was to create a dam wall that would be driven into the ground just behind the chamber. It was to cost *f* 850,000 and the whole operation was to be carried out during a dry period but in view of the scale of the operation it would only be possible to carry off "with a well set up organisation" (Eijsvoogel 1929: 192).

The unforeseen dangerous hollowing out[18] and the huge expenses that needed to be incurred to safeguard the weir constituted reason enough for the editorial team of the "The Public Works engineer" periodical to publish a commentary column on the indispensability of a

[18] In itself this problem was as old as modern irrigation itself, see the "Van Thiel hole" described in **Chapter 3**.

supporting water engineering or "hydrodynamic" laboratory. The Director of Civil Public Works had already proposed, in 1927, establishing such a laboratory at the Technical College in Bandung. The proposed project would cost *f* 180,000. It was not at all clear, however, what kind of savings were to be expected from the introduction of such a laboratory and, in any case, that would only become clear in the future. The above-mentioned editorial team argued that for this reason and also because "the state of the country's finances" was presumed to be poor, the government would not place the required sums on the budget for 1929. The proposal was simplified and thus made cheaper. The Directors of Government Companies and Education and Services really supported the proposals. Despite everything the plans failed to get onto the budget a year later, again because of alleged money shortages (*Redactie Waterstaats-Ingenieur* ["Editors Public Works Engineer"] 1929: 192[19]).

J.W.F.C. Proper who had already lobbied for the establishment of such a laboratory in 1928 repeated that wish in a speech given in 1934 upon becoming Professor of Indies Hydraulic Engineering at the Technical College in Bandung. That was before the laboratory was built. Such a situation was not unusual during the depression of that time. Times started to improve and, by 1936 the hydrodynamic laboratory was opened. Built on the premises of the Bandung Technical College, it was a part of the Department of Transport and Public Works. This laboratory was not the only irrigation laboratory. For some time Civil Public Works had run a materials research laboratory designed to "carry out research and tests and to subsequently provide advice regarding the quality of technical consumption goods" (*Verslag laboratorium BOW* ["Civil Public Works Laboratory Report", 1927: 1). Another laboratory was the hydrodynamic test station at Tanjung Priok: this was where for instance the model tests were made for the outlet sluice in the *Mookervaart* (see **Chapter 9**). The funding of a hydraulic work was something which was then given "ground technical" attention in the Ground Mechanics Laboratory. (Ibid., Vlugter 1949: I. 102; see for an overview of hydrodynamic set ups and studies Vlugter 1941[20]).

The Romijn gate

The laboratory that needs special mention is the Provincial Hydrodynamic Laboratory in Semarang (established in 1927). One of the things worked on there was the creation of a new inlet sluice for the tertiary sections. In the past it was really only the water that was allocated to sugar crops that had been measured. As has been illustrated above, water management did gain more attention over the course of time and that was only reinforced by the crisis which resulted in the extending of water management to plant regulation and detailed culture plans. In striving to achieve a good and precise distribution of water reserves and to use water as economically as possible, ever more attention was given to the measuring out, to allocating the right quantity and that was of course extended to water distribution for agricultural purposes. One of the things that made it possible to implement these plans was the developing of a new sluice.

At first water was measured by means of a measuring gauge placed behind the tapping point (the Cipoletti gauge) consisting of a pipe to let water through and a shutter. The regulating of water supplies and the measuring of the water let through were therefore separate activities. It would obviously have been better if the two things had been combined in one tapping sluice

[19] This "money shortage" did not manifest itself in the spendings made in the field of irrigation which peaked in 1929 and which still remained high in 1930 (see **Appendix C**).

[20] Vlugter (1941: II. 84) argued about all the delays, also in the Netherlands: the Hydrodynamic Laboratory in Delft was opened in 1933 but when it came to constructing the large closing sluice in IJmuiden and the closing off dyke and drainage sluices for the *Zuiderzee* ("South Sea") works it suddenly became necessary to call upon the services of German laboratories! See for this laboratory Dirkzwager (1977).

designed to regulate flows and measure them. Indeed, such a tertiary sluice was finally constructed. Vlugter (1949: I. 102) summarised this piece of history and the refining of technology as follows:

"It was the engineer S.H.A. Begemann, then section engineer at Mojokerto and also professor at Delft who wished to see both these functions combined in one structural work and he maintained that the closed venturi gauge would be the most suitable solution. In '25, '26 and '27 the engineer P. de Gruyter repeatedly demanded, in the journal "*De Waterstaatsingenieur*", that attention be given to a new type of combined tapping and measuring sluice later to be known informally as the Crump-de Gruyter sluice. In the years '29 and '30 work was carried out in the open-air hydrodynamic laboratorium in Semarang which focused on improving the venturi gauge and on creating this module. At the same time, a new type of measuring instrument was developed there that operated with constant flow-through speeds in the pipe. It was the engineer D.G. Romijn who had the last word in 1932 when he recommended using the regulated gauge overflow which was then in common use".

Vlugter subsequently pointed out that many others had also worked on the developing of a new type of tapping sluice. Since he had been one of those people he certainly knew the situation. While working at the laboratory in Semarang he figured in the making of the new sluice that was linked to the development of the referred to measuring instrument facilitating constant flow-through speeds in the pipe. It was because of all the objections made by Vlugter and against him in connection with the proposed tapping sluice that Romijn became determined to develop a sluice that would represent "the last word" in sluice constructions. In the words of Romijn (1932: 287) it had to do with "a regulating and measuring system consisting merely of an overflow fixture with a wide top and a differential gauge scale"[21] (see **Figures 10.7 and 10.8**).

Irrigation and the state

Normal projects

The project undertaken in the Tangerang plain constituted one of the last colonial irrigation projects. The most recent total overview of all the irrigation works projects is to be found in the "Civil Public Works Report" of 1925 (pp. 2-12). There hundreds of irrigation areas were reported: 405 to be exact. In all those areas irrigation works had either been completed, were in progress or were being prepared or considered or even, in some cases, had been halted (e.g. the Solo Works!) or were no longer being considered (see **Appendix I**). The Tangerang plain was registered there as an area where the project was in the preparation phases. Other important projects were the Tanggul-Bondoyudo Works (referred to in **Note 16**), the Cimanuk Works in the Residency of Cirebon (later Indramayu) covering no less than 132,000 *bouws*[22] and, of course, the Krawang Works (see **Box 10.2**).

[21] With the help of Vlugter Romijn, Public Works engineer in Demak, was able to carry out further tests with this shutter in the referred to laboratorium in Semarang (Romijn 1932: 287). The article by Romijn that appeared in "The Public Works Engineer" followed the article by Rietveld on the hundred-year-old Sampean weir!

[22] Statistic obtained from Van der Meulen (1940: 153). According to De Vos (1941: 282) it involved 114,000 *bouws*. The Cimanuk Works was thus to become the biggest colonial irrigation project undertaken in Java (and the whole of the Indies).

Foto 1.
Vooraanzicht bij debiet 0
Meethuisje weggelaten.

Foto 2.
Achteraanzicht bij werking
met stort.

Foto 3.
Achteraanzicht bij werking met
minimum drukverlies.

Foto 4.
Achteraanzicht bij verdronken
toestand.

Figure 10.7: Testing the Romijn sluice (from: Romijn 1932)

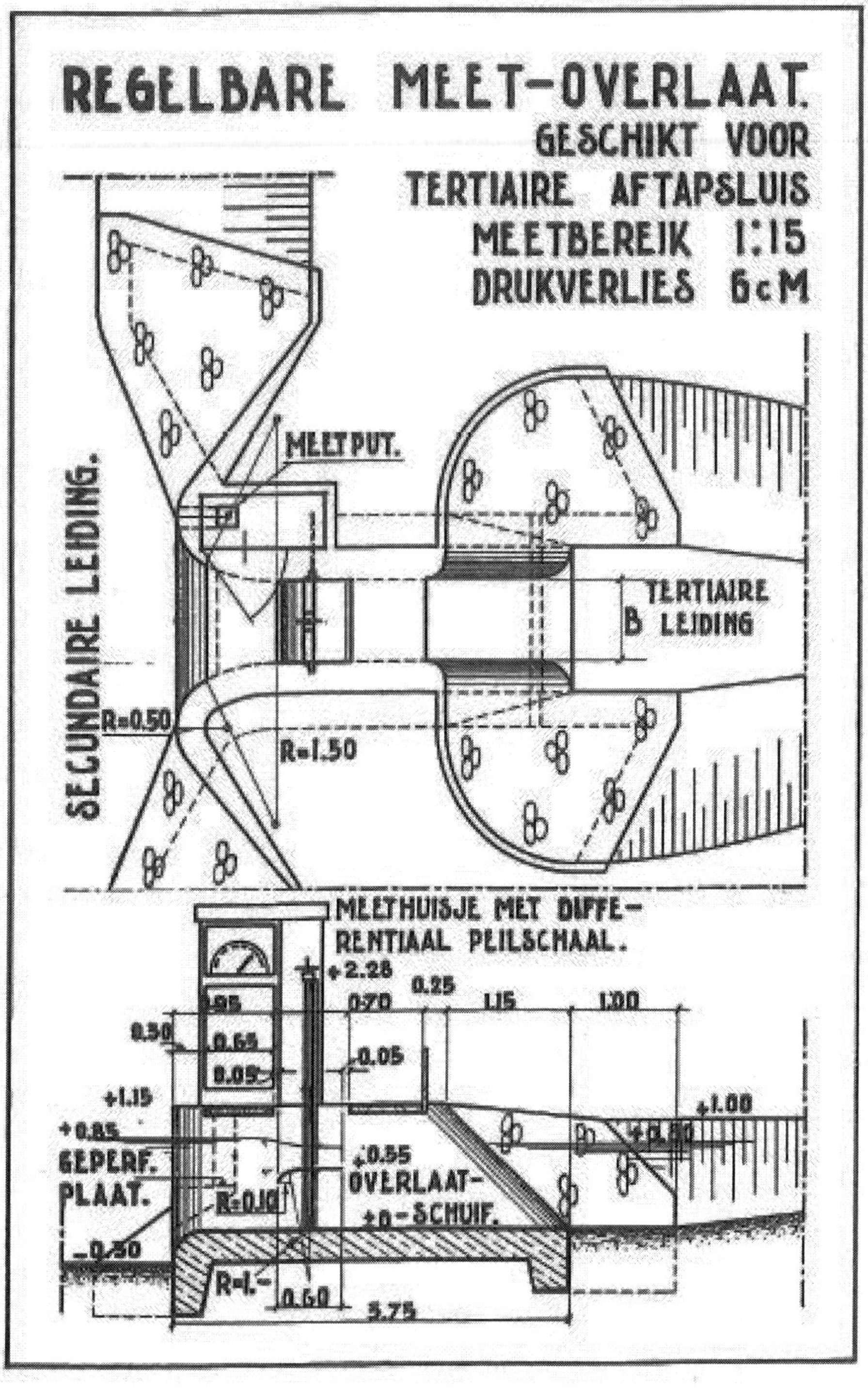

Figure 10.8: Technical drawing of Romijn sluice (from: Romijn 1932)

Box 10.2 The Krawang Works

At the time of the opening of the works in 1925 it was not just the weir but also the 5½-kilometre-long main canal and a secondary channel (with which, together with existing waterways several thousands of *bouws* of land could be watered). Later came the completion of the Eastern and Western branches which were 27 and 52 kilometres long respectively, and all the other channels. By 1936 the works were as good as completed and able to provide irrigation for 101,500 *bouws*. If we calculate the expenses for a number of adjoining areas and also the spendings on roads then we end up with a total sum of 18.8 million guilders.
Interesting detail: in the thirties what was known as the white rice "lodger" appeared in the plain. The "technical perfecting" of the area brought with it very favourable conditions for this particular insect! In the east monsoon season the white rice "lodger" had a "drought sleep" as a caterpillar. It would then be woken by the first rains and later it would change into a butterfly. Finally it would lay its eggs on the young *padi* thus causing great damage to the crop. (*Opening* 1925, Bakhoven 1936).

The Tangerang Works were thus created in a period when many other irrigation works were being completed or were still under construction. At that time irrigation was a routine affair. The "normal character" of the Tangerang Works is, apart from anything else, clear from the plan set up. Van Breen, Polderman and Dumont were evidently taking the same approach as that adopted with the Pemali Works. On the basis of the data collected they determined the structure of the irrigation system that was to be created. When it came to constructing secondary and tertiary channels the engineers basically stuck to the existing drainage canals.[23] There was also another respect in which the influence of the Pemali-Comal Works was noticeable and that was in the sequence of the works' construction, as proposed by Snell (who accounted for the buying back of privately owned land). The Pemali-Comal Works were constructed as separate works and then later linked up together (see **Chapters 5 and 6**). The overall Tangerang Works design was based on the – smaller – Cidurian irrigation works. It was built up in stages and the area to be irrigated was gradually expanded. In that way the irrigation situation in the area in question was improved despite the fact that the original plan was never realised. (Compare this with the activities in the Solo Valley which also replaced the larger first planned project and which are described and compared with the Pemali-Comal Works in **Chapters 7 and 8**[24]).

The creating of large mountain reservoirs was something that characterised the intervention of engineers in irrigation activities in that particular period. So far many reservoirs have been alluded to such as the *waduks* in Penjalin (1934) and Malahayu (1935, see **Figure 11.1**) in the Pemali-Comal area (**Chapter 5**) and the Pacal *waduk* (1933) in the Solo Valley

[23] The concern was thus with "normal projects" (cf. Kuhn 1971, see also the opening quote of **Chapter 9** and **Chapter 2, Note 15**). The term "normal project" also existed in the nineteenth century but then it had the somewhat negative connotation of a (constructional) project that had to be copied when it came to new works (Weijs 1921: 373; cf. Post 1879, e.g. p. 65 ff.).

[24] As we saw in the descriptions of the Solo Works, Snell had been instrumental in decisions by supporting the policy of making small-scale improvements introducing *waduk* irrigation. The partial change method was also followed in the case of the Krawang Works but then not just in terms of securing a gradual entering into use. For instance, in anticipation of the works, various temporary and permanent facilities were introduced, one such example being the so-called Sasa Works. The area involved there (6280 *bouws*) was already set up in the first decade of the previous century as a secondary section for the future Citarum irrigation system. The inbedding finally occurred in 1930. (Bakhoven 1936: VI. 111-112).

(**Chapter** 7[25]). Another reservoir was the Gembong *waduk* (see **Box 10.3**). In all, during the period being discussed, some six large reservoirs were constructed, their capacities varying from 2.4 to 60 million cubic metres. (Vlugter 1949: I. 102-103, Begemann 1936[26]).

Box 10.3 The Gembong reservoir

The irrigation area at the foot of the Muria mountains in Central Java received little rainfall in the east monsoon season, to the detriment of the sugar industry. This was what prompted Public Works to complete the Gunungrowo *waduk* in 1925. The results were good and so the idea was repeated. In 1933 the Gembong *waduk*, which had a capacity to store some ten million cubic metres of water, entered into use. It was therefore twice as big as the Gunungrowo *waduk*. The land area irrigated with water from that reservoir extended to some 10,000 *bouws*. The Gembong *waduk* was closed off with an earthen dam which, at a height of 38 metres, was higher than either the Penjalin (21 metres) or the Pacal (35 metres). The rim of the dam was 380 metres long. The construction of the dam had been preceded by extensive terrain research conducted under the supervision of the Geological Service. The Civil Public Works laboratory for material research in Batavia examined soil specimens. Laboratory research continued, too, when the dam was under construction with tests being carried out by laboratory staff who were on site. The building method opted for by the engineers involved was termed the "hydraulic-fill" method (i.e. the soil was spouted up). Ground in the surrounding area was loosened with water cannons and then transported to the site, still mixed with water. There the mud was floated onto the dam in construction from the two sides.
Apart from having a water tapping outlet the reservoir also had a *banjir* channel. A tapping tower was built in the reservoir so that the shutting system could be operated. The tower was circular, 5.90 metres in diameter and 42 metres high. The tower was connected to the dam by a 123 metre bridge. The entire project cost *f* 885,000 almost half of which was expended on the earthen dam structure. (Van Veen 1935, see also Begemann 1936).

The modern irrigated surface area rose in the 1920-1930 period from 519,000 to 883,400 *bouws* thus representing an increase of 364,400 *bouws* which was more than the 319,000 *bouws* of the decade before (see **Chapter 8**). The irrigated area then rose by 271,000 *bouws* to 1,154,700 *bouws* in 1936. In terms of percentages of the total *sawa* acreage the increase was: from 19.5% in 1920 to 31.1% in 1930 and 39% in 1936. (See **Appendix B**).

---

[25] As was explained in **Chapter 7** (**Note 36**) there was a need, in 1925, in relation to the Solo Valley for a similar improvement plan to that launched in the Tangerang plain. There it also became apparent that despite the study carried out by Snell (1928) and the measures taken in conjunction with that study, like e.g. to create the Pacal *waduk*, this was to lead to no satisfactory solutions in that area. From that point of view the situation in the Tangerang plain was better!

[26] Begemann who embarked on the development of a new type of tapping sluice was, in 1936, at the time of the presentation to which I refer, Head of the Public Works Department in Central Java. Later he also became a Professor in Delft. His inaugural speech there was also on the subject of reservoirs.

Technical and political innovations

Before the Sewan sluice complex was constructed laboratory tests were carried out with scale models. When it came to establishing the irrigation network in the Tangerang plain the Romijn shutter was also implemented. These constituted two important technological innovations, both of which had emanated from the rapid developments in the field of irrigation technology during the period under consideration. The foundations had been laid earlier, both as far as the creation and the management of works was concerned (see **Chapter 8**). It was thus now possible for attention to be devoted to the details. In conjunction with the sluice design for the *Mookervaart* research had resulted in a refined specimen of technology: the cog threshold. Much the same could be said of Romijn's adjustable measurable spillway. In devising a way to let water through while at the same time gauging it, one of the ideals of the engineers had been realised. Obviously, despite all the knowledge and experience, things could still go drastically wrong as was borne out by the weir at Citarum. In time, that weir was in danger of succumbing to the force of the water[27]. Again this problem constituted a huge incentive for further advancements to be made in the laboratory setting. It even led to an empirical moment: with the Tangerang Works the engineers had again learned things from the weir in the Citarum, this time to be vigilant about the tumbling pool.

In 1949 Vlugter, then Professor of Hydraulic Engineering at the Technical College in Bandung, described this technological development phase in a speech (already cited above) commemorating the transfer of the Bandung Technical College, in 1924, "to the State". He claimed that during the first quarter of the twentieth century engineers had managed to achieve a certain degree of unity in the setting up of projects and the designing of structural works. That was to change in the subsequent quarter between 1925 and 1950 which would by contrast "be characterised by a breaking away from such fixed forms and norms and a striving for perfection" (Vlugter 1949: I. 102). This was evidenced, for instance, in the design aspect of irrigation works. To clarify his point Vlugter drew a parallel with the car world:

"Just as the square Ford, rising high up from its chassis had to be modified to meet the streamline form of the modern vehicle, so weirs, distribution works, deluge dams, aqueducts, siphons etc. have had to adapt" (ibid.).

Vlugter suggested that laboratories were able to contribute a great deal to the design improvement process; hydrodynamic laboratories for the water aspect and the Soil Mechanics Laboratory for the ground aspect. Even the structural part above ground and water level was not able to escape improvement ideas. Such "visible sections which, in terms of hydraulic structures comprise only the smallest part, have also moved with their times, architecturally, and have come to stand for 'new professionalism'" (ibid.). Vlugter was indeed proud. He ended his historic description of the Romijn gate (see above) as follows:

"Through this good teamwork [of all concerned, Vlugter included, WR] a way of distributing water has been developed which stands out favourably when compared to what has further been achieved in this area. Though, in America, they are big in big achievements we may certainly claim to have been big in small achievements" (ibid.).

---

[27] The situation repeated itself in a more serious form after independence: at that point the structural work threatened to collapse which meant that "major rehabilitation" was required (M. Memed, personal communication, August 1993). Nevertheless I would still term that weir one of the monuments of colonial irrigation technology (see **Chapter 1**).

Progress in irrigation techniques was, of course, also affected by the various influences of the times. The economic crisis of the thirties was to leave its mark on irrigation efforts. It was to make better distribution and more economical use of water imperative and that, in turn, was to lead to improvements in water management. Such changes first became evident in the water regulating moves, later to be supported by plant regulating thus culminating in elaborate culture plans. With regard to sugar cane cultivation, water distribution was improved when the various alternating watering rulings were improved. However, advancement in the field of technical methods was also very welcome. Here laboratories, which were able to make such technical refinement possible, were instrumental. The Romijn gate was very useful when it came to the matter of optimising water use.

It was the needs of the day that frequently also gave cause for techniques to be otherwise perfected. There were always financial, demographic and sometimes even agricultural objections attached to the building of large reservoirs (see **Chapter 8**). One of the factors that made the *waduks* expensive was the special technical requirements that had to be met. In fact, the geographical circumstances in Java were not favourable for reservoir construction. The deep valleys made it necessary to build high dams. Another problem was the subsoil. Since the terrain was not suitable for concrete dams they had to be built of earth (like the Gembong *waduk*) or mountain shale (like the Pacal). The methods employed, such as the wet building technique used with the Gembong *waduk*, were – up to a point – new[28]. At the end of the day, laboratory research coupled with meticulous on-site field work was unable to take away all the barriers, but it helped, for instance by steering project workers in the right technological directions building-wise as happened with the Gembong *waduk* (Begemann 1936, see **Box 10.3**).

The way in which the government reacted to the depression of the thirties was by intervening in affairs even more. In the field of irrigation that was manifested in all the control-oriented and technological refinements. Undoubtedly matters would also have gone well with less intervention from the irrigation service as proved by the fine example of the successful irrigation system set up in Bali. The *subaks* pointed in the direction of the Pateguan Management Regulation which placed responsibility with the farmers themselves but it was an option that was not given a chance. It was simply the trend to interfere. Developments in the area of irrigation were to culminate in the development of the General Water Regulation but it was an arrangement that was a product of another development as well.

When the Tangerang Works became operational in 1936 it was the Governor of West Java, the Head of the Provincial Public Works Department and the Director of Transport and Public Works who made speeches. It was not without reason that two people from the Province were allowed to speak. The special Irrigation Service for the Tangerang Works had been set up as a section of Civil Public Works but later, once the Provinces had been created and had received their own public works services, it was incorporated into the provincial hierarchy. The Provinces had been created in connection with decentralisation and emancipation and, in the process, water control had become the domain of the Provinces. There were exceptions though and because there were no general water rights the situation remained obscure. The General Water Regulation was seen as the solution. It brought with it the rounding off of administration reform. Administrative changes were also affected by the crisis of the thirties. Water regulation was an example of this: the desire to regulate, prompted by the malaise, was clearly evident here. The depression had other consequences as well. Administrative reform with its idealistic notions was

---

[28] What was also innovatory was the soil improvement method employed in the case of the Pacal *waduk*. While the dam was actually under construction it became apparent that the foundation base on the front side of the dam would need to be made impermeable to water. This was achieved by injecting cement into the structure. The Mining Detection Service (or Geological Service) subsequently published favourable recommendations concerning this technique. Because of the costs that was even turned into a separate project. (Lieneman 1931).

perpetuated in a process of rationalisation in which retrenchment and increased efficiency became the goals. Regardless of all the decentralisation and simplification the government was still able to extend its power. There was another essential factor here: the restless population's striving for autonomy. The government tried to maintain a firm grip and did that by implementing rigid rule.

System

Despite the "serious financial worries" emanating from the depression of the thirties the "major interests of the population" that were vested in the Tangerang Works gave the "Government cause to at least continue with these works". Those were the words of Van Buuren, the Director of Transport and Public Works, spoken at the time of the festive opening of the works in question (*Tangerangwerken* ["Tangerang Works"] 1936: VI. 157). The Krawang Works project also continued even surviving the recession of the early twenties. However, the economic dip, especially the depression of the thirties, was to affect the progress of irrigation works. At first the Tangerang Works idea was abandoned only to be later revived and subjected to delays. One specific problem resided in the buying back of private land. The economic problems were also evident from the government's expenditure on irrigation works in general which dropped in the twenties and fell even more in the thirties. The problems – also in a political sense[29] – were unable to stop the wheel of irrigation intervention that had been set in motion by the Ethical Policy, but why was that?

Because of all the troubles, irrigation concern had become more important than ever and so much was made of all the successes. The economic problems were even referred to in order to highlight the success of the completed works, despite all. The mood was aptly summed up in the words of Fock, the Governor-General at the time of the opening of the weir at Walahar (*Opening* 1925: 13):

"In recent times we have heard much talk of welfare politics. The Government was in agreement with this – it must strive to promote the welfare of the population and, in so doing, all possible influencing factors must be considered. Therefore what better evidence could there be for the fact that the Government has not lost sight of the welfare of the population for one moment than this work which means so very much to the population and which was brought about in the darkest years of economising?"

The government cared for the population and the irrigation works were "living evidence" of this. Undoubtedly it wished to receive no words of thanks from the population because it was simply doing its duty (see the words of Fock cited at the beginning of this chapter) but it did of course hope to in this way legitimise its existence. Amidst all the consternation that awakening nationalism brought with it, the government tried to win over the favour of the population with important irrigation works (compare the "supporting of authority" by Happé 1939, see above).

Pride reverberated in the words of Fock which was something we also saw with Van der Hoek, the Governor of West Java, at the time of the opening of the Tangerang Works (see **Chapter 9**). There was also pride amongst the Public Works engineers. When the Krawang Works became operational the Director of Civil Public Works, J. Blackstone (1925-1927), made it known that this concerned "something special". "Never in Java have irrigation works of the

[29] Although in this context I intend this generally, the political unrest also obviously had a physical effect as is, for instance, evidenced by the following mention made in a description of (a section) of the Tangerang Works in *Verslag BOW* (1926: 89): "The irregularities that occurred in the month of November resulted in a great loss of employees which in turn led to work delays".

size of the Krawang Works been realised" (*Opening* 1925: 3). Blackstone drew a comparison with the Pemali Works, the works in the Brantas delta (of De Bruyn, see **Chapter 4**) and even with the halted Solo Works[30]. Vlugter was proud of the great work at a small sluice (see his quotation above). That self-awareness amongst engineers and administrators was something that was in general a reflection of the way that the development of modern irrigation was presented in the thirties (see **Chapter 1**). With the engineers, these sentiments were not just shown in words, take for instance the monument in honour of Lamminga. It was erected in 1930, nearly thirty years after all his activities in the Pemali-Comal region. Since then engineers, like Van Breen, Polderman and Dumont, had spread out to continue the good work elsewhere. Following in the footsteps of the "great engineer" they designed the Tangerang Works. The monument served to symbolise the deeds of Lamminga but it also bore witness to the actions of those who had come after him, who had emulated him and thus also the success of modern irrigation in general. Even though he was an important link Lamminga was merely a link in a chain. The erectors of the monument were therefore also honouring themselves. The pride in irrigation works reached further than the world of administration and technology. Irrigation works were impressive enough to be included in colonial photo albums alongside of other specimens of technical know-how such as railway bridges and large buildings. The weir of the Krawang irrigation system was a favourite object (see Tien 1938: photo 1, **Figure 10.1** here; a photo of the Citarum weir also in De Vries 1928 and De Vos 1941).

The progress that marked the intervention of engineers in irrigation is not only to be traced to its significance. On the occasions of the openings of major works it always became evident which parties were involved in irrigation affairs. When the Tangerang Works entered into use in 1936 it was Van Buuren, Director of Transport and Public Works, Van der Hoek, the Governor of West Java and J.J. Jonker, the Head of the Provincial Public Works Department in West Java who spoke. Ten years earlier, at the time of the opening of the weir in the Citarum the people who had spoken then had been the Governor-General Fock, the Regent Raden Toemenggoeng Soeriamihardja and the Director of Civil Public Works, Blackstone.[31] In this respect what was quite telling was the unveiling of the Lamminga monument in 1930. Amongst the invited guests were: a Governor-General representative, the Governor of Central Java, the Resident of Tegal, the Mayor of Tegal, the Head of the Provincial Public Works Department, the Head of the Pemali-Comal Irrigation Division and many representatives from the Departments of Civil Public Works and Agriculture, the sugar industry and the engineering associations the Royal Institute of Engineers and the Delft Engineers Society. A number of those guests had also been invited to speak.[32]

---

[30] The Governor-General, Fock (*Opening* 1925: 11-12), also alluded to the Solo Works (see **Chapter 8**). Ultimately the Krawang Works was to become the second biggest irrigation project in the Indies after the Cimanuk Works (see **Note 22** and also Van der Meulen 1940: 153).

[31] The opening speeches indicate which other people were also involved, especially if one studies the votes of thanks (see, for instance, the words of Van Buuren in **Chapter 9**).

[32] There was yet one other party. In the case of the Krawang Works the Governor-General had the honour of opening the works but Blackstone was only allowed to make that known "after the priest had implored the Almighty to bless the works" (*Opening* 1925: 9). When it came to the opening of the Tangerang Works it was reported that there the "*penghulu*" had prayed (*Tangerangwerken* 1926: VI. 157-158). The opening of the Pemali Works, i.e. of the aqueduct at Poncol in 1902 was exuberantly celebrated with representatives from the world of irrigation, Dutch and Javanese internal administration and sugar people as well as the Director of the Semarang-Cheribon Steam Tram Company. Apart from several "emotional speeches" made by individuals who remained nameless and a telegram from the Governor-General, Rooseboom, it was only Lamminga who made an official speech (at least according to *D.* 1902).

As will have become clear, there were – in the twenties and thirties – many groups and institutions involved in the matter of modern irrigation: engineers and their social societies, government organisations at different levels and the sugar lobby. The other parties involved were companies, technical colleges and laboratories and, of course, the population. Over the course of time the role of each of the population in modern irrigation had grown via Javanese administrators (in irrigation committees but also in other respects such as in the opening of irrigation works) and via research consultation such as with the research into night *waduks*. With so many groups involved modern irrigation (as an entirety of infrastructural facilities) had become the cornerstone of a socio-technical complex or system comprising a range of technical and non-technical elements and supported by the many organisations and groups involved (see Hughes 1987, the opening quotation of this chapter and **Chapter 2**)[33].

With the Tangerang Works, the last casus of this study, we returned in the previous chapter to Batavia where state intervention with Javanese water affairs first began even though the first activities had to do with the digging of canals that were not primarily intended for irrigation purposes (see also **Chapter 3**). In this chapter the developments discussed there in concrete terms have been contextualised. I thereby arrived at a theoretical concept presented in **Chapter 2**: the system concept. This linking of empirical and theoretical issues will be continued in the following chapter in which I shall also formulate my conclusions relating to the development of modern irrigation in Java.

[33] See for a comparison of the irrigation network in Java with irrigation situations elsewhere in the world, notably in Japan and America, Meyers (1933). Compare this also with Lintsen (1992) who discussed Hughes' system theory in conjunction with large-scale and small-scale water control in traditional and "hydraulic societies" respectively and in the Netherlands which is dominated by water boards.

11

'Modern!'

Conclusion: a research-based representation of colonial irrigation intervention

> Initially, human emancipation tended to emancipate mankind from the forces of nature. ... The utmost he [man, WR] can achieve is an adaptation of his techniques to the natural environment, in order to take advantage of the natural conditions surrounding him. Even with further progress of technical refinement, the situation does not fundamentally alter – Francis Bacon's adage **non nisi parendo vincitur** (nor is nature to be conquered but by submission) remains valid even in the most advanced stages of technological development.
>
> ...
>
> In order to become part of human evolution, the emancipation process should be broadened to a new dimension: in addition to liberation from the fetters of our natural surroundings it should also encompass a liberation of creative human potentialities from suffocating social structures (Wertheim 1983: 10-11).

It was around 1900 that the modern era hit the Dutch East Indies. "*Modern*! That word speedily echoed throughout Europe ... Bear with me if I also use that word, even though I am unable to fully grasp the meaning of it", commented the writer Pramoedya Ananta Toer (1983:13). Apart from locomotives, perhaps the leading symbols of the modern era (Adas' "Machines as the measure of man", 1989, has a photo of a steam train on the book's front cover), the rise of modernity in the Indies was also marked by impressive irrigation works: monuments of colonial irrigation technology, such as, for example, the weir in the Pemali river.

By about 1890 the knowledge and skill of irrigation engineers had progressed to such a degree that they had become capable of creating whole irrigation systems with headworks, inlet and outlet canals and even smaller canals for more extensive irrigation. To that end other important conditions had also been fulfilled including the establishment of an independent Public Works Organisation. De Vos (1946: 280) wrote in *Daar wèrd iets groots verricht* ("Something Great Was Achieved There") that from "approximately the beginning of this century ... a start [has] been made on the systematic creation of complete technological irrigation works". But here it was really the wish that was father to the thought. Admittedly the development of new technology was an aspect of the rise of a new Indies but it did not go all that smoothly. On the one hand the changing of the irrigation system aided by the implementation of Western techniques was actually ahead of the modernisation wave while, on the other hand, just when the time was ripe for it the civil engineers had little to offer and it was only later that they were able to connect up with the process that was to lead to a modern Indies. That is something that we shall further elucidate here in the conclusion to this whole study.

The questions were:

1. How did modern irrigation actually develop in colonial Java?
2. What were the conditions facilitating that development?
3. How did irrigation development and the developments occurring within the Indies state influence each other?

The answers to all these questions are to be found below. We shall commence with a summary of the development of modern irrigation in Java by tracing the four cases dealt with in this study, followed by sections on conditions and interaction. Ideological facets will be discussed in several places, with concluding remarks in the final section.

Figure 11.1: View from the dam of the Malahayu reservoir in the Pemali area (photo WR)

From headworks to project series

The four cases

The Sampean Works

Our journey through history begins in 1832 when an engineer was sent out to the Sampean area of Eastern Java to replace the temporary dam constructed there with a permanent one. C. van Thiel was a true pioneer. The dam that he constructed consisted of a wooden framework filled with river stones placed between walls built of slate. This framework dam was a success but it would still take almost half a century for a permanent weir to finally be completed. When the wooden dam wore out, another engineer tried to follow it up with a Javanese solution by creating a dam where the water flooded over the weir diagonally (an overspill or *awiran*), but it was soon destroyed by the river. With the temporary dams that were to afterwards dominate the scene for nearly twenty years the Resident and his civil servants were in effect reverting to the old Javanese approach to irrigation. This was followed by the revenge of technologists and the construction of a permanent weir that was completed in 1876. The destructive force of the water made many adaptations necessary. The final deed was the construction of a *banjir* canal around the construction area: in effect the engineers had by then already opted for a stone threshold in the river that would function as a new weir!

Constructing a weir in the Sampean that could stand up to the increasing water force (probably due to the deforestation continuing upstream), was quite a battle and it was only very slowly that the engineers managed to stand up to their natural enemy. All the alterations were also to have adverse effects that were partly to go down in history as "the hole created by van Thiel" but which were in part also attributable to the disturbing crumbling of the riverbed. Another annoying effect noticeable at first was the environmental damage in the form of the depletion of the *jati* forest and later other forests as well. Partly because of this, wood started to disappear as building material and people were forced to turn to brick (originally the famous Dutch Waal bricks used as ballast in Dutch vessels).

It was sugar cane cultivation that really gave rise to the need for the construction of a weir in the Sampean and which was to gain special attention during the time of the Cultivation System in conjunction with exploitation (likewise introduced to the whole of Java in 1832). Through the Cultivation System, the Dutch overlords were able to compel the Indies population to cultivate certain specific crops two of which, sugar (and to a lesser degree) indigo, required irrigation water.

In the case of the Sampean weir there was no evident conflict between civil servants and engineers but generally speaking these two groups did clash. In the case of the Sampean it was the Civil Service which took the initiative for matters that the Bureau or Department of (Civil) Public Works (as of 1854/1866) was unable to take responsibility for due to financial and personnel problems. Because they tackled things in the Javanese way, civil servants provided serious competition for the engineers. Though the engineers were very critical of the traditional techniques the alternatives they had to offer were not, at first, much better. Simultaneous to the Sampean weir trials and tribulations there was also the troublesome rise of the Public Works Organisation. The colonial government established that service in 1854 following a period of starvation in Demak which, earlier on, had given people cause to build dams in the Glapan and the Tuntang. In the earlier days one of the important Directors, who also did much to get Public Works off the ground, was the engineer H. de Bruyn. In spite of all the opposition, Public Works gradually expanded which meant that ultimately the engineers secured for themselves an independent position. Indeed, that happened not long before – in the Sampean area – the final solution materialised in 1887. A new era had begun.

In order to be able to say more about this we shall divert our attention to the Pemali plain on the north coast of Java which provides us with the setting for the second case.

The Pemali Works

The Pemali plain was dry and barren, also to the disappointment of the local sugar refiners. The improvement activities commenced with the erecting of a weir but while that weir was still under construction a general plan was published, in 1896. The plan unfolded ideas for the creation of an entire irrigation system with input and output canals (an improvement in comparison to the Javanese irrigation plans with which these canals coincided) and further minor irrigation works. The plan demonstrated cybernetic tendencies: it revealed backward and forward reasoning from the water input and output view-points. The plan was based on much research into such matters as debits (i.e. the amounts of water in the river at any one time) and rainfall levels. The Pemali Works, covering 44,000 *bouws*, were completed in 1903. They formed a part of the Pemali-Comal Works that was to continue being worked on until the twenties and which, together, were to constitute one of the biggest irrigation systems in Java (170,000 *bouws*).

The Pemali Works were successful – also in relation to other projects in the region (the partial approach!) – and were to form, for that reason, an example (or paradigm) for later works. That also applied from the management angle. After the works had been completed this was followed by the introduction of technological management (on the part of engineers). One important matter was the question of how water was distributed between the local farmers and the commercial sector, between rice and sugar crops. Considerable experimentation was carried out with local farmers, especially where the involvement of the population was concerned. The main point of departure was the traditional management form in which the *Ulu-Ulu* fulfilled an important role. This water master comprised a part of the village council. In the agreement that was finally settled (formally in 1910) he was actually given an independent position. For a long time this Pemali ruling was normative and even today it still applies (see the **Epilogue**).

Someone who was inextricably linked with the Pemali(-Comal) Works was the engineer A.G. Lamminga who was active in the 1895-1903 period. He was to become known as the founder of modern irrigation technology in the Dutch Indies and (for a brief period) he was able to propound his principles in his role as Professor at the Technical College in Delft. Lamminga was honoured with a monument which, unlike his works, was removed when the country gained its independence. However, it would really be a mistake to believe that the creation of modern irrigation works actually started at that time with Lamminga (or perhaps even slightly later as outlined in connection with De Vos here above). Lamminga was no deus ex machina on the stage of modern irrigation. Other than the headworks constructed by the pioneers he also built on earlier works, notably those in the Demak, where after a considerable past (and the threat of a second famine) an entire irrigation system finally emerged in 1894. However, he also built on the works in the Sampean area where, in 1891, the *banjir* canal was followed up by works linked to elaborated irrigation networks (completed in 1906, 15,000 *bouws* big).

Lamminga was not the only one involved in such undertakings at that time. The Pemali Works were part of a larger irrigation programme extending throughout Java known as the General Irrigation Plan drawn up in 1890 and involving some sixteen major projects in densely populated regions. The plan was basically yet another consequence of the improved position that engineers had secured for themselves through the introduction of a new water ruling established in 1885. This ruling represented a turning point in the struggle for emancipation on the part of engineers. The new verve was evidenced in the attitude of the

Irrigation Brigade which was requested to carry out research into the possibility of providing all government land with modern irrigation. Several years later this body was amalgamated with the Civil Public Works bureaucracy (as Technical Division E). In conjunction with technical control the Indies authorities introduced Irrigation Divisions. In other words, during this period the activities of engineers in the field of irrigation underwent a true boom, both from the point of view of projects and management.

Because of all the various fiascos the weir in the Sampean (as well as the Demak Works) constituted a good training ground but, around the turn of the century, there was to be one experience that was to be much tougher (though De Vos – 1941 – fails to mention it) and that was the Solo Valley Works disaster, the third project to be examined in this study.

The Solo Valley Works

The Solo Valley was a region in East Java where, because of all the droughts and floods, the population led a dreadful existence. In order to finally do something about the problem, the engineers launched a massive project affecting 223,000 *bouws* that was too far exceed all previous and future projects in terms of its scope. The project, which also fell under the General Irrigation Plan, was an ambitious sample of engineering technology that could even be termed impressive on an international scale (with a main canal that was 165 kilometres long!). Part of the plan involved diverting the Solo river to the Java Sea. The largest river in Java (also known as the "auspicious Lord of the Water") transported so much silt into the Straits of Surabaya that it was feared that this would hamper shipping movements (involving huge steam ships!)

The project had the potential to make its creator, promoter and executer the greatest hero of engineering intervention in the area of irrigation overnight but history was to take a different turn and Pierson was to become an outcast. When during all the activities it emerged that there was going to be a massive financial deficit it was the Dutch government that decided to suspend the project. Despite all the support received from engineering circles (the Royal Institute of Engineers constituting an important pressure group) the recommendation to continue received from a state commission had no effect and the project was halted in 1903/1905. The alternative option was to embark on a small-scale improvement programme which was to include building large reservoirs (*waduks*; see for an example in the Pemali area **Figure 11.1**). The discussions continued though, also after the "definite" decision to stop in 1929 after follow-up investigations had also been carried out. (Today the Solo Valley is still awaiting a satisfactory decision and the report brought out by the Solo Commission mentioned here is again receiving attention. See in this connection the **Epilogue**).

The Solo Works, just like the Pemali Works and the Sampean Works (with its extensive irrigation network) that were laid down in the 1890 programme, demonstrate to us that the modern approach could also fail. In the first place that could be attributed to all the (financial-)economic concerns. Even though the engineers had been given a free rein in 1885 this freedom started to come to an end in 1897 when something known as the Rentability Commission was set up. As well as engineers, civil servants were involved in that Commission and they were thus given quite a big (structural) say in matters. The Commission had to study the economic viability of proposed projects. It was not the Solo Works that gave rise to this Rentability Commission but they did make its work extra important. According to the majority of people in the Commission the Solo Works did score high but there was also a degree of doubt as far as the Director of Publics Works, the engineer J.E. Meyier, was concerned.

The rentability criterion was given extra weight and content when more interest started being shown in small farming in connection with the Ethical Policy. This political movement was something that emanated from the "reduced welfare" that was becoming evident in the Indies towards the end of the century before last together with a renewed threat of famine in the Demak region. An agricultural expert joined the Rentability Commission. Silt, which also helps to determine the fertility of the soil, became an important area of attention and in this connection new objections started being made to the Solo Works. The question posed was whether in the case of long canals the silt could reach the far away fields. Another problem was of a managerial-technical nature: how could agriculture be coordinated in such a large area? The large-scale approach emphasised in the project was also queried, though that was not to really become public until a decade later. The fact that De Meyier's opinion was to carry so much weight was something that linked up with another aspect of the Ethical Policy which was that in colonial decision-making the interests of the Indies population were starting to carry more weight. (Conversely it was so that later follow-up research was to occur at the instigation of a member of the People's Council). The stopping of the Solo Works project created a crisis in the irrigation world and so from that point of view it became a failure.

Under the new policy and after the abandonment of the Solo Valley project a preference developed for smaller works designed to support rice cultivation. In general, and as far as the Solo Valley in particular was concerned, this policy was propagated by the engineer and Dutch parliamentarian (for the *SDAP*: a former socialist party), H.H. van Kol. Javanese irrigation was reinstated. Plans for large and small reservoirs were developed for the Solo Valley, the engineers partly being influenced by the numerous little water catchments created by the local population. The first large reservoir was completed in 1917 and the second one in 1933. In the smaller-scale approach there was more thought for control (in this respect the situation in the Demak was improved). In practice this led to three-way debate between engineers, civil servants (who had never left control!) and agriculturists. The consequences of the Solo Valley and the effects of Ethical Policy became intermingled, for instance in the matter of the decentralisation of public works affairs where lower level "councils" were given more to say and to do. In the second decade of the twentieth century the creation of modern irrigation works was given a new impetus. By 1920 the General Irrigation Plan projects were (finally) all more or less completed (with extra money having been pumped into the less profitable projects) and the spendings on new projects had reached their zenith. This therefore brings us to the fourth and final project.

The Tangerang Works

The Tangerang Works, which drew irrigation water from the Cisadane and Cidurian rivers fitted in well into the Lamminga school. In comparison to the example of the Pemali Works the works in the Tangerang plain, situated to the west of Jakarta in West Java, constituted a normal project in the Kuhnian sense of the word (which meant that it was not so much pioneering work as the resolving of a puzzle within a certain framework termed by Kuhn a "paradigm") or research accompanied by a well thought out general plan for an area of 74,000 *bouws* in which everything was in order. What formed a problem in that area was the private estates where the respective owners were lord and master and the population was therefore left poverty-stricken. The plan was to buy back that land and to then upgrade the whole region by introducing an irrigation plan and a road plan. The economic problems of the twenties and thirties led to delays but not to an abandonment of the plans, though the colonial engineers were not to see the completion of their works (the works were completed after the time of independence, see the **Epilogue**). The movable weir at Pasar Baru was completed in 1934, thanks to the assistance of an important constructor. It was equipped with electrical sluices because otherwise the Tangerang would overflow at high water.

One of the technical problems concerning the works was the problem presented by the Mookervaart which dated from the seventeenth century (and was older than the *Westerslokkan* and the *Oosterslokkan*). The canal helped with the flushing clean of the canals in Jakarta. If nothing was done then the implementation of the weir, located a little further upstream, would discharge water through the canal to plague Jakarta instead of putting it to good use. However, damming off also had its problems. If that were to be done it would mean that all the *banjir* water would have to be transported away by the Cisadane thus meaning that the river would have to be deepened at great expense. The final solution found was that of closing off the waterway with the help of a couple of sluices: one intended for the *banjir* water and one for shipping. For the benefit of the Sewan sluice point laboratory research was carried out for the first time. Another innovation and something that also emanated from experimentation with water circulation was the Romijn shutter, an adjustable measuring spillway capable of regulating the inflow of water into the *sawas* while at the same time measuring the water volume. One incentive for laboratory research was the arrival of another weir in the Citarum which, in the twenties, almost looked as if it was going to be destroyed by the water force (created by the weir itself: it all had to do with the destructive force of the overflowing water).

During the final phase the headworks in the Tangerang plain were executed under the supervision of the Provincial Public Works Department, an organisation emerging from perpetuated decentralisation. It was in this connection that in 1936 the General Water Regulation also saw the light of day, the preparations for which stretched back to the pioneering age of the development of modern irrigation. This Regulation were marked by the effects of the depression of the thirties and the accompanying interference on the part of government, like for example where it dictated how a detailed cultural plan should be organised. The combined regulations for water and plant control were aimed at improving water management. One reason why this was required was because of falling sugar cultivation attributable to the malaise. Because of this, rice cultivation increased and rice requires more water than sugar cane. The innovation of the Romijn shutter was something that fitted in perfectly with these developments.

The Tangerang Works constituted an example of a new generation of irrigation projects. Instead of simply imitating Lamminga's paradigm these projects were prepared and executed in tremendous detail, even agricultural-economic feasibility studies were carried out and everything, from the larger water volumes in the rivers to the small sluices directing the water to the *sawas*, was examined. In the final period of the colonial era many of these projects were seriously looked into, usually in order to improve existing modern or Javanese irrigation systems.

The development of modern irrigation

In conclusion we may detect the following developments when it comes to the matter of the creation of modern irrigation works in Java. At first the irrigation engineers created individual headworks on a small scale. These were actually permanent works that replaced temporary Javanese works. In the process it was increasingly the case that sustainable materials were used. Things continued like that until about 1885. What then began to emerge were the first projects involving entire irrigation systems with separate feed-in and drainage canals and elaborate irrigation networks. It all involved large works, in the case of most projects the irrigation areas concerned covered more than 7000 *bouws*. The projects were based on extensive research. The economic side (the rentability aspect) was not, however, given all that much attention.

Around 1900 the large-scale approach started to crumble, both on economic and technological grounds. By way of reaction to that attention started being paid to smaller works that corresponded better with small localised farming efforts. The way in which irrigation facilities were managed by engineers also gained more attention – that emerged at the same time as the first irrigation systems. Later it again became possible to embark on larger works. In the period from roughly 1885 to 1920 engineers started to learn how to successfully shape irrigation works from the point of view of building technique, management and revenue. After that the development started to take off and standard projects were executed. In this final phase it became possible to focus upon optimising technical and managerial aspects[1].

This technological outline could be further elaborated. Successes and failures followed each other in a constant succession. The pioneering works provided solutions that were sometimes a success but sometimes not. In the consecutive projects there were extreme results in both directions. Not everything went well with the normal projects in the final phase. Certainly at first, it was hard for the engineers to outdo the Javanese builders. There were elements of traditional irrigation that served to inspire the engineers but the results were of varying success. The part played by administrators in all of this was vital. There were "constructive" facets to it all (they initiated, for instance, the Sampean Works and later, when the engineers went overboard, there was participation in the Rentability Commission and in management) but there were also negative sides to it all (at first there was conflict between engineers and civil servants with the latter relying too heavily upon Javanese technology). Other important involved parties were the sugar refiners and the agricultural experts. On top of that all other kinds of groups and institutes were involved, including contractors, laboratories and technical colleges. The relationship that existed between engineers and the Indies government was not exactly straightforward: the engineers were supported in their work (for example the 1885 ruling) but they were also opposed (the Solo Works). In the relationship that existed between engineers and the government there were moreover other actors at work like particularly (the representatives of) the Civil Service and the Agricultural Department.

The development of modern irrigation in colonial Java – the changes made to the existing irrigation system with the aid of Western means – may be seen as falling into various phases. On the basis of project histories they may be viewed as falling into four phases[2]. What would appear to fit in best with the empirical case material and the information deduced from the contexts would be a three-way division into headworks, initial projects for entire systems and normal projects. This view of the development of modern irrigation more or less corresponds with that sketched by Vlugter (1949) (and with that of Ankum 1984, 1988 as far as dates go, see **Appendix I**). The correspondence with Vlugter's overview only really applies to technical developments in the area of irrigation. Because of its broad view of matters this

---

[1] Booth (1977) maintained that colonial engineers fell short when it came to the developing of tertiary irrigation facilities and the matter of management (see **Chapter 2**). That might in general be said to be correct but there was in fact thought for tertiary supplies as e.g. was demonstrated with the Pemali Works where management was also well organised. It is possible that in the forties and fifties more was lost than she realised (see the **Epilogue**). Another additional possibility was that late colonial engineers were less concerned with tertiary irrigation activities than their predecessors (after the colonial period the adage was "stay out of the tertiary area", G. de Jager's personal communication, September 1996).

[2] The overlap between the Pemali and the Solo Works could be reversed by placing emphasis upon their creation (1893-1903) in the case of the first works and by stressing, with the last works (1903-1917), the matter of their being followed up.

study ultimately provides us with an entirely different idea of the development of modern irrigation than one might gain from the colonial notions outlined in **Chapter 1**. What is really focused on here (and what was lacking in the colonial age) is the thought given to failures, Javanese irrigation, involved parties other than engineers or the Indies government and the complicated relationship between technology and politics. The four cases examined provide us with a great deal of information even though it must be said that information – like the matter of the conflict between civil servants and engineers – on other works and general information (in the contextual chapters) was indispensable

Now that we have gained an idea of how the development of modern irrigation in colonial Java actually progressed we can finally investigate the backgrounds to these developments.

Under certain conditions

In **Chapter 2** I did suggest, upon the basis of the available colonial and post-colonial documentation, what were the various necessary conditions (in the area of Science, Technology and Society) for the development of modern irrigation in Java. The components were: failing traditional systems, (clever) engineers, technological science, welfare policy (rice), exploitation politics (sugar), a strong state, professionalisation and ideologies on the importance of technology. As indicated there, it was not just a matter of developing modern irrigation technology from the point of view of works and projects (the way in which irrigation intervention occurred) – what was also important was the results: the actual modernisation of the existing irrigation network that took place. In that connection the emphasis was upon the significance of technology, namely technology in the sense of material artefacts and infrastructure. That is the approach I shall use here. The question will therefore be: what were the factors that made the development of modern irrigation systems possible in colonial Java? Here below follows a summary of the salient points. The three matters I shall examine will be these: the conditions that were related to the need for irrigation works, to the Indies state and to the engineers.

The social need

Irrigation – artificial watering – is necessary for the cultivation of rice. Since time immemorial Javanese farmers, for whom rice cultivation was the chief source of income, had been making use of various irrigation means, which they themselves had always created and maintained. In fact they had been using irrigation systems since about the beginning of our Christian Era. In addition to that one of the things that characterised the Indo-Javanese past was its big irrigation works tradition. Why, then, should Dutch engineers interfere with this? It is hard to assert, in the light of its long history and the results of the efforts of pioneers (which were not so brilliant), that Javanese irrigation was somehow inadequate.

Sugar cane cultivation provides us with our first answer to this question. In the century before last a modern sugar cultivation movement developed in East Java. In the east monsoon season it was necessary to irrigate those crops and it was for that reason that sugar was cultivated in *sawas* as a crop that alternated with rice. The fields were watered by means of Javanese irrigation systems. The indigenous population had never constructed any large structural works and this was where the Indies state which, from 1830 onwards was in charge of sugar cultivation, stepped in. Civil servants directed the construction of large irrigation works, mainly in the form of dams. To that end, just as Javanese rulers before them had done, they enlisted thousands of labourers to compulsorily do their part in the construction work. These large-scale samples of Javanese technology were of a poor quality and that was what gave rise to the need for modern irrigation works. Over the course of time the nature of this need changed. After 1870 sugar cultivation was transferred to independent sugar refiners who asked the government to provide modern irrigation facilities which they were prepared to financially subsidise. By the twentieth century it had become obligatory for them to contribute to this industry. Even though the sugar industry was to remain important for the whole of the colonial period the international sugar market proved rather changeable which meant that irrigation demands fluctuated between being great and not so great. Around 1885 there was a crisis which continued until 1903. Thanks, though, to the irrigation works that had been constructed in the interim period a period of prosperity was able to follow. The twentieth century saw a period of recession in the early twenties which, after 1929, was even to turn into a depression. As a result sugar cultivation also diminished, especially in the thirties. This was to have consequences for the need for modern irrigation which was to decrease.

There was, however, a second necessity. During the course of the nineteenth century the living standards of the Javanese population deteriorated. Whilst on the one hand the population began to grow, on the other hand the Exploitation Policy, which included the Cultivation System and all kinds of other services imposed on the population (also from the Javanese side), yielded pressure. All of this led to a series of famines, the best known being that of 1849 in Demak. In that same area a new threat followed in the early seventies and a new disaster around 1900.

The state and Public Works

How exactly did the Dutch and Indies authorities react to the needs for irrigation works? Like the mother country, the colonial state had a vested interest in the cultivation of sugar cane. Under the Cultivation System sugar culture became an important source of income for the state and because of this the Indies government began to show interest in modern irrigation. When, later, sugar cultivation became privatised, the Indies government saw it as its obligation to support the various enterprises by providing works and infrastructures but not only for the purposes of sugar cultivation.

When the colonial government was confronted with the worsening living conditions of the population it decided to take measures to improve matters. One of these measures was to create modern irrigation works. It was a measure that was taken both for humanitarian and economic reasons. There was even a link with political survival. The colonial state had economic interests and thus also interests in “peace and order”. Naturally this required a policy that would ensure that the subjects (and employees within the context of the Cultivation System) did not starve to death. In the nineteenth century the interests of the population were placed higher and higher on the political agenda which thus meant that the need for a welfare policy also increased, as did the demand for the creation of modern irrigation works in support of rice cultivation. Disaster prevention made way for welfare promotion. In its irrigation policy the Indies government really anticipated Ethical Policy. Around 1900 the “lessened welfare” of the population started to draw attention and from that time onwards the Netherlands started to see it as its “moral duty” to develop the population. The Exploitation Policy disappeared and the onus came to lie upon the stimulation of small farming. The population’s irrigation requirements were given high priority and this was not to change though the rising population numbers did suppress the efforts while the depression of the thirties made the population’s water requirements only greater.

What the execution of such policies needed was a solid governmental basis. After 1848 ultimate authority remained in the hands of the Dutch government while actual administration in the Indies lay in the hands of the colonial government (notably the power of the Governor-General). The body that administered power locally was the Civil Service (the

Residents and their civil servants). The inland administration service formed the true basis of the colonial administration. However, over the course of time the administrative organisation changed because other services developed alongside of the Civil Service. Indeed, that happened early on in the Cultivation System introduction phase and a special Directorate was set up to that end.

The nineteenth century was to provide a stage for rising liberalism and thus also for the liberalisation of the Netherlands and the Indies. That had consequences for the administrative organisation. In that connection the year 1854 was to see a breaking down of the administrative body into various branches. One such branch was the Public Works. The state constitution further evolved when, in 1886, "general administrative departments" were introduced which included a departmental supplement to the Civil Service and the Civil Public Works Department. The latter was subordinate to the Civil Service. When the colonial administration was to later withdraw from economic life and put all its energy into supporting the interests of enterprise and the population this was to develop parallel to the rise of the Civil Public Works Department. In 1885 the engineers became autonomous in relation to the Civil Service. The tendency which existed towards differentiation and specialisation within the administrative body (which by then had become a proper bureaucracy) was perpetuated after the turn of the century when liberalisation made way for the Ethical Policy. One important new specialist area was agriculture. A technocratic administration developed in which technologists (irrigation engineers, agricultural experts – later agricultural engineers – but also railway, mining and other types of engineers) were the ones who had (or gained) the biggest say. In other words, it turned into a technocracy. What also emerged under the new politics was a decentralisation or democratising policy that was to lead to the development of a People's Council, a more independent Indies state, three Provinces and democratic bodies operating at provincial and lower levels. Nationalism and the depression of the thirties induced a reaction in the form of a tightening up of policy and of the administration system.

The government thus decided that engineers should be allowed to create irrigation works, in the first place for sugar cultivation. At first there was even a separate service for this. As far as the administrative body of the early state was concerned the Civil Service was the most powerful factor. Irrigation works was the responsibility of the Civil Service. Together the Residents and the civil servants determined when irrigation works needed to be constructed. The main concern in that connection was to create larger dams which was not something that the population automatically did. In those circumstances engineers were sometimes called in to help.

After the famine in Demak in 1849 the Indies government started to take things seriously. A separate service was set up for the creation of irrigation works. The Public Works Organisation was given few means and the Civil Service continued to control what did and did not happen in the area of irrigation. Because of this engineers were not able to project themselves very well in their work. In fact it was rather the case that their works were hardly distinguishable from other works: they were washed away just as fast as the structures created by the Civil Service along Javanese lines. For this reason Public Works had difficulty shaking itself loose from the grip of regional administration. But there was a turn around. The goal became that of irrigating all government land according to modern methods. A body known as the Irrigation Brigade was created for the purposes of research and what followed was the General Irrigation Plan. In the interests of management irrigation divisions were created. Towards the end of the century the engineers had all sorts of restrictions imposed upon them in the form of the Rentability Commission established to examine the economic feasibility of all the various proposed projects. The Commission again put the civil servants somewhat in the picture. After the Solo Works fiasco came a new curtailment of technological power, this time because the newly set up Department of Agriculture was given an important say in matters. As far as water management was concerned, a three-cornered relationship developed between Civil Public Works, the Civil Service and Agriculture. Cultural plans were developed in connection with management and ultimately the decentralisation policy led to the development of Provincial Public Works Departments sanctioned by the General Water Regulations of 1936.

Engineers believed as no other group in the superiority of modern technology to traditional Javanese methods. The definition created by the engineers slowly penetrated to the other partners in the irrigation development process and in the first place to the Civil Service employees. For a long time the non-technical civil servants continued to view Javanese irrigation in a positive light even when the colonial government started to listen to the engineers and to give them a position of monopoly in the area of irrigation. After the turn of the century it emerged that the civil servants had really been "converted" and had become convinced of the usefulness of modern irrigation. At the same time Javanese irrigation underwent a certain positive revaluation in engineering circles. The Solo Works were to suffer from this directly and it was moreover so that the focus was on small farming: the agricultural experts were not all that impressed by major works. Even though at the dawn of the modern era the intervention of engineers in irrigation issues found itself in crisis the Indies government had, with its Ethical Policy, effectively taken over the engineers' way of thinking. What had begun in the area of irrigation extended to other sectors. Society was seen as being malleable and progress as being the goal of policy. For the administrators modern technology began to gain significance as an instrument for the development of the country and its people. Within the state the Ethical Policy brought with it a variation on the civilising mission theme in the form of the modernisation mission. Influenced by the national movement this ideology only became stronger.

Engineers and knowledge

The engineers who were preoccupied with public works affairs began serving the Indies state at the beginning of the nineteenth century. When the creation of modern works was raised, the colonial administration was simply able to call upon these engineers and in the course of time new engineers were appointed. In the early days of the development of modern irrigation it was not difficult for the administration to find such technologists: the few such experts required were (apparently) on hand. In that connection we can read that certain engineers were active there for years on end. Towards the end of the nineteenth century, when the need for engineers in the Indies became greater, conscious efforts were made to attract engineers to serve in the colony. In the eighties of that century the conditions offered for engineers interested in pursuing a career in the Indies were most favourable. That led to the arrival of well-known engineers such as Lamminga and C.W. Weijs. Around 1910, when the activities of Civil Public Works were stepped up, the demand for engineers was greater than the availability. Since there were not enough Dutch engineers the colonial government decided to call upon foreign engineers. Later, when such training was offered in the Indies, it became possible to draw upon locally trained engineers.

In conjunction with their striving for power and recognition the engineers developed a certain professional ideology that was to underline the usefulness of their approach and the importance of irrigation concern in general. Engineers were keen to broadcast the scientific basis of their approach. They were quick to dismiss Javanese technology which, to their minds, led to botch jobs and sloppiness. Science was equated with civilisation and engineers were keen to associate civilisation with other things as well. "Technological irrigation" was placed in the light of prosperity and the welfare of the Indies population and in the light of the

Dutch (civilising) obligation to improve such things.[3] Insofar that they possessed any obvious education the first engineers had military backgrounds. However, after the establishment of a college in Delft, in 1842, for the training of engineers, all of this was to change. The engineers who had been educated there possessed a general civil engineering background. Indies hydraulic engineering emerged as a field at the beginning of the last century when the engineering institute in Delft was given technical college status. Engineers who had made their careers overseas were the first to occupy what was initially a temporary but later a permanent academic chair in Delft. The first Professors were Lamminga and Weijs. The Technical College in Bandung was to become an "offshoot" of the Technical College in Delft which also gained a Professor in Indies Hydraulic Engineering.[4]

Another facet of the whole process of professionalisation was that which involved the creation of professional organisations and their accompanying journals. It was in 1851 that Dutch engineers in the Indies first organised themselves into a cohesive group and that was when the Indies Section of the Royal Institute of Engineers was set up. That same institute and also particularly the Dutch head office, manifested itself as a pressure group operating in the interests of engineers. The Dutch-East Indies contingent, which also had its own journal, became independent in 1921. The Indies irrigation engineers were given their own association in 1912 when the Society of Public Works Engineers in the Dutch East Indies was established and "The Public Works Engineer" was the title of its journal.

In this particular study the professionalising of engineers is especially associated with the rise of the Public Works Organisation, especially the Civil Public Works Department. It was this striving for upward mobility that was to form the backdrop to the frantic endeavours of engineers to emancipate themselves from the Civil Service in a conflict that was, to a great degree, all about the position and image of Public Works. The forming of a professional ideology, the setting up and extending of training courses and the establishing of autonomous organisations were all other characteristics of the same process of professionalisation but in this context they were particularly significant because they supported the rise of the Public Works engineers within the framework of the colonial state formation process.

By about the middle of the nineteenth century engineers had a (civil) education behind them and ideologically they were strong but what was the level of their know-how? The first engineers, also those who possessed Delft qualifications operated on a trial and error basis: they would create structures and then wait to see what happened. The fact that this somewhat experimental approach was indeed characterised by trial and error was amply demonstrated in the indecision and plodding on displayed in the Sampean area. In the early phase of the intervention of engineers in irrigation issues engineers possessed general hydraulic knowledge (after all the Dutch had a long tradition in this area) but their knowledge had nothing to do with irrigation and certainly not with irrigating in tropical regions. Up to a point, the Javanese works did serve to inspire the engineers but ultimately little interest was shown in such methods. At that time engineers also looked further afield for their inspiration, they looked especially to Italy and France, both of which were countries with a long irrigation history.

There was hardly any space for the scientific approach, in other words, for creating irrigation works based upon careful fieldwork and other preparatory steps, although all of that was to change in the last quarter of the nineteenth century. What then unfolded in the project-oriented approach that emerged was an interest in thorough preparatory research and in the

[3] In the period around 1900 there was one dissident, the engineer De Meyier. He was keen to emphasise the limitations of modern irrigation.

[4] Agricultural experts originated from Wageningen where there was an agricultural college which, later, was to gain polytechnic status.

creation of elaborate designs. Another thing to emerge was an interest in complete irrigation systems: alongside of the headworks canal networks were systematically created for the distribution of water. By that time knowledge on irrigation matters had expanded considerably and that was particularly attributable to hard practical experience (the many mishaps) but also to the advances being made in hydraulic engineering. It became evident that a scientific approach to irrigation activities was essential, just as it was necessary to view irrigation facilities as part of a cohesive whole and – because of the advances in knowledge – this was also possible. Another aspect of the scientific approach was that it brought with it the creation of a general plan of campaign.

Figure 11.2: Candilima inlet sluice, East Java, 1912 (photo UBL KITLV)

De Meyier's 1891 publication on irrigation in a large manual for hydraulic engineering constituted a milestone. It provided the first major guidelines on the construction of modern irrigation works. Previous to that all that existed was an instruction book for "structural engineers and industrialists" dating from the sixties in which the construction of modern irrigation works, including Van Thiel's framework dam, was described.

A founder was then required to consolidate the principles of modern irrigation technology, especially by means of pragmatic exemplification. Lamminga, the man who fitted the bill, was to especially make his name through his activities in the Pemali-Comal region. He built on the practical experience of others but also made use of theoretical knowledge in the form of research results, calculation methods and formulas relating to rainfall levels, river debits and the dimensions of structural works. For any given irrigation area he would draw up a general plan before going on to examine the designed irrigation system from every possible angle. Lamminga became famous for his Tegalian capacity line for the designing of canals. He launched an idea for the writing of a handbook on the construction of irrigation works (containing numerous practical examples) but the book never materialised. In turn, his successors were likewise to apply and expand his knowledge. Trial and error was also the method that was to be followed with regard to another aspect of irrigation, that of water management, and notably water distribution. Together with Civil Service people, the engineers tried out all kinds of possibilities in which the emphasis was either on engineering intervention or on the participation of the local population. In this respect (and more so than in the building method side) Lamminga also made an important contribution to the finding of an ultimate solution in the form of the Pemali Ruling. In this connection it is worth mentioning his Pemali application line which indicated the varying water requirements of rice crops. Water regulations remained heavily dependent upon practical circumstances which was where agricultural experts were later also to exercise great influence.

Another important publication, consolidating the irrigation knowledge of the time in one particular project, was the 1901 Solo report. The report accounted for the norm developed towards the end of the nineteenth century according to which projects had to be economically sound. Economic considerations led to agricultural research and that led to new knowledge including knowledge on the properties of silt! At the beginning of the twentieth century serious thought was also given to Javanese irrigation and elements of that were incorporated too (*waduks*, see **Figure 10.2**). Van Maanen's 1924 manual (which was revised in 1931) reflected the experience gained from all projects carried out in the 1885-1920 period. It contained the basic principles of modern irrigation science and the related management aspects and consideration was furthermore given to the rentability of works.

After the turn of that century, irrigation science was to see great progress, at that point Indies hydraulic engineering also became a subject taught at the Technical College in Delft. Up until the end of the colonial era empirical knowledge collection would continue to be an important method and the actual knowledge level would continue to rise (the empirical cycle!) That emerged, for instance, from the construction of sluice facilities. The experience gained from the problems posed by silt to the weir and canals of the Pemali irrigation system proved most instructive. The outlet sluice of this irrigation system was therefore adapted accordingly. Later works, such as the Tangerang Works, were thus given entire outlet sluice sections. During the course of the twentieth century scientific research in the field of irrigation received good facilities in the form of laboratories that were especially devoted to hydrodynamic studies. There, too, the importance of empirical evidence prevailed as was evidenced in the development of the laboratory institution itself. In that connection the difficulties experienced with the Walahar weir served to heighten the importance of laboratory research. The process of knowledge acquisition within the laboratories themselves also had a very experimental character; one need only think of the little sluice that let water through while at the same time measuring it (in this respect Van Maanen's 1931 manual provided more information than the 1924 edition).[5]

[5] See for information on agricultural (irrigation) knowledge e.g. Smits (1929) and Metzelaar (1946).

Developmental conditions

It was thanks to the obvious social need for modern irrigation works that the Javanese irrigation system was modernised – by means of headworks, pioneering projects for entire systems and standard projects – and it was also thanks to the Indies state, which gradually offered ever more favourable conditions in terms of policy, administrative organisation and ideology. Last but not least, modernisation was made possible by the irrigation engineers who not only increased in numbers within the state but who also grew in terms of (social) position and recognition and as regards their accumulated knowledge and methodology. The circumstances surrounding the development of modern irrigation slowly improved. Let us therefore examine that more closely according to the three recognisable periods of modern irrigation development which were: the stage of individual works creation (up until around 1885), the period of pioneers' projects (±1885-±1920) and the time when whole series of projects prevailed (±1920-1942).

There was a continued need for modern irrigation works, both for sugar and rice cultivation. At first the colonial administration dealt with this by creating ad hoc policies for occasional works and by tackling disasters. These, then, were two of the important pretexts for the intervention of engineers in irrigation issues, even though in the latter case irrigation activities were only tolerated to a certain extent. There were other factors, though, that made the creation of modern irrigation works possible at that time but which were not at the same time very constructive to the conversion of the existing system. The Indies government established a powerful administrative organisation (the Civil Service being particularly powerful) while at the same time creating an irrigation service that was not very flexible. The Civil Service employees who were lord and master of the Residences had faith in Javanese irrigation and there was, for the time being, nothing that the engineers could say or do to change that view. Engineers were available but the numbers employed by the state remained limited. Though convinced of the validity of their own approach they were not very specialised and their knowledge was too general to guarantee good results. In such circumstances there was a limit to the number of headworks that engineers could be expected to produce.

Slowly the colonial government developed a policy that was more conducive to the creation of irrigation works. In the process, the interests of the population gained some ground though the sugar industry was important enough (and weighty enough) and continued to pressurise the government to serve its interests. The government made Public Works an independent organisation, a step that heralded the arrival of a technocratic administration. This administration and the welfare policy that took root around the turn of the century were supported by the acceptance, in governmental circles, of the ideology of the engineers which equated modern (irrigation) technology with progress and civilisation. Engineers were given the opportunity to create entire irrigation systems. What was also important was that from the end of the nineteenth century engineers were supported in their ambitions by the various powerful professional organisations. In other words, over the course of time, favourable conditions developed for the modernisation of existing irrigation systems and that was to lead, in the second period, to great constructional activity.

At that time the relatively weak links in the chain of favourable circumstances were the knowledge existing in the field of irrigation (also with regard to management), the fact that engineers were not yet very specialised and the shortage of personnel. It was a time when leading figures laid foundations while others blundered. In conjunction with the Solo Works failure and the definite breakthrough made by the Ethical Policy, certain changes began to take place after 1900: rentability calculations became more important and agricultural experts started to emerge. In the end, engineers started to learn from experience and they were given specialised training so that in the final period the development of modern irrigation was given two new enabling conditions. Finally the shortage of personnel problem was resolved by appointing foreign engineers and colleagues with qualifications gained in the Indies. All these favourable circumstances dovetailed so that in the third period engineering intervention in irrigation took the form of irrigation system series construction. Naturally the depression of the thirties was to bring with it certain limitations during the last decade of this final period.

The conclusion to therefore be drawn is that the development of modern irrigation in Java was linked to a whole series of development conditions. To complement Headrick (1988), who listed three prerequisites for the development of modern irrigation in a colonial context (imperialism, a strong state and modern technological know-how), the specific conditions emanating from my analysis regarding Java are the following:

a. there had to be a need for irrigation (sugar cane, rice cultivation),
b. such need(s) had to be recognised by the colonial wielders of power who then had to see it as being in their interests to adopt a relevant policy,
c. an administrative organisation was then required to execute such policy,
d. there also had to be an independent body to execute the irrigation works which needed at the same time to be a part of the administrative body,
e. within the state there had to be an ideological framework to make all these various things possible,
f. irrigation engineers were required with the correct ideologies and appropriate education who were supported by professional organisations,
g. there had to be sufficient knowledge.

These conditions may be variously sketched as being of a social, political, administrative (in two instances), ideological, professional and scientific character. Unlike what Headrick suggests my study demonstrates that in Java these conditions did not all come at once to remain as fixed truisms but that they rather evolved.

Here we may furthermore just explain some of the points of difference surrounding the colonial, post-colonial and theoretical literature discussed in **Chapters 1 and 2**:

1. In various colonial and post-colonial writings there are differences of opinion concerning the social need for modern irrigation works. As far as the state was concerned what was important was the stimulating of sugar cane cultivation and/or rice crops. In the colonial era the importance of rice cultivation was emphasised whilst post-colonial studies stress the importance of sugar cultivation (as does Headrick 1988, on the whole). My conclusion is that in its irrigation intervention the government was interested in both facets: both sugar cane and rice cultivation required irrigation facilities and so the state embarked on creating those facilities for both the crops in question. Put politely that means that all the authors referred to in **Chapter 2** in this connection were, to a degree, right. From a developmental angle, though, this may be further specified.

The state had exploitation interests in sugar but also the desire and the interest to feed its subjects (and employees) and thus keep them quiet and happy. When the state dropped its sugar activities the need for irrigation works – then required for the enterprises – remained. Modern irrigation works were therefore starting to be created before the time of free trade imperialism (after 1870) in the Indies. At that time entire irrigation systems, that is to say according to scientific methods, were subsequently created but that was once again for sugar and rice. In relation to management there was in fact a clearer bias in favour of sugar (irrigation divisions in sugar growing areas). As far as the population was concerned it was no longer just a matter of keeping people contented and alive but it was also a matter of serving people's prosperity and well-being. With the introduction of the Ethical Policy (in 1901) and later the depression of the thirties it even seemed that the interest of the population had come to predominate. When the national movement arose the peace and order perspective gained new significance within the state. Headrick's thesis (1988) linking the rise of modern irrigation to free trade imperialism, a strong state and technological knowledge only therefore gains a certain degree of support (Headrick [1988] also drew attention to the effect of food shortages, see for instance p. 173). In the case of rice there were two main objectives which were to have food and to gain peace and quiet. There was, however, one way in which the colonial and imperialist contexts came to light much more clearly than in the choice of the agricultural goal and that was through the rentability interest. When the state began to intensify its irrigation efforts that was accompanied by the notion that works had to be remunerative. That certainly was the case up until 1901 when the Exploitation Policy predominated but even after that time rentability remained (to an extent) an important criterion.[6]

2. Many colonial engineers emphasised the place of science in the development of modern irrigation. The engineers furthermore maintained that alongside of Javanese irrigation their scientific-based facilities were superior. This is a point that was stressed in **Chapter 1** and elsewhere in the study. There were also colonial writers who underlined the importance of governmental policy. In post-colonial literature on Indonesia the (implicit) emphasis is also upon such policy. My analysis supports this second viewpoint and elaborates upon it.

In practice the superiority of the scientific approach was not as great as one might think. The "permanent" works created by the engineers were at first not much better than the Javanese structures and they had much to stand up to during *banjirs* as was illustrated by, for example, the works in the Sampean area. Though the battle fought there might have been a heroic one the events did not reflect great technological capacity based upon scientific knowledge. In this instance the lack of means may be cited as providing extenuating circumstances. By comparison to the role of knowledge it is the role of the state in the whole development of modern irrigation that is nevertheless of overriding importance. At the time when the government provided a favourable framework the engineers were actually rather lacking in knowledge. In the matter of knowledge on irrigation what was furthermore quite striking was that this knowledge was of a very empirical nature. Progress was especially marked by practical experience and, to a lesser degree, by theoretical development in (technological and irrigation) science[7].

3. Opposed to this moderate knowledge was a strong ideology. The engineers were spurred on by professional ideology and a mission to civilise, two ideologies that underlined the importance of (modern) technology (together the "engineering ideology"). The civilising mission was also borne out by administrators. This was an aspect of the intervention of engineers in irrigation and colonial policy that was introduced in the early chapters of this

[6] I do not have a clear overview of the importance of the rentability criterion in connection with public works in the Netherlands but I understand from verbal reports (e.g. G. de Jager 1996) that less emphasis was placed upon rentability than was the case in the Indies. (Cf. Van Bosse 1901: 361 and Homan van der Heide 1899 and 1901).

[7] Another significant factor in this connection is the observation that irrigation science development was something that particularly took place abroad where Dutch engineers limited themselves to the application side. An example of such development is R.C. Kennedy's canal formula that was developed in India and subsequently taken on board in the Dutch Indies (by e.g. Homan van der Heide and Haringhuizen; Headrick 1998: 186; G. de Jager, personal communication, September 1996). In this connection I should like to remind the reader of my remark in **Chapter 2** (**Note 34**) to the effect that the development of knowledge is not the central theme of this study and to my suggestion that those interested in researching such matters would be well advised to study e.g. the lecture notes of former Professors of irrigation in Delft and Bandung.

book. As was seen in **Chapter 2** Adas (1989) indicated that when evaluating non-Western cultures of the beginning of the eighteenth century one sees that religious factors make way for technological-scientific considerations. From that time onwards non-Western technology started being viewed in a negative light. In this study it has been demonstrated that a similar thing happened in the Indies. While Javanese technology made an impression on non-Western observers others dismissed this "random irrigating" as inefficient. Javanese irrigation was given a bad name in the middle of the nineteenth century which was quite late if one compares this to what Adas described. Where Adas (1989: 203-204) writes:

"Many nineteenth-century writers equated the advance of European colonization with the triumph of science and reason over the forces of superstition and ignorance which they perceived to be rampant in the non-industrialized world".

this is a biased representation of the nineteenth century that I have only seen presented in connection with engineers! The turning point, in the sense of their views being accepted by the colonial administration, did not come until the end of the nineteenth century and the beginning of the twentieth century. That was when the civilising mission (and engineering ideology in general) became the basis of all policy. On top of that there was among engineers in around about 1900 a partially revived appreciation of the traditional approach[8]. That was, in part, related to the Solo Works disaster. The idea had been that these works would amount to a great prestige project in which diverse problems would be tackled using various advanced technological techniques. In that respect they were to be an exceptional sample of nineteenth century belief in progress. When things went wrong and the project failed people began to question the pretensions of engineers thus placing them under pressure and so making way for a slight revival of Javanese irrigation methods (see **Figure 11.2**)[9]. This renewed interest not only served to underline the fact that everything really revolved around ideology but it also proved that there could be an ideological revolution as well or that things could at least be made less black and white!

The reason why the positive image surrounding Javanese irrigation methods stuck for a long time was because those methods were less defective than some would have liked to have pretended as, indeed, was borne out by the fact that certain components were copied. In this respect my findings support those of Pacey (1990) who used concrete examples to demonstrate just how important traditional technology is to the successful development of modern technology[10]. Furthermore, behind the positive impressions created of Javanese irrigation there was a definite link with the conflict between engineers and civil servants. As has been frequently illustrated in **Chapter 1** and elsewhere in this study, engineers glorified their "scientific" approach in their endeavour to improve their position. The Javanese alternative was really a weapon wielded in the battle fought by the civil servants but I shall return to this point later on.

---

[8] That applied especially to technological facilities. Traditional irrigation management or the proportional water division system equated with that (also to be seen as a case of "invention of tradition", cf. Breman 1980; see **Chapter 2, Note 31**) remained, throughout history, a subject of positive attention without ever in fact becoming the one and only example of engineering activity.

[9] Compare with Pfaffenberger (1988: 249) who indicates that it is precisely technological failure that illustrates the social and mythological dimensions of any technology.

[10] See e.g. his analysis of the fight against the dreaded sleeping sickness in Africa (Pacey 1990: 190).

Irrigation development and state formation

Now that the conditions for the development of modern irrigation in colonial Java have been discussed it is time for the last question, that of the interaction between irrigation and the state. The relationship between these two issues has been the subject of much speculation. Headrick (1988: 171) believes that that is not so strange. He claimed that "irrigation and kingdoms arose together in early river valley civilizations" before adding: "So closely have water control and despotism been united that it is tempting to describe the first as the cause of the second". Here below I shall go on to further elucidate the relationship between state formation and irrigation development in colonial Java.

The modernisation of irrigation and the state

In colonial and post-colonial Indonesian publications on the development of modern irrigation in Java there is thought for the importance of the policy (food and exploitation politics) and for Public Works as an operational organisation. Headrick (1988) also pointed to the need for a strong state. In all of these publications (with the exception of that of Van Doorn 1994a, see below) little attention is given to the development of the administrative organisation in relation to the development of modern irrigation. (See **Chapter 2**). My study does consider that and the findings from those considerations are tabulated below.

In **Chapter 2** the modernisation process of the Indies state was divided into three clearly distinguished phases. Those phases may be characterised as follows:

- The early colonial state in which the state adhered to an exploitation policy (the Cultivation System) dictated by the motherland and where a simple administrative body was developed (the Civil Service dominated).
- The modernising state which gave private initiative a chance and which supported that with infrastructural works and which also developed a welfare policy in the interests of the local population (liberalisation and the Ethical Policy). Irrigation works were constructed for sugar and rice cultivation. The administrative body was expanded and differentiated (general administrative departments including Civil Public Works).
- The modern state which had obtained a certain degree of autonomy for itself in relation to the mother country and which involved the population in matters of administration (democratisation with, for instance, the People's Council).

The way in which the Public Works Organization acted was crucial to the development of modern irrigation. As time passed by so the position of Public Works and thereby also its ability to create irrigation works (and maintain them via technical maintenance) improved. There were two important influencing factors behind this, the first of which was the (liberalisation) policy of the Indies (and Dutch) government that had also instigated the establishment of Public Works as a separate service. The striving of the engineers involved, towards power and recognition was the second factor. In the Indies Public Works, especially the Department, was the organisation around which the struggle of the engineers to achieve emancipation occurred and, more generally, it was in conjunction with that organisation that they were able to manifest their drive to become professional. Public Works could be viewed as an "intermediary" between the state and technology. On the one hand the service was part of the state and a representative of the state enabling engineers to carry out their operations. On the other hand, however, the same service was responsible for irrigation development. To put it another way, Public Works was one of the instruments enabling engineers to create irrigation works.[11]

In terms of period division, the development of modern irrigation fitted in well with the process of colonial state formation: headworks were constructed in the early colonial state period, the first projects then followed in the transition period and the modern colonial state became the stage for ordinary projects. Within the framework of the colonial modernisation process of state and technology in Java we might conclude that the development of modern irrigation began with the creation of entire irrigation systems (around 1885). The modern irrigation works that engineers had created in the previous period might therefore be termed pre-modern or semi-modern products of "piecemeal engineering". This corresponds nicely with the terminology used by Brouwer (1991: 48) although he refers in this connection to "semi-technical irrigation systems" (see **Chapter 2**).

Conflict within the state

Within the process of Indies state formation there was an on-going battle between Public Works engineers and Civil Service employees. The entire process may be viewed as an arena within which the various groups involved (or in this case the services) contended – in line with their interests – for intervention in irrigation. At first the establishment of an independent public works service was at stake.

To a significant extent the state formation process in the Indies coincided with the development of the Civil Service. When the colonial state first emerged it consisted of an administration system that was headed by a Governor-General with Residents as kind of viceroys. Beyond that the history of the colonial state really amounted to a process of building up a central administrative organisation and forming specialised professional departments. Later on there was decentralisation in the Provinces. In the process the Civil Service, originally an independent administrative body, gradually lost its powerful position. The fact that at central level it formed one of the branches and later one of the administrative departments did not detract from this. The Civil Service was thus more or less incorporated into the rising central administrative bureaucracy and so gained a subordinate position as a normal department in the midst of an unfolding technocracy. (See Van den Doel 1994 and Van Doorn 1994a, see also Van Doorn 1982).

In tracing the development of modern irrigation it becomes quite clear how the Civil Service gradually disintegrated as Public Works began to gain more power. In early colonial society the administrators were in charge: they determined what happened. Engineers were newcomers on the scene who endeavoured to strengthen their position and simultaneously change the status quo. For a long time the Civil Service employees were in a position to keep the engineers striving for emancipation at bay. Ultimately, though, all of that changed and the technologists were the ones who came off best. These changing positions were the consequence of a process in which a liberal colonial state was seen to develop. When the

---

[11] (Civil) Public Works could therefore be seen as an "external" but also as an "internal" factor in irrigation development (or as a part of the state and as an aid in the creation of irrigation works). At the same time this also indicates how confusing it can be to distinguish between the terms external and internal. This lack of clarity confirms the criticism reported in **Chapter 2** of the involved approaches to technological development. There I asserted that technological development is not an autonomous process and that equally it cannot take place in a vacuum without social influence. Technology is man-made and technologists are guided by all sorts of considerations. In the case of modern irrigation this was effected by state employed engineers dutifully carrying out the instructions of their employer who also (partly) in connection with their striving for professionalisation, wanted to create as many as possible irrigation works, with that adopting their scientific approach and who wanted to rise socially.

engineers started exercising their newly gained freedom by setting up an extravagant and prestigious project the authorities asserted themselves but they did this without curtailing the power of the engineers too much. Agricultural experts appeared on the state stage to further augment the technocracy. Together with these new specialists, the engineers and the civil servants ultimately formed a (specimen) union which, in turn, fitted in well with the transformation that the modern state organisation – influenced by the Ethical Policy – was undergoing.

The rise of the engineers and the demise of the civil servants were thus two things that went hand in hand. Even when the conflict between the Civil Service and Civil Public Works had been sorted out the relationship between both institutions remained important to the way in which modern irrigation developed.

The struggle between the Civil Service and Public Works was also reflected in images. Almost the whole nineteenth century long the civil servants stuck to the notion that alongside of the mess made by engineers, Javanese farmers proved to be good if not outstanding hydraulic experts. Engineers saw modern irrigation works as a necessity while Civil Service employees often thought that such works were a luxury. This study supports the importance of the ideological component within the whole conflict as expressed by Dickson (1981: 191-192, see also **Chapter 2**):

"… not only does technology function politically in a material sense to promote the interests of a dominant social class by maintaining a particular form of social organisation; it also, I suggest, functions politically in a symbolic sense, in that the particular interpretation placed on technology is one designed to support a dominant ideology".

Interaction between the state and technology

The part played by the Indies state in Javanese irrigation development during the consecutive periods of the colonial state formation process may be typified as follows. In the early colonial state period the government of the day allowed a limited number of modern irrigation works to be constructed and it was only here and there that headworks were installed. At this stage civil servants dominated and the room for manoeuvre given to engineers was minimal. Irrigation improvement was given new impetus in the transition period and the nature of the activities also changed. At first the government gave the engineers plenty of freedom and so they embarked on installing entire irrigation systems and on regulating the relevant management. Later the government broadened its scope by involving civil servants, once again, more prominently in the process and by calling in agricultural experts. Under the policies of the day the construction of smaller-scale works and the establishment of technical control facilities were given relatively more weight. After a while all of that changed and once again large new works projects were undertaken. In the modern colonial state period, political and other circumstances were favourable for the realisation of irrigation (control) systems. At the time irrigation involvement was a co-operative enterprise between experts and civil servants. Economic and political problems did, however, lead to certain adjustments.

Conversely irrigation development did have consequences for the state. In the early phases of the state formation process the irrigation engineers who were new on the scene did enter into conflict with the powerful civil servants. It was only slowly that the engineers saw results, notably when their technological innovations became more successful. The opposition they provided did, however, manage to contribute to the dismantling of the Civil Service. During the transition phase the engineers at first enjoyed a certain degree of autonomy but the Solo Valley fiasco, together with the Ethical Policy, changed the position of the engineers and the constitution of the state. The engineers, by now a more or less established group, found themselves competing with the new agricultural experts. The civil servants were also once again given a clear role in irrigation involvement. In addition, responsibility for public works was decentralised which weakened the position of the centralised Public Works Department. Nevertheless, the authorities adopted the ideology of the irrigation engineers which was that modern technology was essential to prosperity and progress and they made this the basis for their new policy. The irrigation development that had manifested itself in previous years now became a model for developments being aimed at throughout society as a whole. In the final state formation stage, rivalry subsided and civil engineers, civil servants and agricultural experts banded together with the government to refine and tighten up water control.

Technology and ideology

Emancipation and modernization

The concepts group, network and system can be used to expose interaction processes but the trouble with all of this and with the new social-constructivist approach to technological development in general, is that a clear sense of direction behind the process of technological development is lacking. It was therefore for this reason that with this approach the view of technological development as an autonomous process did creep in via a back entrance, even though social-constructivists would like to assert that what was involved here was apparent autonomy. People and groups act, such actions lead to networks and ultimately to a system which subsequently goes its own way. (Compare Winner 1993, see also **Chapter 2**). An alternative may be borrowed from the modernisation concept but if we use this exclusively as a descriptive concept, as was done in this study, then the process that we thus refer to and qualify remains in itself unexplained (compare Lintsen 1992-1995).

It would be impossible for me to resolve the question of the relationship between individual actions, group actions and macro-sociological processes in this study but I have at least been able to throw some light on the development of modern irrigation in colonial Java on the basis of the process of Indies state formation. If we wish to define this more clearly we could draw parallels with the views of the sociologist Elias. He (1971) saw society in terms of a developing "configuration" (or "figuration") of acting people (and groups), none of which has the power to individually influence the direction in which the whole goes. Elias (1970) does see a direction: the direction of the civilisation process, but precisely how this process is the result of (inter) actions between people remains unclear. Elias (1972) clearly indicates with "processes of state formation" an important in-between level. In that way state formation emerges as a starting point for the weaving together of micro actions and macro processes. The process of state formation also proved to be an essential intermediate level in the colonial context between the macro processes of the modernising society on the one hand and the struggling and battling engineers at micro level on the other hand.

Irrigation development, state formation and the setting up of a public works service are three processes with clear emancipation sides to them (à la Wertheim, see **Chapter 2** and the opening quotation of this chapter) but my empirical material gives cause for a more differentiated view of the matter. The building of the weir in the Sampean had the character of a fight for emancipation in which people strive to improve their lot by controlling nature (in this case by managing water) and where they ultimately succeeded. Much the same applied to the Pemali and Tangerang Works, both of which reflected human triumph over nature. The Solo Works just went a river too far though, thus supporting the words of Francis Bacon: *non nisi parendo vincitur*, nature can only be conquered by submitting oneself to it.

From the point of view of the local population the rise of the modern colonial state could be seen as a process of emancipation. The colonial authorities became increasingly concerned about the interests of the population and so developed a welfare policy together with a policy to involve people more in decision-making processes. The Netherlands thus unwittingly led the Indies in the direction of independence, the logical outcome of the process of state formation up until then. From the point of view of the population (or, at least, its elite) national independence represented the ultimate aim of the state formation process. For the colonial overlords it was a bitter pill which gave rise to notions of doom (like *Indië verloren, rampspoed geboren* ["Loss of the Indies, Birth of Disaster"], Wesseling 1988, compare Baudet and Fennema 1983). Within the emancipation process of the colonial engineers the newly gained independence of Civil Public Works represented a milestone. Engineers contributed to and profited from the rise of a technocratic administration. The losing party in all of that was the civil servants. They witnessed the shrinking of their irrigation duties and saw their power dwindle within irrigation affairs. Generally the Civil Service workers also saw that their roles diminished and their position of power worsened. With the Civil Service people the emancipation of Public Works engineers and other experts was coupled with a reverse process. As has been explained, the distress for them in the field of irrigation remained limited: they continued to be involved in management and, through their involvement in the rentability of works they remained involved in the creation of systems. The Solo Works certainly did the engineers no good but at least their professionalisation process had by then gathered enough momentum to continue.

These processes of emancipation of the engineers and the population in general were embedded in the broader process of modernization, in which ideological factors were main drivers. The modernisation mission, which manifested itself in the Ethical Policy phase, fitted in nicely with the (developing) modern colonial state, just as modern irrigation technology fitted in smoothly. This was something that was highlighted in **Chapter 2**. My study confirms the theoretical view put forward by Adas (1989: 203-204) who pointed out that the small numbers of Europeans who ruled in colonised regions did this on the basis of their "superior technology", also because this ensured that "they had the 'right', even the 'duty', to police, arbitrate disputes, demand tribute, and insist on deference". Also referred to in **Chapter 2** was Dove (1985) who revealed how within the framework of Javanese (pre) colonial state formation wet rice cultivation was idealised. His conclusion was that agricultural development should not be seen "as a value free process, but as a process carried out by and for specific actors – whether these be governments or peasants" (p. 33). Without applying his productivity analysis of traditional agriculture versus wet rice culture to Javanese and modern irrigation (which would be interesting but I lack the data for this) it is possible to take his conclusion and apply it to irrigation development in colonial Java. The conclusion is that this was not a value free development either but rather a process carried out through and in the interests of actors. Unlike in Dove's case the actors here – apart from the government – were the engineers and the civil servants.

Ultimately, the Dutch empire was managed in the spirit of technological optimism and faith in progress, in which irrigation and other engineers set the tone, technologically, social-politically and ideologically, though always in collaboration with and under the influence of other actors (see for other civil engineering areas than irrigation: Ravesteijn and Kop 2004 and 2008). The Dutch colonial empire was engineered by a variety of actors and increasingly in the spirit of an ideology of emancipation and modernization. Though the Dutch did not particularly desired and planned this, their efforts paved the way for the independent Republic of Indonesia.

A mission-laden legacy

A hundred years after the Indies state had taken its first steps on the road to the realisation of modern irrigation by sending an engineer to the Sampean area, the first movable weir was completed in Pasar Baru. Irrigation engineers designed the weir and all the other works in the Tangerang plain at a time (1916-1920) when the Ethical Policy, which placed the interests of the Indies population above those of colonial gain, was at its height. An optimistic faith in social progress and in the malleability of society were the things that constituted important elements in the underlying philosophy of this policy. This philosophy, inspired by the thinking of engineers about technology and progress, embodied great confidence in modern technology. All of this was expressed in the modernisation mission: the colonial state believed that it was obliged to allow the Indies population to share in enjoying the blessings of Western technology and culture. The expanding of modern irrigation facilities was one of the policy cornerstones and all the financial means made available for that flowed freely. Apart from all the good intentions and the rising expenditure there was also a strong state machine with a close-knit organisation and specialised welfare services including the Civil Public Works Department and the Provincial Public Works Departments. The projects were designed and executed by well-trained and well-developed engineers supported by their professional organisations. The younger generation especially had become acquainted with Indies hydraulic engineering during the course of their studies at the Technical College in Delft where years of experimental knowledge had been condensed into a scientific form.

The technological aspirations and potential of the Indies state exceeded the needs of the times firstly because of a recession and secondly because of a crisis in the world economy. The engineers were given the go ahead for the Tangerang Works, though after various delays and subsequently their work was also delayed. The weir in the Cisadane, together with the adjoining sluice complex was festively opened in 1936. Apart from the economic problems the circumstances surrounding the construction of modern irrigation works had further improved since the time when the works had been in preparation. In the case of the Sewan sluices use was made of laboratory tests. This represented ultra new technology and it was precisely in 1936 that the most important Hydrodynamic Laboratory of the Department of Transport and Public Works (at the Technical College in Bandung) was opened. The ingenious Romijn shutter implemented for the extensive Tangerang irrigation system was a product of laboratory research. The referred to college had furthermore seen to it that engineers from Delft had gained Indies colleagues.

At the time of the design and implementation of the Tangerang Works, which was just one of the many irrigation projects then being worked on or completed in the Indies, the conditions for the creation of modern irrigation works were, in other words, favourable. There was a need for that among the people and within the state (welfare development), there was a policy directed towards irrigation development (Ethical Policy), there was a strong administrative body (the state), there were specialized operational organisations for irrigation works (Civil Public Works and the Provincial Public Works Departments), there were recognised authorities (irrigation engineers) and, last but not least, there was the necessary ideological support (a belief in progress based on modern technology).

A hundred years prior to that things had been different. There had been a need for irrigation works, for sugar culture but only in a limited respect (for the odd headworks). Exploitation was rife and any clear kind of irrigation policy was lacking, just as was professional organisation for irrigation activity. If they were undertaken at all modern irrigation works were generally undertaken at the instigation of the powerful Civil Service. The administrators were entitled and inclined to embark on irrigation works projects themselves. There was a reservoir of hydraulic engineering knowledge but it was not very specific. The technologists did not have a civil engineering background but at most a military training. Unlike the engineers those who possessed power did not have great faith in the modern approach. The (not totally unjustified) idea was that Javanese irrigation was good enough. The conditions for the creation of modern irrigation works were therefore at that time much less favourable. At this point I cannot refrain from giving just one more taste of the colonial atmosphere in which one engineer outlines the trials and tribulations of the first technologists, also from the personal angle:

"The engineers 50 years ago with their inadequate education for a career in the tropics, with their minimal knowledge of Indies affairs, have laboured in the Indies under conditions which they – at the time – regarded as quite normal but which now would appear to be perfectly unbelievable. ... Because of their unabated, long-term stay in the tropics during which they were, towards the end, overworked and exhausted they usually missed out on the opportunity to spend a short time in the higher regions because of the poor communication means. ... Those same defective means of communication were also usually fatal for the rapid completion of works; it was not uncommon to have to wait months for the materials that had been ordered. ... According to modern-day standards they had to cope with the defective resources of the technology of the day" (Van Sandick 1929: 269).

The conditions for the construction of modern irrigation works therefore gradually improved and developments were seen that went from pioneering works to serial projects via trend-setting samples of engineering, and failures. The technologists who had once been sent into the Indies hinterland by the relevant authorities armed with little more than bricks had become respectable monument builders by the end of the colonial period.

That was how irrigation engineers were able to make a substantial contribution to the modernising process in the Indies. This contribution started in 1885 which was relatively early but when, with its Ethical Policy, the colonial state endeavoured to catapult itself into the modern era the engineers went through a period of decline. It was the halting of the Solo Works that proved to be their downfall. All that they could do was take a small-scale approach but that only proved to be a short-term solution. After the necessary measures had been taken to ensure that such things would not be repeated (including the Civil Service and Agriculture) the trend first set by the early and late pioneers of separate and entire works, including those of the "great engineer" Lamminga, was again pursued. Following new and different lines the intervention of engineers in irrigation matters finally took off. From doing pioneering work or balancing on a knife edge and seeing bad projects turn disastrous or good ones prove exemplary, all the work done in the field of irrigation gradually turned into routine technological operations. In other words, it became a normal state of affairs. Thoroughly conversant with all the ins and outs, engineers started to set up good projects. They stuck to Lamminga's paradigm but further elaborated it, partly by streamlining the design side of works projects. Advancements made in the field of technological science opened up new possibilities and facets of projects or of irrigation technology itself started being developed in laboratories. Certain projects, like the Tangerang Works, stood out because of their sheer dimensions but all projects of the late colonial period stood out as feats of modern engineering technology.

With the construction of the weir at Pasar Baru the colonial state managed to harness the forces of one of the biggest rivers in Java amid the stream of worldwide depression. Indeed, an impressive structure had risen up that really served to symbolise the power of technology and the state over nature and human beings. The weir was also a symbol of the modernisation mission of the Indies state, thus contributing to its legitimisation. The relevant structure, clearly visible from the air for anyone flying into or out of Jakarta, was one of the last colonial structural works, a high point in colonial knowledge and capacity, just before the fall. After the economic difficulties of the twenties and thirties a third problem arose in the (sequel to the) construction of the Tangerang Works. This time the problem was of a political nature and it was the power of the colonial state that was at stake. It was for that reason that the works – especially the more elaborate sections designed to channel water to the *sawas* – were not actually completed until after the country gained its independence.

The Republic of Indonesia built on the legacy of Dutch East Indies engineers. Initially, it did so from an ideology of technological optimism and development, which was rooted in the colonial modernization mission. Political independence was a radical break with the colonial past, but the mission of irrigation, with is dual aspect of trust on technology and progress in general, continued to inspire engineering and development efforts.

Epilogue: engineering the republic

> Science and technology cannot be goals in themselves. They may be regarded as society's investment in a more humane existence for everyone. The training and education of engineers is big business; a business with its own particular culture, norms and values. The manner of operation has to be in accordance with its rules and regulations. Their calculations have to be correct. The specialists have to be in mutual agreement as to the content of the speciality they call a profession. Specialization has been promoted to religion, complete with initiation rituals. This poses the danger that the specialist becomes uprooted from his nutritional basis: the reality of everyday people of which society is composed and in whose service he is supposed to be engaged (Riedijk 1986: 6).

It does not take very long for any traveller passing through Java to realise that there are irrigation facilities everywhere and that they are all of vital importance. The facilities exist in all shapes and sizes and are of varying ages. Many of the colonial works are still intact but a great many of the works, such as those of the Jatiluhur reservoir, are new (see **Figures 1-3**). This chapter will illustrate how things further progressed in the field of irrigation after the Indonesians had sent the Dutch back to their homeland and had taken over complete control of matters themselves. We shall examine the irrigation efforts after that juncture, the problems entailed, the topical discussions on irrigation as well as recent developments. In the process, the irrigation areas of the four cases discussed in this study will also be considered.

We shall see that the political rift did not amount to a rift in the area of irrigation and that post-colonial development in the field of modern irrigation entailed continuity beside change. What had begun in the colonial era was perpetuated after the declaration of independence and (up to a point) the same kinds of problems were encountered. The discussions on irrigation that arose in recent decades are also clearly recognisable in the context of the colonial past. I therefore hope to be able to demonstrate that many historical matters on irrigation affairs had implications for post-independent issues and that a knowledge of colonial irrigation activities is still relevant to present and future developments in the field of irrigation in Java and Indonesia (compare De Vries 1961: 271).

1

2

3

Figures 1-3: Jatiluhur reservoir:

1. Reservoir with sharp crested circular (emergency) spillway
2. Head canal
3. Dam and head canal

Nation state formation

Order and reform

"We, the Indonesian people, hereby declare the Independence of Indonesia. Matters relating to the transfer of power, etcetera will be effected as efficiently and as speedily as possible". This was the declaration of independence of 17th August 1945 which was to form, for Sukarno and Hatta, the basis for the creation of a modern Indonesian state (cited in Witjes et al. 1990: 9). The declaration came only days after the Japanese capitulation. The Netherlands was not in agreement with any of this and so it tried to reassert its power over the Indies which, in turn, led to violent struggle. The international community did not react kindly to this turn of events and so pressurised the Dutch to entering into negotiations with the nationalists. In 1946 the Linggarjati convention was signed in which all the parties agreed that a sovereign Indonesian state should be established in 1949. Differences of opinion about the creation of an interim administration led, in 1947, to intervention steps by the Dutch government: the "first police action". However, at the instigation of the United Nations, negotiations were continued. A new agreement was drawn up but it was not sufficient to prevent the Netherlands from once again attempting, in 1948, to turn the situation to its own advantage by means of military force. This time the United Nations intervened, forcing the Netherlands to cease its "second police action" and to instead resume dialogue. This occurred during the round-table conference of 1949 and it was what finally led to the establishment of the independent "United Indonesian States".

For the Netherlands that marked the end of the conflict but not for Indonesia. Most of the states comprising the new nation had been set up by the Netherlands during its final military campaign. The Indonesians therefore saw the federal state form as a Dutch innovation. In 1950 all of that changed when the Republic of Indonesia was created into which all the various states were incorporated. In order to forge one nation state from all the numerous islands, population groups and different political parties and religious groups that made up Indonesia, President Sukarno developed a state ideology known as the *Pancasila*. It embraced a number of principles, including the believe in one God, a united state, democracy and justice. On these grounds a constitution was established which made way for an elected parliament. For the time being, though, the situation remained unstable: various population groups and political factions (including the powerful *PKI* communist party) started to revolt; the army was faced with rebellion (there was, for instance, the *RMS* movement in the Moluccas, striving for independence). The central body of power, the President and the parliament (for which elections were first held in 1955) were therefore also in a weak position. Towards the end of the 1950s Sukarno tried to change the situation. He secured more power for himself and formed a broad-based government. Afraid that the army might mount a coup d'état he decided to leave out any communists but later he relented and decided to allow communists into his government.

In 1965 the army did usurp power, the reason for this being – according to military people – the threat of a communist take-over. Suharto who led the coup, thus making himself the most powerful man in the country, was to become Sukarno's official successor as President in 1968. The military regime altered the political system and created what was known as the "New Order" (*Orde Baru*) which contrasted with the "Old Order" (Sukarno's *Orde Lama*). Those in power basically stuck to the *Pancasila* ideology but just slightly changed the emphasis. One of the main policies was to establish law and order. The army was given important military tasks and the political parties were abandoned. For the military people, political stability was a precondition for a second main objective, that of economic development. (See for the post-war political events, apart from Witjes et al. 1990, also Pluvier 1978).

Following the financial crisis in Asia in the late 1990s, Suharto and his regime fell in 1998 and a new political era started under the heading of "Reform" (*Reformasi*). Democratization and decentralization resulted, though accompanied by social unrest and even terrorism.[1]

Economic development

In the 1940s and 1950s the social and economic conditions of the people worsened. Population numbers continued to rise but rice production fell. With the start of the new government Sukarno decided to take in hand the country's rebuilding and the development of the economy. First of all there was a five-year plan (1956-1960) which was then followed by an ambitious eight-year plan known as the "National Overall Development Plan" (1961-1969). The goals were to industrialise and to improve agriculture. In the meantime there was also a three-year plan, launched by the Department of Agriculture, which was directed at achieving self-sufficiency in the area of rice growing by 1962. In this connection it was especially imported fertiliser that was used. Despite all the efforts made on the part of the Indonesian government the situation did not really improve and that was particularly due to increases in rice production (being roughly 6% higher than in 1965 when compared to 1940) lagged behind population growth (which was at that time 20%). In the latter half of the 1960s there was a serious food crisis: by then rice supplies had been completely depleted and rice prices had risen dramatically (Witjes et al. 1990: 55-56).

In contrast to the "populist" policy adopted by Sukarno (of mobilisation and political participation on behalf of the population) the military people in positions of power pinned all their hopes on a Western-oriented path for economic developments in the post-1967 period. In other words, they aimed to modernise and industrialise under free market conditions. In that way (as an OPEC country) Indonesia was able to profit from all its oil reserves which, notably in the 1970s – when world oil prices rose sharply – attracted much foreign interest. In the 1980s the oil prices fell sharply which meant that savings had to be made also in connection with the falling dollar rate. Under the new order Indonesia came to depend upon foreign investment and foreign aid. The Western countries which supported the military coup because of their aversion to communism – it was, after all, the Cold War era – were really prepared to help Indonesia. In 1967 fourteen donor countries united themselves under the chairmanship of the Netherlands in what was known as the Inter-Governmental Group for Indonesia (IGGI) which, together with the World Bank and the International Monetary Fund, supported Indonesia's development. The relationship with the former coloniser was surprisingly close and cooperative; it was oriented to development. The relation deteriorated, however, with time, mainly because of hobby-ism on the Dutch side and insufficient knowledge of the new Dutch administrators with regard to Indonesian etiquette, culminating in a complete breakage in 1992, when the Dutch government criticised the human rights situation in Indonesia after riots in occupied East Timor.

As far as the development of the economy was concerned, the government began drawing up five-year plans (*Repelitas*) after 1969. At first it was agriculture that was of central importance. Where small-scale agriculture was concerned the aim was to become self-sufficient in the area of rice production and so to this end an agricultural modernisation and rationalisation programme was set up. The state thus introduced the new technology of what was known as the Green Revolution. This comprised varieties of rice ("wonder rice"[2]) developed in Philippine

---

[1] See for the process of decentralization in Indonesia and its implications for flood defence management in Jakarta Simanjuntak et al. (2012).

[2] Compare this with the "wonder cane" introduced in 1925 (see **Chapter 1**). The requirement for new and more productive rice varieties was something that also dated from the colonial era (see e.g. Happé 1939: 42, note 2).

laboratories together with the required production means such as fertilisers, insecticides and such like (see in connection with this *Bimas* programme and other measures, Hüsken 1988: 26-29). Later the accent shifted to the establishing of modern industries and to the constructing of related infrastructural works. The government also tackled the problem of rapid population growth by focusing on such matters as family planning. In order to alleviate pressure on Java the government pursued the policy of stimulating transmigration from Java to other regions within Indonesia such as Sumatra, Kalimantan and Sulawesi. As a result of the policy to economise mounted in the latter half of the 1980s the (costly) transmigration programme was hit by heavy limitations! (Witjes et al. 1990: 90).

Just as had been the case under Sukarno, the regime largely made use of the same avenues as those used by the colonial overlords when it came to executing their five-year plans. As far as the local government was concerned the three Provinces were retained in Java (*Jawa Barat, Jawa Tengah* and *Jawa Timur*). In their position as City Districts Jakarta (formerly: Batavia) and Yogyakarta were respectively given District and special status. The former Residencies continued to exist as political units even though there was a power shift in the direction of the lower Districts and local authorities. Departments, which were subdivided into Directorates General (instead of into divisions) remained important bodies in the administrative bureaucracy. The Department of Civil Public Works (*BOW*) became the *Departemen Pekerjaan Umum dan Tenaga Listrik* ("Department of Public Works and Electric Power", later Electric Power was deferred to another department; abbreviation: *PU*).What was new was the central position fulfilled by the army which, apart from being involved in the parliament (75 military people having been appointed by the government from a total number of 500 members) was also involved in various government services.

The final upshot of all these efforts was that Indonesia underwent a period of rapid economic growth. In the 1979-1989 period the country's Gross National Product rose from 49.2 to 95 thousand million dollars. The size of the population also increased, rising by more than 2% per year in the 1965-1987 period but it then fell from 2.4% in 1980 to 2.1% in the subsequent period. In 1987 the population of Indonesia was 171.4 million people, some 60% of whom lived in Java (Witjes et al. 1995: 304, see also Dirkse et al. 1993). Nevertheless the GNP per head of population increased in the 1965-1987 period by 4½% per year (in the Netherlands that was 2.1%). The agricultural policy, notably the introducing of the technology of the Green Revolution, led to rapidly expanding harvests so that by 1984 the aimed at self-sufficiency in rice production had been achieved.[3]

However, the path followed also had negative effects. Unemployment rose because many of the smaller Indonesian companies were wiped out by foreign companies. That was especially apparent at the time of the New Order. In reaction to protests mounted in the 1970s the government somewhat modified its policy by limiting foreign investments and striving to make the growth more evenly distributed. Transmigration (for more than three million people in the 1969-1984 period) was, for many of them, a radical step that was sometimes badly planned by the government, which did not bring improved living conditions for all involved and which was subject to much criticism (Witjes et al. 1990: 90-94). Admittedly the new technology did at first create more jobs in the rice sector (by increasing the numbers of harvests) but later the employment situation became less favourable and there were fewer job opportunities. Moreover,

---

[3] Agricultural details are to be found in Booth (1988). She speaks of a "success story". In the 1970s the rise in rice production went hand in hand with rising oil incomes which is remarkable in view of the fact that other OPEC countries with significant agricultural sectors were struck by an ailment known as the "Dutch disease", one of the symptoms of which was a production shift to the building and trading sectors. (Booth 1988: 1-2).

many of the smaller farmers found themselves in financial difficulty. Generally speaking the gap between poor and rich farmers widened. One hazard was the excessive use of chemical fertilizers and pesticides, on the one hand, and the problem of draining the soil of all its nutrients, on the other. Another problem – chiefly outside Java – that is linked to intensive farming and also to the wood industry is that of erosion caused by deforestation. In that way the mountain rainwater finds its way to the plains more quickly and so the danger of *banjir* flooding increases. The problem is only intensified by the vast quantities of silt transported by the water which blocks up the rivers.[4]

Over the course of time the population became more included in the economic development process, partly through the creation of village organisations and co-operations. This increased participation was partly instigated by the pressure of Western countries which stipulated that active participation in economic affairs on the part of the population was essential if the country was to receive financial support.

In the post-Suharto period these tendencies continued, though not in a straight line. Indonesia suffered from the Asian financial crisis and consequently from rising oil prices between 1997 and 2006, though high growth figures soon returned, making Indonesia one of the fastest growing economies in the world. Despite continued population growth (to over 250 million people in 2015), GNP per capita rose to some 3.500 US dollars in 2015 (Worldbank 2017). Trade with China increased, while the orientation on Western countries and their aid programmes decreased. Nowadays, still over 40% of the labour force works in agriculture, though the country has become dependent again on rice imports (*Pertanian di Indonesia* 2015). Overall, living standards improved, as unemployment and poverty declined, though the elimination of fuel subsidies took their toll and the great disparity in incomes has remained an issue. Improving the quality of public services, like health care, and infrastructure, including irrigation, are main challenges for the future, in which sub-national authorities like regencies have a key role to play. Another challenge is to combat corruption, which is rampant, despite the disappearance of the military dictatorship. (See, for instance, N. Schulte Nordholt 1991: 31-34 and Berenschot et al. 2016[5]).

---

[4] See for details of the agricultural problems Hüsken (1988: 27-31) and also Witjes et al. (1990: 54-59), see for the consequences of deforestation Witjes et al. (1990: 98). In fact there is as yet no consensus among hydrologists on the matter of the relationship between deforestation and increased incidents of flooding. There are strong indications that forests can generate their own precipitation and also that in agricultural areas "evaporisation" sometimes increases. (G. de Jager, personal communication, September 1996).

[5] See for corruption in relation to irrigation affairs in Southern India Wade (1982).

Irrigation endeavours[6]

Old Order, new works

In the 1940s and 1950s little happened in the field of irrigation for the simple reason that the circumstances were not right and finances were not available. There was a need, though, for continued efforts and that had already been the case at the end of the 1930s. After more than a hundred years of activity in the field of irrigation much had by that time been achieved. The Dutch engineers who had been involved in all of that wrote about it all in quite lyrical terms as was demonstrated in **Chapter 1**. They were not, however, completely divorced from realism and some of them saw that they still had far to go. Happé (1939) for instance demonstrated that the irrigation efforts of that time (a further 40,000 new hectares of modern irrigated *sawa* or rice field per annum) was in actual fact insufficient in relation to population growth (1.73% per year in the 1920-1930 period). It was only thanks to the gradual expanding of the agricultural acreage that it remained possible to guarantee food supplies but that was also to come to an end. Happé saw possibilities in Java for another ten years. After that the modern irrigation expansions would have to stand alone which meant that the construction pace would have to be speeded up. He believed that it would be impossible to suddenly accelerate things in that way, which was why he lobbied for construction activities to be immediately gradually increased. Happé also realised that the Outlying Regions were also significant when it came to irrigation expansion, certainly in the long-term, which was why he argued people should continue to migrate to these areas.[7]

The Japanese did devote attention to the creation of irrigation works (for instance in the Sampean region, see below) and after their departure the tasks in the field of irrigation did not diminish. In its endeavours to restore colonial order the Netherlands saw it as its obligation to take in hand the rebuilding of the country. Public Works was to have a key role in all of this as is evidenced by the installing of the Department of Public Works and Redevelopment. The engineer who was made Head of the Division of Irrigation and Sanitation was W. J. van Blommestein. This Indies engineer had gained his doctorate in 1939 at the Technical College of Bandung under De Vos, his subject being the designing of a mechanical uniaxial unit with impeller and turbine for simultaneous generation of pump lift and water power (Van Blommestein 1939). He drew up a plan for the western part of the North Javan plain: the Federal Welfare Plan for West Java (Van Blommestein 1949). The cause for this was "the serious food situation in Indonesia" and the aim was "to strengthen the economic position of the island [i.e. Java, WR] by improving the water situation". At the heart of the plan was the idea to construct two large water reservoirs in the Citarum river where previously an irrigation system with a movable weir at Walahar had been created (see **Chapter 10**). One of those reservoirs would be designated chiefly for irrigation purposes (the Jatiluhur *waduk* with a capacity of approximately three billion cubic metres, the

---

[6] My main sources for these and the following sections were Booth (1977), Ankum (1988) and Kop et al. (2015). The information gathered was also based on interviews conducted in the Netherlands with e.g. P. Ankum (May 1992 and May 1994) and L. Horst (June 1993). I also drew on information gleaned during my trips to Indonesia in 1993 and 1995. The important interviews there were with: R. Didiek (September 1993 and March 1995), R. Hutapea (March 1995), Loekman Soetrisno (March 1995), Soebandi Wirosoemarto (February 1995), Soenarno (August 1993 and February 1995), J. Sonneveld (August 1993 and February 1995) and M. Zakarijah (September 1993 and March 1995). Where necessary relevant references have been made in the text. Reference is also made to the reports and folders collected in Indonesia that have been consulted in connection with the drawing up of this chapter.

[7] From 1910, the Outlying Regions, especially Sumatra and Sulawesi, were the scene of Dutch irrigation activity (see **Chapter 1**). The Simeloengoen Works in North Sumatra constitute a fine example, with leading contributions from the engineers G.E. Bekkering and G.A.L. Statius Muller (J.H. Kop, personal communication, July 2017). Some information about these efforts can be found in Kop et al. (2015). Dutch irrigation works in the Outer Islands remain an interesting topic for follow-up research.

largest up until then having been 60 million cubic metres!) while the other would be used mainly to generate electricity (the Tarum *waduk* with a capacity of more than a billion cubic metres). The project proposition further involved two canals: one to the west (to Jakarta and on to the Ujung river in the Residency of Bantam) and one to the east (leading to Cirebon and the Pemali river). The total length of this waterway was 385 kilometres (compare this with the main canal of the stopped Solo works originally intended to be more than 165 kilometres long). Particularly during the east monsoon season the reservoirs would make it possible to expand and improve water provision in the plain which covered a total area of some 517,240 hectares. In this way it would be possible to grow two consecutive rice crops in one season throughout the region. In that respect the plan was able to supplement existing irrigation systems including the older Citarum irrigation works (thus alleviating pressure on the weir at Walahar), irrigation in the Tangerang plain (to the west) and a part of the Pemali-Comal irrigation system (to the east).

What was striking about the Welfare Plan was that there were ideas to supplement water shortages in one river area with water surpluses from another area by means of "inter basin transfer". That was not something that was new. In the Pemali-Comal area, for instance, that had been done before (see **Chapter 5**). What was new was the scale of the plan and the way in which it was effected. It was necessary to pump the water up in order for it to be diverted from the Citarum area to other river areas. This project linked up nicely with Van Blommestein's field of interest but this time it was large-scale pumping up of water by means of hydro-electric power that was required. There was another thing that was striking about the project proposition and that was its multifunctional nature. It related to a whole range of water uses for agricultural purposes, drinking water facilities, the generation of electricity, shipping, industry, fisheries and the flushing out of the canals of Jakarta. Other important aspects were: the combating of the danger of flooding and, the reclaiming of land by means of impoldering followed by pumping. It was, in other words, a large, regional and integrated development plan. The costs (500 million guilders) were phenomenal, certainly in that day and age. Van Blommestein (1948/49: I. 82) had great expectations:

"With the execution of this combined project it will be possible to – by producing an extra 600,000 tons of prepared rice on an annual basis – ensure that the people have sufficient rice provisions for a number of years even though the population of Java is rapidly rising. It will thus also be possible to lay the foundations for large-scale industrialisation in the interests of stabilising the welfare".

The Dutch exodus from Indonesia in 1949 suddenly put an end to Van Blommestein's career and all his ambitions but his plan remained intact!

Van Blommestein's plan had been rather global, certainly as far as its hydraulic and economic principles were concerned, but that was not a problem for the new republic. The project finally got off the ground in 1957 in what amounted to the first five-year plan of the 1950s (Jatiluhur 1992: 1). Subsequently the project was also integrated into the next plan programme spanning eight years. In the process the original project plan had been reduced to smaller proportions. It involved creating a weir for the Jatiluhur reservoir and a first section for both main canals. The total area involved was roughly 260,000 hectares. In fact, within that eight-year plan the Jatiluhur project actually constituted the core of all the planned irrigation activities in Java (Booth 1977: 48-49). It also became the basis of a new trend, that of conceiving irrigation or development projects with numerous objectives (i.e. which were multifunctional or "multipurpose") and which linked together various irrigation areas (and therefore even river areas). The body responsible for all of this was the Indonesian Department of Public Works and the project was realised with foreign aid. Since relations with the Netherlands had at that time broken down no support could be sought from those quarters so the Jatiluhur lake was created with French financial aid. The reservoir was completed in 1967 at a time when the New Order was taking over from the Old Order.[8]

Up until then irrigation policy had been chiefly directed towards new projects unfolding in Java, notably the Jatiluhur project and especially away from there in Sumatra and Sulawesi. In effect it was a continuation of the colonial policy that had also been oriented towards expanding modern irrigation facilities. The works that had been developed in the colonial era (largely in Java), however, had become ever more dilapidated in the 1940s and 1950s when maintenance had been neglected. Despite that the rehabilitation of these facilities was given little attention. Under the Old Order this pattern of decline continued so that by about 1965 many of the existing irrigation systems were more or less out of use. This was one of the main reasons for the poor food situation of the day (see above), a situation which thus presented a major challenge to the New Order.

New Order, changing perspectives

Rehabilitation and expansion

The development policy pursued under the military regime took the shape of a large rehabilitation and expansion programme in the field of irrigation. This was launched by the government in 1969 as part of its policy to modernise and rationalise agriculture. The aim was especially to renovate neglected colonial irrigation works. The first plan immediately concerned systems covering a total area of 780,000 hectares, the vast proportion of which (about 90%) were in Java. At the same time new works were prepared and executed, often in order to supplement existing facilities such as those in the Jatiluhur region. The emphasis of the activities gradually shifted from rehabilitation to expansion. The other islands received much less attention.[9] In the 1969-1989 period a total sum of 6½ thousand million dollars was expended on "water resources" development relating to four five-year plan programmes. A fifth of all the financing was in the form of foreign aid. The greatest pillar of support was the International Development Agency (IDA) division of the World Bank and what was known as the *PROSIDA* programme (i.e. *Proyek Irigasi* IDA). Furthermore the Asian Development Bank (in which Japan was an important partner) and various donor countries including the Netherlands (and again Japan) were financially involved. Financial problems (see above) prompted the government to heavily reduce its investments in the last plan (1984/85-1988/89) from a planned 3.9 to 1.4 thousand million dollars, despite extensive mission based improvement plans. (In het Veld 2015, Kop 2015).

---

[8] When the Jatiluhur reservoir was being completed Van Blommestein was busy working in the Dutch colony of Suriname which had not yet gained its independence. There he was responsible for the construction of a similar reservoir in the Suriname river (known as the Brokopondo plan) that was to go down in history as the Van Blommestein lake. The above-mentioned Bimas programme (from *bimbingan massal* meaning a massive operation) started on a small-scale in 1963 in the Jatiluhur area. The construction of the dam prompted students of the Agricultural University in Bogor (Buitenzorg) to commence on an information service programme (Witjes et al. 1995: 56). See for the development of the Citarum River Basin Water Resources Development and the West Tarum canal in particular Yap (2015). See for a biography of Van Blommestein Ravesteijn (2002c).

[9] However, see for irrigation efforts in the Outer Islands Van Nes (2015), Van Diest (2015), Houterman and Haag (2015), Schultz et al. (2015). The irrigation activities were chiefly intended to improve small-farming activities. Sugar cane continued to be cultivated in Indonesia but the world sugar prices no longer guaranteed a secure income.

Figure 4: Silted movable weir at Wilalung, built in 1926 and in use till 1989 (photo WR)

Figure 5: Silted inlet sluice in the Solo Valley (photo WR)

Figure 6: Advanced flood warning system for the Brantas river in Malang (photo WR)

Figure 7: Inflatable rubber dam in Surabaya (photo WR)

For the purposes of the execution of the *PROSIDA* irrigation programme a special *PU* Division was set up within the Directorate General for Water Resources Development. In the Provinces project offices were established which, just like the *PU* Division that was involved, remained relatively independent. These bodies were expected to operate more efficiently than the central Department and the Provincial Public Works Departments due to the fact that – as regards size and standards – the staff of these normal organisations were not equipped for such a massive task. Gradually the situation began to change. The central Department started to gain personnel who were also capable of carrying out major projects and other financial resources and organisations were linked up to *PU* in conjunction with irrigation activities. In 1984 the *PROSIDA* Division became more integrated into the Department's organisation when the Division was incorporated into the new *Irigasi* I Directorate. In the Provinces the offices were transferred to the Provincial Public Works Departments, a move that was preceded by training activities that had taken place since 1975. Apart from receiving a lot of money and logistic support the *PROSIDA* Division also had well-trained irrigation engineers at its disposal. Some of those people were Indonesian engineers who earned better there than in other functions because more was expected of them and they had to work longer hours. *PROSIDA* also employed many foreign engineers, particularly Dutch ones. The Dutch engineers operated under the auspices of an organisation known as *NEDECO*, an umbrella organisation including six engineering bureaux (two of which were *DHV* and *Euroconsult*) and the Dutch state, all of which had been set up in 1950 in order to help returning "tropical" engineers to find work and to deploy their knowledge. It was particularly in the renovating of old works that the engineers made use of data drawn from the colonial past and they obtained maps and other material from the Indies Civil Public Works archives[10].

At first the rehabilitation programme was only directed towards main and secondary works. Policy makers and engineers presumed that the farmers, presented with improved water supplies, would themselves be motivated to develop the tertiary sections. In that way they were sticking to the same strategies adopted by their colonial predecessors. However, the farmers did not contribute sufficiently in the way that was expected of them and they also failed to do their bit when, after the mid-1970s, a start was made on the creation of fields and further irrigation plans were made. The reason for this was the fact that, at village level, the farmers were not well organised. In that respect the effect of the neglecting of irrigation facilities in previous years was being felt. Another problem was the fact that there no subsidies were offered and the farmers did not possess the required technological knowledge. Demonstration projects (see below) had no effect either which was why the government finally took responsibility for rehabilitation at tertiary level. In 1977 the government produced a large programme for tertiary development designed to cater for two million hectares.

Once all the various old irrigation systems had been renovated and new ones had been constructed the next thing to be focused on was the matter of water management in the relevant irrigation areas and, specifically, the distribution of water. At first it was very much the engineers who were involved in this. Just as in the colonial era this technical management was divided into (reactivated) Irrigation Divisions (or regions) and Sections which fell under the provincial authorities. The kinds of problems encountered were: personnel shortages and lack of co-operation on the part of farmers. Another problem was that maintenance, a second important

[10] If I am to believe what my informants told me about this matter things were not always done in an historically correct way and, from time to time, engineers simply removed archive material. When I came across a 1969 (rehabilitation) report in a colonial Civil Public Works file in the Citeureup Archive that convinced me that files had indeed been removed though sometimes they do turn up elsewhere.

management task, was neglected. As far as the tertiary sections were concerned this was left to the farmers but, once again, they failed to comply. Tertiary fields that were improved by the government soon again became areas where *banjirs* (floods) were rife.

The problem with control ("operations and maintenance") made it necessary to mobilise the farmers. In the 1970s the state mounted demonstration projects in which tertiary fields were created and, via the Pemali ruling, the population was involved together with the respective *Ulu-Ulus* who were independent of town administration. One innovation led to the formation of "water users associations" based on the town or village as a unit. (See for these *Dharma Tirta* Duewel 1981). In the 1970s these numbers of organisations were limited but the government saw in all of that an exemplary model. From the participation point of view the organisations were more successful than control had been under the Pemali ruling (Loekman Soetrisno, personal communication, March 1995) and measures aimed predominantly at expanding the users associations followed in the 1980s. In order to stimulate farmers to participate training projects were specially set up for them in the post-1983 period. At District level the government decided to breathe new life into the irrigation committees. Just as had been the case in the past, representatives drawn from all the government services were involved in water management. When budgetary adjustments had to be made in the 1980s the water users had to start paying more. Apart from having to provide physical labour for the purposes of maintenance the farmers were also obliged to provide financial support.[11] On top of that the government tried to introduce a water taxation system (an "irrigation water service fee"). It was to be imposed on top of the existing land rent and the new maintenance contribution. Ankum (1988: 353) listed the following contributions: maintenance payment and land rent both amounting to roughly ten dollars per hectare, water tax at roughly fifteen dollars per hectare. Experiments carried out with such taxes levied upon irrigation water, for instance in the Cidurian and Brantas areas, had proven that this kind of taxation was hard to introduce.

There were positive results. Many of the works were renovated, irrigation was expanded and new irrigation systems were constructed (though not all Dutch works could be saved, see **Figures 4 and 5**). Despite the sharp population growth Indonesia became, as already mentioned, self-supporting where rice was concerned and this was clearly the result of combined efforts to improve agricultural and irrigation facilities.[12] The irrigation policy also brought with it its problems. In the first place the modernisation and rationalisation of agriculture, together with results of improved irrigation provisions, led to a widening gap between rich and poor and to a gradual depletion of the soil nutrients as well as erosion (see above). The other problems arising were more specific. One of the social problems arising when large reservoirs were created was the fact that people had to make way for water. Modern irrigation expansion thus gave rise to one of the more dramatic aspects of the transmigration programme. Also, the expropriation of large tracts of land made necessary by reservoir construction was something that made population migration extra expensive. At environmental level the irrigation programme contributed to the very topical problem of water shortage. Gradually the people of Java reached the maximum available water supply. That had to do with the success of modern irrigation but also with the fact that other water users, industry included, started to make ever-greater demands upon water supplies[13]. In turn that made control extra important.

---

[11] Another economy drive was the idea to give the Province a bigger share in all the management expenses.

[12] See for the results of the post-war *PU* efforts in the field of irrigation and in other areas the jubilee publication entitled *Vijfenveertig* ("Forty Five") (1990).

[13] The extending of industrial areas was something that also led to a physical diminishing of the *sawa* acreage as was seen in the Tangerang plain (see below). In the eyes of the government that was, from the development point of view, not so much a problem but rather a matter of policy.

Just like in the Jatiluhur region the Brantas river area became the setting for extensive project activities (see **Figure 6**). In a first master plan (1961-1973) for the entire Brantas basin the whole area was freed from flooding. Subsequently, under a second plan (1973-1985) rice production was sharply increased which meant that the area was able to contribute to the achieving of national self-sufficiency as far as rice production was concerned. It was a plan that also focused greatly on the generating of electricity. In 1985 a third integral plan (continuing until 2000) was introduced, directing efforts towards supplying water for industrial and domestic purposes. Other objectives related to the plans mentioned here had to do with the areas of tourism and fisheries. The important irrigation works were three large storage reservoirs created in the river's upper reaches, one of which was the Karangkates lake (1972). Other works included a new movable weir at Lengkong (1973) to replace De Bruyn's 1857 weir and an inflatable rubber dam in the Surabaya river (1993, see **Figure 7**). The latter weir was a new type for Indonesia; the presence of rubber tubing that can be pumped up gives such dams variable height possibilities of several metres. Japan provided substantial help when it came to the matter of executing the plans, especially with the reservoirs in the upper river reaches[14].

The modernization approach in discussion

A damper was placed on the success story of irrigation efforts under the New Order, when in 1994 and 1995 Indonesia was once again forced to import rice (some one and a half million tons in 1995). Although this happened before (in the latter half of the 1980s that was also necessary for several years, Witjes et al. 1990: 59), it still prompted one to question how irrigation activities should further progress in Indonesia. Should similar things be done or should there be a change? What characterised the irrigation programme started in 1969 was that it was a modernisation programme dictated from above, that it involved big systems created by engineers and that the role of engineers, also from the angle of control, was essential. These matters were reviewed in Indonesia and among all the foreign experts involved. The disappointing results in relation to the enormous investments being made was one of the main stumbling blocks but not the only one. The modernisation programme was above all else expensive and, increasingly, it has been placed under greater financial pressure. It therefore became attractive to the government to seek alternative and cheaper ways and means as well. In the latter half of the 1980s it was chiefly spending cuts that already triggered off important policy changes in the field of management. At that point the government decided to transfer all irrigation systems for areas of 500 hectares and less to the respective users (within a fifteen-year period). This was termed a "turning over" policy (see, for example, Study 1987)[15]. Now, however, a whole new approach seemed necessary.

Main question in the debate on other approaches to construction and management of irrigation works was how far one should go to in involving the farmers. In the course of time the policy had changed in this regard and the farmers had become more involved in management (and also had to pay more!), but their participation was limited. Following upon the problems that arose in the irrigation activities, a second important issue in the debate was: how to regulate

[14] See for the Japanese aid in general, especially during the Suharto regime Kohama (2004).

[15] The turnover policy is also evidenced in the practice of the transference of larger systems to the provincial authorities. In the past completed projects had also been turned over to the authorities but there the question had always been: when precisely is a project completed? Gradually the awareness grew that works are in fact never completed and so there was the question of which body should be responsible for follow-up work, *PU* or the provincial water services (Ankum 1988: 359). The turning over of larger works was, in part, an answer to this latter question. The new policy was also applied to large works in progress with the result that the relevant Directorate (*Irigasi-I*) was hollowed out.

water management in relation to other water users than farmers and the environment? With regard to four points the debate in the 1990s was reminiscent of discussions in the colonial period.

From the top or from the bottom?

It has been especially engineers who lobbied for a continuation of the modernisation strategy, though with much more attention to non-technological facets. A good example of this is provided by Ankum who upholds the integrated approach by asserting that "a technically perfect system is not automatically a properly functioning system" (1988: 360). In this connection he concluded (ibid.):

"it is essential to include other elements as well, notably in respect of: (i) guidance by the irrigation committee, (ii) improvement of O&M [operation and maintenance, WR] procedures, (iii) strengthening and training of O&M staff, (iv) participation of water users, and (v) co-ordination between all parties".

In the case of perpetuated modernisation there would be two things that are important to observe: improving the efficiency of irrigation systems and the tackling of new projects.

There is, however, another possible angle of approach, the "participatory approach". When, in the 1970s and 1980s, the results of the irrigation policy adopted did not come up to expectations and the issue of co-operation on the part of farmers turned out to be particularly problematic, solutions were not only sought within the existing framework but outside of it as well. There was a motion, in the first place among social scientists and agricultural experts, to not only involve the farmers in management but also in the designing and constructing of tertiary fields. What was rather surprising at that time was the fact that the farmers were not involved in the work of the engineers at all. As far as the structure of an irrigation area was concerned, for instance with regard to the number of tertiary canals and the size of the tertiary fields, the engineers stuck to fixed technical norms. These norms and other more economic criteria relating to the work to be done, like for instance the numbers of man-hours per unit of ground moved and the wage level at which mechanical processing became cheaper stemmed (largely) from the colonial era and so were seen as deriving from the Indies "Civil Public Works manual" (F. Hüsken, personal communication, June 1996). Inspectors saw to it that these norms were abided by in practice. There was, though, no leeway for – where necessary – local adaptations. A project that was set up in the 1980s with the financial support of the Ford Foundation where the farmers participated at every stage demonstrated that positive results did emanate from this approach (R. Hutapea, personal communication, March 1995).

Large scale or small scale?

The executing of large projects is something that fits in with far-reaching modernisation. In that connection one might in the first place think of the development plan for Java and Madura with which Van Blommestein surprised the world in 1979 (Van Blommestein 1979, compare Bienefelt 1981 and Van der Post 1983). This was launched as a "delta plan" for Indonesia. The plan traced the ideology of the Federal Welfare Plan and also elaborated it. It envisaged the connecting up of irrigation systems throughout Java and the transferring of water from West Java (where there is a surplus) to East Java (where there is a shortage) and even from Java to Madura.

At the heart of the plan was the notion that large reservoirs should be formed that would be linked up to series of canals. In this way it would be possible to create electric power-stations that would draw their power from water. The water needed in Madura would derive from the

Solo river and would be conducted under the Surabayan straits by means of a three-kilometre-long culvert. For the Solo Valley area the plan drew on the 1900 Solo report plans for a movable weir at Ngluwak. Van Blommestein expected that his plan would lead to a doubling of the irrigated *sawa* acreage and a doubling (or even a tripling) of the crop sizes in areas where that had previously been unthinkable. Another advantage of the plan was that it offered the prospect of better protection against flooding, both in the Jakarta region and, for example, the Solo Valley area. The diminishing of the silt level would improve matters for the harbour at Jakarta while the various canals throughout Java would also be useful for shipping purposes. What was particularly striking about this plan, the costs of which were estimated at one and a half thousand million dollars, was that it was even more global than the Federal Welfare Plan of 1949 (see above[16]). The Indonesian government was quite enthusiastic about the plan and decided to carry out further research (Development 1981). An evaluation delegation, set up in 1982 by the Dutch Ministry of Foreign Affairs (in particular its *DGIS* division), arrived at the conclusion that Van Blommestein's plan was technically complex but was (as far as could be ascertained) a sound plan which, in the light of the results of the Green Revolution, however, would not need to be implemented (L. Horst, personal communication, June 1993, Bakker et al. 1982/83). Another problem was the transmigration factor. Ultimately therefore the plan was not executed, except for in the case of one reservoir (see below). This was also due to the fact that in the latter part of the 1980s funding for irrigation activities was less abundant[17]. Later, due to further recent rice imports, the situation changed again. This meant that Van Blommestein's plan still stood a chance. However, all the other objections still remained concerning, in other words, the costs and the social problems[18].

Meanwhile the Federal Welfare Plan, also an aspect of the new plan, was pursued. Following the Jatiluhur lake the Tarum and Cirata reservoirs were created in the 1983-1988 period (activities linked to the entire network continued until 1993)[19]. The irrigation area served

[16] The Hydrodynamic Laboratory worked out the details of the 1948 plan in the 1980s and came to the conclusion that it contained many inaccuracies. In fact Van Blommestein also wrote an appendage to the 1979 plan on water power as an aspect of the development of the "integrated perennial irrigation system" in East Java and Madura (1984). See for the Dutch Delta Plan Bijker (1995) and Van de Ven (1993).

[17] The discussions surrounding the plan were extensive and the atmosphere was not always ideal. In 1984 a second visit, involving several of the delegation's members and including L. Horst, was made to Indonesia in response to a request made by the Indonesian government. Talks were held with Indonesian authorities (including of *PU*) and two representatives from the Dutch Embassy, F.E. Schulze of the Agricultural Council and W.G. Wessels of the *DGIS*. The talks only confirmed the conclusions drawn by the delegation to the effect that there should be: "no more large new investments in water works but more emphasis should be placed on making better use of the water generated by existing facilities" (from a letter sent by Wessels on behalf of the Dutch ambassador to the Minister of Foreign Aid, see Remaining archive sources). The findings of the follow-up visit were in fact integrated into the final report dating from 1982/1983! However, Schulze and Wessels were critical about the delegation's work. Remarks made by Wessels in the above-mentioned letter to the effect that the Agricultural Council had detected "a large number of technical failings" and "inconsistencies" in the design report gave rise to amazement on the part of those involved and an exchanging of somewhat angry letters between the various parties (Remaining archive sources). At Delft University of Technology Van Blommestein was viewed as a "man of vision" and his ideas were thought to be certainly worth realising (based on personal remarks made by P. Ankum, June 1992 and a student essay – Van Gorkum and Klein n.d. – written under his supervision and that of Professor J. H. Kop).

[18] The fact that the social problems remain perpetual became clear when, in 1993, a report relating to protest action and three deaths in connection with the proposed construction of a weir in Madura (the Nipah dam) appeared in a Dutch newspaper: "According to a military spokesman shots were released because an estimated five hundred farmers and villagers armed with daggers had threatened a group of civil servants from Jakarta sent out to determine the most appropriate site for the dam" (*de Volkskrant*, 28th September).

[19] From 1979 onwards people in this area also deployed "cloud seeding technology", in other words, the using of planes to create rain clouds (Jatiluhur 1992: 7).

by the Jatiluhur system thus grew to around 300,000 hectares. The Cirata *waduk* which, just like the Tarum *waduk* was intended chiefly for electricity generation purposes had been foreseen in Van Blommestein's Welfare Plan but only as a possibility. However, in the subsequent plan the reservoir did occupy a prominent place.

The alternative to a large-scale approach to the creation of irrigation facilities is a small scale one. Since the 1970s (under its *Repelita* II programme) the government had been experimenting with this "appropriate technology" especially in the (transmigration) areas outside Java. The idea was to improve upon existing works while also constructing new ones, for instance for *sawas* that are dependent upon rainfall levels. Furthermore, there had been a lot of support since 1969 (via subsidies) for rehabilitation and expansion of village irrigation or farming systems, that is to say, simple systems, which were built by peasants and managed without *PU* intervention. In the late 1980s there was research into small-scale irrigation projects (funded by USAID), and the outcomes were favourable (R. Hutapea, personal communication, March 1995). Consequently, the government decided to increase its investments in small-scale activities: in connection with the lost capacity for self-sufficiency, she launched a major improvement programme for village irrigation (300,000 hectares) in 1995. Experts (including Loekman Soetrisno, personal communication, March 1995), however, found this top-down programme not the best way of improving farmer systems. They expected among other things that it would affect the independence of farmers and pleaded for a participatory approach (which had appeared to work well with small works).

Absolute or proportional?

In the 1990s the *DHV* engineering firm was busy designing a computer model for the (computer-guided) distribution of water for irrigation purposes in the Tangerang plain. The experiment failed, however, due to lack of support on the part of those involved (J. Sonneveld, personal communication, February 1995). In a nutshell this is the story of what happens when engineers dominate control. Their water distribution is of an absolute nature, that is to say, based upon the water requirements of the crop. Such control is made possible by a technology of measuring and distributing. It works well, provided the population accepts it (J.H. Kop, personal communication, June 2017). Computer-guided, absolute water distribution is something that fits in well with a perpetuated line of modernisation (Ankum 1991, see also, Study 1987).

The alternative is proportional water distribution that is based upon the size of the land area to be irrigated. The latter system corresponds more closely to the population's traditional forms of water management. In arguments where the innovation of proportional control is advocated it is often the Balinese *subaks* that are alluded to. Recent history well indicates how important such traditional farming organisations are to water control. Towards the end of the 1970s the Indonesian government launched a large development programme for Balinese irrigation. The same approach was used as that adopted in Java. The *subaks* (1300 in all on the island) were not included in the programme which meant that targets were not achieved and upon the initiative (and at the expense) of the *subaks* reconstructions were made (Horst 1996).[20] The interest in proportional water distribution was increasing. As we have seen, it was essential for the population to be involved in control, something which led to the reintroduction of the Pemali

[20] The American anthropologist Lansing endeavoured to prove that where irrigation control in Bali is concerned traditional and modern elements can go together. Following his research into the *subaks* and their religious basis (1991) he initiated a project which required the involvement of Hindu priests and *subaks* in the further development of control. It meant training the priests to use computers. The main idea behind Lansing's project was that water distribution might be optimised in connection with disease and pestilence. The relevant film is entitled: "The Goddess and the Computer".

ruling and, especially, to support for the establishment of water user associations. It was a development that also drew attention to proportional water distribution. At first the users' organisations were modelled on the Balinese *subaks* (Booth 1977: 55-56, see also Duewel 1981: 195). Absolute water distribution remained as a criterion but disappointing results in this direction (noticed at international level by the World Bank), the government's turnover policy (i.e. the transferring of small systems to users) and attention devoted to farmer participation kept the proportional system under consideration. (Horst 1994, 1996: 52).

The critics of the measures taken to improve localised irrigation (see above) pointed out that the available water quantities did not allow for production rises: increased water consumption in the mountainous regions where farming networks are concentrated automatically means less water in the plains with harvest increases in one place leading to harvest decreases in another. In that connection the experiences in the Sampean area were referred to (see below). All of this raised the issue of water use in general. More so than when post-colonial irrigation efforts began, water had become a scarce commodity that needed to be managed and divided up between different kinds of water users. The problems were even more serious than that. Generally rice cultivation in Java was being threatened by salinization as a result of intensive water use and, in coastal areas, intrusion of seawater because of low river discharges and subsidence. Desertification, which has long been predicted, was a serious menace (Van Dieren 1995: 97 onwards). Consequently, an environmental policy directed towards preventing and combating erosion and limiting water consumption became necessary. All of this constitutes an extra burden on the distribution of the water and the way to organize this.

Reforms: management and participation

When one considers the various features of the modernisation approach there were therefore different possible options: as opposed to the top-down approach there is the participation approach; small-scale activities may be embarked upon as opposed to large-scale activities, engineering control may be (partly) replaced by autonomous control and giving priority to management over construction[21]. What actually happened?

One way in which endeavours were made to address all the issues – or at least some of them – is in the setting up of "river basin management", that is, relatively independent organisations for managing water in river basins. In effect this involves extending (and transforming) Irrigation Divisions. All aspects of water management in a river basin, including water and soil conservation (also by reforesting) may be examined and organised in mutual co-ordination. There are 90 different river areas in Indonesia and some of the larger regions, like the Brantas river and the Citarum river, have their own water management organisations. It was therefore no coincidence that in these two areas state companies ("public corporations") were set up for management purposes (Jatiluhur 1992, Jasa Tirta 1993, Asian Development Bank 2016, compare Ankum 1990). New integrated control in these areas followed the execution of large, multifunctional irrigation projects. However, elsewhere, too, the establishing of such units became priority, like for example in the Sampean area (see below). River basin management became the new goal and frame of action, prepared and based on relevant research by, among others, *DHV* (Java 1994).

[21] As we have seen the Agricultural University of Wageningen (L. Horst) and the University of Technology in Delft (P. Ankum) placed different emphasis upon the various facets of this discussion, notably when it comes to the managing of the bigger projects. In **Chapter 2** (**Note 11**) I indicated that they did have rather different views about what were the objectives of the colonial irrigation efforts for sugar cane production or rice cultivation. My research indicated that both objectives were in fact important (see the **Conclusion**). See for experiences with and discussions on various approaches to irrigation development and irrigation management in general Stern (1979) and Coward (1980).

This turn in – and to – management was part and parcel of a new direction that emerged in the domain of irrigation, facilitated if not determined by the political transition of the late 1990s and crystallized in a new water law adopted in 2004. Following democratization and decentralization the new law build on the principles of Integrated Water Resources Management, strengthening for example public participation (Van Beek 2015). The new approach is being tentatively adopted in various project areas, also within the *PROSIDA* project (Van Beek 2015, compare Schrevel 1993[22]). The kinds of irrigation efforts undertaken together with certain of the problems that arose can be well illustrated if one traces the development of the four works projects dealt with in this book.

Revisiting the four cases

Sampean Works

The Sampean delta works were improved in the 1972-1988 period. The irrigation area was moreover extended when, in 1984, a new weir complete with sluices entered into operation. The works also incorporated a 43-kilometre-long main canal. The Sampean *baru* (the new dam) provides some 8600 hectares of land with water. The total area irrigated thus amounts to 19,400 hectares (which, in 1925, was 15,400 *bouws*). The whole Sampean *baru* idea arose in the 1930s because of the frequent *banjir* flooding that had come to plague the area. It was thus concluded that it would be necessary to construct a weir. The job was started in the Japanese period but it was not a great success. The remnants of that dam are still visible today. Apart from rice (and cattle crops) sugar cane is also cultivated in the region irrigated by the Sampean *baru*. All the sugar produced is processed in a sugar refinery that was built during the first half of the nineteenth century. The colonial irrigation facilities are used chiefly for sugar cane cultivation and supply some four sugar refineries. In general, since the main works were completed during the nineteenth century, the hydraulic situation in the Sampean delta has changed in a number of significant ways which is expressed in the way in which the old works are now referred to, partly already since colonial times. The old dam has become a "sluice", another sluice has become a "dam" (the Sampean *lama*, the old dam, opposite to the new one), while the *banjir* canal has taken over the course of the river.

When the new weir in the Sampean area was created the authorities thought that they had finally managed to banish the destruction caused by floods but that was not the case. In 1993 there was another flood in Situbondo at the mouth of the Sampean. On top of that it turned out that there was still water shortage, especially in the dry season. Researchers (from the Gadjah Mada University in Yogyakarta) put this down to the numerous (more than 2000!) small dams in the upper reaches of the Sampean that had been constructed in the 1980s by farmers using government subsidies. The researchers lobbied for a water control system for the whole area so that the water distribution between both modern weirs as well as the links with the inland farming system might be well organised and the crop pattern in the entire area geared to that. (Sahid Susanto and Suprodjo 1987, see also Effendi Pasandaran 1976). The final upshot of all the water problems – flood risk in the wet period and too little water in the dry period – was that the ground in the river area deteriorated. According to local Public Works representatives (in Bondowoso) this came as the result of the expanding of the settlements in the mountains and it was also due to the "bad" way in which farmers had taken to creating rice terraces – pressurised by economic necessity.

[22] The focus on river basin management and Integrated Water Resources Management in general is in accordance with an international trend, see e.g. Ravesteijn et al. (2012).

Figure 8: Dam of the Malahayu *waduk* with traditional weir in the foreground (photo WR)

Figure 9: Bambu water conduits taking their water at the Damarwulan weir in the east monsoon period (photo WR)

Figure 10: Inlet sluice to tertiary canal (photo WR)

There was an experimental river basin management project in the Sampean area in the 1995-2000 period, in which *DHV* was involved, while the basin remained the scene of research and development in follow up work (Asian Development Bank 2016, Van Beek 2015). The area nevertheless remained sensitive to *banjirs* in the following years, for example in 2002 when bridges and houses in the area were destroyed. Then improved flood prevention policies seem to be effective, though further improvements are still possible and even necessary, especially in legal-institutional terms (Wardhono et al. 2012).

Pemali Works

After 1969 many structural works were renovated in the Pemali-Comal area, for example under the *Prosida*-B programme (In het Veld 2015). One such work was the weir in the Pemali river at Notok that was renovated in the 1971-72 period. The present extent of the entire irrigation area is 124,800 hectares (which, in 1925, was 169,500 *bouws*). The government created a tertiary section in the Pemali area for demonstration purposes. Deforestation in the upper reaches of the Pemali has created new problems. In the first place sedimentation has diminished the river's ability to flow freely and, at the same time, the Pemali has high water levels during the wet seasons. The chances of *banjirs* have therefore only increased (and that includes the flooding of other rivers in the area) while there is an even greater shortage of water in the east monsoon season. As far as the Pemali flow rates were concerned the peaks started to vary, thus leading to a different crop pattern with a later rice-planting period. Finally there were problems when it came to distributing water between the upper river regions and the coastal area.

The irrigation area is the place where the Pemali ruling was first created and after independence the ruling remained in force although in the 1970s, in at least a part of the area (in the Brebes regency), a new water control system was introduced and an association of water users (Hutapea et al. 1976) was set up. Beyond that the Pemali-Comal region has always remained an area with a substantial sugar production level. It is especially this sugar region that is known for its conflicts in the matter of distributing water between sugar producers and rice farmers (R. Hutapea, personal report of March 1995).

The Pemali-Comal area has become the scene of River Basin Management Planning, which guided operation and management of the works as well as their institutional embedding (Asian Development Bank 2016). Practical results are unclear, though in addition to *banjirs*, droughts have attracted attention the past decades (Hatmokoa 2015).

Solo Valley Works

When the Dutch withdrew the Solo Valley area was labelled a problem area which meant that subsequently priority was given to the region when it came to the matter of creating new facilities. Following the huge Solo floods of 1966 originating in the upper reaches of the river which affected, amongst other places, the city of Surakarta, the Japanese produced a plan for the river basin area of the Solo as a whole. This plan, produced in 1974, also related to the Solo's main tributary, the Madiun (Master Plan 1974). The idea was to create thirty reservoirs, four of which would be very big (able to hold 86 to 920 million cubic metres of water). The relatively smaller reservoirs (which still provided the capacity for an average of 14½ million cubic metres of water and which would have been termed large in the colonial era) were only intended for irrigation purposes. The big reservoirs had a multi-functional design. They were intended to prevent *banjirs*, to provide water for irrigation and to generate hydro-electricity. What was different about the Japanese plan was that it was not rice growing that was considered but rather the cultivation possibilities allowed by the existing natural situation and the way in which the crop pattern could be adopted to that, with maize as an important option[23].

Part of the Japanese plan was executed like, for instance, the large storage reservoir in the upper reaches of the Solo at Wonogiri (660 million cubic metres, completed in 1982). In that way an extra 28,200 hectares of *sawa* could be provided with irrigation water. In the Solo Valley – the lower reaches of the river – an irrigation reservoir was also created: the Gondang *waduk* (1987). A statue of a departing family group and a waving child at Wonogiri serves to remind one that when the lake was created more than fifty *desas* were lost. The inhabitants were forced to become a part of the transmigration programme. The plan also included a similarly large lake intended for the Solo Valley: the Jipang reservoir which was intended to be built not all that far from Ngluwak (where a weir had been planned in colonial times). It was to be the biggest of all the reservoirs (920 million cubic metres) but it did not materialise. Indeed, since then it has been decided "at top level" that this lake will definitely not be created (Sidarta, personal communication, March 1995). One of the reasons for abandoning the plan was the transmigration factor but there were also other problems too. Financial means were lacking (partly due to the high costs of transmigration) and, in view of the criticism levelled against the programme, it was also hard to secure foreign aid. Another barrier was the fact that the province of Central Java – the main area to be potentially affected by the plans, while East Java would profit – was opposed to the idea.

Canadian engineers developed a new general plan for the Solo Valley (Rutledge 1986) that strongly resembled the Dutch project and other similar smaller plans which had later been developed in the colonial era. For instance, the construction of the drainage canal leading to Sidayu Lawas on the Java Sea constitutes an aspect of this Canadian plan with a colonial past. The excavations through the northern hills to the Java Sea was part of the famous Solo Works and the endeavour to create a new river estuary. The canal was built in the 1990s, that is a narrow version[24]. The Canadian plan furthermore included the construction of a large reservoir along colonial lines, the Kerjo-Cawak(-Lamong) *waduk*. Other important elements were the rehabilitation activities (in the Pacal and Prijetan irrigation areas) and the conversion of a large marsh to a spare basin: the Jabung reservoir. The proposed rehabilitation finally took place in the 1987-1991 period (and it involved 25,000 hectares).

In addition, more small-scale works were undertaken in the Solo Valley such as, for instance, the perpetual dike improvement jobs. Much work has been done in the 1990s, including the execution (with Japanese help) of a programme involving 33 small pumping-stations for irrigation water drawn from the Solo. Other initiatives were: the construction of a series of weirs in small tributaries of the Solo and of a series of larger overflow dams in the Solo and Madiun. These latter dams are of the rubber dam type. One such inflatable dam has been completed in the Solo at Surakarta and at least six have been created in the Madiun river.

Meanwhile, the project management was busy with the development of a "master plan", again for the entire Solo river area (including also once more the Madiun river). Use was made of all the available plans and research, including a study into the devising of a mathematical model designed to optimise the water situation in the Solo river area. The model was created by the Hydrological Laboratory in Bandung in cooperation with the Hydrodynamic Laboratory in Delft (Pengembangan 1992, River 1988 and *Studi* 1993[25]). These on-going activities paved the

[23] This corresponded with De Meyier's point of view as expressed in the Solo report (Telders et al. 1900).

[24] Indonesia hoped that it might be able to rely on Japanese aid and that it might then be possible to widen it. In the 1980s there was mention that the Netherlands might be involved in the (further) continuation of this colonial project (via the State Public Works Organisation [*Rijkswaterstaat*] and not *DGIS*). In this connection a "Claus mission" was set up. (L. Horst, personal communication, June 1993).

[25] The 1900 Solo report did not play a part in the considerations of the project management in relation to the

way for the application of River Basin Management Planning which recently has resulted in new measures and plans, including several new reservoirs (Asian Development Bank 2016).

The city of Surakarta is now free of flood danger but the weir in the upper reaches of the Solo has little effect on the situation in the Solo Valley. Up to now other measures have also not been sufficiently effective. Though the inhabitants of the Bengawan Jero no longer need rafts people there and elsewhere in the Solo Valley still suffer from flooding with every year the threat of renewed *banjirs*. Even the Solo Valley project offices in Bojonegoro and Lamongan were flooded in 1988. Dikes flanking the Solo are usually reinforced after flooding events, but that is like rearranging buckets under the tap. Whether or not the new river basin management will make the difference, remains to be seen.

Cisadane-Cidurian Works

In the Tangerang plain, apart from needing to be rehabilitated the works also had to be completed. Activities undertaken in conjunction with the new policy and immediately begun in 1969 in connection with irrigating from the Cisadane continued until 1987. The area ultimately irrigated covered 36,200 hectares. The viaduct over the Cimanceuri for the purposes of Cidurian irrigation was realised in the 1970s. The existing Cidurian system works were not renovated until the 1988-1992 period (see, for example, Cidurian 1988 and 1989). Once all the work had been completed the size of the irrigation area was 10,400 hectares. The total Tangerang plain land acreage provided with modern irrigation facilities lagged behind the colonial estimates (of 51,800 hectares or 74.000 *bouws*) since some of the land area was designated for other purposes, in other words, for the establishing of various industries and for the building and extending of Jakarta's international airport.[26]

---

creation of a master plan for the entire Solo river. The reason for this was simple. The staff involved in the project did know about the report but it had not been seen at the various project offices in the region, including the head-office at Kartosuro (near Surakarta). The staff were therefore not fully conversant with Dutch ideas as emerged when the canal leading to the sea was excavated. Upon completion of the canal the engineers wanted to allow the little river that flowed into the sea at Sidayu Lawas to link up with the canal. It was presumed that this was what the Dutch had also had in mind but no one was quite certain. Since I had studied the relevant report I was able to become a useful informant for the project workers in question. (See also **Chapter 7**, **Note 2**). The fact that the local population had not forgotten about the Solo Works clearly emerged from the referred to story (referred to in the already-mentioned footnote) told by a project participant to the effect that in the early 1990s the local government had received a letter in which a request had been made for the main canal designed and partly dug by the Dutch to be completed. My informant guessed that the writer of this was undoubtedly a family member of somebody who had originally been involved in the works project in question. As mentioned, the Indonesian authorities (*PU*) asked *DHV* to produce recommendations concerning this same plan. The question is, how did they find out about it? Was the information found in the archives or was it, as one project worker suggested, obtained from the son of one of the engineers involved in the works who had visited Indonesia in the 1980s? The colonial plan was also known to Van Blommestein who, as we have seen, integrated it into his development plan for Java and Madura. Is the colonial Solo report still relevant? The recommendations made by *DHV* are hazy but what is clear is that *DHV* did not offer its unconditional support. The opinion voiced by P. Ankum of Delft University of Technology was favourable (personal communications, May 1992 and May 1994). He maintained that the technical and agricultural objections once made to the plan no longer really held. He mentioned e.g. the availability of fertiliser. One may really question whether the old Solo plan is still relevant to Indonesia today. Shifts in policy would currently point in a different direction (see above and also Ravesteijn 1995). The report could, however, come in useful when drawing up a general plan for the Solo area so that discussions at national level could be short-circuited with activities at project level. In this regard the Solo report illustrates how colonial archive material may be relevant to further developments in the field of irrigation in Indonesia.

[26] The Cidurian area is one of the areas in Indonesia where, in 1992, because of the breakdown in relations with the Netherlands, project activities that had been supported by Dutch funding abruptly came to an end. By then the rehabilitation of the colonial irrigation system in the Cidurian area was, admittedly, as good as completed but activities in the field of organisation and training were not. (M. Boissevain 1992, Kampfraath & Sonneveld 2015).

The works have reduced the danger of flooding in the Tangerang plain but that depends on sufficient drainage, for instance, through the *Mookervaart* ("Mooker channel"), which could threaten Jakarta. This gave rise to conflicts on the matter of whether or not the Sewan drainage sluice should be opened. In the whole Jakarta area the flooding situation has deteriorated over the years, as a consequence of the subsidence of the city resulting from excessive groundwater abstraction and other factors, worsened by sea level rise. At the same time, the implementation of older plans has been delayed, despite – or even as a consequence of – recent institutional and political reforms, though ultimately the Eastern Flood canal has been completed (Kop 2008, Simanjuntak et al. 2012). Recently, the Great Garuda plan emerged to fight flooding from the sea, among others by closing the Jakarta Bay with a dike (Priyambodho et al. 2015). Though this plan does not address flooding from the rivers flowing through Jakarta, it will nevertheless impact the regional water situation enormously, probably including in ways not foreseen.

Continuity and change

What is striking about the new Indonesia is the matter of continuity in relation to many aspects of the colonial past. Naturally that is not surprising. The national state that arose from that archipelago in the 1940s was the end-product of a process of state formation that had begun in the colonial period (see **Chapter 2**). Under the Ethical Policy the Dutch East Indies population became involved in power formation and was increasingly drawn into the state machine and it was education which made that possible. The national movement that subsequently developed simply took over the colonial state after the Japanese occupation. The development policy of the New Order was simply a perpetuation of the Ethical Policy in which the democratic element, however, was limited (but that also occurred in the 1930s). That led to a situation of similar changes in the local agricultural situation. Hüsken (1988: 247) expressed it thus:

"In essence the policy of the New Order looks ... in many respects like a perpetuation of the ideas that colonial economists and civil servants formulated in the 1920s (...). What is even more remarkable than this continuity at the level of political ideology is the fact that this was coupled with a number of similarities in the nature and direction of the changes in the rice economy".

Here the author is referring to such matters as processes of agrarian differentiation (the widening gap between rich and poor farmers) that came as a result of agricultural modernisation and rationalisation. (See also for the issue of continuity N. Schulte Nordholt 1991: 6-7, Moon 2009 and Colombijn and Coté 2015).

Also in the area of irrigation, continuity was perceptible but alongside of that there was also change within the framework of perpetuated development. There are, in this connection, a number of dimensions that can be highlighted:

1. Continuity is revealed in the fact that colonial structural works, rehabilitated or not, remain operational. In general we may assert that the basis for the present-day irrigation system, post-colonial works aside (partly again based upon Dutch design) was laid in the colonial period. But there are also differences. Colonial irrigation engineers worked on separate irrigation projects: a weir in the river with, linked to it, one or two inlets and a canal system. These works are still visible today but they have become part of a greater whole. Many of the irrigation areas are connected. The Citarum irrigation works with the weir at Walahar is part of a much bigger Jatiluhur system. Another example is the Demak works which are included in the Jratunseluna irrigation area embracing the river basins of four rivers (106,100 hectares, Hieselaar 2015, see also Van Hofwegen 2015). Another change resides in the fact that projects were not any longer solely (or chiefly) directed towards irrigation and drainage purposes but were also used to

provide water for other uses (industry, sluicing out and drinking water, electricity generation). Again the Jatiluhur multifunctional project provides us with a good example. In reality, irrigation projects have therefore also become a part of regional development projects in which agricultural irrigation is linked up to other economic activities.

The joining together of various river basins and irrigation projects with various objectives and irrigation works within the framework of (regional) development plans are the elements that have come to typify post-colonial irrigation practices[27]. All these features, however, had their roots in the colonial era. In that respect the development of modern irrigation may be said to have continued after independence. At micro level the developments also continued. That is where the attention given to tertiary sections increased. At management level people fell back on colonial arrangements including the Pemali ruling. In this respect one of the things to instigate change was the introduction of associations of water users which certainly represented progress as far as the participation of farmers was concerned. The introduction of river basin management and the 2004 Water Law constitute follow-up developments, aspiring to reconcile bottom-up influence with top-down intervention.

2. Under the New Order the programme of rehabilitation and expansion in modern irrigation revealed continuity and change with respect to colonial irrigation policy. It was not surprising to see that this programme arose in the 1960s because that was when all the conditions for successful irrigation development were ripe. There was a need for works (because of population growth and neglect), there was a strong state (the New Order), a policy aimed at improving the food situation and stimulating economic growth for which plenty of foreign financial resources were made available, a special organisation (*PROSIDA*), well educated (and paid) Indonesian and foreign engineers and, last but not least, various ideological support (the Pancasila and a strong development ideology). It was *PROSIDA* that did the honours because a state organisation was not at that moment capable of supporting such an extensive programme. Later that was to change.

The affairs surrounding the irrigation programme were, up to a point, reminiscent of the rediscovery of the wheel. Indeed, the way in which the programme was set up and amended displayed parallels with the historic progress of irrigation activities. In the colonial time attention was also first paid to main and secondary works (and at the very beginning only to headworks) and only later to tertiary facilities when water distribution and maintenance were considered after works had been constructed (rehabilitation was then less relevant) and at first control was dominated by engineers (in the Irrigation Divisions) with later the share of the farmers being reinforced (with the Pemali ruling). Under the New Order administrators and farmers came up against the same problems as their predecessors of the colonial past, notably where the relationship between farmers and the irrigation service was concerned. This therefore led to a similar kind of development process. For instance, in the colonial era there had also been the transmigration problem in connection with large reservoirs, like for instance with the Rawa Pening reservoir (225 million cubic metres), though reservoir building was barely affected. In independent Indonesia this problem only became a real obstacle in the latter half of the 1980s (when there was a shortage of finances and heavy protests were mounted). Consequently, the 1979 Van Blommestein plan for the whole of Java, which is in itself a splendid example of the

[27] For Schrevel (1993) it is in the linking of irrigation projects to the general context that the conditions for the successful functioning of irrigation systems are to be found.

further development of colonial irrigation engineering, met with resistance, while his earlier Welfare Plan was embraced with much more enthusiasm.[28]

3. In the republic there is a kind of "parallel hierarchy" reminiscent to that of the colonial administration: a *PU* line of irrigation regions and sections with, within that, various officials and a provincial administration line (with Provincial Public Works Department), Residences, Regencies, (Sub-)Districts and villages. Just like the colonial struggle between Civil Public Works and the Civil Service – which was part of the ongoing struggle between sectional and hierarchical departments – there is still rivalry between *PU* and the Civil Service (*Dalam Negeri*), but since the triumphing of the engineers with the 1885 ruling (see **Chapter 6**) their relationship has not fundamentally changed. It was rather the case that all of this served to consolidate the position existing between irrigation engineers and civil servants. The technocracy of the New Order strongly resembled the technocracy of the colonial order under the Ethical Policy (see **Chapter 8**). Just like the Indies Civil Public Works Department (especially in the 1885-1900 period), *PU* reflected something of a state within a state structure. It is a powerful Department able, to a large degree, to determine what happens in the field of public works. It was the development activities after independence, together with the wide foreign support, which served to make *PU* powerful. When there is conflict concerning irrigation and other affairs in the field of public works it is technologists who have the upper hand. Sometimes problems arise because the dividing up of responsibilities is not always clearly organised. At village level it is the position of the *Ulu-Ulu* in relation to village administration that has, for instance, again been problematic.

4. Recent new developments sprang forth from discussions in the 1990s on the matter of irrigation. These talks were very similar to the kinds of debates continued in the colonial era. Big projects or small projects and support provided to village systems? It was (and probably remained) a discussion that passes through the history of colonial irrigation activities like a main thread. Preference was often given to big projects (especially by the lobby of engineers) but the alternative smouldered under the surface and flared up when problems arose. As far as the 1995 improvement programme for village irrigation is concerned we can see similarities to the situation around 1900. In 1905 the man who was then Director of Civil Public Works distributed a circular in favour of supporting *desa* works. This move was made because one of the biggest irrigation projects of the colonial era – the Solo Valley project (see **Chapter 8**) – had just failed. In the 1990s the results of the widespread efforts were disappointing which once again led to a shift in emphasis in favour of smaller works. In that respect it would indeed seem that history has been repeating itself.

The debate surrounding absolute or proportional water distribution is another case in point. Towards the end of the nineteenth century Civil Public Works experimented with both methods in the Pekalen and Pateguan areas. Ultimately the advantages of the relevant water control rulings were combined in the Pemali ruling with the independent water master being taken from the one system and the absolute distribution from the other one (see **Chapters 5 and 6**). Later the Romijn gate became an important technological innovation in this connection (see **Chapter 10**); something that might be compared to the computer-guided (absolute) distribution system of today. However, just as had been the case with smaller works, proportional water distribution – and thereby also the Balinese *subaks* – remained an attractive alternative in the background and

[28] The turnover policy also revealed colonial parallels, e.g. like when it came to the transferring of large works in progress to the Provinces.

the discussion surrounding this once again became topical, for instance in the 1930s (see **Chapter 10**). In fact controlling water on the basis of given river areas, after construction projects in such areas and even in relation to different river areas had been carried out (controlling after constructing!), goes back to 1870 when a committee including De Bruyn suggested creating such an organisation and forming irrigation districts (see **Chapter 4**). The later Irrigation Divisions, reactivated after independence, constituted the first implementation of this idea.[29]

The main problem in the field of irrigation in Indonesia has always been that of attuning national irrigation services to local rice cultivation requirements, in which we recognize the top-down versus bottom-up debate. The right balance always needs to be found between city and village, between modern technology and traditional methods and between engineers and farmers (for practical solutions, see **Figures 8-10**). This issue, which already existed before the Dutch started focusing upon irrigation in their colony, still constitutes a major challenge for the country's present society. In this connection new (or different) approaches have been and are experimented with in which the participation of farmers remains central. What precisely the best relationship is between a national and a basic level will depend on the context, especially the political-economic context. In many ways the New Order was just a continuation of the colonial order but even then changes have also been seen there as well. Consequently, new forms of approach to irrigation developed, a process that gained momentum after the 1997 political reforms and in which the 2004 Water Law was a highlight.

5. Finally, continuity has also been revealed in the problems surrounding the Solo Valley. The new authorities adopted the same line of approach as that taken in the colonial era after the big project designed to improve the situation in the area had been halted. The idea was to have smaller works and large reservoirs. A general plan failed to be executed despite the availability of new plans and the results of this are clear. In spite of all the post-colonial improvements, including the creation of a new and large reservoir, the Solo Valley today remains one of the few areas in Java where water management is clearly insufficiently organised. Similarly an integral plan to develop the Solo river region as a whole – proposed in one of the new plans – has not come off either, partly because the provincial dividing of the area formed a barrier. Recently however, the preparations for a new master plan found a new context and purpose in the form of river basin management, which might well abolish the political problem. Top-down or a participation approach, large or small-scale activities, absolute or proportional control: these are all questions that could come to fruition in the development of the Solo under the new management structure. From being, in part, a backward area it could become a "test case" for new policy and possibly even a show case for the future (post-modern) Indonesia. The thread of the colonial past might even be picked up if, when new plans are drawn up, the Solo report of 1900 is used as source of knowledge and inspiration (see **Note 25** of this chapter).

---

[29] The environmental problems are not new either and were a matter of contention (in the form of deforestation being cited as a possible reason for the decreasing rainfall) even before the Public Works Bureau was established in 1854. Already, from the events surrounding the Sampean weir in the nineteenth century, the relationship between population growth, deforestation and increased flooding had been demonstrated. Around 1900 it was concluded in the Pemali area that falling water levels could be attributed to deforestation. Appeals to reforest regions has an equally long history. (See **Chapters 3, 4 and 5**).

Appendices

A Overview map of the irrigation areas in Java and Madura around 1940

B Sawa acreage of the governmental land areas in Java and Madura

C Annual government expenditure on irrigation works in Java and Madura

D Annual government expenditure on Indies irrigation works

E Rentability of the irrigation works in the governmental land areas in Java and Madura

F Numbers of civil engineers employed by the Indies Civil Public Works Department

G Relative government spendings devoted to public works and other policy areas in the Indies

H Inflation-corrected government spendings on public works in the Indies

I Justification of the four case choices

J Directors of the Department of Civil Public Works and the Department of Transport and Public Works

K Agricultural acreage in the governmental land areas of Java and Madura 1870-1910, according to field type

L Government land rice production in Java and Madura 1870-1910

M Sugar cane acreage and sugar production in Java 1870-1913

N Annual government expenditure on large and small irrigation works in Java 1890-1909

Note:
Civil Public Works Report = *Verslag BOW*
Colonial Report = *Koloniaal Verslag*

Appendix A

Overview map of the irrigation areas in Java and Madura around 1940

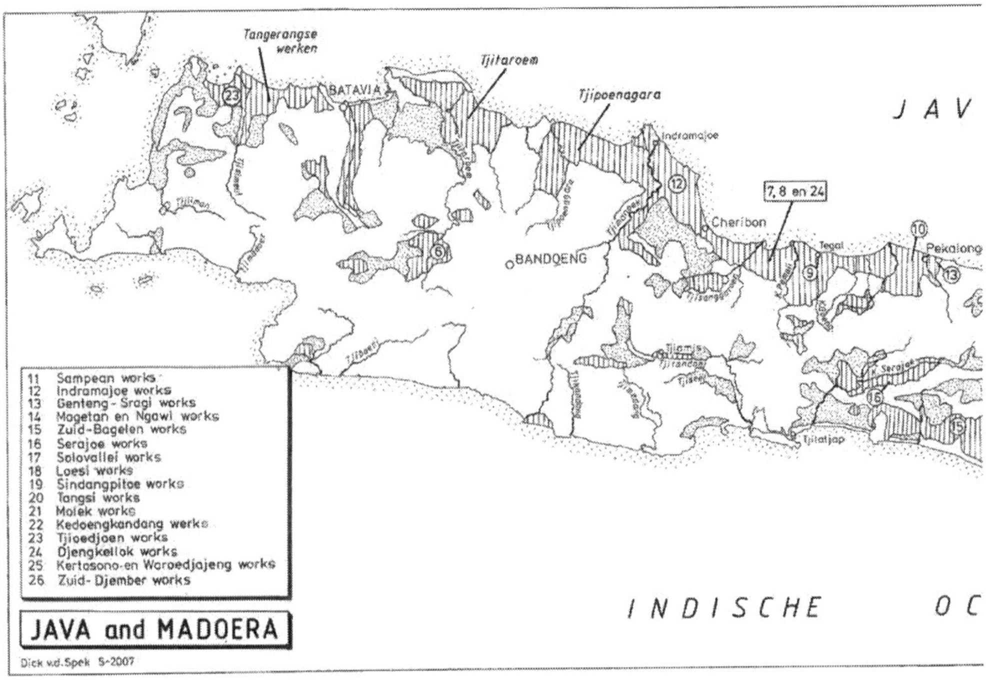

Map of the irrigation areas in Java and Madoera around 1940.

Source: Ravesteijn and Kop (2008)

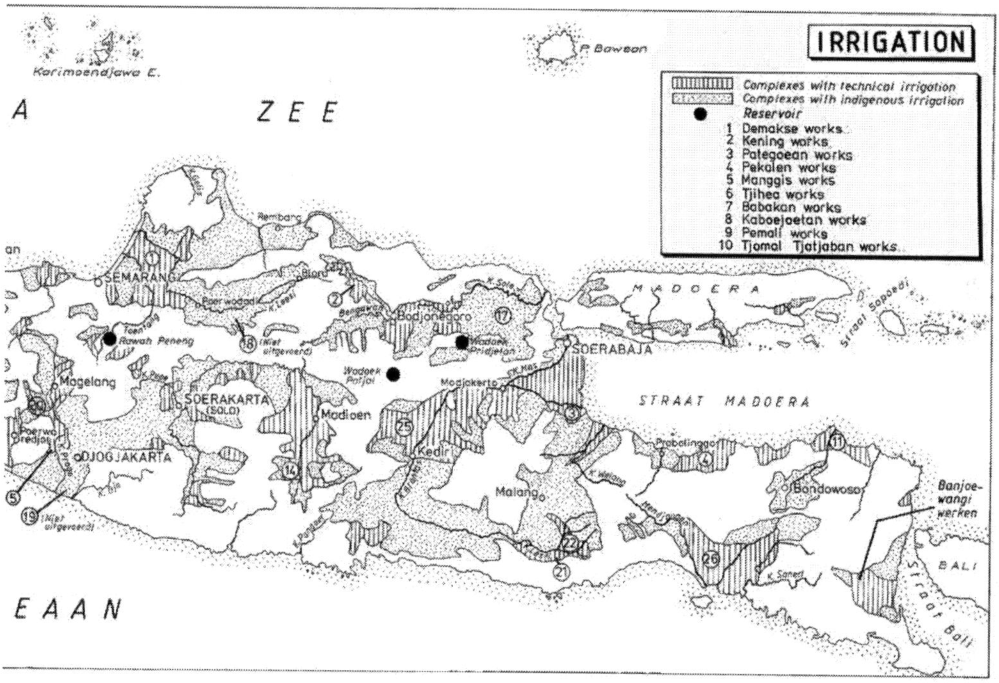
IRRIGATION
Complexes with technical irrigation
Complexes with indigenous irrigation
Reservoir
1 Demakse works
2 Kening works
3 Pategoean works
4 Pekalen works
5 Manggis works
6 Tjihea works
7 Babakan works
8 Kaboejoetan works
9 Pemali works
10 Tjomal Tjatjaban works
Karimoendjawa E.
P. Bawean
A
Z E E
E A A N
SEMARANG
Rembang
Blora
Poerwodadi
Bodjonegoro
Rawah Peneng
Wadoek Patjal
Wadoek Pridjetan
SOERABAJA
M A D O E R A
Straat Sapoedi
STRAAT MADOERA
Magelang
SOERAKARTA (SOLO)
Madioen
Modjokerto
Poerworedjo
DJOGJAKARTA
Kedir
Malang
Probolinggo
Bondowoso
Banjoe-wangi werken
BALI
Straat Bali

Appendix B

Sawa acreage of the governmental land areas in Java and Madura (in 1000 hectares)

Year	Total sawa acreage*	Acreage under modern irrigation**	Percentage
1895	2,365.4	50	
1896	-	60	
1897	-	70	
1898	-	80	
1899	-	90	
1900	2,450.1	100	4.1
1901	2,460.4	110	4.5
1902	2,456.8	120	4.9
1903	2,449.0	130	5.3
1904	2,452.5	140	5.7
1905	2,457.7	150	6.1
1906	2,463.3	160	6.5
1907	2,488.7	170	6.8
1908	2,502.7	180	7.2
1909	2,516.7	190	7.6
1910	2,530.7	200	7.9
1911	2,544.7	232	9.1
1912	2,558.7	264	10.3
1913	2,572.7	296	11.5
1914	2,586.7	328	12.7
1915	2,600.7	360	13.8
1916	2,614.7	391	15
1917	2,628.7	423	16.1
1918	2,642.7	455	17.3
1919	2,656.7	487	18.4
1920	2,670.7	519	19.5
1921	2,684.7	551	20.5
1922	2,699.6	583	21.6
1923	2,732.1	614	22.5
1924	2,747.7	646	23.5
1925	2,745.5	678	24.7
1926	2,767.1	704	25.5
1927	2,770.7	730	26.4
1928	2,756.0	757.7	27.4
1929	2,782.3	814.7	29.3
1930	2,840.2	883.4	31.1
1931	2,859.1	934.2	32.6
1932	2,864.5	944.3	33
1933	2,857.5	987.6	34.5
1934	2,881.0	993.1	34.5
1935	2,903.2	1054.2	36.4
1936	2,964.9	1154.7	39

* These figures are based on land area estimates for the 1907-1920 period. As of 1920 the figures are accurate but figures given for the years prior to that have simply been reconstructed as well as possible.
** The quantities up until 1928 are estimates based on data from the Civil Public Works Report in which 1900, 1910 and 1919 figures were points of departure.

Source: Happé (1936: II. 26)

Appendix C

Annual government expenditure on irrigation works in Java and Madura (in guilders)*

Year	Surveys/construction**		Repair and maintenance**	Private contributions	Total government expenditure
1895	129,897	*300,392*	*128 ...*		558,289
1896	135,540	*823,469*	*164 ...*		1,123,009
1897	154,226	*451,302*	*177 ...*		782,528
1898	125,319	*676,879*	*195 ...*		1,001,170
1899	129,291	*695,934*	*213 ...*		1,034,253
1900	116,565	*398,669*	*226 ...*		741,234
1901	111,928	*1,337,495*	*256 ...*		1,705,423
1902	131,177	*1,792,342*	*295 ...*		2,218,519
1903	156,778	*1,577,190*	*331 ...*		2,064,968
1904	164,591	*1,669,565*	*370 ...*		2,204,156
1905	171,971	*1,404,247*	*404 ...*		1,980,218
1906	195,834	*1,345,840*	*440 ...*		1,981,674
1907	228,918	*1,668,074*	*480 ...*		2,376,992
1908	239,971	1,848,124	378,728		2,466,823
1909	234,509	1,860,624	444,769		2,538,902
1910	244,829	2,885,349	471,136		3,601,314
1911	264,840	3,878,741	451,147		4,594,728
1912	333,527	3,917,606	583,059		4,834,192
1913	336,270	5,355,885	845,182		6,537,337
1914	387,896	5,099,913	784,999		6,272,808
1915	352,826	4,014,009	1,193,239		5,560,074
1916	400,793	4,818,852	1,644,809		6,864,454
1917	304,607	5,769,253	1,488,277		7,562,137
1918	325,351	6,722,567	1,613,021		8,660,939
1919	283,537	6,990,994	1,973,307	166,056	9,081,782
1920	356,793	7,545,443	2,390,956	77,043	10,216,149
1921	344,169	7,663,923	2,249,615	170,269	10,087,438
1922	301,758	5,080,059	2,505,407	210,749	7,676,475
1923	245,220	4,892,284	3,045,180	269,096	7,913,588
1924	257,622	4,880,666	2,447,954	323,687	7,262,555
1925	266,885	6,574,534	2,566,655	2,185,742	7,222,332
1926	236,242	6,796,989	1,977,752	2,561,616	6,449,367
1927	198,641	7,192,349	1,964,702	656,382	8,699,310
1928		7,321 ...	2,929 ...	1,181 ...	9,069 ...
1929		7,417 ...	3,835 ...	381 ...	10,871 ...
1930		7,025 ...	2,959 ...	682 ...	9,302 ...
1931		5,313 ...	2,787 ...	454 ...	7,646 ...
1932		2,716 ...	2,345 ...	353 ...	4,708 ...
1933		2,138 ...	2,389 ...	311 ...	4,216 ...
1934		1,646 ...	2,282 ...	50 ...	3,278 ...
1935		1,264 ...	2,179 ...	35 ...	3,408 ...
1936				183 ...	3,505 ...

* The table is based on data extracted from the Civil Public Works Report.

** For the years 1895-1907 only the total amount spent on construction, repair and maintenance is known. These separate sums have been estimated on the basis of data from the 1908-1927 period. The sums spent on the terminated Solo Valley works are not included in these figures.

Source: Happé (1939: II. 25)

Appendix D

Annual government expenditure on Indies irrigation works (in guilders)*

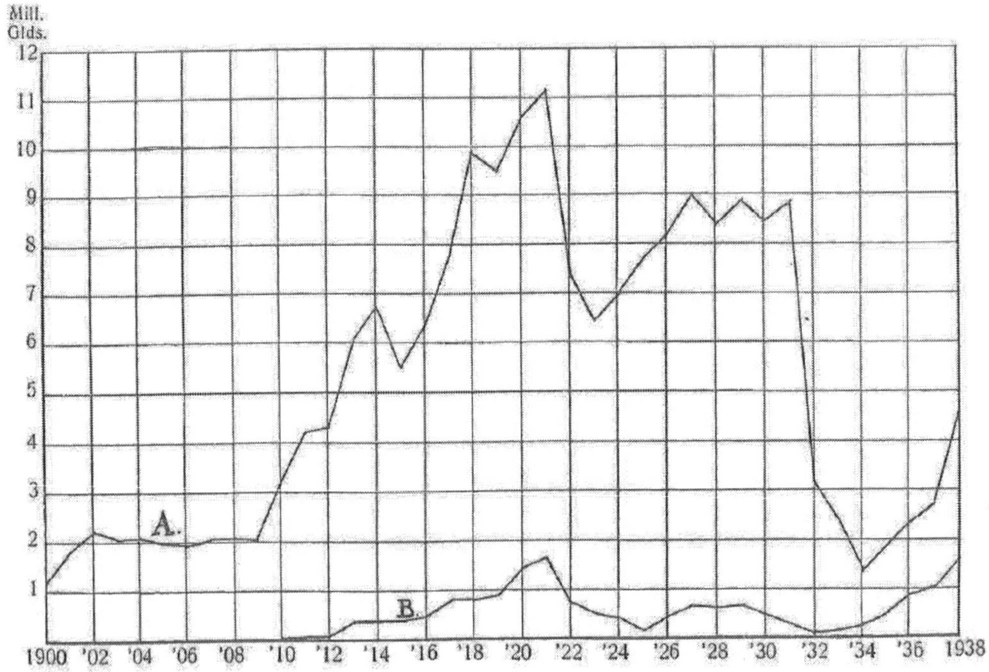

A Spendings on irrigation works in Java

B Spendings on irrigation works in the Outlying Regions, especially Sumatra and Sulawesi

* Sums of money for research and construction of works

Source: Van der Meulen (1940: 149)

Appendix E

Rentability of the irrigation works in the governmental land areas in Java and Madura*

Year	Government spendings on irrigation (in guilders)**	Land rent increases (in 1000 guilders)***/%	Indirect increases in land incomes/%	Total land incomes: the sum of the percentages	Average rent from the Indies fixed debt (%)
1901	14,643,188				
1902	16,861,707	*280*			
1903	18,926,675	*420*			
1904	21,130,831	*560*			
1905	23,111,049	*700*			
1906	25,092,723	*840*			
1907	27,469,715	*980*			
1908	29,936,538	*1120*			
1909	32,475,440	*1260*			
1910	36,076,754	1400 3.88	1700 4.72	8.60	3.06
1911	40,671,482	1540 3.80	1972 4.86	8.66	3.05
1912	45,505,674	1680 3.69	2244 4.93	8.62	3.04
1913	52,043,011	1820 3.50	2516 4.83	8.33	3.03
1914	58,315,819	1960 3.36	2788 4.78	8.14	3.03
1915	63,875,893	2100 3.29	3060 4.78	8.07	3.02
1916	70,740,347	2240 3.17	3323 4.71	7.88	3.84
1917	78,302,484	2380 3.04	3595 4.60	7.64	4.22
1918	86,963,423	2520 2.90	3867 4.45	7.35	3.69
1919	96,045,205	2680 2.79	4139 4.31	7.10	4.34
1920	106,261,354	2800 2.64	4411 4.15	6.79	5.00
1921	116,348,792	3248 2.79	4683 4.03	6.82	5.06
1922	124,025,267	3696 2.98	4955 4.00	6.98	5.89
1923	131,938,855	4144 3.14	5219 3.96	7.10	5.32
1924	139,201,410	4592 3.39	5419 3.89	7.18	5.71
1925	146,423,742	5040 3.44	5763 3.93	7.37	5.51
1926	152,873,109	5474 3.58	5984 3.92	7.50	5.56
1927	161,572,419	5922 3.66	6205 3.84	7.50	5.18
1928	170,641 ...	6370 3.74	6440 3.78	7.52	5.41
1929	181,512 ...	6818 3.75	6924 3.81	7.56	5.33
1930	190,814 ...	7266 3.80	7509 3.93	7.73	5.36
1931	198,460 ...	7714 3.88	7942 4.00	7.88	5.48
1932	203,168 ...	8162 4.02	8027 3.95	7.97	5.10
1933	207,384 ...	8596 4.16	8395 4.05	8.21	4.98
1934	210,662 ...	9044 4.30	8399 4.00	8.30	4.26
1935	214,070 ...	9492 4.43	8961 4.18	8.61	4.03
1936	217,595 ...	9856 4.53	9815 4.51	9.04	3.98

* The table is based on information from the Civil Public Works Report.
** The spendings on the creation of the suspended Solo Valley works are not included.
*** The italicised sums are estimates.

Source: Happé (1939: II. 26)

Appendix F

Numbers of civil engineers employed by the Indies Civil Public Works Department

Year	Delft engineers	Foreign engineers	Engineers from Bandung	Total
1878	60	-	-	60
1888	71	-	-	71
1898	92	-	-	92
1908	109	-	-	109
1913	155	15	-	170
1918	181	20	-	201
1923	195	56	-	251
1928	207	17	30	254
1930	204	14	45	263
1932	191	14	47	252
1934	154	10	38	202

Source: Limburg (1936: 428-429)

Appendix G

Relative government spendings devoted to public works and other policy areas in the Indies (in percentages)*

Policy terrains	1871	1881	1895	1905	1913	1921
Justice	4.2	4.4	4.9	4.5	3.2	2.3
Finance	7.8	8.9	11.7	17.5	19.6	17.0
Income tax service	*3.1*	*3.1*	*2.8*	-	-	-
Pensions etc.	*3.6*	*4.4*	*7.6*	*8.3*	*5.6*	*4.7*
Civil Service	45.3	32.0	22.9	20.1	12.2	9.8
Administration	*7.3*	*6.4*	*9.2*	*7.9*	*3.8*	*1.8*
Cultures	*30.1*	*19.7*	*6.0*	*4.0*	-	-
Education	1.7	2.4	3.4	3.7	4.1	3.5
European	*0.7*	*1.0*	*1.7*	*2.0*	*1.7*	n/a
Javanese	*0.3*	*0.8*	*1.0*	*1.1*	*1.9*	n/a
Health Care	0.8	1.3	1.6	1.7	1.9	1.7
Mining/ industry	4.6	4.2	6.1	7.5	3.4	2.5
Public works**	8.5	17.1	20.4	18.5	37.7	39.2
Railways	*0.7*	*6.8*	*8.1*	*8.9*	*11.3*	*16.4*
War Department	19.2	22.0	21.5	21.7	12.3	11.5
Naval Department	7.9	7.7	6.0	5.6	5.6	4.4
Rent etc.	-	-	1.4	-	-	8.1
Total	100.0	100.0	100.0	100.0	100.0	100.0

* For the years 1871-1895 the figures given are estimates and for the year 1921 the figures are provisional.
** Apart from relating to irrigation works this also relates to road, bridge, public building and government company (such as railways, post and telegraph) expenditures.

Source: Booth (1990: 215, 224)

Appendix H

Inflation-corrected government spendings on public works in the Indies (in millions of guilders)

Year	Irrigation works	Port authority works	Post and transport	Rail and tram transport	Year	Irrigation works	Port authority works	Post and transport	Rail and tram transport
1871	0.1	-	0.1	-	1906	0.5	0.1	0.8	7.5
1872	0.1	-	0.0	-	1907	0.3	0.1	0.3	6.0
1873	0.2	0.1	0.1	-	1908	0.5	0.5	-	8.0
1874	0.2	-	0.0	-	1909	0.2	0.6	0.5	6.9
1875	0.8	-	0.0	0.5	1910	0.2	0.7	0.4	9.2
1876	0.9	0.1	-	4.0	1911	0.3	1.7	1.5	14.3
1877	1.2	5.7	0.0	3.8	1912	0.3	4.0	1.8	16.6
1878	0.9	0.9	-	3.3	1913	0.3	7.7	3.9	38.8
1879	0.3	4.0	0.0	6.8	1914	0.2	13.0	2.0	39.4
1880	0.4	3.4	-	8.1	1915	0.2	13.0	1.5	34.7
1881	0.4	2.7	-	7.9	1916	0.2	10.2	2.5	32.9
1882	2.0	2.1	-	8.1	1917	0.2	8.1	4.8	30.0
1883	1.7	1.7	0.0	5.8	1918	0.4	10.0	6.1	26.0
1884	1.3	1.5	0.1	7.1	1919	0.3	13.1	8.1	37.0
1885	1.1	1.3	-	8.0	1920	4.7	20.3	11.0	54.4
1886	1.1	0.4	-	6.5	1921	5.8	37.1	15.9	69.6
1887	1.1	0.4	0.1	4.1	1922	3.8	25.1	7.9	64.7
1888	1.4	-	1.1	7.1	1923	3.2	15.6	2.6	54.8
1889	1.6	0.3	0.0	6.2	1924	3.5	4.4	1.3	22.8
1890	1.6	0.3	-	7.1	1925	3.9	2.0	1.2	27.1
1891	1.8	0.1	-	9.1	1926	3.8	3.5	6.6	16.7
1892	1.5	4.0	0.8	8.9	1927	3.1	2.3	3.0	15.1
1893	1.9	0.4	-	6.8	1928	3.3	1.9	4.0	21.6
1894	2.9	0.6	-	6.6	1929	3.7	2.1	6.0	19.8
1895	3.2	0.3	-	8.8	1930	3.2	2.8	6.2	14.8
1896	3.4	0.1	-	8.9	1931	2.0	0.7	2.9	12.5
1897	3.0	-	0.3	9.4	1932	0.9	0.1	1.4	2.2
1898	3.4	-	-	14.0	1933	0.7	0.1	1.5	0.9
1899	1.2	-	-	10.7	1934	0.4	0.1	1.2	0.3
1900	0.8	-	-	10.5	1935	0.6	0.2	0.7	0.4
1901	0.8	0.2	0.8	9.3	1936	0.5	0.2	0.8	0.4
1902	1.3	0.3	-	16.4	1937	0.5	0.2	3.1	1.0
1903	1.1	0.2	2.2	19.6	1938	0.4	0.6	1.2	1.7
1904	1.2	0.3	-	9.5	1939	0.6	2.0	1.3	2.3
1905	0.8	0.1	1.2	9.3	1940	0.6	1.9	1.3	-

Source: Mansvelt and Creutzberg (Vol. 3 1977: Table 2)

Appendix I

Justification of the four case choices

The idea of examining in detail the Sampean weir and the Pemali, Solo Valley and Tangerang Works was something that evolved during the course of background research in conjunction with this study. Basically it would seem impossible to create a convincing argument for why these particular irrigation works are so suitable for describing and analysing the development of modern irrigation in Java. The four cases – selected from over 400 – should be particularly representative. However, I shall endeavour to show why the number of cases suitable for study was in fact limited and why my choices certainly were not bad ones.

The 1925 Civil Public Works Report was the last one to give a general overview of irrigation works or of irrigation areas: some 405 irrigation areas which fell into four states. The majority of these irrigation areas had permanent works: 266 (in thirteen regions works were not completed). These works covered 1,465,357 *bouws*[1]. In 34 areas works were under construction (21 of which constituted new irrigation areas). In the remaining areas the works projects were predominantly still in the research or preparation stages and in a few instances this had to do with extending modern existing systems. The smallest report summarised ten works that were completed on paper but where "construction work" had been "temporarily abandoned".

The size criterion was also a great help. Large projects (viewed here as those encompassing more than 10,000 *bouws*, in the text I adhere to a general limit of 1000 *bouws*) comprised in the 1925 report less than 10% of the entire project range of 49 (of which 28 had been completed, six were underway, eleven were being considered and five had been rejected – one of those 28 was related to another project that was being executed in 1925).

If one is to select projects from different periods one then has to divide the period up into phases. Let us just see what the periods were that were witnessed by engineers. If we take the history of events represented by Van Sandick (1912b[2]) then we may supply the following years and data. 1. up until 1872: inland or random irrigation, as of 1832 structural works and the intervention of engineers; 2. 1872-1888: technical surveys and the construction of irrigation works; 3. 1888-? (according to Van Sandick: 1912): technological water management; 4. after 1912 (?): agricultural management. In his speech on "A Hundred Years of Irrigation" Vlugter (1949) distinguished three phases: 1. until 1990: the pioneering phase; 2. 1900-1925: increasing building activity; 3. 1925-1950: breaking away from fixed forms and perfectionism. Ankum (1984 and 1988) gives a postcolonial period division: 1. until 1832: non-technological irrigation; 2. 1832-±1920: the construction period with, in 1890, the first "master plan"; 3. from ±1920: technological management.

Period division is evidently a function of the present: the further one goes in time when reflecting, the longer the pioneering phases appear to have been and the rougher the period divisions become. In the above-given phases the turning points seen in the history of modern irrigation are many: 1872, ±1890, 1900, 1912 and 1925. The actual definitions of the periods are, however, confusing[3]. It is thus difficult to extract from this a usable phase division. From my own research it is the 1885/1890 period that emerges as a turning point. In 1885 the Indies government established a ruling that gave the engineers the go-ahead and this

[1] One *bouw* = 0.7 hectares.

[2] I refer here to (for instance) articles written by various colonial engineers that are referred to in **Chapter 1**.

[3] Irrigation expert, H.J. Schoemaker, makes no general period divisions: he takes the rain observations of Melchior from the middle of the last century and uses that to mark the beginning of modern irrigation. From that point onwards he conceives of history as one continuous flow (personal report, July 1995).

was followed, in 1890, by the General Irrigation Plan for Java (Ankum's master plan, see the 1892 Civil Public Works Report).

From the 1925 Civil Public Works Report it emerges that in the pre-1885/90 era no major irrigation projects had been realised (but there had been smaller works: the irrigation of the Rebuk area of 1931 *bouws* created in 1860 and the Kenning irrigation project, 3440 *bouws*, completed in the 1989-1890 period). Five projects were begun at that time though: the Sampean Works (1875-1901), the Demak Works (1853-1894), the works in the Brantas Delta (the Sidoarjo Delta area, 1857-1919) and the irrigation activity in the Oosterslokkan and Westerslokkan areas (of, respectively, around 1750 to 1900 and around 1800-1900). The last two works took the form of canals and so cannot be regarded as samples of modern irrigation works (**see Chapter 3**). The other three projects did, however, qualify as that. The reason why it took so long for the construction work to be completed was because these three projects all started up as headworks in the form of: the weirs in the Sampean, the weir at Glapan and the movable weir at Lengkong (the first of its kind). Later, when people began creating entire irrigation systems, these headworks were extended.

Of all these headworks it was notably the Sampean weir that drew attention. Construction work on that did not begin in 1875, as stated in the 1925 Civil Public Works Report, but rather as early as in 1832! In 1914 when the first project description of the (history) programme produced by Lamminga appeared in the Royal Irrigation Engineers' journal (Voorduin 1914, see **Chapter 2**), "The Engineer" editorial devoted attention to the Sampean weir (*Bladzijden* 1914 and 1915; previously the weir had been mentioned by Van Sandick 1912b and Lamminga 1910). In 1932 the weir was again given publicity in connection with its 100th anniversary (Rietveld 1932). The weir was also given an important place in Vlugter's (1949) historical overview. This does not mean to say that its construction amounted to a "success story": it constituted half a century of hard labour. Still, and perhaps precisely because of this, (it was heavy going for the pioneers) it would seem that of all the old irrigation works projects it was the development of the Sampean weir that was to become the engineers' showpiece.

If we look further to the period after 1885/90 then we see that the range of works significantly diminishes on the basis of the referred to irrigation plan of 1890 which accounted for nineteen projects. Later a further seven projects were added. By around 1920 almost all of these projects had been completed (this is also a date referred to by Ankum). If we take size as a criterion then it appears that there were, in all, fifteen projects that exceeded the 10,000 *bouws* mark. This number can be further reduced by consulting Lamminga. What did he consider to be the important works? For his description of modern irrigation he thought chiefly of ten works (see the overview of Lamminga's study programme below).

Lamminga himself was involved in the first three projects. The first project listed – constituting one of the five big works – was even his most important one. What might have looked like self-glorification on the part of Lamminga was later rectified by the engineering community: his works had set the trend. The Pemali Works is something we simply cannot ignore (alluded to by, for instance, Vlugter 1949).

In view of his intentions it would seem to be no mere coincidence that Lamminga went for successful projects (with the exception of the Sampean Works, but this was a project that he allowed to start later on). There were other less successful projects as well. The Civil Public Works Report of 1925 lists no less than five large works plans that were aborted in the execution phase. Covering 223,000 *bouws* the project in the Solo Valley constituted the biggest of these five projects and it was part of the General Irrigation Plan. There was no other project that was going to get the colonial pens writing again. After its termination, in 1898, a huge discussion commenced on the project which, with all its ups and downs, had lasted the whole colonial period. In the first period the ten-yearly "The Engineer" register

(1895-1905) alone made many references to it. Indeed, the writings on the Solo Valley Works were considerable. There was the research report of 1900 (Telders et al.) produced by a state commission which, according to Ankum (1984: 10) constituted a good indication of the level of irrigation know-how at that particular time. The project was also referred to by Van Sandick (1912b) and Vlugter (1949) and (though not included in the considerations) by Happé (1939).

What was striking about Lamminga's choices was that he only included projects in Central and East Java: that had to do with the fact that the choices were made in (or around) 1909. The General Irrigation Plan had no plans drawn up for West Java. All the big projects there were embarked on later. According to that same 1925 Civil Public Works Report there were eleven large projects being contemplated in 1925, five of which were in West Java. The biggest of those projects was the one in the Tangerang plain. De Vos (1941) mentioned this project as being one of the three. The Tangerang Works were also referred to by Van der Meulen (1940) and Vlugter (1949).

Despite the fact that I maintain that the four projects picked out here have constituted a good choice, others could also have been considered. Instead of dealing with the Sampean weir I could just as well have looked at the weir at Glapan or at the movable weir in Lengkong. The Krawang Works would have been a good alternative for the Tangerang Works. Ultimately the reader is able to judge for himself what might have been best because these, and other (alternative) projects, are given plenty of attention in the sidelines of this study (in **Boxes**).

Lamminga's study programme*

Works	Residency	Size (in bouws)	Construction period
1 Pemali Works	Pekalongan	43,745	1893-1903
2 Babakan and Kabuyutan Works	Pekalongan	4,516	1890-1902
3 Comal-Cacaban Works	Pekalongan	37,402	1896-1906
4 Manggis Works	Kedu	6,110	1850-1908
5 Tangsi Works	Kedu	3,866 (2,875)	-1909
6 Sampean Works	Besuki	15,387	1875-1901
7 Kedungkandang and Molek Works	Pasuruan	12,604	1901-1915
8 Irrigation works for the districts Warujayeng and Kertosono	Kediri	20,315	1903-1911
9 Singomerto Works	Banyumas	7,441	1880-1919
10 Banjaran Works	Banyumas	1,210	1910: in execution

Sources: Voorduin (1914: 2), supplemented with data from the Civil Public Works Report (1910 and 1925).

Appendix J

Directors of the Bureau of Public works, the Department of Civil Public Works and the Department of Transport and Public Works

Directors of the (Civil) Public Works Bureau and Department 1854-1934*

G.H. Uhlenbeck	04-11-1854 until 13-04-1861
Ir H. de Bruyn	18-04-1861 until 10-01-1868
Ir P.J.G. Beyerinck	30-01-1868 until 03-02-1870
Ir W.H.F.H. van Raders	03-02-1870 until 10-08-1874
Ir H. de Bruyn	10-08-1874 until 02-06-1877
H.J. Bool	05-06-1877 until 23-04-1879
T.C.J. Kroesen	23-04-1879 until 06-1884
B.Th. de Bruyn (interim director)	06-1884 until 28-12-1884
H.L. Janssen van Raay	28-12-1884 until 05-06-1889
Ir M.J. van Bosse	05-06-1889 until 17-09-1892
Ir G. van Houten	17-09-1892 until 25-06-1898
Ir J.E. de Meyier	25-06-1898 until 07-10-1901
Ir H.P. Mensinga	07-10-1901 until 15-06-1905
Ir A.P. Melchior	15-06-1905 until 05-08-1908
Ir W.B. van Goor	05-08-1908 until 18-02-1911
Ir J. Homan van der Heide	18-02-1911 until 26-09-1914
Ir P.J. Ott de Vries	26-09-1914 until 14-07-1920
Ir A.G. Allart	14-07-1920 until 30-05-1922
Ir J.W. de Bruijn Kops	30-05-1922 until 03-05-1925
Ir J. Blackstone	03-05-1925 until 06-09-1927
Ir E.H.M. Uljee	06-09-1927 until 03-05-1930
Mr Dr J.A.M. van Buuren	03-05-1930 until 31-12-1933

* The Department of Civil Public Works, established in 1866, was disbanded on 1st January 1934 and replaced by the Department of Transport and Public Works. This latter department also incorporated the Government Companies Department, established in 1908 from one of the Civil Public Works Divisions.

Note: "Ir" is the Dutch abbreviation for Engineer (± M.Sc.) and "Mr" stands for Master of Law.

Sources: ENI (1917: 715-728), Kielstra (1887: 128, 130, 135, 136), Creutzberg (1972: 732)

Directors of Transport and Public Works 1934-1942

Mr Dr J.A.M. van Buuren	01-01-1934 until 19-10-1936
Ir Ch.F. van Haeften	19-10-1936 until 14-07-1937
Ir C. Hillen	08-09-1937 until 26-03-1938
Ir Ch.F. van Haeften	26-03-1938 until 1942

Source: Creutzberg (1972: 733)

Appendix K

Agricultural acreage in the governmental land areas of Java and Madura, 1870-1910, according to field type (in bouws)

Year	Irrigated sawas* (total %)	Rain supplied sawas	Swamp sawas	Tegalans	Uneven ground areas	Total agricultural acreage
1870	1,302,396 (45%)	687,913	56,407	680,990	179,562	2,907,268
1880	1,493,137 (49%)	817,333	46,345	617,632	51,199	3,025,646
1885	1,677,717 (47%)	967,205	53,631	751,886	119,977	3,570,416
1890	1,692,355 (46%)	1,003,654	51,711	816,041	135,070	3,698,831
1895	1,753,201 (47%)	1,018,517	49,060	888,215	154,120	3,708,993
1900	1,776,015 (42%)	1,085,313	56,274	1,124,133	153,218	4,194,953
1905	1,821,269 (42%)	1,046,941	63,584	1,180,081	186,220	4,298,095
1910	1,953,838 (38%)	1,073,074	65,019	1,608,976	387,100	5,088,007

* The differences from the Happé figures (1939, see **Appendix B**) are, generally, a result of the fact that Happé based his facts on corrected figures (note: the figures given in **Appendix B** are in hectares).

Source: Colonial Report (1871/72-1911/12)

Elucidation

In 1870 the land area in use for agricultural purposes was 2,907,268 *bouws*. By 1900 that acreage had increased to 4,194,953 *bouws* which represented an extra 1,287,685 *bouws* or, 40.3% more. In that same period the acreage provided with irrigation facilities, Javanese and modern, rose from 1,302,396 to 1,776,015 *bouws* thus representing an increase of 473,619 *bouws* or 36.4%. The rise in the area of irrigated land was especially apparent in the period leading up to 1885 when it was 375,321 *bouws*. Despite the absolute increases the relative share of the land area irrigated went down slightly from 45% to 42%. If we further break this down into irrigated *sawas*, rain-dependent *sawas*, swamp *sawas*, *tegalans* (dry land) and land in irregular use then we can ascertain that there was a 36.4% surface increase in irrigated *sawa* land while rain-dependent sawas and *tegalans* rose by 57.8% and 65.1% respectively and the other land types fell by 0.2% and 14.6% respectively. The growth was thus to be seen predominantly in the rain-dependent *sawas* and in the non-irrigated *tegalans*.

Appendix L

Government land rice production in Java and Madura 1870-1910 (in pikols)*

Year	Irrigated sawas – 1st crop	Irrigated sawas – 2nd crop	Total irrigated sawa area (% of total)
1870	32,727,557	1,154,665	33,882,222 (73%)
1875	38,933,726	2,263,316	41,197,042 (73%)
1880	39,521,105	3,284,707	42,805,812 (69%)
1885	49,505,151	2,583,072	52,088,223 (72%)
1890	40,728,000	4,274,300	45,002,300 (74%)
1895	46,814,200	3,861,900	50,676,100 (69%)
1900	47,094,900	5,805,247	52,900,147 (68%)
1905	45,299,221	5,653,866	50,953,087 (68%)
1910	49,663,000	8,018,722	57,681,722 (68%)
Year	Rain sawas – 1st crop	Rain sawas – 2nd crop	Total rain sawas
1870	9,910,740	64,416	9,975,156
1875	11,665,598	43,869	11,709,467
1880	14,330,737	380,428	14,711,165
1885	15,709,609	164,074	15,873,683
1890	12,125,900	420,200	12,546,100
1895	17,615,800	686,100	18,301,900
1900	19,333,950	602,540	19,936,490
1905	16,543,380	971,744	17,515,124
1910	17,737,457	1,413,540	19,150,997
Year	Swamp sawas	Tegalans	Uneven land
1870	1,017,111	481,285	1,348,403
1875	1,294,383	1,210,628	741,191
1880	1,277,716	2,475,739	485,794
1885	1,227,230	1,690,734	1,401,927
1890	997,300	1,434,200	912,700
1895	1,160,200	2,128,900	1,137,800
1900	1,076,491	3,217,669	1,043,612
1905	1,378,153	3,685,043	1,044,764
1910	3,244,781	3,449,661	759,486
Year	Total	Average production level per bouw – planted	Average production level per bouw – successful
1870	46,104,177	21,7	22,43
1875	56,152,711	-	27,58
1880	61,756,226	-	-
1885	72,281,797	-	-
1890	60,892,600	-	-
1895	73,404,900	-	-
1900	78,174,409	24,19	24,99
1905	74,576,171	22,97	24,07
1910	84,286,647	26	-

* A pikol = 61.76 kilo
Source: Colonial Report (1871/72 – 1911/12)

Elucidation
The rice harvest rose in the 1870-1900 period from 46,104,177 to 78,174,409 *pikols*, thus representing an increase of 69.6%. The harvest share of the irrigated sawas rose from 33,882,222 to 52,900,147 *pikols* or, by 56.1%. The production per *bouw* went up in the period in question from 22.43 to 24.99 *pikols*.

Appendix M

Sugar cane acreage and sugar production in Java 1870-1913

Year	Area in sugar (in bouws)	Production in pikols	Average production per bouw
1870	54,176	2,440,000	± 45
1900	128,301	12,050,544	93.75
1913	204,778	23,736,184	116
Increase	873%	278%	158%

Source: Gonggrijp (1957: 121)

Elucidation

The sugar production rose from 2,440,000 *pikols* in 1870 to 12,050,544 *pikols* in 1900 thus representing a rise of 393.9%. This increase was partly attributable to the rise in acreage planted in sugar cane which went from 54,176 to 128,301 *bouws*, or, which rose by 136.9%. For a slightly smaller part the growth came as a result of the production rise per *bouw* which rose from 45 to 93.75 *pikols* or, by 108.3%.

Appendix N

Annual government expenditure on large and small irrigation works in Java 1890-1909 (in guilders)

Year	Large works	Small works	Total*
1890	832,000	-	832,000
1891	1,270,000	-	1,270,000
1892	1,547,000	-	1,547,000
1893	1,496,000	-	1,496,000
1894	896,617	-	896,617
1895	965,260	146,973	965,260
1896	889,628	233,381	1,123,009
1897	782,528	277,263	1,059,791
1898	871,879	234,957	1,106,836
1899	908,934	213,838	1,122,772
1900	606,556	214,188	820,744
1901	1,136,378	388,484	1,524,862
1902	1,647,900	377,248	2,025,148
1903	1,353,447	521,189	1,874,636
1904	1,405,412	494,552	1,899,964
1905	1,331,715	409,532	1,741,247
1906	1,378,650	351,723	1,730,373
1907	1,285,702	405,805	1,691,507
1908	1,205,600	624,547	1,830,147
1909	1,046,425	667,040	1,713,465

* Compare **Appendix C**. Sometimes the amounts correspond but sometimes they do not! The sums expended on the Solo Works are not included in this table either.

Sources: Van Bosse (1901: 360), Thal Larsen (1912: 930) (based upon the Civil Public Works Report)

Sources

Introductory note

In this study I have made use of materials drawn from a range of sources. In the first place unprinted and unpublished information has been used from the *National Archief* ("National Archives of the Netherlands", denoted as the "National Archives"; until 2002: *Algemeen Rijksarchief* [*ARA*] or "General State Archive") in The Hague where, for instance, the *Archief van het Ministerie van Koloniën, Oost-Indië* ("Archives of the Ministry of the Colonies, East Indies") and the *Verzameling Haringhuizen-Schoemaker* ("Haringhuizen-Schoemaker Collection") were consulted. A second archive where relevant information (printed and unprinted) was found was the *Archief van het Departement van Burgelijke Openbare Werken / Verkeer en Waterstaat* ("Archives of the Department of Civil Public Works / Traffic and Public Works") in Citeureup in Indonesia (in references this has been shortened to "*BOW* Archives", "*BOW*" being the abbreviation of the Department). That archive was not well inventoried. There I had to work with provisional inventories that had been created within the framework of courses given in archive management. For further archive documentation use was made of Creutzberg's sources publication (1972-1975). Another source for this study was the details drawn from a file created by L. Horst on W.J. van Blommestein's plans. The material contained there related predominantly to the post-1945 period.

Much information was derived from printed sources, in particular the *Verslag van het Departerment van Burgerlijke Openbare Werken* ("Report of the Department of Civil Public Works") in the Dutch East Indies (known as and referred to as the *Verslag BOW* ["Civil Public Works Report"] created for the different specific years that were dealt with; the years given refer to the years that the Report deals with, not to the year of publication). In the post-1892 period that report was published annually by the Civil Public Works Department. The section I consulted most often (usually Part V) was the one that dealt with irrigation, watering and dam control (after 1910 that was published in a separate volume). That report continued to be published until 1927. For the period after that I was able to make use of the annual publication of the *Voorlopige cijfers en gegevens omtrent de werkzaamheden van het Departement der Burgerlijke Openbare Werken* ("Provisional figures and data surrounding the activities of the Department of Civil Public Works", 1927-1933, also published for 1924; these reports were compiled at the request of the *Volksraad* ["People's Council"]) as well as *the Jaarverslag van het Departement van Verkeer en Waterstaat* ("Annual Report of the Department of Transport and Public Works", 1938-1940), both available in the National Archives ("Haringhuizen-Schoemaker Collection") and consulted there (denoted here as the *Voorlopige cijfers* and the *Jaarrapport* together with the relevant year). This collection also contains registers of the "Civil Public Work Reports" (under no. 98). A usable survey of these and several other sources in the National Archives is to be found in Schokkenbroek (1988).

Official reports brought out by the government, including several volumes of the report on the *Onderzoek naar de mindere welvaart der Inlandsche bevolking op Java en Madoera* ("Research into the Reduced Prosperity of the Indigenous Populations of Java and Madura", published by the *Mindere Welvaartscommissie* ["Lesser Welfare Committee"]), constituted other printed and useful sources. In addition I also made use of *Het Verslag van de Handelingen der Staten-Generaal* ("The Report on the Proceedings of the States-General") and the relevant appendices, especially the "Colonial Report" that started appearing annually after 1849 (these are referred to respectively as *Handelingen* and *Koloniaal Verslag*, together with the particular year in question; occasionally these quotations were taken from *De*

Ingenieur ["The Engineer"]). Another source consulted was the *Staatsblad van Nederlandsch-Indië* or *Indisch Staatsblad* ("Dutch East Indies Bulletin" or "Indies Gazette").

I furthermore made frequent use of book publications dating from the colonial era, especially concerning the non-technological aspects after that period. The technological/scientific journals frequently referred to were these: *De Ingenieur*, *De Waterstaats-Ingenieur* ("The Public Works Engineer") and the *Tijdschrift van het Koninklijk Instituut van Ingenieurs* ("Journal of the Royal Institute of Engineers"). A non-technical journal that provided me with much useful information was *De Indische Gids* ("The Indies Guide"). The various registers and bibliographies that served to simplify my searches through the different journals were notably these: the ten-yearly listings of *De Ingenieur* and the Hartmann (1895-1906), Schalker and Muller (1912-1928), Sepp (1934-1935) and Nagelkerke (1974) series.

One final source was that of the interviews carried out with engineers and other experts in the field of irrigation development, including sociologists, during the course of my two research trips to Indonesia in 1993 and 1995. During my travels I also collected many unpublished reports and brochures drawn up by government bodies and engineering bureaux on the subject of irrigation (i.e. projects) in the period after 1945.

Here below is a list of the various sources. The primary sources, printed as well as the unpublished reports and brochures and dating from the post-1945 period, are included in the literature list which, apart from these and other source listings, also includes my references to other writings. Insofar as published sources and other literature has (also) been consulted in the National and *BOW* Archives, reference has been included to the archive section (much the same applies to the items derived from the Horst file). Several unpublished reports that I only came across in the archives and to which I refer a number of times, are nonetheless mentioned in the literature list and are also linked to the archival material by means of cross-referencing.

Archival

National Archives (of the Netherlands)

(Archive of the) Ministry of the Colonies (East Indies)

- Resolutions 1886, 13-15 January, inventory no. 3922; Ruling on the control and supervision of public works and all the country's civil public works 1885.
- Mail report 1886, no. 71, Letter from Gallois, the Government's Secretary, to the Director of Civil Public Works, Buitenzorg, 23 January 1886 (no. 70/c).
- Resolutions 1898, 4-7 November, no. 76 (7 November), inventory no. 5320; Documents on the Solo Valley Works including:
  1. Memo on the Solo Valley Works derived from the commission established by governmental decree on 28 September 1897 and consisting of the 1st Class Chief Engineers L.H. Slinkers and H.P. Mensinga, 13 April 1898.
  2. Memo pertaining to the works for the irrigation of the Solo Valley written by the Director of Civil Public Works, J.E. Meyier, Batavia, 8 August 1898.
  3. Memo from Division A3 of the Ministry of the Colonies on the Solo Valley Works.
  4. Telegraph message from the Minister of the Colonies, J.T. Cremer, to the Governor-General in Batavia (no. 76).
- Mail report 1922, no. 841, Report concerning the flooding of the River Solo and the relevant damage caused by that flooding (see also nos. 874 and 981).
- Mail report 1924, no. 2686, Research into the possible resumption of the Solo Works (see also nos. 994, 2090 and 2815).

The J. Haringhuizen/H.J. Schoemaker Collection (list number 2.22.07)

No. 44	File XXXIX: Archivalia from the engineer A.G. Lamminga concerning the Solo Valley. 1899-1904. Including: Report concerning research conducted in connection with the plans for a possible resumption of the irrigation works in the Solo Valley produced by D.C.W. Snell (Surabaya, May 1928).
No. 54	File XLIX: Documents concerning the Tangerang Works in the Cisadane. 1916. With: An elucidation of the general improvement and expansion plans for the road network in the Tangerang plain compiled by the Chief Engineer and Head of the Works D. Snell (Weltevreden, 9 February 1925).
No. 62	File LVII: Various papers written by the engineer A.G. Lamminga relating to works in Tegal. 1896-1897. Including: Preliminary design for the improvement of water drainage and irrigation between Comal and Cacaban (Regency Pamalang and district Maribaya) 1895-1897, by Lamminga, with a postscript written in 1896.
No. 76	Documents by the engineer A.G. Lamminga on irrigation works in Pemali Brebes. 1902.
No. 79	Report concerning the Observation Service for the Surabaya Navigation Routes. The Hague, 1906.
Nos. 87-96	Reports published by the Department of Civil Public Works in the Dutch East Indies. 1892-1928.

No. 97 Provisional figures and data relating to the activities of the Department of Civil Public Works. 1924, 1926-1933, 1938.
Also containing: Annual Report of the Department of Transport and Public Works for the year 1938 (and not: Provisional figures for 1938).

No. 98 Indices and filings of the reports on Civil Public Works.

No. 111 Annual Reports of the Department of Transport and Public Works in the Dutch East Indies for the years 1939 and 1940, 1940, 1941. Contains the reports for 1939 and 1940.

No. 124 Various reports concerning the irrigation division Pemali-Comal by W.G. van der Meulen, 1919.

The A. Groothoff Collection (list number 2.21.076)

No. 165 File on a lecture given concerning irrigation and drainage improvements between the Comal and the Cacaban rivers (Pekalongan) 1905.
With various newspaper articles dealing with the matters of sugar cane cultivation reductions and food provision, 1919.

No. 167 Documents relating to irrigation in Java. 1916. Including: Rulings on the use and distribution of water in the Pemali area. Established according to a resolution by the resident of Pekalongan, dd. 25 January 1910 no. 593/34.

The W. Cool Collection (list number 2.21.038)

No. 93 Cool's incoming documents received in his position as member of the "Commission for the investigation of the economy of irrigation and drainage works" set up by the Royal Institute of Engineers 1932-1937.
Including various articles in/for *De Ingenieur* ("The Engineer") and the *Tijdschrift voor Economische Geographie* ("Journal for Economic Geography").

BOW Archives (Archives of the Department of Civil Public Works/Transport and Public Works in Citeureup, Indonesia)

E I-28 Documents on the Tangerang Works (1934). Including:

1. A memo concerning the improving of irrigation and drainage in the Tangerang plain, drawn up by the 3rd Class Engineers H.W. Dumont, L.J. Polderman and the engineer and Head of the Works, H. van Breen, Batavia, Weltevreden, February 1919.
2. Letters on the progress being made with the Tangerang Works:

- Letter from the Director of Civil Public Works addressed to the Head of the Irrigation Works in Bantam and Batavia in the Centre of Batavia, Batavia-Central, 3 October 1933 (no. E 10/3/7).
- Letter from the Director of Civil Public Works to the Head of the Irrigation Works in Bantam and Batavia in the Centre of Batavia, Batavia-Central, 30 October 1933 (no. E 10/3/16).
- Letter from the Head of Irrigation Works in Bantam and Batavia, F.G. Dumas, to the Director of Civil Public Works in Bandung, Batavia-Central, 11 December 1933 (no 3273/301).

- Letter from the Director of Transport and Public Works to the Head of the Irrigation Works in Bantam and Batavia in the Centre of Batavia, Batavia-Central, 19 January (no. E 10/1/5).
- Letter from the Head of the Tangerang Works, F.G. Dumas, to the Head of Provincial Public Works in Batavia, Batavia-Central, 28 June 1934 (no. 1039/301).

E II-92 Documentation on the Solo Valley Works (1898). Including:

1. Imprints of articles by Van Sandick (1898b and c) from "Insulinde" of 22 November 1898.
2. The irrigation of the Solo Valley. Memo for the Civil Service Director pertaining to the improving of water supplies and water drainage in the Solo Valley written by the Inspector of Cultures, Liefrinck, Batavia, 25 May 1892 (no. 41/c).

E VI-27 Documentation on the Pacal (waduk) Works (1940).
Including: Memo of Explanation to go with the project concerning the creation of part XV of the Pacal Works: "The conversion of a section of the main canal of the former Solo Valley Works between the K. Besuki (Pohkenep dessa) and the K. Mekuris (Barong dessa) into the Pacal main channel", written by Termeulen, the Section Engineer. Bojonegoro, 22 October 1934.

E VIII-99 Documentation relating to research into the efficient management of the Provincial Public Works Departments (1934).

- Letter from the Director of Transport and Public Works, J.A.M. van Buuren, to His Excellence the Governor-General of the Dutch East Indies, Bandung, 10 July, 1934 (no. E 59/1/1). With appendices.
- Letter from the Director of Civil Public Works, J.A.M. van Buuren, to the Governor of the Province of West Java in Batavia, the Governor of the Province of Central Java in Semarang and the Governor of the Province of East Java in Surabaya, Batavia-Central, 30 December 1932 (no. E 63/8/9).
- Letter from the Governor of the Province of East Java to the Head of Provincial Public Works of East Java in Surabaya, Surabaya 21 June 1933 (no. C 70/10/25).
- Letter from the Director of Civil Public Works, J.A.M. van Buuren, to the Governor of the Province of West Java in Batavia, Batavia-Central, 30 June 1933 (no. E 59/1/1).
- Letter from the Governor of the Province of East Java to the Director of Civil Public Works in Batavia-Central, Surabaya, 20 July 1933 (no. C 70/9/15).
- Letter from the Director of Civil Public Works, J.A.M. van Buuren, to the Board of Representatives for the Province of Central Java in Semarang, Batavia-Central, 21 August 1933 (no. E 59/1/2).
- Memo relating to a proposal for far-reaching moderations and reorganisations of the Public Works Department for the Province of Central Java, compiled by the Head of the Provincial Public Works Department, Van Batenburg, Semarang, 4 November 1933. (With an accompanying letter from the Governor of the Province to the Director of Civil Public Works, dd. 18 December 1933 – no. A 73/24/6).
- Letter from the Director of Transport and Public Works, J.A.M. van Buuren, to the Director of the Civil Service in Batavia-Central, Bandung, 3 March 1934 (no. E 57/1/2).

- Report from the inter-provincial commission concerning the making of recommendations in conjunction with the possible reorganisation of the Provincial Public Works Departments. The commission comprised the following engineers: J.M. Gasille, Head of Provincial Public Works for East Java, S.H.A. Begemann, Head of Provincial Public Works for Central Java, J.J. Jonker, Head of the 2nd District of Provincial Works for West Java. (Undated).

Remaining archive sources

- The "Van Blommestein" file in the possession of L. Horst, retired professor from the Agricultural University of Wageningen and member of the Van Blommestein plan evaluation commission. Some of the information used from this file was the following:
  - Letter from W.G. Wessels, written on behalf of the Dutch Ambassador, to the Minister for Development Co-operation, dd. 10 February 1984.
  - Letter from L. Horst to P. Unger (DAL/OA DGIS bureau), dd. 6 March 1984.
  - Letter from F.E. Schulze, engineer, (of the Agricultural Council for the Dutch Embassy in Jakarta) addressed to P. Unger (DAL/OA DGIA bureau), dd. 9 May 1984.
  - Letter from F.E. Schulze (Agricultural Council) to L. Horst, dd. 10 May 1984.
  - Letter from L. Horst and W.H. van den Toorn to R.R. Smit, M.Sc. (head of the DAL/OA DGIS bureau), dd. 3 July 1984.
- All the other documents consulted from this file which are included in the literature list concern: Bienefelt (1981), Van Blommestein (1979 and 1984), Development (1981) and Van der Post (1983).

Interviews

In the Netherlands

- P. Ankum, engineer, Delft University of Technology (May 1992 and May 1994)
- Professor R. Brouwer, engineer, Delft University of Technology (October 1994)
- Professor L. Horst, engineer, Wageningen Agricultural University (June 1993)
- H.J. Schoemaker, engineer and former Professor, Delft University of Technology
- (July 1995)
- Dr. N. Schulte Nordholt, Twente University of Technology (July 1993)
- Dr. J. Wuisman, former DGIS staff member (July 1993)

In Indonesia

- R. Didiek, engineer and Brantas project co-worker (September 1993 and March 1995)
- Dr. Effendi Pasandaran, Director of the Agency for Agricultural Research and Development within the Department of Agriculture (February 1995)
- Dr. R. Hutapea, Satya Wacana University in Salatiga (March 1995)
- Professor Dr. Loekman Soetrisno, Dean of the Gadjah Mada University in Yogyakarta (March 1995)
- Mohammed Memed, engineer and Director of the Hydrological Laboratory in Bandung (August 1993)
- Roedjito, engineer and former manager of the Brantas project and President-Director of the Brantas Management Authority (September 1993)
- Sidarta, engineer and manager of the Solo project (March 1995)
- Soebandi Wirosoemarto, engineer and former Director-General of Water Resources at PU (February 1995)
- Soenarno, engineer and Director of Irigasi-1 at PU (August 1993 and February 1995)
- J. Sonneveld, engineer and DHV co-worker (August 1993 and February 1995)
- Muhammed Zakarijah, engineer and Solo project co-worker (September 1993 and March 1995)

Bibliography

Abbreviations of journals:

DG	= De Gids ("The Guide")
DI	= De Ingenieur ("The Engineer")
DINI	= De Ingenieur in Nederlandsch-Indië ("The Engineer in the Dutch Indies")
DII	= De Ingenieur in Indonesia ("The Engineer in Indonesia")
DWI	= De Waterstaats-Ingenieur ("The Public Works Engineer")
IGS	= Indisch Genootschap, Verslag der Algemeene Vergadering ("The Indies Society", General Meeting Reports)
IG	= De Indische Gids ("The Indies Guide")
JGBT	= Jaarboek voor de Geschiedenis van Bedrijf en Techniek ("Yearbook on the History of Business and Technology")
TBB	= Tijdschrift voor het Binnenlandsch Bestuur ("The Civil Service Periodical")
TC	= Technology and Culture
TKIVI	= Tijdschrift van het Koninklijk Instituut van Ingenieurs ("Journal of the Royal Institute of Engineers"), Not.: Notulen van de vergaderingen ["Meeting minutes"], Verh.: Verhandelingen ["Proceedings"])
TKIVI (NI)	= Tijdschrift van het Koninklijk Instituut van Ingenieurs, Afdeeling Nederlandsch-Indië (Verhandelingen) ("Journal of the Royal Institute of Engineers, Dutch Indies Section" ["Proceedings"])

Adas, M.

1981 From avoidance to confrontation: Peasant protest in precolonial and colonial Southeast Asia. *Comparative Studies in Society and History* 32: 217-247.

1989 *Machines as the measure of men. Science, technology, and ideologies of western dominance*. Ithaca/Londen: Cornell University Press.

Alexander, J. and P. Alexander

1978 Sugar, rice and irrigation in colonial Java. *Ethnohistory* 25: 207-223.

Alvares, C.A.

1980 *Homo faber. Technology and culture in India China and the West from 1500 to the present day*. The Hague etc.: Martinus Nijhoff Publishers.

Andriessen, J.H.

1991 *Onder voorwaarden. Mens en organisatie als context voor nieuwe tele-informatie technologie*. Delft: Faculty of Philosophy and Technical Social Sciences, Delft University of Technology. (Inaugural Lecture).

Angoedi, A.

1984 *Sejarah irigasi di Indonesia 1*. Komite Nasional Indonesia, International Commission on Irrigation and Drainage (ICID).

Ankum, P.

1984 Irrigation management. Review, present conditions and prospects. Republic of Indonesia, Ministry of Public Works, Directorate of Water Resources Development, Directorate of Irrigation II (together with NEDECO, P.T. DESERCO and DHV).

1988 Management of irrigation rehabilitation projects. An experience from Indonesia. Wallingford, Oxfordshire, England: Overseas Development Unit of Hydraulic Research Ltd. (Paper for the Asian Regional Symposium on the modernisation and rehabilitation of irrigation and drainage schemes, the Development Academy of The Philippines, 13-15 February 1989).

1990 River basin management on Java, Indonesia. In: J. Wessel, L.C. Grijns and P. Ankum (eds.), Short course on integrated river basin management. Delft: Faculty of Philosophy and Technical Social Sciences (Law and Public Administration Section), Faculty of Civil Engineering (Irrigation Section), Centre for Comparative Studies on River Basin Administration (RBA), Delft University of Technology. Pp. 91-115.

1991 Flow control in irrigation systems. Delft: International Institute for Hydraulic and Environmental Engineering (IHE), Delft University of Technology (Irrigation & Polder Management).

Arends, G.J.

1994 *Sluizen en stuwen; de ontwikkeling van de sluis- en stuwbouw in Nederland tot 1940.* Delft: Delft University Press.

Asian Development Bank

2016 River basin management planning in Indonesia: Policy and practice. Mandaluyong City, Philippines: Asian Development Bank.

Baal, J. van

1976 Tussen kolonie en nationale staat; de koloniale staat. In: H.J.M. Claessen, J. Kaayk and R.J.A. Lambregts (eds.), *Dekolonisatie en vrijheid.* Assen/Amsterdam: Van Gorcum. Pp. 92-108.

Bakhoven, H.G.A.

1936 De bevloeiing van de vlakte van Noord-Krawang uit de Tjitaroem. *DINI* 3 (7): VI. 107-135.

Bakker, A.J., Soedjito, Soemarwoto, F.S. Bertrums, L. Horst, L.F. Kortenhorst, F. Kuipers, W.H. van den Toorn and H. Westerhout

1982/1983 Preliminary assessment of the need for and the possibility of integrated water resources development on Java. Jakarta/Wageningen: Directorate General of International Cooperation, Ministry of Foreign Affairs, The Netherlands and Directorate of Water Resources, Ministry of Public Works, Indonesia.

Bakker, M.S.C.

1989 *Ondernemerschap en vernieuwing. De Nederlandse bietsuikerindustrie 1858-1919.* Amsterdam: NEHA.

Basalla, G.

1988 *The evolution of technology.* Cambridge etc.: Cambridge University Press.

Baudet, H.

1991 *Delft en Indië.* In: Een veranderende wereld. Liber amoricum ter gelegenheid van de zestigste verjaardag van Ferdinand van Dam. Amsterdam: Thomas Rap.

Baudet, H. and I.J. Brugmans (eds.)

1961 *Balans van beleid. Terugblik op de laatste halve eeuw van Nederlandsch-Indië.* Assen: Van Gorcum/Prakke & Prakke.

Baudet, H. and M. Fennema

1983 *Het Nederlands belang bij Indië.* Utrecht/Antwerpen: Uitgeverij Het Spectrum.

Baudet, H. and J.H. Makkink

1992 *De lange weg naar de Technische Universiteit Delft. 1. De Delftse ingenieursschool en haar voorgeschiedenis.* The Hague: SDU Uitgevers.

Beek, E. van

2015 Water management on West-Java (1965-2000). In: J.H. Kop, W. Ravesteijn and K.J. Kop (eds.), *Irrigation revisited: An anthology of Indonesian-Dutch cooperation* 1965-2014. Delft/Jakarta: Eburon. Pp. 263-274.

Beerling, R.F.

1962 *Heden en verleden. Denken over geschiedenis.* Arnhem: Van Loghum Slaterus.

Begemann, S.H.A.
1935 Voordracht over reservoirdammen ten behoeve van bevloeiingen op Java (verslag). *DI* 17: A. 141-142.
Bemmelen, W. van
1908 *Regenval op Java, 1879-1905*. Onderzoek naar de mindere welvaart der Inlandsche bevolking op Java en Madoera. Weltevreden: F.B. Smits. Volume VIIb.
Benda, H.J.
1955 The communist rebellions of 1926-1927 in Indonesia. *The Pacific Historical Review* 24: 139-152.
Bentum, M. van
1995 *Water, water en waterwerken. De ontwikkeling van irrigatietechnologie in het stroomgebied van de Segura, Zuidoost-Spanje*. Wageningen: Ponsen en Looijen BV.
Berenschot, W., H. Schulte Nordholt and L. Bakker
2016 *Democratization and citizenship in Southeast Asia*. Leiden: Brill.
Berger, L.G. den
1915 *Landbouwscheikundige onderzoekingen omtrent de irrigatie op Java*. Delft: Technische boekhandel en drukkerij J. Waltman Jr.
Bericht
1854 Bericht over "het ontwerp van verbetering der distrikten, waardoor de Poorongrivier en de Soerabaia stroomen". *TKIVI (Not.)* meeting 14-2-1854, pp. 68-70.
Berkel, K. van
1985 *In het voetspoor van Stevin. Geschiedenis van de natuurwetenschap in Nederland*. Meppel/Amsterdam: Boom.
Berkhout, F.M.C.
1956 Vijftig jaar bouw- en waterbouwkunde in Nederlands-Indië en in Indonesië en Nederlands Nieuw-Guinea. In: *Koninklijk Instituut van Ingenieurs, Afdeling voor Bouw- en waterbouwkunde, Herdenking van het vijftigjarig bestaan van de afdeling voor Bouw- en Waterbouwkunde van het Koninklijk Instituut voor Ingenieurs*. Pp. 30-41.
Bertels, K.
1973 *Geschiedenis tussen struktuur en evenement. Een methodologies en wijsgerig onderzoek*. Amsterdam: Wetenschappelijke Uitgeverij.
Bestuur ("Administration")
1930 De onthulling van het Lamminga-monument. *DWI* 18 (4): 120-124.
Bienefelt, Th.
1981 Nederland en Indonesië gaan "deltaplan" voor Java en Madura bestuderen. *Internationale Samenwerking*. (In: Horst file on Van Blommestein).
Blackstone, J.
1925 De opening van de Tjitaroemwerken. *DWI* 13 (12): 347-349.
Bladzijden ("Pages")
1914 Eenige bladzijden uit de geschiedenis van het irrigatiewezen op Java. *DWI* 2 (6): 151-156.
1915 Eenige bladzijden uit de geschiedenis van het irrigatiewezen op Java (vervolg). *DWI* 3 (1): 17-23.
Blok, A.
1977 *Antropologische perspectieven*. Muiderberg: Dick Coutinho.
Blommestein, W.J. van
1939 *Een nieuw pompstation in Ned.-Indië voor irrigatie en ontwatering*. Tegal: J.D. de Boer. (Dissertation Bandung Polytechnical College).

1948/1949 Een federaal welvaartsplan voor het westelijk gedeelte van Java. *DII* 1 (4): I. 50-53, (5): I. 61-82. (In: Horst file on van Blommestein).
1979 A development project for the islands of Java and Madura (Indonesia). Voorburg. Appendix of Development 1981, see there.
1984 Hydro-power as the prominent feature for the development of integrated perennial irrigation system in Eastern Java and Madura. Abstract. (Paper).
Bodemeijer, Ch.E.
1904 Een irrigatie-praatje. *DI* 19 (12): 204-205, *TBB* 26: 24-30.
Boeke, J.H.
1941 Van vier tot vierenveertig millioen zielen op Java. In: W. H. van Helsdingen and H. Hoogenberk (eds.), *Daar wèrd wat groots verricht .... Nederlandsch-Indië in de xxste eeuw*. Amsterdam: Elsevier. Pp. 346-356.
Boes, J., W. Ravesteijn and W. Riedijk (eds.)
1989 *Appropriate technology in industrialized countries*. Delft: Delft University Press.
Boissevain, J.
1974a *Friends of friends*. Oxford: Basil Blackwell.
1974b Towards a sociology of social anthropology. *Theory and Society* 1: 211-230.
Boissevain, J. and J. Friedl (eds.)
1975 *Beyond the community: Social process in Europe*. The Hague: Department of Educational Science of the Netherlands.
Boissevain, M.
1992 “Snotterig om zo maar weg te lopen”. De Nederlandse ontwikkelingswerkers nemen met weemoed afscheid van hun projecten in Indonesië. *De Volkskrant* 25 April, Het Vervolg p. 9.
Boomgaard, P.
1980 Bevolkingsgroei en welvaart op Java (1800-1942). In: R.N.J. Kamerling (ed.), *Indonesië toen en nu*. Amsterdam: Intermediair Bibliotheek. Pp. 35-52.
1987a *Children of the colonial state. Population growth and economic development in Java, 1795-1880*. Dissertation Vrije Universiteit Amsterdam.
1987b The welfare services in Indonesia, 1900-1942. In: L. Blussé, A. Booth a.o., *India and Indonesia from the 1920s to the 1950s: the origins of planning*. Leiden: E.J. Brill.
Booth, A.
1977 Irrigation in Indonesia. *Bulletin of Indonesian Economic Studies* 13 (1): 33-74 (part I), (2): 45-77 (part II).
1988 *Agricultural development in Indonesia*. Sydney/Wellington/London/Boston: Allen and Unwin.
1990 The evolution of fiscal policy and the role of government in the colonial economy. In: A. Booth, W.J. O’Malley and A. Weidemann, *Indonesian economic history in the Dutch colonial era*. New Haven, Connecticut: Yale University Southeast Asia Studies.
Bordes, J.P. de
1880 Review of C.L.T. Post, “Over den waterstaat in Nederlandsch-Indië”, 1879. *DG* 44, III: 186-206.
Bosch, J. van den
1934 Eenige zakelijke Extracten. In: *Indisch Staatsblad* 1934 no. 22: 51-76. (Supplement A).
Bosse, M.J. van
1893 De werkkring van den ingenieur van den waterstaat in Ned.-Indië. *DI* 8 (7): 65-72, (8): 79-85.
1901 Discussiebijdrage. In: H.H. van Van Kol, Een algemeen irrigatie-plan voor Java. *DI* 16 (22): 358-367, (25): 414-418.

1912 J.A. de Gelder in het tijdperk van de bouw der haven van Tandjong Priok. *DI* 27 (39): 786-789.
Breen, H. van, L.J. Polderman and H. W. Dumont
1919 Nota betreffende de verbetering der bevloeiing en afwatering van de Tangerangsche vlakte. (In: BOW Archives E I-28, 1).
Breman, J.C.
1976 Modernisering en emancipatie in de koloniale en post-koloniale samenleving. In: H.J.M. Claessen, J. Kaayk and R.J.A. Lambregts (eds.), *Dekolonisatie en vrijheid.* Assen/Amsterdam: Van Gorcum. Pp. 109-118.
1980 *The village on Java and the early-colonial state.* Rotterdam: Erasmus University Rotterdam, CASP (1).
Broek d'Obrenan, R. van den
1918 Bevloeiïng in Nederlandsch-Indië. In: R.A. van Sandick (red.), *Onze kolonien.* Serie III, no. 2. Baarn: Hollandia-Drukkerij. Pp. 3-47.
Brooshooft, P.
1887 Het productieve van bevloeijingswerken. *IG* 9, I: 1020-1032.
1901 *De ethische koers in de koloniale politiek.* Amsterdam: J.H. de Bussy.
Brouwer, R.
1991 Irrigatie. Delft: Delft University of Technology, Faculty of Civil Engineering. (Lecture notes).
Brouwer, R. and P. Ankum
1992 Irrigatie. Delft: Delft University of Technology, Faculty of Civil Engineering. (Lecture notes).
Brummelhuis, H.C.F. ten
1995 *De Waterkoning. J. Homan van der Heide, staatsvorming en de oorsprong van moderne irrigatie in Siam, 1902-1990.* Dissertation University of Amsterdam.
Bruyn, H. de
1858 Memorie tot betoog van de noodzakelijkheid eener uitbreiding van den waterstaat in Nederlandsch Indië, en voornamelijk op Java. In: I Kielstra 1887, Levensschets van H. de Bruyn, *TKIVI (Verh.)*, pp. 118-121 (brief description), II De Bruyn 1863 (see below): 61-65 (the section on "rivers and water works").
1863 Verslag van een reis naar Frankrijk en Noord-Italië. *TKIVI (Verh.)* 1862-1863, 3e issue, pp. 60-179.
1870 *Iets over bevloeijingen op Java.* Leyden: De Breuk & Smits.
Bruyn, H. de, Verploegh, D. de Paulij and W. van Raders
1875 *Rapport omtrent het irrigatiewezen op Java en Madura.* Batavia: Landsdrukkerij.
Buiter, H.
1993 *Nederlands-Indië (1830-1949). Een kolonie in ontwikkeling.* Utrecht/Antwerpen: Kosmos – Z&K Uitgevers.
Burger, D.H.
1975 *Sociologisch-economische geschiedenis van Indonesië.* Amsterdam: KIT. (Two volumes).
Bijker, W.E.
1984 Techniekgeschiedenis: een mogelijke basis voor theorieën over techniekontwikkeling? *JGBT* 1: 44-65.
1987 De sociale constructie van netwerken en technische systemen; nieuwe perspectieven voor de techniekgeschiedenis. *JGBT* 4: 7-24.
1995 Sociohistorical technology studies. In: S. Jasanoff, G.E. Markle, J. C. Petersen and T. Pinch (eds.), *Handbook of science and technology studies.* Thousand Oaks/London/New Delhi: SAGE Publications, Inc. Pp. 229-256.

Bijker, W.E., Th.P. Hughes and T. Pinch (eds.)
1987 *The social construction of technological systems. New directions in the sociology and history of technology*. Cambridge, Mass./London, England: MIT Press.
Bijker, W.E. and J. Law
1992 *Shaping technology/building society. Studies in sociotechnical change*. Cambridge, Mass./London, England: MIT Press.
C.
1873 De dam in de Sampean-rivier. *Nederland en Java. Veertiendaagsche Courant, uitgegeven door de Maatschappij tot Nut van den Javaan*. No. 23: 90-91.
Campo, J.N.F.M. à
1986 Wereldsysteem in bedrijf; scheepvaartconcurrentie in Indonesië 1891-1914. *JGBT* 3: 252-269.
1992 *Koninklijke Pakketvaart Maatschappij. Stoomvaart en staatsvorming in de Indonesische archipel 1888-1914*. Hilversum: Verloren.
2005 *Engines of empire. Steamshipping and state formation in colonial Indonesia*. Hilversum: Verloren.
Casimir, H.B.G.
1984 Mijn visie op wetenschap en researchmanagement, Wetenschapsontwikkeling, een spanningsveld tussen wens en werkelijkheid. In: A. Sarlemijn, *Tussen academie en industrie. Casimirs visie op wetenschap en researchmanagement*. Amsterdam: Meulenhoff Informatief. Pp. 19-73 and pp. 181-189.
Charité, J. et al. (eds.)
1989 *Biografisch woordenboek van Nederland*. Third volume. The Hague: Instituut voor Nederlandse geschiedenis.
Childe, V. Gordon
1951 *Man makes himself*. New York: New American Library.
1963 *Social evolution*. London: C.A. Watts & Co.
Cidurian
1988 Cidurian Upgrading and Water management Project B-130. Inception Report, Volume 3, Annexes F-I. DHV Consultants in associationn with: ISSAS, Delft Hydraulics, P.T. Deserco, P.T. Indah Karya.
1989 Irrigation and development in the regency of Tangerang. Report of the Joint Evaluation Mission to the Cidurian Upgrading and Water Management Project in West Java, Indonesia (13-11-88 – 2-12-88).
Clason, E.W.H.
1936 Economische beschouwingen over de irrigatie op Java en Madoera. *DINI* 3 (1): VI. 1-25.
Clemens, A.H.P. and J.Th. Lindblad
1989 *Het belang van de buitengewesten. Economische expansie en koloniale staatsvorming in de buitengewesten van Nederlands-Indië 1870-1942*. Amsterdam: NEHA.
Cohen Stuart, H.G.C.
1930 De vaarwaters van Soerabaja. *DI* 45 (3): B. 17-29.
Colombijn, F. and J. Coté
2015 *Cars, conduits, and kampongs: The modernization of the Indonesian city, 1920-1960*. Leiden/Boston.
Coward, E.W. (ed.)
1980 *Irrigation and agricultural development in Asia*. Ithaca/London: Cornell University Press.

Cramer, Ch. G. C.
1914 *De ingenieur in Ned.-Indië op technisch en sociaal gebied.* Amsterdam: F. van Rossen.
1919 *Verslag over de in 1917 genomen proeven met het opzamelen van bevloeiingswater gedurende den nacht in wadoeks van beperkten omvang teneinde dit water voor bevloeiingsdoeleinden te benutten.* Weltevreden: Landsdrukkerij.
1920 Het beheer van bevloeiingswerken. Algemeen Ingenieurs Congres Batavia, 8-15 Mei 1920. 2e Section, Irrigation sanitation. Announcements and pre-advices. Part 2. Pp. 1-47.
1927 Wadoekstelsel. In: *Encyclopaedie van Nederlandsch-Indië.* The Hague: Martinus Nijhoff; Leiden: N.V. v/h E.J. Brill., Volume V: 461-466.
Creutzberg, P.
1972-1975 *Het ekonomisch beleid in Nederlandsch-Indië.* Three volumes. Groningen: Wolters Noordhoff/Tjeenk Willink.
Cutcliffe, S. H.
1995 A hitchhiker's guide to STS. Review of S. Jasanoff et al. (eds.), "Handbook of science and technology studies", 1995. *TC* 36 (4): 1015-1020.
D.
1902 Feestelijke opening van het aquaduct te Pontjol. *DI* 17 (49): 867-871.
Deal, T.E. and A.A. Kennedy
1982 *Corporate cultures: The rites and rituals of corporate life.* Reading, MA: Addison-Wesley.
Demographics of Indonesia
2016 Wikipedia, retrieved 5-15-2016.
Development
1981 Development project of Java and Madura. Republic of Indonesia, Ministry of Public Works, Directorate General of Water Resources Development. (In: Horst file on Van Blommestein).
Deventer, C.Th. van
1899 Een eereschuld. *DG* 63 (3): 205-257.
1904 *Overzicht van den economischen toestand der Inlandsche bevolking van Java en Madoera.* The Hague: Martinus Nijhoff.
Deventer, S. van
1865 *Bijdragen tot de kennis van het landelijk stelsel op Java.* Zalt-Bommel: Joh. Noman en zoon. (Three volumes).
Dickson, D.
1981 *Alternative technology and the politics of technical change.* Glasgow: William Collins Sons and Co Ltd. (Fontana).
Diemer, G.
1990 *Irrigatie in Afrika. Boeren en ingenieurs, techniek en cultuur.* Amsterdam: Thesis Publishers.
Diemer, G. and J. Slabbers (eds.)
1992 *Irrigators and engineers. Essays in honour of Lucas Horst.* Amsterdam: Thesis Publishers.
Dieren, W. van
1995 *Het groene universum.* Amsterdam: Van Gennep.
Diest, W.J. van
2015 Rawa Seragi non-tidal swamp development project, Lampung province (1975-1979). In: J.H. Kop, W. Ravesteijn and K.J. Kop (eds.), *Irrigation revisited: An anthology of Indonesian-Dutch cooperation* 1965-2014. Delft/Jakarta: Eburon. Pp. 165-172.

Dirkse, J.P., F. Hüsken and M. Rutten (eds.)
1993 *Development and social welfare. Indonesia's experiences under the new order.* Leiden: KITLV Press.
Dirkzwager, J.M.
1977 *Water. Van natuurgebeuren tot dienstbaarheid.* The Hague: Martinus Nijhoff.
Dixon, R.
2003 Review of R. Mrázek, "Engineers of happy land: Technology and nationalism in a colony", 2002. *Social History* 28 (3): 401-403.
Doel, H.W. van den
1994 *De stille macht. Het Europese binnenlands bestuur op Java en Madoera, 1808-1942.* Amsterdam: Bert Bakker.
Does de Bije, A.H.E. van der
1919 Bevloeiing in de Solovallei. *DI* 34 (28): 509-515.
Doorn, J.A.A. van
1982 *The engineers and the colonial system, technocratic tendencies in the Dutch East Indies.* Rotterdam: Erasmus University Rotterdam, CASP (6).
1994a *De laatste eeuw van Indië. Ontwikkeling en ondergang van een koloniaal project.* Amsterdam: Bert Bakker.
1994b De eerste spoorweg op Java. In: M.L. ten Horn-van Nispen, H.W. Lintsen and A.J. Veenendaal jr. (eds.), *Nederlandse ingenieurs en hun kunstwerken. Twee honderd jaar civiele techniek.* Zutphen: Walburg Pers, Stichting Historie der Techniek. Pp. 80-88.
Dove, M. R.
1985 The agroecological mythology of the Javanese and the political economy of Indonesia. *Indonesia* no. 39: 1-36.
Driesen, G.L.
1900 Verslag der commissie van advies nopens de werken in de Solo-vallei. *DI* 15 (46): 700-709, (47): 715-721, (48): 730-735, (49): 754-758, (50): 770-774, (51): 785-790.
1901 De al- of niet-hervatting der Solowerken. *DI* 16 (1): 14.
Duewel, J.
1981 Dharma tirta: The growth and cultivation of water users associations in two villages of central Java, Indonesia. In: T. Wickham (ed.), *Irrigation management: Research from Southeast Asia.* Agricultural Development Council, Inc. Pp. 187-203.
Dumas, F.G.
1929 De bevloeiing in de Tangerangsche vlakte. *DWI* 17 (7): 199-209.
Edge, D.
1995 Reinventing the Wheel. In: S. Jasanoff, G.E. Markle, J. C. Petersen and T. Pinch (eds.), *Handbook of science and technology studies.* Thousand Oaks/London/New Delhi: SAGE Publications, Inc. Pp. 3-23.
Effendi Pasandaran
1976 Water management decision-making in the Pekalen Sampean irrigation project, East Java, Indonesia. In: D.C. Taylor and T. H. Wickham (eds.), *Irrigation policy and the management of irrigation systems in Southeast Asia.* Bangkok: Agricultural Development Council, Inc.
Eerenbeemt, H.F.J.M. van den
1989 *In het spoor van de vooruitgang. Het moderniseringsproces in de Nederlandse samenleving 1730-1980.* Tilburg: Tilburg University Press.
Elenbaas, W.
1902 De verlegging van de Solorivier naar Sidajoe Lawas en de werken ter bevloeiing van de Solovallei. *DI* 17 (44): 792-796. Naschrift van R.A. van Sandick, p. 796.
1923 De Solovallei. *Indisch Bouwkundig Tijdschrift* pp. 162-163.

Elias, N.
1970 Inleiding tot Über den Prozess der Zivilisation. In: G. van Benthem van den Berg en J. Godschalk, *Sociologie en geschiedenis*, Amsterdam: Van Gennep.
1971 *Wat is sociologie*. Utrecht/Antwerpen: Het Spectrum.
1972 Processes of state formation and nation building. Transactions of the 7th World Congress of Sociology, Varna, Bulgaria, September 1970. Geneva: International Sociological association.
Ellul, J.
1980 *The technological system*. New York: Continuum.
Elson, R.E.
1979 Cane-burning in the Pasaruan area: An expression of social discontent. In: F. van Anrooij, D.H.A. Kolff, J.T.M. van Laanen and G.J. Telkamp (eds.), *Between people and statistics. Essays on modern Indonesian history presented to P. Creutzberg*. The Hague: Martinus Nijhoff. Pp. 219-234.
1984 *Javanese peasants and the colonial sugar industry. Impact and change in an East Java Residency, 1830-1940*. Singapore: Oxford University Press.
Encyclopaedie ("Encyclopedia")
1917-1939 *Encyclopaedie van Nederlandsch-Indië*. The Hague: Martinus Nijhoff; Leiden: N.V. v/h E.J. Brill. (Eight volumes).
Ende, J. van den
1994 *The turn of the tide. Computerization in Dutch society, 1900-1965*. Delft: Delft University Press. (Dissertation).
Ende, J. van, W. Ravesteijn and D. de Wit,
1993 Waarom geen Nipkowschijf in elke huiskamer? *Jaarboek Mediageschiedenis* 5: 131-161.
Ertsen, M.
1993 An experimental waterdistribution method in the Netherlands East Indies (1890-1910). Wageningen Agricultural University, Department of Irrigation and Soil and Water Conservation. (Master Thesis).
2005 *Prescribing perfection. Emergence of an engineering irrigation design approach in the Netherlands East Indies and its legacy, 1830-1990*. Delft: Delft University of Technology. (Dissertation).
Ertsen, M. and W. Ravesteijn
2004 Levend water. Ontwikkeling van irrigatietechniek en waterkracht. In: W. Ravesteijn and J.H Kop (eds.), *Bouwen in de archipel. Burgerlijke openbare werken in Nederlands-Indië en Indonesië 1800-2000*. Zutphen: Walburg Pers 2004, pp. 159-175.
2008 Living water. The development of irrigation technology and waterpower. In: W. Ravesteijn and J.H. Kop (eds.), *For profit and prosperity: The contribution made by Dutch engineers to public works in Indonesia 1800-2000*. Zaltbommel/Leiden: Aprilis/KITLV Press 2008, pp. 238-271.
Etemad, B.
2007 *Possessing the world: Taking the measurements of colonisation from the 18th to the 20th century*. New York/Oxford: Berghahn Books.
Es, D.J.F. van
1931 "De nachtwadoeks", door Prof. Ir. J. Haringhuizen. *DWI* 19 (11): 382-383.
Essen, E.A.C.F. von
1910 J.L. Pierson. *DI* 25 (14): 253-256.
Eijsvoogel, W.F.
1929 De beweegbare stuwinrichting in de Tjitaroem nabij Walahar. *DWI* 17 (6): 191-192.

Fasseur, C.
1975 *Kultuurstelsel en koloniale baten. De Nederlandse exploitatie van Java 1840-1860.* Leiden: Universitaire Pers Leiden.
1995 *De weg naar het paradijs en andere Indische geschiedenissen.* Amsterdam: Uitgeverij Bert Bakker.
Feestelijke opening ("Celebratory opening")
1925 Feestelijke opening van de bevloeiingswerken voor Noord-Krawang. Reproductiebedrijf Topografische Inrichting.
Forbes, R.J.
1959 *Mensenwerk. Vijfduizend jaar techniek in twee delen.* Amsterdam: Querido.
Frank, A.G.
1971 *Capitalism and underdevelopment in Latin America.* Harmondsworth: Penguin Books.
Fukuyama, F.
2005 *State building: Governance and world order in the 21st century.* London: Profile Books Ltd.
Furnivall, J.S.
1939 *Netherlands India. A study of plural economy.* Cambrigde: Cambridge University Press.
Galtung, J.
1980 *The North/South debate: Technology, basic human needs and the new international economic order.* New York: Institute for World Order.
Geertz, C.
1963 *Agricultural involution. The processes of ecological change in Indonesia.* Berkeley: University of California Press.
Gendt, G.J. van
1868 Aarden dammen door ravijnen. *TKIVI (Verh.)*, 1867-1868, pp. 1-13.
Gerlings, J.Th.
1901 Discussiebijdrage. In: H.H. van Kol, Een algemeen irrigatie-plan voor Java. *DI* 16 (22): 358-367, (25): 414-418.
Gerst, E.
1901 Discussiebijdrage. In: H.H. van Kol, Een algemeen irrigatie-plan voor Java. *DI* 16 (22): 358-367, (25): 414-418.
Go Gien Tjwan
1966 *Eenheid in verscheidenheid in een Indonesisch dorp.* Amsterdam: Sociologisch-Historisch Seminarium voor Zuidoost Azië (publikatie no. 10).
Gonggrijp, G.
1938 De westersche cultures in Nederlandsch-Indië. In: *Het bedrijfsleven tijdens de regeering van H.M. Koningin Wilhelmina 1898-1938.* Amsterdam: J. Frijda. Pp. 418-422.
1957 *Schets ener economische geschiedenis van Indonesië.* Haarlem: F. Bohn. (First edition 1928).
Goor, J. van (ed.)
1986 *Imperialisme in de marge. De afronding van Nederlands-Indië.* Utrecht: H&S Uitgevers.
Goor, W.B. van
1898 De stuw in de Solorivier te Ngloewak. *DI* 13 (20): 257-261.
1898 De stuw in de Solo-rivier te Ngloewak. *DI* 14 (11): 127-129.
Gorkum, U. van, and M. Klein
n.d. Over Van Blommestein, de geestelijke vader van het Javaanse integraal waterbeheer. Student Paper Delft University of Technology.

Goss, A.
2009 Decent colonialism? Pure science and colonial ideology in the Netherlands East Indies, 1910–1929. *Journal of Southeast Asian Studies* 40 (1): 187–214.
Graadt van Roggen, J.F.
1932 Het instituut van den oeloe-oeloe-pembagian in de irrigatieafdeeling "Pemali-Tjomal". *DWI* 20 (4): 122-130.
1935 Plant- en waterregelingen in de provinciale waterstaatsafdeling "Pemali-Tjomal". *DINI* 2 (4): VI. 47-56.
Graaf, M.H.K. van der (ed.)
1984 *De crisis van de technocratie en het alternatief van de sociocratie.* Amersfoort: De Horstink.
Grinwis Plaat, P.
1895 Bevloeiingen in Noord-Italië en Spanje. Verslag uitgebracht op last van Zijne Excellentie den Minister van Koloniën.
Gruyter, P. de
1933 De teelt van oostmoessonpadi (gadoe) met intermitterende bevloeiing. *DWI* 21 (12): 321-325.
1934 Vischteelt en -kweek met behulp van bevloeiingswater. *DINI* 1 (6): VI. 69-78.
Gijn, H. van
n.d. *De verwaandheid van de technici contra de kommiezerij.* Rotterdam: Van Meurs & Stufkens.
Haasse, H.S.
1992 *Heren van de thee.* Amsterdam: Querido.
Handelingen ("Proceedings")
Handelingen der Staten-Generaal, Eerste en Tweede Kamer. With: Supplement B: *Begrooting van Nederlandsch-Indië.* Supplement C: *Koloniaal Verslag.*
Happé, P.L.E.
1916 Inlandsche bevloeiingswerken in Zuid-Bali. *DWI* 4 (10): 449-456.
1935 Waterbeheer en waterschappen. *DINI* 2 (11): VI. 135-140.
1936a Waterbeheer en waterschappen. Repliek. *DINI* 3 (8): VI. 139-145.
1936b Slotwoord (waterbeheer en waterschappen). *DINI* 3 (8): VI. 148.
1939 Eenige beschouwingen over bevloeiingswerken op Java en Madoera. *DINI* 6 (1): II. 13-26, (2): II. 33-42.
Hargrove, E.C.
1994 *Prisoners of myth. The leadership of the Tennessee Valley Authority, 1933-1990.* Princeton, New Jersey: Princeton University Press.
Hatmokoa, W., Radhikaa, B. Raharjab, D. Tollenaar and R. Vernimmen.
2015 Monitoring and prediction of hydrological drought using a drought early warning system in Pemali-Comal river basin, Indonesia. *Procedia Environmental Sciences* 24, pp. 56-64.
Haringhuizen, J.
1919 *De Indische waterbouwkunde.* Wageningen: H. Veenman.
1920 Het "Lamminga-fonds". *DI* 35 (51): 976.
1931 De nachtwadoeks. *DWI* 19 (10): 335-353.
Hartmann, A.
1895-1906 *Repertorium op de literatuur betreffende de Nederlandsche koloniën, voor zoover zij verspreid is in tijdschriften en mengelwerken.* The Hague: Martinus Nijhoff. (Including First and Second Sequel).

Hasselman, C.J.
1914 *Algemeen overzicht van de uitkomsten van het welvaart-onderzoek gehouden op Java en Madoera in 1904-1905*. The Hague: Martinus Nijhoff.
Headrick, D.R.
1981 *The tools of empire. Technology and European imperialism in the nineteenth century*. New York: Oxford University Press.
1988 *The tentacles of progress. Technology transfer in the age of imperialism*. New York/Oxford: Oxford University Press.
Helsdingen, W.H. van and H. Hoogenberk (eds.)
1941 *Daar wèrd wat groots verricht .... Nederlandsch-Indië in de XXste eeuw*. Amsterdam: Elsevier.
Herinnering ("Reminder")
1892 Een herinnering aan een irrigatieplan. *IG* 14, I: 106.
Heslinga, J.H.
1923 Irrigatie en wetgeving op Java. *DWI* 11 (2): 35-42.
Hieselaar, W.
2015 Jratunseluna basin development project (JBDP) Central Java (1970-1976). In: J.H. Kop, W. Ravesteijn and K.J. Kop (eds.), *Irrigation revisited: An anthology of Indonesian-Dutch cooperation* 1965-2014. Delft/Jakarta: Eburon. Pp. 37-90.
Hobsbawm, E.J.
1989 *The age of empire 1875-1914*. New York: Random House, Vintage.
Hofstede, K. ter, and J. van Santbrink
1979 Koloniaal waterbeheer. Een onderzoek naar het ontstaan en de ontwikkeling van het technisch beheer van irrigatiesystemen met als ingang de schakelfunctie tussen projectorganisatie en bevolking. Master Thesis Landbouw Hogeschool Wageningen.
Hollick, M.
1982 The appropriate technology movement and its literature: A retrospective. *Technology in Society* 4: 213-229.
Hofwegen, P. van
2015 SEDEKU, WISMP, IWIRIP: Description, developments and expectations (1976-2014). In: J.H. Kop, W. Ravesteijn and K.J. Kop (eds.), *Irrigation revisited: An anthology of Indonesian-Dutch cooperation* 1965-2014. Delft/Jakarta: Eburon. Pp. 91-97.
Homan van der Heide, J.
1899 *Beschouwingen aangaande de volkswelvaart en het irrigatiewezen op Java in verband met de Solovalleiwerken*. Batavia/The Hague: G. Kolff & Co./W.P. van Stockum en Zoon.
1900 Over de bemestende werking van irrigatiewater. *DI* 15 (7): 104
1901 *Economische studiën en critieken met betrekking tot Java*. Batavia/The Hague: G. Kolff & Co./W.P. van Stockum en Zoon.
1905 Het slibbezwaar in de Britsch-Indische irrigatiekanalen en de middelen die men aanwendt om dit te overwinnen. *DI* 20 (11): 152.
Horn-van Nispen, M.L. ten, H.W. Lintsen and A.J. Veenendaal jr. (eds.)
1994 *Nederlandse ingenieurs en hun kunstwerken. Twee honderd jaar civiele techniek*. Zutphen: Walburg Pers/Stichting Historie der Techniek.
Horst, L.
1994 Irrigation water division structures in Indonesia. A case of ambivalent technology development. Wageningen: Wageningen Agricultural University, Department of Irrigation and Soil and Water Conservation. (Draft).

1996 Intervention in irrigation water division in Bali, Indonesia: a case of farmers' circumvention of modern technology. In: G. Diemer and F.P. Huibers (eds.), *Crops, people and irrigation*. London: Intermediate Technology Publications. Pp. 34-52.

Houterman, J. and A. Haag

2015 Dutch involvement in tidal swamp development (1930s-2014). In: J.H. Kop, W. Ravesteijn and K.J. Kop (eds.), *Irrigation revisited: An anthology of Indonesian-Dutch cooperation* 1965-2014. Delft/Jakarta: Eburon. Pp. 173-218.

Hughes, Th.P.

1983 *Networks of power: Electrification in western society, 1880-1930*. Baltimore: Johns Hopkins University Press.

1987 The evolution of large technological systems. In: W.E. Bijker, Th.P. Hughes and T.J. Pinch (eds.), *The social construction of technological systems. New directions in the sociology and history of technology*. Cambridge, Mass./London, England: MIT Press. Pp. 51-82.

Hüsken, F.A.M.

1988 *Een dorp op Java. Sociale differentiatie in een boerengemeenschap, 1850-1980*. Overveen: ACASEA.

Hutapea, R., Prajarta Dirjasanyata and N.G.S. Nordholt

1976 The organization of farm-level irrigation in Indonesia. In: D.C. Taylor and T. H. Wickham (eds.), *Irrigation policy and the management of irrigation systems in Southeast Asia*. Bangkok: Agricultural Development Council, Inc.

Idema, H.A.

1924 *Parlementaire geschiedenis van Nederlandsch-Indië 1891-1918*. The Hague: Martinus Nijhoff.

Ilcken, J.

1891 Irrigatie in Nederlandsch-Indië. *DI* 6 (45): 411-414, (46): 421-424.

Indisch Staatsblad (Staatsblad van Nederlandsch-Indië). Especially:

1834 No. 22 Besluit van den Gouverneur Generaal ad interim van Nederlandsch Indië, van de 28sten Maart 1834, no. 1. Stelsel van cultures.

1854 No. 100 Besluit van den Gouverneur-Generaal van Nederlandsch-Indië, van de 29sten December 1854 no. 13. Bestuur en toezigt over den waterstaat en de burgerlijke openbare werken.

1855 No. 17 Besluit van den Gouverneur-Generaal van Nederlandsch-Indië, van den 12den Maart 1855 no. 6. Waterstaatsdienst in Nederlandsch-Indie.

1865 No. 30 Koninklijk besluit d.d. 26 December 1864 no. 70. Reorganisatie van het personeel en van hetgene daarmede in verband staat.

1866 No. 87 Ordonnantie d.d. 12 Augustus 1866. De djatibosschen in de residentie Bezoekie, Probolingo en Pasoeroean onder geregeld beheer gebragt.

1867 No. 85 Besluit van den Gouverneur-Generaal van Nederlandsch-Indië, van de 28sten Junij 1867, no. 3. Reglement op het beheer van en toezigt over de burgerlijke openbare werken in Nederlandsch-Indië.

1877 No. 238 Besluit van den Gouverneur-Generaal van Nederlandsch-Indië van 25 November 1877 no. 39. Nieuw reglement op het beheer en toezigt over de burgerlijke openbare werken.

1885a No. 82 Koninklijk besluit d.d. 10 Februari 1885 no. 10. Organisatie van het personeel van den waterstaat en 's lands burgerlijke openbare werken.

1885b No. 173 Besluit van den Gouverneur-Generaal van Nederlandsch-Indië van 22 October 1885 no. 18. Reglement op het beheer en toezicht over den waterstaat en 's lands burgerlijke openbare werken.

1889 No. 39 Besluit van den Gouverneur-Generaal van Nederlandsch-Indië van 7 Februari 1889 no. 8. Reglement op het beheer en toezicht over den waterstaat en 's lands burgerlijke openbare werken.

1890a No. 60 Koninklijk besluit d.d. 13 Januari 1890 no. 74. Nieuwe formatie van het technisch personeel bij den waterstaat en de burgerlijke openbare werken.

1890b No. 199 Besluit van den Gouverneur-Generaal van Nederlandsch-Indië van 24 September no. 17. Intrekking van de 2de alinea van artikel 3 van het Reglement op het beheer en toezicht over den waterstaat en 's lands burgerlijke openbare werken.

1910 No. 177 Besluit van den Gouverneur-Generaal van Nederlandsch-Indië van 3 Maart 1910 no. 36. Reglement op den dienst van 's Lands waterstaat.

1925 No. 378 Ordonnantie van 14 Augustus 1925. Instelling van een provincie West-Java.

1934a No. 547 Ordonnantie van 11 September 1934. Aanvulling van de Provincie-, Regentschaps- en Stadsgemeente-ordonnantie.

1934b No. 548 Ordonnantie van 11 September 1934. Bepalingen betreffende het toezicht op de uitvoering van openbare werken van openbare gemeenschappen, waarvoor van Landswege subsidie is verleend.

1934c No. 550 Ordonnantie van 11 September 1934. Wijziging van de instellingsordonnanties der provincies West-, Midden- en Oost-Java, en intrekking van de ordonnantie in Staatsblad 1926 no. 177.

1934d No. 578 Besluit van 6 October 1934 no. 32. Voorschriften in verband met de opheffing van den Dienst voor Waterkracht en Electriciteit.

1934e No. 603 Besluit van 25 October 1934 no. 22. Nadere wijziging van den werkkring van de departementen van algemeen bestuur in Nederlandsch-Indië.

1936 No. 489 Ordonnantie van 26 September 1936. Vaststelling van een Algemeen Waterreglement voor de Gouvernementslanden van Java en Madoera.

Irrigatie ("Irrigation")

1888 Irrigatie in Indië. *DI* 3 (2): 11-12, 3 (3): 19-20, 3(5): 37-38.

Jaager, C.J. de

1901 Beschouwingen over rentabiliteit van waterwerken. With a foreword by Prof. J. Kraus. *IG* 23, I: 1-30.

Jaarverslag ("Annual Report")

1938-1940 Jaarverslag van het Departement van Verkeer en Waterstaat over 1938. (In: National Archives, Haringhuizen-Schoemaker Collection nos. 97 and 111).

Jasanoff, S., G.E. Markle, J.C. Petersen and T. Pinch (eds.)

1995 *Handbook of science and technology studies*. Thousand Oaks/London/New Delhi: SAGE Publications, Inc.

Jasa Tirta

1993 Jasa Tirta Public Corporation. Summary. Malang.

Jatiluhur

1992 Jatiluhur Authority Public Corporation.

Java

1994 Java irrigation improvement and water resources management project. Summary. DHV Consultants. Republic of Indonesia, Ministry of Public Works, Directorate general of Water Resources Development, Directorate of Planning and programming. Summary.

Jong, J. de

1989 *Van batig slot tot ereschuld. De discussie over de financiële verhouding tussen Nederland en Indië en de hervorming van de Nederlandse koloniale politiek 1860-1900*. The Hague: SDU Uitgevers.

Jong, J.J.P. de
1998 *De waaier van het fortuin. Van handelscompagnie tot koloniaal imperium. De Nederlanders in Azië en de Indonesische Archipel 1595-1950*. The Hague: SDU Uitgevers.
Jonge, J.A. de
1978 Het economisch leven in Nederland 1873-1895. In: D.P. Blok et al. (eds.), *Algemene geschiedenis der Nederlanden*. Volume 13: *Nieuwste tijd: Nederland en België 1840-1914, tweede helft*. Haarlem: Fibula – Van Dishoeck.
Kampfraath, A.A. and J. Sonneveld
2015 The Cidurian upgrading and water management project (1985-1992). In: J.H. Kop, W. Ravesteijn and K.J. Kop (eds.), *Irrigation revisited: An anthology of Indonesian-Dutch cooperation* 1965-2014. Delft/Jakarta: Eburon. Pp. 317-325.
Kat Angelino, A.D.A. de
1929 *Staatkundig beleid en bestuurszorg in Nederlandsch-Indië*. First Part. The Hague: Martinus Nijhoff.
Kesteren, C.E. van
1896 Ter gedachtenis van K.F. Holle. *IG* 18, II: 1003-1007.
Kielstra, E.B.
1886/87 Levensschets van H. de Bruyn. *TKIVI (Verh.)*, pp. 108-139.
Kleinman, D.L. and K. Moore (eds.)
2014 *Routledge handbook of science, technology, and society*. Abingdon, Oxon and New York: Routledge.
Kloppenburg, W.H.
1914 Evenredige verdeeling bij de detailbevloeiing van de Pemali-werken. *DI* 29 (52): 1018.
Knight, G.R.
1993 *Colonial production in provincial Java. The sugar industry in Pekalongan-Tegal, 1800-1942*. Amsterdam: VU University Press/CASA.
Koens, A.J.
1934a Rentabiliteit van bevloeiingswerken van overheidsstandpunt. *IG* 56, I: 348-350.
1934b Uitbreiding van de technische verzorging der irrigatie in Ned.-Indië. *IG* 56, II: 704-707.
Kohama, H.
2004 The significance of Japan's official development assistance in Indonesia's agricultural development: The case of increased rice production. In: Kohama, H. (ed.), *Asian development experience, Vol. 1: External factors for Asian development*. Singapore: Institute of Southeast Asian Studies.
Kol, H.H. van
1901 Een algemeen irrigatie-plan voor Java. *DI* 16 (21): 341-348, discussie: (22): 358-367, (25): 414-418.
1903 De Solo-werken en de haven van Soerabaja.
1911 *Nederlandsch-Indië in de Staten-Generaal van 1897 tot 1909. Een bijdrage tot de geschiedenis der koloniale politiek in Nederland*. The Hague: Martinus Nijhoff.
Koloniaal Verslag ("Colonial Report")
Handelingen der Staten-Generaal, Eerste en Tweede Kamer. Supplement C.
Kop, J.H.
2008 Water in the city. Drinking water, sanitation and flood control in urban areas. In: W. Ravesteijn and J.H. Kop (eds.), *For profit and prosperity: The contribution made by Dutch engineers to public works in Indonesia 1800-2000*. Zaltbommel/Leiden: Aprilis/KITLV Press 2008, pp. 309-343.

2015 Irrigation sector mission Indonesia (1984). In: J.H. Kop, W. Ravesteijn and K.J. Kop (eds.), *Irrigation revisited: An anthology of Indonesian-Dutch cooperation* 1965-2014. Delft/Jakarta: Eburon. Pp. 245-262.

Kop, J.H., W. Ravesteijn and K.J. Kop

2015 *Irrigation revisited: An anthology of Indonesian-Dutch* cooperation 1965-2014. Delft/Jakarta: Eburon.

2017 *Tapak tilas irigasi: Bunga rampai kerja sama Indonesia-Belanda 1965-2014*. Jakarta: Netherlands Embassy.

Korving, H.

1947 *Het Koninklijk Instituut van Ingenieurs in Indië*. In: Koninklijk Instituut van Ingenieurs. Jubileum 1847-1947. Supplement to *De Ingenieur* of September 12th.

Koster, D.A.

1899 Beschouwingen aangaande de volkswelvaart en het irrigatiewezen op Java in verband met de Solovallei-werken. *DI* 14 (47): 577-579, (48): 593-595, (49): 603-606.

Kothari, R.

1980 Foreword. In: C.A. Alvares, *Homo faber. Technology and culture in India China and the West from 1500 to the present day*. The Hague etc.: Martinus Nijhoff Publishers. Pp. IX-XIII.

Kroesen, J.C.Th.

1871 Rapport der commissie, belast met een onderzoek omtrent het in de regentschappen Grissee, Sidajoe en Lamongan werkende stelsel van irrigatie door middel van wadoeks en de wenschelijkheid om dat stelsel in de afdeeling Grobogan toe te passen. *Tijdschrift voor Nijverheid en Landbouw in Nederlandsch-Indië* 17: 144-158.

Kuhn, T.S.

1970 *The structure of scientific revolutions*. Chicago/London: University of Chicago Press.

Kuitenbrouwer, M.

1985 *Nederland en de opkomst van het moderne imperialisme; koloniën en buitenlandse politiek 1870-1902*. Amsterdam/Dieren: De Bataafsche Leeuw.

1994 Drie omwentelingen in de historiografie van het imperialisme: Engeland en Nederland. *Tijdschrift voor Geschiedenis* 107: 559-585.

Kunstmeren (“Artificial lakes”)

1882 Daarstelling van kunstmeren voor irrigatie. *IG* 4, II: 216-219.

Lakerveld, A. van, and Brocx

1863-1871 *Handleiding voor bouwkundigen en industrieelen in Nederlandsch-Oost-Indië*. The Hague: Gebroeders Van Cleef. (Four volumes).

Lakoff, S.A.

1977 Scientists, technologists and political power. In: I. Spiegel-Rösing, I. and D. de Solla Price (eds.), *Science, technology and society. A cross-disciplinary perspective*. London and Beverly Hills: SAGE Publications. Pp. 355-392.

Lammers, W.

1929 Invloed van de bestuurshervorming op den dienst van ‘s lands waterstaat in Nederlandsch-Indië. *DWI* 17 (2): 28-44.

1939 Het “Provinciaal Waterreglement Oost-Java”. *DINI* 6 (2): II. 43-50, (3): II. 51-64, (4): II. 91-99.

1942 *De beteekenis van cultuurplannen voor den inheemschen landbouw op Java en Madoera*. Rede uitgesproken bij de aanvaarding van het ambt van buitengewoon hoogleraar aan de landbouwhogeschool te Wageningen op 18 Februari 1942. Wageningen: H. Veenman & Zonen.

Lamminga, A.G.
1885/1886 Irrigatie uit de rivier Pekalen. Bijdrage tot de kennis van het irrigatiewezen in de residentie Probolingo. *TKIVI (NI)*, pp. 55-76.
1894/1895 Werken tot verbetering van de bevloeiing en den waterafvoer der districten Gending, Gading en Padjarakan, afdeeling Kraksaän, residentie Probolinggo. *TKIVI (Verh.)*, pp. 93-179.
1900 Reorganisatie van den Indischen waterstaatdienst. *IG* 22, II: 1349-1367.
1902 Feestrede bij de opening van het aquaduct te Pontjol. *DI* 17 (49): 867-870.
1905 Pekalen-irrigatiewerken in de afdeeling Kraksaän der residentie. *DI* 20 (46): 758-766.
1911 Gewijzigde inzichten in den bouw van prises d'eau in Indische rivieren sedert 1887. *DI* 26 (1): 108-117.
1910 *Beschouwingen over den tegenwoordigen stand van het irrigatiewezen in Nederlandsch-Indië*. The Hague: Gebrs. J. & H. van Langenhuysen.
Landbouwatlas ("Agricultural Atlas")
1926 *Landbouwatlas van Java en Madoera*. Mededeelingen van het Centraal Kantoor voor de Statistiek no. 33. Weltevreden: Departement van Landbouw, Nijverheid en Handel.
Lansing, J.S.
1991 *Priests and programmers: Technologies of power in the engineered landscape of Bali*. Princeton, N.J.: Princeton University Press.
Layton, E.
1977 Conditions of technological development. In: I. Spiegel-Rösing and D. de Solla Price (eds.), *Science, technology and society. A cross-disciplinary perspective*, London and Beverly Hills: SAGE Publications. Pp. 197-222.
Leakey, R.E.
1981 *Op het spoor van de mens*. Utrecht/Antwerpen: Het Spectrum.
Leidelmeijer, M.
1992 Technische ontwikkeling in de suikerindustrie op Java, 1795-1870. *JGBT* 9: 95-123.
Lemaire, T.
1976 *Over de waarde van kulturen*. Baarn: Ambo.
Lente, D. van, H.W. Lintsen. M.S.C. Bakker, E. Homburg, J.W. Schot and G.P.J. Verbong
1992 Techniek en modernisering. In: H.W. Lintsen (ed.), *Techniek in Nederland. De wording van een moderne samenleving 1800-1890*. Volume I. Zutphen: Walburg Pers. Pp. 19-36.
Leon, M. de
1851 *Oost-Indische mysteriën. De toestand der civiele genie in Nederlandsch Indië*. Rotterdam: H. Nijgh.
Liefrinck, F.A.
1886/1887 De rijstcultuur op Bali. *IG* 8, II: 1033-1059, 1213-1237, 1557-1568; 9, I: 17-30, 181-189, 364-385, 515-552.
1892 Nota voor den Directeur v. Binnenl. Bestuur betreffende de afwatering van den watertoevoer en den waterafvoer in de Solo-vallei. (In: BOW Archives E II-92, 2).
1896/1897 De verbetering van het irrigatiewezen op Java. *IG* 18, II: 1165-1205; 19, I: 311-336, 473-498.
Lieneman, B.
1931 Grondverbetering door cement-injectie bij den wadoekdam Patjal. *DWI* 19 (11): 366-377.
Limburg, J. et al.
1936 *De toekomst der academisch gegradueerden*. Groningen/Batavia: J.B. Wolters.

Lindblad, J.Th.
1989 The economic history of colonial Indonesia: An historiographical survey. *Economic and Social History in the Netherlands* 1: 31-47.
Lintsen, H.W.
1980 *Ingenieurs in Nederland in de negentiende eeuw*. The Hague: Martinus Nijhoff.
1982 Review of M. Pieterson (ed.), "Het technisch labyrint", 1981. *Wetenschap en Samenleving* no. 9: 40-46.
1985 *Ingenieur van beroep*. Den Haag: Ingenieurspers.
1992 Grootschaligheid versus grootschaligheid. *Erfgoed van Industrie en Techniek* 1 (1): 3-7.
Lintsen, H.W. (ed.)
1992-1995 *Geschiedenis van de techniek in Nederland. De wording van een moderne samenleving 1800-1890*. Zutphen: Walburg Pers. (Six volumes).
Lintsen, H.W. and E. Homburg
1995 Techniekgeschiedenis in Nederland. In: H.W. Lintsen (ed.), *Techniek in Nederland. De wording van een moderne samenleving 1800-1890*, Volume VI. Zutphen: Walburg Pers. Pp. 255-266.
Locher-Scholten, E.
1981 *Ethiek in fragmenten; vijf studies over koloniaal denken en doen van Nederlanders in de Indonesische archipel 1877-1942*. Utrecht: Hes.
1994 *Sumatraans sultanaat en koloniale staat. De relatie Djambi-Batavia (1830-1907) en het Nederlandse imperialisme*. Leiden: KITLV Uitgeverij.
2004 *Sumatran sultanate and colonial state: Jambi and the rise of Dutch imperialism, 1830-1907*. Ithaca, N.Y.: Southeast Asia Program Publications, Southeast Asia Program, Cornell University
Lorenz, C.
1990 *De constructie van het verleden. Een inleiding in de theorie van de geschiedenis*. Meppel/Amsterdam: Boom.
Lucas, A.
1977 Social revolution in Pemalang, Central Java, 1945. *Indonesia* 24: 87-122.
Loekman Soetrisno
1980 *The sugar industry and rural development: The impact of cane cultivation for export on rural Java: 1830-1934*. Ph. D. Thesis Cornell University.
Maanen, Th.D. van
1924 *Irrigatie in Nederlandsch-Indië*. Weltevreden: Visser & Co.
1931 *Irrigatie in Nederlandsch-Indië*. Batavia-Centrum: Visser & Co. (Second revised and increased edition).
MacLeod, R.
1977 Changing perspectives in the social history of science. In: I. Spiegel-Rösing and D. de Solla Price (eds.), *Science, technology and society. A cross-disciplinary perspective*, London and Beverly Hills: SAGE Publications. Pp. 149-196.
Mansvelt, W.M.F. and P. Creutzberg (eds.)
1975-1978 *Changing economy in Indonesia. A Selection of statistical source material from the early 19th century up to 1940*. Four volumes. The Hague: Martinus Nijhoff.
Marel, J. van der, Ch.G. Cramer and J.E. van der Stok
1919 *Voorstel betreffende eene algehele doorvoering van het wadoekstelsel en eene daarmee gepaard gaande afschaffing van de zogenaamde dag- en nachtregeling*. Weltevreden: Landsdrukkerij.
1921 *Verslag betreffende de toepassing van het wadoekstelsel over 1918 en 1919*. Weltevreden: Landsdrukkerij.

Marle, J.W. van
1894 Irrigatie in de residentie Tegal. *DI* 9 (51): 619-623, (52): 635-637.
Master Plan
1974 Master plan of Sala river basin development. Republic of Indonesia, Ministry of Public Works and Electric Power, Directorate of Water Resources Development. Overseas Technical Cooperation Agency Japan.
Maurits (P.A. Daum)
1982 *H. van Brakel, ing. B.O.W.* Amsterdam: Querido. (First edition 1890).
McVey, R. T.
1965 *The rise of Indonesian communism.* Ithaca, New York: Cornell University Press.
McVey, R. T. (ed.)
1978 *Southeast Asian transitions. Approaches through social history.* New Haven/London: Yale University Press.
Mededeelingen ("Announcements")
1924 *Mededeelingen der regeering omtrent enkele onderwerpen van algemeen belang.* Weltevreden: Landsdrukkerij.
Melchior, A.P.
1897 De bevloeiingswerken op Java. *IG* 19,II: 1181-1208, 1288-1316.
1914 J.E. de Meyier. *DI* 29 (5): 87-91.
Menenteng
1888 De Menenteng waterleiding in het district Losarie, residentie Cheribon. *TKNI* Verhandelingen en mededeelingen, pp. 42-48.
Metzelaar, J.Th.
1946 Irrigatie. In: C.J.J. van Hall and C. van de Koppel, *De landbouw in den Indischen archipel.* The Hague: W. van Hoeve. Pp. 201-238.
Meulen, J.H.F. ter
1918 De geschiedenis van eene regeling tot exploitatie van irrigatiewerken op Java. *De Indische Mercuur* 41 (37): 721-723.
Meulen, W.A. van der
1940 Irrigation in the Netherlands Indies. *Bulletin of the Colonial Institute of Amsterdam* 3: 142-159.
Meyers, A.A.
1929 De aanpassing van eenige onzer openbare werken zoowel aan de in Nederlandsch Oost-Indië aanwezige natuurlijke, als aan de gegroeide koloniale, omstandigheden. *DWI* 17 (9): 264-273.
1933 Schets, waarin de zich op Java voordoende irrigatievraagstukken op economisch, sociaal, landbouwkundig, technisch, financieel en beheers-gebied vergeleken worden met de omstandigheden elders. *DWI* 21 (9): 226-232.
Meyier, J.E. de
1891 Bevloeiingen. In: N.H. Henket, Ch. M. Schols and J.M. Telders (eds.), *Waterbouwkunde*, First Part, Section VII. The Hague: Gebroeders Van Cleef.
1891/1892 Aantekeening A Geschiedkundig overzicht, B De stuw te Glapan, C De stuw te Sedadie. *TKIVI (NI)*, pp. XII-XXI. (In: Slinkers 1891/92).
1898a Studie over vaste stuwdammen in verband met de voorgenomen opstuwing der Solo-rivier. *DI* 13 (3): 23-26, (4): 33-37.
1898b Nota omtrent de werken ter bevloeiing van de Solovallei, van de Directeur der Burgerlijke Openbare Werken, Batavia, 8 Augustus 1898. In: National Archives, Ministry of the Colonies, Resolutions 1898, 4-7 November, no. 76 (7 November), inventory no. 5320.
1902 Irrigatie-fanatisme. *IG* 24, I: 172-195.

1910 De legende der Solovallei-werken. *IG* 32, I: 822-823.
1912a De hervatting der Solovallei-werken. *IG* 34, I: 662-664.
1912b Een "ingenieur" over de Solo-vallei-werken. *IG* 34, II: 1228-1230.
1913 Een inlandsch oordeel. *IG* 35, I: 245-246.
1920 *De technische vraagbaak voor Nederland en Koloniën*. Deventer: A.E. Kluwer.
1921 Waterstaat. In: *Encyclopaedie van Nederlandsch-Indië*. The Hague: Martinus Nijhoff; Leiden: N.V. v/h E.J. Brill.Volume IV: 700-731.

Mindere Welvaartscommissie ("Lesser Welfare Committee")
1905-1914 *Onderzoek naar de mindere welvaart der Inlandsche bevolking op Java en Madoera*. Weltevreden: F.B. Smits. (12 Volumes). Especially:
1908 *Overzicht van de uitkomsten der gewestelijke onderzoekingen naar den Landbouw en daaruit gemaakte gevolgtrekkingen*. Volume VA (First Part). Batavia: H.M. van Dorp & Co.
1910 *Overzicht van de uitkomsten der gewestelijke onderzoekingen naar de irrigatie en daaruit gemaakte gevolgtrekkingen*. Volume VIIA.
1914 *Voorstellen en besluiten der welvaartscommissie in 1914*. Volume XI. Batavia: Papyrus.

Minister
1902 Minister van Asch van Wijk en de Solo-quaestie. *DI* 17 (40): 707.

Moon, S.
2004 Empirical knowledge, scientific authority, and native development: The controversy over sugar/rice ecology in the Netherlands East Indies, 1905–1914. *Environment and History* 10 (1): 59–81.
2007 Technology and ethical idealism: A history of development in the Netherlands East Indies. Leiden: Leiden University Press.
2009 Justice, geography, and steel: Technology and national identity in Indonesian industrialization. *OSIRIS* 24 (1): 253–277.

Mrázek, R.
2002 *Engineers of happy land: Technology and nationalism in a colony*. Princeton, N.J.: Princeton University Press.

Mumford, L.
1967 *The myth of the machine: Vol. 1. Technics and human development*. New York: Harcourt-Brace-Jovanovich.
1972 Technics and the nature of man. In: M. Kranzberg and W.H. Davenport (eds.), *Technology and Culture*. New York etc.: New American Library. Pp. 200-215.

Muijzenberg, O. van den, and W. Wolters
1988 *Conceptualizing development*. Dordrecht: Foris Publications (CASA).

Naerssen, F.H. van
1938 Historische techniek. *DI* 53 (7): A. 65-66.
1976 Tribute to the god and tribute to the king. In: C.D. Cowan and O.W. Wolters, *Southeast Asian history and historiography*. Ithaca and London: Cornell University Press.

Nagelkerke, G.A.
1974 Bibliografisch overzicht uit periodieken over Indonesië 1930-1945. Leiden: Bibliotheek Koninklijk Instituut voor Taal-, Land- en Volkenkunde.

Nelkin, D.
1977 Technology and public policy. In: I. Spiegel-Rösing and D. de Solla Price (eds.), *Science, technology and society. A cross-disciplinary perspective*, London/Beverly Hills: SAGE Publications. Pp. 393-442.

Nes, A. van
2015 Luwu/Pompengan: Development of an irrigated area (1975-1992). In: J.H. Kop, W. Ravesteijn and K.J. Kop (eds.), *Irrigation revisited: An anthology of Indonesian-Dutch cooperation* 1965-2014. Delft/Jakarta: Eburon. Pp. 133-144.
Niel, R. van
1981 The effect of export cultivation in nineteenth-century Java. *Modern Asian Studies* 15 (1): 25-58.
Noble, D.F.
1984 *Forces of production: A social history of industrial automation*. New York: Alfred A. Knop.
Nota ("Memorandum")
1857 Nota over den waterstaat der afdeelingen Soerabaya en Modjokerto en over de kanalisatie der Porrongrivier. *TKIVI (Not.)* Supplement XI, meeting 11-11-1856, pp. 56-61.
Numans, J.G.
1916 De bevloeiing in het tertiaire vak. *DWI* 4 (8): 337-344.
Oostinjer, H.
1898 De vaste stuwdam in de Solo-rivier op Java. *DI* 13 (7): 80-81.
Ott de Vries, P.J.
1922 De werkkring en de taak van den ingenieur in Nederlandsch-Indië. *DI* 37 (37): 736-744.
1933 Ir. Rudolf Adriaan van Sandick. *DWI* 21 (4): 81-83.
1936 Prof. ir. C.W. Weijs, 80 jaar. *DI* 51 (33): A. 269-271.
Overzicht ("Overview")
1916 *Overzicht der geldmiddelen van Nederlandsch-Indië van 1967 af*. The Hague: Martinus Nijhoff.
Pacey, A.
1990 *Technology in world civilization. A thousand-year history*. Oxford: Basil Blackwell.
1992 *The maze of ingenuity. Ideas and idealism in the development of technology*. Cambridge, Massachusetts/London England: MIT Press.
Pareau Dumont, H.W.
1940 Eenige technische en economische mededeelingen over het gebied der voormalige Solovalleiwerken. *DI* 55 (9): A. 75-76. (Verslag van een lezing).
Pengembangan
1992 Pengembangan wilayah sungai Bengawan Solo. Departemen Pekerjaan Umum, Direktorat Jenderal Pengairan, Proyek Induk Pengembangan, Wilayah Sungai Bengawan Solo.
Pertanian di Indonesia
2015 http://www.indonesia-investments.com/id/budaya/ekonomi/ikhtisar-struktur-ekonomi/pertanian/item378, retrieved January 2017.
Pfaffenberger, B.
1988 Fetishised objects and humanised nature: Toward an anthropology of technology. *Man* 23: 236-252.
1990 The harsh facts of hydraulics: Technology and society in Sri Lanka's colonization schemes. *TC* 31 (3): 361-397.
Pierson, J.L.
1891/1892 De plannen tot verbetering der bevloeiing en afwatering van de Solo-vallei. *TKIVI (Verh.)*, pp. 58-71.

Pieterson, M. (ed.)
1993 *Technisch labyrint. Een maatschappijgeschiedenis van drie industriële revoluties.* Amsterdam: Boom.
Pluvier, J.
1978 *Indonesië: kolonialisme, onafhankelijkheid, neo-kolonialisme.* Nijmegen: Socialistische Uitgeverij Nijmegen.
Poirier, R.
1957 *L'épopée des grands travaux; de la tour de Babel à la cité de l'atome.* Vol. II. Paris: Plon.
Polderman, L.J.
1935 Voorloopige gegevens betreffende de exploitatie van het reservoir Pendjalin. *DINI* 2 (7): VI. 91-104.
Polderman, L.J., W. Swaan and A.M. Verschoor
1935 Voorloopige richtlijnen voor de exploitatie van het reservoir Pendjalin. *DINI* 2 (12): VI. 149-159.
Polderman, L.J. and J.F. Graadt van Roggen
1936a Waterbeheer en waterschappen. 2. Is invoering op Java van waterschappen in den geest van de Balineesche soebaks gewenscht? *DINI* 3 (2): VI. 33-41.
1936b Dupliek (waterbeheer en waterschappen). *DINI* 3 (8): VI. 145-148.
Posno, M.M.C.
1935 Het sluizencomplex Sewan nabij Tangerang. *DINI* 2 (8): VI. 105-116.
Post, C.L.F.
1879 *Over den waterstaat in Nederlandsch-Indië.* Amsterdam: Schuitemaker & Co.
Post, W. van der
1983 Delta-plan voor Java. *Algemeen Dagblad* 27 August, p. 35. (In: Horst file on Van Blommestein).
Pijnacker Hordijk, J.M.
1901 Discussiebijdrage. In: H.H. van Kol, H.H. van, Een algemeen irrigatie-plan voor Java. *DI* 16 (22): 358-367, (25): 414-418.
Priyambodho, B.A., C. Qin and W. Ravesteijn
2015 Under the wings of the great Garuda: responsible port innovation in the Jakarta Bay area. *Coastal Cities and their Sustainable Future* 148 (2015), pp. 82-93.
Q.
1932 B.O.W. en de provincie. *DS* 3: 13-16.
Quant, J.F.
1899 De Solowerken. *DI* 14 (32): 407-410, (33): 417-418.
Radder, H.
1992 Normative reflexions on constructivist approaches to science and technology. *Social Studies of Science* 22: 141-173.
Ramaer, J.W.
1914 Antwoord op Ypelaar 1914. *DWI* 2 (6): 159-163.
Ravesteijn, W.
1989 Technology and culture: Impulse towards a cultural-anthropological approach to approriate technology. In: J. Boes, W. Ravesteijn and W. Riedijk (eds.), *Appropriate technology in industrialized countries.* Delft: Delft University Press. Pp. 3-34.
1991 Pretensions and failures: Irrigation engineers in the Netherlands Indies 1870-1910. Paper Annual Meeting of the Society for the History of Technology, Madison, Wisconsin (USA), 30 October – 3 November 1991.
1992 Wheel of technology: Irrigation in Java. Paper 4S/EASST-Joint Conference on Science, Technology and "Development", Gothenburg, Sweden, August 12-15, 1992.

1993 Failed or continued development? Social construction of irrigation in the Solo Valley, Netherlands East Indies. Paper Irrigation seminar, Wageningen Agricultural University, 15 April 1993.

1995 Mega-irrigatieproject op koloniaal Java. *DI* 107 (15): 17-19.

1997 *De zegenrijke heeren der wateren. Irrigatie en staat op Java, 1832-1942* ("The auspicious lords of the waters. Irrigation and the colonial state in Java, 1832-1942"), 1997). Delft: Delft University Press. (Dissertation).

2000 Irrigatie en koloniale staat op Java: de gevolgen van de hongersnoden in Demak ("Irrigation and the colonial state in Java: the consequences of the famines in Demak"). *Jaarboek voor Ecologische Geschiedenis* Vol. 4 (2000): 87-112.

2002a Dutch engineering overseas: The creation of a modern irrigation system in colonial Java. *Knowledge, Technology and Policy* 14 (2002) 4: 126-144.

2002b Irrigation development in colonial Java: The history of the Solo Valley works from a regime perspective. *International Journal of Technology, Policy and Management* 2 (2002) 4: 361-386.

2002c Een ingenieur met visie. Prof. Dr. Ir. Willem Johan van Blommestein (1905-1985). *Tijdschrift voor Waterstaatsgeschiedenis* 11 (2002) 1: 6-11.

2006 Water control and the colonial state: The case of Dutch irrigation engineering in the Indonesian island of Java, 1832-1942. *Journal of the International Committee for the History of Technology* Vol. 11 (2006): 197-211.

2007a Controlling water, controlling people: Irrigation engineering and state formation in the Dutch East Indies. *Itinerario. International Journal on the History of European Expansion and Global Interaction* 31 (2007) 1: 89-118.

2007b Between globalisation and localisation. The case of Dutch civil engineering in Indonesia, 1800 – 1950. *Comparative Technology Transfer and Society* 5 (2007) 1: 32-65.

2010 Ideology and practice of colonial engineering. In: H. de Jonge and T. van Meijl, *On the subject of labour: Essays in memory of Frans Hüsken*. Nijmegen: In de Walvis publishers, 2010, pp. 90-95.

Ravesteijn, W, L. Hermans and E. van der Vleuten (eds.)

2002 Water systems. Special issue of *Knowledge, Technology and Policy* 14 (2002) 4.

Ravesteijn, W. and J. H. Kop (eds.)

2004 *Bouwen in de archipel. Burgerlijke openbare werken in Nederlands-Indië en Indonesië 1800-2000* ("Building in the archipelago. Civil public works in the Dutch East Indies and Indonesia 1800-2000"). Zutphen: Walburg Pers 2004.

2008 *For profit and prosperity: The contribution made by Dutch engineers to public works in Indonesia 1800-2000*. Zaltbommel/Leiden: Aprilis/KITLV Press.

Ravesteijn, W., X. Song and R. Wennersten

2012 European and Chinese integrated river basin management: Experiences and perspectives. In: S. Mambretti (ed.), *Flood risk assessment and management*. Southampton, UK / Billerica, USA: WIT Press, 2011, pp. 59-70.

Redactie Ingenieur ("Editors Engineer")

1888 Irrigatie in Indië. *DI* 3 (2): 11-12, (3): 19-20, (5): 37-38.

Redactie Waterstaats-Ingenieur ("Editors Public Works Engineer")

1929 Heeft Indië een hydrodynamisch laboratorium noodig? *DWI* 17 (6): 192-193.

Reddy, M.A.

1990 Travails of an irrigation canal company in South India, 1857-1882. *Economic and Political Weekly* March 24: 619-628.

Rees, D.W.F. van, and S. de Graaff
1900 *Nota over den invloed van de particuliere suikerriet-cultuur op de teelt van Inlandsche voedingsgewassen*. Batavia: Landsdrukkerij.
1907 *Vervolg der nota over den invloed van de particuliere suikerriet-cultuur op de teelt van Inlandsche voedingsgewassen*. Batavia: Landsdrukkerij.
Ribbers, J.C. and H. van Gelderen
1906 Rapport omtrent den Waarnemingsdienst der Vaarwaters naar Soerabaia. The Hague: F.J. Belinfante, voorh. A.D. Schinkel. (In: National Archives, Haringhuizen-Schoemaker Collection no. 79).
Riedijk, W.
1986a *Technology for liberation*. Delft: Delft University Press.
1986b *Techniek op maat. Aangepaste technologie en nieuwe werkgelegenheid*. Meppel/Amsterdam: Boom.
Riedijk, W. (ed.)
1982 *Appropriate technology for developing countries*. Delft: Delft University Press.
Rietveld, J.Th.
1932 De Sampeanstuw honderd jaar. *DWI* 20 (9): 277-287.
Ringers, J.A.
1938 Onze waterbouwkundige prestaties. In: P. Lieftinck (ed.), *Het bedrijfsleven tijdens de regeering van H.M. Koningin Wilhelmina 1898-1938*. Amsterdam: J. Frijda. Pp. 249-262.
River
1988 River basin development of Wonogiri dam. Department of Public Works, Directorate general of Water Resources, Bengawan Sala River Basin Development Project.
Robbers, C.
1913 De wadoek Pridjetan, een belangrijke vergaarkom in de Solovallei. *DI* (23): 449-461.
Rochussen, J.J.
1853 *Toelichting en verdediging van eenige daden van mijn bestuur in Indie*. The Hague: Gebroeders Van Cleef.
Rokkan, S.
1975 Dimensions of state formation and nation-building: A possible paradigm for research on variations within Europe. In: Ch. Tilly (ed.), *The formation of national states in western Europe*. Princeton: Princeton University Press. Pp. 562-600.
Romijn, D.G.
1932 Een regelbare meetoverlaat als tertiaire aftapsluis. *DWI* 20 (9): 287-292.
Rutledge, S. E.
1986 Basin development plan. Lower Solo river development project. Montreal Engineering Company. (Summary).
Rybczynski, W.
1980 *Paper heroes*. Garden City, New York: Anchor Press/Doubleday.
Sahid Susanto and Suprodjo
1987 Surface water utilization at the Sampean watershed area, East Java, Indonesia. (Paper).
Saltet, A.H.
1896 Het beheer der burgerlijke openbare werken in Nederlandsch-Indië. *IG* 18, I: 1-36.
1912 Nogmaals "irrigatie en landbouw op Java" en een woord over het overbrengen der Irrigatie-afdelingen naar het Departement van landbouw. *TBB* 42: 67-73.
Sandick, R.A. van
1898a Bevloeiing uit schrik? *IG* 20, I: 150-158.
1898b De werken in de Solo-vallei geschorst. Offprint from: *Insulinde*, 22 November. (In: BOW Archives E II-92, 1).

1898c De Nieuwe Rotterdamsche Courant en de Indische Waterstaat. Offprint from: *Insulinde*, 22 November. (In: BOW Archives E II-92, 1).
1900a Het verslag de commissie van advies nopens de werken in de Solo-vallei aan den Minister van Koloniën. *DI* 15 (31): 466-470, (32): 481-483, (33): 493-496, (34): 509-515, (35): 525-527.
1900b Een brief uit Indië over de Solo-zaak. *DI* 15 (51): 790-791.
1900c Het verslag van de commissie van advies nopens de werken in de Solo-Vallei. *IG* 22, II: 1007-1016, 1333-1348.
1901a Openbaarmaking gewenscht van het advies der Commissie voor de Solowerken over de reorganisatie van den Indische Waterstaat. *DI* 16 (33): 537.
1901b Discussiebijdrage. In: H.H. van Kol, Een algemeen irrigatie-plan voor Java. *DI* 16 (22): 358-367, (25): 414-418.
1905 Irrigatie en landontginning (reclamation) in het westen der Vereenigde Staten van Noord-Amerika. *DI* 20 (15): 231-253.
1911 Landbouw en irrigatie op Java. *DI* 26: 946-950.
1912a Ter herinnering aan J.A. de Gelder. *DI* 27 (39): 785-786.
1912b Irrigatie op Java. *DI* 27 (46): 914-923.
1918a Ir. M.J. van Bosse. *DI* 33 (9): 152-154.
1918b Ir. G. van Houten. *DI* 33 (35): 659-660.
1926a Ter herdenking. Ir. M. Ypelaar. *DI* 41(9): 169-171.
1926b Ter herdenking. Ir. H.H. van Kol. *DI* 41 (51): 1025-1028.
1929 De Indischen ingenieur, 50 jaren geleden en thans. *IG* 51 (1): 265-269.

Schaik, A. van
1986 *Colonial control and peasant resources in Java. Agricultural involution reconsidered.* Amsterdam: University of Amsterdam.

Schalker, W.J.P.J. and W.C. Muller
1912-1928 *Repertorium op de literatuur betreffende de Nederlandsche koloniën in Oost- en West-Indië, voor zoover zij verspreid is in tijdschriften en periodieken.* The Hague: Martinus Nijhoff. (Third to Sixth Sequel).

Schalij, J.
1903 Het zelfstandig bestaan van de verlegging van den Solo-mond. *DI* 18 (2): 24

Schoemaker, H.J.
1983 Wateraanvoer, -verdeling en afvoer. Delft: Technische Hogeschool Delft, Afdeling der Civiele Techniek. (Lecture notes).

Schoemaker, H.J. and A. Figee
1982 Hydraulic engineering in irrigation and drainage. Appropriate technology in developing countries. In: W. Riedijk (ed.), *Appropriate technology for developing countries*. Delft: Delft University Press. Pp. 151-181.

Schokkenbroek, J.C.A.
1988 De Nederlands-Indische regering en irrigatie op Java, ca. 1900-1942. Manuscript.

Schoor, W. van der
1994 Biologie en landbouw. F.A.F.C. Went en de Indische proefstations. *Gewina* 17: 145-161.

Schot, J.W. (ed.)
1998-2003 *Techniek in Nederland in de twintigste eeuw*. Zutphen: Walburg Pers. (Seven volumes).

Schrevel, A.
1993 *Access to water. A socio-economic study into the practice of irrigation development in Indonesia*. Dissertation Utrecht University.

Schulte Nordholt, H.G.C.
1988 *Een Balische dynastie. Hiërarchie en conflict in de Negara Mengwi 1700-1940*. Haarlem: Multi Print Noord.
Schulte Nordholt, N.G.
1991 *Indonesië*. Amsterdam/The Hague/Brussel: Koninklijk Instituut voor de Tropen/Novib/NCOS.
Schultz, B., R.H. Susanto, F.X. Suryadi and A. Sidik Waskito
2015 Analysis of water management in reclaimed tidal lowlands of Indonesia. Experiments in the Telang I scheme, Musi Delta, South Sumatra (2004-2008). In: J.H. Kop, W. Ravesteijn and K.J. Kop (eds.), *Irrigation revisited: An anthology of Indonesian-Dutch cooperation* 1965-2014. Delft/Jakarta: Eburon. Pp. 219-244.
Schumacher, E.F.
1978 *Small is beautiful*. London: Sphere Books LTD.
Scott, J.
1995 *State simplifications. Some applications to southeast Asia*. Amsterdam: CASA.
Sepp, D.
1934-1935 *Repertorium op de literatuur betreffende de Nederlandsche koloniën, voor zoover zij verspreid is in tijdschriften, periodieken, serie- en mengelwerken*. The Hague: Martinus Nijhoff. (Seventh and Eighth Sequel).
Setten van der Meer, N.C. van
1979 *Sawah cultivation in ancient Java*. Canberra: Australian National University Press.
Shrum, W. and Y. Shenhav
1995 Science and technology in less developed countries. In: S. Jasanoff, G.E. Markle, J. C. Petersen and T. Pinch (eds.), *Handbook of science and technology studies*. Thousand Oaks/London/New Delhi: SAGE Publications, Inc. Pp. 627-651.
Sibinga Mulder, J.
1912 De irrigatie in verband met de Javasuikerindustrie. *IGS* (12 Maart), pp. 177-199.
Simanjuntak. I, N. Frantzeskaki, B. Enserink and W. Ravesteijn
2011 Evaluating Jakarta's flood defence governance: The impact of political and institutional reforms. *Water Policy* 14 (2012): 561–580.
Slamet, I.E.
1968 *De Indonesische dorpssamenleving*. Amsterdam: Universiteit van Amsterdam, Antropologisch-Sociologisch Centrum, Afdeling Zuid- en Zuidoost-Azië.
Slinkers, L.H.
1891/92 De Waterwerken in de afdeeling Demak. *TKIVI (NI)*, pp. I-XII.
Slors, J.E.V.A.
1936 Waterbeheer op Java. *DINI* 3 (8): VI. 137-138.
Smits, M.B.
1929 *Over den landbouw in Nederlandsch-Indië*. Groningen/Den Haag/Weltevreden: J.B. Wolters.
Snell, D.C.W.
1928 Verslag nopens het onderzoek verricht in verband met de plannen tot eene eventueele hervatting van de bevloeingswerken in de Solovallei. In: National Archives, Haringhuizen-Schoemaker Collection no. 44.
Soest, G.H. van
1869/71 *Geschiedenis van het kultuurstelsel*. Rotterdam: H. Nijgh (& Van Ditmar). (Three volumes).
Sollewijn Gelpke, J.H.F.
1885 *Gegevens voor een nieuwe landrente-regeling. Eindresumé der onderzoekingen bevolen bij Gouvts. Besluit van 23 Oct. 1879 no. 3*. Batavia: Landsdrukkerij.

Spiegel-Rösing, I.
1977 The study of science, technology and society (SSTS): Recent trends and future challenges. In: I. Spiegel-Rösing and D. de Solla Price (eds.), *Science, technology and society. A cross-disciplinary perspective*, London and Beverly Hills: SAGE Publications. Pp. 7-42.

Spiegel-Rösing, I. and D. de Solla Price (eds.)
1977 *Science, technology and society. A cross-disciplinary perspective*. London and Beverly Hills: SAGE Publications.

Stand ("Status")
1903 Stand van het irrigatievraagstuk der Solovallei. *DI* 18 (47): 824.

Stapel, F.W.
1941 Hoe uit de Oost-Indiën Nederlandsch-Indië werd. In: W.H. van Helsdingen and H. Hoogenberk (eds.), *Daar wèrd wat groots verricht .... Nederlandsch-Indië in de XXste eeuw*. Amsterdam: Elsevier. Pp. 27-65.

Steinberg, Th.
1993 "That world's fair feeling": control of water in 20th-century America. *Technology and Culture* 34 (2): 401-409.

Stern, P.H.
1979 *Small scale irrigation. A manual of low-cost water technology*. London/Bet Dagan, Israel: Intermediate Technology Publications/International Irrigation Information Center.

Stoppelaar, J.W. de
1930 Bemoeienis van de desa met bevloeiingswater. *Koloniaal Tijdschrift* 19: 441-449.

Studi
1993 Studi pengembangan sumber daya air terpadu wilayah sungai Bengawan Solo. Volume I Laporan Utama. Badan Penelitian dan Pengembangan Pekerjaan Umum. Republik Indonesia.

Study
1987 Study of irrigation management in Indonesia. Phase I. Draft Final report. International Irrigation management Institute (IIMI), Digana Village via Kandy, Sri Lanka. (Technical Assistance Agreement no. 673 INO/IIMI-ADB-GOI).

Swaan, W.
1931 "De nachtwadoeks", door Prof. Ir. J. Haringhuizen. *DWI* 19 (12): 408-410.
1935 Irrigatie in Ned.-Indië in crisistijd. *DI* 30 (46): A. 410-411. (Report of a speech).

Tangerangwerken
1936 Ingebruikstelling der Tangerangwerken. *DINI* 3 (9): VI. 153-158.

Telders, J.M., W.F. Leemans, J. Kraus and J.E. de Meyier
1900 *Verslag van de commissie van advies nopens de werken in de Solovallei*. Delft: Waltman.

Teeuwen, H.H.A.
2015 The role of the legal framework in implementing water resources development projects during the second part of the 20th century. In: J.H. Kop, W. Ravesteijn and K.J. Kop (eds.), *Irrigation revisited: An anthology of Indonesian-Dutch cooperation* 1965-2014. Delft/Jakarta: Eburon. Pp. 17-35.

Telkamp, G.J.
1981 Aangepaste technologie in koloniale context. De textielindustrie in Indonesië van 1930 tot 1942. In: P. Boomgaard, L. Noordegraaf, H. de Vries, W.M. Zappey, *Exercities in ons verleden*. Assen: Van Gorcum. & Comp. B.V. Pp. 224-245.

Teng Sioe Tjhan
1933 *De landrente-belasting*. Rotterdam: De Banier. (Dissertation Nederlandsche Handelshoogeschool Rotterdam).
Thal Larsen, J.H.
1912 Naar aanleiding van "De hervatting der Solovalleiwerken" in de "Indische Gids". *DI* 27 (46): 927-930.
1932 *Grepen uit het verleden en het heden van het irrigatiewezen*. Wageningen: H. Veenman en Zonen.
Tien ("Ten")
1938 *10 Vervlogen jaren. Uitgegeven ter gelegenheid van het tienjarig bestaan van de Koninklijke Nederlandsch-Indische Luchtvaartmaatschappij*. 1 November 1928-1938. Batavia-C.: De Unie/K.N.I.L.M.
Tilly, Ch.
1994 Entanglements of European cities and states. In: Ch. Tilly and W. P. Blockmans, *Cities and the rise of states in Europe A.D. 1000 to 1800*. Boulder/San Francisco/Oxford: Westview Press.
Tilly, Ch. (ed.)
1975 *The formation of national states in western Europe*. Princeton: Princeton University Press.
Toer, Pramoedya Ananta
1983 *Aarde der mensen*. Amsterdam/Weesp: Manus Amici/Het Wereldvenster. (NOVIB/NCOS).
Tubergen, J. van
1901 Opmerking naar aanleiding van het verslag der Solovalleicommissie. *DI* 16 (49): 800-803.
1902 Verslag der Solo-vallei-commissie. *DI* 17 (5): 77-81.
Veen, P.A.F. van and N. van der Sijs
1990 *Etymologisch woordenboek*. Utrecht/Antwerpen: Van Dale Lexicografie BV.
Veen, F.M. van
1935 De reservoirdam Gembong. *DINI* 2 (2): VI. 7-26.
Veer, P. van 't
1980a *De Atjeh-oorlog*. Amsterdam: Arbeiderspers/Wetenschappelijke Uitgeverij.
1980b Vogelvlucht door de geschiedenis van Indonesië (1800-1979). In: R.N.J. Kamerling (ed.), *Indonesië toen en nu*. Amsterdam: Intermediair Bibliotheek. Pp. 9-33.
Veld, W. in het
2015 Prosida-B irrigation rehabilitation project (1970-1974). In: J.H. Kop, W. Ravesteijn and K.J. Kop (eds.), *Irrigation revisited: An anthology of Indonesian-Dutch cooperation* 1965-2014. Delft/Jakarta: Eburon. Pp. 99-111.
Ven, G.P. van de (ed.)
1993 *Leefbaar laagland. Geschiedenis van de waterbeheersing en landaanwinning in Nederland*. Utrecht: Matrijs.
Verbetering ("Improvement")
1899 De verbetering van den waterafvoer in West-Brebes. *DI* 14 (18): 215-217.
Verbong, G.
1988 *Technische innovaties in de katoendrukkerij en -ververij in Nederland 1835-1920*. Amsterdam: NEHA.
Verburgh, S.
1884 De inkrimping van de afdeeling burgerlijke openbare werken in de Indische ontwerp-begrooting voor 1885. *IGS* (November), pp. 136-184.

Verrips, J. (ed.)
1995 *Transactions. Essays in honor of Jeremy F. Boissevain.* Amsterdam: Spinhuis.
Verschoor, A.M.
1934 Intensiveering van de landbouw, een irrigatietaak. *DINI* 1 (8): VI. 87-89.
1935 De herstellingen van de stuw Kaliwadas. *DINI* 2 (4): VI. 56-60.
Verslag BOW ("Civil Public Works Report")
1893-1927 *Verslag over de Burgerlijke Openbare Werken in Nederlandsch-Indië over het jaar ....* Batavia/The Hague. Especially Part V: Bevloeiing, afwatering en waterkering. (In: National Archives, Haringhuizen-Schoemaker Collection no. 87-96).
Verslag laboratorium BOW ("Civil Public Works Laboratory Report")
1927 *Verslag der werkzaamheden in het laboratorium B.O.W. 1917-1925.* Weltevreden: Landsdrukkerij.
Vink, G.J.
1941 De inheemsche landbouw. In: W. H. van Helsdingen and H. Hoogenberk (eds.), *Daar wèrd wat groots verricht .... Nederlandsch-Indië in de XXste eeuw.* Amsterdam: Elsevier. Pp. 357-369.
Vlugter, H.
1941 12½ Jaar hydrodynamisch onderzoek aan waterloopkundige modellen in Ned.-Indië en hydraulisch research-werk in het algemeen. *DINI* 8 (9): II. 82-93.
1949 Honderd jaar irrigatie. *DII* 1 (7): I. 99-105.
Vogel, J.E.A.
1924 Voorwoord. In: Th. D. van Maanen, *Irrigatie in Nederlandsch-Indië.* Weltevreden: Boekhandel: Visser & Co. Pp. VII-XIV.
Voorduin, J.C.
1914 De werken ter bevloeiing van een deel der afdeeling Brebes (Residentie Pekalongan) uit de Pemalie-Rivier. *TKIVI (Verh.)*, pp. 1-132.
Voorlopige cijfers ("Provisional figures")
1924, 1926-1933 Voorlopige cijfers en gegevens omtrent de werkzaamheden van het Departement der Burgerlijke Openbare Werken. (In: National Archives, Haringhuizen-Schoemaker Collection no. 97).
Vos, H.C.P. de
1926 Bevloeiing, welvaart en cultuur. *DWI* 14 (6): 183-190.
1946 De strijd om en tegen het water. In: W. H. van Helsdingen and H. Hoogenberk (eds.), *Daar wèrd wat groots verricht.... Nederlandsch-Indië in de XXste eeuw.* Amsterdam: Elsevier. Pp. 273-286.
Vries, E. de
1933 Landrente en irrigatie. *DS* 4: 258-262.
1961 De welvaartsdiensten. In: H. Baudet and I.J. Brugmans (eds.), *Balans van beleid. Terugblik op de laatste halve eeuw van Nederlandsch-Indië.* Assen: Van Gorcum/Prakke & Prakke.
Vries, H.M. de (ed.)
1928 *The importance of Java seen from the air.* Batavia: H.M. de Vries/G. Kolff & Co.
Vijfenveertig ("Forty Five")
1990 *45 Tahun Departemen Pekerjaan Umum.* Jakarta: Departemen Pekerjaan Umum.
Wade, R.
1982 The system of admistrative and political corruption: Canal irrigation in South India. *Journal of Development Studies* 18: 287-328.
Walbeehm, A.H.J.G.
1901a Eenige cijfers betreffende de Keningwerken. *TBB* 20 (3): 191-198.
1901b Nog eens de Keningwerken. *TBB* 21 (4): 323-337.

Wallerstein, I.
1974 *The modern world-system I: Capitalist agriculture and the origins of the European world-economy in the sixteenth century*. New York etc.: Academic Press.
1980 *The modern world-system II. Mercantilism and the consolidation of the European world-economy 1600-1750*. New York etc.: Academic Press.
Wanders, A.J.M.
1971 *Het raadsel Mars*. Utrecht/Antwerpen: Het Spectrum N.V.
Wardhono, A., G. Pratomo, B. Prakoso and C. Gema Qori'ah
2012 Countermeasures flood disaster Sampean river policy in Situbondo district. *GSTF International Journal of Law and Social Sciences* 2 (1): 118-122.
Watson-Verran, H. and D. Turnbull
1995 Science and other indigenous knowledge systems. In: S. Jasanoff, G.E. Markle, J. C. Petersen, T. Pinch (eds.), *Handbook of science and technology studies*. Thousand Oaks/London/New Delhi: SAGE Publications, Inc. Pp. 115-139.
Weatherford, J.
1988 *Indian givers. How the Indians of the Americas transformed the world*. New York: Fawcett Columbine.
Weber, E.
1976 *Peasants into frenchman. The modernization of rural France 1870-1914*. Stanford: Stanford University Press.
Weijer, G.A.Ph.
1941 De groote cultures. In: W. H. van Helsdingen and H. Hoogenberk (eds.), *Daar wèrd wat groots verricht .... Nederlandsch-Indië in de XXste eeuw*. Amsterdam: Elsevier. Pp. 286-322.
Weijs, C.W.
1900 Irrigatie-afdeelingen op Java; de inrichting en werking en het nut, dat van deze instellingen verwacht mag worden bijzonder voor verbetering van bevloeiingstoestanden daar te lande. *IGS* (Februari), pp. 7-139.
1913 *Schets van de ontwikkeling van technische bemoeienis met irrigatie in Indië*. Delft: J. Waltman Jr.
1921 Ir. A.G. Lamminga. *DI* 36 (20): 372-379.
Welderen baron Rengers, W.J. van
1905-1907 *Schets eener parlementaire geschiedenis van Nederland van 1849 tot 1891*. The Hague: Martinus Nijhoff. (Three volumes).
Wertheim, W.F.
1956 *Indonesian society in transition*. The Hague: Van Hoeve.
1972 *Evolutie en revolutie. De golfslag der emancipatie*. Amsterdam: Van Gennep NV.
1983 *Emancipation in Asia: Positive and negative lessons from China*. Rotterdam: CASP 10.
Wessel, J.
1996 *Dimensies van waterbeheer*. Delft: Delft University Press. (Farewell Speech).
Wessel, J., L.C. Grijns and P. Ankum (eds.),
1990 Short course on integrated river basin management. Delft: Faculteit der Wijsbegeerte en Technische Maatschappijwetenschappen (Sectie Recht en Bestuurskunde), Faculteit der Civiele Techniek (Sectie Irrigatie), Centre for Comparative Studies on River Basin Administration (RBA), Delft University of Technology.
Wesseling, H.L.
1988 *Indië verloren, rampspoed geboren*. Amsterdam: Bert Bakker.

Winner, L.
1993 Upon opening the black box and finding it empty: Social constructivism and the philosophy of technology. *Science, Technology and Human Values* 18 (3): 362-378.
Wisseman Christie, J.
2001 Irrigation in Java and Bali before 1500. Paper for the KITLV Jubilee workshop on "Water as a life giving and a deadly force", Leiden, 14-16 June 2001.
Witjes, B., F. Hüsken and J. Banning
1990 *Indonesië*. Utrecht: Teleac/Terra Uitgeverij.
Wittfogel, K.A.
1957 *Oriental despotism. A comparative study of total power*. New Haven and London: Yale University Press.
Witzenburg, J.H. van
1936a Waterbeheer en waterschappen. 1. Statistische gegevens en eenige kritische beschouwingen omtrent invoering van bevloeiingscorporaties op Java. *DINI* 3 (2): VI. 27-33.
1936b Dupliek (waterbeheer en waterschappen). *DINI* 3 (2): VI. 145.
Wolf, E.R.
1969 *Peasant wars of the twentieth century*. New York etc.: Harper & Row.
1982 *Europe and the people without history*. Berkeley etc.: University of California Press.
Wong Tanie (R. Huygen van Raal)
1900 Op- en aanmerkingen op het werk van den ingenieur J. Homan van der Heide, over volkswelvaart en irrigatiewezen op Java. *IG* 22, II: 874-883.
Worldbank
2017 http://data.worldbank.org/indicator/NY.GNP.PCAP.CD?locations=ID, retrieved January 2017.
Wijn, P.J.A. and E.W.H. Clason
1935 De economie der Tanggoel-Bondojoedowerken. *DINI* (3): VI. 29-38.
Yap, J.
2015 The West Tarum canal (1970-2014). In: J.H. Kop, W. Ravesteijn and K.J. Kop (eds.), *Irrigation revisited: An anthology of Indonesian-Dutch cooperation* 1965-2014. Delft/Jakarta: Eburon. Pp. 275-295.
Ypelaar, M.
1914 Irrigatie. *DWI* 2 (6): 156-159.

Index of colonial engineers

Curriculum vitae

Wim Ravesteijn is Associate Professor of Responsible and Sustainable Innovation affiliated to the Ethics and Philosophy of Technology Section within the Department of Values, Technology and Innovation, Faculty of Technology, Policy and Management (TPM), Delft University of Technology. He has been a part-time Contract Professor at Harbin Institute of Technology (HIT, China), in the framework of a joint TPM-HIT Engineering and Policy Analysis student exchange and double degree master programme. He has also taught Technology and Management at Beijing Information Science and Technology University where he was appointed Honorary Professor. His broad field of learning is Science, Technology and Society studies focused on public works and urban planning from historical, cultural and global perspectives. He has done research (including dissertation research) into the design, construction and management of civil engineering works in the Netherlands East Indies and Indonesia and into Integrated Water Resources Management in the Netherlands, Europe and China. Consequently, he embarked on a research project about Responsible Port Innovation in the Netherlands, Indonesia and China. He has published several books and numerous journal articles and conference papers on these and other topics. Together with other researchers, especially from China, he is currently preparing a collection of papers on Responsible Port Innovation in relation to the new Maritime Silk Road.

Made in United States
Orlando, FL
04 November 2026

90209953R00240